DATE DUE			
Apr 15 78			
Aug 15 79			

RIGHT & LEFT

Robert Hertz
1881–1915

Essays on
Dual Symbolic
Classification

RIGHT & LEFT

Edited and with
an Introduction by
Rodney Needham

Foreword by
E. E. Evans-Pritchard

The University
of Chicago Press
Chicago and London

RODNEY NEEDHAM, Fellow of Merton College, is University Lecturer in Social Anthropology at Oxford. He is the author of *Structure and Sentiment* (1962), *Belief, Language, and Experience* (1972), and numerous papers on the ethnography of Southeast Asia, social classification, and symbolism. His distinctions include the Monograph Prize of the American Academy of Arts and Sciences, the Rivers Memorial Medal, and the degree of Doctor of Letters of the University of Oxford. [1973]

THE UNIVERSITY OF CHICAGO PRESS, CHICAGO 60637
THE UNIVERSITY OF CHICAGO PRESS, LTD., LONDON

Printed in the United States of America
International Standard Book Number: 0-226-56995-0
Library of Congress Catalog Card Number: 73-82982

To the Memory of
Robert Hertz
(1881–1915)

Contents

Foreword

Dr. Needham has done me the kindness, and the honor, again of asking me to write a foreword. I do so with the greatest satisfaction because it enables me to express once more my admiration for Robert Hertz, two of whose essays—the one here reproduced, that on the Right Hand, and the other on the Representation of Death—are for me two of the finest essays ever written in the history of sociological thought. The conclusions he reached in both may now seem obvious, but it is Hertz who made them so. Even when the conclusions appear erroneous, it is Hertz who has led towards a truer conception of dualism.

This contrast of right and left may teach us all a lesson; and here I may be allowed to take a bit of credit to myself, for what Hertz wrote seems, except here and there, to have been forgotten—I suppose totally passed by in the English-speaking world—until I brought him into circulation again. (It is so long ago that I cannot remember when I first became acquainted with his writings, which have been an inspiration to me in my ethnographical researches, especially among the Nuer.) I included a lecture on Hertz every year at Oxford during my entire tenure of the Chair of Social Anthropology at that University. It is therefore most gratifying to see in this volume what a rich harvest has sprung up from the seed sown. Once the symbolism of right-left had been brought back to the notice of anthropologists it was found all over the world, and Hertz has been vindicated over and over again.

Now it is elementary that concepts derive their meanings in relation to their opposites, that *X* means something in relation to non-*X*. We have been made familiar with this idea from Heraclitus to Hegel. So it is not surprising that we find in the languages of the peoples we study words which can be set forth in pairs of complementary opposites, e.g., dark and light, hot and cold, good and bad, and so on—the number is limitless. How could it be otherwise? Right and left are such a pair. We need not, however, discuss this further, for it is not only obvious but also not to the point with regard to the contents of this book, which goes beyond language or the structure of the mind into the whole question of collective representations and their generality. What we have to find out is what in each society we study is associated with the pairs of opposites. In every language I know, for example, certain qualities, moral and spiritual, are associated with the opposites of hot and cold. This was what Hertz was trying to discover in his research into the notions of right and left; and his discoveries were original and brilliant. But we have to go further and ask whether these associations are restricted to particular cultures or are universals or near universals (as Hertz would suggest). This collection of essays takes us a long way along that road, but there is still a long road ahead.

There is nothing more I can say. Dr. Needham and his brilliant team of collaborators have said all that can at the present time be said, and have said it very well. I only wish to join a hand with them in laying a wreath on Hertz's tomb.

E. E. EVANS-PRITCHARD

All Souls College, Oxford

Introduction

Rodney Needham

Das Zwei *verdient Aufmerksamkeit.*
G. C. Lichtenberg

I

On 13 April 1915, at the age of thirty-three, Robert Hertz was killed in what Marcel Mauss was bitterly to describe as the "useless attack" on Marchéville.[1] It was a wretched affair, quite doomed, and the officers knew that they were leading their men to their deaths. There were three hundred yards of open country to be crossed, at 2:50 in the afternoon of a clear spring day, and covered by German machine guns.[2] The company commander went first over the parapet and within ten paces was dead. He was followed by his two second-lieutenants—one of them Hertz—and they were at once shot down by his side.[3]

This was the end of a young academic who was already recognized as a "master among masters," [4] and who had produced work of an unmistakable excellence. There was every prospect that he would become a considerable scholar, and in retrospect it seems likely that he would have proved greater than that. Evans-Pritchard has suggested that Hertz might have become the equal of Durkheim,[5] and there are indeed grounds to argue that, had he lived, he would have assumed with Mauss the leadership of an *Année sociologique* group which could have transformed sociological thought. As it was, this gifted team of Durkheim's pupils was practically destroyed by the war, and the only substantial works that Hertz left in print were three essays. One of them was on the pre-eminence of the right hand.

Alice Hertz has told us that her husband was preoccupied with ambidexterity before he ever saw a sociological problem in the matter. He had become acquainted with certain new pedagogical methods which developed both the right and the left hand of children, and these interested him. Also, he had a baby son. What became the focus of his investigation, from a sociological point of view, was that it was a contribution to the analysis of our representation of space.[6] Mauss later saw the essay as an appendix to Hertz's larger investigation into what he regarded as the most difficult and least studied aspect of religious and moral phenomena: crime and sin, punishment and pardon—"the dark side of humanity."[7] According to this view, the essay on the superiority of the right hand is actually a study of the impurity of the left side, and as such it is incidental to "the total study of impurity in general."[8] Within the essay itself, however, Hertz's own emphasis falls explicitly on dualism. This is prominently seen in his conclusion: "The obligatory differentiation between the sides of the body is a particular case and a consequence of the dualism which is inherent in primitive thought." The central theme, to judge by this and other statements of the kind, is that of "polarity," or opposition, as manifested in symbolic classification.

This is the theoretical theme of the present collection of papers, and in bringing them together the initial motive is to indicate how much is due to Hertz's now classic essay. More generally, the volume demonstrates also how much novel and rewarding research can derive from the inception and application of one fundamental idea. In this case, there is weighty and decisive evidence of such progress; but it is another lesson of the collection that a theoretical advance, however inspired, may be only very belatedly recognized, and that the potential of an idea may have to wait decades for effective exploitation. Hertz's essay, moreover, languished in general neglect in spite of the prominent support and professional advertisement that his work early received. It is true that during his lifetime the essay on the right hand supplied a definitive example in the introduction to Durkheim's study of the elementary forms of religious life: "The distinction of right and left . . . , far from being implicit in the nature of man in general, is very probably the product of representations which are religious and therefore collective."[9] Shortly after the war, too, Mauss drew attention to the essay in his introduction to "Le Péché et l'expiation," and he republished it in his edition of Hertz's collected papers, *Mélanges de sociologie religieuse et folklore.*[10] But even the promotion of Hertz's analysis on the part of such distinguished scholars as Durkheim and Mauss was not enough at the time to secure its adoption into the general concerns of sociologists and social anthropologists. Thousands have read Durkheim on the elementary forms of religious life, especially since the publication in 1915 of an English translation,[11] but Durkheim's reference to Hertz in making his essential case did not, it appears, induce his readers to turn to the authority on whom he relied. Not only was the essay itself largely ignored, and its intrinsic interest thus unrealized, but more seriously its academic neglect had the consequence that it was delayed in exerting its full benefit on the inquiries of ethnographers and other students of civilization.

Nevertheless, Hertz's article did not remain entirely disregarded. In 1933 Marcel Granet, a colleague and friend of Mauss, delivered to the Institut Français de Sociologie, in Paris, a communication on right and left in China (below, chap. 3). The topic was chosen, as he declared, partly because it provided an occasion to recall the fine work of Hertz.[12] In 1934 Ira S. Wile published a long survey of the literature on handedness[13] in which he acknowledged a direct stimulus from Hertz's paper: a quotation from this formed the epigraph to the book, and Hertz's views were repeatedly called upon in the argument. Wile's book in turn led Wieschhoff, in 1938, to make a study of concepts of right and left in African cultures (below, chap. 4); he did not cite Hertz himself, but the source of the theoretical interest remained clear. In 1941 Kruyt opened his report on right and left in central Celebes (below, chap. 5) with a summary of Hertz's argument, and it was from this basis that he conducted a quite new ethnographical investigation into the topic.

The turning point, however, in the redirection of anthropological attention to the subject of lateral values, was Evans-Pritchard's paper, published twelve years later, on Nuer spear symbolism (below, chap. 6).[14] Here too the acknowledged analytical authority was Hertz. But it was not this paper alone that was to arouse a wider and more consequential interest among social anthropologists: it was Evans-Pritchard's teaching at Oxford which gave an unprecedented impetus to such studies, and which was the chief occasion of the production of the present volume. His lectures brought Hertz's ideas into circulation again,[15] and the added importance that his own eminence imparted to the topic of right and left led directly to a noteworthy series of investigations into systems of dual symbolic classification. Great credit accrues to Evans-Pritchard on this count, and his name deserves to stand with that of Hertz for having led so far towards the new recognition of a fundamental feature of thought and imagery.

After Evans-Pritchard's lectures a further step forward, of a practical kind, was the production of an English translation of Hertz's essays on death and on the right hand. Evans-Pritchard suggested their inclusion in the series of translations of French sociological classics being brought out, under his aegis, from the Institute of Social Anthropology at the University of Oxford, and the title appeared in 1960 with an introduction by himself.[16] The same year also saw the publication of "The Left Hand of the Mugwe" (below, chap. 7), and this was quickly followed by a remarkable burgeoning of anthropological interest, displayed in a succession of papers directed intensively to the topics, in lateral symbolism in particular and dual classification in general. Some of these articles were based, as had been that by Hertz, on the analysis of published sources; but a cardinal feature of most of them was that they were the products of original ethnography, and they showed with reiterated force how revelatory an inquiry into the polarity of values isolated by Hertz could prove to be in the analysis of field materials. This volume includes a number of such studies, both literary and ethnographical, down to the year 1971, by which time the theme of right and left had achieved a gratifying and widespread recognition.[17]

II

Preparations for a handbook on the symbolism of right and left were initiated in 1962, and the plan was that it should consist of papers that had already been published. This procedure promised the advantage that each modern paper would have been subjected to scholarly scrutiny before being reprinted, and that in the interim each surviving author would have had the opportunity to make improvements. The version of each such paper to appear in this place was likely, therefore, to be superior to that first published, or at least to have been found still correct by its author. A further intended advantage, from an editorial point of view, was that there would be no need to keep any author waiting for publication while the rest of the collection was made up.

As it turned out, the majority of the recent papers retained their original form. Dr. Beidelman, however, wrote a new paper that was merely based on a much shorter article, "Right and Left Hand among the Kaguru"; Dr. Cunningham made substantial revisions to his paper on the Atoni house; Professor Littlejohn considerably extended his article on Temne right and left; and Dr. Beck added a new analysis, employing a new method, to her study of castes in South India. Dr. Fox wrote an entirely original study, about Roti, especially for the handbook; this paper, "On Bad Death and the Left Hand," is printed here for the first time.[18]

One paper in the body of the book, that by La Flesche on right and left in Osage ceremonies (first published in 1916), has no patent connection with the prior work of Hertz.[19] It is reprinted here, not only for its intrinsic value as an apparently independent investigation of the topic among an American Indian people, but also because it came out originally in a privately published work of which only two hundred copies were printed, so that it is now scarce and hard to come by. In addition to the detailed analyses and reports, it seemed also well worth while to reproduce, as an appendix, Alice Warner's note of 1904 on the terms used for "right hand" and "left hand" in Bantu languages.

The essays collected here are not by any means all that might have been included, and there is much else in print on the ideas and values attaching to right and left. For instance, if intrinsic relevance and resonant exposition were all that counted, Sir Thomas Browne's observations "Of the Right and the Left Hand"[20] would surely be included; and there is a great deal more in European literature that could swell into a huge anthology. Also, as the preparation of the volume advanced there appeared in journals, or were offered to the editor, new anthropological investigations which in their own right amply deserve notice. But the intention behind the present collection was in the first place to compile a kind of symbolic handbook which would provide a manageable conspectus of the theoretical issues, together with a useful body of pertinent evidence, and a limit had to be drawn.

Already, it may seem, the provocative character of the problems may tend to be rather overwhelmed by the weight of the combined papers and the repetition of common findings. In this field one cannot in any case strive for completeness, and a superabundance of corroboration by ethnographic illustrations could well turn wearisome. The first object, then, is to record the conception of a problem in the study of collective representations, and then to show how it has been explored and to what results it has led. The handbook is meant to be a stimulus to thought, not an encyclopedia, and even its present large compass should still permit that use.

III

It had been projected that the essays should be preceded by an analytical introduction: not in order to assess the papers individually, for the authors already say perfectly clearly what they wish to say, but to abstract from the collection (and also from the vast background literature) a quintessential account of the topics under examination, and to put a general theoretical construction upon them. There are questions of method, too, which deserve technical attention; and ultimately there should be room also for a more philosophical consideration of the implications of the study of right and left for the interpretation of the collective forms of human experience.[21] But as the volume grew, and the investigations deepened, it became apparent that to do so much in an introduction was not feasible. Notes and references and illustrations had accumulated far beyond any economical treatment, and the issues discerned were so fundamental that they should not be barely sketched out in an editorial prologue.[22] So the decision was taken to furnish a more ordinary introduction, and to let the collection itself serve rather as a mine for theoretical exploitation.

Nevertheless, there are two aspects of this work as a whole which call for some mention with regard to the different kinds of theoretical interest that they have. The first is that the collection is probably unique in its arrangement. The ordinary practice in compiling a joint work is to model it on a symposium: a topic is chosen, and a group of coeval authors address themselves in common to the discussion of this; or, in the case of a Festschrift, the honorand is named and the writers direct their essays convergently on him or his work. In principle this is an excellent procedure, since the differing views of the contributors can be expected to reflect various parts of the complexity of the subject. In practice, too, this method of composition has proved repeatedly to possess advantages, derived from contemporary cooperation, in gaining a more panoptic and critical depiction of the matter or work under examination. But in the present instance the collaboration is not contemporaneous:

it is sequential. Hertz's classic essay marks the inception of a theoretical concern, and the rest of the papers (to the seeming exclusion of that by La Flesche) are all inspired, directly or indirectly, by Hertz. They are ordered chronologically, so as to show the successive influences and the increasing intensity of the investigations. (Those papers that were rewritten or specially composed are placed according to the year of original publication or the date of writing respectively.) It is not often that the birth and subsequent fortunes of an idea can be so readily and clearly traced, and in these regards the present volume has an unusual interest for the history of thought.

One of the incidental sources of interest to be found in it, if a rather perturbing one, is the large factor of accident that can be seen to affect the survival of an idea. Even the early support of Durkheim and Mauss did not give Hertz's paper any real fame, and it is easily to be imagined that it might simply have dropped out of sight. There are thousands of articles in French learned periodicals of the first decades of this century, most of them yellowing unread on brittle pages, and Hertz's essay might well have moldered unrecognized in their company. That it was in the event taken up by Granet may have been due primarily to the fact that he was a friend of both Durkheim and Mauss. Wile, from whose book Wieschhoff takes his start, is evidently a different case: it was his practice to read anything at all that had any bearing on handedness, and his thorough industry was most likely to discover Hertz's essay sooner or later. Kruyt does not say where he learned of Hertz's argument, but possibly he was directed to it by the preponderant interest of the Leiden school of social anthropologists, under the leadership of the late Prof. Dr. J. P. B. de Josselin de Jong, in the tradition of the *Année sociologique*. Thereafter, the recognition accorded to Hertz was brought about by Evans-Pritchard, who, in addition to the implicit testimony of his own works, has explicitly declared his intellectual allegiance to the *Année* school.[23] Among the present authors who published their analyses after the date of his "Nuer Spear Symbolism," half were at Oxford under Evans-Pritchard, and the rest have in turn had more or less close personal and academic connections with these.

For the most part, therefore, the transmission of theoretical influence can easily be traced, and the impulse behind a noteworthy conjunction of effort can be identified. But, as in the charting of most such lines of thought, the question still remains why Hertz's essay did not have a yet wider success, and why the application of his ideas has been demonstrated in the main by scholars who had happened to be brought into professional association. There have been many others who worked under Evans-Pritchard at Oxford yet did not respond to this stimulus, just as there must be even more who have encountered Hertz's translated essay in print but have made nothing of it. Admitted, receptivity to an idea or to a style of thought is hard to account for, and many contingencies of personality and circumstance may be responsible for an ideological stance; but behind an actual resistance or disparagement there can sometimes be detected certain deleterious predispositions, and it should be helpful to comment on some of these here.

IV

The papers in this collection, however disparate they may be in some ways, all agree in two basic analytical regards: that oppositions can validly be established, and that these can be systematically interrelated.

At a number of places below, these premises are given expository expression in the form of binary schemes of symbolic categories in which the terms are drawn up in two columns. Clearly, however, in the analysis of collective representations no theoretical premises can be taken for granted, and a method is not justified merely by the fact that it can frame a consistent account of otherwise disorderly particulars. Ultimately, the style of analysis typified in this volume calls for a formal explication, and in default of such a validation we must concede that persuasiveness in the practical analysis of individual cases is not enough.[24] It is the more understandable, also, that among social anthropologists there should be a number who, as one understands from common report, are very suspicious of attempts to establish instances of dual symbolic classification. Such wariness may easily be accepted in principle, but usually there is considerable difficulty in practice when one tries to make sure of the precise grounds on which objections are to be encountered. Whereas there are many dualistic analyses of symbolism, which are open to inspection in printed sources, it is generally hard indeed to discover anything more than isolated allusions that can be set against them. In these circumstances it is scarcely feasible to be clear even about the terms in which a theoretical debate might be conducted. But there has recently appeared one critical paper which actually sets out at some length a number of forthright objections to the kind of work represented in the present collection,[25] and it does so moreover with specific reference to one of the constituent papers.[26] It is therefore doubly to the advantage of the collection that, by so fortunate a concurrence, certain forms of objection should have been displayed with an admirable clarity and in time for useful adduction here. To examine the article quite as closely as it richly deserves would be disproportionate with an editorial introduction,[27] but even a brief attention to some of its features will be instructive.

The paper's main concern is announced as simply "to set the Nyoro ethnographic record straight,"[28] but its real interest is to be found in its analytical premises and in the interpretation that is placed upon the method of exposition displayed in the work under criticism. Let us take up just four such points. To rectify them will do much to prevent unnecessary misunderstanding of the theoretical implications of the handbook as a whole.

First, there is the question "whether the classifications expounded in studies of this kind exist in the minds of the people studied, and if so, at what level of explicitness, or only in the mind of the observer."[29] The critic concludes in this case that since the title of the analyst's paper (i.e., chap. 15 below) "specifies Nyoro symbolic classification, . . . it may be assumed that he is imputing the scheme he advances to the Nyoro themselves." This assumption would appear almost calculated to impede understanding, for in general it is certainly important, on the contrary, not to impute the formal representation of a symbolic classification to the individual consciousnesses of the people under study:

> From the fact that a society subscribes to a dual classification . . . that is analyzable systematically by reference to a general relation of complementary opposition, it does not at all follow that the members of that society shall individually conceive their experience in oppositional terms. That an equally general relation of analogy is also analytically necessary in order to compose the pairs of opposites into a system does not entail, either, that the thoughts of any individual shall perpetually follow a dialectical zig-zag between the two sets of opposed cultural categories by which the ideology can be schematized.[30]

What liaisons may exist between collective representations and the conceptual apprehensions of individuals is indeed a hard question;

but methodologically it has been a commonplace since Durkheim's earliest writings, at the end of the nineteenth century, that they are not to be confused. The parallel between an analytical scheme and the grammar of a language (of which the speakers may similarly be unconscious) should be too hackneyed to be drawn yet again, but apparently even this thumb-marked primer may well be brought out once more if the point is to be made. It can also be made by comparison with the study of social organization, where (strangely enough, perhaps) the analytical distinction is not usually found so difficult to see. A system of asymmetric prescriptive alliance, for example, can be represented schematically in a great many ways haveing varying degrees of simplicity. The myriad phenomenal complexities of such a form of social life, among the Purum or the Batak or the Sumbanese, can to a considerable extent be instructively subsumed under a relational figure so simple as $A \rightarrow B$. But no social anthropologist would dream of imputing this very scheme itself to the people under study. For that matter, it is a perplexing matter to conjecture just what such an imputation could possibly entail; for even if a Nyoro had learned to write out columns of opposites, or a Sumbanese had learned to draw arrows to stand for alliances, in neither case could any immediate inference be made from the form of the scheme to the process of the individual's conceptions. So, in the chapters that follow, it should be clearly understood that the binary schemes do not in themselves carry this implication.

Second, "The imputation to Nyoro symbolic thought of a pervasive binary quality on the scale suggested by [the] table has no warrant in the ethnography" (p. 438); "the principle of dual symbolic classification relates to a very much narrower range of Nyoro collective representations . . ." (p. 439). Here a distracting consideration of dimension has been gratuitously introduced. The analysis under criticism nowhere makes any reference to a degree of pervasiveness or to the scale of the symbolism. It represents a dual principle wherever this can apparently be discerned in the ethnographic record, and it says nothing at all about any other symbolic features or about other institutions. Nor, for that matter, does the delineation of a dual classification imply that this is the only possible order to be found in the facts, or that the people themselves subscribe to no other conventional division of phenomena. In general, then, it should be taken that a binary scheme applies directly only to those aspects of thought and imagery from which it is derived. How characteristic it may be of the culture as a whole, beyond the limits of the analysis, must wait upon further demonstration or investigation. Not, however, that the question of scale is in itself inconsiderable, only it must be reflectively treated. It is in fact often quite practicable, and revealing, to trace the extent to which an implicit premise, or mode of representation, pervades a given culture; and such an assessment of the scale of employment is inseparable from the attempt to characterize a form of social life. A striking example is to be found in Gregory Bateson's subtle study of Iatmul thought, in which he isolates the distinctive "motifs" of pluralism, monism, direct dualism, diagonal dualism, and seriation.[31] Whereas the motifs are held to be characteristic, they are nevertheless of different and even opposed types; yet the fact that Iatmul collective thought can be termed monistic does not prevent it from being concurrently pluralistic as well, one dualism does not exclude the other, and neither dualism is incompatible with seriation. In addition, one may instance from the study of this fascinating society (and one described by so gifted an observer) the general importance of alternation in Iatmul classification, both symbolic and jural, as isolated by Francis Korn.[32] As for an analytical principle of complementary opposition, it may in a given society be a general motif or it may be limited to certain aspects of social life. More narrowly, the symbolism of right and left may be radical to a society, as among the South Indians studied by Beck, or it may be comparatively insignificant, as among the Lugbara studied by Middleton. These are not matters for dogma or presumption: they are issues for empirical analysis, and only a demonstration specifically directed to such ends can determine questions of scale. The essays in this volume are about dual symbolic classification: they do not maintain that there is nothing else.

This leads us to the third objection, namely, that this style of analysis resorts to a "prefabricated schema of binary opposition" (p. 439). This charge is very much at fault. The binary scheme is the result of the analysis of ethnographical particulars, and in these respects it cannot be "prefabricated." The analyst seeks an order in the data, and the principle of opposition is simply one of the formal notions to which he has recourse in doing so. Whether he represents the facts examined in the form of a binary scheme depends on whether he thinks the several contrasts that he isolates have an intrinsic significance of the kind. The values of lateral symbolism are often the readiest means of initiating such an inquiry.

Thus the Nyoro bury the afterbirth of a male child to the right side of the house door, and that of a female child to the left. Similarly, they bury a man lying on his right side and a woman on her left. These reports show that a definite contrast is made such that, in these contexts, male is associated with right and female with left. This, moreover, is an exhaustive discrimination: there is no intermediary or residual category, and the binary quality is therefore not prefabricated. The same conclusion follows from the examination of the procedure of a diviner at a consultation. The ethnographer explicitly says that the diviner places a wand on the left shoulder of the client and says, "Sickness be gone, . . . sorrow be gone, barrenness be gone"; and that he then places the wand on the right shoulder and says, "Come wealth, come children, come long life, . . . come all goodness." Here again there is an extreme and undeniable contrast of values associated consistently with the left and with the right. Again, to cite one more simple example, the ethnographer reports a myth in which God points up with his right hand and says, "This is heaven"; he points down with his left hand and says, "This is earth."[33]

In such instances the evidence is clear and incontrovertible: its significance has nothing to do with any theoretical predisposition on the part of the analyst, but is that of the values expressly and conventionally symbolized by right and left in Nyoro tradition. It is mutually exclusive contrasts such as right/left, male/female, fertility/barrenness, sky/earth, etc., which then permit the construction of a columnar scheme of oppositions. But this scheme says nothing, of course, about any other contexts and it does not yield any further oppositions. Each symbolic contrast has to be established individually, and a certain incidence of oppositional values does not in itself justify the conclusion that the principle of opposition orders other collective representations as well. Oppositions must be demonstrated: they cannot be proved by inference.

As for those oppositions that have been established, however, and registered in a binary scheme, there is one simple test of the validity of the analysis. This is to re-examine the symbolic values in question, in their several contexts, and to try to order them consistently in some other scheme that is not binary and does not call upon a principle of opposition. This alone is not a decisive test, and if it cannot be done by a particular analyst[34] it does not show that another scheme is in principle not possible, but it does tend to show a degree of cogency in the binary scheme. On the other hand, if a new ordering did prove possible, this would not necessarily mean that the principle of opposition was invalidated, but only that the symbolism in question was constituted by some principle in addition to that of opposition. A society need not, after all, employ only a single mode of classification.[35] In either case, whether the evidences can or cannot be reordered in a nonoppositional scheme, there will still remain a considerable problem; namely, to explain how it is, in that event, that the ethnographical evidence permits a coherent dual interpretation, a fact which would be difficult to accept as merely fortuitous.[36]

Finally, we come to the fourth objection, and that which embodies the most serious mistake. It is a defect which runs right through our critic's reconsideration of Nyoro symbolism, and it quite nullifies the attempted refutation of an oppositional analysis. It is clearly expressed in the opening deposition (pp. 414–15), where we find these telling lines:

> There is no evidence that diviners, mediums and mystical office are regarded by Banyoro as being in themselves inauspicious rather than auspicious . . . ; there is no evidence that odd numbers are considered as inauspicious. . . . In a great number of cases auspiciousness and inauspiciousness are aspects or stages of things or events; they are not absolute qualities of them, on the basis of which things and events can be neatly classified as either one thing [*sic*] or the other.

There follow a number of other allusions to the same effect: e.g., "there is little suggestion in the literature that there is anything particularly inauspicious about girls or the 'queen' as such . . . , or about subjects, huntsmen, or sexual intercourse, all of which . . . are associated with the left hand" (p. 416); that huntsmen receive the left portion of the animal killed "does not necessarily suggest that huntsmen are 'inauspicious'" (p. 416, n. 2); "Banyoro do not think that there is anything inauspicious about cooking in itself" (p. 436); and so on throughout.

We need not dwell on the details of the fact that nowhere in the oppositional analysis under criticism is it actually said that diviners, mediums, odd numbers, girls, subjects, hunters, or cooking are "inauspicious." [37] The point at issue is not the misrepresentation in itself, but to show that the misrepresentation is (in part, at least) the product of a mistaken conception of the method of analysis. What the critic is doing is to take a number of items that are listed in the "left" column of the binary scheme of Nyoro symbolic classification, and then to assert that none of them is thereby inauspicious. The assumption appears to be that all of the terms in the column of the left are represented as inauspicious, and all of those in that of the right as auspicious.[38] To show that certain of the "inauspicious" items are not regarded by the Nyoro as inauspicious then shows, it seems to be supposed, that the general dichotomy does not obtain. Why, though, does our critic think that the argument does rest on a partition of Nyoro symbolic values into auspicious and inauspicious? It is simply because the results of the analysis are summed up in a table composed of two columns. The critic himself makes plain that this is the source of his miscomprehension: it is this "mode of representation" (p. 433) that suggests to him the "implications" by which he is so far led astray. Chief among these is the supposed implication that "all the things or qualities listed in the same column are thought . . . by Banyoro to be like one another . . . in virtue of this shared quality" (pp. 433–34). It is this prejudicial construction which underlies the general condemnation (p. 435) of the oppositional analysis:

> It is in fact not the case that all the terms listed in the column headed by the word "right" . . . are thought of as good, auspicious, and esteemed; all those in the column headed by the word "left" as bad, inauspicious, and "hated."

Here, most advantageously, we have an unambiguous instance of a grave source of possible misunderstanding against which readers of this volume deserve to be placed especially on their guard.

The first rectification to be made is that a two-column scheme, listing the oppositions in what is analyzed as a dual symbolic classification, is not a total and systematic depiction of a complete body of thought and imagery. It is a mnemonic and suggestive device which simply brings together in a convenient and apt fashion the series of oppositions that have been established; and these are usually listed (as they are specifically in chap. 15 below) simply in the order in which they make their appearance in the course of the analysis. In itself the scheme neither states nor implies any boundaries or liaisons other than those that have already been demonstrated. It is, to repeat this crucial point, no more than an expository convenience: a conventional figure that helps one to recall the cumulative effect of the argument.

The second necessary rectification is that to draw up such a table by no means implies that all of the terms in either column are "thought of" in any particular way by these whose symbolism is in part given this diagrammatic form. The terms stand for collective representations, i.e., conventional modes of speech and action, and unless there is specific ethnographical evidence to such effect it cannot be assumed that the participants themselves think of their symbolism at all, let alone that they think of the matters denoted by the terms in any unifying order.

It is not suggested, therefore, that a binary scheme of the kind in question "exhibits a 'total' character, based on the division of all of the things and qualities listed into two opposed and mutually exclusive spheres" (p. 437). This is certainly not so, and equally certainly it is not suggested by the form of the table that "all of the things or qualities listed in each of [the] two columns are thought . . . to belong to a single category" (p. 437). Rather, it is this misguided interpretation of the scheme that must resolutely be avoided.

Two distinct fallacies are responsible for this miscomprehension. The first is to ignore the overriding importance of context. To register a particular opposition, e.g., white/black or even/odd, in the table does not imply that the contrast of values pertains to any context other than that in which it is demonstrated to be significant. Nor, accordingly, does the listing of a term in one column of the table mean that it belongs to an exclusive sphere, by an ascription so absolute that it cannot be listed (in another context) in the opposite column. Nyoro symbolic categories are indeed concerned with *aspects* of certain things and situations rather than with these things and situations considered as a totality (cf. pp. 418–19); and this is in fact a notion that guides the whole of the analysis under criticism. It is only by disregarding the crucial factor of context, then, that it seems possible to a critic to belabor the points that in Nyoro culture sheep are not opposed to cattle as inauspicious, that there is no evidence that chickens are thought to be inauspicious, that there is no evidence that alien dialect is thought to be inauspicious, that there is no evidence that sexual intercourse is thought to be inauspicious (p. 436), and so on persistently. These critical contentions are entirely irrelevant, since nowhere in the argument in question is it even hinted that these terms of the "left" column share any quality at all, let alone that of being inauspicious. (Actually, on sexual intercourse in particular it is even expressly said in the analysis [sec. V] that what perhaps counts in one context is the destructive and impure "aspect" of sexuality.) It is only the arbitrary and fallacious construction put upon the table that imputes a common quality to all the terms in one column. Such a construction is not merely unjustified by the particular analysis from which the table in question derives, but on more scholarly grounds it is in addition a quite needless mistake. To make this point let us turn to a field of study where such matters are usually far better understood, namely, the investigation of Vedic symbolism.[39]

Originally there was neither day nor night, until the gods said to Mitra and Varuṇa: "Make a separation." Mitra produced the day, Varuṇa produced the night. Hence the day belongs to Mitra, the night belongs to Varuṇa.[40] Concordantly, Mitra is associated with the sun, Varuṇa with the moon. By one account, "Mitra (the Sun) inseminates Varuṇa (the Moon)."[41] However, when they are joined together into a couple they are one and the other gods of both day and night; Varuṇa, even when he is alone, retains a bright side, though he still has also a dark side by which he remains contrasted with Mitra.[42] The contexts in question are matters for textual demonstration and need not be reported here. The chief point, rather, is that Mitra and Varuṇa, even though unequivocally associated respectively with day and night, sun and moon, are in other contexts not so contrasted. It cannot therefore be said that either deity possesses, in an absolute and fixed manner, any one of the contrastive values. The same kind of lesson emerges from a consideration of Mitra and Varuṇa in relation to the moon. There are many indications which combine to associate Varuṇa with the moon, together with night, magic, the awesome, and the feminine. In a binary table these terms can all be listed together, let us say in the "left" column. But that does not mean that the moon as such shares with the other terms some common quality such that it must find its place only in that column, and in association exclusively with Varuṇa; for the opposition between Mitra and Varuna themselves is assimilated to that between the waning moon and the waxing moon. As for right and left, specifically, we are plainly told that "Mitra is the left and Varuṇa the right, or else Mitra is the right and Varuṇa the left (according to whether the right is considered as the *strong* side or as the *just* side)."[43] Again, Mitra is associated with the sun and the sky, and Varuṇa with the moon and the earth; Mitra is masculine, Varuṇa feminine. The sky itself, therefore, might be expected to be considered masculine, and hence to find its place in the "right" column of our hypothetical table. Yet in fact, "from one point of view the Sky is feminine to the Sun, but from another the Sky is no less masculine to the Earth."[44] In other words, whether the sky is regarded as masculine or as feminine depends on the context, and the column in which it should be listed alternates with the particular opposition in question. Finally, to take another example from the same field, the god of fire, Agni, is by some features associated with values pertaining characteristically to Mitra, yet by others he is associated with those pertaining rather to Varuṇa. Hence one text declares: "O Agni, you are Varuṇa when you are born, you become Mitra when you are alight."[45] So Agni too cannot be rigidly assigned to one column of terms or to the other, but belongs in either according to context.

These examples, taken briefly from a classical system of symbolic classification, show not only the importance of keeping the context of opposition perpetually in view, but also how it is that the dual scheme does not necessarily effect a total and exhaustive partition of all things and qualities into two mutually exclusive spheres. It is the more readily understandable, furthermore, that the terms in one column of a binary table should not be assumed to share any attribute or to belong to a single category. As Dumézil writes, in comparing the Mitra-Varuṇa idiom of opposition with that of traditional China, "it is vain to try to start from one element . . . in order to deduce the others from it."[46] These points are also made in one of the essays in this volume (chap. 7, sec. III),[47] in relation to the status of the Mugwe. This personage is indirectly associated, it is argued, with the feminine; yet the ethnographic source states that the Mugwe is "higher" than the elders and is "above" them, a fact which appears inconsistent with the plain inferiority of women to men in this society. "But we have to remember . . . the matter of context: ritually . . . the Mugwe is superior to the elders, but politically he is definitely not." It cannot therefore be said that the Mugwe is absolutely superior to the elders, or that he is inferior to them, but only that he has one or the other standing according to the particular relationship in which his office is opposed to theirs. As for the question of a shared quality, "it has to be kept in mind that the ascription of terms to one series in the scheme does not entail that they all share the particular attributes of any one term. . . . One does not say, therefore, that the Mugwe *is* feminine, any more than one would say that night or south or the subordinate age-division is feminine." Similarly, in the Nyoro case, it should not need repeating that the things or qualities listed in one column of the table are certainly not represented as sharing any one quality, let alone as composing one category. Even if the term "inauspicious" did appear in the left column, therefore, the scheme would by no means imply that the other terms listed in the column—e.g., diviner, odd numbers, subject, hunter, sexual intercourse, sheep, chickens, or alien dialect—were thereby to be regarded as inauspicious. Put formally, $a : b :: c : d$ does not entail that $a \equiv c$ or that $b \equiv d$.

There will presumably be some significant similarities among the terms listed in one column, such that in certain contexts a relationship of homology of the type $a \equiv c$ can indeed be demonstrated; but the homology must be established by specific evidence in each case and cannot be simply inferred. Moreover, there are in fact forms of symbolism in which it can be said that a series of homologous symbolic terms do share something of a common quality. This is so most prominently in the dual classification by *yin* and *yang* in Chinese tradition. According to Granet, these are "two Emblems, richer than all others in power of suggestion," and this embracing opposition can evoke all the other couples of emblems. *Yin* and *yang* have a power of evocation that is truly indefinite and "total," and they thus serve as "rubrics for two opposed classes of symbols." They "preside over the classification of all things," and in turn all things and all ideas are "divided between Yin and Yang." [48] Even this is far from the consubstantial construction that we have had to argue against, but it does show that in a dual symbolic classification it is in fact possible for one opposition to stand for and to subsume all the rest. A similar case, though more restricted, is to be found in the ancient Indian classification. Mitra and Varuna do not determine a general bipartition of the universe, at all levels, but at the level of sovereignty they too serve as emblems or rubrics for the oppositions with which they are formally homologous.[49] At the same time, however, the difference in extent of application between the Chinese and the Indian rubrics demonstrates once more that associations within a series or set of homologous terms (i.e., those represented by one column in a table of opposites) have to be established by particulars and that they cannot be presumed by a general inference.

With this point made, we may turn finally to the second and more damaging of the two radical fallacies under discussion. The contention that a table of opposites implies a total division of things and qualities into two opposed and mutually exclusive spheres, each characterized by one distinctive quality, rests at once on a disregard of the function of analogy in a dual classification and also on a misunderstanding of the nature of analogy.[50] We have noted, at the beginning of this section, the premise that the oppositions to be established in any discrete classification are systematically interrelated; and a crucial part of the task of analysis is to determine how the various contextual opposites can be consistently connected into an ideological whole. There are a number of sources to be called upon in justifying the premise,[51] but for the present purpose it must suffice to make a summary case. In a dual classification the pairs of symbolic categories are related by, in Dumézil's phrase, "dialectical analogy." Or, in the explanation proposed in chap. 7 below (sec. III), "The association of [the] terms rests on analogy, and is derived from a mode of categorization which orders the scheme, not from the possession of a specific property by means of which the character or presence of other terms may be deduced." This is what is conveyed, too, by the statement in chap. 15 (sec. VII) that the scheme of Nyoro symbolic classification is "made unitary by analogy." Liaisons are made indirectly, by analogy, not by the positing of direct resemblance or equivalence or identity. There is thus not an absolute assortment of things and qualities into classes which define their symbolic significance once and for all. Instead, there is a constant "classificatory current," as Dumézil puts it; the "equilibria are unstable," and the symbolic categories are ascribed different values according to the "perspectives" in which they are viewed.[52] A single complex system is built up in which, as Lloyd similarly writes, "the dominant motif is . . . *recurrent antithesis.*"[53]

The essential fact is that it is not the function of analogy to establish a kind or degree of direct resemblance. The similarity between any two homologous terms does not depend on the common possession of any distinctive property: it is relational. Kant wrote long ago, after all, that analogy does not mean an imperfect similarity between two things, but a perfect similarity of relations between quite dissimilar things.[54] This formulation is itself open to logical revision, and it certainly admits of more precision, but the essential argument is correct and of immediate relevance to the study of symbolic classification. To revert to our Nyoro test case, there is accordingly no occasion to consider "the highly dubious hypothesis that diviners are regarded as in some manner feminine." [55] Through his left hand the diviner is evidently associated symbolically with the feminine, but this analytical inference does not assert or depend on a direct resemblance: it is "derived analogically from the association of masculine with right and feminine with left." To the extent that a diviner's office is characterized by his resort to the left hand, he is indirectly associated with the feminine by the elementary analogy right : left : : male : female. There is abundant evidence to establish the component opposites (right/left, male/female) in this formula, and it is the analogical relations among these symbolic terms which lead to the inference that the use of the left hand indicates an association with the feminine. This indication of one aspect of his status is reinforced, moreover, by further analogical connections defined by oppositions between colors and between numbers. But one does not therefore say that the Nyoro diviner *is* black or that he *is* odd (uneven), any more than one could say that he *is* in any manner feminine. Under each aspect, the symbolic characterization does not depend on an absolute and direct qualitative resemblance, but upon a relative and indirect analogical relationship to statuses, things, and ideas with which the diviner may share (in these contexts) no specific and common property.

Thanks therefore to an unusually explicit and determined attempt to invalidate the style of analysis exemplified in this volume, we have been furnished with a providential occasion to obviate certain fundamental misapprehensions in the analysis of dual symbolic classification.[56] With these precautions, the case for oppositional analysis may confidently be left to the authors of the papers below, in studies covering a period of more than sixty years of developing expertness. Negative objections must of course be accorded some value in academic discourse, but no positive advance in understanding can be expected from grudging derogations. To discern order in the collective representations of human experience calls for original and intensive work in the imaginative apprehension of exotic modes of thought and imagery. On this score there is a great deal to be said for Revel's austere injunction: "Let there be no discussion about methods except by those who make discoveries." [57]

V

It is a question, though, to what extent the papers in this volume do actually make discoveries. They certainly demonstrate many positive advances, both ethnographical and analytical, but ultimately there is still an uncertainty about the intrinsic significance of the dual schemes and their constituent principles.

A general implication is that they refer to constant tendencies of the human mind, and one analysis further concludes (chap. 15, sec. VIII) that what may have been discerned in the investigation of symbolic categories are certain primary factors of human experience. But when we try to justify the analytical constructs on which such propositions rest, and to assess their real correspondence with natural modes of thought and apprehension, we rapidly pass the limits of proof.

This is a deeply problematical situation, but not one that is peculiar to the study of lateral symbolism. It is a central issue in any humane discipline, and as an essentially philosophical problem it may not admit any definite resolution. It has to do with the variable meanings attached to such abstractions as "fact" and "theory," and with the uncertain relations which are variously held to obtain between these. In such regards the essays presented here can in themselves have no decisive effect, even though they can be claimed to have a special demonstrative value in the consideration of the problem. Yet, all the same, it is still an unavoidable concern to ask how, or in what degree, oppositional analysis can ever be said to be right.

The first possible source of validation is the judgment of the participants, of those whose classification the analyst is trying to understand. An immediate ground of difficulty, however, is the commonplace observation that not all members of a society have a clear or comprehensive view of the collective representations that they recognize and express, and that none may have an abstract relational conception of their classification as a scheme of order. There are indeed some societies, or some individuals within certain societies, of such an analytical bent that indigenous formulations can be had. This appears to be the case with the South Indians, for example, and not surprisingly since their social organization is ordered and even named by the values of right and left. In Kodi, also, on the island of Sumba (eastern Indonesia), one skeptical and extremely intelligent aristocrat has even analyzed the dual symbolic classification of his society by reference to the principle of "balance" between opposites.[58] But difficulties proliferate when one tries to assess the probative weight of such indigenous formulations. The symbolic categories are collective representations, and the local commentators did not produce them. To the extent that the classifications are autonomous social facts, given by tradition, even those who frame their lives by them are still much in the position of the foreign analyst when they put an abstract construction upon the categories. If in doing so they report a conventional exegesis, a kind of local metaphysics, they are in effect simply reporting the symbolism in question, only at a level of greater generality, and the explication is itself part of what the social anthropologist has to account for. If, on the other hand, they independently excogitate certain principles on which they conclude the classification is based, their analysis does not gain a decisive authority merely by reason of the fact that they are members of the society under study. In the more common case, moreover, the principles that are argued by anthropologists to account for a system of dual classification, or even to inhere in it, are not explicitly recognized as such by those who employ the symbolic categories of which it is composed. Even if the more analytically minded members of the society can be brought to see the logic of the external analysis, this proves nothing about the validity of the abstract notions resorted to, or about the correctness of the scheme in which the indigenous categories are framed. Conversely, if members of the society deny that the analyst's construct is right, there are numerous grounds on which it can be countered that their denial is insufficient reason to think the analysis wrong.

A second form of possible validation proposes itself when a social anthropologist makes an analysis of published ethnographic data on a society with which he himself has no direct acquaintance. In this case, a special interest naturally attaches to the response of the ethnographer responsible for the data, or to the judgment of someone who has subsequently been in a position to test the analysis in the field. For instance, the argument of "The Left Hand of the Mugwe" (chap. 7 below) has been investigated among the Meru themselves by Dr. Jurg Mahner, and he is recorded as having found that his evidence "clearly confirms the structural analysis proposed by Needham."[59] It can certainly be conceded, at any rate, that in certain particular regards some confirmation can be had, especially perhaps when the analyst has isolated what appears to be an inconsistency in the literature which the later inquiry proves able to resolve.[60] More generally, a prominent opposition may be thought confirmed by the original ethnographer, as when Fr. Bernardi, after a return to the Meru, reported that the religious function of the Mugwe is "integrated with the essentially political function of the elders."[61] But it does not take a very sophistical mind to see grounds on which these agreeable confirmations can be subverted. If an investigation is carried out in the light of a published analysis, the apparent confirmation is made in terms which are those of the analysis itself, and for the most part the new ethnographic support will thus merely extend the evidential grounds on which the analysis was worked out. This will then show simply that the analysis is in fact consistent with the published ethnographic evidence, whereas the consistency is precisely the quality that makes the analysis worth testing. If, however, a number of relevant evidences are discovered which are not consistent with the analysis, these do not invalidate the respects in which the analysis does fit the facts. And if the reinvestigation leads the ethnographer to the conclusion that the oppositional method of analysis is incorrect, or at least is not readily applicable to the society in question, this finding will itself remain in principle an alternative analysis and will not constitute a final refutation. To the extent that the analysis under test is not riven by methodological flaws, is consistent with the ethnographical facts, and does not pass over any contradictory facts, it represents an ideological order which cannot be simply adventitious or insignificant. It may not be the sole construction that can be put on the evidence, and it may not provide the key to the classification, but so far as it justifiably fits the evidence it presumably corresponds to something. So if a restudy in the field cannot definitely prove the cogency of an oppositional analysis, it cannot fundamentally disprove it either.

The third means of validation to be mentioned dispenses entirely with the consideration of cultural signification and rests instead on the formal comparison of oppositional analyses of classifications from different civilizations. The present collection provides abundant material for the assessment of this issue, but once again it cannot provide a firm resolution. This wide comparison creates the strong impression that human beings all over the world tend to order themselves and their environments in remarkably similar ways, and by implicit recourse to classificatory principles so general and adaptive as to appear natural proclivities of the human mind.

But the comparison can have such force only to the extent that each particular analysis be granted to have established the individual operation of those principles, and on this score there is no final assurance. It could be contended, also, that the principles ascribed to a number of classifications in common were just as factitious in comparative analysis as in the study of singular ideologies; so in this respect as well no superior confirmation can be had simply on the ground of generality. Certain constant values, contrasts, and associations can certainly be demonstrated, of course: e.g., the near-universal pre-eminence of the right hand, the opposition of life to death, or the association of the sides with the sexes. But it could still be argued that these were no more than isolated features, and that they had no systematic significance for the study of classificatory propensities in general. They might rather be assimilated to such matters as mother-in-law avoidance, the magical power of iron, or a characteristically human activity like dancing. These features of culture are intrinsically interesting, and they have a high degree of incidence throughout the world; yet they are not systematically integrated, or mutually coherent, and their frequent appearance in different cultures does not signal the employment of a distinct and consistent mode of symbolic classification. For that matter, it could further be contended that the mutual reinforcement of the essays below is not the reflection of general cultural phenomena, or the product of a revelatory mode of analysis, but that the correspondences among them have to do instead with the connections among the investigators and with the pressures of theoretical influence that can be traced from one to another. Here again, it must be conceded that there is no way of making a decisive refutation of such objections, for they relate to the interpretation and abstract analysis of collective representations, or the history of ideas, and not finally to decidable questions of logic and fact.

There are certainly logical grounds on which it can be argued that "the organization of concepts by contrasted couples seems indeed to be an original and permanent form of thought";[62] but matters of logic are not to be decided by cultural particulars, and conversely the ordering of ethnographic evidence by logical criteria does not prove that these are intrinsic to collective representations. In these regards the comparative study of dual symbolic classification, as expressed especially through the values of lateral symbolism, constitutes a paradigm of the difficulties that must beset any attempt to arrive empirically at a theory of thought and action.[63] It might be said, for that matter, that the materials in the present volume set up a test case of the very feasibility of social anthropology as a theoretical discipline.

VI

The textual editing of this volume has consisted mainly in the collection and arrangement of the papers. On only one point has any attempt been made to influence their presentation. In their original versions the essays featured binary tables in which the disposition of comparable terms varied from one paper to another: in some the "right" (or positive, etc.) column appeared on the right side of the page, towards the end of the line, and in others it appeared on the left side. It was thought desirable to make the form of the tables consistent throughout, and in accordance with heraldic and iconographic practice it was proposed that the column containing the term "right" should be placed on the proper right of the page (i.e., on the left as one looks at it). By this means the scheme of classification would be presented as though it were a blazon or a work of religious art, turned towards the reader, and exhibiting by the very disposition of its categories the oppositional mode of evaluation that it was intended to depict. The tables have where necessary been adapted to this convention.

Profound thanks are due to Sir Edward Evans-Pritchard for the original impulsion to concentrate on the study of right and left, for his encouragement of the present embodiment of that interest, and for his valued cooperation in contributing a foreword.

The frontispiece is reproduced from a photograph of Robert Hertz kindly presented by his friend, the late Sir Alan Gardiner, to Professor Evans-Pritchard and now in the possession of the Institute of Social Anthropology at the University of Oxford.

Notes

1. Marcel Mauss, "In Memoriam: l'oeuvre inédite de Durkheim et de ses collaborateurs," *Année sociologique,* n.s., 1 (1925): 7–29 (see p. 23).

2. Alice Hertz, preface to Robert Hertz, *Mélanges de sociologie et folklore* (Paris: Alcan, 1928), p. xiv.

3. Emile Durkheim, obituary of Robert Hertz, in *L'Annuaire de l'association des anciens élèves de l'école normale supérieure,* 1916: 116–20. (Dr. Steven Lukes kindly provided the reference to this moving but little-known memorial.)

4. Mauss, "In Memoriam," p. 23.

5. E. E. Evans-Pritchard, introduction to Robert Hertz, *Death and the Right Hand* (London: Cohen & West, 1960), p. 24.

6. Alice Hertz, preface, p. x.

7. Mauss, "In Memoriam," p. 24. The introduction to the work that Hertz had undertaken was published by Mauss, under the title "Le Péché et l'expiation dans les sociétés primitives," in the *Revue de l'histoire des religions* 86 (1922): 1–60.

8. Mauss, in R. Hertz, "Le Péché et l'expiation," p. 2.

9. Emile Durkheim, *Les Formes élémentaires de la vie religieuse: le système totémique en Australie* (Paris: Alcan, 1912), p. 17.

10. (Paris: Alcan, 1928), pp. 99–129.

11. *The Elementary Forms of Religious Life: A Study in Religious Sociology* (London: Allen & Unwin, n.d.).

12. It may be recalled also that Granet had early been influenced by the work of Emile Durkheim and Marcel Mauss on the social determination of categories, "De quelques formes primitives de classification," *Année sociologique* 6 (1903): 1–72. See *Primitive Classification,* ed. and trans. Rodney Needham (Chicago: University of Chicago Press, 1963), editor's introduction, p. xxxii. Cf. Granet's assertion below (p. 48): "the macrocosm is explained by the social structure. . . ."

13. *Handedness: Right and Left* (Boston, Mass.: Lothrop, Lee, & Shepard, 1934).

14. Reprinted as chap. 9 in E. E. Evans-Pritchard, *Nuer Religion* (Oxford: Clarendon Press, 1956), pp. 231–47.

15. See Foreword above, p. ix.

16. Robert Hertz, *Death and the Right Hand,* trans. Rodney and Claudia Needham, intro. E. E. Evans-Pritchard (London: Cohen & West, 1960).

17. Dr. Beck's paper on South India (below, chap. 18) was printed in 1970; the substantial added comments, "A Reanalysis," were submitted to the editor in 1971.

18. It is much regretted that Dr. Fox alone, and he in particular (considering his further contribution by way of the translation of Chelhod), should have had to wait since 1968 for the appearance of his paper.

19. It is possible that a colleague in the Bureau of American Ethnology, or some other anthropological acquaintance (such as Alice Fletcher, with whom La Flesche collaborated for over twenty years), knew of Hertz's writings and directed his attention to this aspect of the Indian life to which he himself belonged.

20. *Pseudodoxia Epidemica: or, Enquiries into very many Received Tenets and commonly presumed Truths* (London, 1646), bk. 4, chap. 5.

21. Cf. below, chap. 15, sec. VIII.

22. It is conceivable that the occasion may eventually be made to present a separate study of these matters.

23. Introduction to Hertz, *Death and the Right Hand,* p. 24.

24. This handbook is in fact meant to supply, in a compendious form,

precisely such a corpus of comparative materials as will facilitate theoretical studies.

25. "Aspects of Nyoro Symbolism," *Africa* 38 (1968): 413–42.

26. Chap. 15: "Right and Left in Nyoro Symbolic Classification." Ideally it would be advantageous to read this essay, and then to refer to the criticism, before continuing through the present section of this introduction. The difficulties raised by the critic have a fundamental importance in that they attach methodologically to all of the papers in this collection; and since they can be appreciated only through a command of particular arguments it would be well to have first some acquaintance with the matters specifically brought to issue.

27. There may in some other place be occasion to make a detailed examination of this unusually valuable case.

28. "Aspects," p. 413; cf. p. 439. The author has indeed uncovered one minor error of fact. With due appreciation, this has been acknowledged and corrected below (chap. 15, n. 7).

29. "Aspects," p. 415, n. 1. (Further references, where unambiguously to this paper, will be made simply by page numbers in parentheses.)

30. Rodney Needham, *Belief, Language, and Experience* (Oxford: Basil Blackwell; Chicago: University of Chicago Press, 1972), p. 156.

31. Gregory Bateson, *Naven,* 2d ed. (Stanford: Stanford University Press, 1958), p. 235.

32. "A Question of Preferences: The Iatmul Case," in Rodney Needham, ed., *Rethinking Kinship and Marriage,* A.S.A. Monographs, no. 11 (London: Tavistock Publications, 1971), chap. 5.

33. These examples of lateral symbolism in birth, death, divination, and myth are to be found below, in chap. 15, at the end of sec. III.

34. Cf. Aspects," p. 439: "I have not been concerned to develop an alternative 'scheme' for the analysis of Nyoro ritual and symbolism."

35. Durkheim and Mauss, *Primitive Classification,* editor's introduction, pp. xviii–xix; cf. pp. 48–54. Cf. also the Iatmul example cited above.

36. Chap. 7, sec. V.

37. See below, chap. 15, passim.

38. It must be allowed that this is really rather curious, since the words "inauspicious" and "auspicious" do not appear anywhere in the table either.

39. It may be apposite to suggest that the views of social anthropologists, in the analysis particularly of symbolism, are influenced to a degree by whether they study great civilizations or else comparatively rude and simple cultures in, for instance, "tribal" Africa. No student of Indian or Chinese civilization, at any rate, would be likely to fall into such analytical blunders as have called for attention here.

40. Abel Bergaigne, *Les Dieux souverains de la religion védique* (Paris, 1877), pp. 116, 117.

41. Ananda K. Coomaraswamy, *Spiritual Authority and Temporal Power in the Indian Theory of Government* (New Haven: American Oriental Society, 1942), p. 30.

42. Bergaigne, p. 117.

43. Georges Dumézil, *Mitra-Varuṇa: essai sur deux représentations indo-européennes de la souveraineté,* 2d ed. (Paris: Gallimard, 1948), p. 84; cf. p. 110. (A new and enlarged version of this genial work is to appear, in an English edition translated by Rodney Needham, from the University of Chicago Press.)

44. Coomaraswamy, p. 49.

45. Bergaigne, p. 138.

46. Dumézil, p. 207.

47. First published, incidentally, eight years before "Aspects of Nyoro Symbolism," which actually cites it.

48. Marcel Granet, *La Pensée chinoise* (Paris: Albin Michel, 1950; 1st ed., 1934), pp. 124, 126, 137; cf. p. 143. It may also be remarked, in connection with the issue of "scale" treated above, that Granet goes on to write: "The Chinese are not at all condemned to find order only where bipartition reigns" (p. 147). Cf. Durkheim and Mauss, *Primitive Classification,* pp. xix, 68, 73.

49. Dumézil, p. 210.

50. Cf. A. M. Hocart, *Kings and Councillors: An Essay in the Comparative Anatomy of Human Society,* ed. and intro. Rodney Needham (Chicago and London: University of Chicago Press, 1970), editor's introduction, pp. xlv–xlvi.

51. Modern treatments of this question in the study of symbolism can be traced back to the eighteenth century, and the classical authorities of antiquity are also directly relevant. A proper consideration of the matter calls for a much larger exposition than is feasible here.

52. Dumézil, pp. 94, 206.

53. G. E. R. Lloyd, *Polarity and Analogy: Two Types of Argumentation in Early Greek Thought* (Cambridge: At the University Press, 1966), p. 41.

54. Immanuel Kant, *Prolegomena . . .* (Riga, 1783), sec. 58.

55. "Aspects," p. 422. In this instance, at any rate, our critic is quite correct: the hypothesis is indeed, so far as the published evidence goes, highly dubious. Even more certainly, however, it is a hypothesis that is nowhere advanced in the analysis of which it is purported to form a central part (see below, chap. 15, esp. sec. V).

56. The critical paper in question calls for much further attention, on scholarly, ethnographical, and analytical grounds. The present purpose, however, is not to substantiate an interpretation of Nyoro symbolism but to explicate by contrast certain theoretical premises and points of method. On this score, and in response to another critic of a very similar persuasion, see also Professor Beidelman's observations below (chap. 8, n. 45).

57. Jean-François Revel, *Pourquoi des philosophes* (Paris: Pauvert, 1957), p. 119.

58. M. Màru Mahemba to the editor, 1955.

59. Bernardo Bernardi, "Il Mugwe dei Meru (Kenya): da istituzione sociale a valore culturale," *Africa: Rivista trimestrale di Studi e Documentazione dell' Istituto Italiano per l'Africa* 26 (1971): 427–42 (see p. 432).

60. Thus in chap. 7 below, at the end of sec. III, it is seen as a puzzle that the elders share with the Mugwe the symbolic color black. In an unpublished report, "The Outsider and the Insider in Tigania Meru" (Discussion Paper no. 5, Cultural Division, Institute for Development Studies, University College, Nairobi, May 1970), Dr. Mahner explains that it was the first European district commissioner in Meru who gave black coats to the elders as a sign of distinction (p. 4). It is thus not a traditional feature of Meru life that elders wear black.

61. Bernardi, "Il Mugwe," p. 440. He continues: "Questa integrazione risulta assai bene anche dall' analisi dal Needham." Cf. below, chap. 7, secs. II and VI.

62. Robert Blanché, *Structures intellectuelles: essai sur l'organisation systématique des concepts* (Paris: Vrin, 1966), p. 15.

63. The skeptical comments made in this section should indicate, at any rate, that fundamental issues are at test and that they are not to be decided by any doctrinaire manipulation. It is easy enough to defend the analyses below from certain methodological imputations (sec. IV above), but this should not lead to an undue confidence about the extent to which they can be accepted as correct.

RIGHT & LEFT

The Pre-eminence of the Right Hand: A Study in Religious Polarity

1

Robert Hertz

What resemblance more perfect than that between our two hands! And yet what a striking inequality there is!

To the right hand go honors, flattering designations, prerogatives: it acts, orders, and *takes*. The left hand, on the contrary, is despised and reduced to the role of a humble auxiliary: by itself it can do nothing; it helps, it supports, it *holds*.

The right hand is the symbol and model of all aristocracies, the left hand of all plebeians.

What are the titles of nobility of the right hand? And whence comes the servitude of the left?

I. Organic Asymmetry

Every social hierarchy claims to be founded on the nature of things, *physei, ou nomō:* it thus accords itself eternity, it escapes change and the attacks of innovators. Aristotle justified slavery by the ethnic superiority of the Greeks over barbarians; and today the man who is annoyed by feminist claims alleges that woman is *naturally* inferior. Similarly, according to common opinion, the pre-eminence of the right hand results directly from the organism and owes nothing to convention or to men's changing beliefs. But in spite of appearances the testimony of nature is no more clear or decisive, when it is a question of ascribing attributes to the two hands, than in the conflict of races or the sexes.

It is not that attempts have been lacking to assign an anatomical

---

"La Prééminence de la main droite: étude sur la polarité religieuse," *Revue philosophique* 68 (1909): 553–80. Newly translated by Rodney Needham.

cause to right-handedness. Of all the hypotheses advanced [1] only one seems to have stood up to factual test: that which links the preponderance of the right hand to the greater development in man of the left cerebral hemisphere, which, as we know, innervates the muscles of the opposite side. Just as the center for articulate speech is found in this part of the brain, so the centers which govern voluntary movements are held to be also mainly there. As Broca says, "We are right-handed because we are left-brained." The prerogative of the right hand would then be founded on the asymmetric structure of the nervous centers, of which the cause, whatever it may be, is evidently organic.[2]

It is not to be doubted that a regular connection exists between the predominance of the right hand and the superior development of the left part of the brain. But of these two phenomena which is the cause and which the effect? What is there to prevent us turning Broca's proposition round and saying, "We are left-brained because we are right-handed"? [3] It is a known fact that the exercise of an organ leads to the greater nourishment and consequent growth of that organ. The greater activity of the right hand, which involves more intensive work for the left nervous centers, has the necessary effect of favoring its development.[4] If we abstract the effects produced by exercise and acquired habits, the physiological superiority of the left hemisphere is reduced to so little that it can at the most determine a slight preference in favor of the right side.

The difficulty that is experienced in assigning a certain and adequate organic cause to the asymmetry of the upper limbs, joined to the fact that the animals most closely related to man are ambidextrous,[5] has led some authors to deny any anatomical basis for the privilege of the right hand. This privilege would not then be inherent in the structure of *genus homo* but would owe its origin exclusively to conditions external to the organism.[6]

This radical denial is at least bold. The organic cause of right-handedness is dubious and insufficient, and difficult to distinguish from influences which act on the individual from outside and shape him; but this is no reason for dogmatically denying the action of the physical factor. Moreover, in some cases, where external influence and organic tendency are in conflict, it is possible to affirm that the unequal skill of the hands is connected with an anatomical cause. In spite of the forcible and sometimes cruel pressure which society exerts from their childhood on people who are left-handed, they retain all their lives an instinctive preference for the use of the left hand.[7] If we are forced to recognize here the presence of a congenital disposition to asymmetry we must admit that, inversely, for a certain number of people, the preponderant use of the right hand results from a bodily disposition. The most probable view may be expressed, though not very rigorously, in mathematical form: in a hundred individuals there are about two who are naturally left-handed, resistent to any contrary influence; a considerably larger proportion are right-handed by heredity; while between these two extremes oscillate the mass of people, who if left to themselves would be able to use either hand equally, with (in general) a slight preference in favor of the right.[8] There is thus no need to deny the existence of organic tendencies towards asymmetry; but apart from some exceptional cases the vague disposition to right-handedness, which seems to be spread throughout the human species, would not be enough to bring about the absolute preponderance of the right hand if this were not reinforced and fixed by influences extraneous to the organism.

But even if it were established that the right hand surpassed the left, by a gift of nature, in tactile sensibility, strength, and aptitude, there would still remain to be explained why a humanly instituted privilege should be added to this natural superiority, why only the better-endowed hand is exercised and trained. Would not reason advise the attempt to correct by education the weakness of the less favored member? Quite on the contrary, the left hand is repressed and kept inactive, its development methodically thwarted. Dr. Jacobs tells us that in the course of his tours of medical inspection in the Netherlands Indies he often observed that native children had the left arm completely bound: it was to teach them *not to use it*.[9] We have abolished the material bonds—but that is all. One of the signs which distinguish a well-brought-up child is that its left hand has become incapable of any independent action.

Can it be said that any effort to develop the aptitude of the left hand is doomed to failure in advance? Experience shows the contrary. In the rare cases in which the left hand is properly exercised and trained, because of technical necessity, it is just about as useful as the right; for example, in playing the piano or violin, or in surgery. If an accident deprives a man of his right hand, the left acquires after some time the strength and skill that it lacked. The example of people who are left-handed is even more conclusive, since this time education struggles against the instinctive tendency to "unidexterity" instead of following and exaggerating it. The consequence is that left-handers are generally ambidextrous and are often noted for their skill.[10] This result would be attained, with even greater reason, by the majority of people, who have no irresistible preference for one side or the other and whose left hand asks only to be used. The methods of bimanual education, which have been applied for some years, particularly in English and American schools, have already shown conclusive results:[11] there is nothing against the left hand receiving an artistic and technical training similar to that which has up to now been the monopoly of the right.

So it is not because the left hand is weak and powerless that it is neglected: the contrary is true. This hand is subjected to a veritable mutilation, which is none the less marked because it affects the function and not the outer form of the organ, because it is physiological and not anatomical. The feelings of a left-hander in a backward society[12] are analogous to those of an uncircumcised man in countries where circumcision is law. The fact is that right-handedness is not simply accepted, submitted to, like a natural necessity: it is an ideal to which everybody must conform and which society forces us to respect by positive sanctions. The child which actively uses its left hand is reprimanded, when it is not slapped on the over-bold hand; similarly the fact of being left-handed is an offense which draws ridicule on the offender and a more or less explicit social reproof.

Organic asymmetry in man is at once a fact and an ideal. Anatomy accounts for the fact to the extent that it results from the structure of the organism; but however strong a determinant one may suppose it to be, it is incapable of explaining the origin of the ideal or the reason for its existence.

II. Religious Polarity

The preponderance of the right hand is obligatory, imposed by coercion, and guaranteed by sanctions; contrarily, a veritable prohibition weighs on the left hand and paralyzes it. The difference in value and function between the two sides of our body possesses therefore in an extreme degree the characteristics of a social institution; and a study which tries to account for it belongs to sociology. More precisely, it is a matter of tracing the genesis of an imperative which is half aesthetic, half moral. Now the secularized ideas which still dominate our conduct were born in a mystical form, in the realm of religious beliefs and emotions. We have therefore to seek the explanation of the preference for the right hand in a comparative study of collective representations.[13]

One fundamental opposition dominates the spiritual world of primitive men—that between the sacred and the profane.[14] Certain beings or objects, by virtue of their nature or by the performance of rites, are as it were impregnated with a special essence which consecrates them, sets them apart, and bestows extraordinary powers on them, but which then subjects them to a set of rules and narrow restrictions. Things and persons which are denied this mystical quality have no power, no dignity: they are common and, except for the absolute interdiction on coming into contact with what is sacred, free. Any contact or confusion of beings and things belonging to the opposed classes would be baneful to both. Hence the multitude of prohibitions and taboos which, by keeping them separate, protect both worlds at once.

The significance of the antithesis between profane and sacred varies according to the position in the religious sphere of the mind which classifies beings and evaluates them. Supernatural powers are not all of the same order: some work in harmony with the nature of things, and inspire veneration and confidence by their regularity and majesty; others, on the contrary, violate and disturb the order of the universe, and the respect they impose is founded chiefly on aversion and fear. All these powers have in common the character of being opposed to the profane, to which they are all equally dangerous and forbidden. Contact with a corpse produces in a profane being the same effects as sacrilege. In this sense Robertson Smith was right when he said that the notion of *taboo* comprises simultaneously the sacred and the impure, the divine and the demoniac. But the perspective of a religious world changes when it is regarded no longer from the point of view of the profane but from that of the sacred. Thenceforth, the confusion that Robertson Smith referred to no longer exists: a Polynesian chief, for example, knows very well that the religious quality which imbues a corpse is radically contrary to that which he himself possesses. The impure is separated from the sacred and is placed at the opposite pole of the religious universe. On the other hand, from this point of view the profane is no longer defined by purely negative features: it appears as the antagonistic element which by its very contact degrades, diminishes, and changes the essence of things that are sacred. It is a nothingness, as it were, but an active and contagious nothingness; the harmful influence that it exerts on things endowed with sanctity does not differ in intensity from that of baneful powers. There is an imperceptible transition between the lack of sacred powers and the possession of sinister powers.[15] Thus in the classification which has dominated religious consciousness from the beginning and in increasing measure there is a natural affinity and almost an equivalence between the profane and the impure. The two notions are combined and, in opposition to the sacred, form the negative pole of the spiritual universe.

Dualism, which is essential to the thought of primitives, dominates their social organization.[16] The two moieties or phratries which constitute the tribe are reciprocally opposed as sacred and profane. Everything that exists within my own phratry is sacred and forbidden to me; this is why I cannot eat my totem, or spill the blood of a member of my phratry, or even touch his corpse, or marry in my clan. Contrarily, the opposite moiety is profane to me; the clans which compose it supply me with provisions, wives, and human sacrificial victims, bury my dead, and prepare my sacred ceremonies.[17] Given the religious character with which a primitive community feels itself invested, the existence of an opposed and complementary segment of the same tribe, which can freely carry out functions which are forbidden to members of the former group, is a necessary condition of social life.[18] The evolution of society replaces this reversible dualism with a rigid hierarchical structure: [19] instead of separate and equivalent clans there appear classes or castes, of which one, at the summit, is essentially sacred, noble, and devoted to superior works, while another, at the bottom, is profane or unclean and engaged in base tasks. The principle by which men are assigned rank and function remains the same: social polarity is still a reflection and a consequence of religious polarity.

The whole universe is divided into two spheres: things, beings, and powers attract or repel each other, implicate or exclude each other, according to whether they gravitate towards the one or the other of the two poles.

Powers which maintain and increase life, which give health, social pre-eminence, courage in war, and skill in work, all reside in the sacred principle. Contrarily, the profane (in so far as it infringes on the sacred sphere) and the impure are essentially weakening and deadly; the baleful influences which oppress, diminish, and harm individuals come from this side. So on one side there is the pole of strength, good, and life; while on the other there is the pole of weakness, evil, and death. Or, if a more recent terminology is preferred, on one side gods, on the other, demons.

All the oppositions presented by nature exhibit this fundamental dualism. Light and dark, day and night, east and south in opposition to west and north, represent in imagery and localize in space the two contrary classes of supernatural powers: on one side life shines forth and rises, on the other it descends and is extinguished. There is the same contrast between high and low, sky and earth: on high, the sacred residence of the gods and the stars which know no death; here below, the profane region of mortals whom the earth engulfs; and, lower still, the dark places where lurk serpents and the host of demons.[20]

Primitive thought attributes a sex to all beings in the universe and even to inanimate objects; all of them are divided into two immense classes according to whether they are considered as male or as female. Among the Maori the expression *tama tane,* "male side," designates the most diverse things: men's virility, descent in the paternal line, the east, creative force, offensive magic, and so on; while the expression *tama wahine,* "female side," covers everything that is contrary of these.[21] This cosmic distinction rests on a primordial religious antithesis. In general, man is sacred, woman is profane; excluded from religious ceremonies, she is admitted to them only for a function characteristic of her status, when a taboo is to be lifted, i.e., to bring about an intended profanation.[22] But if woman is powerless and passive in the religious order, she has her revenge in the domain of magic: she is particularly fitted for works of sorcery. "All evils, misery, and death," says a Maori proverb, "come from the female element." Thus the two sexes correspond to the sacred and to the profane (or impure), to life and to death. An abyss separates them, and a rigorous division of labor apportions activities between men and women in such a way that there can never be mixing or confusion.[23]

If dualism marks the entire thought of primitive men, it influences no less their religious activity, their worship. This influence is nowhere more manifest than in the *tira* ceremony, which occurs very often in Maori ritual and serves the most diverse ends. The priest makes two small mounds on a sacred plot of ground, of which one, the male, is dedicated to the Sky, and the other, the female, to the Earth. On each of them he erects a stick: one, called the "wand of life" and which is placed to the east, is the emblem and focus of health, strength, and life; the other, which is placed to the west, is the "wand of death" and is the emblem and focus of all evil. The detail of the rites varies according to the end sought, but the fundamental theme is always the same: on the one hand, to repel towards the pole of mortality all impurities and evils which have penetrated the community and which threaten it; on the other, to secure, strengthen, and attract to the tribe the beneficent influences which reside at the pole of life. At the end of the ceremony the priest knocks down the wand of Earth, leaving the wand of Sky standing: this is the sought-after triumph of life over death, the expulsion and abolition of evil, the well-being of the community and the ruin of its enemies.[24] Thus ritual activity is directed by reference to two opposite poles, each of which has its essential function in the cult, and which correspond to the two contrary and complementary attitudes of religious life.

How could man's body, the microcosm, escape the law of polarity which governs everything? Society and the whole universe have a side which is sacred, noble, and precious, and another which is profane and common; a male side, strong and active, and another, female, weak and passive; or, in two words, a right side and a left side—and yet should the human organism alone be symmetrical? A moment's reflection shows us that this is an impossibility. Such an exception would not only be an inexplicable anomaly, it would ruin the entire economy of the spiritual world. For man is at the center of creation: it is for him to manipulate and direct for the better the redoubtable forces which bring life and death. Is it conceivable that all these things and these powers, which are separated and contrasted and are mutually exclusive, should be confounded abominably in the hand of the priest or the artisan? It is a vital necessity that neither of the two hands shall know what the other doeth:[25] the evangelical precept merely applies to a particular situation this law of the incompatibility of opposites, which is valid for the whole world of religion.[26]

If organic asymmetry had not existed, it would have had to be invented.

III. The Characteristics of Right and Left

The different way in which the collective consciousness envisages and values the right and the left appears clearly in language. There is a striking contrast in the words which in most Indo-European languages designate the two sides.

While there is a single term for "right" which extends over a very wide area and shows great stability,[27] the idea of "left" is expressed by a number of distinct terms, which are less widely spread and seem destined constantly to disappear in the face of new words.[28] Some of these words are obvious euphemisms,[29] others are of extremely obscure origin. "It seems," says Meillet,[30] "that when speaking of the left side one avoided pronouncing the proper word and tended to replace it by different ones which were constantly renewed." The multiplicity and instability of terms for the left, and their evasive and arbitrary character, may be explained by the sentiments of disquiet and aversion felt by the community with respect to the left side.[31] Since the thing itself could not be changed, the name for it was, in the hope of abolishing or reducing the evil. But in vain; for even words with happy meanings, when applied by antiphrasis to the left, are quickly contaminated by what they express and acquire a "sinister" quality which soon forbids their use. Thus the opposition which exists between right and left is displayed even in the different natures and destinies of their names.

The same contrast appears if we consider the meaning of the words "right" and "left." The former is used to express ideas of physical strength and "dexterity," of intellectual "rectitude" and good judgment, of "uprightness" and moral integrity, of good fortune and beauty, of juridical norm; while the word "left" evokes most of the ideas contrary to these. To unite these many meanings, it is ordinarily supposed that the word "right" meant first of all our better hand, then "the qualities of strength and skill which are natural to it," and by extension diverse analogous virtues of the mind and heart.[32] But this is an arbitrary construction. There is nothing to authorize the statement that the ancient Indo-European word for the right first had an exclusively physical connotation; and more recently formed words such as our *droit*[33] and the Armenian *adj*,[34] before being applied to one of the sides of the body, expressed the idea of a force which goes straight to its object, by ways which are normal and certain, in opposition to ways which are tortuous, oblique, and abortive. It is true that the different meanings of the word in our languages, which are the products of an advanced civilization, are distinct and juxtaposed; but if we trace them back by the comparative method to the source from which these fragmentary meanings derive, we find them originally fused together in one notion which encompasses and confounds them all. We have already met this notion: for the right, it is the idea of sacred power, regular and beneficent, the principle of all effective activity, the source of everything that is good, auspicious, and legitimate; for the left, the ambiguous conception of the profane and the impure, something feeble and incapable which is also maleficent and dreaded. Here, physical strength (or weakness) is only a particular and derivative aspect of a much vaguer and more fundamental quality.

Among the Maori the right is the sacred side, the seat of good and creative powers; the left is the profane side, possessing no virtue other than, as we shall see, certain disturbing and suspect powers.[35] The same contrast reappears in the course of the evolution of religion, in more precise and less impersonal forms: the right is the side of the gods, where hovers the white figure of a good guardian angel; the left side is dedicated to demons, or to the devil, and a black and wicked angel holds it in dominion.[36] Even today, if the right hand is still called good and beautiful, and the left bad and ugly,[37] we can discern in these childish expressions the weakened echoes of designations and religious emotions which for many centuries have been attached to the two sides of our body.

It is a notion current among the Maori that the right is the "side of life" (and of strength) while the left is the "side of death" (and of weakness).[38] Fortunate and life-giving influences enter us from the right and through our right side; and, inversely, death and misery penetrate to the core of our being from the left.[39] So the resistance of the side which is particularly exposed and defenseless has to be strengthened by protective amulets; the ring that we wear on the third finger of the left hand is intended primarily to keep temptations and other bad things from us.[40] Hence the great importance in divination of distinguishing the sides, both of the body and in space. If I have felt a convulsive tremor while sleeping it is a sign that a spirit has seized me, and according to whether the sign was on the right or on the left I can expect good fortune and life or ill-fortune and death.[41] The same rule holds in general for omens which consist in the appearance of animals thought to be bearers of fate; sometimes these messages are susceptible of two contradictory interpretations, according to whether the situation is seen from the point of view of the person who sees the animal or of the animal which he encounters;[42] if it appears on the left it presents its right side, therefore it can be considered favorable. But these divergences, carefully sustained by the augurs for the confusion of the common people and the increase of their own prestige, only show in a still clearer light the affinity that exists between the right and life, and between the left and death.

A no less significant concordance links the sides of the body to regions in space. The right represents what is high, the upper world, and the sky; while the left is connected with the underworld and the earth.[43] It is not by chance that in pictures of the Last Judgment it is the Lord's raised right hand that indicates to the elect their sublime abode, while his lowered left hand shows the damned the gaping jaws of Hell ready to swallow them. The relation uniting the right to the east or south and the left to the north or west is even more direct and constant, to the extent that in many languages the same words denote the sides of the body and the cardinal points.[44] The axis which divides the world into two halves, the one radiant and the other dark, also cuts through the human body and divides it between the empire of light and that of darkness.[45] Right and left transcend the limits of our body to embrace the universe.

According to a very widespread idea, at least in the Indo-European area, the community forms a closed circle at the center of which is the altar, the Ark of the Covenant, where the gods descend and from which place divine aid radiates. Within the enclosure reign order and harmony, while outside it extends a vast night, limitless and lawless, full of impure germs and traversed by chaotic forces. On the periphery of the sacred space the worshippers make a ritual circuit round the divine center, their right shoulders turned towards it.[46] They have everything to hope for from one side, everything to fear from the other. The right is the *inside,* the finite, assured well-being, and certain peace; the left is the *outside,* the infinite, hostile, and the perpetual menace of evil.

The above equivalents would in themselves allow us to presume that the right side and the male element are of the same nature, and likewise the left side and the female element; but we are not reduced to simple conjecture on this point. The Maori apply the terms *tama tane* and *tama wahine* to the two sides of the body, terms whose almost universal extension we have already noted: man is compounded of two natures, masculine and feminine; the former is attributed to the right side, the latter to the left.[47] Among the Wulwanga tribe of Australia two sticks are used to mark the beat during ceremonies: one is called the man and is held in the right hand, while the other, the woman, is held in the left. Naturally, it is always the "man" which strikes and the "woman" which receives the blows; the right which acts, the left which submits.[48] Here we find intimately combined the privilege of the strong sex and that of the strong side. Undoubtedly God took one of Adam's left ribs to create Eve, for one and the same essence characterizes woman and the left side of the body—two parts of a weak and defenseless being, somewhat ambiguous and disquieting, destined by nature to a passive and receptive role and to a subordinate condition.[49]

Thus the opposition of right and left has the same meaning and application as the series of contrasts, very different but reducible to common principles, presented by the universe. Sacred power, source of life, truth, beauty, virtue, the rising sun, the male sex, and—I can add—the right side: all these terms are interchangeable, as are their contraries; they designate under many aspects a single category of things, a common nature, the same orientation towards one of the two poles of the mystical world.[50] Is it believable that a slight difference of degree in the physical strength of the two hands should be enough to account for such a trenchant and profound heterogeneity?

IV. The Functions of the Two Hands

The different characteristics of the right and the left determine the difference in rank and functions which exists between the two hands.

It is well known that many primitive peoples, particularly the Indians of North America, can converse without saying a word, simply by movements of the head and arms. In this language each hand acts in accordance with its nature. The right hand stands for *me,* the left for *not-me, others.*[51] To express the idea of *high* the right hand is raised above the left, which is held horizontal and motionless; while the idea of *low* is expressed by lowering the "inferior hand" below the right.[52] The raised right hand signifies *bravery, power,* and *virility*; while on the contrary the same hand, carried to the left and placed below the left hand, signifies, according to context, the ideas of *death, destruction,* and *burial.*[53] These characteristic examples are enough to show that the contrast between right and left, and the relative positions of the hands, are of fundamental importance in "sign-language."

The hands are used only incidentally for the expression of ideas; they are primarily instruments with which man acts on the beings and things that surround him. It is in the diverse fields of human activity that we must observe the hands at work.

In religious ceremonies man seeks above all to communicate with sacred powers, in order to maintain and increase them, and to draw to himself the benefits of their action. Only the right hand is fit for these beneficial relations, since it participates in the nature of things and beings on which the rites are to act. The gods are on our right, so we turn towards the right to pray.[54] A holy place must be entered right foot first.[55] Sacred offerings are presented to the gods with the right hand.[56] It is the right hand that receives favors from heaven and which transmits them in benediction.[57] To bring about good effects in a ceremony, to bless or to consecrate, the Hindus and the Celts go three times round a person or an object, from left to right, like the sun, with the right side turned inwards. In this way they pour upon whatever is enclosed within the sacred circle the holy and beneficent virtue which emanates from the right side. The contrary movement and attitude, in similar circumstances, would be sacrilegious and unlucky.[58]

But worship does not consist entirely in the trusting adoration of amical gods. Man would willingly forget the sinister powers which swarm at his left, but he cannot; for they impose themselves on his attention by their murderous blows, by threats which must be eluded, and by demands which must be satisfied. A considerable part of a religious cult, and not the least important part, is devoted to containing or appeasing spiteful or angry supernatural beings, to banishing and destroying bad influences. In this domain it is the left hand that prevails: it is directly concerned with all that is demoniacal.[59] In the Maori ceremony that we described it is the left hand that sets up and then knocks down the wand of death.[60] If greedy spirits or souls of the dead have to be placated by the making of a gift, it is the left hand that is specified for this sinister contact.[61] Sinners are expelled from the church by the left door.[62] In funerary rites and in exorcism the ceremonial circuit is made "in the wrong direction," presenting the left side.[63] Is it not right that the destructive powers of the left side should sometimes be turned against the malicious spirits who themselves generally use them?

Magical practices proliferate on the borders of regular liturgy. The left hand is at home here: it excels at neutralizing or annulling bad fortune,[64] but above all in propagating death.[65] "When you drink with a native [on the Guinea Coast] you must watch his left hand, for the very contact of his left thumb with the drink would suffice to make it fatal." It is said that every native conceals under his left thumbnail a toxic substance that possesses almost "the devastating subtlety of prussic acid."[66] This poison, which is evidently imaginary, symbolizes perfectly the murderous powers that lie in the left side.

It is clear that there is no question here of strength or weakness, of skill or clumsiness, but of different and incompatible functions linked to contrary natures. If the left hand is despised and humiliated in the world of the gods and of the living, it has its domain where it commands and from which the right hand is excluded; but this is a dark and ill-famed region. The power of the left hand is always somewhat occult and illegitimate; it inspires terror and revulsion. Its movements are suspect; we should like it to remain quiet and discreet, hidden if possible in the folds of the garment, so that its corruptive influence will not spread. As people in mourning, whom death has enveloped, have to veil themselves, neglect their bodies, and let their hair and nails grow, so it would be out of place to take too much care of the bad hand: the nails are not cut and it is washed less than the other.[67] Thus the belief in a profound disparity between the two hands sometimes goes so far as to produce a visible bodily asymmetry. Even if it is not betrayed by its appearance, the hand of sorcery is always the cursed hand. A left hand that is too gifted and too agile is the sign of a nature contrary to right order, of a perverse and devilish disposition: every left-handed person is a possible sorcerer, properly to be distrusted.[68] To the contrary, the exclusive preponderance of the right, and a repugnance for requiring anything of the left, are the marks of a soul unusually associated with the divine and immune to what is profane or impure: such are the Christian saints who in their cradle were pious to the extent of refusing the left breast of their mother.[69] This is why social selection favors right-handers and why education is directed to paralyzing the left hand while developing the right.

Life in society involves a large number of practices which,

without being integrally part of religion, are closely connected with it. If it is the right hands that are joined in a marriage, if the right hand takes the oath, concludes contracts, takes possession, and lends assistance, it is because it is in man's right side that lie the powers and authority which give weight to the gestures, the force by which it exercises its hold on things.[70] How could the left hand conclude valid acts since it is deprived of prestige and spiritual power, since it has strength only for destruction and evil? Marriage contracted with the left hand is a clandestine and irregular union from which only bastards can issue. The left is the hand of perjury, treachery, and fraud.[71] As with jural formalities, so also the rules of etiquette derive directly from worship: the gestures with which we adore the gods serve also to express the feelings of respect and affectionate esteem that we have for one another.[72] In greeting and in friendship we offer the best we have, our right.[73] The king bears the emblems of his sovereignty on his right side; he places at his right those whom he judges most worthy to receive, without polluting them, the precious emanations from his right side. It is because the right and the left are really of different value and dignity that it means so much to present the one or the other to our guests, according to their position in the social hierarchy.[74] All these usages, which today seem to be pure conventions, are explained and acquire meaning if they are related to the beliefs which gave birth to them.

Let us descend lower into the profane. Many primitive peoples, when they are in a state of impurity—during mourning, for example—may not use their hands, and in particular they may not use them for eating. They must be fed by others putting the food into their mouths, or they seize the food in their mouths like dogs, since if they touched the food with their polluted hands they would swallow their own death.[75] In this case a sort of mystical infirmity affects both hands and for a time paralyzes them. It is a prohibition of the same order that bears on the left hand, but as it is of the same nature as this hand itself the paralysis is permanent. This is why very commonly only the right hand can be actively used at meals. Among the tribes of the lower Niger it is even forbidden for women to use their left hands when cooking, evidently under pain of being accused of attempted poisoning and sorcery.[76] The left hand, like those pariahs on whom all impure tasks are thrust, may concern itself only with disgusting duties.[77] We are far from the sanctuary here; but the dominion of religious concepts is so powerful that it makes itself felt in the dining room, the kitchen, and even in those places haunted by demons and which we dare not name.

It seems, however, that there is one order of activity at least which escapes mystical influences, viz., the arts and industry: the different roles of right and left in these are held to be connected entirely with physical and utilitarian causes. But such a view fails to recognize the character of techniques in antiquity: these were impregnated with religiosity and dominated by mystery. What more sacred for primitive man than war or the hunt! These entail the possession of special powers and a state of sanctity that is difficult to acquire and still more difficult to preserve. The weapon itself is a sacred thing, endowed with a power which alone makes blows directed at the enemy effective. Unhappy the warrior who profanes his spear or his sword and dissipates its virtue! Is it possible to entrust something so precious to the left hand? This would be monstrous sacrilege, as much as it would be to allow a woman to enter the warriors' camp, i.e., to doom them to defeat and death. It is man's right side that is dedicated to the god of war; it is the *mana* of the right shoulder that guides the spear to its target; it is therefore only the right hand that will carry and wield the weapon.[78] The left hand, however, is not unemployed; it provides for the needs of profane life that even an intense consecration cannot interrupt, and which the right hand, strictly dedicated to war, must ignore.[79] In battle, without actually taking part in the action, it can parry the adversary's blows; its nature fits it for defense; it is the shield hand.

The origin of ideas about right and left has often been sought in the different roles of the two hands in battle, a difference held to result from the structure of the organism or from a sort of instinct.[80] This hypothesis, which is refuted by decisive arguments,[81] takes for the cause what is really the effect. None the less, it is true that the warlike functions of the two hands may sometimes have reinforced the characteristics already attributed to them and the relations of one to the other. Consider an agricultural people who prefer peaceful works to pillage and conquest, and who never have recourse to arms except in self-defense: the "shield hand" will rise in popular estimation, while the "spear hand" will lose something of its prestige. This is notably the case among the Zuni, who personify the left and right sides of the body as two gods who are brothers: the former, the elder, is reflective, wise, and of sound judgment; while the latter is impetuous, impulsive, and made for action.[82] But however interesting this secondary development may be, which considerably modifies the characteristic features of the two sides, it should not make us forget the primary religious significance of the contrast between the right and the left.

What is true of the military art applies also to other techniques; but a valuable account from the Maori enables us to see directly what makes the right hand preponderant in human industry. The account concerns the initiation of a young girl into the craft of weaving, a serious affair wrapped in mystery and full of dangers. The apprentice sits in the presence of the master, who is both artisan and priest, in front of two carved posts which are stuck in the ground and form a sort of rudimentary loom. In the right post lie the sacred virtues which constitute the art of weaving and which make the work effectual; the left post is profane and empty of any power. While the priest recites his incantations the apprentice bites the right post in order to absorb its essence and to consecrate herself to her vocation. Naturally, only the right hand comes into contact with the sacred post, the profanation of which would be fatal to the initiate; and it is the same hand that carries the thread, which is also sacred, from left to right. As for the profane hand, it can cooperate only humbly and at a distance in the solemn work that is done.[83] Presumably this division of labor is relaxed in the case of rougher and more profane pursuits. But none the less it remains the case that, as a rule, techniques consist in setting in motion, by delicate manipulation, dangerous mystical forces: only the sacred and effective hand can take the risk of initiative; the baneful hand, if it actively intervenes, will only dry up the source of success and vitiate the work that is undertaken.[84]

Thus, from one end to the other of the world of humanity, in the sacred places where the worshipper meets his god, in the cursed places where devilish pacts are made, on the throne as well as in the witness-box, on the battlefield and in the peaceful workroom of the weaver, everywhere one unchangeable law governs the functions of the two hands. No more than the profane is allowed to mix with the sacred is the left allowed to trespass on the right. A preponderant activity of the bad hand could only be illegitimate or exceptional; for it would be the end of man and everything else if the profane were ever allowed to prevail over the sacred and death over life. The supremacy of the right hand is at once an effect and a necessary condition of the order which governs and maintains the universe.

V. Conclusion

Analysis of the characteristics of the right and the left, and of the functions attributed to them, has confirmed the thesis of which deduction gave us a glimpse. The obligatory differentiation between the sides of the body is a particular case and a consequence of the dualism which is inherent in primitive thought. But the religious necessities which make the pre-eminence of one of the hands inevitable do not determine which of them will be preferred. How is it that the sacred side should invariably be the right and the profane the left?

According to some authors the differentiation of right and left is completely explained by the rules of religious orientation and sun-worship. The position of man in space is neither indifferent nor arbitrary. In his prayers and ceremonies the worshipper looks naturally to the region where the sun rises, the source of all life. Most sacred buildings, in different religions, are turned towards the east. Given this direction, the parts of the body are assigned accordingly to the cardinal points: west is behind, south to the right, and north to the left. Consequently the characteristics of the heavenly regions are reflected in the human body. The full sunlight of the south shines on our right side, while the sinister shade of the north is projected on to our left. The spectacle of nature, the contrast of daylight and darkness, of heat and cold, are held to have taught man to distinguish and to oppose his right and his left.[85]

This explanation rests on outmoded naturalistic conceptions. The external world, with its light and shade, enriches and gives precision to religious notions which issue from the depths of the collective consciousness; but it does not create them. It would be easy to formulate the same hypothesis in more correct terms and to restrict its application to the point that we are concerned with; but it would still run up against contrary facts of a decisive nature.[86] In fact, there is nothing to allow us to assert that the distinctions applied to space are anterior to those that concern man's body. They all have one and the same origin, the opposition of the sacred and the profane; therefore they are usually concordant and support each other; but they are none the less independent. We are thus forced to seek in the structure of the organism the dividing line which directs the beneficent flow of supernatural favors towards the right side.

This ultimate recourse to anatomy should not be seen as a contradiction or a concession. It is one thing to explain the nature and origin of a force, it is another to determine the point at which it is applied. The slight physiological advantages possessed by the right hand are merely the occasion of a qualitative differentiation the cause of which lies beyond the individual, in the constitution of the collective consciousness. An almost insignificant bodily asymmetry is enough to turn in one direction and the other contrary representations which are already completely formed. Thereafter, thanks to the plasticity of the organism, social constraint [87] adds to the opposed members, and incorporates in them, those qualities of strength and weakness, dexterity and clumsiness [*gaucherie*], which in the adult appear to spring spontaneously from nature.[88]

The exclusive development of the right hand has sometimes been seen as a characteristic attribute of man and a sign of his moral pre-eminence. In a sense this is true. For centuries the systematic paralyzation of the left arm has, like other mutilations, expressed the will animating man to make the sacred predominate over the profane, to sacrifice the desires and the interest of the individual to the demands felt by the collective consciousness, and to spiritualize the body itself by marking upon it the opposition of values and the violent contrasts of the world of morality. It is because man is a double being—*homo duplex*—that he possesses a right and a left that are profoundly differentiated.

This is not the place to seek the cause and the meaning of this polarity which dominates religious life and is imposed on the body itself. This is one of the most profound questions which comparative religion and sociology in general have to solve; we ought not to tackle it indirectly. Perhaps we have been able to bring certain novel elements into this research; in any case, it is not without interest to see a particular problem reduced to another that is much more general.

As philosophers have often remarked,[89] the distinction between right and left is one of the essential articles of our intellectual equipment. It seems impossible, then, to explain the meaning and genesis of this distinction without taking the part, at least implicitly, of one or the other traditional doctrine concerning the origin of knowledge.

What disputes there were formerly between the partisans of innate distinction and those of experience! And what a fine clash of dialectical arguments! The application to human problems of an experimental and sociological method puts an end to this conflict of dogmatic and contradictory assertions. Those who believe in the innate capacity to differentiate have won their victory: the intellectual and moral representations of right and left are true categories, anterior to all individual experience, since they are linked to the very structure of social thought. But the empiricists were right too, for there is no question here of immutable instincts or of absolute metaphysical data. These categories are transcendent only in relation to the individual; replaced in their original setting, namely, the collective consciousness, they appear as facts of nature, subject to change and dependent on complex conditions.

Even if, as it seems, the different attributes of the two hands, the dexterity of one and the clumsiness of the other, are in great part the work of human will, the dream of a humanity gifted with two "right hands" is not at all chimeric. But from the fact that ambidexterity is possible it does not follow that it is desirable; the social causes which led to the differentiation of the two hands might be permanent. However, the evolution that we are now witnessing hardly justifies such a view. The tendency to level the value of the two hands is not, in our culture, an isolated or abnormal fact. The ancient religious ideas which put unbridgeable distance between things and beings, and which in particular founded the exclusive preponderance of the right hand, are today in full retreat. Neither aesthetics nor morality would suffer from the revolution of supposing that there were weighty physical and technical advantages to mankind in permitting the left hand to reach at least its full development. The distinction of good and evil, which for long was solidary with the antithesis of right and left, will not vanish from our conscience the moment the left hand makes a more effective contribution to human labor and is able, on occasion, to take the place of the right. If the constraint of a mystical ideal has for centuries been able to make man into a unilateral being, physiologically mutilated, a liberated and foresighted society will strive to develop the energies dormant in our left side and in our right cerebral hemisphere, and to assure by an appropriate training a more harmonious development of the organism.

Notes

1. Some of which are set out and discussed in Wilson 1891: 149; Jacobs 1892: 22; and Jackson 1905: 41.

2. See Wilson 1891: 183; Baldwin 1897: 67; and van Biervliet 1899: 276.

3. Jacobs 1892: 25.

4. Bastian and Brown-Sequard, in Wilson 1891: 193–94.

5. Rollet 1889: 198; Jackson 1905: 27, 71.

6. Jacobs 1892: 30, 33.

7. Wilson 1891: 140, 142.

8. Wilson 1891: 127–28; Jackson 1905: 52, 97. The latter author estimates those who are naturally right-handed at 17 percent; but he does not explain how this figure is arrived at. Van Biervliet (1899: 142, 373) does not admit "the existence of truly ambidextrous persons"; according to him, 98 percent of people are right-handed. But these reckonings apply only to adults; and he assigns a far too narrow meaning to the word "ambidexterity." What matters here is not so much the dimensions of the bones or the strength of the muscles as the possible use of one or the other member.

9. Jacobs 1892: 33.

10. Wilson 1891: 139, 148–49, 203. A left-handed person benefits from the inborn dexterity of the left hand and the skill acquired by the right.

11. See Jackson 1905: 195; Lydon 1900; Buyse 1908: 145. An "Ambidextral Culture Society" has existed in England for some years.

12. Cf. (on peasants in Lombardy and Tuscany) Lombroso 1903: 444. Lombroso believes himself to have justified scientifically the old prejudice against left-handed people.

13. Most of the ethnographic facts on which this study is based come from the Maori, or more exactly from the very primitive Tuhoe tribe, whose conceptions have been recorded with admirable fidelity by Elsdon Best in his articles in the *Transactions of the New Zealand Institute* and the *Journal of the Polynesian Society*.

14. Our account of religious polarity is intended to be no more than a rapid sketch. Most of the ideas expressed here will be familiar to the reader who knows the works published by Durkheim, Hubert, and Mauss in the *Année Sociologique*. As for certain novel views which this account may obtain, these will be taken up again elsewhere, with the necessary elaboration and proofs.

15. Some examples of this necessary confusion will be given below. See what is said later about the inferior class, earth, woman, and the left side.

16. On social dichotomy, see McGee 1900: 845, 863; Durkheim & Mauss 1903: 7.

17. On this last point, see chiefly Spencer & Gillen 1904: 298.

18. Note that the two moieties of the tribe are often localized, one occupying the right and the other the left (in camp, during ceremonies, etc.). Cf. Durkheim & Mauss 1903: 52; Spencer & Gillen 1904: 28, 577.

19. The outline of which exists from a primitive stage: women and children, in relation to men, form an essentially profane class.

20. On the identification of the sky with the sacred element and the

earth with the profane or sinister, cf. (for the Maori) Tregear 1904: 408, 466, 486; Best 1905a: 150, 188; 1906: 155. Compare the Greek opposition of celestial to chthonian divinities.

21. See especially Best 1905b: 206 and 1901: 73.

22. Best 1906: 26.

23. See, on the Maori, Colenso 1868: 348, and cf. Durkheim 1898: 40; Crawley 1902.

24. Best 1901: 87; 1906: 161–62; Tregear 1904: 330, 392, 515. Cf. Best 1898a: 241.

25. Matt. 6: 3. For the reciprocal interdiction, cf. Burckhardt 1830: 282.

26. McGee has described the dualistic structure of primitive thought from a point of view and in terms rather different from mine. He considers the distinction between right and left as an addition to a primitive system recognizing only the opposition between before and behind. This assertion seems arbitrary to me. Cf. McGee 1900: 843.

27. This is the root **deks-* which is met with in different forms from the Indo-Iranian *dákšina* to the Celtic *dess,* passing through Lithuanian, Slavonic, Albanian, Germanic, and Greek. Cf. Walde 1905–6 s.v. *dexter.*

28. Concerning these terms (Skr. *savyáh,* Gr. *laios,* Gr. *skaios,* etc.) cf. Schrader 1901 s.v. *Rechts und Links;* Brugmann 1888: 399.

29. Gr. *euònumos* and *aristeros,* Zend *vairyāstara* (= better), OHG *winistar* (from *wini,* friend), Arabic *aisar* (= happy, cf. Wellhausen 1897, 2: 199), to which should be added, according to Brugmann, the Latin *sinister.* According to Grimm 1818, 2: 681, 689 and more recently Brugmann 1888: 399 the left was originally the favorable side for the Indo-Europeans; these philologists have been deceived by linguistic artifices intended to conceal the true nature of the left. It is certainly a question of antiphrasis.

30. In a letter which he has been so kind as to send me, and for which I express my thanks, Meillet had already suggested this explanation (1906: 18).

31. Similarly, and for the same reason, "the names of illnesses and infirmities such as lameness, blindness, and deafness differ from one language to another" (Meillet 1906: 18).

32. Cf. for example Pictet 1863: 209.

33. From the low Latin *directum;* cf. Diez 1878, 5: 272 s.v. *ritto.*

34. Connected with the Skr. *sādhyá,* according to Lidén 1906: 75. Meillet, to whom I owe this note, considers the etymology to be irreproachable and very probable.

35. Best 1902: 25; 1904: 236.

36. Meyer 1873: 26. Cf. Gerhard 1847: 54; Pott 1847: 260. Among the Greeks and Romans the right is frequently invoked in formulas of obsecration; cf. Horace *Ep.* 1. 7. 94—*quod te per genium dextramque deosque penates obsecro et obtestor:* see Sittl 1890: 29, n. 5.

37. Cf. Grimm 1818: 685.

38. Best 1898a: 123, 133.

39. Darmesteter 1879, 2: 129 n. 64.

40. The custom goes back to very ancient times (Egyptian, Greek, Roman). The metal (originally iron, later gold) is endowed with a beneficial

virtue which protects from witchcraft: characters engraved on the ring add to its power. The names given to the third finger of the left hand prove its magical character and function: it is the finger "without a name," "the doctor," and in Welsh "the charm finger." See the articles "Anulus" and "Amuletum" in Daremberg & Saglio 1873; Pott 1847: 284, 295; Hofmann 1870: 850. On the word *scaevola* (from *scaevus*, left), meaning a protective charm, see Valeton 1889: 319.

41. Best 1898a: 130; Tregear 1904: 211.

42. Or, what amounts to the same thing, the god who sends the message. This explanation, already proposed by the ancients (Plutarch *Quaestiones Romanae* 78; Festus 17 s.v. *sinistrae aves*), has been definitely proved by Valeton (1889: 287). The same uncertainties are found among the Arabs: cf. Wellhausen 1897: 202 and Doutté 1909: 359.

43. The whirling dervishes keep the right hand raised with the palm upwards, in order to receive from heaven blessings which the left hand, held low towards the earth, transmits to the world below. Simpson 1896: 138. Cf. p. 104.

44. See Gill 1876: 128, 297. The Hebrew *jamîn*, Skr. *dakshina*, Irish *dess* mean both right and south; see Schrader 1901 s.v. *Himmelsgegenden*. For the Greeks the east is the right of the world and the west the left; cf. Stobaeus *Eclogae* 1. 15. 6.

45. This is why the sun is the right eye of Horus and the moon his left. The same in Polynesia (Gill 1876: 153). In Christian representations of the crucifixion the sun shines on the region to the right of the cross, where the new Church triumphs, while the moon illuminates the side of the impenitent thief and the fallen synagogue. See Mâle 1898: 224, 229.

46. See Simpson 1896; and below p. 15.

47. Best 1898a: 123; 1902: 25; Tregear 1904: 506.

48. Eylmann 1909: 376. (I am indebted to M. Mauss for this reference.)

49. A contemporary physician has naïvely formulated the same idea: see Liersch 1893: 46.

50. The table of contraries which, according to the Pythagoreans, balance each other and constitute the universe comprises finite and infinite, odd and even, right and left, male and female, stable and changing, straight *(euthu)* and curved, light and shade, good and evil, high and low; see Aristotle *Metaphysics* 1. 5; and cf. Zeller 1876: 321. The correspondence with the table that I have set out is perfect: the Pythagoreans have simply defined and given shape to extremely ancient popular ideas.

51. Wilson 1891: 18–19.

52. Mallery 1881: 364.

53. Mallery 1881: 414, 416, 420. Cf. Quintilianus 11. 3. 13 in Sittl 1890: 358 (on the gesture expressing abomination).

54. See Schrader 1901 s.v. *Gruss*. Cf. Bokhâri 1903: 153.

55. Bokhâri 1903: 157. Conversely, places haunted by *djinn* are entered left foot first (Lane 1836: 308).

56. When the left hand intervenes it is only to follow and duplicate the action of the right (White 1887: 197). It is still often ill-regarded (Sittl 1890: 51 n. 2, 88; Simpson 1896: 291).

57. See Gen. 48: 13.

58. On *pradakshina* and *deasil,* see Simpson 1896: 75, 90, 183, and especially the monograph by Caland (1898). Traces of this observance are found in the entire Indo-European area.

59. See Plato *Laws* 4. 717a—*tois khthoniois theois . . . aristera nemōn orthotata tou tēs eusebeias skopou tugkhanoi;* cf. Sittl 1890: 188.

60. Gudgeon 1905: 125.

61. Kruyt 1906: 259, 380 n. 1.

62. Martène 1736, 2: 82; cf. *Middoth* in Simpson 1896: 142.

63. Simpson 1896; Caland 1898; Jamieson 1808 s.v. *widdersinnis.* Sorceresses present the left to the devil, to do him homage.

64. Best 1904: 76, 236; 1905: 3; 1901: 98; Goldie 1904: 75.

65. See *Kauśika sūtra* 47. 4 in Caland 1900: 184. Blood extracted from the left side of the body causes death (Best 1897: 41). Contrarily, blood from the right side gives life, regenerates (the wounds of the crucified Christ are always in his right side).

66. Lartigue 1851: 365.

67. Lartigue 1851; Burckhardt 1830: 186; Meyer 1873: 26, 28.

68. This is why beings, real or imaginary, which are believed to possess dreadful magical powers are represented as left-handed: such is the case with the bear among the Kamchadal and the Eskimo (Erman 1873: 36; J. Rae in Wilson 1891: 60).

69. Usener 1896: 190–91. When the Pythagoreans crossed their legs they took care never to place the left on top of the right. Plutarch *De vit. pud.* 8. Cf. Bokhâri 1903: 75.

70. On the Roman *manus,* see Daremberg & Saglio 1873 s.v. *manus;* Sittl 1890: 129, 135. The Romans dedicated the right to good faith; in Arabic the oath is called *jamîn,* the right (Wellhausen 1897: 186).

71. In Persian, to "give the left" means to betray (Pictet 1877, 3: 227). Cf. Plautus *Persa* 2. 2. 44—*furtifica laeva.*

72. See Schrader 1901 s.v. *Gruss;* Caland 1898: 314–15.

73. Cf. Sittl 1890: 27, 31, 310 (*dexiousthai,* dextrae).

74. On the importance of right and left in Christian iconography, see Didron 1843: 186; Mâle 1898: 19.

75. Cf. (for the Maori) Best 1905a: 199, 221.

76. Leonard 1906: 310. Neither may a woman touch her husband with the left hand.

77. On the exclusive use of the left hand for cleansing the apertures of the body "below the navel," see Lartigue 1851; Roth 1899: 122; Spieth 1906, 1: 235; Jacobs 1892: 21 (on the Malays); *Laws of Manu* V, 132, 136; Bikhâri 1903: 69, 71; Lane 1836: 187.

78. Best 1902: 25; Tregear 1904: 332.

79. Tregear 1904.

80. For example, Carlyle, cited by Wilson (1891: 15); similarly, Cushing 1892: 290.

81. An account of these is to be found in Jackson 1905: 51, 54. But the weightiest argument has escaped him. It is extremely probable, as has been shown by Deniker (1900: 316) and Schurtz (1900: 352), that the shield derives from a parrying-stick, the manipulation of which required great

dexterity. Moreover, there are many peoples who do not know the use of the shield; such indeed are the Maori (Smith 1892: 43; Tregear 1904: 316), among whom the distinction between right and left is particularly pronounced.

82. Cushing 1892; 1883: 13. Cf. a curious passage on Hermes the Thrice-Great in Stobaeus *Eclogae* I. 59; and Brinton 1896: 176–77 (on the Chinese).

83. Just as it may not be touched with the left hand, so the sacred post must not be surprised in its upright state by night or by a (profane) stranger. See Best 1898b: 627, 656 and Tregear 1904: 225, who follows him.

84. The thread worn by a Brahman must be plaited from left to right (cf. above, p. 19); plaited the opposite way, it is consecrated to the ancestors and cannot be used by the living (Simpson 1896: 93).

85. See Meyer 1873: 27; Jacobs 1892: 33.

86. (1) The system of orientation postulated by the theory, though very general and probably primitive, is far from being universal; cf. Nissen 1907. (2) The heavenly regions are not characterized uniformly: e.g., for the Hindus and the Romans the north is the *regio fausta* and inhabited by the gods, while the south belongs to the dead. (3) If ideas about the sun played the part attributed to them, the right and the left would be inverted among the peoples of the southern hemisphere; but the Australian and Maori right coincides with ours.

87. This constraint is exercised, not only in education properly speaking, but in games, dances, and work, which among primitive peoples have an intensely collective and rhythmic character (Bücher 1897).

88. It could even be that constraint and social selection should at length have modified the human physical type, if it were proved that the proportion of left-handers is greater among primitives than among civilized peoples; but the evidence on this point is vague and of little weight. Cf. Colenso 1868: 343; Wilson 1891: 66; and, on Stone Age man, Wilson 1891: 31 and Brinton 1896: 175.

89. In particular, Hamelin 1907: 76.

References

Baldwin, James Mark
1897 *Développement mental dans l'enfant et dans la race.* Paris.

Best, Elsdon
1897 Tuhoe land. *Transactions and Proceedings of the New Zealand Institute* 30: 33–41.
1898a Omens and superstitious beliefs of the Maoris. *Journal of the Polynesian Society* 7: 119–36.
1898b The art of the Whare Pora. *Transactions and Proceedings of the New Zealand Institute* 31: 625–58.
1901 Maori magic. *Transactions and Proceedings of the New Zealand Institute* 34: 69–98.
1902 Notes on the art of war as conducted by the Maori of New Zea-

land. *Journal of the Polynesian Society* 11: 11–41, 47–75, 127–62, 219–46.
1904 Notes on the custom of *rahui*. *Journal of the Polynesian Society* 13: 83–88.
1905a Maori eschatology. *Transactions and Proceedings of the New Zealand Institute* 38: 148–239.
1905b The lore of the Whare-Kohanga (Part 1). *Journal of the Polynesian Society* 14: 205–15.
1906 The lore of the Whare-Kohanga. *Journal of the Polynesian Society* 15: 1–26, 147–65, 183–92.

BIERVLIET, J.-J. VAN
1899 L'homme droit et l'homme gauche. *Revue Philosophique* 47: 113–43, 276–96, 371–89.

BOKHÂRI, EL, TRANS. OCTAVE HOUDAS AND W. MARCIAS
1903–8 *Les traditions islamiques*. Paris.

BRINTON, DANIEL G.
1896 Lefthandedness in North American aboriginal art. *American Anthropologist* 9:175–81.

BRUGMANN, KARL
1888 Lateinische Etymologien. *Rheinisches Museum für Philologie* 43:399–404.

BÜCHER, CARL
1897 Arbeit und Rhythmus. *Abhandlungen der Königlich Sächsischen Gesellschaft der Wissenschaften* 39, no. 5. Leipzig.

BURCKHARDT, JOHN LEWIS
1830 *Arabic proverbs*. London.

BUYSE, OMER
1908 *Méthodes américaines d'éducation générale et technique*. Paris.

CALAND, W.
1898 Een Indogermaansch lustratie-gebruik. *Verslagen en Mededeelingen der Koninklijke Akademie van Wetenschappen,* Afd. Letterkunde, 4e reeks, 2:275–325. Amsterdam.
1900 Altindisches Zauberritual. *Verhandelingen der Koninklijke Akademie van Wetenschappen,* Afd. Letterkunde, nieuwe reeks 3, no. 2. Amsterdam.

COLENSO, WILLIAM
1868 On the Maori races of New Zealand. *Transactions and Proceedings of the New Zealand Institute* 1 [separate pagination].

CRAWLEY, ERNEST
1902 *The mystic rose: a study of primitive marriage*. London.

CUSHING, FRANK HAMILTON
1883 Zuñi fetishes. *Annual Reports of the Bureau of Ethnology* 2:1–45.
1892 Manual concepts: a study of the influence of hand-usage on culture-growth. *American Anthropologist* 5:289–317.

DAREMBERG, C. V., and SAGLIO, E.
1873 *Dictionnaire des antiquités grecques et romaines*. Paris.

DARMESTETER, JAMES
1879 *Zend-Avesta*. London.

DENIKER, (J.)
1900 *Races et peuples de la terre.* Paris.
DIDRON, ALPHONSE NAPOLÉON
1843 *Iconographie chrétienne: histoire de dieu.* Paris.
DIEZ, FRIEDRICH CHRISTIAN
1878 *Etymologisches Wörterbuch der romanischen Sprachen.* Bonn.
DOUTTÉ, EDMOND
1909 *La société musulmane du Maghrib: magie et religion dans l'Afrique du nord.* Alger.
DURKHEIM, ÉMILE
1898 La prohibition de l'inceste et ses origins. *Année Sociologique* (Paris). 1 (1896–97):1–70.
DURKHEIM, E. and MAUSS, M.
1903 De quelques formes primitives de la classification. *Année Sociologique* 6 (1901–2):1–72.
ERMAN
1873 [Comment on Meyer 1873.] *Verhandlungen der Berliner Gesellschaft für Anthropologie, Ethnologie und Urgeschichte,* p. 36. Berlin.
EYLMANN, ERHARD
1909 *Die Eingeborenen der Kolonie Süd-Australiens.* Berlin.
GERHARD, EDUARD
1847 *Ueber die Gottheiten der Etrusker.* Berlin.
GILL, WILLIAM WYATT
1876 *Myths and songs from the south Pacific.* London.
GOLDIE, W. H.
1904 Maori medical lore. *Transactions and Proceedings of the New Zealand Institute* 37:1–120.
GRIMM, JACOB LUDWIG CARL
1818 *Geschichte der deutschen Sprache.* 2 vols. Leipzig.
GUDGEON, W. E.
1905 Maori religion. *Journal of the Polynesian Society* 14:107–30.
HAMELIN, O.
1907 *Essai sur les éléments principaux de la représentation.* Paris.
HOFMANN, F.
1870 Ueber den Verlobungs- und den Trauring. *Sitzungsberichte der Kaiserlichen Akademie der Wissenschaften,* Phil.-Hist. Klasse 65:825–63. Vienna.
JACKSON, JOHN
1905 *Ambidexterity: two-handedness and two-brainedness, an argument for natural development and rational education.* London.
JACOBS, JACOB
1892 *Onze rechthandigheid.* Amsterdam.
JAMIESON, JOHN
1808 *Etymological dictionary of the Scottish language.* Edinburgh.
KRUYT, ALB. C.
1906 *Het animisme in den Indischen Archipel.* The Hague.
LANE, EDWARD WILLIAM
1836 *Modern Egyptians.* London.

LARTIGUE
1851 Rapport sur les comptoirs de Grand-Bassam et d'Assinie. *Revue Colonial* 2 ser., 7:329–73.
LEONARD, ARTHUR GLYN
1906 *The lower Niger and its tribes.* London and New York.
LIDÉN, EVALD
1906 Armenische Studien. *Göteborgs Högskolas Arsskrift,* vol. 12.
LIERSCH, L. W.
1893 *Die Linke Hand: eine physiologische und medizinisch-praktische Abhandlung.* Berlin.
LOMBROSO, C.
1903 Lefthandedness. *North American Review* 177:440.
LYDON, F. F.
1900 *Ambidextrous and free-arm blackboard drawing and design.* London.
MCGEE, W. J.
1900 Primitive numbers. *Annual Reports of the Bureau of American Ethnology* 19:821–51.
MÂLE, ÉMILE
1898 *L'art religieux du XIIIe siècle en France.* Paris.
MALLERY, GARRICK
1881 Sign-language among the North-American Indians. *Annual Reports of the Bureau of Ethnology* 1:269–552.
MARTENE, EDMOND
1736–37 *De antiques Ecclesiae ritibus.* 3 vols. Antwerp.
MEILLET, PAUL JULES ANTOINE
1906 *Quelques hypothèses sur des interdictions de vocabulaire dans les langues indo-européennes.* Chartres.
MEYER, VON
1873 Ueber den Ursprung von Rechts und Links. *Verhandlungen der Berliner Gesellschaft für Anthropologie, Ethnologie und Urgeschichte* 5:25–34.
NISSEN, HEINRICH
1906–10 *Orientation: Studien zur Geschichte der Religion.* 3 vols. Berlin.
PICTET, ADOLPHE
1859–63 *Les origines indo-européennes.* 2 vols. Paris.
POTT, AUGUSTUS FRIEDRICH
1847 *Die quinare und vegisimale Zählmethode bei Völkern aller Welttheile.* Halle.
ROLLET, ETIENNE
1889 La taille des grands singes. *Revue Scientifique* 44:196–201.
ROTH, H. LING, ed.
1899 Notes on the Jekris, Sobos and Ijos of the Warri District of the Niger Coast Protectorate. *Journal of the Anthropological Institute* 28:104–26.
SCHRADER, OTTO
1901 *Reallexicon der indogermanischen Alterstumskunde.* Strassburg.
SCHURTZ, HEINRICH
1900 *Urgeschichte der Kultur.* Leipzig and Vienna.

SIMPSON, WILLIAM
1896 *The Buddhist praying-wheel.* London and New York.
SITTL, CARL
1890 *Die Gebärden der Griechen und Römer.* Leipzig.
SMITH, S. PERCY
1892 *Futuna: Horne Island and Its people, Western Pacific. Journal of the Polynesian Society* 1:33–52.
SPENCER, B., AND GILLEN, F. J.
1904 *Northern tribes of central Australia.* London.
SPIETH, JAKOB
1906 *Die Ewe-Stämme.* Berlin.
TREGEAR, EDWARD
1904 *The Maori race.* Wanganui, N.Z.
USENER, HERMANN
1896 *Götternamen.* Bonn.
VALETON
1889 De modis auspicandi Romanorum. *Mnemosyne* 17:275–325.
WALDE, ALOIS
1905–6 *Lateinisches Etymologisches Wörterbuch.* Heidelberg.
WELLHAUSEN, JULIUS
1897 *Reste des arabischen Heidenthums.* Berlin.
WHITE, JOHN
1887–90 *Ancient history of the Maori: his mythology and traditions.* 6 vols. Wellington.
WILSON, DANIEL
1891 *Lefthandedness.* London.
ZELLER, EDUARD
1876 *Die Philosophie der Griechen.* Leipzig.

Right and Left in Osage Ceremonies

2

Francis La Flesche

The habitat of the Wazházhe Indians, better known as the Osage tribe, was in the country now included in the states of Missouri and Kansas. Like many of the tribes which made their homes along the Missouri River, the Osage maintained themselves partly by hunting and partly by cultivating the soil.

The purpose of this paper is to set forth some of the peculiar thoughts of the ancestors of the Osage, when the ancient leaders were organizing the people as a tribe. These thoughts are expressed in the rituals, ceremonial forms, symbols, and myths that have been transmitted orally through a long line of generations.

Early in this formative period the Osage had become imbued with the idea that all forms of life proceeded from the united fructifying powers of two great forces, namely, the sky and the earth, and that the continuity of all forms depended absolutely on the unity of these two. This idea the ancient leaders figuratively expressed in the complex organization of the tribe and in the rites that were formulated as a means by which to perpetuate the tribal life. They divided the groups of families composing the tribe into two great divisions, one to represent the sky and to be known by the name *Tsízhu,* and the other to represent the earth, and to be known by the name *Hónga.* By the interlacing relations between these two great divisions the leaders united the people into one ever-living body.

As the inseparable unity of the sky and the earth made possible the continuity of the life that proceeded from them, so must the

Reprinted from *Holmes Anniversary Volume* (Washington: James William Bryan Press [privately printed], 1916), pp. 278–87.

two great tribal divisions be inseparably united to make possible the continuity of the tribal life. This idea of the bringing together of the two great symbolic divisions of the tribe to form one body was, in its turn, likened to a living man. This symbol was further carried out by the ceremonial positions of the two great divisions in the tribal rites. The left side of this man, who faced the east, is the Tsízhu division, representing the sky, and his right side is the Hónga, representing the earth with its land and water.

In performing the ceremonies connected with the tribal rites, the members of the two divisions sit facing each other in two parallel lines extending east and west; this arrangement is always observed whether the place of meeting be in a wigwam or outdoors. The space between the two parallel lines represents the space between the sky and the earth, through which lies the path traveled by the sun.

This symbolic arrangement of the positions of the two great tribal divisions governs the movements in ceremonies and the places the symbols must occupy—as to whether they belong to the right side or to the left. For example, when a candidate is to be initiated into the mysteries of the tribal rites, two pairs of symbolic moccasins are made, one to be worn by the initiator and the other by his official messenger. While the two great divisions are represented in the use of these two pairs of moccasins, another symbol, denoting the living unity of the tribe, appears in con-

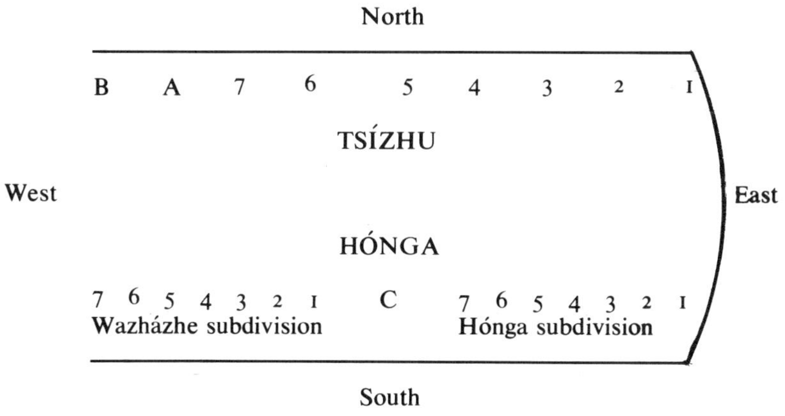

Diagram of the dual division of the Osage

nection with the making of the moccasins, namely, that of a young buffalo bull. The knife employed in cutting the material for the moccasins is spoken of as a "horn" of this symbolic buffalo. If the ceremony is being given by a gens on the Hónga side, the knife is spoken of as the "right horn," and if given by a gens of the Tsízhu side, the knife is spoken of as the "left horn" of the buffalo.

The downy feather, an under-tail covert of the eagle, worn by the initiator in the ceremony, symbolizes one of the sun-pillars, sometimes seen on both sides of the sun as it begins to rise above the horizon. This feather is spoken of as the sun-pillar at the right or the one at the left side of the sun, according to the side of the tribal division to which the initiator and the candidate belong.

CEREMONIAL ORDER OF THE OSAGE GENTES *

HÓNGA

Hónga Subdivision

1. Waçabeton (Black Bear)
   Waçábeçka (White Bear), Shóka (Official messenger)
2. Ingthónga (Puma)
   Hinwáxaga (Porcupine), Shóka (Official messenger)
3. Opxon (Elk)
   Ta He Shabe (Dark-horned Deer), Shóka (Official messenger)
4. Móninkagaxe (Earth Maker)
5. Hónga Gthezhe (Spotted Eagle)
6. Xutha (Golden Eagle)
7. Hónga Zhínga (Little Hónga)
   Íbatse Tadse (The Gathered Winds)

C. Hónga Utanondsi (Isolated Hónga, the Earth)
   Monhinçi (Arrowpoint), Shóka (Official messenger)

Wazházhe Subdivision

1. Wazházhe çka (White Wazházhe, or Real Wazházhe)
   Ingthónga Ni Montse (Puma in the Water), Shóka (Official messenger)
2. Kek'in (Turtle)
   Bak'a Zhoigatha (Cottonwood Tree People), Shóka (Official messenger)
3. Mikethestsedse (Cat-tail)
   Káxe Wahuça (Crow), Shóka (Official messenger)
4. Wátsetsi (The Star that came to the Earth)
   Xuthá Paçon Zhoigatha (Bald Eagle People), Shóka (Official messenger)
5. Oçúgaxe (They Who Make the Path Straight)
   Monshódsemonin (Those Who Walk in a Mist), Shóka (Official messenger)

6. Tatháxi, or Ṫaçindseçka (Deer People).
   Wadsúta zhinga Zhoigatha (Small Animal People), Shóka (Official messenger)
7. Ho Inikashiga (Fish People)
   Enonmindse ton (They Who Alone Own the Bow), Shóka (Official messenger)

Tsízhu

1. Tsízhu Wanon (Elder Tsízhu), also Wakon'da Nonpabi (The God Who is feared by All, the Sun)
   Wabaxi (meaning lost), Shóka (Official messenger)
2. Çindse Agthe (The Wearers of the Wolf Tail on the Scalp-lock)
   Shónge Zhoigatha (Wolf People), Shóka (Official messenger)
3. Péton Tonga Zhoigatha (Great Crane People)
4. Tsedóga Indse (Buffalo Bull Face People), related to the Tsízhu Wanon
   Tseákon (meaning uncertain), Shóka (Official messenger)
5. Mik'ín Wanon (Elder Sun People)
6. Hon Zhoigatha (Night People)
   Tapá Zhoigatha (Deer Head or Pleiades People), Shóka (Official messenger)
7. Tsízhu Uthuhage (Tsízhu Who are the Last in the Order)

Tsi Hashi (Those Who were the Last to Come)

1. Níka Wakondagi (Men of Mystery, or Thunder People)
   Xondse Watse (Cedar Star), Shóka (Official messenger)
2. Thóxe (archaic name for the buffalo bull)

---

*This order of the Osage gentes was given by Shóntonçabe to Miss Alice C. Fletcher in 1896.

At the initiation of a candidate into the mysteries of the tribal rites, the officers and the candidate, in ceremonially approaching their place within the ground marked out for the ceremony, observe certain rules as to the right and left. If the initiator, his assistants, and the candidate belong to the Hónga side, they will go from left to right, around the eastern end of the place to the western end, cross the space and enter on the Hónga or right side. If they belong to the Tsízhu division, they will go around the eastern end of the place, from right to left, to the western end, cross the space and enter on the Tsízhu or left side.

On arriving at their place at the eastern end of the ground, the men sit side by side in the middle, facing the west. They put down on the ground before them a bag of woven buffalo-hair. This bag was made with reference to the position of the two great divisions, for when the bag was being made for one of the gentes of the Hónga division, the hair used is taken from the right shoulder of the buffalo, and when the bag is made for a gens of the Tsízhu, the hair is taken from the left shoulder.

There is also a right and a left end to the buffalo-hair bag, indicated by the mouth and the flap, which must always be placed toward the west, with the flap on the upper side of the bag.

Within the buffalo-hair bag is another bag made of deerskin, which is so placed that its mouth and flap must be in the same position as the outer bag, so that it also may be said to have a right and a left end.

Inside the deerskin bag is a case made of woven rush. This also is placed so that its mouth and flap may be toward the west. This case, however, has other marks to distinguish the right end and the left. The uninitiated would not think to look for these marks, but one who has been properly instructed would examine the fastenings at an end of the case, and, finding there six, would say, "the left end," and on examining the other and finding seven fastenings, he would say, "the right end."

These three envelopes constitute a portable shrine, which they are in reality. Each of the envelopes is called *waxóbe,* a sacred article, because it has been made ceremonially and for the purpose of protecting the sacred bird-hawk which forms the central figure of all the war rituals and ceremonies. The sacred bird-hawk is placed within the case made of woven rush with its head toward the end having the seven fastenings, and its feet toward the end having six. This bird represents life and death—life for the Osage and death for all their enemies. The upper side of this woven rush case represents the sky and the lower side the earth. The inner part of the case, where the bird-hawk lies, represents the space between the sky and the earth, into which all life comes and never departs except by death.

The portable shrine used in the initiatory ceremonies is the property of the gens to which the candidate belongs, and at the close of the ceremony is transferred to the keeping of the initiate, who puts it in a given place in his home. This place has reference to the positions of the two great tribal divisions, so that on entering a house in which there is a portable shrine, if it is seen hanging at the left of the door, as one faces the door from within, it will be known that the master of the house belongs to the Tsízhu division; if the shrine hangs at the right of the door, then it will be known that he belongs to the Hónga division.

So also as to the sacred burden-strap of the mistress of the house, which is regarded by some of the people as even greater in sanctity than the sacred bird-hawk. If the gens in which the mistress of the house was born belongs to the Tsízhu division, her burden-strap hangs at the left of the door. Where master and mistress both belong to the same division, the shrine and the burden-strap will be seen hanging side by side on the same side of the door. Nor is this the only instance in which the positions of right and left are considered with reference to the sacred burden-strap. When the burden-strap is made, the material is taken from the left side of the buffalo skin, if the woman for whom it is intended belongs to the Tsízhu; if she be of the Hónga, it is taken from the right.

In one of the seven degrees of the Osage rites there is a spoken part in the ritual relating to the gourd rattle used for beating time to the music of the songs. There are two versions of this spoken part: in one the gourd rattle symbolizes the head of a man of the enemy; in the other, the head of a puma. The gravels within the gourd that is shaken to make the sound, symbolize the teeth. When a Hónga recites this spoken part, he will say, "The seeds of this rattle [meaning the gravel] are the teeth of the right jaw of the man." If a Tsízhu recites it, he will say, "The seeds of this rattle are the teeth of the left jaw of the man." The handle of the gourd represents the right or left fore-arm of the man, this being determined by the division to which the man reciting the words belongs.

When a man goes through the rite of fasting, he is forbidden to lie down to rest during the seven days' period of fasting. He is, however, permitted to sit down, and when he does so, he must sit facing the south, which is the right side of the division, if he be a Hónga; if he be a Tsízhu he will sit facing the north, which is the left side.

In the ritual of two of the degrees of the Osage tribal rites there is a spoken part that is mythical in character and relates to the limitation in the number of certain prescribed warlike deeds to be performed by a man in order to win rank as a warrior. This story is in two parts and has two animals for its heroes. It should be remembered in this connection that the division on the right side, symbolizing the earth, is divided so as to represent the dry land and the water. One of the animal heroes is the black bear, a land animal; the other is the beaver, a water animal. The subdivision toward the east on the earth side, representing the dry land, retained the name of the whole division, Hónga, and that toward the west, representing water, was given the name Wazházhe.

The story of the black bear, in brief, is as follows: After rushing madly about, when in due season, during the month of September, the hibernating spell seized him, he came to a cave and made his way into the opening, being careful to enter at the right side. He found a comfortable place within and lay down to sleep for seven lunar months. When he awoke, he felt of his body and found that he had lost all his fat, and that his skin hung in wrinkles upon his bones. He dragged himself to the entrance of his cave, taking care to keep to the right side. As he stood in the open air he heard all around him the singing of birds and the humming of insects; he also heard the sighing of the mild winds among the branches of the budding trees and saw the mists of spring floating in the air. When he felt revived by the life-giving air of springtime, he moved forward and took seven steps, making seven footprints in the soft earth. Turning back, he looked thoughtfully at his footprints and then said, "When my children, the Wazházhe and the Tsízhu, go forth against their enemies who dwell toward the setting of the sun, they shall strive to win honors, equal in number to these seven footprints." Then he moved back to the opening of the cave and across to the space on the left side, and strode forward, making six footprints in the soft earth. As before, he turned back and looked at the marks of his feet upon the ground, and said, "When my children, the Wazházhe and the Tsízhu, go forth against their enemies, who dwell toward the setting of the sun, they shall strive to win war-honors, equal in number to these six footprints." (Note the correspondence of these numbers to the fastenings of the ends of the woven rush case—seven on the right end and six on the left.) The bear, revived in strength by the warm, wavering atmosphere of spring, went on. The growing grasses rustled musically at every step he took. At last he came to the banks of a river, where stood the house of the beaver. There his story ends, and that of the beaver begins.

To the middle of the river the beaver swam and made his way up the stream, against the strong current, rippling the surface as he pushed forward. He came to a bend of the river where, on its low banks, a willow sapling stood; this he cut so that it fell toward the setting of the sun, where dwelt the enemies of the Osage. He carried the sapling to his house and laid it at the door, the butt-end resting within the entrance at the right, and then he said: "This act of mine is not without a purpose. My children, the Tsízhu and the Hónga, shall use this sapling to count their war-honors." Again and again he repeated this act, bringing each time a sapling from a bend of the river until he placed seven at the right side of the door of his house. He continued his work in the same manner and brought home six more saplings which he placed at the left side of the door of his house. Thirteen honors in all each warrior of both the right and the left side must risk his life to win in order to count. Seven and six are the numbers fixed by the black bear and the beaver, and these are the sacred numbers.

In the ceremonies of two of the seven degrees of the Osage rites, this story is pictured by the placing of a black-bear skin and a small mound of earth, to represent the beaver's house, in front of the place where the warrior who is to recount his war-honors must sit. The candidate who is being initiated conducts the warrior to this seat and then brings to him the thirteen willow saplings with which he is to count. These saplings are divided into two parts, one containing seven and the other six. In bringing the two bundles of saplings, the candidate grasps in his left hand the bundle containing seven, and in his right that containing six, so that when placing them before the warrior, who sits facing the east, the seven saplings will be at his right and the six at his left. The bunches of saplings are so arranged that the butt-ends of the six rest on the butts of the seven.

In fixing the number of war-honors to be won by the warriors, the sky was not outdone by the earth, for it took from the sun thirteen of its rays—seven from the right side and six from the left—for the use of the warriors in counting their warlike deeds.

It may be well to mention here that on the further division of the two great divisions into smaller groups, the left division was divided into seven sacred fireplaces, each having a separate name representing some object of nature. To the right division fourteen sacred fireplaces were given—seven for the part representing the dry land of the earth, and seven for the part representing the water part of the earth. The twenty-one sacred fireplaces stood for groups of families—divisions in a tribe that are termed gentes or clans by ethnologists.

As has been stated, the Osage of the olden time, when forming their tribal organization, divided the families of the people into two parts to represent the interdependent sky and earth, finally they molded the two parts into an inseparable body and made it to symbolize a man standing in a position facing the sun. They did not leave him there like an immovable statue, but attributed to him a mind capable of thinking and a body having the power of motion, as shown in the movements of the people when performing the great war ceremonies.

In organizing a war-party to include the warriors of both of the two divisions, certain preliminary ceremonies are performed in connection with the selection of the leader, the selection of a man to act as ceremonial director for him, and the appointment of the commanders and other officers of the party. When these ceremonies have been concluded, the people pull down their wigwams and, dividing themselves into two great divisions, reset them in a ceremonial order, that is, in two great squares with a dividing avenue extending east and west. It is at this movement that the change of the position of the symbolic man takes place: instead of facing the east he now faces the west, thus bringing the Tsízhu division, which represents the left half of his body, to the south, and the Hónga division, which represents the right half, to the north side.

After setting up the wigwams in ceremonial order, other ceremonies are performed—the preparation of the sacred charcoal with which the warriors paint themselves when about to make an attack, the making of the feathered crooks for the commanders, and the making of the rawhide straps for tying the captives if any should be taken: seven for the Hónga and seven for the Tsízhu. The straps for the Hónga are made of the skin of the right hind leg of the buffalo, and those for the Tsízhu are made of the skin of the left leg.

On the day the warriors are to depart, they move out of the camp, going westward, and when they have gone about a quarter of a mile they halt for the final ceremonies. The warriors sit in two groups with a space extending east and west between them, the Hónga at the north and the Tsízhu at the south. The old men who are to remain at home form two half-circles around the warriors, those of the Hónga at the north and those of the Tsízhu at the south. When all have settled down, the old men form two processions, each marching around the two groups of warriors, the Hónga going around by the left and the Tsízhu by the right, singing the final songs of the ceremony. When this is done the leader steps forward a few paces, in the line of the space dividing the warriors, and recites three rituals, standing with his face toward the west. He then takes from a pile of grass, placed at his feet by a servant, a handful, and holding it toward the sky, makes a prayer. Four times he does this, at each time laying down a bunch of the grass, so that all four bunches lie in a row along the line of march. This done, the leader returns to his place and the warriors march out, each group in single file, over the four bunches of grass. When a man of the Hónga division arrives at the four bunches of grass he does not forget to put forward his right foot to step upon the first bunch of grass when taking his four sacred footsteps in marching out, and a man of the Tsízhu will remember to put forward his left foot first as he takes his four sacred footsteps.

The teaching of the symbol, expressed in the ceremonial arrangement of the tribe, as that of a man and his going forth, as acted out in the war ceremonies, became so fixed in the minds of those who had been initiated into these rites that they repeated the acts of the "going forth" of the symbolic man when they were about to enter upon the duties of their daily life, as when a man of the Hónga side, on arising in the morning, always puts on his right moccasin first, and a man of the Tsízhu side puts on the left moccasin first, so that his steps might follow those taken by the symbolic leader.

When the men who planned the organization subdivided each of the two great divisions into smaller groups, they declared two of them to be peace-makers, one for the Hónga and one for the Tsízhu. The one for the Hónga was called Pónka Washtage, the Gentle Pónka, and the one for the Tsízhu was called Tsízhu Washtage, the Gentle Tsízhu. From the minds of the people of these two gentes were removed all thoughts of vengeance, bloodshed, and acts of violence.

From among the people of these two groups were chosen two chiefs, one from each group. It was the duty of these two chiefs to maintain peace within the tribe and to sentence to exile any member of the tribe who became unruly and defied authority. It was also their duty to conduct the buffalo hunt, during which one chief issued the orders for the march one day and the other chief those for the next day, and so on through the entire journey, thus making it appear as though the tribe was moving on two legs. The position of each of the two chiefs was hereditary. If a murderer fleeing from vengeance should happen to run into the house of a member of one of these two groups, he would be given protection by all.

When a war-party returned, bringing home a captive, all the members of the tribe who had been initiated into the mysteries of the tribal rites assembled to decide the fate of the captive. The two chiefs were also called to the council. If the warriors, ignoring the presence of the peace-makers, decided to take the life of the captive, these did not interfere; but if the captive were referred to either one of the chiefs, he would say, "Since you have referred the captive to me, I can only say, let him live." No one could then offer harm to the stranger, for to take his life would be murder, and the murderer would have been punished. When the chief thus passed his word, the ceremony of adopting the captive into the tribe proceeded. A member of the Black Bear gens was called on to draw a little of the captive's blood, a symbolic elimination of his natural relation to the tribe in which he was born. Then a member of the Water gens was summoned to give him water to drink, symbolizing the life of the Osage. Corn was also given him to eat, by a member of the Buffalo gens, which also symbolized Osage life. The captive's face was then painted with yellow clay furnished by the Elk gens, after which two narrow black lines, close together, were drawn upon his face, beginning at one corner of his forehead and ending at a point under the ear on the opposite side. The drawing of the two lines on his face meant that from that time he was the official messenger of the two great divisions at the performance of the ceremonies of the tribal war rites, and that he should be accorded the respect due to his position. If his captor were a Hónga, the two lines commenced at the left corner of his forehead and ended below his ear on the right side. If the captor were a Tsízhu, then the two lines began at the right corner of the captive's forehead and ended below his ear on the opposite side of the face.

The decree of the chief that the captive should live, and the performance of the adoption ceremony, not only made him a member of the tribe but of the gens to which his captor belonged, with all the rights and privileges to which a native Osage was entitled; and he became a member of the family of his captor, who treated him as his own son. This addition to the tribal family was purely by ceremonial acts; nevertheless, it was regarded as sacred, as an addition by natural birth, and did not affect the unity that was vital to the tribal organization.

Right and Left in China

3

Marcel Granet

I must begin by offering my excuses to those who may have been misled by the title of my paper and who will be disappointed by it. It is not about right and left in the political senses of these words. I shall not take it upon myself, thankfully, to explain Chinese politics. There is more than enough to do in expounding the mythology of Right and Left in China.

The facts that I shall have to set out are fairly complicated, and I should offer my apologies on this score also. I have chosen this topic partly because Henri Lévy-Bruhl asked me for a paper on it, at rather short order, and partly because it provides an occasion for me to recall the fine work of the late and lamented Robert Hertz on the pre-eminence of the right hand.

In the latter study, Hertz maintained two theses. One, which was concerned with physiology, tried to explain the pre-eminence of the right hand, from a physiological point of view, by reasons of a social kind; the other, which was more general, dealt with the classification of religious facts. Hertz postulated an absolute opposition between left and right analogous to that between pure and impure, an opposition which he considered to be more essential than that between sacred and profane. Left and right are opposed absolutely as that which is *right* to that which is *sinister,* as good is to bad, i.e., in a diametrical opposition. Hertz was therefore led to speak, in this connection, of religious polarity.

"La droite et la gauche en Chine." Communication to the Institut Français de Sociologie, 9 June 1933. Reprinted, by arrangement with the publishers, from Marcel Granet, *Études sociologiques sur la Chine* (Paris: Presses Universitaires de France, 1953), pp. 261–78. Translated by Rodney Needham.

The Chinese facts have no bearing of interest upon the physiological part of Hertz's thesis, and I shall leave this to one side. At most, I might be able to tell you that if the Chinese are right-handed this has to do with the very reason that Hertz gave: the Chinese are *obligatorily* right-handed—at least in certain respects.

But what may give their case a special interest is that *whereas the Chinese are right-handed, the honorable side for them is the left.* Hertz mentioned this difficulty in his work. Without going into this very complicated question, he simply suggested the idea that since China had an agricultural civilization the reason that the Chinese, though right-handed, preferred the left might perhaps be sought in the techniques of agriculture.

In fact, if there are technical reasons for the preference (which is limited in any case) of the Chinese for the left, these reasons might perhaps better be sought, not in the techniques of agriculture but in military techniques.

The point on which the Chinese case presents a particular interest is related to the mythology of right and left: the latter is preferred to the right, but the right is not absolutely inauspicious, nor is the left always auspicious. The diametrical opposition or polarity of which Hertz spoke is not found in China.

The Chinese attribute values to left and right which are unequal, and relative to the circumstances, but are always comparable. There is never question of an absolute pre-eminence, but rather of an alternation. This has to do with a number of characteristics of Chinese civilization and thought. There is nothing abstract in Chinese categories, and it would be vain to look among them for diametrical oppositions such as Being and Non-being. Space and time are conceived as a collection of domains, each with its own conventions; instead of absolute oppositions there are only correlations, so that formal indications or counter-indications are recognized, no absolute obligations, no strict taboos. *Everything is a matter of convention, because everything is a matter of what is fitting.*

The problem of right and left has to do with the very general issue of *Etiquette.* In China, etiquette governs both cosmography and physiology. It expresses the structure of the world—and this is no different from the structure of the individual; the architecture of the universe and that of the individual rest on exactly the same principles. It is therefore the anatomy of the world which will explain the alternate pre-eminence of the right and of the left.

I shall start with the most simple facts. The representations concerning the right and the left are strictly obligatory. They have to do with rites, which means that they are part of a body of rules by which attitudes, gestures, modes of existence, and conduct are imposed upon individuals.

The first of these rules or ritual attitudes favors the right. The right hand is the hand for eating with. Let us note at this point an indication in support of Hertz's thesis: as soon as children are capable of picking up food, they *must* be taught to eat with the right hand. The right is thus educated in a way which is intended to give it a certain preeminence. This education bears in the first place on activities relating to food. The fact that the right hand is the hand for eating with is well confirmed by the name that the Chinese give to the index finger: this is not the finger for pointing with (something which is dangerous and forbidden); it is the finger for eating with. In order to taste a sauce one dips the index finger into it and sucks this finger.

But next there is a fact which seems to point in the opposite direction (we are in the domain of etiquette, i.e., of complication). When children grow up, they are taught how to greet people. The ritual of salutation is different for boys and for girls. Boys cover the right hand with the left when they bow: they *conceal* the right and present the left. Girls, on the contrary, and no less obligatorily, pay their respects by covering the left hand with the right.

It will already be seen that left and right form part of that great system of bipartite classification, the classification by Yang and Yin. The left is *yang,* it belongs to the male; the right is *yin,* it belongs to the female. *Yang* and the left are male, *yin* and the right are female.

But the ritual of greeting leads us to a new complication. In time of mourning, men make their salutations as though they were women, i.e., in this case they do not present the left hand but the right; the right hand must then cover and conceal the left. An inversion is produced by which the left is associated with the auspicious and the right with the inauspicious. Another rite of greeting and respect consists in uncovering the shoulders, or more exactly in uncovering one shoulder. When one is to be punished one uncovers the right shoulder, and when one attends a joyful ceremony one uncovers the left shoulder. Here again, and in a number of other cases of the same kind, the left is the auspicious side whereas the right is the inauspicious side.

Let us now pass on to another ritual, one of the present day. At this point things begin to get complicated. In general, one gives to the left and one takes on the right. Hence a juridical custom: when two persons make a contract, they divide a slip, a cutting; the left half is kept by the one who has the advantage of the other, i.e., by the creditor, and the right half is kept by the one in the inferior position, i.e., by the debtor. Here again the left is pre-eminent. When it is a question of presents consisting of living things, the ritual is very complicated and there is a tendency to explain it by reasons of convenience which are not in fact at work. Sheep, horses, dogs, and prisoners of war must be presented on a leash and by giving this leash (for it is by giving the leash that possession is transferred). For sheep and horses, the giver has to hold the leash in his right hand, because (it is explained) sheep and horses are inoffensive animals. In order to give a dog, which may bite, the right hand must be free, ready for defense, so the leash is held with the left hand. The reason is the same, it is said, in the case of prisoners of war. But it is hard to believe that the alleged motive of convenience is the true reason. As a matter of fact, prisoners of war whom one gives while holding them by the left hand are persons from whom one has cut, or from whom one is about to cut, the left ear. Presumably, therefore, the ritual is inspired by complex reasons governed by certain religious conceptions.

Some of the most important facts about the etiquette of left and right are to be found in the ritual of oath-taking, of which there are two forms. First there is the oath that is concluded by clasping the right hands (and which is symbolized in writing by the image of two *right* hands). The right, in this case, seems to predominate, and it might be thought that it predominates because it is auspicious, but the facts demand a closer inspection. To swear by gripping in this way is an oath of conjugal or military companionship. It corresponds to a peace-making after a feud. For this reason it seems most often to be completed by the conclusion of a blood-pact, the *blood* being taken from the *right* arm. But in the second type of oath it is the left that prevails. When a solemn oath, one that is binding in law, is sworn under the eyes of the gods, a little blood has to be taken from the victim. This blood must be taken from close to one of the ears, which is obligatorily the *left* ear. The blood is used to anoint the lips, and it is sniffed (sometimes, instead of being taken from the ear of the victim, it is made to flow from the nose of the swearer). The facts differ from those concerning the oath by gripping, in that it is not the *blood* that is the essential thing but the *breath.* What counts is the animation of the oath-taker's word by the breath taken from the victim through the mediation of its blood. This is why the blood is taken (with the aid of a knife with bells on it) from near the organ of hearing, and in this case the left ear is preferred.

We can say, then, that as far as oath-taking is concerned there is a kind of pre-eminence of the right when the hands are involved, and a pre-eminence of the left when it is the ears. If the Chinese favor the right in the case of the hands (and also the feet), they favor the left in the case of the ears (and also the eyes). This is because the upper part of the body and the lower part are opposed, for reasons which the doctors will be able to make clear. In China, more than elsewhere, it is necessary for doctors to have (in addition to a technical knowledge, which in itself would not be sufficient) not only a classical education but also a universal science. The principles of their art are based primarily on a knowledge of the macrocosm, and their knowledge of the human body is derived from this.

Now the world does not differ in its structure from the chariot or the house of the Chief. It consists of a roof, which is round (this is the Sky), and a rectangular base (which is the Earth). Between the sky and the earth, connecting them, are one or more columns. A solitary column represents the chief himself; when there are a number of columns (usually four) they stand for ministers, pillars of the state, or for mountains situated at the four corners of space. One of the best known Chinese myths is that of Kong-Kong, an evil minister who rebelled against his sovereign and uprooted a pillar, either the main column or one of the corner columns. He broke Mount Pou-Tcheou, which is a mountain, or a column, situated at the northwest of the Universe. This had grave consequences: Sky and Earth, being no longer joined by a column to the west, tipped over *in opposite directions.* The Sky leaned towards the west, while the Earth leaned to the east. This explains why it is that the stars move towards the west, and that the rivers of China all flow to the seas to the east. Furthermore, the phenomenon of tipping was complicated by a phenomenon of slipping, so that Sky and Earth are no longer placed one exactly over the other.

This myth has been given learned explanations of an astronomical kind. There is a quite simple explanation, namely, that the myth is intended to account for the fact that the capital, which *ought* to be at the center of the world, is *nevertheless* so situated that at midday on the summer solstice the gnomon still throws a shadow. If the world had not been displaced, the gnomon should make no shadow at all at the place which is that of the Chief.

But here, now, are the consequences as far as the human body is concerned. Part of the Earth is missing to the west, whereas the Sky is deficient to the east. The Sky is the Above, the Earth is the Below. Now the human body is composed of an above and a below. The head (round) represents the Sky, the feet (rectangular) represent the Earth which they touch. (This is the reason that it has long been forbidden for Chinese sovereigns to display in their court dancers doing the head-stand, for to perform this is precisely to turn the world upside down.) Since the head is the Sky, there is a deficiency in the head, as in the Sky, to the west, whereas close to the Earth, in the lower part of the body, there is a deficiency to the east. *It is enough to know that there is an equivalence between west and right, and between east and left,* to see that the right eye must be less good than the left eye, the left ear better than the right ear, and that inversely man must favor the right as far as the feet are concerned—and *also the hands.*

You should not see all this as a simple invention due to scholastic fantasy. The doctors have invented nothing. The idea belongs to ancient folklore and has been translated into the rituals. The practice of cutting off the left ear of prisoners of war is significant; and it may be added that when a bow is drawn at an enemy it is the left eye that is aimed at.

The structure of the microcosm depends exactly, as we have seen, on the structure of the macrocosm. But how is the structure of the latter to be explained? I shall surprise no one here when I say that the macrocosm is explained by the social structure—which is rather complicated. It is from this complication that there arises the alternative preference for the Right or for the Left.

The social structure is ordered by two great principles: (1) by oppositions governed by the category of sex and which are symbolized by the opposition of the Yin and the Yang; (2) by oppositions resulting from the hierarchical organization of the society and corresponding to the opposition between inferior and superior. Here therefore are two couples—Yin and Yang, High and Low—in which the opposition is of a cyclic type and results in an alternation. With these couples is combined the couple Left-Right (not to speak of other couples such as Before and Behind).

Let us start with the opposition of Above and Below, i.e., of superior and inferior. The image of Space, the image of the World, is formed after the representation of the assemblies held by the Chief when he receives his vassals. The Chief holds his reception standing on a dais with his back to the north and his face to the south, i.e., facing the light or the Yang; the vassals prostrate themselves facing north, towards the Yin, and instead of holding their heads up to the Sky they must press their faces against the Earth. Hence a series of equivalences: the Above is equivalent to the Sky, and also to Yang, for when the Chief stands facing the south he receives the full rays of the sun; he thus assimilates the Yang, the luminous principle. It follows also that the *front* of the body is *yang,* that the chest is *yang.* Inversely, the Below is equivalent to Earth, which is equivalent to *Yin,* which is equivalent to Behind, which is equivalent to the back.

All of this evokes an extremely important myth which bears on an essential theme in Chinese mythology, namely, the theme of hierogamy. Sky, Yang, and male are characterized by the fact that they cover, that they embrace and press against their *chest;* Earth, Yin, and female, on the contrary, present the *back* and carry on the back. I should mention here that Earth is a mother and Sky is a father, that the mother supplies the *blood* and the father the *breath.* Hence a series of equivalences which are most important in Chinese medicine: the Yang corresponds to the chest, and in the chest is the heart, which is the organ of the *breath.* Thus the doctors know that the heart is a simple vital organ, the Yang corresponding to the uneven. Conversely, the back is Yin: it is associated with the blood, or rather with all the fertile humors, and the vital organs corresponding to the back are the kidneys. The kidneys thus form a double vital organ (even = double) which is associated, moreover, with dancing and with the feet, which are made for touching the Earth (=Yin). . . .

For the rest, Yang and Yin, in their hierogamies, are not reduced to any single position (and this has happily permitted the doctors to adopt a very large number of other equivalences useful for arriving at diagnoses). In one of the most famous books of medicine the back becomes yang, through an inversion in location, and the heart thereby shifts to the back, for it could not remain in the chest and thus become yin (even) without being duplicated.

Here we see a primary opposition, namely, the opposition of Above and Below, Chief and Vassal. The Chief is associated with the south, the Vassal with the north. You will notice that it is he who stands to the north but faces south who is under the influence of South, whereas he who is to the south and faces north is under the influence of North.

The other opposition is that between men and women. Men place themselves to the west, i.e., facing the direction of the rising sun; they are thus equivalent to the east even though they are placed to the west. Women, conversely, who are placed to the east, are equivalent to the direction of the setting sun, the west, a fact which gives rise to a number of ambiguities and complications in etiquette. The Chief, who stands with his face to the south, *has the east to his left,* from which it follows that East equals Left and that West equals Right; these are absolute equivalences which are always valid. The Chief is not limited to holding receptions, standing on his dais. The Chief is an *archer* (which is the title of Chinese lords), and by this title he is mythologically a Sun, especially a rising sun. Consequently, though he faces the south, he is a person of the east. Conversely, the vassals opposite him, while being people who turn their faces to the north, are also people of the west. Hence an essential correlation, viz., the connection of east with south (Yang), and of west with north (Yin).

The Chief is an archer, and when he moves from one place to another he goes by chariot. This is where facts concerning military techniques become relevant. The Chief, when he is in his chariot, must never face anywhere but south. The army is a camp on the march, always turned towards the south. This is very easily done. All that is needed is to have a red flag carried at the head of the army, for red is equivalent to the sun. The Chief, since he marches directly towards his red flag, thus always has the east to his left wherever he goes. In all religious diagrams, the north is placed at the bottom and the south at the top, so that *west is to the right and east is to the left.*

The Chief, who is an archer, does not drive his chariot. Chinese chariots are occupied by three men: the driver, naturally, has to be in the middle, where he is flanked by his two companions, namely, the archer, chief of the chariot, and a spearman who is the vassal or supporter of the Chief. Now the spearman, since he is *right-handed,* has to wield his spear with his right hand; he can only employ it usefully so long as he is placed on the right side of the chariot. This leaves for the Chief only the place on the left. The left is the place of the Chief, and consequently the place of honor. These facts have their effect on the system of ideas concerning Left and Right.

When the Chief holds a reception, his court is drawn up facing him. The arrangement of the vassals in court assemblies serves to mark the different regions of space. Among the vassals there are three who are as it were a projection of the Chief: these are called the Three Dukes. This trinity represents the Chief: his left and his right, plus the Center. The three dukes, whose mission it is to double for the Chief, are oriented, even though they are vassals, as is the Chief himself: they are considered as facing south, and consequently the *duke of the left* is the first among them. He governs over the East, i.e., *the left of the world,* and is thus the most honored of the three.

But the collectivity of vassals are opposed to the Chief. They are considered as actually facing the north. Since the east is the left of the Chief, and since the left is the honorable side, the east will be the side of honor for the vassals who are placed facing the Chief; among them, the most highly honored will therefore be he who is on the right, and the inversion is thereby absolute.

Vassals do not stay all the time at the court; they travel. But when they are on the road they do not at all abandon their attitude as vassals: just as the Chief marches with his face always towards the south, so the vassals always face north. The side of honor thus remains for them the right and hence the west. It will be seen that etiquette, by a pleasing *tour de force,* has succeeded in combining the two principal formulas of classification: the inferior placed to the south and facing north, and the male placed to the west and facing east. The vassal takes the west (right) part of the road, where he marches under the influence of the east. The eastern (left) part of the road is reserved exclusively for women, who there receive the influence of the west.

The vassals present themselves as Chiefs when they return to their own homes; there they are the masters. Everything is changed once they are seated in the attitude of Chiefs in their houses. The place of the master of the house, who faces south on his platform, is to the east, i.e., to the left; the place of the mistress of the house is to the west, i.e., to the right.

All of this has important consequences; for example, the palace of the prince who is heir-presumptive must be built to the east, whereas the dowager has necessarily to live to the west, in the palace of the west—or, as they prefer to say, "the palace of a thousand autumns," for the west is autumn, just as east is spring.

Here we see a new feat on the part of etiquette; it has succeeded in connecting woman with autumn, i.e., with the harvest, whereas it links man to the spring, i.e., to the tasks at the beginning of the year. This leads to further correlations which are endlessly complicated: women make the crops grow, something that is also done by means of the game of the Swing. The swing and autumn (or the harvest) are equivalent: the palace of a thousand autumns, palace of the swing, and the dowager herself—all these are equivalent.

But let us pass on to the ritual of retiring for the night. In his own home the husband is the east, and when he retires to sleep he keeps to the east; the wife belongs to the west, and when night comes she stays in the west. But the husband has to change position, since he is a sun who comes from the east and sets in the west; yet his mat is nevertheless placed to the east of that of his wife. Here a curious complication intervenes: when one lies down, one has to place oneself against the earth, in an attitude which is completely different from the standing posture in which one receives heavenly influences from Above. At night, a ritual of an inauspicious type is appropriate: to lie directly on the earth is to assume an attitude comparable to that of the dead. This imposes several precautions. When husband and wife lie down, they have to place their heads to the north, and should not extend their feet towards the north; only the dead do this, for they have to direct their feet towards the cemeteries which are situated to the north of villages and towns. To sleep with one's feet to the north would be like committing suicide. During the night, therefore, the head has to be kept to the north and the feet to the south. The woman, who stays on the west, occupies the left side, whereas the man, who remains to the east, occupies the right. The alternation of left and right, with regard to their ritual preeminence, is constant.

The structure of the world does not in itself explain the facts concerning the etiquette of Right and Left. The world has a structure, a morphology, which depends on the social structure. It has also a physiology, the essential law of which is a *principle of rotation,* namely, the rhythmic and cyclic alternation of the Yin and the Yang. The principle of etiquette is therefore to render manifest the structural identity of the macrocosm and the microcosms, while taking into account the physiological modifications of the macrocosm, which correspond to different eras, and to changes in the world order, which means in the order of civilization. There are times at which the Yang governs, and there are times which are ruled by the Yin, and at each alternation the principles of etiquette are completely reversed; where the Right previously dominated, the Left comes into the ascendant, and vice versa.

Thus we find in China none of that distrust or hatred of left-handers which is characteristic of other cultures. A left-hander is worth as much as a right-hander. More exactly, there are cultural eras, or physiological phases of the Universe, in which it is fitting to be left-handed, and other phases in which it is appropriate to be right-handed. There are several instructive myths on this point. There are generally six in the family of Suns, and when they give birth it happens that three are born on the left and three on the right. Those who emerge from the right of the maternal body are entirely right-handed, and those who come out of the left are all left-handed. This is to be understood in the most absolute sense. The hero is right-handed, or left-handed, to the point of being hemiplegic. He is alive on only the right, or the left, side of the body. He will be a spirit of the Left or a spirit of the Right.

Here are some examples in which the rules of etiquette will be seen to function with a rigorous precision. The first royal dynasty, that of the Hià, the founder of which was Yu the Great, was a dynasty which reigned under the sign of the Earth. From this fact the historians have been able to *deduce* all the physical characteristics of the founder of the Hià, including the details of his birth. Yu the Great emerged from the body of his mother through the *back,* for the back is yin and the earth is yin. He reigned by virtue of the Earth, so he had big feet, and he was right-handed. When he walked, he continually dragged his left leg; only his right foot advanced.

T'ang the Victorious, the founder of the Yin dynasty, which followed that of the Hià, appeared in history as a rising Sun.· He reigned by virtue of the Sky. Therefore he was very tall, stretched towards the Above. He emerged from the body of his mother by her chest, which is yang, and he made contact with the earth only through feet which were minuscule. He was entirely of the left, and walked with his left foot always in front. Right-handed or left-handed, Yu and T'ang are both hemiplegic. They are so in consequence of their several dedications: one is dedicated to the Sky, the other to the Earth, one to the spirit of Rain, the other to that of Drought.

Such are the ideas which govern mythology and history—for what I have called mythical facts are regarded by a fair number of our contemporaries as historical. But what is valid for mythology or for history is also valid for medicine. Here is the way children are born. The principle of conception corresponds to the point which represents true north, midnight, and the winter solstice. Both male and female come from this and depart from this. The male (Yang) sets off to the left, and the female to the right. Men marry at thirty, women marry at twenty. If we count thirty stations to the left on the chart of the twelve cyclic characters, starting from *tseu* (child, midnight, the first cyclic character), we arrive at the cyclic character *sseu,* and if we count twenty stations on the other side, to the right, we arrive again at the same cyclic character: the female and the male thus meet at the ages of twenty and of thirty respectively, at the character *sseu.* This character represents the embryo; it marks the station appropriate to *real* conceptions. Children, male and female, are therefore born at *sseu.* If the child is a male, it will continue to turn towards the *left,* and as it has to be born at ten months (the Chinese include the first month in their reckoning) the place of its birth will be the cyclic character *yin;* the place of birth of a girl (this time we go to the *right*) will be the cyclic character *chen.* On the chart of the cyclic characters the decimal numbers corresponding to the cyclic numbers *chen* and *yin* are 7 and 8. The entire life of a woman is dominated by the number 7: girls teethe at 7 months, and lose their milk-teeth at 7 years; they are nubile at 14, and the menopause occurs at 49. Boys are dominated by the number 8: their teeth appear at 8 months and are lost at 8 years; they arrive at puberty at 16, and become impotent at 64. This is not a simple invention, either, resulting from the scholastic ingenuity of the doctors, but is implicit in many very ancient rites and a long-lived folklore. You have seen that the one who goes towards the right is the female; the one that goes to the left is the male. When Chinese doctors are asked to discern the sex of a child while it is still in the womb, they can answer without hesitation. All they need to do is to see whether the embryo lies to the left or to the right in the mother's belly. If it is to the left, it is a boy; if it is to the right, it is a girl. When an embryo moves towards the right, this is because it belongs on the right. One that belongs to the left has to move to the left.

Let us at this point pass on to a theme of etiquette which is quite different, namely, the ritual of reception. When one receives a guest, one goes to receive him at the door to the court of honor in the house, and one conducts him to the reception room by way of two series of steps, one series to the east and the other to the west. The master of the house, who has to take the eastern steps, places himself, when he receives his guest, facing north and to the *right* of the door, after which he advances, still facing north and turning towards the right, towards the steps on the east. The guest, placed on the left, walks towards the left. We have no information on how their feet are moved as they walk in the courtyard, but we do know how they climb the steps of the eastern and western stairways. The guest, who is a man of the left, has to mount each step with the left foot, the right never doing anything other than follow. The master of the house, to the right, makes each pace with the right foot. Conversely, when the guest is seen off, the positions are reversed (and both of them face south): the master of the house, who is to the east (*left*), walks on the left, while the guest, who occupies the right (*west*), moves by walking with the right foot.

On the chart of the cyclic characters, the progress towards the left corresponds to the order of time and of the characters, to the course of the Sun: this is what the Chinese call the order that is *fitting*, whereas the movement to the right, opposite to the course of the Sun, is known as the *inverse* order. The inverse order is what is appropriate to a sorcerer. The founder of the Hià dynasty, Yu the Great, who was integrally of the right, is one of the patrons of sorcerers. His step, the step of Yu, is still danced by sorcerers; it consists in starting off with the right foot and moving forward with the right side of the body continually in front.

There is, as you see, an alternate pre-eminence of Left and Right, but this does not alter the fact that the right hand is the more used. It is for this very reason, perhaps, that the left preponderates. This is shown by a number of important rules of etiquette.

One of these rules is particularly significant. When an heir is born, and when he is given a personality (this has to do with ensuring the connection between the breath-soul and the blood-soul), the child is welcomed by the name of its father; this is done by two of the father's principal vassals, his head cook and his chief musician. The cook places himself to the right, and this agrees with the fact that the right is the hand for eating with, but very probably also with the fact that the right is the hand of *blood*. The chief musician, on the contrary, stands to the left, in the place of honor, and this presumably accords with the fact that the Yang, the Sky, and the *Breath* belong to the Left.

When people return from a war, and a celebration is held, the victorious general leads the triumphal pomp armed with a flute and a battle-axe (this is the time when the captives will have their left ears cut off). The general holds the battle-axe in his right hand, and the flute with his left. In military affairs, which are considered as inauspicious, the right is preponderant, but the triumph is regarded as a peace-ceremony, and in this case it is the left which is preferred. The right is only a supporting hand, it is the hand which acts; it is also the hand which kills and which spills blood, the hand of the soldier. But it is not the soldier (placed on the right in the war-chariot) who wins the battle; it is the Chief, who is placed on the left. The Chief animates the entire battle with his *breath*, while the soldier does nothing but shed *blood*. The place of honor corresponds to the hand which does not act, not to the hand, charged with low tasks, which does the work.

The characters which designate left and right are formed with the aid of an element which portrays the hand, to which is added another element which supplies the meaning: for the right, this is a sign which formerly stood for something round. This may evoke two ideas: the right is the hand of the mouth and of food, and it is also the hand of round things such as circle or compass. The left, on the contrary, is specified by means of a sign standing for a set-square. There is a bas-relief, dating from the second century A.D. but which is inspired by more ancient traditions, which represents two mythical personages, heroic founders who form a primordial couple. They are Fou-Hi and Niu-Koua, husband and wife, but also brother and sister, a couple who are both hierogamous and incestuous. They are interlaced at the lower part of the body, but the woman, who is placed to the right, holds in her right hand a compass for making circles; and the man, on the left, holds in his left hand a set-square for making a square.

The rhythmic alternation of right and left can be understood in connection with the idea of hierogamy. The set-square is the badge of the sorcerer. The word for "set-square" also means "art," especially "musical art" (still in relation to the left). All the arts, with magic in the first place, are evoked by the set-square. The reason that Fou-Hi, head of the primordial household from which marriage originated (the expression "compasses and set-square" refers to correct sexual behavior), has a set-square as his token is that he is considered as the inventor of divination and the first sorcerer. In the ancient language there was a word which meant both "sorcerer" and "sorceress," but there was yet another word which designated the sorcerer in particular. Etymologists explain this fact by saying that there was a need for a special word for a sorcerer, who had to be both yang and yin: the Chief, the magician, contains in himself the Yang and the Yin, which are resorbed in him.

This theme agrees with the Chinese theories on even and uneven. The uneven, which is yang, is a synthesis of even and uneven, of Yin and Yang. Similarly, the sorcerer, because of the hierogamies which he knows how to effect, is both man and woman, and a woman when he wishes to be (the theme of change of sex is common). Moreover, when the sorcerer holds the set-square which produces the square, he possesses the round (Chinese geometers think that the square engenders the round). The round figures the Sky, the square figures the Earth. The set-square, badge of the sorcerer, who holds it in his left hand, thus evokes the Yin, but it is considered to conceal and to produce the Yang: the theme of exchange of attributes is always associated with that of hierogamy.

There is thus a certain pre-eminence of the left, just as there is a certain pre-eminence of the set-square, symbol of the magical arts. But this pre-eminence is only occasional; the left issues from the right, as the round issues from the square, in consequence of a complete change, a total mutation; the left is transformed into the right, just as when the sorcerer is transformed into a sorceress he remains nothing other than a woman. There is a cycling and alternation, or an alternating pre-eminence. There is no fixed predominance, no absolute opposition.

This assemblage of facts regarding the mythology of Left and Right brings out the structural correlation which is established in China between the Universe, the human body, and society; all of this, the morphology and physiology of the macrocosm and the microcosms, forms the domain of Etiquette.

Never do we find absolute oppositions: a left-hander is not sinister, and neither is a right-hander. A multitude of rules show the left and the right as predominating alternately. The diversity of times and places imposes, at any point, a very delicate choice between left and right, but *this choice is inspired by a very coherent system of representations.*

Let me illustrate this point with a final example, taken this time from the ritual of serving at table. How should fish be served? According to whether the fish is fresh or dried, matters are entirely different. If it is dried fish, the head must be turned towards the guest. But if it is fresh fish, it is the tail which must be turned towards the guest. Nor is this all: the season has to be taken into account also. If it is summertime, the belly of the fish must be turned to the left; if it is winter, to the right. This is why: winter is the reign of Yin, and Yin, as we have seen, corresponds to the Below; the belly (even though it forms part of the front) is the underneath of the fish; therefore it is *yin.* During winter, in which the Yin reigns, the belly should be the best-nourished part, the fattest and most succulent. The fish is placed with its belly to the right in winter because one has to eat with the right hand, and one begins by eating the good parts. The most succulent morsel must therefore be to the right. In summer, when Yang reigns, everything changes.

We can see, then, how minute are the rules of etiquette. The preeminence of the right or of the left depends always on events, on the occasional circumstances of time and place. I have been able to explain the rule governing service at table because I have found an analysis of it in a competent author of antiquity: it would have been impossible to reconstitute by an act of the imagination the reasons which serve to justify these rules. I shall conclude, therefore, by remarking that when it is a question of etiquette, i.e., of symbolism, any attempt at an ideological interpretation is dangerous. There is only one valid interpretation, namely, that which is given by those who combine a practice of the etiquette with a direct knowledge of the system of symbols by which it is inspired.

Concepts of Right and Left in African Cultures

4

Heinz A. Wieschhoff

I

Questions connected with right and left in their physiological and psychological aspects have been treated extensively in the book *Handedness, Right and Left* by Ira S. Wile.[1] According to his special frame of interest he devotes a few pages to the treatment of material touching this problem as applied to the African continent. I cannot consider it to be my task to adopt a critical point of view towards the author's data and its interpretation, although his views, as I regard them, are not generally sustainable throughout in an anthropological sense. This, however, is not important for the validity of his thesis in general. Here I shall only present the material itself in an ordered manner. The "right and left" problem will be offered in its cultural confines, and no attempt will be made to discuss the question of handedness physiologically.

As may be expected, the material available in the literature is rather poor, not only in that information is lacking from many parts of Africa, but that many references are not trustworthy and may consequently be eliminated.

It may be well to arrange the data on the basis of the following classification:

1. Right side associated with men, left with women
2. Right equivalent to "good," left to "bad" (inferior)
3. Right connected with good luck, left with misfortune; or, correspondingly, happenings on the right side being good omens, those on the left bad omens

Reprinted from the *Journal of the American Oriental Society* 58 (1938): 202–17, with the permission of the American Oriental Society.

4. Left representing fortune; right misfortune
5. Right side preferred, left considered inferior
6. Color associations with right and left
7. Right and left denoting orientation

There exist furthermore a number of statements in the literature which do not fit very well into these groups and which apparently have no bearing upon the question at large.

1. Right side associated with men, left with women

The close association of right with male and left with female has been recorded from various parts of the African continent. Attention may be drawn to the fact that the same associations are very strongly predominant in the Western world. In respect to the Bantu-speaking parts of Africa, Werner[2] makes the general statement that the right hand is often called "the male hand" or sometimes "the strong hand," and the left, although less frequently, is called or referred to as the "female hand" or the "inferior hand." In particular Weeks[3] states that among the Boloki of the northern Congo area, the ears of newborn infants are pierced, the left ear lobe in the case of a girl, the right of a boy. The author emphasizes the fact that as a rule the left side is considered inferior. From the Loango Peschuel-Lösche notes that every person in leaving a hut or a bed is very careful to touch the floor with the right foot first, and that among these people the right leg is called in the native language, the "man-leg."[4] In the same book we find the statement that left-handed persons, who form the same proportion of the population as elsewhere, are referred to as using the "other hand" or "woman-hand."[5] The secret society of the Ekoi in Cameroon has a sacred drum, upon the right side of which is carved the figure of a man, on the left side a woman's (Talbot).[6] The author mentions, in connection with the strings worn by medicine men of the same tribe, that those on the right side are regarded as male and those on the left, female.[7] And again the same author states that twitching of the sole of the right foot announces the visit of a strange man, of the sole of the left foot, however, the visit of a strange woman.[8]

From the area around Lake Tchad, Frobenius[9] in describing the founding of a town and the ceremonies which are connected therewith, reports that after certain rituals a virgin—the representation of the female—is buried to the left of the east entrance, and a bull—the symbol of the male—to the right of it.

In the provinces of Dar Fur as well as in Wadai, Nachtigal [10] found that the right is always connected with man and the left with woman. The A-Kamba in East Africa (Lindblom) [11] consider the expression "on the right hand" as equivalent to "men's hand," while "on the left hand" means "women's hand." In respect to burial practices the author reports a similar attitude. The corpse of a dead man is placed on the right side with the hands under the head, that of a woman on the left side. That the left arm is called "woman's arm" is stated by the author in another place.[12] Hobley [13] also affirms this association of left and female from the East African Kavirondo.

The same concept seems to be prevalent among the Bakitara of the Victoria Nyanza. They bury a dead queen as well as the wives of their more prominent tribesmen in such a way that their hands are placed under the left side of the head and the wives of the latter dignitaries are buried on the left side of their huts. Ordinary men and women are buried with their hands under the right side of the head (Roscoe).[14]

This association of left with women and right with men in respect to burials seems rather widely distributed in Africa. I found it to be the case for all the tribes in Mashonaland, Southern Rhodesia. Of the Bavenda in Northern Transvaal Stayt [15] mentions that "when the deceased is a man the body is arranged in a sitting position, with the right side of the head resting on the clasped hands." A few examples are given by Seligman of the Nilotic tribes of the Eastern Sudan. The Acholi buried a man on the right side of the door and a woman on the left.[16] A similar report is given of the Bari: ". . . the grave being dug in front of the house of the deceased – on the right of the door for a male, on the left for a female." [17]

The Konde of the northern Nyassa area, upon visiting the grave of a relative, touch it with the elbow, the body, and the forehead (Fülleborn).[18] If the buried person is a woman, the women touch the grave with their right side, if a man, they touch it with the left; the men, however, observe the same custom in the reverse. Baumann [19] informs us that among the Wambugwe in East Africa the bodies of deceased women are carried from their huts with the left side downward, male corpses in the reverse manner. The Wa-Chagga (Merker) [20] cut a piece of skin from the hide of a sacred bull and wear it around the middle finger. This piece is worn on the right hand when the person to whom the bull was sacrificed belonged to the father's family, but on the left if the person thus honored was a member of the mother's family. If the sacrifice was made for an undetermined male ancestor the string was tied around the big toe of the right foot, around the big toe of the left foot instead when a female ancestor was honored.

Concerning the Bushmen of the Cape Colony, Dornan [21] narrates that at initiation ceremonies the little finger had to be cut off, boys losing one from the right hand, girls one from the left.

The only exception to this rule is reported by Schinz [22] from the Hottentot of South Africa, among whom women occupy the right side of the huts. It is naturally difficult to decide how much emphasis can be placed upon this remark.

2. Right equivalent to "good," left to "bad" (inferior)

Similarly distributed throughout the African continent we find the belief that right is equivalent to good and left to bad. Its expressions are as manifold as those of the beliefs mentioned above.

Repulsion from use of the left hand is especially strong in respect to food. For the Mohammedans of the Sudan, Junker [23] states that, generally speaking, they are not allowed to eat with the left hand, as it is considered *negis,* or "impure," in the religious sense. Therefore it is well to sit with the right side towards the food, especially if space should be limited. In respect to the inhabitants of Morocco Westermarck [24] says in more detail: "The disfavour with which a left-handed person is regarded is due to the notion that the left side is bad and the right side is good, which is found among so many other peoples and also prevailed among the ancient Arabs. It is bad *fäl* to use the left hand for good acts, which in accordance with custom are performed with the right, such as eating, giving alms, offering and receiving food or drink or other things, greeting a person, telling the beads of one's rosary; whereas the right hand should not be used for dirty acts, such as cleaning one's anus or genitals or blowing one's nose, and when you spit you should do it to the left."

The Jekris of the Lower Niger area use the left hand for cleansing purposes and therefore eat only with the right hand (Roth).[25] They present objects and shake hands only with the right. Winterbottom [26] says, similarly, that the natives of Sierra Leone consider it an unpardonable offense to offer the left hand, which also is never used for eating. The Tim call the right hand the "eating hand" and the

Suru of the same area name it the "good hand." Also the Ashanti of the West African Gold Coast are very careful not to touch food with the left hand and to clean the right hand before they eat with it (Bowdich).[27]

The tribes of the Lower Niger area do not allow women to touch kitchen implements with the left hand, nor are they allowed to touch them at all during the period of menstruation (Leonard).[28] In general, remarks the recorder in a footnote, the right hand is regarded as good, the left as bad. The right hand indicates friendship, the left animosity. The Ija as well as the natives of Brass observe the rule that in no case may a woman touch her husband's face with the left hand, or cook or eat food except with the right. From the Ibo and other tribes of this area the same author reports that only warriors who have killed men with their own hand may drink with the left, apparently as a sign of distinction.

Of the Pangwe in Cameroon Tessmann[29] records that the bodies of prominent sorcerers are placed so as to lie on the left side in burial, which means, as the author himself emphasizes, with the right side uppermost. Evil magicians, those who practice witchcraft, are buried on the right side, or with the left above.

The Bakitara of the Victoria Nyanza hate left-handed people and no one is allowed to give anything to another person with the left hand (Roscoe).[30] Exactly the same is reported by Baumann[31] for the Waseguyu who consider it bad manners to eat with the left, as this is used for all kinds of impure actions. The Ovambo in Southwest Africa avoid passing an object to a person with the left hand, and regard a greeting made with the left hand as an offense (Schinz).[32] Perhaps also what Irle[33] reports from the Herero, the southern neighbors of the Ovambo, belongs to this group of concepts. When, during a fight, the leader has a cramp in the left cheek below the eye, it indicates that the fight will be lost and that important persons will be killed. In contrast to this belief, it may be added here, itching in the right foot denotes an approaching death in the family. Among the Ovimbundu of Southern Angola "a very insulting sign is made in this way. The left arm is held up with the fist closed. The left wrist is grasped with the right hand. The left fist is then shaken while the right hand is still grasping the left wrist" (Hambly).[34] Apparently what we have here is an indication that left is equivalent to bad.

A belief may perhaps be indicated in Halkin's[35] report about the

Ababua of Central Africa, who during an ordeal, put a liquid into a person's left eye to determine his innocence or guilt. Unquestionably, however, what Trilles[36] reports of the Central African Pygmies also belongs in this group. He writes: "Les doigts de la main gauche représentent l'étranger, l'ennemi, le gibier chassé, l'objet convoité, ou dans un autre ordre d'idées, la femme, les enfants, c'est-à-dire, en somme, comme toujours pour le coté gauche l'être inférieur, d'où malheur et calamité, tandis que les doigts de la main droite représentent l'homme lui-même, l'hôte, le chef, les hommes du clan, c'est-à-dire l'être supérieur, d'où bonheur, chance etc."

3. Right connected with good luck, left with misfortune

As far as literary information is concerned the most consistent data on association of right with good luck and left with misfortune are found in North and East Africa. I should like to quote here Westermarck's observations in respect to the inhabitants of Morocco:[37] "Twitching of your right eyelid indicates that some absent member of your family will come back or that some other pleasant event is in store for you, but a twitch of your left eye means that a member of your family will die or that you will have some other sorrow. . . . According to a scribe from the Ait Wäryäger, itching of the right palm, the right side of the face, or the right eyebrow indicates happiness, but itching of the left palm, the left side of the face, or the left eyebrow indicates sorrow."

The A-Kamba in East Africa believe that if a hyena or jackal crosses one's path from right to left, it is a bad omen, but from left to right, a good one (Hobley).[38] But there are some instances from this tribe which point in the opposite direction, as will be seen later. Nigmann[39] reports of the Wahehe that sacrifices are interrupted when the bird *ngulung ulu* cries on the left side of the road, but that the same cry heard from the right side is a good omen. Of the Masai, Fuchs[40] notes that a man on a visit to a sick woman, hearing the call of the bird *ol-tilo* on the left, knows that the woman is very ill, but if the bird calls on the right side of the road it is a sign that she feels better. If, however, somebody wishes to visit a sick man and hears the bird cry on the left side, it is a sign that the illness is not serious; the bird call coming from the right side, however, means that the man will die. Here it is of course interesting to note that we find a sex-association, as pointed out above, that refers to visiting a sick man or woman. If a man departing for war hears the bird *tilo* crying on the right, he knows that he will be successful, but if the bird calls on the left quarter, he immediately turns home to avoid defeat.

Among the WaChagga a left-handed man is not allowed to accompany a party of warriors, as it is believed that he would bring misfortune. The same recorder (Gutmann)[41] adds that if a person when traveling hits his right foot against something it is a good omen and that good news and good food may be expected at the journey's end; the same occurrence in regard to the left foot, however, would be regarded as a warning not to continue the trip. The Washamba interpret the cry of the black monkey on the right side of a traveler as a good omen, on the left as a bad one (Karasek and Eichhorn).[42] Müller[43] tells of a similar belief from Fetu. The call of the bird *obruku* on the right side signifies good fortune, on the left, evil, and a person starting on a journey will instantly turn back, however far he may have walked, should he hear the call on the left side. Also among the Amhara of Abyssinia this belief is found (Harris).[44]

Among the natives of the Kilimanjaro areas Dundas[45] observed the wearing of rings of sheepskin around the third finger of the right hand. After the sacrifice of an animal they wear it on the big toe of the right foot. These skin-pieces are considered to be charms. Thus if a man travels at night and a dangerous animal approaches him, he spits on the ring and asks his ancestors for help.

The Bedouin north of Agazi postpone a journey if they see a (black) bird on the right and an old woman on the left of the road. Here again we note the association of women and left (Munzinger).[46]

Des Marchais,[47] reporting on the Gold Coast in the early part of the eighteenth century, remarks that the natives, upon leaving the hut for trading purposes, note the direction in which the head is turned. If to the right, they regard the day as a fortunate one and do not hesitate to risk everything, but if the head turns to the left, it foretells misfortune, and they do not leave the hut under any circumstances.

The Ekoi believe that the twitching of the upper lid of the left eye indicates that something bad will soon be seen, for example, an ordeal by boiling water; twitching of the lid of the right ėye announces the prospect of a pleasant sight, such as a dance. Twitching in the top of the left arm at the beginning of a journey indicates that disagreeable things are in store and that friendly powers are trying to hold one back. The same feeling in the top of the right arm, however, is a good omen "and foretells that a friend's arm will soon lie within one's own" (Talbot).[48] In respect to the call and flight of birds, the Ekoi have a different interpretation as will be seen later.

Tönjes[49] remarks of the Ovakuanjama, a tribe of the Ovambo group, that the call of a bird on the right side means luck, but when heard on the left, misfortune. Thus if one goes to visit the chief, a bird call on the left signifies that one will not have the success desired. The neighboring Herero believe that misfortune is imminent when a rabbit or buck runs through the settlement from right to left (Irle).[50] In the religion of the Bushmen, Campbell[51] finds the belief that there exists a kind of devil who has made everything with the left hand.

A report may be added here which has no direct bearing upon this question and which cannot be interpreted according to the classification here offered. The Mountain-Dama in Southwest Africa bury a dead man with his sandal on the left foot only. The one from the right foot is given to his brother or relative (for luck?) (Irle).[52]

4. Left representing fortune; right, misfortune

The geographic area representative of the belief that the left side represents luck and fortune is rather limited. Aside from the Ekoi in Cameroon we find evidence of this association predominating widely throughout Northeast Africa. Regarding the Ekoi we have already noted that prominence is generally given to the right side, which symbolizes the male principle as well as good fortune. But in respect to the flight and calls of birds it is the opposite. Talbot[53] cites five different types of birds which are regarded as important for predictions. Some of them indicate good fortune if they are heard on the left side, but bad if they call on the right. Other birds bring luck when they cross a road or path from right to left, misfortune when they fly in the opposite direction. With these remarks the general tendency to regard the left as favorable, although not exclusively so, is evident, as has been shown above.

Also from the East African A-Kamba we have already mentioned the predominant importance of the right for omens of good fortune. In respect to the calling of birds, however, these natives make certain exceptions. Thus Hobley[54] reports that the call of a red-headed woodpecker on the left side of the road is a good omen and is believed to be a sign leading to a dead elephant, a great "find" for these people. But the same call heard on the right side is a bad omen. This is confirmed by Lindblom.[55] He says of the same tribe that the call of a bird on the left side is a good omen and that the hearer will have future opportunities to acquire women, cattle, and other wealth, but that a twitching of the left arm, in A-Kamba terminology synonymous with "woman's arm," signifies that one may be compelled to give something away. This latter part of the report indicates the primary importance of, and emphasis upon, the right, as discussed above.

The Wageia-Kavirondo consider the right hand to be unlucky, the left, however, to be lucky (Weiss).[56] The result of a journey was therefore predicted according to whether a bird cried on the left or right side. If a traveler struck the great toe of his right foot against a stone or a root twice, it indicated bad luck; the same happening with the left foot meant that the journey would be successful. To stumble with the right first and then with the toe of the left foot was considered to be without significance. Here may be added the statement of Gutmann[57] on the WaChagga. As mentioned above these natives interpret the hitting of the left foot as a bad omen, but if somebody should continue a journey in spite of such warnings he might discover that his left foot is the lucky one and would in future regard it as such, providing that he does not make discoveries to the contrary. The personally favored foot or leg is referred to as the "nice one," although ordinarily this term is given to the right leg or foot.

The Danakil in the northeastern parts of Africa considered the flight of birds from left to right as a bad omen (Harris).[58] The same is reported for the Wateita (Rebmann)[59] and the Bogos when making a journey regarded a bird's call on the right as a sign of safe return, on the left of success in their plans (Munzinger).[60] Here we note a slight difference in the interpretation.

Perhaps in line with the general understanding of left as being favorable is the custom of the Masai who at new-moon throw a stone or branch with the left hand and say: "Give me a long life," or "Give me strength" (Fuchs).[61]

5. Right side preferred, left considered inferior

It is generally understood that almost universally the right side is the superior or preferred one, so it might seem superfluous to cite such evidence for Africa. There are not very many remarks in the literature, but such testimony speaks of this preference for the right.

Herodotus[62] mentions that Psammetichus I favored foreign, especially Ionian, soldiers and gave them the place at his right. In the kingdom of Wadai in the central parts of the Sudan the highest official was called *Dsherma toluk* and the next in rank *Dsherma luluk.* The modifier *toluk* means right and *luluk* left, so that the highest official has the title "to the right" (Nachtigal).[63] From the province of Dar Fur the same author[64] mentions that the newly crowned king when inducted into office in an inaugural procession first took the road *Orre de,* which means the "route of man," then the *Orre beja,* the "route of woman," which are associated respectively with right and left. In Abyssinia the seat on the right of the emperor was considered the superior one, the one on the left of less importance (Salt).[65] A similar report is given by Bruce,[66] although the preference for right is not specifically expressed.

The highest officials next to the king, the Bale, in the town Ibadan, Yorubaland, have the title right- and left-handed Bale (Ellis).[67] They were the principal councillors of the king. The author makes at this place no definite statement as to which is the higher in rank. Referring to the Magba or high priest of the god Shango, however, he remarks[68] that this priest had twelve assistants who were called according to their rank and authority the "right hand," "left hand," third, fourth, etc., which seems to indicate a preference for the right hand.

The Masai, writes Fuchs,[69] called the boys who were circumcised first the "right hand circumcised," those subsequently circumcised the "left hand circumcised." Of the Boloki, Weeks mentions[70] that the first-born of twins was carried on the right arm, the second-born on the left arm. Among the Waguha of the eastern parts of the Belgian Congo, the father's brother takes the newborn child from the hut and lifts it first to the right, then to the left, and finally towards all those mountains which are thought to be occupied by spirits (Schmidt).[71]

Krapf[72] and others[73] remark that the Zulu distinguish between three houses in a family: (1) The house of the first married woman, called the house of the right hand; (2) the house of the great woman; and (3) the house of the third woman, or the house of the left hand.

Here perhaps may be added Irle's[74] statement about the Herero, who call the Kunene river the right-lying river and the smaller river, the Okavangu, the left-lying river. It is uncertain as to whether these names were adopted because the Herero on their migration first encountered the Kunene on their right. It is, however, possible that Kunene and right have been identified through the idea of size, a suggestion that is perhaps strengthened by the circumstance that the name Kunene sometimes has been interpreted as "great river."

6. Color associations with right and left

The association of colors with right and left is a topic which I intended to treat in a special study, since it involves questions which have no direct bearing upon the problem raised here. In general, however, I should like to state that among many tribes right is associated with light (white) and left with dark (particularly red) colors. There are, as might be expected, exceptions to such a rule. Thus Fuchs [75] reports from the Masai that those warriors who have killed enemies paint the right part of the body red, the left white. The Baluba Hembe of the Congo region color the left eyelid of a deceased person with white earth (Colle).[76] On other occasions this same tribe uses the customary colors, i. e., white for right and red for left (Colle).[77] Or, to give an example which indicates sex association, Lichtenstein [78] who visited South Africa at the end of the eighteenth century states that the female sorcerer of the Xosa painted the left eyelids, arm, and thigh white and the corresponding members on the right, black.

7. Right and left denoting orientation

In the literature only one reference could be found to indicate that words for right and left are unknown. From the Waniaturu, von Sick [79] reports that right and left are expressed in terms of orientation. Thus in saying to a man "turn to the right" they say "go to the east," and so on, according to the general direction intended.

In Wadai as well as in Dar Fur right is very definitely associated with west and left with east (Nachtigal).[80] It seems as if such an association is quite frequent in the Eastern or Anglo-Egyptian Sudan. And moreover here the concept of left and east is closely connected with women, right and west with men.

In the region of Shoa in Northeast Africa left is associated with south and right with north (Krapf).[81]

In this connection a report might be added which may have some bearing upon this question. Holub [82] says of the Barotse of the

Upper Zambesi the following (in free translation): "Some of the king's wives and children are always invited to attend the morning meal of the king. At this occasion the wives as well as strangers (referring only to Europeans) sit down in the direction of the *rising sun,* while at evening meetings the same persons are placed at the *left* of the king. Invited dignitaries of the tribe sit at the right of the king, if the meal is taken in the interior of the house, at the left, however, if taken outside." It seems quite obvious that Holub emphasizes the contrast between the direction of the rising sun (east) and left. If he actually means this to be a contrast, we can then believe that in the Barotse area right and east as well as left and west are synonymous. This interpretation will, however, not be stressed here.

II

According to the material offered in this study the predominant importance of the concept of right is quite obvious. Scattered over most parts of the African continent are indications that the right is considered the superior side and is associated with such beliefs as are understood to be good and favorable. In a rather limited area of Northeast Africa and among the Ekoi of Cameroon we found a few cases in which the left side was preferred, but the same tribes considered the right more favorable in other relations, so that we do not have an area with exclusive left preference. The material in respect to this interesting problem, as far as the African continent is concerned, is certainly not sufficient to enable us to offer any definite theory. It may, however, be pointed out that most of the references dealing with right-predominance come from East Africa, the Sudan, Nigeria, and Southwest Africa, the last being closely connected culturally with East Africa. Only a few references can be found from among tribes inhabiting the central parts of the continent, such as the Boloki, Loango, Ababua, etc.

This distribution of right-preference, despite the incompleteness of our survey, seems to point to outside influences. As the clearest description was obtainable from those tribes which had more or less close cultural contacts with Arabs and Islam, it seems to me that such an influence might be suggested. The long-lasting Arabic influence upon North as well as East Africa, going back at least for a period of a millennium, cannot be overestimated. Such cultural influences may even have reached the tribes of the Congo area.

Such an introduction of culturally confined right-preference must have had a considerable influence upon handedness in general. That is the point I should like to emphasize in connection with the material presented: perhaps handedness is to a greater extent determined by custom and belief, so that even for primitive groups it is almost impossible to obtain data concerning the biological confinement of handedness. Among most of those African tribes which have an outspoken right-preference as shown above, we find the occurrence of most rigorous customs to "cure" left-handedness. So Kidd[83] writes: "If a child should seem to be naturally left-handed the people pour boiling water into a hole in the earth, and place the child's left hand in the hole, ramming the earth down around it; by this means the left hand becomes so scalded that the child is bound to use the right hand."

It seems to me that most of those tribes which live outside the area discussed above are rather indifferent toward the question of right or left. It would be too premature to make more definite statements as long as the available material is as scanty as it is now. Another important culture trait for right and left questions is the system of counting, i. e., whether the right or the left hand is used for expressing numbers. Although this problem is not discussed here, it is well to emphasize that, while in the East African region the right hand is predominantly used for counting, in the central parts of the continent the left is preferred. This is true for the Pygmies of the Congo area and for the Bushmen.[84]

Notes

1. I. S. Wile, *Handedness, Right and Left* (Boston, 1934).
2. A. Werner, "Right and Left Hand in Bantu," *Journal of the African Society* (London), 1904, pp. 112–16.
3. J. H. Weeks, *Among Congo Cannibals* (Philadelphia, 1913), p. 100.
4. E. P. Peschuel-Lösche, *Volkskunde von Loango* (Stuttgart, 1907), p. 325.
5. Ibid., p. 39.
6. P. A. Talbot, *In the Shadow of the Bush* (London, 1912), p. 218.
7. Ibid., p. 174.
8. Ibid., p. 324.
9. L. Frobenius, *Monumenta Africana* (Frankfurt a. M., 1929), p. 125.
10. G. Nachtigal, *Sahara und Sudan* (Leipzig, 1889), 3: 55, 341, 429.
11. G. Lindblom, *The A-Kamba in British East Africa* (Uppsala, 1920), p. 104.
12. Ibid., p. 291.

13. C. W. Hobley, *Ethnology of A-Kamba and Other East African Tribes* (Cambridge, 1910), p. 104.
14. J. Roscoe, *The Bakitara* (London, 1923), p. 323.
15. H. A. Stayt, *The Bavenda* (London, 1931), p. 161.
16. C. G. and B. C. Seligman, *Pagan Tribes of the Nilotic Sudan* (London, 1932), p. 133.
17. Ibid., p. 290.
18. F. R. Fülleborn, *Das Deutsche Nyassa- und Ruwuma-Gebiet* (Berlin, 1906), p. 328.
19. O. Baumann, *Durch Massailand zur Nilquelle* (Berlin, 1894), p. 187.
20. M. Merker, *Die Masai* (Berlin, 1904), p. 20.
21. S. Dornan, *Pygmies and Bushmen of the Kalahari* (London, 1925), p. 159.
22. H. Schinz, *Deutsch-Südwestafrika* (Oldenburg and Leipzig, 1891), p. 82.
23. W. Junker, *Reisen in Afrika* (Vienna and Olmütz, 1890), 1: 222, 223.
24. E. Westermarck, *Ritual and Relief in Morocco* (London, 1926), 2: 14.
25. H. L. Roth, "Notes on the Jekris," *Journal of the Anthropological Institute of Great Britain and Ireland* 28 (1899): 122.
26. T. H. Winterbottom, *Nachrichten von der Sierra Leone Küste* (Weimar, 1805), p. 164.
27. T. E. Bowdich, *Mission from Cape Coast Castle to Ashantee* (London, 1819), p. 490.
28. A. G. Leonard, *The Lower Niger and Its Tribes* (London, 1906), p. 310.
29. G. Tessmann, *Die Pangwe* (Berlin, 1913), 2: 131, 378, 379.
30. Roscoe, p. 20.
31. Baumann, p. 37.
32. Schinz., p. 277.
33. J. Irle, *Die Herero* (Gütersloh, 1906), p. 133.
34. W. D. Hambly, *The Ovimbundu of Angola,* Field Museum of Natural History Anthropological Series, vol. 21. 2 (Chicago, 1934), p. 253.
35. J. Halkin, *Les Ababua* (Brussels, 1911), p. 385.
36. R. P. Trilles, *Les Pygmées de la forêt équatoriale* (Paris, 1932), p. 202.
37. Westermarck, 2: 35.
38. Hobley, p. 104.
39. E. Nigmann, "Die Wahehe," *Baessler Archiv* (Berlin, 1908), p. 37.
40. Fuchs, in A. C. Hollis, *The Masai* (Oxford, 1909), p. 119.
41. B. Gutmann, *Dichten und Denken der Dschagga Neger* (Leipzig, 1909), p. 153.
42. A. Karasek and A. Eichhorn, "Beiträge zur Kenntnis der Waschambaa IV," *Baessler Archiv* 8 (Berlin, 1923–24): 34.
43. Müller, *Fetu,* p. 100. (Exact title unavailable at present.)
44. Sir John Hobbis Harris, *Gesellschaftsreise nach Schoa* (German edition) (Stuttgart, 1845), 2: 58.
45. C. H. Dundas, *Kilimanjaro and Its Peoples* (London, 1924), p. 212.

46. M. Munzinger, *Ostafrikanische Studien* (Basel, 1883), p. 159.
47. Des Marchais, *Voyage en Guinée, isles voisines et à Cayenne* (Paris, 1730), 1: 353.
48. Talbot, p. 324.
49. H. Tönjes, *Ovamboland, Land, Leute . . .* (Berlin, 1911), pp. 207, 208.
50. Irle, p. 132.
51. J. Campbell, *Travels in South Africa* (London, 1822), 2: 13.
52. Irle, p. 155.
53. Talbot, p. 324.
54. Hobley, p. 104.
55. Lindblom, p. 291.
56. M. Weiss, *Die Völkerstämme im Norden Deutsch-Ostafrikas* (Berlin, 1910), pp. 232, 233.
57. Gutmann, p. 153.
58. Harris, 1: 134.
59. Rebmann, in Krapf, *Reisen in Ostafrika* (Kornthal, 1858), 2: 5.
60. W. Munzinger, *Über die Sitten und das Recht der Bogos* (Winterthur, 1859), p. 90.
61. Fuchs, in Hollis, p. 80.
62. Herodotus, 2: 36.
63. Nachtigal, 3: 233.
64. Ibid., p. 440.
65. Salt, in *Neue Bibliothek der Reisen* (Weimar, 1814), 4: 241.
66. J. Bruce of Kinnaird, *Die Quellen des Nils* (Leipzig, 1790–91), 3: 265.
67. A. B. Ellis, *The Yoruba-speaking Peoples* (London, 1894), pp. 169–70.
68. Ibid., p. 97.
69. Fuchs, in Hollis, p. 5.
70. Weeks, p. 99.
71. R. Schmidt, *Les Waguha* (Brussels, 1911), p. 140.
72. Krapf, pp. 161, 164.
73. G. Fritsch, *Die Eingeborenen Südafrikas* (Breslau, 1872), p. 92.
74. Irle, p. 50.
75. Fuchs, in Hollis, p. 106.
76. B. Colle, *Les Baluba* (Brussels, 1913), 2: 430.
77. Ibid., p. 586.
78. H. Lichtenstein, *Reisen im südlichen Afrika* (Berlin, 1811), 1: 415.
79. H. von Sick, "Die Waniaturu," *Baessler Archiv*, vol. 5, 1. 2 (Leipzig, 1915): 54.
80. Nachtigal, 3: 227, 230, 341, 419 n., 429.
81. Krapf, 1: 72.
82. E. Holub, *Sieben Jahre in Südafrika* (Vienna, 1881), 2: 323.
83. D. Kidd, *Savage Childhood* (London, 1906), p. 296.
84. I. Schapera, *The Khoisan Peoples of South Africa* (London, 1930), p. 220; Trilles, p. 201.

Right and Left in Central Celebes

5

Alb. C. Kruyt

Robert Hertz, in his study "La Prééminence de la main droite" (1928), concedes that the origin of the customary use of the right hand in the ordinary activities of life must be sought in the human organism. But the complete subordination of the left hand to the right, whereby the former is not only left undeveloped but is also less regarded than the right, must be sought in causes lying outside the human organism.

The author traces the preference for the right hand over the left to primitive man's conception of the cosmos. This is seen as divided into two halves, masculine and feminine. In the former is found everything that conduces to the welfare and good fortune of man; the latter is identified with everything that brings harm and misfortune. One half is sacred, the other is profane. Man grasps at everything that comes from the former and repels everything which is thought to issue from the other side.

This division of the macrocosmos into a sacred half and a profane, the one beneficial and the other destructive, is applied by primitive man to himself, the microcosm. The right hand, which as a result of the human organism is naturally employed more than the left, is identified with the sacred and life-giving half of the cosmos, and the left is identified with the profane, impure, and death-dealing half. Man therefore does everything with his right hand, for he thinks that he will bring disaster upon himself if he uses the left.

"Rechts en Links bij de Bewoners van Midden-Celebes," *Bijdragen tot de Taal-, Land- en Volkenkunde van Nederlandsch-Indië* 100 (1941): 339–56. By permission of the Koninklijk Instituut voor Taal-, Land- en Volkenkunde. Translated by Rodney Needham.

It is very possible that the conception described here reflects the process of development by which over the whole earth the right has acquired a more prominent and more favored position than the left. Most peoples in the world have outgrown this primitive conception of the cosmos, but customs still exist here and there which point in that direction.

The inhabitants of central Celebes recognize the same differences in value between the right hand and the left as we do. There are persons among them who by preference use the left hand, and such people are said by the Toradja to be stupid. But in daily life this opinion is frequently belied. One of the divine heroes of the Mountain Toradja is known by the name of Guma Ngkoana, "he who wears his sword on the right side of his body," from which it appears that he was left-handed. When looking at pictures, the Toradja were immediately struck by anyone who was doing something with the left.

The Toradja have also reflected upon how it has come about that men do everything with the right hand, and why it is that the left has such unfavorable connotations. From conversations with the people about this subject it emerged that they explain the phenomenon by reference to the opposition which they make between the living and the dead. In what follows I shall set out the relation between right and left as they conceive it, without wishing to align myself with those who maintain that this concept evolved in the opposite way to that proposed by Hertz, namely, that the preference for right over left first arose through physical causes and that primitive man thereafter applied this distinction to his cosmology.

As has been stated above, the Toradja base their conception of right and left on the sharp opposition which they make between the living and the dead. The former live on earth, the latter have their abode in the underworld. Although the Toradja speak of themselves as "dark people," the living are white in comparison with the dead. The latter are pitch-black, in agreement with the night in which they live, whereas the living are white in agreement with the daylight in which every day they rejoice.

During the burning of the felled trees when forest land is cleared, if anyone becomes really black from contact with the charred wood he will repeatedly hear people say, "You look just like a dead person." When watch is being kept over a corpse, no one may sleep, for the vital spirit, which leaves the body during sleep, might easily come under the harmful influence of the deceased, or as the Toradja put it: the deceased can easily seize the roaming spirit of life and take it away to the realm of shadows. In order to prevent this, in fact, there is someone ready to blacken the face of the sleeper with soot in order to give him the appearance of a dead person, so that the deceased will leave him alone.

In the addresses which are made to the deceased, it is often said: "Thou art different from ourselves"; "thy way goes left, ours goes right"; "take no further notice of us, for we have nothing further to do with each other." Expressions of this kind make it plain that the deceased is a different kind of being from a living person.

This idea is also expressed in the stories which tell that the dead do everything precisely the other way around from the living. It is demonstrated, to begin with, in a number of mourning usages, which are intended to effect a temporary assimilation of the living to the dead so that the latter shall leave the former unmolested. For instance, on the occasion of a death it is forbidden to do anything that makes a noise. The explanation usually given is that people do not want to attract the attention of the deceased, but the basic idea underlying this prohibition is the opposition between the living and the dead. The living rejoice in their life, and they therefore laugh, sing, dance, and are noisy; the deceased leads a somber and joyless existence, wandering still over the earth but having no share in the pleasures of the living. Man carries out his daily occupations for the support of the body: he husks rice, chops wood, and pounds sago, while women weave their cotton. The deceased no longer does any of this, so the living must also stop. Tasks which produce no noise can still be performed unnoticed, but those just mentioned are noisy and can thus only be carried out at a fair distance from the house of the deceased.

In the Bada' district, during the period of mourning, people go so far as to turn the husking-blocks upside down and place them under the houses, simply to show that the dead do things in a way that is opposed to the custom of the living. Fresh vegetables, green leaves, and newly chopped wood may not be brought into the village at this time, but only dry wood and dry leaves.

When the living go to draw water, they lay the bamboo containers on their shoulder, but the dead behave differently: they carry the bamboos in the hand. For as long as the living are still in contact with the deceased, it is safer for them also to do so, and it is therefore a custom of mourning that the bamboos are carried in the hand when water is fetched. – When it was still the custom for men to carry spears as they walked, they carried them on the shoulder, and when they climbed up into a house they stuck the lower end of the shaft into the ground so that the spear stood upright. The dead behave differently; they hold the spear in the hand while they walk, and when they go up into a house they set the spear against one of the house poles. The living also have to do this during the mourning period. – Among many Toradja tribes the most usual way of carrying loads is to bear them on the back in a basket. The dead are different; they hang the burden from the end of a stick over the shoulder, and this is therefore the only permitted way during mourning.

In Bada' a small bundle of spare garments in a cloth is tied on to the chest of a corpse, for the dead have the chest at the back, and the calves of the leg in the place of the shinbones, all quite differently from living people. This idea is carried to such an extent that spirits are thought of as having the face and the feet turned backwards. There are earth-spirits of which it is said that their nose is upside down, with the nostrils on top. All these fantasies spring from the desire to give a tangible expression, as it were, to the idea that the dead are the antipodes of the living. In order that quite absurd oppositions such as a reversed face, an upside-down nose, or feet turned backwards might not be associated with the memory of the dear departed, these characteristics are transferred to nature-spirits (very often it cannot be made out whether people have the souls of the dead or nature-spirits in mind when they speak of such matters).

It is a general custom among the Toradja to make a field for the dead: a small patch of land, one or two square meters in extent, is cleared and planted with all sorts of crops such as are cultivated in dry fields, viz., maize, rice, yam, cassava, sweet potato, sugar cane, banana, pumpkin, and various vegetables. But because the dead do everything just the other way around from the living, the plants are put in upside down, with the top in the earth and the roots up. Among some tribes no plants are put in the field of the dead, but they plant instead the kernels or seeds of maize, gourds, cucumber, and Job's tears. Since these are all for the dead, the germ is cut out of the seeds in order to express in this fashion the opposition between living and dead. Of course, nothing flourishes in these little fields, but the living never go near them.

Such miniature gardens are not intended as a form of sacrifice, gift, or tribute to the dead; they are supposed to keep the dead away from the fields of the living, for any intervention by the dead would be fatal to the crops. This is particularly clear among those tribes which plant nothing in the patch of land cleared for the dead. When this is ready, the dead are enjoined: "Plant anything that you like here, but stay away from my field."

At the making of the fence for the garden of the dead, also, the opposition living/dead is not forgotten. When the living fence their fields, they take care that the posts which keep the fence firm are set into the ground with the root end, or the part where the branch had joined the tree, down. This is because if a post were stood the other way up, this would form a weak point in the fence where buffaloes and pigs would break through. When the miniature field for the dead is laid out, however, things have to be done in the reverse way: it is then the top ends of the posts which are driven into the ground.

The opposition between the living and the dead extends also to the language spoken. The dead speak the same language as the living, only the meanings given to the words are the reverse of those ascribed to them by the living. "Yes" on earth means "no" in the underworld. When the living say "forwards," the dead understand this as "backwards" or as "stand still." In the many tales of meetings between the living and the dead, such as are found throughout the Archipelago, these differences between words are referred to as a source of continual misunderstanding. This peculiarity of speech is not confined to the dead, but all sorts of other spirits can also be recognized by it.

There are also tribes which maintain that not only the meanings of the words change in the mouths of the dead, but that also the syllables of the words are reversed, so that the first and last syllables are transposed. Thus the dead speak of *nora* when the living say *rano,* "lake"; in the mouths of the dead, *madago,* "good," is pronounced as *godama.* Both linguistic forms have the same meaning: the former expresses the opposition in the meanings of the words, the latter in their forms.

It is clear from the above how the inhabitants of central Celebes naively make it plain that a dead person is a quite other being than a living. The people pursue this idea in the reasoning that: We living do everything with our right hand, therefore the dead do everything with the left. Or, as it is otherwise put: what for the living is right, for the dead is left. This is very quickly conveyed to the understanding of someone who has just died. As soon as the deceased starts on the journey to the land of the dead, he comes to a point where the path forks into two. In his living state he ought to choose the right-hand path, since right is then more favored than left. But if he did so in this case he would return to earth among the living. If, as a dead person, he wishes to arrive at the abode of the deceased ancestors, then he must take the left-hand path.

A remarkable application of this idea is provided by the Sa'dan Toradja in their story of Tato' Pondang. This man lost his daughter, and was inconsolable over the loss. One day, a stranger came to him and said that he was able to take him to his daughter in the land of the dead. After Tato' Pondang had accepted this offer, the stranger poured water three times over his head, turned him three times around to the left, and had him walk backwards out of his compound. By doing this, Tato' Pondang became a dead person, and invisible to the living. – Once arrived in the town of the dead, Tato' Pondang did indeed see his daughter again, but she forced her father after a short stay to return to earth. When Tato' Pondang had returned among the living, he had the gift of seeing right through people: he could see their brains, their lungs, intestines, and all of their internal organs. He became so sick and tired of this sight that he begged his guide to turn him into an ordinary man again. Thereupon the stranger brought Tato' Pondang to his house and had him stand at the bottom of the steps. Then he took a white hen and slaughtered it over the head of the spell-bound man so that the blood ran down over his face. Then the stranger turned him three times around to the right and pushed him backwards off the yard of the house. By this means Tato' Pondang became once more an ordinary man.

All sorts of customs relating to a corpse, so long as it remains above ground, show clearly that account is taken of the fact that the deceased uses his left hand in place of his right. During this period the deceased is thought to be still among the living. Therefore there is a general custom that whenever the living have a meal, they set a plate or bowl with food in it next to the corpse. The plate is usually placed at the left side of the corpse, which is lying on its back; Toradja have often told me that they do so because the deceased eats with his left hand. In some districts the food is set down at the right side of the body, probably in view of the fact that the deceased is still counted among the living. The uncertainty about whether a dead person belongs among the living or among the dead, during the time when the corpse lies in the house, is presumably the reason that some families have been led to place the food on the chest or between the legs of the body, whereby the deceased can reach it with either the right or the left hand.

Among the Bare'e-speaking Toradja, nothing made of iron may be given to the deceased. Among other Toradja groups, however, this is permitted, so that a man is provided with his sword and a woman with her gardening-knife. These objects are always laid at the right side of the corpse, so that he or she may be able to grasp them with the left hand.

The idea that the deceased has to be prepared to do things with his left emerges sometimes in even the smallest matters. Thus there is a custom among the To i Rampi' to cross the arms of the corpse (which lies on its back), in contrast to the general usage of stretching the arms along the sides. (This crossing of the arms is presumably a survival of the practice of burying the corpse in a squatting posture.) The right arm is crossed under the left, doubtless in the intention that the deceased shall be ready to use the left arm.

A custom which agrees with the idea that the dead do everything with the left hand is that the living employ the left whenever they do anything for or in connection with the dead. It has been described above how the Toradja make little gardens for their dead. All the work involved is done with the left hand. – When food is set aside for the deceased, at a mealtime, this is done with the left hand. The plate is put down by the corpse, so long as this is still in the house, with the left hand. – Offerings of food are laid down before the dead in various circumstances; frequently an offering for the dead is dropped through the floor boards. These acts are all performed with the left hand.

Among practically all of the Toradja it is forbidden for a widow or a widower, and often for certain close relatives of the deceased as well, to eat rice during the period of strict mourning. This period is brought to a close with a ceremonial meal, at which the widow (or widower) takes some cooked rice in each hand; that which is in the left hand is cast through the crevices in the floor with the words, "Eat thy rice." Simultaneously, the rice that is in the right hand is thrust into the mouth. Others place a little rice on the left elbow, with which they throw it away for the dead, after which they themselves eat. There are still other ways of terminating the prohibition on eating rice, but the deceased is always served with the left hand.

The Toradja frequently make offerings of strips of *fuya* [bark-cloth] to the souls of the dead and to spirits. When these strips are to keep the souls of the dead at a distance they are held in the left hand, or they are cast in the direction of the dead with this hand. In Bada' the person who removes the afterbirth holds a piece of white *fuya* in the left hand; elsewhere it is used to cover the head; the intention is that the souls of the dead shall be kept away by it.[1]

The idea that left is connected with the dead and right with the living allows us to see the significance of the division of a number of phenomena into death-dealing and life-giving, according to whether they are perceived to our left or to our right.

It is a general rule concerning birds of omen that the cries of auspicious birds, when heard only on the right, bring good fortune. If the same sound is heard to the left, this means misfortune, sickness, or death. The meaning of this opposition appears the most clearly in the observation of bird-cries when on the warpath. If an auspicious noise is heard to our right, this brings life and success, i.e., we shall defeat our enemy. If the sound comes from the left, the enemy hear the same noise as an auspicious sign to their right; this means good fortune and life for them, i.e., they will kill us. The situation can be expressed as follows: we hear to our left the sounds which are auspicious for our enemies. Here again, left is death, right is life.

In the case of birds whose cries are by nature inauspicious, the idea is precisely the reverse: if they are heard on the right they have a harmful influence on my life, but if they are heard on the left they can do no harm; in the latter event they favor us, for to the enemy these ill-boding sounds are on the right, and they therefore attack their life-force.

Even if one does not have to deal with human enemies, there are still lots of spirits which are after our life and thus have to be put on a par with souls of the dead. So the opposition right = life, and left = death, is involved in the observation of ominous sounds in everyday life as well. This is so in working in the fields, when traveling, and when out hunting. One of the most highly regarded and auspicious birds is the kingfisher (Sauropatis chlorus). The Toradja are delighted to hear it, particularly when they are hunting. It is said in general of its cries that they are strengthening when heard on the right and weakening when heard on the left.

It is not only the cries of omen-birds which have meaning for men, but also their flight. If we enter into the ideas of the Toradja, it is clear that when a bird of good fortune, i.e., a bird whose cries are in themselves auspicious, flies across our path from left to right, this means prosperity or success for us, since it transfers death and evil from the left to the right, i.e., it changes these into good fortune and life. If the bird flies from right to left, then it changes life into death, and turns our good fortune into adversity, our health into sickness.

In the case of birds whose cries in themselves exert an evil influence, the matter has once more to be turned round. If they fly from the left to the right they bring the harm which they naturally cause over to the side of good fortune, and this turns our well-being into adversity. The Posso Toradja express the situation as follows: the bird takes away life (the life-force). If the bird goes in the opposite direction, it transfers the evil that it bears out of our life and into the sphere of death, thereby rendering us a great service.[2] Whenever it happens to someone from the Pu'umboto district (Posso) that an "evil" bird crosses his path from left to right, he quickly runs seven times around a tree, apparently with the aim of transferring to the tree the evil that the bird has brought into his life.

What has been said here about the flight of omen-birds applies also to the direction in which a snake crosses our path. Here too there is a difference of opinion, such that some people regard the movement from left to right as auspicious while others believe the opposite; this results from the vague ideas which are entertained about the snake, according to which it is sometimes considered as the bearer of good fortune and sometimes again as the bringer of adversity.

The principle of right and left applies to many other omens. In former times, when the Toradja went on the warpath and heard the grumbling sound of a wild pig on the right side, this was taken as a lament for the lives which some members of the party were to lose; if this noise was heard on the left, it meant a lamentation over the enemy and was thus favorable to the war party. If the pig was startled and let out a squeal, this was a cry of coming triumph over the enemy if heard on the right, and a sign of victory for the enemy if heard on the left. – The shrieks of monkeys heard on the right foretold our good fortune; heard on the left, they meant success for the enemy.

One of the most dreaded omens is the fall of a tree when there is no direct cause to be seen. Trees hold off in the air all the afflictions which can injure man; they are the brooms of the air; illnesses and misfortune are transferred to trees. If a tree falls, it shows that it is no longer able to contain the evil: it lets the evil loose, so that it spreads and works harm on men, causing them to fall sick and die. If the tree falls to the right of us, the evil "feeds" on our life. If it falls to the left, then it is other people who will be afflicted, not us.

If anyone dreams that he loses a tooth, this means that a member of his family will die; if it is a right molar, he has to fear the loss of his wife or child; if it is a left molar that falls out in the dream, he has not much to worry about, since this signifies the death of a distant relative.

The same is the case with the terrifying phenomenon sometimes presented by a corpse, that one or both of its eyes will not stay shut. It is said of this that the deceased is looking around for one of the survivors, whose life-force he will take away with him to hell. If it is the right eye that stays open it is more serious than the left, for in the former case a very close member of the family will die, whereas in the latter case it is a distant relative of the deceased who will be affected.

When a Toradja mother has recuperated after giving birth, she looks very closely at the little body of the newborn child in order to see whether it has any red or black birthmarks on its skin. Each spot will have something to say to her about the future fate of her child, according to the place on the body where it is found. In general, spots on the right side of the body have a favorable significance, whereas those on the left side foretell misfortune and adversity.

We can no longer be surprised at the fact that right and left play a great part in all important circumstances of life; in order to ensure life, one must do everything with the right, because left means death. When a bridegroom goes up into the house of his bride on the wedding day, he and his escort have to set their right foot on the first rung of the steps, so that they shall also enter the house with the right foot (for this reason the number of steps is always uneven). As he climbs up, he counts: life (right), death (left), life, death, and so on, until with "life" (right) he arrives in the house. Others count: *pone,* "ascend" (a long life), *na'u,* "descend" (a short life), and so on, so that they will enter the house with *pone.*

When a shaman has completed her efforts to procure life-force, she receives as her fee the right forefoot of the pig that is sacrificed.[3]

Right and left play an especially great part in the harvesting of rice, which supports human life, for the force of this precious foodstuff must not be impaired by being brought into contact with the left. Previously, at the distribution of the seed-rice to the planters, these have to take care that the rice stays on the right side of the women who plant it. If they were to hold it on the left, people say that the workers would get a pain in the back. *Sirih-pinang* is constantly brought around to women as they reap the harvest; the helpers must stay on their right. When the leader of the harvest cooks the first new rice, she has to take care to do nothing with her left hand.[4] – If she (the leader) wishes to bathe in the course of the harvesting (in some tribes it is forbidden to do so at this time), when she gets to the water she sets her right foot on a stone which is covered with fern (*siro*). As a rite of transition before the bathing of the entire body, she sprinkles water over her foot and thereafter bathes.[5]

Among the Toradja, the purpose of divination is not so much to find out whether something is good or bad, whether it will bring good or ill-fortune, but to impart strength to man and to fortify his life. This is the reason that the test is repeated many times until the desired result has been obtained. It is only to be expected that right and left will be decisive in divination, since right brings life and left brings death. In the form of divination which involves the killing of a dog or a hen, the auspicious or inauspicious character of the sacrifice is determined by the position of the animal as it dies; if it lies on its right side it brings strength and life, whereas if it is on its left it brings misfortune.

One of the most common forms of divination among the Toradja is the string-oracle: four cords or long stems of grass which are woven together and wound round the hand with the eight ends knotted two by two to each other. From the figure that is formed by the knotted string after it is unwound, it is divined whether prosperity or adversity is foretold. If a traveling party have consulted the oracle in this way after the observation of an evil omen, all the members of the party have to touch the hand of their leader in which the oracle is held in order to partake in the favorable consequences which neutralize the operation of the bad omen. This they have to do with the left hand, for, as the Toradja say, if they did so with the right hand the evil effect of the omen would return, i.e., its power would be restored. In the light of what has been discussed above, we can say that our life is threatened anew with death by contact with the right hand.

If it is learned that a sickness is approaching, an offering-place is set up at the entrance to the village, on the left-hand side of the path as one leaves. What is in question here is death, and thus the left side of man. If it is done to the right, the people of Posso say: *maewa dju'a,* i.e., resist the sickness. This is because the disease must have the offering on its right side as it enters the village in order to receive it (to experience its effect and to pass on without causing harm).[6]

Ritual activities often feature the right and the left. The former is intended to strengthen human life, and the latter is supposed to disarm the evil powers which bring death. At the end of a period of sickness, when all the evil which is thought to be the cause of the illness is expelled from the village, sweeping is first done with a broom held in the right hand, in order to gain strength, and then with the left hand, in order to remove the evil, the death.

When the priest of agriculture carries out the ritual at the commencement of work in the fields, he holds in his left hand a bundle of grass on which everything that brings evil is collected, while he holds in his right hand a bunch of life-sustaining (sacred) plants which give life and strength to men.

Every year a ceremony of sacrifice is carried out at which the buffaloes are blessed, so that they will suffer no harmful consequences from their labor in the wet rice-fields, where they churn up the ground with their clumsy hooves. On this occasion they are sprinkled with water in which life-giving herbs have been placed. The officiant sprinkles this water once with the left hand in order to expel all evil (*bui*) from the animals, and he then sprinkles water five times with the right hand in order to strengthen their lives.

The husking of the first rice of the new harvest always takes place with some ceremony. As a preliminary act, the person in charge of the work in the fields brings down his left elbow seven times on to the bundle of rice, as though he were husking with it. Then he does the same thing with the right elbow. The former action is supposed once more to render the evil harmless and to prevent it removing the nutritional value from the rice; the latter action, performed with the right, is thought to strengthen its power of sustenance.

When a woman in childbirth goes to bathe for the first time after her delivery, she takes a burning length of twisted barkcloth in her hand in order to keep at a distance, with its smoke and its smell, the malicious spirits which lie in wait for her. When she arrives at the water, she sticks a stem of reed from the bank into the ground as a sacrificial stake; to the right side of it she ties a small strip of barkcloth as an offering to beg life; the burning length is laid on the ground to the left of it.

It is difficult to say what precisely are the thoughts of a Toradja mother when she puts her baby to the breast for the first time; but always she makes it suck first at the left breast, apparently in order to prevent any interference on the part of the dead, for when there is insufficient milk this is always ascribed to the influence of the dead (in such cases the milk is "bought" from the dead). If the mother were to give her child to suck from the right breast first, it would subsequently suffer from continual hunger and would perpetually cry at the breast.

We have already seen how great is the significance which is attached to the flight of birds as foretelling the future: from right to left puts our fate in the realm of death, whereas from left to right presages life. The former is thus inauspicious, the latter is auspicious. The same principle is applied by man in his ritual activities, which take place frequently at all kinds of ceremonies. It would make up a long list if I were to mention everything that I have noted down concerning these rites, and I shall give just a few examples.

When a band of warriors had returned successfully from an expedition against the enemy, before entering the temple they had to make seven circuits of the building from left to right: the scalps of the defeated enemy, which had been brought back, provided life for the tribe.

When rice is planted, the planters have to go always from left to right. When the mature rice is cut, the leader of the harvesters so arranges them that they stand in a row which forms the radius of a circle, as it were, moving from left to right over the field.

Rituals of the kind are particularly prominent at the sacrifices, performed by shamans, which are thought to procure life for men, animals, and plants. The dances performed repeatedly by the shamans go firstly a certain number of times (usually four) from right to left, in order to expel all evil and all disruptive influences, and then an odd number (usually seven) from left to right, in order to bring life and prosperity to men.

One of the ceremonies in the shamanic ritual as held in Bada' goes as follows: The officiating shamans, with a number of elders, sit down together in a circle around a winnow containing some husked rice. The chief shaman has some knives (four or seven) in her hand. At a certain moment she drops these in front of an old man who is seated to her left. This man picks them up with his left hand, and then in his turn drops them before his own left-hand neighbor. In this way the knives are passed twice around the complete circle. After this the knives are passed around to the right with the right hand; this also is done twice. In answer to my questions about the meaning of this, the people said that in the circulation from right to left the knives were grasped by the souls of the dead, and that the latter were thereby prevented from making the shamans ill. In the circulation from left to right the knives are the "bridge" along which the spirits (*anitu*), who give life, furnish the shamans with spiritual and physical force.

The post to which the sacrificial beast (a buffalo) is to be tethered in order to be killed is brought ceremonially to the spot where it is to be set in the ground. Before this happens, the shamans make three rightwise circuits of the trunk of the tree. When the post is standing in the hole, the shamans each take a handful of husked rice and swing their arm seven times up the length of the wood, releasing the rice on the seventh swing. Then they dance around it twice from left to right. In this way the post is charged with life and power.

One of the sins which are visited upon the entire people is the perpetration of incest. At the rite which serves to expiate a lesser degree of this sin, the officiant twice walks seven times around the guilty pair, sprinkling the while with cooling water from a bunch of life-giving plants: first he walks seven times from right to left in order to remove the sin from the couple and to cast it out, then he walks seven times from left to right in order to supply them with strength so that they will not succumb to the evil that they have committed.—The villagers are also decontaminated in the same way. The officiant goes three times round the group of villagers, sprinkling the water into the air, and four times in the opposite direction, letting the life-giving water fall on the people.

The same is seen at the death-dance in Napu, on the occasion of the *ende*-ceremony: the dance goes three times from left to right, and four times the other way. At the dedication of the buffaloes, which we have mentioned above, the (sevenfold) circumambulation with the offerings is made from left to right, so that in this case the strength and life shall be conferred on the beasts. When the people are asked the reason for this, they can only answer that it is not good to go in the opposite direction. In some areas the circumambulation is carried out in both directions; going to the left is then supposed to remove all evil *(bui)* from the animals, and going to the right obtains life-force.

In order to remove the weakening influence of someone's death from his surviving relatives, the members of the family of the deceased form a row and, holding each other's hands, walk a number of times under a small gateway, on which the contamination of the death is supposed to remain. They go seven times through it from right to left, and three times in the opposite direction.

In the district of Rampi', in order to fortify the vitality of small children they are passed seven times in a circular motion over the buffalo which is to be killed for them. This movement is made from left to right, "so that they shall have a long life," as is said in explanation.

In building a house it may well happen that somebody drops part of the material. This is not good, for the house is thereby made unhealthy. In order to nullify the deleterious result of such an event, a hen is killed inside the house and its head is then thrown from right to left over the ridge of the roof. The threatened ill consequences are thus returned to the place where they belong—to the left.

Finally, one more example from hunting practices. It may happen that the dogs are bewitched in one way or another, or that they come under a spell. This is shown by the fact that they no longer catch anything. Among the western Toradja, one of the means of removing the magic or the spell from the animals consists in mixing a certain medicine with their food. As this remedy is stirred into the food, the hand must turn seven times from left to right and three times from right to left.

NOTES

1. On Timor, a Belu mother, soon after the rites marking her delivery, places a coconut shell with some ash at the intersection of two paths, a place where souls of the dead and other spirits are to be found (the ash is taken from the hearth of the fire at which the woman warmed herself while she was lying-in). Then she kicks the coconut shell far away with the heel of her left foot. According to the source, she "thus kicks away from herself any further consequences of the child-birth." Perhaps it might be more correct to say that by scattering the ash she prevents the dead and the other spirits from approaching her. (Grijzen 1904: 51.)

2. The same differentiation between bird-cries heard on the right and the left, or in the flight of birds to the right or in the other direction, is also reported from other peoples, e.g., the Dayak. Hose and McDougall report that the flight of birds from right to left is auspicious, which we may take to refer to birds which are thought of as bringers of evil (Hose and McDougall 1912, 2: 58). Thus Gomes says that the calls of the *nendak, katupong,* and *beragai* must be heard to the left; if they are heard on the right "they are not propitious." The calls of "sacred" birds must be heard on the right side. (Gomes 1911: 153.)

3. Grijzen reports of the Belu that at a marriage a cut is made in the right forefoot of the sacrificial pig. The blood from the wound is collected in a small container, and everybody present is then dabbed with it. (Grijzen 1904: 59.)

4. On the Minahassa, Adam writes: "When a house is built, the beams must be set in place and measurements made always on the left (i.e., while remaining oneself on the right side of the house) . . . ; in the same way Tontemboan agricultural priests and diviners from the calls of birds, when they circumambulated the village stone, had to keep this on their left" (Adam 1925: 431).—When a man in Minahassa was clearing land, he had to keep the area that was to be worked on his left, for he had to keep to the right side of the plot that was to be planted (Schwarz 1907: 159).

5. Among the Dayak also the right foot and the right arm have a special significance for the whole body. Thus Hose and McDougall write that eight days after a child is named the shaman comes to ask for blessings on it. On this occasion the child is brought out on to the front gallery and is displayed to all the inhabitants of the house. One of the members of the family makes a cross with charcoal on the right foot of the child, who is then taken to the door of each apartment in order to receive a gift. The charcoal cross protects the life of the infant from malevolent forces; the sign on the right foot holds good for the entire body. (Hose and McDougall 1912, 2: 163.)—Among the Kenya Dayak, at the head-hunting ceremony which gave life and health to the tribe, blood from the sacrificial animal was smeared on the right arm alone of the participants (Elshout 1926: 294).—At the sacrifice held for a newborn baby, the infant is smeared on the right arm with blood from the slaughtered animal in order to transfer to the baby the purificatory (life-strengthening) effect of the blood (Elshout 1923: 204).—It is noteworthy, also, that in Kenya society people of high birth are called *dia tau,* i.e., those of the right (Elshout 1923: 186).

6. Mallinckrodt relates that the Dayak of south Borneo distinguish two sorts of *karuhai,* magical objects. "These *karuhai* are differentiated in the first place as those of the left side, those which put into effect evil intentions such as black magic or fornication, etc., and those of the right side, which are employed in right ways, e.g., to be profitable in trade, to become a great plaiter, and so on" (Mallinckrodt 1927: 637). Here once more, therefore, left brings ruin and death, right brings success and life.

Geurtjens describes a sacrifice of atonement for evil committed on the Kei Islands. The priest begins his invocation of the gods with: "I bless away all evil, sin, impurity, and adversity, so that this shall all pass by God and vanish at his left side." Later in the rite, after he has rubbed oil into the band which he wears on his head, he prays that "all evil shall pass by the left side of the place of sacrifice and disappear." The priest then breaks off the points of his head-band and throws them away to his left. (Geurtjens 1921: 93, 94.)

I have found an interesting application of right and left reported by van den Berg in connection with the installation of a new ruler on Buton. The Koran is opened at a random place; the number of times that the letter *kh* appears on the right-hand page is then counted, and the number of times that *sh* appears on the left-hand page. If there are more of the former than of the latter, the decision is good, otherwise not. Here, too, once more: right brings life, left brings death. (Van den Berg 1939: 472.)

References

Adam, L.

1925 Zeden en Gewoonten en het daarmee samenhangend Adatrecht van het Minahassische Volk. *Bijdragen tot de Taal-, Land en Volkenkunde van Nederlandsch-Indië* 81: 424–99.

Berg, E. J. van den

1939 Adatgebruiken in verband met de Sultansinstallatie in Boeton. *Tijdschrift voor Indische Taal-, Land- en Volkenkunde* 79:469–528.

Elshout, J. M.

1923 *Over de Geneeskunde der Kĕnja-Dajak in Centraal-Borneo in verband met hunnen Godsdienst.* Amsterdam.

1926 *De Kĕnja-Dajak uit het Apo-kajangebied: bijdragen tot de kennis van Centraal-Borneo.* 's-Gravenhage.

Geurtjens, H.

1921 *Uit een Vreemde Wereld: of, het leven en streven der inlanders op de Kei-eilanden.* s'-Hertogenbosch.

Gomes, E. W.

1911 *Seventeen years among the Sea Dyaks of Borneo.* London.

Grijzen, H. J.

1904 Mededeelingen omtrent Beloe of Midden-Timor. *Verhandelingen van het Batavisaasch Genootschap van Kunsten en Wetenschappen,* vol. 54.

HERTZ, R.
1928 *Mélanges de sociologie religieuse et folklore*. Paris. ["La Prééminence de la main droite," pp. 99–129; see chap. 1 above.]
HOSE, C., AND MCDOUGALL, W.
1912 *The pagan tribes of Borneo*. 2 vols. London.
MALLINCKRODT, J.
1927 Het Begrip *djawi* bij de Dajak van Zuid-Borneo. *Koloniaal Tijdschrift* 16: 629–50.
SCHWARZ, J. A. T.
1907 *Tontemboansche Teksten*. 3 vols. Leiden.

Nuer Spear Symbolism

6

E. E. Evans-Pritchard

When I think of the sacrifices I have witnessed in Nuerland there are two objects I see most vividly and which sum up for me the sacrificial rite: the spear brandished in the right hand of the officiant as he walks up and down past the victim delivering his invocation, and the beast awaiting its death. It is not the figure of the officiant or what he says which evokes the most vivid impression, but the brandished spear in his right hand.

The *lam* or invocation states the intention of the sacrifice. Its words are a projection of the will and desire of the person as he turns towards Spirit; and an essential part of the action is the brandishing of the spear. As the man who discharges the priestly office walks up and down delivering his oration the movements of the spear in his right hand emphasize his words: opening and closing his fingers on it, poising it in his hand, raising it as though to strike, making little jabs with it into the air, and so on. These movements are an integral part of the expression of intention, and there is more to the action than meets the eye.

In Nuer ritual the meaning of the symbolism is generally at once evident to ourselves, at any rate in its main import, for there is an intrinsic relation between the symbol and what it stands for. When an animal is cut in half in cases of incest, to allow intermarriage between distant kin, before a man takes his dead brother's wife in leviratic union, at the closing of an age-set, in mortuary ceremonies, and on other occasions, we can at once perceive how the purpose of the rite is expressed in the severing of the carcass. A relationship of

---

Anthropological Quarterly 1 (1953): 1–19. Reprinted with the permission of the editors.

one kind or another between persons is being severed.[1] Likewise the symbolism of the rite, common among primitive peoples, of putting out fires and relighting them at a man's mortuary ceremony, and in the case of the rehabilitation of a homicide the relighting of them with firesticks, is at once evident for us. The past is finished with; one begins anew. Likewise the shaving of the head of a bride at her marriage, of a boy at his initiation, of a kinsman at a mortuary ceremony, and of a homicide at the settlement of a feud expresses, and brings about, by symbolic action the passing from one state to another as obviously for us as for the Nuer. Again, we can see immediately also the appropriateness of the action to the situation and purpose in the ritual making of a line or boundary (*kee*). A leopard-skin priest cuts a line between opposing factions to forbid combat. The dominant lineages of the Gaagwong and Lek tribes may not, for a mythical reason, tether their cattle in a common kraal, but if they cannot conveniently avoid doing so a line of earth is thrown up between the sections of the kraal occupied by each. On the other hand, whilst there is generally a ridge of raised earth dividing adjacent gardens of neighbors this is absent when the owners of them are members of the same *ric* or age-set. Another, and final, example is that of a man who leaves the tribal territory where he was born and brought up to reside in the territory of a different tribe. He may then—it may not be a regular practice—take a pot of earth from his natal territory and mix it in an infusion with earth from the territory of his adoption, and drink the infusion, on each occasion adding more of the new earth and less of the old, thereby slowly making the transference from his old to his new home. We have no difficulty at all in understanding and entering into this symbolism.

Since we at once perceive the meaning of the symbolism of the ritual action we may suppose that Nuer also perceive its logical fitness to its purpose; and, indeed, it is often certain that they do so, for if asked to explain what they are doing they interpret the symbolism of a rite in terms of its purpose. The symbolism is manifest to them, as it is to us. But there is a deeper symbolism which is so embedded in ritual action that its meaning is neither obvious nor explicit. The performer may be only partly aware or even be unaware that it has one. Interpretation may then be difficult for a person of alien culture, and the door is open for every kind of extravagant guesswork to enter. Nevertheless if it be rash in such circumstances to put forward symbolic interpretations of ritual acts, or features of them, we are sometimes compelled to make the attempt, as in this excursus on the spear, by the very emphasis given to them by the culture we are trying to understand.

Spear symbolism figures prominently, in one way or another, among the Nilotic peoples. Among the Shilluk, the spears of Nyikang are emblems of the sacral kingship.[2] Ancient spears figure also among the royal emblems of the Anuak.[3] Among the Lango, spears, some of great age, play an important part in the ritual of rain-making; and spears are also offered to God in one of his refractions and are placed in his shrines.[4] The clans and lineages of the Luo of Kenya have their sacred spears, known as "spears of sacrifice," which are heirlooms used ritually on occasions of war and general calamity.[5] The rain-maker chiefs of the Acholi likewise possess sacred spears.[6] The religious leader of a Dinka community possesses ancient spear emblems and is known as "the master of the fishing spear."[7] In all these instances the spears are sacred relics and for the most part also emblems of office. Among the Nuer we are not so much concerned with relics or office as with the idea of vitality, vitality of the individual and of the lineage.

Since we have no spears ourselves and nothing which takes their place in our lives it is difficult for us to appreciate their importance for Nuer. Nuer have no knives, other than that (*ngom*) used for cutting the marks of manhood at initiation, so that their fighting spears, besides their use as weapons, have to serve where other peoples use knives.[8] A man's fighting spear (*mut*) is constantly in his hand, forming almost part of him—when he is fighting, hunting, traveling, herding, dancing, displaying himself with his oxen, playing with his comrades, and so on—and when he lays it down it is within his reach; and he is never tired of sharpening and polishing it, for a Nuer is very proud of his spear. In writing a preliminary account of Nuer age-sets many years ago and without reference to the symbolic significance of the spear I wrote that "one is surprised at the real feeling a Nuer expresses for his spear, almost as though it were animate and not a mere weapon."[9] Later I came to realize better that in a sense it is animate, for it is an extension of the right hand, which stands for the strength, vitality, and virtue of the person. It is a projection of the self, so when a man hurls his spear he cries out either "my right hand" or the name of the ox with which he is identified.

The spear, being an extension of the right hand, stands for all that the right hand stands for. Robert Hertz has shown us in a brilliant essay how in primitive societies the polarities of thought and values divide the person also into two contrasted and opposed sides, the right and the left, the right being associated with strength, goodness, and life, and the left with weakness, evil, and death.[10] A slight organic asymmetry is made the symbol of absolute moral polarity. For the Nuer also the right arm stands for what is strong, virile, and vital and consequently for masculinity and hence for the paternal kin and the lineage. Therefore during the discussions about bridewealth in the byre of the bride's home on her wedding day the bridegroom's people sit on the right side of the byre and the bride's people on the left side. Therefore also, when the carcasses of oxen sacrificed at marriage ceremonies are divided among the kin, the right fore and hind legs are the portions of the father's brothers and sisters and the left fore and hind legs are the portions of the mother's brothers and sisters.[11] The left side symbolizes evil as well as femininity, and there is here a double association, for the female principle is also associated with evil directly, as it were, and not merely through the convergence of femininity and evil in the concept of the left side. Thus we have two opposites, the one comprising the left side, weakness, femininity, and evil, and the other comprising the right side, strength, masculinity, and goodness.

I give a few examples of the association of the right side with good and the left side with evil. When a fruit or animal is cut in two at sacrifices the left half may be either thrown or given away and only the right half be consumed by the people of the home. It is propitious for a sacrificial ox stabbed with the spear to fall on its right side and unpropitious for it to fall on its left side. A dead man is buried to the left of his hut or windscreen, the side of misfortune. A woman is said to warn her son that when he visits his bride to cohabit with her she may crouch to the right side of the entrance to the hut so that he has to enter by the left side. If she does this he must order her to the other side lest some ill come to him.[12] If a man stubs his "good foot" it is a good omen and if he stubs his "bad foot" it is a bad omen. I was told that either foot may be the good or bad one—experience showing any individual which is which for him—but there is a convention that if a man's first child is a boy the right foot, and if it is a girl the left foot, becomes the good one.

When I was in Nuerland I was only half aware of the significance of left and right for Nuer. When writing this paper I found therefore that in several respects my observations, or at any rate what I had recorded, were insufficient to answer certain questions that arose from a further consideration of the left-right polarity. It occurred to me that if the representations were as I supposed them to be then, for example, when Nuer deform the horns of their favourite oxen, with which they identify themselves, it should be always the left, and never the right, horn which is trained downwards. Or again, when Nuer erect the sacred pole, associated with the spirits of their lineage and also with its ghosts, at the entrance to their windscreens, which is their practice, it should always be to the right of the windscreen (taking, in this case, bearings from within it). My recollection, confirmed by the evidence of my photographs, supported these conclusions, but I asked Dr. Lienhardt and Dr. Howell to verify them, which they have been able to do. It should follow also that a husband sleeps on the right side of the hut and his wife on the left side, and here again Dr. Lienhardt has been good enough to confirm that this is the invariable practice. He has made a further and very important observation. I was aware that the west is associated with death and the east with life, but I did not know, till he told me, that east is identified with right and west with left, thus bringing into the left-right polarity the polar representations not only of life and death but also of the cardinal points east and west.

It is entirely in accord with what we have learnt of the associations with the left and right hands in Nuer thought, and also with what Hertz has told us in his essay, that Nuer youths should emphasize the contrast between the two hands by putting the left arm out of action together for months or even a year or two. This they do by pressing a series of metal rings into the flesh of the left arm from the wrist upwards so tightly that sores and great pain result and the arm is rendered useless for any purpose other than the display of fortitude and as a passive instrument for the right hand to play upon. A ring on a finger of the right hand is rubbed up and down the discs on the imprisoned left arm to accompany the compliments and endearments of courtship. Such a mutilation is only fully intelligible in terms of symbolic associations—or with what Hertz calls the collective consciousness. Here the fact that it is only the left horn of favorite oxen which is debased (if the right is trained at all it is trained upwards) is of great significance, for a man and his favorite ox are identified. What he does to his left hand he does to his ox's left horn: what he does to the ox he does to himself.

It is perhaps important to add, before proceeding further, that the ideas of weakness, femininity, and evil do not derive from any possible organic inferiority of the left hand. If anything, as Hertz suggests, it is the other way around. That Nuer do not think of the left hand as being in a material sense evil is shown by the fact that left-handed persons suffer no disabilities at all and are not considered in other respects as different from other people.[13] Nuer do not, in my experience, attach any importance to the matter, but simply say of a left-handed man that his left hand is his right hand. It is as a symbol, not as a thing in itself, that the left hand has significance for them. Similarly, the left half of the severed carcass of a sacrificial animal is not intrinsically evil. It is always eaten by someone. It is bad symbolically, not in itself.

It is suggested that the spear as a projection of the right hand symbolizes the vitality of man, of the manhood of man with all the associations of lineage values and of blessedness that go with them. It is within the logic of the representation that we speak only of men. The spear stands for masculinity. Women do not bear fighting spears. The spear does not go with femininity. Hence also boys do not bear fighting spears till at their initiation to manhood they are given them by their fathers. Before this event they are something in between men and women, and this is shown by the fact that they milk the cows, a feminine task that men may not undertake. That neither women nor boys bear spears means that they do not go to war and also that they do not sacrifice. It is not just that a woman may not slaughter the sacrificial victim—it is not, in any case, important who slaughters it—but that, not being able to bear the spear, she cannot make the sacrificial invocation, which is made by the spear in the right hand as well as by the mouth. She can indeed address Spirit at sacrifices but if she does so she prays *(pal);* she does not invoke *(lam)*. This is understandable when we think of the spear as an extension of the right hand and hence representing strength, masculinity, and goodness. Sacrifice, like war, belongs to that side of life, what we ourselves call the spear-side.[14]

It is important here, and before we proceed further with the argument, to note that the spear we are concerned with is the *mut,* a metal fighting spear (or, in a more restricted sense, spear-head). It is not a *bidh,* a metal fishing spear, and it is not a *giit,* a fighting spear fashioned out of substances other than metal. We have further to bear in mind that though spears are now easily obtained by purchase from Arab traders this is a very recent development. There is no iron in Nuerland and what metal spears the Nuer used to possess were procured in one way or another from neighboring peoples, and it is certain that till recently there were very few of them. The Nuer made up for the deficiency by fashioning spears from horn and bone and hard wood. Spears fashioned from these materials were still plentiful when I was living in Nuerland, though they were taking on more and more a purely sentimental and ceremonial value, being often used in dances but seldom for fighting and hunting. Since, however, the spears of the ancestors, the names of which are cried out in invocations, were iron fighting spears there must always have been a certain number of them, and also a certain number of iron fishing spears (for which horn, bone, and wood substitutes are unsuitable), but, as Dr. Howell has pointed out, they were few in number, this accounting, in his opinion, for the high value—several head of cattle—placed upon them.[15] I agree with him that it must have been very rare for a man to have had more than one *mut*, the *giit* spears being regarded as supplementary to it. This must consequently have been a very valuable possession and, if lost, most difficult to replace; and it was not just a private possession but a family hierloom passed from father to son down the generations. This does not mean that it was a relic. It was for practical use and therefore when worn was presumably replaced; otherwise one would see these ancestral spears today. However, the age of a spear has no great significance for Nuer. For them, even if the spear a man's father gives him at his initiation has been bought from an Arab merchant, and is not in fact the spear the father received from his father and the father's father from his father, it is ideally so regarded and thus serves as a symbol of filiation. The spear is thus a point at which two complex social representations meet, that of the personage and that of the lineage. Consequently I do not think that the high assessment of spears in cattle can be reduced to scarcity alone or even that scarcity was at any time the primary consideration. Spears, both fighting and fishing spears, were something more, and fighting spears something much more, than weapons of war or of the chase. They were almost parts of the person. I have seen Nuer enraged when neighbors have borrowed their spears without permission, especially if they have lost them, their anger being out of all proportion to the offense if we think of the matter solely in terms of economic value, for the economic value of spears is quite negligible at the present day. It is the audacity and the insult which outrage the owner, as though someone had taken, and perhaps lost, part of his person; and all the more so in the case of the fighting spear, with which are bound up his manhood and his participation in his lineage, as we see from the manner of his receiving it at his initiation.

I have discussed elsewhere [16] the ritual of initiation. All that need be said here is that when a boy is initiated into manhood and takes on the full responsibilities of that status he is presented by his father with a *mut*, a metal fighting spear, and an ox—the two objects in which, as I have said, the whole drama of sacrifice is centered. I discuss here only the spear. A boy may before initiation possess a fishing spear, but even today he is most unlikely to own a fighting spear. Even should he do so, he would still be presented with a spear by his father at his initiation for it is a ceremonial gift expressing formal recognition of his manhood and all that that means in the social life of the Nuer, and also the handing over by one generation to another. It is not just a spear, but a new status also that he is being given. The boy is now a boy no longer but man and warrior and soon to be husband and father. He now takes part in feuds and wars and raids. He also for the first time engages in dances and displays with oxen, both of which among the Nuer are martial exercises as well as play intimately associated with courtship; and also in the pursuits of herding and hunting. All these activities require the use of the spear, but it is important that we recognize that it is not the acquisition of a weapon, whatever its economic value might have been in the past, nor even its utility, great though that may be, that gives a crucial significance to the gift of a spear at initiation. Its significance is moral, not merely utilitarian. It is not the spear itself, nor its possession, which is stressed but the activities associated with it: war and raiding, dancing and display, and herding. The uses of the spear itself and the evaluations of its uses as an index of social personality are blended, so that the spear is not just a weapon but also something which stands for a very complex set of social relations.

But the investment of a youth with a spear at his initiation would seem to be something more, for initiation is not only into the social life of adults but also into a new relationship with the cattle which has an important religious side to it. There is now established an identification, deriving from the sacrificial situation, between the initiates and cattle and, looked at from this point of view, the rites of initiation may be said to have a sacramental character. The boy enters into communion with the spirits and ghosts of his lineage through the cattle. "The spear of initiation" is thus a symbol of a sacramental change as well as of a change in social status. In both symbolic aspects it is an extension of, and stands for, the right arm and represents strength, strength of the soul as well as strength of the body of the person; and, as I shall attempt to show, in both the symbolism is also a representation of the collective strength of the lineage to which the person belongs and of its soteriological relationship to its common herd.

I have suggested that the fighting spear has a symbolic meaning for Nuer besides what it means to them as a weapon and tool—that it is a projection of the self and stands for the self. This is most important for an understanding of the nature of Nuer sacrifice. Its manipulation in the most common sacrifices, the piacular ones, expresses, if our interpretation is right, the throwing of the whole person into the intention of the sacrifice. It is not only said but also thought, desired, and felt. Not only the lips make it but also the mind, the will, and the heart. This interpretation makes the miming with the spear intelligible for, as an extension of the right arm, it stands for the whole person. It is for this reason that a spear must be carried during the invocation and not in order to slay the animal at the end of it. Other invocations by other men may follow before that is done, and the quick dramatic thrust into its heart which concludes the rite may be made by anyone and not necessarily by a man who has made an invocation or by a spear used in the invocation.

But we have also to note that on many sacrificial occasions—those of a confirmatory kind held in structural situations—when a man makes an invocation he does so as the representative of his clan (where "clan" is used in this context clan or lineage is to be understood—a man may be speaking in reference to his maximal lineage). He identifies himself with the clan by identifying his spear with that of the ancestor of the clan. It is his own spear which he brandishes but the name of the spear he shouts out as he does so is that of the spear of the ancestor of the clan, the clan spear-name.

Each of the Nuer clans has a spear-name and sometimes a large lineage of a clan has a secondary name which is different from that of another lineage of the same clan. This spear-name is shouted out by a representative of the clan, while he brandishes a spear in his right hand, in war, at weddings, and on other public occasions when the clan as a whole is concerned—ideally, that is, and never actively and corporately; and especially as an exordium to sacrificial invocations. It is *"mut gwara,"* "the spear of our fathers." On such occasions as require the services of a leopard-skin priest he calls out the spear-name *"mut Geeka,"* "spear of Gee." Gee is regarded as the common ancestor of most of the true Nuer clans, and to the east of the Nile of them all, so this spear-name combines the representation of the priestly office with that of the Nuer as a whole.

It is essential to note that, with two exceptions, no actual spears of the ancestors of the clans exist, and it is not held by Nuer that they ever did exist, except in the sense that the ancestors had their own spears. The virtue is in the idea of "the spear of our fathers," not in any material clan relic. Consequently, in invocations any spear will serve the purpose of the rite and represent that of the ancestor of the clan and hence symbolize the clan as a whole. Any spear will do, but, for the reason I have stated, there must be a spear; and when Nuer sitting in my tent recounted to me what is said in invocations they gestured with their right hands as though they held spears in them, for they found it difficult to speak the words without making the gestures; just as in recounting what is said in prayers *(pal)* they found it difficult to do so without moving their outstretched hands up and down.

Published literature on the Nuer, and also my own notebooks, record information about only one actual spear of a clan. This is the spear, called *wiu,* of the Gaatgankir clan, who are regarded by all, including themselves, as being of Dinka origin; and the spear is a Dinka, and not a Nuer, type of spear. A mysterious origin and power are attributed to it. It is believed to have been held by Kir, the ancestor of the clan, when he was cut out of the gourd in which he was found, and it is also associated with the air-spirit *wiu,* which is regarded as being in some sense immanent in it. When I was in Nuerland it was in the charge of a family of leopard-skin priests of the Tar lineage of the Eastern Gaajak tribe. I did not myself see it, but it has been described by Mr. Jackson, who saw it in March 1922 near the Pibor river.[17] He records that it was decorated with cowrie shells and beads and was housed in a special grass hut where visitors treated it with great deference. He says that it was prayed and sacrificed to, especially before raids on the Dinka and Burun peoples;[18] that if two sections of the Nuer wished to engage in fighting among themselves it would be placed between them to prevent an engagement; and that oaths were taken on it. I was told that only old people would look upon it. The importance of this spear to our discussion of clan spear-names is that, as I will explain later, all such spear-names have an association with the spirit *wiu* through the further association of this spirit with lightning and thence with the idea of striking, so that the spear *wiu,* perhaps also because it has a material existence, has become the prototype of clan "spears." Dr. P. P. Howell tells me that the Thiang clan of Zeraf Island, a part of Nuerland I have not visited, also possess an ancestral spear, called *mut bar thiang* in invocations. He has not seen it but Nuer have described it to him as being nearly worn through with much polishing. It is unknown whether any cultic practices like those I have mentioned above are connected with it.

Apart from the Gaatgankir and the Thiang spears the "spears" of the Nuer clans and lineages are only names which are symbols of these descent groups. Through the association of a tribal community with the clan dominant in it the spear-name of this clan is shouted out in invocations uttered when the whole tribe goes to war but, except in this context, which I discuss below, in which a political group is merged conceptually with a clan or a lineage, the spear-name is only invoked in reference to a descent group as an exclusive group. Thus, when I asked a Wot tribesman whether the Wot tribe had a tribal spear he replied: "We have many spears. One lineage *(gol)* has one spear, another lineage has another spear, a third lineage has a different spear, and so on." By "spear" he meant a spear-name, not an actual spear. Consequently, if two persons have the same spear-name there is likelihood of agnatic relationship, and spear-names are therefore often spoken of in connection with proposed marriages. One hears Nuer saying in discussions about the permissibility of a proposed marriage "what about their spears?" or "they have the same spear, they cannot marry," "their spear is different to ours, we can marry their daughter"; and at a wedding the masters of ceremony on the bride's side and on the bridegroom's side, each acting as representative of his clan, begin their invocations by shouting out their clan spear-names.[19] The spear-name is, I believe, also shouted out by the master of ceremonies when a Dinka boy is adopted into the lineage of the man who has given him domicile; at mortuary ceremonies when the lineage has lost a member; in settlement of blood-feud, when the lineage receives cattle through which its lost member may be replaced; and at initiation, when a link is added to the chain of lineage descent. When, as mentioned above, clan and tribe are identified politically in war and raiding a representative of the dominant clan of the tribe brandishes a spear and calls out the spear-name of his clan on behalf of the whole tribe. This man, called *ngul,* is usually, perhaps always, a leading man of the senior lineage of the dominant clan, that descended from the eldest son of the ancestor of the clan. Thus this rite in the Lou tribe is performed by a man of the Gaaliek lineage of the Jinaca clan. Likewise the Tar lineage who have charge of the *wiu* spear are descendants of Thiang, the eldest son of the founder of the clan; and the Thiang who own the *thiang* spear are descended from Thiang, the eldest son of Gee.

I cannot always explain the meaning of these spear-names or even translate them, and Nuer themselves cannot always say for certain what they mean, for they arose in ancient days. It is clear, however, that they are charged with symbols expressing the unity and continuity of clans and lineages. I give a few examples, choosing those in which the meaning is more or less evident. The Jiruet lineage have *mut tora,* spear of the monorchid. This lineage respect monorchids, whether they be man or beast. The Gaatiek clan have *mut yier,* spear of the stream, because their ancestor came out of a stream. The Gaatnaca clan have *mut ghama,* spear of the thigh. This seems to refer to the loins of the ancestor from which they sprang. The Gaaliek lineage of this clan have the secondary spear-name *mut tang,* spear of the spear-shaft, because the *ngul,* whom I have referred to above, of the Lou tribe is of this lineage. He uses a spear-shaft in war ritual. The Gaatleak clan have *mut leak,* the word *leak* being simply, it would seem, taken from the clan name itself. Many leopard-skin priests are members of this clan and, as I have explained, they use *mut Geeka,* spear of Gee, as an equivalent expression. The Thiang lineage have a secondary spear-name *mut Thiang,* spear of Thiang, which is the name of their ancestor.

When a man calls out his spear-name he often does so with embellishments, which are further symbolical representations of the lineage. They refer to the ancestor of the clan or lineage, to its spirits, to its totems, to its ghosts, to its cattle, or to its origin and traditions. Thus a Gaatgankir clansman in making invocations adds to *mut wiu* such expressions as *mut kwe, mut jangemo me coali Kir,* and *mut gwara. Kwe* is the fish-eagle and also a color distribution of cattle.

The shining of the spear is likened to the white face of the fish-eagle against its black body and to the white splash on the head of a dark colored cow or ox. *Jangemo me coali Kir* means "that Dinka who is called Kir" and refers to the Dinka origin of the clan. *Mut gwara* means "spear of our fathers." The spear in the hand of the speaker, the spear *wiu,* the spear used to cut open the gourd in which the ancestor was found, and the spirit *wiu* all seem to be fused in the representation. In a similar manner the Gaawar clan may add to their spear-name *mut wang,* spear of the eye (I think) such expressions as *mut nhial, mut puara,* and *mut kwoth nyuota.* I do not know why the spear is called "spear of the eye" (if that is the right translation). *Nhial* is the firmament and *puar* is a cloud. The imagery is derived from the clan myth of origin. Their ancestor fell from the sky and the clan is therefore associated with sky, clouds, and rain. When he fell he had in his hand a sprig of the *nyuot* tree, a tree associated with rain. Hence the *kwoth nyuota,* the spirit of the *nyuot* tree.

Thus the spear-name is either that of the ancestor of the lineage or clan or in some way signifies him, and the elaborations of it, such as by reference to a spirit or a totem, are also just different ways of denoting the lineage or clan as a whole; for the name of the ancestor stands for the whole clan, both here and elsewhere. In myths a lineage is personified for the purpose of the action of the story, the name of the lineage being used to indicate its ancestor. Nuer sometimes even insert the name of a lineage into a genealogy as its founder, though the form of the word shows that it is the name of a group and not of a person; or they give the founder a composite name, appending the name of the lineage to the personal name, for example, Nyang Gaaliek, Nyang being the name of the person and Gaaliek the name of the lineage of his descendants.

I have attempted to show that the spear brandished in sacrificial invocations stands for the person and that when this person speaks as a representative and on behalf of the clan or lineage it stands for the clan or lineage. In the one case it is the right hand (vitality) of the individual and in the other the right hand (vitality) of the ancestor (the clan) which is emphasized. In the second case the spear is closely associated with the idea of the clan as a battle host.

When we ask why clans should be symbolized by a spear, or rather by the idea of a spear contained in a spear-name, and not by something else, we cannot give an acceptable answer in terms of the scarcity, and therefore high value, of iron nor in terms of simple utility. The symbol is not *you,* iron. Nor is it the *bidh,* the fishing spear, which is perhaps even more essential for Nuer than the fighting spear, for they have no substitute for it and could not survive without a good supply of fish. It is the *mut,* the iron fighting spear. The fact that the wood, horn, and bone pointed spears do not figure as symbols might suggest that it is because it is made of iron, which lasts longer and makes a more efficient weapon, that the *mut* is the symbol of clans, but it appears to me to be a more satisfactory explanation that it is because the *mut* not only stands for the right hand and hence vitality but also as the symbol of going to war and of making sacrifice.

The word *mut,* besides meaning a fighting spear, has a general sense of taking part in war and raiding: *"ce Nath wa mut,"* "the Nuer went raiding"; *"ca mut nang Jaang,"* "war was made (by the Nuer) against the Dinka." The idea expressed by the word *mut* in these examples is not so much the general idea of war and raiding as the idea of a collectivity, the clan or lineage in its political or tribal embodiment, going to war or going on a raid. Hence Father Kiggen correctly translates *"te ke mud mediid"* (his spelling) as "they have a big army."[20] By synecdoche "spear" stands for "battle host."

It is, I believe, in some such sense of the clan militant that we should interpret the spear symbolism of the clans. Nuer always speak of "spear" where I have used the expression "spear-name." However, not only are there in almost all cases no actual spears, but it is not even the idea of any particular spear that they have in mind. What they have in mind is the clan as a whole for which the spear stands as a symbol not just as a spear but as representing the collective strength of the clan in its most conspicuous corporate activity, for clans and lineages are most easily and distinctly thought of as collectivities in relation to war. That the representation is of the clan as a battle host is shown by the Nuer statement about their clan spears that they only exist in the sense that "they are in the mouths of men when they go to battle." Two remarks made by Nuer give further support to an interpretation along these lines. One man said of all clan spears that *"twokdien e wiu,"* "their origin is *wiu,"* and that *wiu* is the *kwoth,* spirit, of all clan spears. There was some discussion about this remark among Nuer present and I gathered from it that all clan spears in this wide and symbolic sense of the word *mut* as the battle host signify the clan as a social group in relation to God in the conception of him as Lord of Hosts. The man could not have meant that other clan spears were derived or copied from the spear *wiu*. That would have made no sense, both because there are no actual spears and also because the Gaatgankir clan who own the spear *wiu* are regarded by everybody as a Dinka clan of later origin than the true Nuer clans. That a spiritual conception of *wiu* was meant is further evident from a remark made to me by another Nuer, a man of exceptional ability, that when the Gaatgankir clan reach ten generations from their ancestor Kir—when they have grown up, so to speak—they will doubtless cease to respect *(thek)* the spear *wiu*, as they do at present, and will respect (the word is here used only to balance the statement and not literally) only its name. As we would put it, they will not then feel the need for a material symbol of the spiritual relationship, and a verbal or ideational symbol will suffice. The association of clan spears with the spirit *wiu* is clear to us when we recall that the spirit is also associated with lightning with which, in this hypostasis, God strikes as man strikes with the spear.

In invocations in which clans are involved as such God is appealed to, as I have explained earlier, in some refraction by which he is figured as its patron. This is the *"Kwoth gwara,"* "the God of our fathers." It is on such occasions also that the spear-name of the clan is shouted out as an exordium to the invocation. This is the *"mut gwara,"* "the spear of our fathers." I would suggest that we have here in the spear-name a symbolic representation of the clan in its relation to God.

If this interpretation is right, then in those sacrifices in which the clan as a whole is concerned the calling out of the clan spear-name by the officiant identifies the whole clan with the intention of the sacrifice as spoken in the invocation. The sacrificial spear in his hand becomes through the exordium the clan sacrificial spear through which in symbol the whole clan offers up the victim to God. The officiant in such sacrifices must therefore be a representative of the clan, what the Nuer call a *gwan buthni;* whereas in the commoner sacrifices, the piacular ones, in which appeal is made on behalf of an individual, anyone can officiate and the officiant is usually a senior member of his family or kin. The intention, and therefore character, of the sacrificial act is different in the two cases. In the first it is of the nature of a validation, in the second of the nature of a *piaculum;* though in some situations there may be a broad overlap. Religion has always these two sides, the one concerned chiefly with the social life and the other with the relation of the individual soul to its God.

Notes

1. We are familiar with a similar rite in the Old Testament and elsewhere, though it does not everywhere have the same meaning as it has for the Nuer (Gen. 15: 9–21; Jer. 34: 18–20; W. Robertson Smith, *The Religion of the Semites,* 3d ed., [1927], pp. 480–81; Sir James Frazer, *The Folklore of the Old Testament* (1918), pp. 391 ff.; H. C. Trumbull, *The Blood Covenant,* 1887, p. 322).

2. W. Hofmayr, *Die Schilluk,* 1925, p. 49.

3. E. E. Evans-Pritchard, *The Political System of the Anuak,* 1940, pp. 55–56.

4. J. H. Driberg, *The Lango,* 1923, pp. 238 and 248 ff.

5. E. E. Evans-Pritchard, "Luo Tribes and Clans," *Journal of the Rhodes-Livingstone Institute,* 1949, p. 31.

6. C. G. and B. Z. Seligman, *Pagan Tribes of the Nilotic Sudan,* 1932, p. 129.

7. Ibid., pp. 181–182 and 196.

8. Being the only thing they have which cuts and is therefore suitable for shaving—their other spears only pierce—the verbal form of the word for fighting spear, *mut,* besides its meaning of "to spear" means "to cut, or shave, hair." When used in this sense it often refers to ritual shaving of the head and it may then be used to refer to the whole ceremony of which shaving of the head forms part, as the final marriage ceremony of consummation and ceremonies in connection with death.

9. E. E. Evans-Pritchard, "The Nuer: Age-Sets," *Sudan Notes and Records* 19 (1936): 256.

10. Robert Hertz, "La prééminence de la main droite," *Revue philosophique,* vol. 68 (1909) (reprinted in *Mélanges de Sociologie Religieuse et Folklore,* 1928).

11. Cf. the custom of the Thonga people (W. C. Willoughby, *The Soul of the Bantu,* 1928, p. 359).

12. Left and right are of course relative to the orientation of the person. Thus when a man takes his bearings from the entrance to hut or windscreen what is left from the inside will be right from the outside. I do not think, however, that the point of orientation affects the argument for it is conventional that in reference to any particular matter the one side is left and the other right.

13. I have heard of only one occasion on which a man is asked to perform an action on account of his being left-handed. If the afterbirth of a calf does not fall it is preferably a left-handed man who is asked to place a grass ring over the dam's left horn—and they may also give it medicines to drink. The symbolism here would seem to be that of *similia similibus curantur.*

14. I was told that a wife may make an invocation at a wedding. This is not, however, a sacrificial invocation in the ordinary sense but something of a rather different kind, known by Nuer as *twoc ghok*. It must in any case be a very rare occurrence, can probably only be done with a wedding stick, and not a spear, in the hand, and by an old woman.

15. P. P. Howell, "On the Value of Iron among the Nuer," *Man*, 1947, no. 144.

16. E. E. Evans-Pritchard, "The Nuer: Age-Sets," *Sudan Notes and Records*, vol. 19 (1936).

17. H. C. Jackson, "The Nuer of the Upper Nile Province," *Sudan Notes and Records*, 1926, pp. 168 and 179–81.

18. We are probably to understand, in view of Nuer religious conceptions in general, that Nuer respect (*thek*) the spear and pray and sacrifice to the spirit *wiu*, which is in the sky as well as in the spear. It is true that they may speak of *"kwothda, mut wiuda,"* "my spirit, spear of my *wiu*," but I take this to be an example of synecdoche, the spear which represents the spirit being substituted in speech for the spirit itself, as is the case with totems. Mr. R. T. Johnston reached the same conclusion with regard to a similar spear among the Bor Dinka. He observes that "the spear by itself, except by association and as a symbol, is not sacred." ("The Religion and Spiritual Beliefs of the Bor Dinka," *Sudan Notes and Records*, 1934, p. 127.)

19. Should the two clans have the same spear-name this is not always and necessarily a bar to the union, for secondary spear-names may indicate that they belong to different clans, or other circumstances may be taken into consideration. These are complications I need not discuss here.

20. J. Kiggen, *Nuer-English Dictionary*, 1948, p. 206. One may ask, in the light of this discussion about the *mut*, why it is that the title of spiritual leaders in Dinkaland is taken from the fishing spear (*bith*) instead of from the fighting spear. An explanation might be put forward in terms of the analysis I have presented. Whereas among the Nuer the fighting spear is the symbol of the clan because what is being symbolized is exclusiveness and opposition, among the Dinka the fishing spear is the symbol of spiritual leadership because what is being symbolized is inclusiveness and unity. This is a guess but it receives some support from the fact that among the Nuer, at any rate in western Nuerland, when a leopard-skin priest goes to settle a feud he is accompanied by a kinsman called the *gwan biedh*, the master of the fishing spear, which is the title of the Dinka spiritual leaders. However, this may be a loan from the Dinka.

The Left Hand of the Mugwe: An Analytical Note on the Structure of Meru Symbolism

7

Rodney Needham

I

In his admirable study of the Mugwe, a religious dignitary among the Meru of Kenya, Bernardi reports a singular fact which raises a problem of comparative and theoretical interest: viz., that the left hand of the Mugwe possesses and symbolizes his ritual power.

The issue is best seen, to begin with, in the following passage:

> Among the Imenti [a sub-tribe] an unusual aspect of the people's conception of the Mugwe concerns his left hand. It is this hand . . . that should always hold the *kiragu* [insignia] and be used only to bless. It is a most sacred member of the Mugwe's body and no one is allowed to see it. During the day, the Mugwe spends his time playing *kiothi,* the Meru draughts, but even while he plays, he must always keep his left hand covered and no one must see it. Sudden death would overtake anyone who dared to look at the left hand of the Mugwe.[1]

Neither in this place, nor in any other of the references to this hand, does Bernardi offer an explanation. The object of this note is to suggest a possible answer.

That the position of the left hand of the Mugwe does raise a problem hardly needs demonstration. Hertz showed fifty years ago the universality of a symbolic differentiation of right and left, and examined in his classic paper[2] the grounds for the pre-eminence of the right; and Wile has brought together in his work on handedness[3] an overwhelming amount of evidence on the distinction of the sides and the practically universal privilege of the right. These

Africa 30 (1960): 20–33. Reprinted by arrangement with the International African Institute.

two works alone show that in every quarter of the world it is the right hand, and not the left, which is predominant; and this is so whether in the great civilizations of Europe and India, or among the most primitive and isolated peoples known. The issue can be studied in such varied fields as the Homeric poems, alchemy, and thirteenth-century French religious art, in Hindu iconography, classical Chinese state ceremonies, emblem books and bestiaries, as well as in Maori ritual, Bornean divination, and the myths of the most disparate cultures. This differentiation and opposition of right and left is the very type of symbolic classification, and its logical simplicity and universal distribution make it a fundamental concern in the social anthropologist's study of symbolism. If, then, we are clearly told by a reliable authority that the *left* hand of a certain personage is sacred and used exclusively for his religious functions, we have every reason to be surprised and to look for an explanation.

Let me begin by compounding the remaining evidences in Bernardi's monograph relating specifically to the left hand of the Mugwe. Enemies try to strike the left hand of the Mugwe of the Imenti "because it was said to hold the power of the Mugwe"; the *kiragu,* insignia of power, the things by which the Mugwe is made to be the Mugwe, are held in his left hand, and for this reason the Mugwe of the Imenti keeps his left hand always under cover of his mantle; a very special power in connection with his blessings is popularly attributed to his left hand, and anyone going to him is advised above all never to look at this hand; in it the Mugwe holds the power of his blessing; it is enough for him to lift his left hand in order to stop any enemy attacking his people; it is a source of great awe; respect and fear are felt for this hand, and no one may look on it without dying.[4]

The facts are thus quite clear. The most valuable relate to the Imenti sub-tribe, but I draw whatever usable evidence I can from other sub-tribes also, and my interpretation should essentially apply to the Meru in general. It would be inappropriate for me, as an orientalist, to introduce ethnographic or cultural considerations by pursuing a comparative study of the matter in other Bantu societies, and I base my analysis entirely on the evidence presented by Bernardi in his monograph. The theoretical problem is one which may properly be tackled by any social anthropologist, whatever the area of his special competence, but I should nevertheless feel hesitant about advancing my interpretation if it were not for the fact that any proposed answer is readily testable by Africanists and by persons in Africa in close touch with the Meru. What I present, therefore, is not merely a speculative exercise of some technical interest, but a testable hypothesis. If correct, it may add to our understanding of the Meru; and in any case it will permit a test, in a new field, of a method of inquiry which has already proved illuminating in others.

There are now two elucidatory matters, one cultural and the other structural, to be examined before dealing with the evidence. The first is that the Meru have been influenced by Christianity. A number of Meru informants in Bernardi's work bear Christian first names, and Christian elements have clearly been introduced into Meru mythology. This, so far as one can see in the monograph, is the most considerable extraneous cultural influence powerful enough to affect their symbolic notions. However, it is certain that the attributes of the left hand of the Mugwe have nothing to do with Christian belief or teaching; for in all the references to the right and left hands in the Bible which Wile has listed, "in no single instance is the left hand given a position of honor, superiority or righteousness."[5] Also it is common knowledge that in western cultural notions in general (such as might have influenced the Meru) it is the right, where any differentiation is made, which is pre-eminent and not the left. The position of the left hand of the Mugwe is not, therefore, due to influence by western culture or by Christianity in particular.

The second, structural, matter is that in societies based on descent such symbolic representations may be expected to correlate with the type of descent system. Roughly, in cognatic societies the relation of symbolic to social order may be indefinite or minimal; in lineal systems the relationship may be discernible in a limited range of particulars but not commonly in a comprehensive manner; and in lineal systems with prescriptive affinal alliance there is usually a correspondence of structure between the two orders such that one may speak of a single scheme of classification under which both are subsumed.[6] Meru society is at present based on exogamous patrilineal descent groups, so that we may therefore expect some elucidation of their symbolic notions by examining their social structure, though not so certainly or profitably as if we were dealing with a system of prescriptive alliance. There is, furthermore, certain evidence on the social system (which I shall examine below) which brings Meru society closer to one form of prescriptive system and makes such an approach even more promising.

What I shall do now is to abstract from Bernardi's account isolated evidences of a scheme of symbolic classification by which the Meru may be taken to order their universe, and within which the peculiar character of the Mugwe's left hand may make sense. This involves the establishing of analogical connections between very different institutions and situations; and this type of analysis brings with it, I fear, the likelihood of a rather disjointed exposition. However, as the evidence accumulates and the conceptual connections are elicited a certain coherence should emerge, the key to which I shall try to set out clearly and briefly towards the end.

II

According to Bernardi, all Meru believe they came from the land of Mbwa, to the north. The word by which they designate the north is *urio,* which "literally" means the right hand.[7]

There are distinct traces in Meru society, connected with their myth of origin, of a dual division. This has now lost its significance, but appears to have been typical of all the nine sub-tribes. Clans in the Imenti sub-tribe have names which refer to the intensity of the light while they were crossing the great water in the tribe's exodus from Mbwa: some are called "black," some "red," and some "white." Those who crossed during the night are black; those who crossed at dawn, red; and those who crossed when the sun was up, white. The elders say, however, that there was "really no distinction" between red and white, and that these formed a single group. The clans may thus be distinguished simply as "black clans" and "white clans." It seems certain, says Bernardi, that this distinction had in the past some effective territorial, social, and probably political significance.[8]

This division of the clans is concordant with a division of the Imenti into two groupings, the Nkuene and the Igoki. These were territorial, Nkuene being on the south and Igoki on the north. Igoki seems to have included all the white clans, and the two designations appear to have become synonymous. The divisions were also referred to geographically, as those of *urio,* north, and those of *umotho,* south. The Igoki are said by the elders to have been "always very proud; they wanted always to be first in grazing and watering their cattle."[9]

In the Tharaka sub-tribe there was a similar division, and the Mugwe came from the *umotho* (southern) group. Only the people of Umotho were privileged to take part in full array at his ceremonial blessings. Those of Urio are described as "alien to the Mugwe," and were not expected to visit him at his residence. "It seems there was, or could be, some kind of friction between the two divisions." The divisions were not exogamous.[10]

In the Tigania sub-tribe the divisions were named Athwana and Igoki: the former was also referred to as *umotho* and the latter as *urio*. The Mugwe of the Tigania resides among the Igoki, i.e., in the northern grouping, a fact which will acquire some significance later. Bernardi reports that the Athwana are described (like the Urio of Tharaka) as alien to the Mugwe, and regards his presence in a specified division as indicative of a former social and political significance to the dual division in this sub-tribe also.[11]

In the Igembe sub-tribe the only mention of *urio* and *umotho* refers not to moieties but to the location of the huts of wives in a polygynous household: "the first wife is always *Urio,* the right."[12]

Another institutionalized duality is seen in the age-set system: all the age-sets were related in a dual division, sets of alternate division being successively in power.[13]

Men and women are differentially evaluated. An Imenti elder, to affirm that "to be circumcised is nothing," says that "even women are operated upon," clearly implying a depreciation of women. More explicitly, elders use the term "woman" to describe their present subordinate political condition: "We are all *women:* the real *man* is the government," expressing also the superiority of man over woman. Further, at the official ceremonies of the Mugwe, on which the stability and continuity of Meru society are said to rest, women and children are not allowed.[14]

"The sun rises at the place of Mukuna-Ruku and sets at the place of the Mugwe." Mukuna-Ruku is a name applied by Meru to a legendary ivory-trader, probably an Arab. His residence is said to have been Mombasa, "i.e. the east, where the sun rises." Mukuna-Ruku is also a mythical figure with a body that is all eyes and gives light to the sun. The obvious inference is that the Mugwe is symbolically associated with the west, but Bernardi says that this "cannot so easily be implied." The elucidation he presents is that the house of the Mugwe cannot come to an end, the Mugwe cannot die; and it is therefore at his dwelling that the sun sets.

"The sun, as the Mugwe, cannot fail to give its light and warmth, it cannot die, and therefore it sets at the dwelling of the Mugwe in order to renew its power for the next day. There is a parallel between the two figures of Mukuna-Ruku and the Mugwe, both possessing a very special character and a very special power: light and immortality."[15] Bernardi does not cite here, as he usually does elsewhere, Meru statements to show that this interpretation is that of the people themselves, and it has the air of being his own. I think, in any case, that it is inconsistent with what else can be discerned of Meru symbolism, and shall try to show why later. For the moment, I suggest that Mukuna-Ruku is associated with east and light, and the Mugwe with west and darkness. This is supported, to give a brief indication, by the color of the sacrificial bull, which must be black, "a color sacred to God," and by that of the Mugwe's staff, which is "the ritual black,"[16] permitting the inference that darkness is not symbolically incompatible with the Mugwe's ritual position.

We have already seen that the Mugwe keeps his left hand concealed while he plays "draughts," and although there is no other information on his right hand the tenor of the evidence is that this is his profane hand. His left hand is reserved for his sacred function, viz., to bless, which is described as his "essential work." His authority, in fact, is "basically religious"; while it is the elders who control all forms of social and political activity and are "the real masters of the country." "The external machinery of tribal government and of social life would appear to work satisfactorily even without the Mugwe," and this is underlined by Bernardi's discovery that, apparently until very recently, the very existence of the Mugwe had entirely escaped the Administration. The Meru are admittedly described as looking up to the Mugwe as their father, and the elders say that before the European administration there was no other "chief" but the Mugwe; but these statements do not really conflict with the clear distinction of function between the Mugwe and the elders, especially when we further learn from the elders themselves that they protect the Mugwe as though he were a queen bee. The Mugwe was in a literally singular position, the one person on whom the society could be said to focus, and whose presence and (ritual) services could be regarded as essential; and in view of his functions it is easily comprehensible that he should be referred to in such terms. The fact is clear, I think, that there was a distinct partition of sovereignty into the religious authority of the Mugwe, seen in his indispensable blessing in the major social institutions, and the political power of the elders, seen in their effective jural and administrative control.[17] The apparently conflicting evaluations of the respective status of Mugwe and elders are made within different contexts and are characterized by different criteria.

Finally, the possible significance of temporal succession deserves some attention. In the myth of the exodus of the Meru from Mbwa the people come to the water and their leader (= Mugwe) divides it with his staff to make a passage for them. He first sends across a small girl and a small boy, and then a young woman and a young man; and only when they have crossed does he take the main body over. This suggests the possibility that those who are first, the forerunners, are of inferior status, and that those whom they precede, the main body, are of superior status. It would probably be going too far to infer that the order in which the sexes are mentioned —first female, then male—makes the same point; but if this is a culturally conventional order it is at least consistent with the fact that first the younger cross and then the older, and with the relative status of women and men.[18] The second illustration also comes from myth. All peoples are said to come from the same place, but the first to be born was a black man, and after him a white [19] man. In this case the predecessors are (whatever their other qualities and however they regard themselves in other respects) political inferiors, and their successors are superiors, an opposition explicitly made by the elders quoted above. Related to this theme, also, is the myth of the origin of the exploitation of natural resources: first came the age-set with the Mugwe, and this is the one which started honey-collecting; next came the set which was the first to cultivate. We cannot be sure of the relative evaluation of these two subsistence activities, but one would think that basic sustenance would depend more on the latter than on honey, which is described merely as one of the staple elements of diet among the Tharaka. Moreover, we can see here another instance of the theme of complementary functions, for sacred honey-beer is one of the insignia of the Mugwe, and the rite of blessing itself consists in the Mugwe sipping some honey-beer and gently spitting it on to the people; whereas according to Laughton (to cite another authority for once) all rights in land lie with the elders, and it is they who control its preservation and exploitation.[20]

III

Having completed a survey of the evidence, we are now in a position to make a systematic interpretation by which the position of the left hand of the Mugwe may be comprehensible.

The first step is to construct a table such as that which follows:

TABLE: SCHEME OF MERU SYMBOLIC CLASSIFICATION

right	left
north	south
Urio	Umotho
Igoki	Nkuene
white clans	black clans
day	night
first wife	co-wife
senior	junior
dominant age-division	subordinate age-division
man	woman/child
superior	inferior
east	west
sunrise	sunset
sun	——(moon?)
light	darkness
sight (eyes)	(blindness)
–	black
elders	Mugwe
political power	religious authority
successors	predecessors
older	younger
white man	black man
cultivation	honey-collecting

This represents a symbolic classification in which pairs of opposite terms are analogically related by the principle of complementary dualism.[21] It relates specifically to the Imenti, though the principle exhibited appears valid for at least some of the other sub-tribes. The oppositions are listed seriatim as they have been elicited in the exposition of the relevant facts. It will readily be seen that the scheme is coherent, and that it displays a systematic order which can immediately be apprehended. A few clarificatory notes may, however, be helpful, and there are also certain difficulties which have to be discussed.

A matter which may occasion some reserve is that the Mugwe should be associated, however indirectly, with feminine. This may be thought in conflict with his paternal authority and with the statements that the Mugwe is "higher" then the elders and "above" them.[22] But we have to remember, firstly, the matter of context: ritually, as a symbol of the unity of Meru society, the Mugwe is superior to the elders, but politically he is definitely not. Even this is misleading, though. It is the *complementarity,* I think, which should be emphasized, rather than differential status in opposed contexts.

Secondly, it has to be kept in mind that the ascription of terms to one series in the scheme does not entail that they all share the particular attributes of any one term. The association of these terms rests on analogy, and is derived from a mode of categorization which orders the scheme, not from the possession of a specific property by means of which the character or presence of other terms may be deduced. One does not, therefore, say that the Mugwe *is* feminine, any more than one would say that night or south or the subordinate age-division is feminine.

Nevertheless, the association in any way of religious authority with feminine may still seem to call for an explanation. This question, it seems to me, can be resolved by comparison with other societies. I select two particularly clear parallels from widely separated and disparate cultures, in which a symbolic association of religion with feminine is quite explicitly and directly made. Among the Ngaju of south Borneo, most religious functionaries are priestesses, and religious matters are so intimately associated with the feminine that men who professionally assume such functions also assume feminine status. They wear women's clothes and dress their hair like women; they are commonly homosexual or impotent, and they even marry men. A man who has thus assumed femininity is thought to be more efficacious in the supernatural sphere than a woman.[23] Among the Chukchi of Siberia, there are four stages in becoming a particularly prominent kind of shaman, each marked by an increased assumption of feminine attributes. In the first, the man adopts woman's hair-style; in the second he wears woman's dress; in the third he throws away all his masculine appurtenances and undertakes woman's tasks, his voice changes and his body acquires the helplessness of a woman; and in the final stage he "changes sex," taking a lover and after a time a husband, and may even claim to give birth to children. Such a shaman has a special relation with the supernatural, marked by the protection and guidance of a guardian spirit, and he is dreaded, even by untransformed shamans.[24] On the most general grounds, therefore, and taking the most extreme cases, the inclusion of the Mugwe in a category which includes feminine may be considered not at all unusual. I may now adduce a superficially isolated and otherwise incomprehensible fact, reported in connection with sexual intercourse, which also associates the Mugwe (of the Imenti) with feminine. An elder says: "Another wonder for the common people: the Mugwe never asks for his wife; it is his wife who asks for him." [25] This very unusual practice can now be seen as an elaboration on a symbolic classification which gives it meaning.[26]

These points made, we may now understand from the scheme why the Igoki were so proud, and why they demanded always to be first in grazing and watering their cattle; for by analogical inference they were the senior of the moieties (Igoki : Nkuene : : north : south : : senior : junior), and these may well have been their traditional and distinctive rights. To take another case, it is even possible that the scheme may give a lead as to whether the Meru came from the north, as Bernardi reports, or from the east, as is said by Lambert, Holding, and, by implication, Laughton.[27] In addition to the equation north = right, which is consistent with an eastern origin, there are the elements of white, day, sun, and light in the right-hand (dominant, privileged) series—all commonly assigned, not to the north, but generally and naturally to the east. One might therefore tend to think (assuming some connection between traditions of origin and Meru symbolic classification) that they came from the east rather than the north. Finally, historical questions aside, it may be seen on what grounds I suggested above that predecessors may be classed as junior. Whether moving from the north or from the east, the children and young people are the first to the south or west; and they are therefore associated with the juniority of the co-wife and the inferiority (asserted, it appears, by the Igoki) of the Nkuene.

However, this last matter brings us now to some difficulties. The predecessor in the advancement of the age-sets is not junior but senior; the predecessor in marriage to a man is not a junior co-wife but the senior; and the elders, similarly, are predecessors to all their younger juniors. Meru ethnography is not extensive or detailed enough to permit useful speculation on my part about these points. It may be that my formulation of the defining relation is mistaken, or that the formal resemblance between the situations from which I elicited it is misleading, e.g., that it is not simply predecession that is decisive, but that some other kind of distinction is symbolically significant. This one couple of terms (predecessors : successors) aside, though, the subsequent and derivative couples remain consistent with the scheme.

Though it is only the Mugwe who is clearly associated with black in a ritual context, it is not only he who wears a black mantle, but the elders as well.[28] If black were a sign of superior social status there would be no difficulty in seeing that the Mugwe and the elders might together be distinguished in this way as social leaders; but in the face of the ritual associations of black, the ritual office of the Mugwe, and the secular status of the elders as a body, this fact creates a contradiction to the scheme which does not seem resoluble by resort to the published ethnography. [See however Introduction above, p. xxxix, n. 60.]

There are other points, too, which cause difficulty, such as the relationships focusing on the concept of *ntindiri*.[29] I have not felt sure enough to include them in the scheme: the ethnography on these points is too slender for any compelling logic to emerge as directive, and a speculative review of the formal possibilities would not be decisive.

IV

The only assumption I have made in constructing the scheme of classification is that Meru symbolism is consistent; and so far as I know I have not omitted from the account any relevant facts which are contradictory to the scheme, or which would lend another interpretation to the significance of the facts to which it relates. I now proceed to the problem.

The resolution which I propose is that it is in accordance with this symbolic order, and consistent with the total scheme of relations between the particular terms, that the left hand of the Mugwe should be regarded as sacred. By a conceptual dichotomy operative in a number of contexts he is symbolically assigned to the category of the left, and it is consistent with this that in some cases his own left should symbolize his status.

There is one point, however, to be made directly. Given that the Mugwe himself belongs symbolically to the category which includes left, it does not necessarily follow that his sacred hand shall also be his left. It is perfectly conceivable that his right hand should be endowed with this value, without contradiction to the classification; and Bernardi's account gives reason to suppose that in most of the nine sub-tribes this is indeed the case. Of the five references which he makes to the left hand, three (comprising the greater and most explicit part of the evidence) relate specifically to the Imenti, and one appears to relate to earlier statements about them; while only the remaining one refers to other sub-tribes as well. This is that in which is described the Mugwe's power to halt enemy attacks by raising his left hand: "This belief was common with the Tharaka, the Chuka, the Igembe and the Imenti; but it is especially with the Imenti that the left hand of the Mugwe has become a source of great awe."[30] We are told, furthermore, in the quotation first cited, that among the Imenti the people's conception of the Mugwe's left hand is "unusual." In most of the sub-tribes, then, the Mugwe's sacred hand may well be his right; while in some, and typically the Imenti, it is his left. This situation has to be taken into account when we try to relate the sacred left hand to the scheme of classification.

It is thus evident that in this context the fundamental distinction to be registered in the scheme must be that between the profane hand of the Mugwe and the sacred hand. By analogical inference we have had no choice about the series to which they must respectively be assigned: the sacred, efficacious hand must enter the series on the "right" side of the scheme, in company with what is socially and mythically dominant and superior; while the profane hand must be assigned to the complex of opposite and complementary terms. Note that this is a purely symbolic ascription: which of the hands, organically speaking, shall be reckoned sacred, and which profane, is indeterminate. In fact, among most of the sub-tribes the sacred hand will apparently be the right (as on the most universal grounds we should anticipate), and it is the right hand which will be assigned to the right-hand series in the scheme, where it will be explicitly associated with "right." But among the Imenti (to take them as typical of the other sub-tribes in this respect, and among whom this symbolic elaboration is most marked) it is the left hand of the Mugwe which, exceptionally, is sacred; and in accordance with its determining character it must be assigned to the right-hand series in the scheme, in company with the generally dominant hand among the other Mugwe. This may seem puzzling at first, but it is obvious that to assign the left hand of the Imenti Mugwe to the left-hand series simply because of the common feature of leftness, which is a *factual* but not necessarily a symbolic attribute, would reverse the ascription of *symbolic* value and constitute a direct contradiction to the symbolic order. The association of the Imenti Mugwe's left hand with the terms of the right-hand series is therefore analogically valid. For Meru in general, I take it, the formula is profane hand : sacred hand :: common left : common right. But in the case of the Mugwe of the Imenti the profane hand is his physical right, so that as far as symbolic attributes are concerned his right hand is his left.

The point is made, I hope, that the selection of one hand or the other as sacred (efficacious, pre-eminent) is not necessarily determined, and certainly not by matters of physical fact; and, in general, that the categorization of a term is not in principle deducible from any one of its properties. Symbolic attributes are not necessary, and one's task in elucidating them is not to claim that they have been determined but to show their coherence. I have tried to explain the symbolic attributes of the Mugwe by relating them to the system of ideas of which they are part, and to the mode of classification by which the ideas are ordered. It still remains to say something about why, in the exceptional case of the Mugwe of the Imenti, the left hand should be pre-eminent.

It may be claimed that the position of his left hand is consistent with the classification in a peculiarly satisfactory way. Even in the scheme I have constructed, which must be a very attenuated version of what might be detected in field investigations directed specifically to the issue, the symbolic reinforcement of the Mugwe's position is striking. He belongs to the left, the south (= left), and he is connected with the black clans (he is theirs), the night (in which he and they crossed the water), the west, sunset, darkness, and the color black. It may be thought appropriate and intellectually satisfying, then, that the ascription of the Mugwe to the left-hand series should be symbolically intensified, among the Imenti, by the value attached to his left hand.

This contention is not a sophistical expedient adopted to give plausibility to an argument, for such re-emphasis of symbolic value has been recorded from other cultures. I shall mention two cases, one from another part of Africa and the other from the Indo-Burma border.

In a recent account of the pastoral Fulani, the following oppositions are recognizable: [31]

right	left
west	east
front	back
south	north
masculine	feminine
senior homestead	junior homestead
genealogical senior	genealogical junior

There is no need to expatiate on this scheme, which is easily confirmed by reference to the source. One recognizes in it a differentiation between the two series of terms similar to that of the Meru classification, and even without recounting the ethnographic evidence a consistency of character can be seen between a number of the terms in each series. The point I wish to make concerns the relations north : south :: junior : senior. Within the homestead the bed-shelters of the wives are ranged north to south according to rank. At first sight one would expect the senior wife to be associated with south; but instead, within the feminine part of the homestead, her shelter is placed to the *north,* and the shelters of her junior co-wives in descending order of seniority to the south. Moreover, the senior wife is explicitly called "north-one," and any junior wife "south-one." Here we have, then, an intensification of symbolic character precisely similar to that of the Mugwe's left hand among the Imenti.[32]

The second example relates to the Purum of Manipur. They seek augury by sacrificing a fowl and observing the relative positions of its legs: if the right rests on the left the augury is good, and if the left rests on the right it is bad. (Right is generally regarded as superior to left among all the Kuki tribes of this area, and this kind of symbolic distinction is radical to their culture.) At the name-giving ceremony for a boy a cock is sacrificed and the above rules of interpretation are followed, but at the ceremony for a girl there is a reversal of the symbolism: a hen is sacrificed this time, and it is the left leg resting on the right that is accounted good augury for her.[33]

These examples from very distant and different cultures demonstrate that the symbolic process which I have posited to explain the case of the left hand of the Imenti Mugwe is not a forced interpretation or a cultural singularity. On the contrary, it is an understandable manipulation of symbolic concepts which has its own validity, and which depends for its effect on the categorization with which at first it appears to be in conflict.

It might be emphasized, finally, that in proposing my explanation I do not intend to claim that for Meru in general the left hand has anything of the value which is attached to that of the Imenti Mugwe. Indeed, although Bernardi's ethnography says nothing on this point, I feel sure that for them it is the right hand (as one would expect) that is pre-eminent. I should think, also, that it is the exceptional status of the Imenti Mugwe's left hand, in contrast to the general evaluation of the right, which in his case marks particularly his exceptional personal status and the nature of his authority.[34]

V

There is one possible objection to the type of analysis that I have made which I should like to comment on briefly. Hertz has written that dualism is of the essence of primitive thought; [35] and I should go further to say that the symbolic opposition of right and left, and a dualistic categorization of phenomena of which this opposition is paradigmatic, are so common as to seem natural proclivities of the human mind.[36] Does this sort of analysis then have any explanatory merit? That is, if we are dealing with a fundamental mode of thought, the demonstration of the existence of a dualistic classification among the Meru might be thought nugatory or tautological.

But this is not the case. Firstly, even a fundamental feature of thought is not necessarily formally manifested in a scheme which is based upon it. Secondly, whatever their logical grounds, symbolic classifications are not everywhere of this dualistic kind: some are triadic, and others feature four, five, or more major categories. They may be reducible, but they are formally distinct from the Meru scheme. Thirdly, although it is possible to maintain that in certain contexts there is a "natural" symbolism which is immediately apprehensible, irrespective of culture, the particulars of a classification are not necessary; so that to elicit from an ethnographic description the symbolic classification and mode of conceptual relation characteristic of a culture is in fact informative. Finally, the construction of this sort of scheme does not depend simply on ingenuity in relating concepts and values which one has some reason to expect in any case. To the extent that the ethnography is comprehensive and reliable, the form of the classification by which a people order their world imposes itself on the analytical construction: "Le système est vraiment dans les faits" (Dumézil).

If, in spite of these considerations (which are advanced, after all, in an excessively summary manner for such a large topic), it is still thought that the approach is faulty, there will yet remain a considerable problem: viz., to explain how it is, in that case, that the ethnography permits the coherent interpretation which I have put upon it, and which I would decline to think fortuitous. And a sociological enterprise would still remain to be carried out, viz., to determine the range of symbolic significance in social systems of different type, and to explain the correlations of social and symbolic structure.

VI

I conclude with an indication of the wider theoretical significance of this inquiry. It derives from the work of Durkheim and Mauss [37] and of Hertz, and nearer to our time takes as models the publications of the Leiden school [38] and Hocart,[39] and latterly the stimulating analyses of Lévi-Strauss.[40] A particular issue connected with the continuing theme of these studies, and to which I wish to draw attention in connection with the Mugwe, is that of the dual nature of sovereignty: the complementary functions of priest and king, the ordering of social life by dualistic notions of religious authority and secular power of which these figures are exemplars. Dumézil has with fascinating effect exploited this type of opposition, compendiously represented by the couple Mitra–Varuṇa, in his analysis of sovereignty in Indo-European society; [41] and Coomaraswamy has similarly, and more minutely, examined the ancient Indian theory of government in terms of the complementary opposites of spiritual authority and temporal power.[42] In contrast to the superficially rather trivial interest of the left hand, it is to these studies that I should wish to relate this modest and tentative note on the Mugwe.

If we are to understand his position in Meru society, it may be more illuminating, it seems to me, and potentially less misleading, to make a structural analysis of the sort I have proposed rather than to try to decide whether he is best described, in our language and symbolic ambience, as leader, public figure, judge, diviner, priest, bishop, prophet, God, chief, or king. All these various appellations, severally applied in order to define one or other aspect of his status, are, as Bernardi himself points out, inexact and misleading. The Mugwe is the Mugwe. What this means may best be understood, I suggest, by concentrating on the functions, attributes, and conceptual associations of the Mugwe in terms of the structure, symbolic as well as social, which gives his office its proper significance. The most general notion by which this structure may be defined is that of complementary dualism, which appears to be a pervasive feature of traditional Meru culture. In the context of the present problem this is expressed in the opposition of secular and religious status: political power is complemented by religious authority.[43]

The distinction of the hands is the commonest manifestation of the mode of classification isolated by this inquiry, and it is the pursuit of an explanation for the singular attributes of the left hand of the Mugwe of the Imenti which has permitted this glimpse of the conceptual order of Meru society.

Notes

1. B. Bernardi, *The Mugwe, a Failing Prophet* (London, 1959), p. 74.

2. Robert Hertz, "La Prééminence de la main droite: étude sur la polarité religieuse," *Revue Philosophique* 68 (1909): 553–80.

3. Ira S. Wile, *Handedness: Right and Left* (Boston, 1934).

4. Bernardi, pp. 61, 103, 110, 120. At the ritual of accession among the Imenti the new Mugwe runs with an old woman, keeping hold of her hand: if she dies, he is a fit successor (p. 93). It is not stated by which hand the Mugwe holds hers; and it is unclear if it is because of the touch of his left hand that she dies, though one might infer so, since she is supposed to be overwhelmed by his supernatural power.

5. Wile, pp. 339–40.

6. R. Needham, "A Structural Analysis of Purum Society," *American Anthropologist* 60 (1958): 75–101.

7. Bernardi, pp. 2–3. It is not clear why Bernardi isolates a literal meaning, implying that only by a kind of extension does the word mean "north." (Cf. Sanskrit *dakshina,* Hebrew *jamīn,* Irish *dess,* "right, south.")

8. Bernardi, pp. 9, 58. Though the clear statement about the equation of red and white clans is highly satisfactory for my present purpose, the triadic division presumably "means" something, and is possibly connected with the number of other contexts in which three seems to have a special significance: see Bernardi, pp. 21, 25–26, 58, 68, 90. Also, W. H. Laughton, *The Meru* (Nairobi, 1944), pp. 11, 14, 15; H. E. Lambert, *Kikuyu Social and Political Institutions* (London, 1956), p. 27. Laughton, p. 2, says that it is the red and the black clans which have "merged into one group."

9. Bernardi, p. 9. *Umotho* or one or other cognate word means "left" in at least some neighboring Bantu languages. See, e.g., M. B. Davis,

Lunyoro-Lunyankole-English . . . Dictionary (Kampala-London, 1938), p. 95, s.v. *moso.*

10. Bernardi, pp. 10, 42.

11. Bernardi, pp. 11, 76.

12. Bernardi, p. 10.

13. Bernardi, pp. 21–23. See also Laughton, p. 4: "There is a traditional and ceremonial antipathy between successive age-sets."

14. Bernardi, pp. 17, 39, 90.

15. Bernardi, pp. 73, 74.

16. Bernardi, pp. 92, 99.

17. Bernardi, pp. 160, 161, 150, 155, 136, 174, 142, 151, 161. This is not to say that the Mugwe is quite without political influence, and we are indeed told that his religious authority is capable of "political extension" (p. 139) and is a source of political power which a strong and ambitious man could exploit (p. 161); but this is a contingent matter of fact, whereas I am concerned with a conceptual system.

18. In one myth, God is described as creating man and then woman; but this is said by Bernardi (pp. 52, 55) to be Christian. However, there is still one clear contrary indication: in an invocation by the Mugwe, he refers to his people as "male, female . . . boys and girls," which tends to dispose of the idea. Bernardi, pp. 192, 121.

19. Bernardi, pp. 193–94. "White": lit. *umutune,* red; cf. the equation of red and white clans.

20. Bernardi, pp. 100–101, 110; Laughton, pp. 3, 5.

21. Cf. Needham, 1958, pp. 97, 99.

22. Bernardi, pp. 139, 152–53.

23. A. Hardeland, *Dajacksch-Deutsches Wörterbuch* (Amsterdam, 1859), pp. 53–54, s.v. *basir;* M. T. H. Perelaer, *Ethnographische Beschrijving der Dajaks* (Zalt-Bommel, 1870), p. 35; Schärer, *Die Gottesidee der Ngadju Dajak in Süd-Borneo* (Leiden, 1946), pp. 64–67.

24. W. Bogoras, *The Chukchee* (Leiden–New York, 1909), pp. 449 ff.

25. Bernardi, p. 107.

26. Bernardi at one place even suggests that a reference to a certain woman could have been "an indirect way of referring to the Mugwe" (p. 39). Note that these cases relate to the Imenti. I do not overlook the possible relevance of the theme of reversal which so often characterizes ritual; but this is an enormous topic which I cannot broach here.

27. H. E. Lambert, *The Systems of Land Tenure in the Kikuyu Land Unit,* Communications, School of African Studies, no. 22 (Cape Town, 1950), p. 7; E. M. Holding, "Some Preliminary Notes on Meru Age-grades," *Man* 42 (1942): 58; Laughton, p. 2.

28. Bernardi, p. 95.

29. Bernardi, pp. 13, 39, 60, 91, 94, 138, 139, 159.

30. Bernardi, p. 110.

31. D. J. Stenning, *Savannah Nomads* (London, 1959), pp. 39–40, 104–5, 106–8. Stenning himself appears not to have paid particular attention to Fulani ideology, and I should like to suggest that a structural analysis to elicit its ruling ideas might prove sociologically illuminating.

32. Unfortunately, we are not told whether the traditional Meru home-

stead is oriented or whether the relative positions of its members within it are of any significance. Laughton (p. 9) reports merely that the hut of the owner of the homestead is on the right as one enters, and that the huts of his wives are disposed counterclockwise from this; but this, though it suggests a conventional arrangement, is not symbolically informative.

33. T. C. Das, *The Purums: An Old Kuki Tribe of Manipur* (Calcutta, 1945), pp. 195, 234; cf. Needham, 1958, pp. 90–91, 97.

34. There is a weaker, because less singular, parallel to this among the Ibo. The right hand is clearly superior and the use of the left is prohibited; but a warrior who has killed a man with his own hands is permitted, as a privilege, to drink with his left. A. G. Leonard, *The Lower Niger and Its Tribes* (London, 1906), p. 310.

35. Hertz, 1909, p. 559.

36. Needham, 1958, p. 97.

37. E. Durkheim and M. Mauss, "De quelques formes primitives de classification: contribution à l'étude des représentations collectives," *Année Sociologique* 6 (1903): 1–72.

38. e.g. W. H. Rassers, *De Pandji-Roman* (Antwerp, 1922). (It is not generally realized that the Leiden school of anthropology inherited and effectively exploited French sociological ideas at a time when they were all but ignored in Britain and the United States.)

39. Especially *Kings and Councillors* (Cairo, 1936); new edition, edited and with an introduction by Rodney Needham, foreword by E. E. Evans-Pritchard (University of Chicago Press, 1970).

40. C. Lévi-Strauss, "The Structural Study of Myth," in T. A. Sebeok, ed., *Myth: A Symposium* (Philadelphia, 1955), pp. 50–66; "La Geste d' Asdiwal," *Annuaire* 1958–9, *Ecole Pratique des Hautes Études* (Section des Sciences Religieuses) (Paris, 1958).

41. G. Dumézil, *Mitra-Varuṇa: essai sur deux représentations indo-européennes de la souveraineté* (Paris, 1948; 1st ed. 1940). At the end of his examination of Indo-European notions of sovereignty, Dumézil makes a brief comparison with the Chinese philosophy of *yin-yang* and concludes with the observation: "Il sera intéressant de confronter le mécanisme indo-européen ici dégagé avec d'autres mécanismes que le *yang* et le *yin*" (p. 211). It is satisfying and intriguing, then, to note how clearly we find in the present African context a Mitra-Varuṇa type of representation of sovereignty: elders = Mitra, the jurist, associated with this world, the day, masculine, senior, and the right; Mugwe = Varuṇa, the magician, associated with the other world, night, feminine, junior, and the left. Cf. also Dumézil, *Les Dieux des Indo-Européens* (Paris, 1952), chap. 2.

42. A. K. Coomaraswamy, *Spiritual Authority and Temporal Power in the Indian Theory of Government* (New Haven, 1942).

43. To pursue an indication of the former constitution of Meru society which I have already touched upon, I should guess that Igoki was the politically dominant moiety, while Nkuene possessed the complementary religious authority of which the presence of the Mugwe was the sign. Cf. also the balance between the social superiority of the wife-givers and the ritual indispensability of the wife-takers in certain systems of asymmetric alliance (Needham, 1958).

Kaguru Symbolic Classification

8

T. O. Beidelman

The right hand of the Lord hath the pre-eminence.
Psalm 118: 16

This paper presents the general features of dualistic symbolic classification among the Kaguru, a Bantu-speaking people of east-central Tanzania, East Africa. It is a revised and expanded version of a paper previously published under a different title (Beidelman 1961b). Elsewhere, I develop some of the ideas presented here in regard to the medial aspects of Kaguru dual symbolic classification (1966b).*

I

The original version of this paper was written in response to Needham's stimulating article, "The left hand of the Mugwe" (1960). Using Bernardi's ethnographic data on the Meru (1959), Needham isolates a dualistic symbolic classification of those people. The result is a very striking illustration of the order and understanding gained by the social anthropologist once this important feature of Meru ideology is shown. Needham then goes on to indicate some of the relations which such a symbolic classification may have to certain structural divisions of a society. Reading Needham's article as well as the recent English translation of Hertz's "The pre-eminence of the right hand" (1960), one is surprised that little such analysis deals with African data. That Hertz's essay has no African sources is perhaps understandable since it was written over fifty years before the great work in African ethnography had begun.

Written especially for this volume.

Wile's fascinating study of handedness (1934) cites Hertz and many African sources, but it is concerned essentially with physiological or psychological, rather than sociological problems. Nonetheless, Wile's work contains an enormous amount of sociologically pertinent data.[1] Hocart's studies on the topic of dualism refer to very few African groups: the Jukun and Yoruba of Nigeria, the Galla of Ethiopia (1936: 161–62; 1954: 87, 90, 92). In a short note, Werner discusses certain meanings of right and left hands in various Bantu languages, but only within a linguistic context (1904). Her study also prompted a short comment on the topic by Stapleton (1905). Perhaps the most original of the early papers on such symbolism in Africa is a little-known work by Wieschhoff (1938)[2] in which he surveys the known literature in order to determine the attributes which various African societies assign to right and left. Wieschhoff appears to be ignorant of Hertz's work but observes that handedness may, to a greater degree than first suspected, be a sociological rather than a biologically determined characteristic (p. 126). Wieschoff's article has been neglected by most anthropologists likely to be concerned with this problem. This is a matter of considerable regret, for although Wieschhoff does not appear to have been a trained social anthropologist, his article is filled with many useful and stimulating sociological insights into the problems involved and contains a useful bibliography of source material. Both Needham and Wieschhoff cite a number of African peoples among which further analyses would probably prove useful. To my knowledge, until recently only the extensive discussion of such classification in Africa, besides Needham's, is Evans-Pritchard's study of symbolism of the right and left among the Nuer (1956: 142, 184, 212, 233–45, 296; 1953).[3] However, since the preparation of the first version of the present paper, Turner has presented a masterly and detailed series of analyses of symbolism among the Ndembu of Zambia (1961a, 1961b, 1962a, 1962b). Although these have not described an essentially dualistic symbolic classification, Turner's full analysis of Ndembu symbolism is still in preparation and seems likely to disclose some such features. Despite its title, "Dualism in western Bantu Religion and social organization," Torday's early paper (1923) provides very little information on the problem with which this collection of essays is concerned. In his publications which appeared subsequent to Needham's work on the Mugwe, Gulliver takes note of this problem of dual classification but is at pains to point out that such categorizations do not seem to occur among the Nilo-Hamitic Arusha, although one might have expected that the case would be otherwise (Gulliver 1961: 32–33; 1963: 145–46). However, some of Gulliver's findings seem inconsistent with this view (e.g., 1963: 31) and Gulliver himself expresses the view that "the generalized, ideal type version tends to conceal or distort the active principles of the system and its real operation" (1963: 36), a view which hardly indicates a predisposition toward the study of symbolism, cosmology, or ideology.

The fact that the study of dualistic symbolic classification in Africa is limited to very few papers might lead one to suppose that this is an unusual phenomenon not found in most of Africa. However, even a cursory examination of the African literature shows that this is not the case and reveals that such analysis would seem to be especially important for the better understanding of some African societies about which considerable information has already been published.[4] I have tried to show how this may be done in my examination of the published Swazi material (1966a). Some years ago Jeffreys published a paper (1946) which, although unclear, suggests several areas in which such analysis would be very fruitful and which indicates the rather widespread occurrence of such classifications in African societies. Less helpful discussions prompted by Jeffreys's paper were later presented elsewhere (e.g., Haekel 1950). A short paper by Straube (1957) indicates that some peoples in southern Ethiopia would provide especially valuable data on these problems. He deals mainly with Ometo dual political organization but clearly indicates that this has cosmological and symbolic counterparts as well (pp. 350–51).

I now turn to an examination of the data for a particular African people, the Kaguru, and consider whether such analysis provides useful insight into the belief and actions of that people.

II

The Kaguru are sedentary hoe-cultivators with small herds of sheep and goats and some cattle. They live in small, dispersed settlements in northern Kilosa and Mpwapwa Districts, east-central Tanzania. Kaguru settlements are said to have been formed in the precolonial period around one matrilineage, often members of a clan with certain religious and political rights to the land concerned. Today various political factors have caused the settlements to become even smaller—two to twenty huts, with single houses frequently occurring. The elimination of raids by neighboring peoples has been one of the most important causes of this disintegration. The few large Kaguru settlements which still exist are not formed about matrilineal descent groups; instead, these are merely aggregations of huts at sites favorable to trade or employment or settlements of cognatic kin closely related to a local political official in tribal administration who resides in such a village. Marital residence is virilocal. In the past, however, brideservice was often required and until this was completed residence was uxorilocal. Kaguru fathers usually encouraged their married sons to live near them, but it is difficult to describe any one combination of relatives as typical of most Kaguru settlements today. Settlements usually comprise close kin such as parents and their married sons and/or daughters, married siblings and their households, households of a man and of his sisters' sons. However, there are also many settlements in which non-kin live together.

Kaguru are organized into approximately one hundred matrilineal clans *(ikungugo,* pl. *makungugo;* also *kolo, lukolo,* or *ng'holo,* pl. *sing'holo* or *kolo).* Each clan is associated with one or more areas. In its area a clan possesses certain rights in the distribution of land and in organizing local rainmaking and fertility rituals. While members of many clans reside in an area, they are all subject to certain controls by the clan which is associated with that area. Colonial administrations recognized some of these clans and from them chose leaders of local "native authorities."

Kaguru symbolic classification is closely related to certain aspects of Kaguru social structure. This classification does not appear to be so comprehensive as the systems described for some societies, such as those with prescriptive alliance. Nevertheless, some understanding of this classificatory system is helpful if we wish to comprehend the terms which Kaguru use in speaking of alliance between social groups and how such groups function in marriage, inheritance, and relations between the sexes. Most important of all, such understanding is required if we wish to appreciate the symbolism of Kaguru ritual and belief. In short, it is essential if we are to have any true appreciation of the way in which Kaguru themselves view their world.

III

The Kaguru conceive of certain rights and obligations, social groups, attributes, and directions in oppositive terms. These terms form a dualistic symbolic classification which is best considered under the categories of either "male" and "female" or "right" and "left." In the earlier version of this paper, I noted that nearly all of the terms presented in such categories also involved some kind of association with the common attributes of right and left. However, I suggested that it might not be possible to subsume a fuller set of terms under such categories. Subsequently, I spent two shorter field-stays with the Kaguru and my findings from these visits cannot be fitted under the headings which I previously used. However, each item listed in a set of categories is not only in opposition to its corresponding item in the other category or column but shares some attributes with several other items in its own category. Thus, for example, fluidity, water, blood, red, danger, all seem to share some attributes also held by femininity, in Kaguru eyes. The nature of these interlinked, complex, and subtle associations of attributes will be clearer later. However, in one sense, at least, the terms "right" and "left" still retain their primacy, even now that we have a more detailed account of this system; these are still the two oppositive terms most frequently heard in Kaguru speech in instances when Kaguru refer to such opposition, even though this embraces categories far wider than just right and left.

Kaguru call the right hand or right side, *kulume;* the left, *kumoso*.[5] They consider the right hand to be clean *(-ela)* and to have strength *(ngufu);* the left to be unclean *(mwafu)* and weak *(ngufu hechaka,* there is no strength). Masculine qualities are thought to be of the right, feminine of the left. When I asked Kaguru why this should be, some said that male *(mugosi* or *-ume)* creatures are always physically stronger than female *(mwanamuke* or *-ike)* and that likewise the right hand is stronger than the left. Others said that this was due to the way persons were fashioned in the womb; they said that a person was made of two joined sides, the right half deriving from the father, the left from the mother.[6]

Kaguru often draw a parallel between the conception and birth of a child and the mythical origin of the Kaguru people and their matri-clans. They recount tales of a great trek of the Kaguru and neighboring matrilineal peoples to their present homeland where they divided into their clans at a place called Chiwepanhuka. Some say that this myth also represents the birth of a child whereby a clan is perpetuated by the addition of a new member and Kaguru tell this tale at the initiation of adolescents with this interpretation in mind. The name *chiwe* (small rock) *panhuka* (fall out or away from a larger mass) may have a triple meaning. It may refer to a rock which has fallen away from a larger formation; it may refer allegorically to a clan which has broken away from the undifferentiated tribal group or to an infant which has broken away from its mother, viz., been born. Kaguru go on to say that by *chiwe* (small rock) people may sometimes actually mean "buttocks" or "vagina," or the female fundament. (We shall later see how this might fit in with another set of complementary opposites associated with the Kaguru house.) In this myth of the great trek, the Kaguru are said to have come from the west, which appears to be associated with the womb, and trekked eastward, a direction apparently associated with the outer world. Not only were the marchers' right sides turned to the south and their left sides turned to the north, but the people are said to have marched in double files, the men in a file on the right and the women in a file on the left. Thus west and north would appear to be associated with women, and east and south with men. This idea of emergence and birth in an eastward, outward direction is repeated even in death, as if all natural processes were oriented in this way, for Kaguru bury their dead so that they are pointed to continue this journey with their feet toward the east. Here it is not an association of east with the lower part of the body but rather an association of east with the onward movements of a journey. Furthermore, in Kaguru burial men lie on their right sides, women on their left. Likewise, it is said that during sexual intercourse a man should lie on his right side, a woman on her left.[7]

During cultivation, at least in the remote mountain areas, Kaguru hoeing parties formed to clear fields sometimes separate into groups of men and women, the men on the right of the column, the women on the left, and the entire column hoeing toward higher ground. Thus in another form the great trek model may here be repeated and in this sense perhaps the orientation of a hoeing party may have a further dualistic implication. In some contexts, Kaguru associate high ground and mountains with certain attributes related to masculinity[8] and valleys with femininity, a point I discuss later.

Further possible indication of the dualistic classification of east and west may, perhaps, be seen in certain Kaguru practices associated with sorcery and counter-sorcery. Thus, a man wishing to perform counter-sorcery is said to cut a *mwiyegea* tree's bark (sausage tree, *Kigelia pinnata*), first on its west side, then on its east side, whereas a person practicing sorcery is said to cut first the east side and then the west. It appears here that normal or right processes are associated with a progression from west to east, whereas abnormal or wrong processes are associated with a progression from east to west, although this point is far from clear.[9] It may, however, be that this cutting is associated with the passage of the sun and not with the trek-birth motif. Unfortunately, I could not determine this to my satisfaction.

Right and left also seem to be associated with certain magical acts. In divination (*maselu* or *mulamuli*) it is said that the signs must appear on both the right and left before the prognostication may be regarded as complete. Unfortunately, I could not secure further details on actual divination techniques. In a text which I collected, a Kaguru is instructed to turn to the right in performing what appears to be anti-witchcraft magic (see Beidelman 1964a: 746). It seems also to be implied that in this magic, which involves the healing of the man's injured hands, his right hand should be treated first, then his left, although the text is not very clear on this.

In omens (*ndege,* sing. and pl.), the general significance of these dual categories is clear (Beidelman, 1963d). If, on a journey, a person hears a turacu *(ng'hulukulu, Turacu spp.)* cry out on the right side, it is thought that something important will soon happen to his paternal kin; if on his left, to his maternal kin; if directly ahead, to his own household (the social unit which unites both groups).[10] If a man is on a journey and he stubs his right toe, something important may be about to happen; if the left, nothing important will happen. I was told that this did not indicate whether the impending event would be good or bad; here the right was said to be associated with strength or importance and the left with weakness or unimportance. If a man sets out on a journey and encounters a lone man, or two or more persons, regardless of their sex, this is an omen of good luck. However, encountering a lone woman signifies misfortune, at least if one continues with one's journey.[11] Most Kaguru speak of the auspiciousness of the left, in connection with the good and bad qualities of omens. However, it is said that some individuals regard the reverse as true.[12]

The opposition of the right (male) and left (female) hands may be seen in many everyday Kaguru practices which clearly indicate the association of the right with cleanness, strength, auspiciousness, and the left with uncleanness, weakness, inauspiciousness. Kaguru encourage all children to use the right hand. A child who grows up to favor his left hand is in no way punished, but people may sometimes jokingly comment on this and, if it is a left-handed boy, they may sometimes say that he is "like a wife" *(kama muke)* in this respect. Kaguru eat with the right hand; they use it for greeting persons and for shaking hands. None of these acts would be performed politely with the left. Although gifts should be given and received with both hands, the right sometimes may be used alone, but never the left. When both hands are used for these purposes, the left should be placed somewhat behind and beneath the right. In bathing together, Kaguru men usually cover the penis with the left hand if moving about but more often prefer to conceal it by hiding it between the legs which are kept together as they stand. Thus, the left hand is used to handle unclean material or to perform unpleasant tasks. It is the hand used in cleaning after defecation. It is also the hand favored in sex play. Kaguru men sometimes speak of their positions of lying on the right side during coitus as being advantageous to them because it enables them to conceal their right hands, keep their left hands free, and force a woman to lower herself into using her right hand in such performances.[13] When a Kaguru visits a doctor for treatment, he makes the first payment to the doctor with his right hand. When the treatment has been successfully completed and the patient is cured, the final payment is made with the left. The right hand precedes the left in most sequences, just as it usually is placed above the left. This, in turn, is consistent with the association of right with males, left with females. During the great trek, the west (womb?) was behind, the east was ahead. Likewise, Kaguru men precede women when walking on paths,[14] in entering rooms, in being served, and Kaguru paternal kin usually (although not always) precede maternal kin in performing various rituals or duties in which both groups take part. Some Kaguru say that when God created the world, he created man first and then woman, but, of course, this idea may well be the result of biblical teaching by Christian missionaries.

The Kaguru apply the divisions of right (male) and left (female) to their beliefs concerning the physiology of kinship and to the terms and activities associated with the two major kin groups which compose each individual's relatives—the paternal and maternal kin. Kaguru consider two apparently contradictory principles of physiological kinship which they themselves do not seem to find contradictory at all. As I noted above, some Kaguru speak of the right side of the body being formed from the father, the left from the mother. Most, however, speak of the father's sperm *(udoko)* combining with the mother's blood (*sakame* or *sakami*) [15] to form a pregnancy. The blood and the sperm feed the pregnancy and for this reason a couple should have frequent sexual intercourse after conception. The sperm is also believed to circulate through a woman's body and contribute to her physical sexual development. Thus, a nubile girl's breasts and buttocks are thought to develop steadily with her sexual experience with men and the resultant circulation of their sperm through her body. A child is believed to have been formed of both paternal and maternal elements, the bone, cartilage, teeth and hair, the hard, solid parts of the body, coming from the father; the blood, the fluid parts, coming from the mother. Presumably, the flesh, insofar as it, too, is red and not firm like bone, may be considered to fall into the latter, liquid category. Before discussing the dual aspects of Kaguru kin groups, we must consider some of the symbolic aspects of the blood-female-left/bone-male-right, categories mentioned above. In doing so we may discern a number of other dual sets of attributes, some of which, particularly those involving color (red/white), matter (fluid/solid), and temperature (hot/normal or cool), seem to be among the most pervasive and evocative symbols in Kaguru life.

It was stated above that a Kaguru child is the product of paternal sperm and maternal blood, these producing a child which is an amalgam of solid paternal and fluid maternal parts. A detailed consideration of the various attributes associated with blood/sperm-bone is a convenient way of approaching the complex problem of Kaguru masculine and feminine symbols. The most contrasting attributes of blood and bone are their colors and physical states, the redness and fluidity of blood and the whiteness and solidity of bone. To a lesser extent, this is also found in the contrast between sperm and vaginal blood.

For Kaguru, the fluidity of blood has several important characteristics readily associated with femininity. First of all, it conveys the idea of flowing, of continuity, of perpetuity and, indeed, it is through women that continuity is achieved in Kaguru society. It is perhaps for these reasons that some Kaguru attempt to derive the word *lukolo* (matri-clan) from a similar archaic word meaning "a place where water flows." As Kaguru say, men have no proper descendants and it is only through women that a matri-clan continues. Obviously, too, fluidity is associated with fertility. Kaguru society is based on agriculture and depends upon the annual rains and upon the few semipermanent valley streams for its economic survival. The most important areas of Kaguru cultivation are in the river valleys. Various Kaguru initiation songs firmly establish the symbolic implications of this point beyond doubt. These songs are in the form of riddles whose hidden meanings concern various aspects of sex. During initiation, Kaguru of both sexes are taught these riddle songs and are taught these hidden meanings. From the Kaguru's explanations of such meanings we gain invaluable information from Kaguru themselves concerning their symbolic thought.[16]

One song goes: *Malangilisi gemite mwigenge galangilila ng'holongo, sikoga;* "those standing on the river bank look to see those bathing (below)." The meaning given to this is: the testicles do not enter inside the vagina during intercourse although the penis does. Here the riverbank *(mwigenge)* and the channel of the stream (*ng'holongo,* pit) are associated with the female (fluid-below). Similar imagery is found in the song: *Kunyika kuya kutonyila fula; yakulilisa fileuwa fowele;* "there in the bush it rained; it washed away the maize stalk." This is said to mean: the blood at childbirth washes out the afterbirth. Here, the fertility of women is associated with their blood and with rain *(fula)*. There is little doubt that the Kaguru euphemism for the blood of childbirth, "rain" *(fula),* is a play on such concepts.[17] However, the song above also hints at the destructive or dangerous aspects of the rain and thus of women's fertility and the process of birth, for it calls attention to its violence, comparing it to the sudden destructive rain which sometimes erodes valuable valley land and washes away crops. (I return to this point shortly.) The word *kunyika* (in the bush) is a common euphemism in songs, referring to the genitals; the analogy is between two wild, dangerous, disorderly areas. Finally, Kaguru say: *Mafula gose kutonya fula dya mihili chimola magenge;* "all rains rain, but the rain of January *(mhili)*[18] erodes riverbanks." This is said to mean: the blood of menstruation and the blood of childbirth are similar, but the blood of childbirth is shockingly great. Again, the blood of childbirth and menstruation are compared to rain, and here, also, the destructive and dangerous aspects of female sexuality and fertility are emphasized. I have noted that one of the Kaguru expressions for blood of childbirth is *fula* (rain), calling attention to the fertile aspect; but another term for childbirth is *ng'hondo* (battle) which emphasizes this dangerous aspect as well. Kaguru also sing: *Muke mutumbe*[19] *kwilage mwitembe, nokwila ule fula ikutonya;* "mother's brother's wife, climb on top the house; how can I climb there myself when it is raining outside?" Kaguru say that this means: a menstruating woman soils anything which touches her. The singer of the song is here, figuratively, a woman although youths also learn the song. The singer cannot climb on top of her hut, presumably to secure food or tools, because she is menstruating, and she asks her mother's brother's wife to do this.[20] Here the symbol of rain *(fula)* itself is assigned an unclean or negative association. This idea of the uncleanness associated with female fertility may be suggested in: *Pula dya ng'ombe dili munakano mwaka no ukwija dili munakano;* "the nose of the cow is moist, all through the year it is moist." This is said to mean: a woman's vagina is always moist. Here, the reference to moistness *(munakano)* refers to her fertility but also, perhaps, to her uncleanness although this second point is only conjecture on my part.[21] The dangerous aspect of sexuality is very clearly indicated in the Kaguru expression *chitwi che duma* (head of a wildcat) which is sometimes used to refer to the vagina and the penis, as is the euphemis *mumwiko* (that which is forbidden or prohibited).[22] The term *kunyika* (in the bush), with its disorderly and wild implications, also refers to male genitals: *Kunyika huya kusina nhungu setu singi sememila singi simapinga;* "in the bush, there are our calabashes, some full, some partly full"; this is said to mean that depending upon the frequency of sexual intercourse, a man's testicles are full or not full of semen. The Kaguru also sing: *Mutema mhato temela mwitumba ya musingisi ng'hameka mhate;* "you cut the stubble in the Itumba Mountains, but in Musingisi lowlands one never sees that the stubble has been cut." This is said to have two meanings: *(a)* One can always tell whether a boy has been circumcised, but one cannot always tell by looking whether a girl has undergone some kind of labiadechtomy. *(b)* Circumcising boys makes them clean, but cutting a girl really does not do much good as far as cleanliness is concerned since she continues to become unclean at each menstruation. (The purpose of cutting a girl is said to be to facilitate her abilities to bear children and not to cleanse her.) The utilization of the mountain/lowland motif is clear enough; but here there is also a suggestion of uncleanness. The stubble seems to stand for hair (see Beidelman 1963g: riddle 10). For Kaguru, hair, especially pubic hair, seems to be associated with uncleanness and perhaps, therefore, with failure to observe the proper conventions in human relations. I was told that a proper person would not want to have sexual relations with someone who had neglected to pluck or shave his or her pubic hair because such persons are unclean.

The Kaguru sometimes refer to the human penis as *mukila* (tail), apparently with a notion of the wild or animalistic attributes of the genitals. Man's penis is that extension of himself which links him through copulation with his unruly counterpart, woman; it is the source of pollution. This attribute of a tail is often emphasized by Kaguru in their folklore; for example, there are many popular Kaguru tales in which baboons don clothing and try to dupe humans into accepting them into society, but eventually their tails, their hairiness, and their rough eating habits (eating uncooked food and eating in a slovenly manner) betray them and lead the humans to drive the baboon back into the bush.[23]

The Kaguru speak of the dirtiness *(mwafu)* of the foreskin *(usubu),* sometimes also called *amakunja* or *kusika* (lower part) (Swahili, *ngovi*), which should be removed. The root *-sika* (outside) seems to have associations both of moistness and of lowness: *kusika* also means downward, lowland, the direction in which streams flow, low (in both a physical and moral sense) and genitals —in contrast to *kuchanya,* upward, highland, direction from which streams flow; *masika* is the term for the rainy season. The uncleanness associated with the foreskin is, in part, also associated with immaturity; thus, a wife who wishes to abuse her husband in a very serious manner may tell him in public that he is not circumcised, that he still has a foreskin, viz., that he does not act like a man.[24] Kaguru themselves do not speak often of this contrast between the cleanness of male genitals and the repeated uncleanness of women's, but they do explicitly make this distinction at times of abuse and with reference to the alleged purpose of male circumcision.[25] It is clear that once the foreskin is removed, men no longer suffer from uncleanness in the sense that women do each month until menopause. However, Kaguru seem to associate the sexual act itself with uncleanness, sometimes even calling it bad *(fiha),* although here I think that word could better be translated into the English term "dirty." It is sometimes associated with shame *(chinvala).*[26] After sexual intercourse, a person should wash before meeting others and the act should most appropriately be done in the dark when the participants cannot see each other. Finally, the act itself seems to partake so strongly of the uncontrollable and passionate (*moto,* heat), see later, that it should not be performed by persons involved in any difficult or important undertakings, e.g., by persons going to hunt, to fight, to travel, to propitiate the ancestral ghosts, to brew beer, to nurse a child, to tend a sick person, or by persons whose children are being initiated.[27]

In discussing the songs above, I refer to the dangerous aspect of feminine fertility, an aspect expressed in the cited texts through the themes of the violence of rain and floods. In this sense, fluidity not only signifies continuity and fertility but also uncontrollability. As I publish further data on Kaguru society, I hope that it will become clearer why these concepts are consistent with the social roles of Kaguru women.

The dangerous and uncontrollable aspects of blood and of women in general are symbolically represented in still other ways by Kaguru. The color red serves admirably in this respect, not only because of its association with the shedding of menstrual blood and birth, but also because of its association with the shedding of blood in battle *(ng'hondo)* and some forms of death in which unusual quantities of blood have been expelled from the body for no obvious reason (perhaps some internal hemorrhage such as may be found in some forms of advanced tuberculosis, cancer, and dysentery) are considered extremely inauspicious and the bodies of persons dying in this way are deposited in the bush and not given ordinary burial.[28] The Kaguru also associate red with fire *(moto),* which, like blood, is useful and important but requires careful control if it is not to be dangerous. Thus, the expression *kuhegesa* (to make fire by fire-sticks, to consume with fire) may also mean "to have sexual relations." The active, upper firestick is known as *lukegeso lugosi* (male firestick) or *mulume* (husband) and the lower, passive one as *luhegeso lufele* (female firestick) or *muke* (wife). Furthermore, the color red is associated, through both fire and blood, with heat *(moto),* both literally and figuratively. However, the notion of fire is a complex one. The hearth is the center of a home and the idea of a fire as a place about which a social group lives is a most important one for Kaguru. It is the place where food is cooked and thus made different from the food of wild animals. The Kaguru term *umoto* (at the fire, at the hearth) is best translated as "custom" or social practice. There is also a probable parallel between the Kaguru references to redness as an allusion to sexuality and their association of the redness of baboons' sexual areas with baboons' disorderly, antisocial nature (Busse 1936: 64). It also parallels the association of baboons with improperly initiated humans (discussed below):

village (society)	bush (Nature)
hairless	hairy
tailless	tailed
orderly	disorderly
initiated	uninitiated
cooked food	uncooked food

Kaguru believe that a woman's menstrual flow (*kutumika,* to menstruate, to be taken up with something) is associated with the height of her fertility and passion to a degree that the woman is not only unclean but dangerous and must not come into contact with certain objects, e.g., she should not sleep in her husband's bed but should sleep on the floor and she should not cross a field full of crops, or brew beer, or climb above others as she might do if she were to fetch goods from the roof granary and storeroom or were she to try to repair a roof, etc. Stakes of the *msane* tree, which exudes a red sap, are sometimes placed in gardens to ward off the baneful influence of any menstruating woman who might pass nearby. Kaguru believe that were a man to touch menstrual blood, he would run a serious risk of contracting leprosy or some serious skin disease. This idea also seems the basis of two euphemisms for menstruation: *na hasi* (be under) and *nhamu* (sick, unclean, menstrual blood). The association of red with passion may be seen in a well-known Kaguru song: *Wadodo nvenve musame ukilawa mwija fikamisa, mhela mukahembe, sikihoma na kisajangu sikivonesa kudung'hu wao;* "youngsters, don't go out early or you may meet a rhinoceros with a horn and it will be stabbing and showing their [*sic*] red parts." This is said to be an admonition to adolescent Kaguru not to enter their parents' huts without first carefully announcing themselves because otherwise they might find their parents having sexual intercourse, a situation which would have implications of incest and the parental curse.[29]

The color red is closely associated with death. When members of a matrilineal group decide to execute a criminal, an inauspicious child, or a leper (Beidelman 1963d), this task is delegated to a member of another clan which stands in a ritual joking relation *(utani)* to it. Such an executioner was given a string of red beads which were then cut so that the beads were scattered on the ground symbolizing the blood to be shed in this execution. Likewise, a great diviner and doctor may decorate his calabashes of medicine with red and white beads. The red beads are said to stand for the dangerous powers under his control.

The association of the uncontrollable aspects of blood with heat is expressed in Kaguru beliefs concerning menstruation and certain types of incest. The term *kuhosa* or *kuhola* (to cool) may be used to describe the fanning of any hot food or hot substance.[30] It is also used in the ceremony *(imhosa)* held after a girl's first menstruation when the first hot blood of menstruation is cooled by the elderly women. It is also used in reference to a cleansing ceremony in which a couple guilty of certain sexual offenses (e.g., certain types of forbidden sexual unions) are cooled of this guilty passion. The name of the plant used in preparing the medicine for this also derives from this cooling operation (*luhosa,* a vine, *Crassocephalum bojeri*).[31]

In contrast to these feminine attributes are the masculine ones of solidity, land, mountains, white, and normal (not hot). The association of men with mountains and land has already been made clear through the examples already cited in my discussion of valleys and fluidity; thus, mountains-land/valleys-water; solid/fluid; upper/lower; male/female. The attributes of solidity and coolness refer essentially to normality or regularity, so that perhaps the term *kuhosa* would more appropriately be translated as "to remove undue hotness," or "to return to normal." It is an attempt to change a dangerous condition into a safe and normal one. In this same sense, one of the Kaguru words for health and fitness is *mheho* (coolness, wind, breeze, air).

White also symbolizes safety, peace, and normality. Thus, white beads figure in the medicinal equipment at boys' circumcision and white beads may be pulverized to form a medicine to stanch the flow of blood from the circumcision wound.[32] White beads decorate a renowned doctor's medicine calabashes to indicate the control he has over his powers and thus their safe nature. Sperm is also sometimes compared, because of its whiteness, to nourishing milk *(mele)*.

Earlier in this paper I mentioned that the Kaguru believe that long ago they divided into their matri-clans at a mythical place called *Chiwepanhuka* (*chiwe,* small stone; *panhuka,* breaking away from a larger mass). I went on to note that in this tale Kaguru consider that the stone represents the female fundament. For reasons I have not been able to determine, the Kaguru seem to associate stones with females, at least in some situations, even though one might assume that the solidity of stone would lead Kaguru to associate it with males instead. In any case, another possible set of opposites should be tentatively suggested, although I neglected to secure conclusive corroboration for this when I worked among the Kaguru. This involves the three hearthstones *(mafiga)* which are located at the center of a Kaguru house and the center-pole (*nguzo* or *nguso*) which stands near them. For Kaguru, the association seems to be hearthstones : center-pole :: vagina : penis :: female : male. The hearthstones form a low place where fire is kept and where containers of food are placed, various containers and food itself having the same sexual connotations for Kaguru that they have for many Europeans. All of these characteristics of the hearth are feminine attributes. In contrast, the height, shape, and strength of the pole suggest masculine attributes. The association of this center-pole with masculine attributes is clear in the following initiation song: *Dikungu mwelu digosi dititu dikola nyumba ne migamba;* "small black bird, it is a giant which holds up the house and the poles of the roof." I was told by Kaguru that the small bird was the penis which, like the center-pole, supports a house (*nyumba,* house, households, a matrilineage).[33] The color black here refers to the smoke-blackened center-pole, darkened by its close proximity to the fire below.[34]

The symbolic coitus suggested by the center-pole standing near the hearthstones is repeated in many other combinations of everyday objects whose shapes and uses take on certain sexual attributes. These paired objects or tools are often mentioned by Kaguru, both in the context of initiation ritual and in general conversation when euphemisms for sexual intercourse are required. Thus, the penis *(mbolo)* may be alluded to by terms for stick, spear *(mugoha)*, stone pestle *(isago)*, wooden pestle *(mtwango)*; vagina *(ng'huma)* may be referred to by the terms for stone mortar *(luwala)*, wooden mortar *(ituli)*, or other containers such as calabashes and baskets.

In these cases, it is not merely the shape involved, but, as in the case of the tools used for preparing food, it is the description of a pair of tools, one active and one passive, which produce something together. This is also clear in the case of firesticks which I have already noted. Thus, too, the action of these tools becomes a euphemism for sexual intercourse: to pound flour *(kutwanga),* to grind flour *(kusajila),* to make fire *(kuhegesa).* Similarly, other expressions of this nature involve spearing animals, poking sticks into holes to flush out game, etc. In terms of shape and use, perhaps the most important single material object associated with a Kaguru man is his bow *(uta).*[35] It is associated with his adult status and with his bravery and dominance. The corresponding object for women is the oil-calabash *(mukomba)* which usually contains castor oil. Such oil is used for beautification and as a sexual lubricant and is therefore sometimes associated with a woman's sexual desirability and receptivity. A man's bow is handed down to his eldest son while a woman's oil-calabash is, along with her jewelry, handed down to her eldest daughter. On such occasions the recipient is reminded of the past traditions associated with the clan of the father or mother.[36]

Kaguru, like Ngulu, divide many plants and animals into two oppositive groups with masculine and feminine connections. It is said that long ago, God gave men and women various plants and animals which they could domesticate and tend. Women, being uncontrollable, neglected theirs and these soon became wild and unusable. But men, being orderly, tended theirs carefully. For this reason, there are many wild plants and animals which resemble those used by men, e.g., women : men :: guineafowl : chickens :: zebras : donkeys :: eland : cattle :: certain grasses : grain :: wild plantain : bananas, etc. This association of the bush and wild animals with disorder and the settlement with order is well illustrated in two Kaguru tales about baboons (Beidelman 1965a: 22–24; and an unpublished MS) which relate the blurring of such distinctions with confusions of other categories. Thus, failure to obey certain rules (involving the separation of the proper and improper seasons for initiation) led to the existence of baboons, themselves representing a confusion between the categories of humans and animals, both in terms of their appearance and behavior. Furthermore, it is also said that one of the reasons why baboons have unusual (confused) tastes in food (they are animals but prefer leaving the bush and raiding the crops of men) is that the original separation between bush (the domain of animals) and gardens (the domain of humans) was not observed by humans. Humans were not content with their crops from gardens and with letting baboons and the other animals enjoy the fruits of the bush; instead, humans entered the bush and consumed these foods as well. In revenge for this intrusion, some of the animals, those which were most offended, assumed their present habits as vermin to humans and entered humans' fields to eat crops in addition to the foods of the forest. Kaguru also believe that excessive incursions of wild predators into the space of society, viz., either into fields or homesteads, may be due to a moral disturbance of the ancestral ghosts or God himself (see Beidelman 1966b: 359). This is thought often due to the immoral acts of the living (failure to observe social rules and categories) which in turn lead to a breakdown between the boundaries separating the living from the dead and the world of the bush from the world of humans. Wild animals or beasts are associated with destruction and also with sexuality. I have already noted that *nhanu* (wild cat) is associated with genitals. Sexually voracious women are sometimes referred to as *makala* (man eaters) (see especially, Beidelman 1964d: 11–13). Kaguru often tell children that persons who have died were devoured by a beast *(dikoko)* of the bush. The dead themselves are the epitome of the potential disorder (and hence their power). Note such terms for the dead as *kaga,* the lost; *matete,* the finished; and *kwaga,* to be lost (die); and *kabanika,* he is broken or put in disorder (he dies). The ghosts of the dead are propitiated only in the bush and the sweeping of their graves is thought to set them in order, the clearing and ordering of the site in the bush corresponding to a temporary ordering of the disturbed shades in the nether world.

The bush is associated with many dangerous and polluting acts: children who are inauspicious *(vigego),* witches, and persons with polluting diseases (such as leprosy or dysentery where body boundaries are blurred through loss of flesh or bloody exudation) are slain or abandoned there. Propitiation of ancestral ghosts and the cutting of initiates must take place in the bush, as does the preparation of certain dangerous medicines such as those used in making rain. Persons should defecate in the bush and most trash and household dirt is thrown in heaps at the borders between a settlement and the bush. Conversely, sexual relations should never take place there, presumably because these must occur within the safe and constraining order of the home.

Kaguru also explain the restriction of boy initiates to the bush as their separation, while in a disordered and medial state, from the village (order). But neither can initiates gaze on nubile women. Kaguru explain that girl initiates are brought back to the confines of a village hut after being cut in the bush, because girls must be hidden and not seen, whereas boys in the bush should be seen and exposed to other men. The manipulation of conceptual categories here seems very complex and is not wholly clear to me.

These are not then entirely consistent patterns of contrasts yet all indicate the danger but also the potency of combining a confusion of such opposed categories. Two curious Kaguru medical practices are probably best explained in this way: (1) The scales of the pangolin *(nghwasuli)* are placed on the backs of sterile sheep and goats to make them bear. These scales are also sometimes boiled in water and then the fluid is used to wash ailing infants' heads to soften the fontanel suture, which, if thought to have hardened prematurely, is considered a cause of illness. The pangolin is a classic object of confusion and thus potency in much of Africa (see Douglas 1957); the Kaguru observe that it has scales but is an animal of dry land and not a fish; they also note that it is a wild animal of the bush but does not run away when it is found by a hunter, as other animals do, but dutifully curls up so that it may be conveniently taken home and eaten. (2) A person's genitals and umbilical cord must be kept separate. If they touch, as in delivery, the child is thought to become sterile. However, it is also believed that if a person is sterile, he or she may steal the umbilical cord of a newborn child and boil it in water and drink this to regain fertility at the expense of that of the infant. I suggest that the umbilical cord is that aspect of a child which links it to the land of the ghosts *(kusimu)* and that it is this ambiguous aspect of it which necessitates its separation from the generative organs.

Yet another aspect of the complementary differentiation of male and female attributes may account for the concept of *chimhenu* (Swahili, *kisukumi, kigwaru,* or *kinvakuzi*). A *chimhenu* is said to be a growth upon a woman's clitoris or upon a man's anus, which leads them to be sterile or to produce unhealthy children or to have unhealthy livestock. Although I could not secure a clear exposition of this, it was stated that these growths interfered with the normal fertility and health of the couple and that once such growths were cut away, the couple's normal sexuality and health of their dependents would return. It would seem that such growths confuse the sexual attributes of the couple, a growth on the man's anus being a kind of clitoris and a growth increasing the size of the clitoris being a kind of female penis; the Kaguru themselves did not, however, explicitly say this.

Finally, I suggest that more detailed study of Kaguru language and thought might reveal certain important dual categories in time and space which could be incorporated into the system. In an earlier paper I suggested that day/night and rainy season/dry season might possibly fit this, but owing to the lack of better data, I am unable to pursue this point further (Beidelman 1963: 18–19).

IV

I have noted that the Kaguru apply their categories of right (male) and left (female) to their major social groups and to many of the various activities and rights and obligations which these involve. Let us now consider this aspect of Kaguru dual classification in more detail.

A Kaguru considers his own matri-clan and his matrilineage (*kiungugo* or *lukolo*)[37] to be of the left *(kumoso);* his father's matri-clan *(welekwa)*[38] of the right *(kulume).* Appropriately, a mother's father may thus sometimes be referred to as *kumoso kwangu* (my left). The reason given for this association of clan group with handedness is that one's matri-clan derives from a female (left) and one's father's matri-clan derives from a male (right). Yet this does not mean that Kaguru consider affiliation to one's own matri-clan to be weaker or less important than affiliation to one's father's clan; quite the reverse is true, even though this may well seem an inconsistency on the part of the Kaguru since they do assign primacy of strength and cleanliness to the right hand. Kaguru are absolutely agreed that the left hand and women have no strength (*ngufu hechaka,* there is no strength), but they also say: *awang'ina munhu mu wakagulu weja wapata singufu kusume wababa munhu,* "among the Kaguru persons' mothers have got strength (plural) more than persons' fathers"; *kosoko iyo weja wakong'haga iminviko*[39] *yose yo lwandi lwa wang'ina munhu,* "because they (persons) followed all the prohibitions of their mothers' side." While I was among the Kaguru, I tried to get an explanation for this apparent contradiction, but probably because of my own linguistic limitations, I did not succeed.

Until modern disintegrative factors intruded, Kaguru society seems to have been organized about the matrilineages which compose the various Kaguru clans. Paternal kin were of only secondary importance. Both *ikungugo* (own matri-clan) and *welekwa* (father's matri-clan) are matrilineal groups. The distinction between these two groups is based not upon the principle of their internal composition (matrilineality) but upon the way in which a group is related to an individual, i.e., maternally (left) or paternally (right).

Kaguru often speak of the sharp opposition between the interests of matrilineal and paternal kin.[40] This division is especially clear at marriages and funerals, the two occasions which Kaguru consider to be the most important events in the career of any individual. The most important concern in the contraction of any Kaguru marriage is the collection, transfer, and distribution of bridewealth. The bridewealth paid by a youth's matrilineage is said to be of the left hand, that paid by his father is of the right. Kaguru carefully differentiate between left and right hand bridewealth. These two types of payments are deposited in two separate containers, for Kaguru say that the wealth of the left and right should never be mixed. The wealth by the left (groom's matrilineage) goes to the left (bride's matrilineage); that paid by the right (groom's father) goes to the right (bride's father). The payments of the matrilineage (left) involve *wegasi* or *bulai* or *kolo* (terms for mother's brothers); those of the father's matrilineage (right) involve the *webaba munhu* (fathers of the person). The payments distinct for the two groups are:

right	left[41]
chibanyo (payment for transfer of rights to a woman	*mukowa* (cloth for carrying the child, viz., the placenta)
mbena manvemba (breaker of the castor stalks)	*mulume we kolo* (mouth of the matri-clan or root)

There are other payments besides these, but the other payments are divided into left and right portions which must be combined to form a total payment. For example, the payment *ndama ndafa mwana* (the calf taken for the child) was, in one marriage which I witnessed, a cash payment in which 150 shillings were paid by the boy's father's matrilineage and 120 shillings by the boy's own matrilineage.

Funerals display a similar division of property. Kaguru wryly observe that the favorite topic of conversation at funerals tends to be marriage, because inheritance involves the reallotment of any bridewealth which may have been collected and held by the deceased from the marriage of his kinswomen. Thus, we should not be surprised to find the same divisions reached concerning the nature of the deceased's death and the division of his wealth. These concern members of both sides of the deceased's kin, and representatives of both these groups must be present. In the same sense, both sides should contribute the burial cloth *(sanda)* in which the corpse is wrapped. The most serious problem confronting Kaguru at funerals is the division of property of the deceased, and, of course, this includes far more than bridewealth. While Kaguru women may possess property, it is more usual for this to be held by men. Most funerals for women are therefore not complicated by such difficulties. Like bridewealth, inheritance is divided into right and left. Property associated with a matrilineage is said to be of the left; that with paternal kin is of the right. Political rights to land and to the conduct of certain rituals associated with the land are inherited matrilineally, and are spoken of as of the left. Until 1963, the holders of the posts of official headmen and chiefs were also determined by membership in certain matri-clans. Kaguru say, "Land is of the left," meaning that political rights to economic use of the land are inherited through women. On the other hand, property such as livestock, planted crops, beehives, and cash may be distributed paternally. While these may be given to a man's children, this need not be the case and such goods may be given to the deceased's father's kinsmen or his sisters' children. I have already noted that a man's bow is given to his eldest son, or, if the boy is still an infant, to the father's eldest daughter or some other kinsman to be held for the son until he is an adult; if there is no son, the bow should be destroyed. Other personal possessions are classified as *chipe*-wealth of inheritance and should be divided into left and right portions, although there is a tendency here for favoring the deceased's matrilineage. Thus, at least in the past, a man's shotgun or other important tools would probably be successfully claimed by one of his sisters' sons, although this might be resented by his own sons.

Kaguru believe that witchcraft may be inherited matrilineally (Beidelman 1963f: 67–68). A person of either sex may be suspected of being a witch.[42] Such persons are said to have inherited this by the left, just as rights to control land or to fertility ritual. However, persons may become witches without inheriting such evil power, although transmission by inheritance is in Kaguru eyes the most likely way. This association of witchcraft with the left therefore does not seem to be based on any negative connotation of witchcraft as unclean or weak or feminine but rather upon the fact that it is associated with a matrilineage, a social group of the left.

In the past the division into right- and left-hand payments also seems to have involved the collection and distribution of bloodwealth *(chimba)* made in the case of a kinsman's murder of a neighbor. The nature of such payments cannot be clearly understood since they are no longer made today.

When Kaguru speak of these various payments and obligations, they sometimes stretch out first one hand then the other, as they mention the right and left obligations, as though to make it absolutely clear what is meant. Nothing could more clearly demonstrate the dualistic character of their thought on such topics.

Both the right and left are concerned at initiation. When a youth returns to his home from his confinement in an initiation hut, he should be greeted by representatives of both his own and his father's clan. He is given small gifts and then his father or one of his father's matrilineal kinsmen rubs castor oil onto the boy from the top of his head to his right shoulder and then downward, applying it with his chin. This is done first to the left side, then to the right: up/down; right/left. After this, a member of the boy's own matrilineage does the same to the boy's left side: first/second; right/left; father's matrilineage/own matrilineage.

Kaguru names are divided into the categories of right and left. Every Kaguru receives several names, usually over half a dozen. He or she receives these names at a ceremony held after initiation. These names are given by both matrilineal and paternal kin and sometimes by others as well. Some of these names must be of ancestors of one's own matrilineage; others of ancestors of one's father's matrilineage. The former are called names of the left, the latter, names of the right. In the same sense, names of ancestral ghosts are divided into left and right categories. These names may be invoked as part of certain rituals related to fertility, illness, etc. Most rites concern matrilineal kin and therefore concern names of the left, and Kaguru themselves state that names of the left are more important names in ritual. However, Kaguru believe that there are important names in both these categories and that both types of names should be used on different occasions in seeking supernatural aid in times of crisis. In the same ceremonies, sheep are sometimes slain and their blood sprinkled as part of the rites of propitiation to the ghosts of the ancestors and to God. On such occasions, the ritual joking partners *(watani)* [43] who perform these rites of sacrifice cut the sacrificial animal's hide into small rings which are then worn on the left wrists of the members of the matrilineage for whom the ceremony has been held.

V

In summary, I present a list of the oppositive terms which constitute Kaguru dualistic classification:

right *(kulume)*	left *(kumoso)*
right hand	left hand
right half of the body	left half of the body
hand used in eating, greeting, in making gifts	hand used after defecation and for unpleasant tasks
hand used in completing payments	hand used in initiating payments
upper hand	lower hand
hand female is encouraged to use in sex play	hand male prefers to use in sex play
side male tends to lie upon during coitus	side female tends to lie upon during coitus
masculine	feminine
first	second
ahead	behind
above	below
upstream	downstream
strong	weak
settlement	bush
regular or stable	difficult to control
(life?)	death
auspicious omens	inauspicious omens
important omens	unimportant omens
sperm *(udoko)*	blood of conception *(sakami)*
bones *(maguha)*, teeth, hair	blood of body *(sakami)*
——	blood of menstruation and of circumcision *(nhamu)*
solid	fluid
land	water (rain)
mountain or hill	valley
white	red
normal or cool	warm or hot
east	west
south	north
single man or several persons	single woman
side of column on which men made the trek to Kaguru-land	side of column on which women made the trek to Kaguru-land

side of column on which men hoe	side of column on which women hoe
domesticated plants and animals	wild plants and animals which resemble domesticated ones
ideally active, dominant	ideally passive
outside?	womb?
father's matri-clan *(welekwa)*	matri-clan (*ikungugo* or *lukolo*)
father *(baba)*	mother (*ng'ina* or *mai*)
father and his brothers *(baba)*	mother's brother (*bulai, kolo* or *mwegosi*)
bridewealth received by clan of girl's father	bridewealth received by clan of girl
bridewealth given by youth's father	bridewealth given by clan of youth
property inherited outside clan	property inherited through clan
rights to usufruct	political rights to land
——	rights to certain fertility ritual
——	wrist on which sacrificial object is worn after propitiatory rites [44]
——	inheritance of witchcraft
formal or respectful relations associated with kin	joking relations *(utani)* and sexual relations
purity	pollution
bow	woman's oil-calabash
bloodwealth paid by father	bloodwealth paid by matri-clan
bloodwealth received by father	bloodwealth received by matri-clan
names associated with father's matri-clan	names associated with matri-clan
side anointed by father's brother	side anointed by mother's brother
first group in ritual	second group in ritual
center-pole	hearthstones
cooked	uncooked
initiated	uninitiated

VI

The Kaguru data are scant, but they form a consistent whole taken from a fairly wide range of Kaguru beliefs and practices. The Kaguru's explanations about the meaning of the various symbols which they employ are not only consistent with such a dual classification but make little sense without it. The full impact of many Kaguru terms and expressions can only be appreciated once their full symbolic or cosmological context is understood within terms of this system of dual symbolic classification. It is certainly unrealistic to expect all peoples to be so articulate about their cosmology and symbolic beliefs that a complete system of their ideas and symbols is presented by the people themselves without requiring the analytical synthesis of the social anthropologist; were this the case, social anthropologists would have few tasks. However, Kaguru themselves do go surprisingly far in such interpretation and synthesis.[45] In initiation songs, the range of Kaguru symbolic abstraction is clearly indicated, and, most important of all, the meaning of the symbols and, to some extent, some of the principles behind the selection and use of these symbolic terms are discussed by Kaguru themselves as part of their explanations to initiates about the meanings of these riddles. However, it must be remembered that, just as all western European Christians are not equally aware of the symbols employed in the liturgy and architecture of their churches, not all Kaguru are equally aware of the full implications of some of their symbolic acts and terms. For example, not all Kaguru see an allegorical meaning in the myth of the great trek, although some Kaguru do. Likewise, new initiates do not know the full meaning of all the ceremonies and songs which they learn at initiation. These are taught gradually through the years at successive ceremonies. While the rudiments are learned at a person's own initiation, added knowledge is gained at successive initiations at which he serves as assistant to the persons in charge or as guardian to the boys. Initiation and inculcation of symbolic lore are gradual and complicated processes which not all Kaguru learn equally and which only the old have mastered. Some Kaguru are uninterested in helping at further initiations, while others are unable to remember such lore; thus, we must not expect all Kaguru, even of one age, to be comparably versed in symbolism and although they participate in certain rituals and ceremonies, some may be only dimly aware that these have deeper, esoteric meanings. In this sense, some of the symbolic acts and beliefs of some Kaguru are held "on faith." We must then picture Kaguru dual symbolic classification as a system of beliefs grasped in varying degrees by the members of Kaguru society and not uniformly meaningful to all. The dualistic symbolic classification which I present here is, of course, not an ideological system constructed, as such, by Kaguru themselves; but this does not mean that the principles behind such a categorization have no meaning for Kaguru. It merely indicates the lack of interest which Kaguru have in carrying out intensive and full synthetic analysis of the various different aspects of their beliefs and actions. They have very great insight into their own society and beliefs, but they are not social anthropologists.[46]

Whether any individual Kaguru sees these various oppositive attributes forming a single system is very doubtful. But there is no doubt that many Kaguru see various sets of attributes in interrelationship with one another and that they are very aware of the principles of thought operative in such categorization. For example, the association:

right	left
male	female
father's matri-clan	matri-clan
fathers	mother's brothers
father	mother
strong	weak
first	second
father's matri-clan's rights and obligations	matri-clan's rights and obligations

may be found in one ritual situation and the terms right/left and strong/weak are sometimes used in reference to some of the various groups, persons, properties, and rituals involved. Similarly:

sperm	blood of conception
white	red
regular	uncontrollable
bone	blood
solid	fluid

This cluster of attributes is found in certain rituals and songs and is explicitly stated by Kaguru. Although the oppositives uncontrollable/regular are not readily associated with some of the terms in the first cluster presented, e.g., mother's brothers/father, etc., there are other terms which do form a bridge between these two sets of terms. Thus, some Kaguru do speak of the blood of conception forming the left of the body. All associate weakness with fluidity or blood and find these both attributes of femininity; in this way, the interconnected attributes of one cluster may be said to be connected with those which form another such cluster. In short, we may see the system as a group of clusters of associated terms with some common terms in each cluster serving as intermediary links between these subgroups, even though certain terms in any one cluster may never be explicitly linked with certain terms in another.

The term utilized on any symbolic occasion is evocative because of the wide number of attributes implicit from the symbols used.

It is as though each such symbolic instance were a subtle epigram whose point depended upon an associative chain-reaction of symbols triggered off by the one or two terms actually presented.[47] Thus, in the song "All rains rain, but the rain of January erodes the riverbanks," the attributes of red/white and unclean/clean are not mentioned at all, and yet the answer to the riddle, the blood of menstruation and birth, makes this implicit association absolutely clear. The subtlety and complexity of these symbols involve the associations of fluidity : solidity :: uncontrollability : stability :: danger : safety, and the ambivalent concept of femininity in which fertility and continuity are also associated with danger, destruction, death, and the quarrels of men. And yet the manifest terms simply involve rainwater streaming down a valley during the planting season.

In this paper I have indicated the general character of Kaguru dual symbolic classification and tried to support my construction with examples from a wide range of Kaguru activities. I am aware of my own linguistic inadequacies in coping with such problems. However, with even a rough appreciation and understanding of such a system, we are better able to understand Kaguru rituals and songs which otherwise would probably appear somewhat irrational or, perhaps, even perversely exotic. We also gain understanding of the frequent use of the Kaguru terms "right" and "left" which occur without fail at any important social occasion involving an assembly of the various kin associated with any Kaguru individual. On such occasions, these terms serve as important pointers to the kinds of values attached to these groups. Most important of all, through such an analysis we can appreciate the ideas concerning the various attributes of the two sexes which form the very core of Kaguru beliefs about their society and which affect almost all aspects of Kaguru behavior, from marital relations, care of menstruation and pregnancy, adultery beliefs, and ideas about kinship relations, to details concerning the nature of ancestral propitiation, inheritance, funerals, and categorization of modes of death.

Notes

* I am grateful to Drs. R. Downs, L. Faron, R. Needham, V. Turner, and W. Whiteley for reading and commenting on various drafts of this essay; however, responsibility for errors remains my own. Dr. Whiteley has indicated the need for further contextualization of the distinctions

postulated in my paper; unfortunately, my grasp of the Kaguru language is not sufficient to allow this on the scale he suggests. The present form of this paper owes much to the essays of Dr. Turner, who has set a standard of ethnographic and analytical excellence which others must be hard put to approach (Turner 1961a, 1961b, 1962a, 1962b).

I did initial fieldwork among the Kaguru in 1957–58 under a research assistantship provided by the Department of Sociology and Anthropology, University of Illinois. Since the first version of this paper appeared, I have benefited from three shorter stays with the Kaguru. The first, in 1962–63, was part of a longer research study of intertribal relations in eastern Tanzania. This was possible through a Ford Foundation postdoctoral grant awarded under the auspices of the University of Oxford. The others, in 1965 and 1966, were through a National Science Foundation grant awarded under the auspices of Harvard and Duke Universities.

1. For example, "Philology and hands," pp. 30–57; "The luck idea and hand preference," pp. 197–232; "Magic and hand values," pp. 233–97; and "Religion and hand symbolism," pp. 298–342; cf. also the curious and interesting work of Wolff (1946), and Fritsch's survey (1964); for a survey of some of the early literature on the physiological aspects of the topic, cf. Cunningham (1902).

2. I am indebted to Professor John Middleton for bringing this work to my notice; cf. also Smith 1952: 22.

3. However, these two works do not seem to convey the full extent to which such symbolism is put by the Nuer. For example, cf. Evans-Pritchard 1956: 56, 57, 61; I have dealt with some of the Nuer data elsewhere (1966c).

4. For example, the Fulani and the Masai (Needham 1960: 30 [above, p. 122]; Fosbrooke 1948; Gulliver 1963: 145–46). The Nilo-Hamitic Baraguyu would also merit such an analysis; unfortunately, my data on these people are at present not sufficient to make such an analysis (Beidelman 1960: 260, 263, 270). Cory reports an especially fine example of dualistic symbolism with reference to social organization (1960). Such concepts also seem to be especially important among the Tonga (Colson 1958: 130, 160, 166, 217, 272). Kronenberg (1961) describes this among the Topotha. Kidd (1906: 296–97) devotes an appendix to the problem of right and left among the Zulu. Although Wilson (née Hunter) does not specifically discuss the problem for the Pondo, such observations are scattered throughout her study (1961: 16, 17, 36, 37, 53, 156, 168, 171, 242, 248, 251, 257). There are rich data also for the Tembu of South Africa (Laubscher 1937: 3–4, 73, 74, 75, 86, 100, 101, 118, 119, 121, 122, 125, 140, 145, 148, 152, 158, 185, 186, 192). Gray (1963: 121) neglects such discussion although it seems clear that his interpretation of the Sonjo priesthood would benefit from such an analysis. The Nyoro seem outstandingly rich in such symbolism and, although these people are well covered in some other respects, no research has ever presented the cosmological aspects of their society and thought in a systematic and analytical manner (Roscoe 1923: 23, 35, 36, 45, 50, 97, 100, 121, 134,

143, 149, 155, 158, 168, 174, 175, 184, 187, 193, 261, 269, 292, 293, 296, 318, 320, 321, 329). The Ganda seem to resemble the Nyoro but the ethnographic data are less detailed (Roscoe 1911: 45, 63, 107, 197). Lindblom cites examples for the Kamba and discusses the problem in a footnote (1920: 104, 140, 291). One of the most interesting and original accounts of such symbolism in West Africa is Frobenius's study of Yoruba divination and cosmology (1913: 228–64); related to this, cf. Morton-Williams (1960: 363, 368, 369, 372). There is no doubt that a great many more references to this problem would be found if the literature were carefully surveyed; my purpose here is not that but only to indicate briefly some of the wide and geographically divergent areas for future work. At a later date, I hope to survey the symbolic classification systems of other matrilineal peoples in east-central Tanzania, notably the Luguru and Ngulu. Some indication of the nature of this material may be found in McVicar 1941: 18–22; 1945: 32; Baxter 1943: 50–1; and in my own work (1964c; 1965b).

5. The term *kulume* derives from *-ume* or *-lume* which is a masculine stem, e.g., *mwanalume,* man (Swahili, *mwanamume* or *mwanaume*); *mulume,* husband. The prefix *ku-* denotes place. The term *kumoso* appears also to have a relation to words in other Bantu languages: *umotho, moso* (Needham 1960: 23n.; also Werner 1904; Stapleton 1905). The Kaguru terms I cite are slightly different from those used in Last's study of this language. Last gives *mkono wa kulumi* (right hand) and *mkono wa kumuno* (left hand) 1886: 123, 133).

Many Kaguru use Swahili words for right and left rather than the Kaguru ones. The Kaguru language is being rapidly replaced by Swahili through the schools, courts, and trade. These Swahili words are often very similar in both sound and meaning to Kaguru words and often seem to involve the same attributes and associations which Kaguru words for right and left have: the right hand is called *mkono wa kulia,* hand for eating; *mkono wa kuume,* hand of male. The left hand is called *mkono wa kuke* or *mkono wa kike,* both meaning hand of female, and *mkono wa kushoto,* an obscure expression of undetermined origin. One Swahili-speaking Kaguru derived this last from *kushota,* to drag one's buttocks on the ground when one is in a crouched position. Perhaps then this signifies "hand of abasement"; I am told, however, that such a derivation is not accepted by Swahili scholars. I did not hear such Arabic-Swahili forms as *yamini,* right (*twa yamini,* to take an oath), and *shemali,* left. Some Swahili dictionaries list an additional expression for right hand which I did not encounter: *mkono wa mlio.* The meaning of this is not clear. Some authorities derive this expression from the verb *kulia,* to cry; *mli* noise. They then suggest that this expression means hand for making noise, viz., for drumming or playing a musical instrument. However, Rev. L. Harries informs me that this expression may perhaps derive from *kula,* to eat. He states that the term *mlo,* food, and the term *mlio,* eating vessel, are used at Lamu on the northern Swahili-speaking coast.

6. Dr. Turner reports similar beliefs for the Ndembu (private communication). This may also be the reason for the Konde (Nyakyusa)

custom related by Mackenzie: "If the *post mortem* reveals tokens of witchcraft on the left side, it has come from the mother; if on the right, from the father" (1925: 252).

7. A similar account of such positions in both burial and coitus is reported for a number of geographically widely dispersed African peoples.

8. Mountains are also associated with the land of the dead (*kusimu*) but in this respect it is not the shape or solidity of mountains which are concerned, as here, but the distance of their summits, the most distant points within the Kaguru's purview are associated with the most distant cosmological region, the land of the dead. This land is inhabited by the ghosts (*wasimu*) of all men and women of all Kaguru clans (cf. Beidelman 1964b: 116, 136).

9. A similar belief is reported among the Lamba (Doke 1931: 217).

10. A somewhat similar situation is reported for the Hehe (Wieschhoff, 1938, p. 209 [above, p. 64]).

11. Similarly, for the Nyoro (Roscoe 1923: 201), for the Ganda (Roscoe 1911: 17), and for the Kamba (Lindblom 1920: 292).

12. In regard to the data on the Chagga of Tanzania, Wieschhoff writes: "As mentioned above, these natives interpret the hitting of the left foot as a bad omen, but if somebody should continue a journey in spite of such a warning he might discover that his left foot is the lucky one and would in the future regard it as such" (p. 212 [above, p. 67]); see also Lantis 1940: 151, 152; Farsi 1958: 26–27.

13. In actual practice, of course, Kaguru use other positions as well. The right-left position related here in only an ideal position mentioned to me by male informants. Lévi-Strauss (1963: 190–91) cites this point but gives an incorrect meaning which runs counter to the reported ethnographic facts. Kaguru women do not, as he suggests, use the right hand in sex play because that is their "impure" hand. As I have stated, they are forced or maneuvered by their lovers into using that hand, the "pure" hand for them as well as for men, as a further expression of their subordinate position. Thus, women must use the "pure" hand for a polluting act while men use their "impure."

14. A few Kaguru men, when asked about this, said it was because women did not want men to see any menstrual blood which might drop as they walked. This is revealing, not as a basis for a custom, but as an insight into certain denigrating attitudes about women which are held by some Kaguru men.

15. For a discussion of some of the implications of this principle of classification, cf. Lévi-Strauss 1949: 486–502; 1963: 185–93.

The Kaguru sometimes distinguish between the blood of the body (*sakame* or *sakami*) and the blood of menstruation or from a circumcision wound (*nhamu, tamu* or *nhume*), but it is not clear to me how precisely these are distinguished in terms of forming a pregnancy. Kaguru relate menstruation (*kutumika,* to be involved, taken up with something) to female fertility and yet it is clear that the blood which leaves the body during menstruation is considered unclean, hot, and dangerous and that it plays no part in forming a child. The Kaguru concept of blood is complex and yet crucial to our problem. I have discussed it at some length elsewhere (1963b).

16. I hope eventually to publish a monograph dealing with such texts and related topics.

17. The term *ifuli* (pudenda), however, does not seem to derive from this root, but from *kufula,* to fart. The notion associates vagina and anus and the unpleasant sounds emitted from them. There are several Kaguru songs alluding to the embarrassing sounds of sexual congress.

18. *Mhili,* the first major rains which occur in January (Beidelman 1963c: 16).

19. The Ngulu term is used here, rather than the Kaguru term *bulai* or *kolo.* Perhaps this term is used to rhyme with *mwitembe* (on the tembe-type house).

The reason for the choice of mother's brother's wife is not clear. It may, however, be worth noting that such a woman is a potential threat to the members of her husband's matrilineage, since it is to her own interest to encourage him to provide for his own (their) children, rather than for the children of the women of his own matrilineage. In this sense, perhaps we should not be surprised that such a person is mentioned in this rather negative context.

20. Thatching and repair of roofs is a household chore which women never undertake, because it is said that their impurity, due to menstruation, makes it bad for them to be above men.

21. Dr. Turner, discussing the Ndembu, states that he finds a similar attitude concerning aversion to the moistness of the vagina (private communication). This idea of moist uncleanness also seems reflected in certain Swahili obscene slang words for vagina: *kora* (snail), *kenye* (the unpleasant smell of the body, as in dirty underclothes), *kinengwe* and *papa* (words for shark, said to be applied because this refers to "food" with an unpleasant, fishy odor); and *mnyevu* (dampness, moistness, but with many more negative associations, cf. *-nya* in a Swahili dictionary).

22. Similarly, the term *ng'hanu* (lynx) is sometimes used to refer to the genitals of either sex, apparently associating this with the danger of sexual relations. I could not determine clearly whether these terms *duma* and *ng'hanu* refer to the same animal in some situations. The association of such fierce feline animals with sexuality and initiation appears to be fairly common in East and Central Africa.

There seems to be a tendency is some societies for an inversion to take place in the application of such sexual slang. Thus, we find the term *cock* widely used in obscene reference to penis, in English, yet among some American Negro groups, it is used as an inverted referent to vagina, apparently to accentuate sexuality and promiscuity (see Abrahams 1964: 264).

23. Elsewhere (1966c) I discuss in some detail similar phallic symbolism among the Nuer; this extensive or exuvial attribute of both tails and penises may also account for their being symbolically homologous in certain other African societies, such as the Swazi (cf. Beidelman 1966a).

24. It is said that an initiated Kaguru woman would refuse sexual rela-

tions with an uncircumcised youth. In many cases this is probably true though there are instances of Kaguru women having intercourse with men of tribes which do not circumcise, although it is sometimes said that these would not be married by such men unless the men were first cut. Kaguru sometimes explain their joking relations (*utani*) with such tribal groups by saying that since they are uncircumcised, they fall into an abusive category (Beidelman 1966b).

Turner reports for the Ndembu an association of the foreskin with femininity and uncleanness (1962b: 161).

A very striking illustration of a similar mode of association may be found in the dramatically pivotal section of Ferdinand Oyono's superb novel *Houseboy* (p. 33) where the young African hero loses his awe and respect for his white employer when he sees him naked and finds him to be uncircumcised.

While in the field I failed to inquire regarding the following point which may be of significance: there is a dramatic contrast in the color of the male glans before and after circumcision. Before circumcision, this is reddish, in strong contrast to the brown or blackish color of the rest of the genitalia and body. After the circumcision wound has healed, the glans takes on the dark color characteristic of the rest of a Kaguru's body. In this respect, it may be that circumcision not only removes feminine "wetness" but also "redness," with all that this implies.

25. For a Kaguru text on the origin of circumcision as a cleansing act, see Beidelman 1964a: 758–60. The text is similar to an Ndembu tale reported by Turner 1962b: 165–66.

26. This negative aspect of the sexual act is clearly seen in the association of sexual relations with joking relations (*utani*) and, indeed, a euphemism for sexual intercourse is *kutania* (to joke, to abuse, to insult). It is among those toward whom one stands in some kind of *utani*-relationship that one can act in a manner which ignores the usual rules of propriety. It is said to be on account of this sexual connotation of joking relations that a wife is sometimes allowed to perform *utani*-rites for her husband when his usual joking partners (*wtani*) are absent. However, the problem of Kaguru joking relations is exceedingly complex and cannot be dealt with here (see Beidelman 1966b).

With regard to the "badness" of sexual relations, Swahili slang sometimes refers to genitals as *ubaya* (badness).

27. Although redness and fluidity are Kaguru attributes of the uncontrollability of femininity, the attribute of left itself does not seem to be utilized by Kaguru to express this. This contrasts with the Fanti of Ghana who, my friend Mr. George Abban informs me, sometimes associate left-handedness with hypersexuality in both sexes.

Some idea of the concept of sex and "dirtiness" may also be seen in certain Kaguru riddles in which a grandmother (a person with whom one has a sexual joking relationship) is associated with stench and uncleanness (see Beidelman 1963g: riddles 15 and 17).

28. I was not able to gain extensive information on this point.

29. For a discussion of incest and cursing, see Beidelman 1963e.

30. I have secured more explicit examples of the association of fire-red-blood-menstruation in my work on Ngulu female initiation. I cannot discuss these here, but I should note that Kaguru seem aware of most Ngulu customs and seem to find many of these very similar to their own (see Beidelman 1964c).

31. I am grateful to the East African Herbarium, Nairobi, for identifying this for me.

32. It is also reported that hyena's or hare's feces are used, but I could not learn why. A hyena's feces are unusually white but a hare's are not.

33. I have collected further data concerning the symbolism of the center-pole and hearthstone among the Ngulu, who very closely resemble the Kaguru in many beliefs and who also have the Chiwepanhuka myth (1964c: 379–80).

34. As far as I can tell, the color black does not seem to have any sexual associations. It is associated with rainmaking and with witchcraft, problems outside the scope of this paper. I was, however, told that menstruating women should wear black and not bright clothing because they should not try to appear attractive to men.

35. This is even more true among the Gogo, the Kaguru's neighbors to the west. My friend, Dr. Peter Rigby, relates many such instances for these people.

36. It also appears likely that the bow and oil-calabash figure very prominently in Kaguru female initiation ceremonies, but, unfortunately, my material is scant on this topic. I do possess extensive information on such ceremonies for the Ngulu, and, in that case, these objects are used in combination and are recognized as male and female sexual objects.

37. From *kuleka,* to bear.

38. From *kulekwa,* to be born.

39. More commonly, the singular, *mwiko,* is used.

40. Although Kaguru matrilineages are the most important corporate groups for Kaguru, this need not mean that they are regarded with unmixed evaluation. For this reason, Kaguru association of matrilineages with certain attributes of left, and thus possibly of disorder, may well conform to other aspects of their attitudes related to the "matrilineal puzzle," viz., their contradictory evaluation of both virilocality and settlements formed around matrilineages. (Of course, such conflicting values need not characterize every matrilineal society; e.g., the Ashanti and Nayar, in the past, did not prize both settlements based upon a matrilineage and also stable households of husband and wives.) Dr. Turner has commented brilliantly on a situation very similar to the one here mentioned for the Kaguru (1957: 67, 77–78, 228–30).

41. The terms associated with the matrilineage clearly symbolize feminine attributes; those associated with the father's matrilineage are more difficult to interpret, although there is some indication that the castor stalk is associated with males because of its upright shape. Such association has explicit symbolic meaning for Ngulu (see Beidelman 1964ç: 376).

42. When I was in Kaguru-land, witchcraft allegations and suspicions seemed to be directed about evenly against men and women. I had hoped

that this point would be clear from my recent essay on this topic, but I repeat the point here since the editors of the symposium in which my essay appears have unaccountably misinterpreted my statements (see Middleton and Winter 1963: 17).

43. Elsewhere (1966b) I analyze Kaguru *watani* and their medial nature between certain Kaguru complementary polar categories.

44. I could not obtain such information for Kaguru, but the neighboring Ngulu, whom Kaguru very closely resemble, wear such leather on the left wrist if their own clan has sacrificed, and on the right wrist if their father's clan has sacrificed and they have attended.

45. In a recent article, Dr. Goody writes somewhat critically of the analysis of dual systems of thought: ". . . such radical distinctions sometimes appear to be seen as having explanatory power in themselves, when an association is made between two or more sets of 'oppositions.' Secondly, just because the elucidation of these relationships is given explanatory force, there is a tendency to assume the presence of such concepts on evidence of a rather slender kind" (Goody 1961: 160–61). These remarks are far from clear. Naturally, theories should be supported by as much evidence as possible, although some of the most stimulating work in anthropology is sometimes prompted at some stage by adventurous speculation on rather slim evidence (surely not an entirely bad thing so long as it is clearly indicated that this is what has been done). But it is clear in such cases as the Kaguru that only by such analysis can we hope to see the full range of meaning associated by Kaguru themselves with particular symbols. Kaguru go far in providing us with the principles of their classification, but we can hardly expect them to do our work for us as social anthropologists. One can only assume that any analysis or heuristic device which enables us to think more clearly about a particular society and which remains consistent with all the known facts, must, until shown otherwise, be an advance in the right direction.

46. I did not succeed in speaking with any Kaguru ritual experts although I did talk with a number of men with more than average knowledge of such matters. I also talked with a few women about symbolism. It was from these persons that my most useful information was obtained. Unfortunately, I never succeeded in gaining the confidence of old women whom most Kaguru consider to be the best experts on such lore.

47. In other papers I go further in trying to account for such symbols: Beidelman 1964c: 386–88; 1966a: 401–4.

Bibliography

Abrahams, R. D.

1964 *Deep Down in the Jungle* . . . Hatboro: Folklore Associates.

Baxter, H. C.

1943 Religious practices of the Pagan Wazigua. *Tanganyika Notes and Records* 15: 49–57.

BEIDELMAN, T. O.
1960 The Baraguyu. *Tanganyika Notes and Records* 55: 245–78.
1961a Hyena and rabbit: a Kaguru representation of matrilineal relations. *Africa* 31: 61–74.
1961b Right and left hand among the Kaguru: a note on symbolic classification. *Africa* 31: 250–57.
1963a Further adventures of hyena and rabbit: the folktale as a sociological model. *Africa* 33: 54–69.
1963b The blood covenant and the concept of blood in Ukaguru. *Africa* 33: 321–42.
1963c Kaguru time reckoning: an aspect of the cosmology of an East African people. *Southwestern Journal of Anthropology* 19: 9–20.
1963d Kaguru omens: an East African people's concepts of the unusual, unnatural and supernormal. *Anthropological Quarterly* 36: 43–59.
1963e A Kaguru version of the sons of Noah: a study of the inculcation of the idea of racial superiority. *Cahiers d'études africaines* 3: 474–90.
1963f Witchcraft in Ukaguru. In *Witchcraft and sorcery in East Africa*, eds. J. Middleton and E. Winter, pp. 57–98. London: Routledge, Kegan Paul.
1963g Some Kaguru riddles. *Man* 63: 158–60.
1964a Five Kaguru texts. *Anthropos* 58: 737–72.
1964b Three tales of the living and the dead: the ideology of Kaguru ancestral propitiation. *Journal of the Royal Anthropological Institute* 94: 109–37.
1964c Pig (*guluwe*): an essay on Ngulu sexual symbolism and ceremony. *Southwestern Journal of Anthropology* 2: 359–92.
1964d Ten Kaguru tales. *Journal of African Languages* 3: 1–37.
1965a Six Kaguru tales. *Zeitschrift für Ethnologie* 90: 17–41.
1965b Notes on boys' initiation among the Ngulu of East Africa. *Man* 65: 143–47.
1966a Swazi royal ritual. *Africa* 36: 373–405.
1966b *Utani:* Kaguru notions of sexuality, death and affinity. *Southwestern Journal of Anthropology* 20: 359–92.
1966c The ox and Nuer sacrifice. *Man* 1 (n.s.): 453–67.
1968 Some Nuer notions of nakedness, nudity and sexuality. *Africa* 38: 113–31.
BERNARDI, B.
1959 *The Mugwe: a failing prophet.* London: Oxford Univ. Press.
BUSSE, J.
1936–37 Kaguru-Texte. *Zeitschrift für Eingeborenen-Sprachen* 27: 61–75.
COLSON, E.
1958 *Marriage and the family among the Plateau Tonga.* Manchester: Manchester Univ. Press.
CORY, H.
1960 Religious beliefs and practices among the Sukuma/Nyamwesi tribal groups. *Tanganyika Notes and Records* 54: 14–26.

CUNNINGHAM, D. J.
1902 Right-handedness and left-handedness. *Journal of the Royal Anthropological Institute* 32: 273–96.
DOKE, C.
1931 *The Lambas of Northern Rhodesia.* London: Harrap.
DOUGLAS, M.
1957 Animals in Lele symbolism. *Africa* 27: 46–58.
EVANS-PRITCHARD, E. E.
1949 Burial and mortuary rites of the Nuer. *African Affairs* 48: 56–63.
1953 Nuer spear symbolism. *Anthropological Quarterly* 26: 1–19. [See chap. 6 above.]
1956 *Nuer religion.* Oxford: Clarendon Press.
FARSI, S.
1958 *Swahili sayings: book two.* Dar es Salaam: East African Literature Bureau.
FOSBROOKE, H.
1948 An administrative survey of the Masai social system. *Tanganyika Notes and Records* 26: 1–50.
FRITSCH, V.
1964 *Links und Rechts in Wissenschaft und Leben.* Stuttgart: Kohlhammer.
FROBENIUS
1913 *The voice of Africa.* Vol. 1. London: Hutchinson.
GOODY, J.
1961 Religion and ritual: the definitional problem. *British Journal of Sociology* 12: 142–50.
GRAY, R.
1963 *The Sonjo of Tanganyika.* London: Oxford Univ. Press.
GULLIVER, P. H.
1961 Structural dichotomy and jural process among the Arusha of Northern Tanganyika. *Africa* 31: 19–35.
1963 *Social control in an African society.* London: Routledge, Kegan Paul.
HAEKEL, J.
1950 Die Dualsysteme in Afrika. *Anthropos* 46: 13–24.
HERTZ, R.
1960 The pre-eminence of the right hand: a study in religious polarity. In *Death and the right hand,* trans. R. and C. Needham. London: Cohen & West. [Newly translated, chap. 1 above.]
HOCART, A.
1936 *Kings and councillors.* Cairo: Printing Office Paul Barbey. [Edited and with an introduction by Rodney Needham, Univ. of Chicago Press, 1970.]
1954 *Social origins.* London: Watts.
HUNTER, M.
1961 *Reaction to conquest.* 2d edition. London: Oxford Univ. Press.
JEFFREYS, M.
1946 Dual organization in Africa. *African Studies* 5: 82–104.

KIDD, D.
1906 *Savage childhood.* London: Black.
KRONENBERG, A.
1961 Age sets and "Bull Classes" among the Topotha. *Man* 61: 89.
LANTIS, M.
1940 Fanti omens. *Africa* 13: 150–59.
LAST, J. T.
1886 *Grammar of the Kaguru language.* London: Society for Promoting Christian Knowledge.
LAUBSCHER, B.
1937 *Sex, custom and psychopathology.* London: Routledge, Kegan Paul.
LEVI-STRAUSS, C.
1949 *Les Structures élémentaires de la Parenté.* Paris: Presses universitaires de France.
1963 *La Pensée sauvage.* Paris: Plon. [*The savage mind,* Univ. of Chicago Press, 1966.]
LINDBLOM, G.
1920 *The Akamba.* Upsala: Appelbergs.
MACKENZIE, D.
1925 *The spirit-ridden Konde.* London: Seeley Service.
MCVICAR, T.
1941 Wanguru religion. *Primitive Man* 14: 13–20.
1945 Death rites among the Waluguru and Wanguru. *Primitive Man* 18: 26–35.
MIDDLETON, J., AND WINTER, E. H.
1963 Introduction to *Witchcraft and sorcery in East Africa.* London: Routledge, Kegan Paul.
MORTON-WILLIAMS, P.
1960 The Yoruba Ogboni cult in Oyo. *Africa* 30: 362–74.
NEEDHAM, R.
1960 The left hand of the Mugwe: an analytical note on the structure of Meru symbolism. *Africa* 30: 28–33. [See chap. 7 above.]
OYONO, F.
1966 *Houseboy.* London: Heinemann.
ROSCOE, J.
1911 *The Baganda: their customs and beliefs.* London: Macmillan.
1923 *The Bakitara or Banyoro.* Cambridge: Cambridge Univ. Press.
SMITH, E.
1952 African symbolism. *Journal of the Royal Anthropological Institute* 82: 13–37.
STAPLETON, W. H.
1905 The terms for 'right hand' and 'left hand' in the Bantu languages. *Journal of the African Society* 16: 431–33.
STRAUBE, H.
1957 Das Dualsysteme und die Halaka-Vergassung der Dorse als alte Gesellschafts-Ordnung der Ometo-Völker Süd-Äthiopiens. *Paideuma* 6: 342–53.

TORDAY, E.
1923 Dualism in western Bantu religion and social organization. *Journal of The Royal Anthropological Institute* 58: 225–46.
TURNER, V. W.
1957 *Schism and continuity.* Manchester: Manchester Univ. Press.
1961a *Ndembu divination: its symbolism and techniques.* Rhodes-Livingstone Papers no. 31. Manchester.
1961b Ritual symbolism, morality and social structure among the Ndembu. *Rhodes-Livingstone Journal* 30: 1–10.
1962a *Chihamba the White Spirit.* Rhodes-Livingstone Papers no. 33. Manchester.
1962b Three symbols of passage in Ndembu circumcision ritual. In *Essays on the ritual of social relations,* ed. M. Gluckman. Manchester: Manchester Univ. Press.
WERNER, A.
1904 Notes on the terms used for "right hand" and "left hand" in the Bantu Languages," *Journal of the African Society* 13: 112–16. [See Appendix to this volume.]
WIESCHHOFF, H.
1938 Concepts of right and left in African cultures. *Journal of the American Oriental Society* 58: 202–17. [See chap. 4 above.]
WILE, I. S.
1934 *Handedness: right and left.* Boston: Lothrop, Lee & Shepard.
WOLFF, C.
1946 *The human hand.* New York: Knopf.

Right and Left in Greek Philosophy

Geoffrey Lloyd

9

The purpose of this article is to consider how the symbolic associations which right and left had for the ancient Greeks influenced various theories and explanations in Greek philosophy of the fifth and fourth centuries B.C. The fact that certain manifest natural oppositions (e.g., right and left, male and female, light and darkness, up and down) often acquire powerful symbolic associations, standing for religious categories such as pure and impure, blessed and accursed, is well attested by anthropologists for many present-day societies.[1] Robert Hertz, in particular, has considered the significance of the widespread belief in the superiority of the right hand, in his essay "La prééminence de la main droite: étude sur la polarité religieuse" (Hertz 1909; cited according to the translation by R. and C. Needham, 1960). It is, of course, well known that the ancient Greeks shared some similar beliefs, associating right and left with lucky and unlucky, respectively, and light and darkness with safety, for example, and death. Yet the survival of certain such associations in Greek philosophy has not, I think, received the attention it deserves. I wish to document this aspect of the use of opposites in Greek philosophy in this paper, concentrating in the main upon the most interesting pair of opposites, right and left. Before I turn to the evidence in the philosophers themselves, two introductory notes are necessary. In the first, I shall consider briefly some of the evidence in anthropology which indicates how certain pairs of opposites are associated with, and symbolize, religious categories in many present-day societies. The second con-

---

Revised version of a paper published under the same title in the *Journal of Hellenic Studies* 82 (1962): 56–66. Printed with permission of the Hellenic Society.

tains a general summary of the evidence for similar associations and beliefs in prephilosophical Greek thought.

I

The superiority of the right hand might be thought to rest on purely anatomical factors. That there is a functional asymmetry of the brain—the left cerebral hemisphere being more developed, in some respects, than the right—is agreed (though whether this is the cause, or an effect, of the superior development of the right hand, is still an open question).[2] Yet even if we assume that there is a definite anatomical basis for the superiority of the right hand, this does not determine why many societies insist that the difference between the two hands should be not only maintained, but emphasized. The mutilation of the left arm is a practice which is reported in a number of societies. Evans-Pritchard, noting how Nuer youths put their left arm out of action for long periods by binding it with metal rings, said that the belief that underlies this and other Nuer practices is that "the right side is the good side and the left side the evil side."[3] According to Hertz (1960: 100), the right is often thought to be the seat of sacred power, "the source of everything that is good, favourable and legitimate," while the left is the profane side, "possessing no virtue other than . . . certain disturbing and suspect powers." It is interesting to note that the right is not invariably the sacred side. Although the great majority of societies hold the right to be the honorable side, there are some instances of peoples who are predominantly right-handed, but who nevertheless consider the left the nobler side: among the Zunis[4] the left and right sides are personified as brother gods, of which the left is the elder and wiser, and among the ancient Chinese,[5] the left was *yang* and therefore superior, the right *yin* and inferior. This reversal of the usual associations indicates, to my mind, the part played by social, rather than purely physiological, factors in determining the attitude to right and left.

Many primitive peoples identify the right-hand side with what is sacred and pure, the left with the profane and the impure, and other pairs of opposites also acquire similar associations. Hertz (1960:97 [p. 9 above]) has already discussed the associations which male and female have for the Maori, for example. The association of day, light, and east with the powers of life and strength, and of night, darkness, and west with the contrary powers of death and weakness, is very common. Further, as perhaps the natural resultant of this tendency to identify certain pairs of opposites with the sacred and the profane, we find that such pairs as day/night, right/left, and male/female are often themselves correlated or identified, even where there is no manifest connection between them. A single example of this may be mentioned.[6] Evans-Pritchard notes that for the Nuer there are two sets of opposites, the one comprising the left side, weakness, femininity, and evil, and the other the right side, strength, masculinity, and goodness: east is associated with life, and west with death, but then east is also identified with right and west with left "thus bringing into the left-right polarity the polar representations not only of life and death but also of the cardinal points east and west."[7]

II

The evidence in anthropology shows quite clearly that in many present-day societies certain natural oppositions (especially right and left) are often associated with, or symbolize, important spiritual categories, e.g., "sacred" and "profane," "pure" and "impure." Some of the associations which various natural oppositions had for the ancient Greeks are, no doubt, well known and need little comment. One antithesis of great importance is that between *sky* and *earth*, for with these are associated two fundamental religious distinctions, (1) the distinction between Olympian and chthonian deities,[8] and (2) the general distinction between gods and men, between the *epouvanioi* (heavenly ones) and the *epichthonioi* (earthly ones).[9] Another important pair of opposites is *light* and *darkness*. As has been shown by Bultmann (1948) especially, light, for the ancient Greeks, was the symbol of well-being, happiness, success, and glory in life, and of life itself (while darkness and night were generally associated with the contraries of these). Among other pairs of opposites connected with sky and earth, or with light and darkness, *up* and *down* and *white* and *black* certainly have important symbolic values from an early stage.[10] Although there appear to be no good grounds for believing that in early Greek religious practices *male* and *female* stood in an unvarying relationship of "sacred" and "profane" to one another (as Hertz suggested is the implication of Maori cults), it may be noted that women are usually thought of as inferior; and Hesiod, at least, repeatedly describes the first woman,

Pandora, as an evil (e.g., *Th.* 570, 585, 600; *Op.* 57, 89), and even implies that she is the source of all evil for mankind.[11]

The associations which *right* and *left* themselves have in Homer and Hesiod may be considered in a little more detail. The fact that the right is the lucky, the left the unlucky, side for the Greeks, is well known: omens on the right are auspicious, those on the left inauspicious, in Homer, for example (e.g., *Il.* xxiv 315–21; *Od.* ii 146–54).[12] But then the lucky direction, from left to right, was observed in many different activities, such as in the serving of wine round a group of guests (*Il.* i 597; cf. Plato *Smp.* 223c, etc., and *Od.* xxi 141 ff., where the suitors try Odysseus' bow, going from left to right of their company), and in the drawing of lots (at *Il.* vii 181 ff., the lot which has been cast is taken around the group of warriors from left to right until it is claimed by its owner). The right hand is used to greet people (e.g., *Od.* i 120 f.), to pour a libation (e.g., *Il.* xxiv 283 ff.) and to give a solemn pledge (e.g., *Il.* iv 159).[13] Conversely the left hand is unlucky. Two of the words for left *(euōnumos* and *aristeros)* are euphemisms, and a third *(skaios)* comes to mean "ill-omened" (as in Sophocles *Aj.* 1225) and "awkward" (e.g., Aristophanes *V.* 1265 f.), like the French "gauche," the opposite of *dexios* meaning "clever" or "skillful" (literally "right-handed").

Many natural oppositions had strong symbolic associations for the ancient Greeks. Although we cannot, of course, speak of any developed or systematic Table of Opposites in Homer or Hesiod, it is interesting to consider the correlations which are made between the positive poles of many of these pairs of opposites on the one hand, and between their negative poles on the other. The identification of light and east and white, and sky and up, on the one hand, and of darkness and west and black, and earth and down, on the other, corresponds to certain facts of observation. Again the conception of the earth as female (or a mother), and of the sky as a generating male, is based on an obvious analogy between the growth of plants and sexual reproduction. On the other hand, at *Il.* xii 238 ff. we find that *right* is identified with *east* and the sun, and *left* with the "misty *west.*" This identification seems more arbitrary,[14] though, as was noted above, there are parallels for it in other societies.

III

Having considered very briefly the symbolic associations of certain pairs of opposites in early Greek literature as a whole, I must next discuss how some of these beliefs may have influenced the theories of the Greek philosophers; and here I refer not only to religious or ethical doctrines, but also, and more especially, to some of the explanations which they put forward to account for various complex natural phenomena. In this context, the use of the opposites right and left is particularly remarkable.

The pairs right and left, male and female, light and darkness appear, of course, in the Pythagorean Table of Opposites *(sustoichia)* given by Aristotle at *Metaph.* A 5 986a 22 ff.[15] It is not certain which group or groups of Pythagoreans may have held this doctrine, nor can we date the table in the form given by Aristotle with any great degree of assurance. One thing which is clear, however, is that the arranging of right, male, and light on one side, the side of the good, and of left, female, and darkness on the other, the side of the bad, corresponds to notions which are implicit, to a greater or lesser extent, in the earliest Greek writers. This feature of the Pythagorean table could be seen as the explicit expression, or rationalization, in ethical terms, of very early Greek beliefs.[16] Elsewhere too in Greek philosophy some of these pairs of opposites are correlated together in passages which have a religious or mystical context. In the eschatological myth in the *Republic* (614c f.), for example, the souls of men are imagined as divided by their judges into two groups: the just travel to the *right, upwards* through the *sky,* carrying tokens of their judgment on their *fronts,* and the unjust go to the *left, downwards* (into the *earth)* bearing their tokens on their *backs.*[17] But some of these opposites also figure in Greek philosophy in contexts where the purpose of the writer is to account for certain phenomena: we must now consider to what extent the theories and explanations based on these opposites are influenced by earlier beliefs and associations of ideas.

First we may deal with a group of theories which aim to account for the differentiation of the sexes at birth.[18] The theories which are attributed to Parmenides and to Anaxagoras were both based on the idea of a correlation between male and right, and between female and left. Parmenides apparently held that the sex of the child is determined by its position on the right or left side of the mother's womb (males are on the right, females on the left). Galen quotes Fr. 17 "on the right, boys; on the left, girls" and interprets it in this sense (*in Epid.* VI 48, *CMG* V 10,2,2 119 12 ff.; cf. Aristotle *GA* 763b 34–764a1, where, however, no specific author is mentioned). Of Parmenides' immediate successors, Empedocles held that the determining factor was the heat of the womb,[19] but Anaxagoras again referred to a difference between right and left, though, unlike Parmenides, he suggested that the determining factor is the side of the body from which the father's seed comes (Aristotle *GA* 763b 30 ff.; cf. *GA* 765a 3 ff.). A variant of this theory appears in the Hippocratic treatise *On Superfetation,* which implies quite specifically that the right testicle is responsible for male children, and the left for females (ch. 31, Littré VIII 500 8 ff.).[20] Other Hippocratic treatises make use of Parmenides' version of the theory,[21] or suggest other correlations between the male embryo and the right-hand side of the mother's body.[22] This is, surely, a remarkable series of theories. Although alternative suggestions are made on which part of the body, or which parent, determines the sex of the child, all these writers assume that *male* and *right* are connected, and so too *female* and *left.* We noted above the tendency to identify the positive poles of various pairs of opposites on the one hand, and their negative poles on the other (for which there is evidence not only from the ancient Greeks but from other peoples as well). It is interesting, then, that these attempted explanations of sex took the form of different applications of the theory that male and female derive from right and left respectively. It is impossible to determine what evidence (if any) Parmenides and others may have appealed to, in order to confirm their theories (it may well be that fictitious evidence was sometimes claimed to corroborate them, see below on Aristotle *GA* 765a 25 ff.), but it seems likely that the earlier symbolic associations of these pairs of opposites contributed to fortify the belief in a connection between the positive or superior terms, male and right. In contrast to the Greek theory, it may be noted that among the ancient Chinese (who held the left to be more honorable than the right) there were theorists who believed that an embryo on the left of the womb would be a boy, one on the right, a girl, proposing a theory opposite to that of the Greeks but in keeping with their own associations for left and right.[23]

One group of theories put forward by some Presocratic philosophers and Hippocratic writers consists of attempted correlations between male and right, female and left. But we may now show how similar theories continued to appear in fourth-century philosophy, in Aristotle himself. Aristotle, it is true, rejects the idea that right and left in some way determine the sex of the child. He criticizes the theory that the two sexes are formed in different parts of the womb in *GA* IV 1,[24] and in so doing, he refers to the decisive evidence of anatomical dissections: "moreover male and female twins are often found in the same part of the uterus: this we have observed sufficiently by dissection in all the Vivipara, both land-animals and fish" (*GA* 764a 33 ff.). His criticisms of the theory that sex is determined by whether the seed comes from the right or the left testicle are also interesting. He says at *GA* 765a 25 ff. that some theorists claimed that when one of the testicles of a male parent animal was excised, certain results followed (i.e., their offspring were all of the same sex): "but they lie; starting from what is likely, they guess what will happen, and they presuppose that it is so, before they see that it is in fact so." These passages clearly mark an important step forward. Aristotle here insists on the careful use of evidence to verify or falsify the theories which were put forward. Where others had been content to assume that males were formed in the right side of the womb, and females in the left, Aristotle uses dissection to prove that this does not hold as an absolute rule.[25] It might be thought, on the basis of these passages, that Aristotle himself was free from preconceptions on the subject of right and left and other such opposites. But in point of fact, this is certainly not the case. His use of the pairs right and left, above and below, and front and back, in particular, is worth considering in detail.

In Aristotle's theory, right and left, above and below, front and back are not merely relative terms. Right, above, and front are said to be the *archai,* the starting-points or principles, not only of the three dimensions, breadth, length, and depth, respectively (*Cael.* 284b 24 f.), but also of the three types of change, locomotion, growth, and sensation, in living beings (*Cael.* 284b 25 ff.). In *IA* ch. 4, 705b 29 ff., for example, Aristotle attempts to establish that all locomotion, in animals, proceeds from the right. The main evidence for this which he brings is (1) that men carry burdens on their left shoulders, (2) that they step off with the left foot—in both cases, according to Aristotle, the right is the side which initiates movement —and (3) that men defend themselves with their right limbs.[26] Because he assumes that the motion of the heavenly sphere (which he thinks of as alive) must be "from the right" and *epi ta dexia* ("to the right" or "rightwards"),[27] he infers at *Cael.* 285b 22 ff. that the northern hemisphere, the one in which we live, is the lower of the two hemispheres. Again, because "upwards" is defined in relation to the place from which food is distributed and from which growth begins (e.g., *IA* 705a 32 f.), the "upper" portion of plants will be where their roots are, and Aristotle accordingly speaks of plants as "upside down" (e.g., *PA* 686b 31 ff.; *IA* 705b 6; cf. *PA* 683b 18 ff. on the Testacea). Right, above, and front are, then, defined by certain functions, but Aristotle holds that these are *more honorable* than their opposites. Thus at *IA* 706b 12 f. he says that "the starting-point is honorable, and above is more honorable than below, and front than back, and right than left." Furthermore, this notion becomes an important doctrine in anatomy, for Aristotle believes that "as a whole, unless some more important object interferes, that which is better and more honorable tends to be above rather than below, in front rather than behind, on the right rather than on the left" (*PA* 665a 22 ff.). He uses this principle to explain such facts as the relative positions of the windpipe and the esophagus (*PA* 665a 18 ff.), and of the "great blood-vessel"[28] and the aorta (*PA* 667b 34 ff.),[29] as also to give an account of the function of the diaphragm (to separate the nobler, upper parts of the body from the less noble, lower parts, *PA* 672b 22 ff.). The faithfulness, one may almost say stubbornness, with which Aristotle adheres to his conception of the essential superiority of right to left, can be seen in his account of the position of the heart. This organ he considers to be the principle of life and the source of all movement and sensation in the animal (*PA* 665a 11 ff.). At *PA* 665b 18 ff., he says that the heart, in man, "lies about the middle of the body, but rather in its upper than in its lower half, and more in front than behind. For nature has established the more honorable part in the more honorable position, where no greater purpose prevents this." Faced with the obvious difficulty that the heart lies on the left side of the body, and not on the more honorable right, Aristotle argues that this is to "counterbalance the chilliness of the left side" (*PA* 666b 6 ff.). On this occasion, when he encounters an obvious and important fact which apparently runs counter to this theory of the superiority and greater nobility of the right-hand side, he does not abandon that theory but refers to a second arbitrary assumption, the (purely imaginary) general distinction between the temperature of the two sides of the body.

In explaining the position of the heart in man, Aristotle refers to a difference in heat between the right and left sides of the body. In man, the heart is slightly inclined towards the left because the left side of the body is particularly cold in his case (e.g., *PA* 666b 9 f.). Elsewhere too, he refers to differences in the heat and purity of the blood in accounting for the general superiority of the upper parts of the body over the lower, of the male animal over the female, and of the right side of the body over the left (*PA* 648a 2–13). At *PA* 670b 17 ff., he accounts for the "watery" quality of the spleen in some animals partly by referring to the generally "wetter and colder nature of the left side" of the body.[30] He then goes on: "Each of the opposites is separated according to the column *(sustoichia)* which is akin to it, as right is opposite left and hot opposite cold: and they are coordinate *(sustoicha)* with one another in the way described" (i.e., right and hot are in one column, left and cold in the other) (*PA* 670b 20 ff.). It is interesting that this theory that the right side of the body is hotter than the left is mentioned in *GA* IV 1 where Aristotle discusses what determines the sex of the embryo. Although, as already noted, he argues strongly in that chapter against earlier theories that the sex of the child is determined by the part of the womb in which it is conceived, yet at the end of his discussion of his predecessors' ideas, at *GA* 765a 34 ff., he grants that "to suppose that the cause of male and female is heat and cold, or the secretion (*apokrisis,* i.e., seed) which comes from the right or the left side of the body, *is not unreasonable (echei tina logon)":* the right side of the body is hotter than the left, and hotter semen, being more "concocted," is more fertile than cold and therefore more likely to produce males. Though he goes on to say (b 4 ff.) that "to speak in this way is to seek the cause from too great a distance," he does, to some extent, accommodate earlier views to his own theory.[31] Yet if we examine this theory of the greater heat of the right-hand side of the body more closely, the weakness of Aristotle's argument is apparent. At *PA* 666b 6 ff., the heart is said to be on the left, in man, to counteract the chilliness of the left-hand side of the body. Yet elsewhere Aristotle suggests that the factor on which this difference in temperature depends is the heart itself. According to the account in *HA* and in *PA*,[32] the heart, in most of the large animals, has three chambers, of which the right-hand chamber is the largest and contains the most abundant and hottest blood,[33] and at *PA* 667a 1 f., for example, he refers to this fact as the reason for the whole of the right-hand side of the body being hotter than the left. There would seem to be an anomaly in arguing (1) that in man the heart is on the left to counteract the excessive chilliness of that side, when (2) the difference in temperature between the two sides of the body is itself seen as the result of a difference in the temperature of the blood in the left and right chambers of the heart. Man is far from being the only species which is said to have a heart with chambers of unequal sizes, yet in man alone (Aristotle believes) the heart is displaced towards the left. Other things being equal, we should expect that the effect of the heart being displaced from the central position which it occupies in all other species of animals would be to *warm* that side towards which it was displaced. Yet so far from concluding that in man the left-hand side is rather *hotter,* relative to the right-hand side, than is the case in a horse or an ox, Aristotle believes that the left-hand side, in man, is *particularly cold.* He holds that the difference in temperature between the two sides of the body is especially great in man, but while this idea is in line with his general doctrine that right/left distinctions are pronounced in humans, it remains, of course, an unfounded assumption.

Aristotle takes right, above, and front to be starting-points or principles, and so superior to, and nobler than, their opposites. He believes, further, that the right-hand side is naturally more active and stronger than the left, not only in man, but also, as a general rule, throughout the animal kingdom. At *PA* 684a 27 f., he generalizes: "all animals naturally tend to use their right limbs more in their activities." [34] We may now consider to what extent Aristotle qualified his theory of the distinction between right and left in the light of his detailed observations of various biological species, or how far he went beyond, or misrepresented, the facts, in stating his conclusions. Although he states it as a general rule that limbs on the right are stronger than those on the left, he notes certain exceptions. He remarks at *PA* 684a 32 ff. that in the lobsters it is a matter of chance whether the right or the left claw is the bigger; but he goes on to say that the reason for this is that lobsters are deformed and do not use the claw for its natural purpose but for locomotion (a 35–b 1).[35] Again, such passages as *IA* 714b 8 ff. show that he recognizes the fact that right and left are not clearly distinguished in such classes as the Testacea (although he does attempt to establish a *functional* distinction between right and left in his analysis of their method of locomotion); [36] but again the reason which he gives for the lack of differentiation between right and left in the Testacea, is that they are a deformed class (e.g., *IA* 714b 10 f.). However, some of Aristotle's statements on the subject of the distinction between right and left in animals are in need of qualification. Ogle noted that the remark at *PA* 684a 26 f. that "in all the Crawfish and the Crabs the right claw is bigger and stronger" (than the left) is "too absolute a statement." [37] Perhaps more important is Aristotle's failure to recognize that the heart inclines to the left-hand side of the body in other species besides man, for he firmly believes that this is so in man alone (*PA* 666b 6 ff.; cf. *HA* 496a 14 ff., 506b 32 ff.). Aristotle undoubtedly had detailed first-hand knowledge of the internal organs of a number of species of animals. It is strange, then, that there are several species, including some with whose internal anatomy he claims to be acquainted,[38] in which the heart inclines to the left, as it does in man.[39]

Aristotle's knowledge of both the external and internal organs of animals, and of their behavior, is vastly greater than that of any of his predecessors. One of the results of the many dissections which he carried out was to establish that male and female embryos are formed in either part of the uterus, right or left, in all the Vivipara. His observations of many lower species (especially of the Crustacea) are remarkably accurate and detailed. Yet one of the theories which he constantly maintains is that right is naturally and essentially superior to left. He believes that this is true in man, and man is the norm by which he judges the rest of the animal kingdom. As he puts it at *IA* 706a 19 f., for example, man is "of all animals, most in accordance with nature," and at *PA* 656a 10 ff. in man alone, "The natural parts are in their 'natural' positions, and his upper part is turned towards that which is upper in the universe."[40] The reason that he gives for the absence of any marked distinction between right and left in some species is, then, that they are imperfect or "deformed" animals. He believes not only that there is what we might call a physiological distinction between right and left—the right side is hotter than the left—but also that in making this distinction nature fulfills an important purpose. The distinction between right and left is an *ideal* which is most fully exemplified in man: as he puts it at *IA* 706a 21 f. "the right is 'most right-sided' *(malista dexia)* in man." It might be said, then, that Aristotle's great knowledge of different biological species served rather to confirm than to weaken his belief in the natural superiority, and the greater nobility, of the right-hand side.

The history of this belief in the inherent superiority of the right-hand side has now been described with evidence from a variety of Greek thinkers down to Aristotle.[41] The Pythagoreans placed right on the side of limit and good, left on the opposite side of the unlimited and evil. Parmenides, Anaxagoras, and several Hippocratic writers assumed that the difference between male and female was to be derived from a difference between right and left, correlating the superior, and the inferior, poles of these two pairs of opposites. Aristotle explicitly states that right is the origin of locomotion, and is better and nobler than its opposite, and he uses this theory quite extensively in accounting for such facts as the position of various organs in the body. Not all the theorists who appear to have assumed the essential superiority of the right-hand side, are normally thought to have been influenced by Pythagoreanism. Though Parmenides' relation to the Pythagoreans may well have been close, Anaxagoras' theories bear few signs of direct Pythagorean influence. The Hippocratic treatises *On Epidemics* II and IV are generally free from Pythagorean conceptions. Aristotle's use of the word *sustoicha,* "coordinate," in connection with his own theory of the pairs right and left and hot and cold at *PA* 670b 22 is obviously reminiscent of the way in which he refers to the Pythagorean principles as arranged in coordinate columns (*kata sustoichian, Metaph.* 986a 22 f.), and yet on several occasions he explicitly contrasts his own account of these and other related opposites with that of the Pythagoreans;[42] and many of his detailed biological theories based on the distinction between right and left are clearly original. It seems, then, that the belief in the inherent superiority of the right-hand side is not an exclusively Pythagorean doctrine. Indeed in some of its elements the Pythagorean Table of Opposites itself merely defined and made explicit extremely old, and no doubt widespread, Greek beliefs.

Whether or not we accept Hertz's general theory that in primitive thought certain natural oppositions often stand for the categories of the "sacred" and the "profane," it will be granted that for the ancient Greeks, as for many other peoples, such antitheses as sky and earth, light and darkness, up and down, right and left, have powerful symbolic associations. The values which attached to the opposites right and left in particular seem to influence some of the theories in which they figure in fifth- and fourth-century Greek philosophy. It was often assumed that right is essentially different from, and superior to, left, the one good, the other evil; or the one connected in some way with masculinity, the other with femininity; or the one thought to be honorable, the other not honorable. The social factors which are involved in the greater development of the right hand itself do not pass unnoticed by Greek philosophers: Plato, especially, remarked how childhood training contributes to the greater usefulness of the right hand.[43] But the belief persisted that right is "naturally" superior to, stronger and nobler than, the left. In Aristotle, the distinction between right and left is conceived not merely as a physiological fact, but as an *ideal*, to which the animal kingdom aspires, but which is most fully exemplified in man. Even a detailed knowledge of different biological species, in many of which there is no distinction, or no marked distinction, between right and left, did not uproot Aristotle's belief that right is naturally stronger and more honorable than left: on the contrary, that knowledge led him to conclude that the differentiation between right and left is a mark of man's superiority to the animals, and of his greater perfection.

The two elements, of dogmatic belief, and of empirical observation, are closely interwoven in the history of theories based on right and left. The element of dogmatic assumption appears first of all in the superstitious belief that right is "lucky" and left "unlucky," but we have seen that the assumption that right is essentially different from, and nobler than, left persists in Greek philosophy right down to Aristotle. Yet many Greek philosophers and medical theorists carried out extensive observations, particularly in biology. Sometimes these observations led to the rejection of a particular theory based on the belief in the superiority of the right-hand side, as when Aristotle's dissections established that males and females are not always formed in the right and left sides of the womb respectively. More often, however, when the results of observations did not tally with preconceived opinions (for example, when it was seen that the heart inclines to the left side of the body in man), those opinions were not abandoned: on the contrary, they were retained, and further dogmatic assumptions were introduced in order to account for the phenomena. It is, perhaps, particularly remarkable that Aristotle, who conducted the most extensive and rigorous biological investigations in antiquity, should nevertheless have firmly and constantly maintained a theory of the distinction between right and left which owes much to the traditional symbolic associations which those opposites had for the ancient Greeks.

Abbreviations

CMG refers to the several volumes of *Corpus Medicorum Graecorum* (ed. Heiberg and others, Leipzig).

DK refers to *Die Fragmente der Vorsokratiker,* edited by Diels, revised by Kranz, 6th edition, 1951–52.

L refers to Littré's edition of the Hippocratic treatises (Paris 1839–61).

The abbreviations used for the works of classical authors are those in the Greek Lexicon of Liddell and Scott, 9th edition revised by Jones, 1940.

Notes

1. I must express my gratitude to Professor Meyer Fortes and Dr. Edmund Leach, Professor and Reader in Social Anthropology in the University of Cambridge, for their help on several questions of anthropology connected with this paper.

2. See Hertz 1960: 90, and Needham's note *ad loc.* [See also p. 4, above.]

3. Evans-Pritchard 1956: 234 ff., where a number of other practices illustrating this belief are given.

4. As Evans-Pritchard notes (1960: 22), Hertz mentions this example only to dismiss it as a "secondary development." The fact that the Zuni are a peaceful agricultural people no doubt contributes to the relative estimation in which they hold the right, or spear, hand, and the left, or shield, hand.

5. See Granet 1934 361 ff., and 1953: 263 ff. The Chinese attitude to this antithesis is complex, for while the left is generally superior and *yang,* and the right inferior and *yin,* yet in the sphere of what is itself common or inferior, the right in some sense has precedence over the left. Thus the right hand is used for eating (Granet 1934: 364) and the right side is the appropriate side for women (while the left belongs to men, Granet 1934: 368).

6. Many primitive societies appear to classify things generally into groups of opposites (often corresponding to opposite groups in the society itself). A number of notable examples of such classifications are given by van der Kroef (1954: 847 ff.), among them that of the people of Amboyna in Indonesia who, according to this authority, correlate pairs of opposites in the following way:

Right	Left
Male	Female
Land or mountain-side	Coast or sea-side
Above	Below
Heaven or sky	Earth
Worldly	Spiritual
Upwards	Downwards
Interior	Exterior
In Front	Behind
East	West
Old	New

7. Evans-Pritchard 1956: 234 f.

8. These two categories of gods are often referred to in invocations, e.g., Aeschylus *A.* 89, *Supp.* 24 f.; Euripides *Hec.* 146 f.; Plato *Lg.* 717ab. The importance of the distinction between them has been particularly

stressed by Guthrie 1950, chaps. 8 and 9, e.g., p. 209: "The distinction between Olympian and chthonian, aetherial and sub-aetherial, or to put it more simply, between gods of the heaven and gods of the earth, is one which I hold to be fundamental for the understanding of Greek religion."

9. On this distinction, see Guthrie 1950: 113 ff.

10. White is associated with good luck: a white vote was used, in classical times, for acquittal (e.g., Luc. *Harm.* 3) and the expression *leukē hēmera* (literally "white day") is used for a lucky day. Conversely, black is the color of death (e.g., *Il.* ii 834) and is associated with various things and personifications of evil omen: in Aeschylus, for instance, it is used of the Furies (e.g., *A.* 462 f.), of misfortune (*Supp.* 89), of Recklessness (*A.* 770) and of a curse (*Th.* 832). It may be that as a general rule the color of the victim sacrificed to an Olympian deity was white, that of the chthorians' sacrificial victims black (cf. *Il.* iii 103 ff., where a white ram and a black ewe are sacrificed to the sun and to earth). Other general distinctions between the rites associated with the Olympians and those of the chthonian deities have been collected by Guthrie (1950: pp. 221 f.), and several of these reflect the symbolic associations of such pairs of opposites as up and down, high and low.

11. At *Th.* 591 ff. the whole race of women—Pandora's offspring—is called "deadly," a "great bane" to men, and at *Op.* 90 ff. it is said that before Pandora, men lived on earth free from evils, suffering, and disease. The idea of the innate inferiority of women recurs, of course, in Greek philosophy: in the *Timaeus* 90e f., it is suggested that cowardly and unjust men become women in their second incarnation, and Aristotle considers the female sex a deviation from type, a "natural deformity," *GA* 767b 6 ff., 775a 14 ff.

12. This is the general rule. But that Greek diviners disagreed among themselves on this and other questions is clear, for example, from a passage in the Hippocratic treatise *On regimen in acute diseases,* chap. 3, Littré II 242 4 ff.

13. These usages are reflected in the use of the verb *dexiousthai* for "to greet" and of the noun *dexia* for "pledge."

14. It has been suggested that Hector's words at *Il.* xii 238 ff. ("Nor do I trouble myself or care at all whether the birds of omen fly to the right, towards the dawn and the sun, or to the left, towards the misty west") refer simply to the position of the Trojan lines, which happen to face north, but it is surely much more likely that they describe the usual method of interpreting omens, in which "to the right" is identified with towards the east. The theory (taken up more recently by Cuillandre, 1943) that right is identified with light because the worshipper faces the rising sun, which then passes to his right on its transit westwards, was rightly dismissed by Hertz (1960, n. 86 [above p. 27]). A decisive argument against the theory is that we should expect the *opposite* correlation to be made by many peoples in the *southern* hemisphere (for if they face the sun at its rising, it passes, of course, to their left) whereas this is not found to be the case: for the Maori and Australian aborigines, for example, right is the good side and is associated with life and light, as for the ancient Greeks.

15. The complete list of opposites is: limit/unlimited, odd/even, one/plurality, right/left, male/female, at rest/moving, straight/curved, light/darkness, good/evil, square/oblong.

16. See Hertz 1960, n. 50 [above p. 25]. Several of the sayings known as the *akousmata* or *sumbola* which are attributed to certain Pythagoreans emphasize a ritual distinction between various pairs of opposites, e.g., "Putting on your shoes, start with the right foot; washing your feet, start with the left" (Iamblichus *Protr.* 21, *VP* 83); "Do not sacrifice a white cock" (Iamblichus *VP* 84, and cf. the gloss on this in Diogenes Laertius VIII 34, "white is of the nature of the good, and black of evil"). Diels-Kranz, 58 C, provide a selection of such sayings.

17. Cf. *Laws* 717ab, where "even" and "left" are assigned as honors to the chthonian deities, and their superior opposites "odd" and "right" to the Olympians.

18. Cf. the excellent monograph by Lesky, 1951, especially pp. 39 ff.

19. Galen, who quotes Fr. 67 (*in Epid.* VI 48, *CMG* V 10,2,2 119 16 ff.), probably took Empedocles' theory to be that males are formed in the hotter parts of the womb, females in the colder (he compares it directly with Parmenides' theory which also referred to different *parts* of the womb). But Aristotle, who quotes the equally ambiguous Fr. 65 at *GA* 723a 24 ff., took Empedocles to be referring to variations in temperature in the womb as a whole over the monthly cycle (the womb is hotter at the beginning of the cycle just after menstruation has occurred, cf. 764a 1 ff.). Censorinus' interpretation, 6,6 DK 31 A 81—that Empedocles, like Anaxagoras, held that males were formed by seed from the right-hand side of the body, females by seed from the left—should probably be ruled out: Aristotle clearly differentiates the two types of theories referring to "hot and cold" and "right and left" respectively and attributes the former to Empedocles, cf. *GA* 765a 3 ff.

20. Cf. also the theory attributed to a certain Leophanes and others by Aristotle at *GA* 765a 21 ff. This text appears to suggest that Leophanes' theory was that if the *right* testis is tied up, *males* will be produced. Yet either we should transpose the words *arrenotokein* and *thēlutokein,* or they have been mentioned in that order (males first) without due regard for their correlation with what has gone before (right mentioned before left at 765a 23). That the theory in question was that the right testis is responsible for males (which are, then, produced when the *left* testis is tied up) is clear not only from the passage in *Superf.* L VIII 500 8 ff., and other texts in ancient writers in which the right testis is connected with male offspring (e.g., *Epid.* VI sec. 4, ch. 21, L V 312 10 f., and Pliny *Nat. Hist.* VIII 72 188), but also from Aristotle's own subsequent remarks. At *GA* 765a 34 ff., he says that the earlier theories which took hot and cold, or right and left, to be the causes of male and female, were not altogether unreasonable, and it is clear that he correlates male with right (and hot), female with left (and cold) and not vice versa: seed from the right side will be hotter, more concocted, and therefore more fertile than seed from the left.

21. E.g., *Epid.* II sec. 6, ch. 15, L V 136 5 ff.; *Epid.* VI sec. 2, ch. 25,

L V 290 7 f.; *Aph.* sec. 5, ch. 48, L IV 550 1 ff.; cf. *Prorrh,* II ch. 24, L IX 56 19 ff.

22. E.g., *Aph.* sec. 5, ch. 38, L IV 544 11 ff.

23. See Granet 1934: 370 and 1953: 273 f. [above pp. 54–55].

24. The evidence from dissections is first introduced at *GA* 764a 33 ff. when Aristotle is criticizing Empedocles' theory (that hot and cold are the causes of male and female), but it is also relevant to Parmenides' theory that males are produced on the right of the womb, females on the left, and Aristotle refers to it again when criticizing that theory later, at *GA* 765a 3 ff. (cf. 16 ff.).

25. A passage in *HA* VII 3 (583b 2 ff.) is interesting, for there Aristotle says that the first movement of male embryos usually takes place on the right side of the womb on the fortieth day, that of females on the left on the ninetieth, although he goes on to qualify or correct this statement: "yet it must not be supposed that there is any exactness in these matters." If authentic, this passage might, perhaps, be taken as evidence that, at one stage, Aristotle may have been rather less critical of the theory that males are on the right, females on the left, of the womb.

26. Aristotle also notes (*IA* 705b 33) that it is easier to hop on the left leg, and elsewhere (*PA* 671b 32 ff.) he says that men raise their right eyebrows more than their left. Some of his evidence seems to be contradictory: while he states that men step off with the left foot (*IA* 706a 6 ff.), he believes that horses step off with the off-fore (712a 25 ff.). His interpretation, too, of much of the evidence which he adduces appears to be quite arbitrary.

27. On the complex problems of the meaning of the phrase *epi ta dexia* as applied to circular motion in general, and of its interpretation in *Cael.* 285b 20 in particular, see especially Braunlich 1936: 245 ff., and cf. Boeckh 1852: 112 ff., Darbishire 1895: 65 ff., and Heath 1913: 231 ff. Whether "to the right" applied to circular motion meant the direction which we call "clockwise," or the direction we call "counterclockwise," the association with *right* marks it clearly as the *more honorable* direction.

28. The "great blood-vessel" corresponds to the superior and inferior Venae Cavae: whether we take it also to include the right auricle of the heart itself will depend on how we interpret the three chambers of the heart which Aristotle recognizes. See further n. 32.

29. Cf. also *HA* 496b 35 ff., and *PA* 671b 28 ff., on the relative position of the two kidneys: Aristotle believes that the right kidney is always higher than the left (although in fact this is not so, for example, in man himself, where the left kidney is usually higher), and he gives the reason that motion starts from the right, and organs on the right push upwards above their opposites. He also believes that the right kidney is less fat than the left (*PA* 672a 23 ff.) and again explains this by referring to the right side being better suited for motion. Several more instances in which he explains the relative positions of organs, and other phenomena, by referring to the superiority of right, front, and above over their opposites, are given by Ogle (1912, note to *PA* 648a 11).

30. Aristotle believes that the spleen on the left in some way balances the liver on the right, e.g., *PA* 669b 26 ff., 36 ff.

31. According to Aristotle's own theory, stated at *GA* 765b 8 ff., male and female are distinguished by their ability or inability to concoct and discharge semen, yet because concoction works by means of heat, males must be hotter than females (b 15 ff.). Moreover it is due to a lack of heat that females are formed (the male element is too weak to master the female, 766b 15 ff.: Aristotle believes that young people, those in old age, and people of a "wet" or "feminine" constitution are all more likely to produce female children, *GA* 766b 27 ff., and these are all people in whom the "natural heat" is weak, b 33 f.).

32. There is some doubt as to which are the three chambers of the heart to which Aristotle refers (e.g., *HA* 513a 27 ff.; *PA* 666b 21 ff.; cf. *Somn. Vig.* 458a 15 ff.). Ogle (1912, note to *PA* 666b 21 ff.) took them to be the two ventricles and the left auricle (he thought the right auricle was taken to be part of the "great blood-vessel," see n. 28 above). D'Arcy Thompson (1910, note to *HA* 513a 27 ff.) on the other hand, took "the largest of the three chambers" (*HA* 513a 32; cf. *PA* 666b 35 f.) to refer to the right auricle and ventricle combined, which would account for the statement that the other two chambers are "far smaller" (*HA* 513a 34 f.) than the third. The suggestion that traditional or mystical ideas have influenced Aristotle in ascribing three chambers to the heart cannot be ruled out, although many features of his account show, as Thompson said, "clear evidence of minute inquiry."

33. Ogle (1912, note to *PA* 666b 35 f.) pointed out that "in an animal, especially one killed by strangulation, as recommended by Aristotle . . . , the right side of the heart and the vessels connected with it would be found gorged with dark blood and contrasting strongly with the almost empty left side and vessels." (At *HA* 511b 13 ff., Aristotle discusses the difficulties involved in making observations of the vascular system, and at 513a 12 ff., he recommends that the animal to be examined should be starved and then strangled.)

34. From *PA* 671b 30 f. and 672a 24 f., it appears that Aristotle held that the right side is naturally stronger than the left. But in several passages he notes that the degree to which right and left are differentiated varies in different species, e.g., *HA* 497b 21 f.; *IA* 705b 21 ff.

35. Cf. *HA* 526b 16 f., and a description of the two claws (chelae) at 526a 15 ff. It is not true that the chelae are used solely for locomotion (*PA* 684a 35 f., see Ogle's note *ad loc.*): indeed Aristotle himself remarks at *HA* 526a 24 f. that they are naturally adapted for prehension.

36. In some animals, right and left are distinguished not in form, but in function alone (cf. *Cael.* 285a 15 f., b 3 ff.). As regards the stromboid Testaceans, he says that they are "right-sided" (*dexia*) because they do not move in the direction of the spire, but opposite to it (*IA* 706a 13 ff.; cf. *HA* 528b 8 ff., and Thompson's note). He appears to argue that because they move in the direction opposite to the spire, *therefore* the spire must be assumed to be on the right-hand side.

37. Cf. *IA* 714b 16 ff. Elsewhere, however, Aristotle is somewhat more cautious in his statement of the difference between right and left in the crabs, at least, e.g., *HA* 527b 6 f. "*for the most part* they all have the right claw bigger and stronger," and cf. 530a 7 ff., 25 ff.

38. At *HA* 502b 25 f., Aristotle remarks that the monkey and suchlike animals (e.g., ape and baboon, cf. 502a 16 ff.) are found *on dissection* to have similar internal organs to those of man. Yet in these animals (as also, for example, in the mole) the heart is on the left. Cf. Ogle, 1912, note to *PA* 666b 6 ff.

39. Aristotle's statement that in all animals which have kidneys the right one is higher is another inaccuracy; see n. 29 above.

40. Cf. *HA* 494a 26 ff. It is interesting that elsewhere Aristotle states that man alone of all the animals can learn to be ambidextrous (*HA* 497b 31 f.; cf. *EN* 1134b 33 ff.; *MM* 1194b 31 ff.), yet he continues to believe that the right is "most right-sided" in man (*IA* 706a 21 f.) and that the right is naturally better than the left and separated from it (*IA* 706a 20 f.).

41. Lesky 1951: 62 ff., has traced the survival of beliefs in various connections between the right-hand side and male children in later writers. Although there were other theorists besides Aristotle who were skeptical about certain such connections (for example Soranus *Gyn.* I 45, *CMG* IV 31 26 ff.), several writers subscribed to them in late antiquity, including Pliny (*Nat. Hist.* VIII 70 176; 72 188), Varro (*Rer. Rust.* II 5 13), and Galen (*UP* XIV ch. 7, Kühn IV 172–75; *De Semine* II ch. 5, Kühn IV 633 f.). Pliny, in particular, is a mine of information concerning the survival of superstitions involving right and left.

42. This is so especially in *Cael.* II 2, where Aristotle agrees with the Pythagorean idea that right and left apply to the universe as a whole (284b 6 ff.), but adopts the opposite view to theirs, saying that we live in the lower of the two hemispheres, and on the "left," not, as the Pythagoreans said, in the upper hemisphere and on the "right" (285b 23 ff.). He also criticizes the Pythagoreans for not having recognized above and below, and front and back, as principles, as well as right and left (285a 10 ff.; cf. his own view, expressed at 284b 20 ff.).

43. A radical view of the effects of training and habit on the use of the two hands is expressed in the *Laws* (794d–795d) where Plato recommends that children should be taught to use both hands equally. He criticizes the view that right and left are naturally different in their usefulness, pointing out that this is not the case with the feet and the lower limbs (794d 5 ff.). He says that it is "through the folly of nurses and mothers" that "we have all become lame, so to speak, in our hands." He notes that athletes can become quite ambidextrous, and he says that the Scythians are in fact so. Cf. further Schuhl 1948: 174 ff., and Lévêque and Vidal-Nacquet 1960: 294 ff., especially 302 ff., who also compare the recommendation of the Hippocratic treatise *In the surgery (Off.)* that the surgeon should learn to use either hand equally (ch. 4, L III 288 1 ff.). With Plato's view, contrast that of Aristotle, who also recognizes that we can become ambidextrous, but says that the right side is still *naturally* stronger than the left (texts in n. 40).

References

Boeckh, A.
1852 *Untersuchungen über das kosmische System des Platon.* Berlin.

BRAUNLICH, A. F.
1936 "To the Right" in Homer and Attic Greek. *American Journal of Philology* 57: 245–60.
BULTMANN, R.
1948 Zur Geschichte der Lichtsymbolik im Altertum. *Philologus* 97: 1–48.
CUILLANDRE, J.
1943 *La Droite et la gauche dans les poèmes homériques*. Rennes.
DARBISHIRE, H. D.
1895 *Reliquiae philologicae*. Cambridge.
EVANS-PRITCHARD, E. E.
1956 *Nuer Religion*. Oxford.
1960 Introduction to Hertz 1960.
GRANET, M.
1934 *La Pensée chinoise*. Paris.
1953 La Droite et la gauche en Chine. *Etudes sociologiques sur la Chine*, pp. 263–78. Paris. [See chap. 3 above.]
GUTHRIE, W. K. C.
1950 *The Greeks and their Gods*. London.
HEATH, T. L.
1913 *Aristarchus of Samos*. Oxford.
HERTZ, R.
1960 La Prééminence de la main droite: étude sur la polarité religieuse. *Revue philosophique* 68 (1909): 553–80. Translated by R. and C. Needham in *Death and the right hand* (London 1960), pp. 89–113 and 155–60. [See chap. 1, above.]
KROEF, J. M. VAN DER
1954 Dualism and symbolic antithesis in Indonesian society. *American Anthropologist* 56: 847–62.
LESKY, E.
1951 *Die Zeugungs- und Vererbungslehren der Antike und ihr Nachwirken*. Wiesbaden.
LÉVÊQUE, P., AND VIDAL-NACQUET, P.
1960 Epaminondas Pythagoricien ou le problème tactique de la droite et de la gauche. *Historia* 9: 294–308.
OGLE, W.
1912 *Aristotle, De partibus animalium*. Vol. 5 of *The works of Aristotle translated into English*. Oxford.
SCHUHL, P. M.
1948 Platon et la prééminence de la main droite. *Cahiers Internationaux de Sociologie* 4: 172–76.
THOMPSON, D'A. W.
1910 *Aristotle, Historia animalium*. Vol. 4 of *The works of Aristotle translated into English*. Oxford.

Symbolic Values and the Integration of Society among the Mapuche of Chile

10

Louis C. Faron

I. Introduction

The Mapuche are best known to anthropologists by the generic term "Araucanian," under which are subsumed the now extinct Picunche, the heavily acculturated Huilliche, and the Mapuche, the "people of the land." The Mapuche live on more than 2,000 small reservations in southern Central Chile, where they engage in field agriculture and raise cattle, horses, sheep, and other animals. Their population is estimated at 200,000, and they occupy an area roughly the size of Delaware. After resisting white soldiers and settlers for approximately three hundred years, they were finally defeated in the Rebellion of 1880–82 and placed on reservations. Their society underwent numerous important structural changes, and cultural modifications took place as well, as a result of the reservation system (see Faron 1956, 1961a, 1961c); but they have survived as one of the largest functioning indigenous societies in the New World. In this paper I would like to analyze a most significant aspect of the cultural and social ambient of the contemporary Mapuche, one which has considerable implications for any consideration of social stability or change.

Following Durkheim, Radcliffe-Brown wrote long ago that "it is in ancestor-worship that we can most easily discover and demonstrate the social function of a religious cult" (1952: 163). Since the propitiation of ancestral spirits is central to the scheme of Mapuche morality (see Faron 1961b), it could possibly be argued that concern with ancestral spirits in some way conditions most aspects of

American Anthropologist 64 (1962): 1151–64. Reprinted by arrangement with the American Anthropological Association.

Mapuche social life. However, this line of inquiry might easily bog down in a morass of tortuous evaluations and judgments, as does Durkheim's classification of phenomena into sacred and profane categories, and, in any case, would not seem to result in the creation of a total impression of the relationship between Mapuche ideational and social systems. But it may be possible to discover a more fundamental principle than ancestor propitiation in Mapuche society, in which the total structure of symbolic values may be related to the social order. This is the line of inquiry pursued here.

In Durkheim's treatment of the sacred and profane, one encounters a consideration of what are clearly moral values of society. It is according to these values that the sacred and profane categories are defined. But one is confronted with much a priori reasoning and tortuous argument to the end of establishing all phenomena in categories or either sacred or profane dimensions. The pervasive notion of dualism among the Mapuche, at least at first glance, would seem to lend itself to orthodox Durkheimian classification. A sacred-profane dichotomy certainly exists in Mapuche thought. But by no means all Mapuche values, even paired as they are in sets of complementary opposites, are amenable to dichotomization in Durkheim's terms. Thus, the sacred-profane classification is not fully applicable to the Mapuche system of values or, at least, does not encompass it. This, it might be said, is well enough—interpretative difficulties serving to indicate the empirical limits of analysis in the framework of a sacred-profane dichotomization of the Mapuche world view. But this actually leaves very much to be desired, because the limits of analysis seem to be reached or approached at the outset.

From a number of examples of this kind of difficulty which suggest themselves, I select the possible classification of shamans as sacred and sorcerers as profane. With respect to the Mapuche, this is a pointless classification, since both shamans and sorcerers have a numinous quality, and since even sorcerers, clearly evil on most occasions and in most contexts, at times have the important role of operating on the positive side of the moral universe when called upon to exact vengeance. Durkheimian thinking would probably deny this interpretation, but the alternative route it suggests is, I feel, unattractive and dangerous. It would take one entirely outside the limits of Mapuche thinking, the relationship between the conceptual model and its empirical foundation becoming most tenuous. Sacred phenomena are viewed as good by the Mapuche, but not all good is sacred. Sacred-profane and good-evil concepts actually cut across one another when unadulterated Durkeimian reasoning is brought to bear on them.

The value of any anthropological concept is measured by its usefulness in understanding and ordering social and cultural phenomena. Since these phenomena are social and cultural and do not exist in a vacuum, they must be ordered in correspondence to the manner in which they are viewed by the people themselves. This is not to say that the Mapuche need visualize a total structural order, but that their partial, piecemeal, and seemingly orderless views be consistent with whatever conceptual order is imposed upon their social and cultural system by the anthropologist. I take my cue, therefore, from the Mapuche themselves.

The interpretative difficulties of the sacred-profane approach are resolvable once it is recognized that the underlying motif of Mapuche thought is not a comprehensive good-evil or sacred-profane set of references but, rather, a dualistic world view into which good/evil, sacred/profane, and other antithetical categories are subsumable as relative and partial expressions of the total order of society. Numerous sets of value symbols are amenable to arrangement consistent with Mapuche notions of this dualistic ordering of the universe, and, of especial interest here, the structure of symbolic values may be related significantly to the ordering of social institutions.

II. The Concepts of "Handedness" and Complementary Dualism

The most comprehensive theoretical framework for this kind of analysis has been suggested by Robert Hertz, a student of Durkheim, and more recently has been refined and applied to great advantage by Rodney Needham [1] in the analysis of Southeast Asian, Indonesian, and African material. Hertz dealt with the phenomenon of complementary opposition in his essay, "The Preeminence of the Right Hand: A Study of Religious Polarity" (1960), and noted that in many if not all societies "honors, designations, prerogatives" were accorded to the *right* hand, whereas the *left* hand held an ancillary if not despised position. Enlarging on this theme, Needham writes:

> The symbolic opposition of right and left and a dualistic categorization of phenomena are so common as to seem natural proclivities of the human mind. What is to be noted here is the particular way to which these notions are symbolically related to the divisions of . . . [a particular] society . . . (1958: 97).

The theoretical interest which underlies this kind of analysis is phrased by Needham as follows:

> . . . to determine through a consideration of symbolic usages whether or not there are more abstract structural principles underlying both social relations . . . and other aspects of . . . culture which are not obviously connected with them (1958: 89).

The result may provide a "total structural analysis."

Whether it does or not would seem to depend on the type of descent system and the structural relations surrounding marriage. Needham suggests that the relationship between value system and social structure is most complete and significant in societies organized around systems of prescriptive alliance and that "marriage preferences . . . have no structural entailments in the total social system comparable to those of a prescriptive system . . ." (1958: 75). The Mapuche have a system of strongly preferential matrilateral alliance. It is my contention that the symbolic and social order of the Mapuche are related in a most significant manner and that they, therefore, may be viewed as representations of a single conceptual scheme—one in which the dualism noted in the ideational construct of complementary opposition is reflected in a dualistic ordering of social institutions. I feel also that these notions of dualism are revealed in the system of *preferred* matrilateral marriage.

If the phenomenon of complementary dualism in association with a right-left polarity of symbolic values is to be used as an analytic tool, it must be able to satisfy certain requirements. For one thing, it must comprise a symbolic arrangement of sets of socially significant polarities. That is, the polar opposites must be logical constructs which together form some sort of conceptual unit. If this much is satisfied, a cultural analysis of the value system is possible. But more than this is needed for the sort of interpretation attempted here. These conceptual units must in turn have some significant relationship to the institutions of society as conceived by the people themselves. In the case of the Mapuche, this relationship is most clearly seen in the area of ritual belief and action where there exists an association of numerous ideas and values with right and left hands, which enable a Hertzian type of analysis to be made. Handedness serves to symbolize the polarity in thought, values, and their social correlates. By analogy, this dualism is discoverable outside the immediate ritual sphere.

The general problem at hand is that of relating seemingly disparate ethnographic data to one another so that they make sense taken singly or together. Now, in Mapuche society, as in many others, it is apparent that the system of kinship and marriage largely dominates the field of social relationships (see Faron 1961a, 1961b, 1962); that the nature of the marital bond, therefore, is a significant factor in social interaction. Mapuche marry kin in a strongly preferential system which is matrilateral and which involves sets of relatively stable wife-giving and wife-receiving, patrilineal descent groups. It is clear that this system entails prohibitions which constitute moral rules. There is also a further connection between marriage-linked lineages (reservation groups) and ritual congregationalism which, over and above a number of obvious concordances between marriage and other social institutions, is expressive of a unified system of morality (see Faron 1961c, chaps. 8, 9). In order to make more than a series of piecemeal functional statements of the relationship between Mapuche morality and its expression in various social institutions an integrating concept, such as complementary dualism, is needed.

Mapuche social relationships are in fact shot through with notions of complementary opposition. Many of these are clearly discernible, some as sacred/profane, good/evil, superior/inferior, and so forth—all in analogic or explicit association with a right-left dichotomy. Where the pre-eminence of the right hand exists as a concept of symbolic importance in society, we may expect to find notions of superior, good, health, and so forth, associated with the right. The logic of dualistic reasoning places complementary notions of inferior, sickness, and so on, with the left. Even in the absence of unmistakable (i.e., verbalized) association with handedness, an ordering of other values may be obtained by analogy with reference to right and left. Indeed, a Hertzian analysis is possible even in the absence of specific mention of handedness (cf. Needham 1960a: 115).

III. Symbolism and Social Structure in Mapucheland

Perhaps the clearest association between phenomena which belong on the right and those which belong on the left is seen in the symbolic attachments of good and evil in the Mapuche scheme of religious morality. Some of the most obvious of these are tabulated below and then discussed for exemplification.

Table I. Mapuche Symbolic Attachments to Right and Left Hand

Right	Left
good	evil
life	death
day	night
health	sickness
ancestral spirits	*wekufe* (evil spirits)
shaman	sorcerer
afterworld *(wenumapu)*	underworld *(reñu)*
tren tren	*kai kai*
abundance	poverty
fullness	hunger

In Araucanian, *kuk* means "hand," *wele* means "left," and *man* means "right." *Welekuk* and *mankuk*, or simply wele and man, with kuk understood, signify respectively "left hand" and "right hand." There is an unmistakable and literal connection between left and evil, and right and good. For example, *piukeman* (*piuke,* heart) is an expression equivalent to *kume piuke* (*kume,* good) and means "pure in heart," "free from evil." *Wesa* (evil) and *wele* (left) are also used interchangeably. *Welenkin,* for example, refers to leftness and means a heart palpitation which forebodes evil or misfortune. Similarly, *welethungun* (left talk) means to speak evil (especially of one's self in contemplation of suicide). An "evil-headed" or "crazy" person (possessed of evil forces) is alternately called *wesa lonko* (*lonko,* head) or *wele lonko.* In a small number of other words, there is also this literal connection between handedness and qualities of good and evil, but permissible improvisations actually would extend the number of such words infinitely. For the most part, however, the association is analogical in a conceptual scheme in which phenomena associated with evil are linked to the left "half" of the universe and those associated with good linked with the right. The right hand column in table I contains obviously good phenomena and the left their complementary opposites, as these entries are paired by the Mapuche. They constitute a partial expression of the overall dualistic order of the Mapuche universe.

There are other clear-cut right-left associations from which analogies may be drawn. When, for example, ancestral spirits appear as Hawks of the Sun, in answer to a ritual summons or in a dream, they may make peculiarly significant gyrations to indicate the propitiousness of some act or plan or the effectiveness of ritual supplication. Whatever the motivation, if they circle to the right it is taken as a good omen, as an indication that events will go well, that prayers have been or will be answered. If they circle to the left, prayers will not be answered, evil is foreshadowed.[2] Some human error, some sin, is indicated. Perhaps a sorcerer remained undiscovered at a funeral or fertility rite. If so, further propitiation is called for, the stigma of impurity or ritual imperfection lingering until a compensatory ritual is held. The Mapuche do not, however, erect insurmountable barriers to their own well-being. Bad omens or visions of evil usually occur before or during, rather than after, the staging of some ceremony, their mitigation providing one of the motives for holding the ceremony, or prolonging and perfecting it.

A similar association of right and left with good and evil occurs when anyone is startled by a bird's song near at hand. If the bird is to one's right, it signifies the presence of an ancestral spirit and presages good fortune. If on the left, it is taken to represent the embodiment of evil and to presage evil. When one dreams of taking a left fork in the road, instead of a right turn, this is also interpreted as an evil omen. Stories of moral import are geared to this left-right theme, insofar as persons who turn right enjoy riches, huge quantities of food served in banquet style, and general good fortune. Those who take the left turn suffer poverty, hunger, and general misfortune. Not until the steps are retraced (similar to the reception of ritual prayer) and the right fork gained do persons throw off the aura of evil and come to enjoy the blessing of good fortune.

The ritual priest *(ñillatufe)* cuts off the right ear of the sacrificial sheep and holds it aloft in his right hand, while offering prayer to ancestors and the pantheon of Mapuche gods. The blood of the sheep is placed in a special wooden bowl to the right of the main altar, the sacred leaves of which are periodically aspersed with it during the *ñillatun* fertility rite. Likewise, the sheep's heart is cut out and held aloft in the right hand of the *ñillatufe,* who passes it to his chiefly assistants lined up along his right (and the right of the altar), who, as the *ñillatufe,* bite into it, hold it up in their right hands, and offer ancestral prayer. By the time the heart has stopped twitching, it is placed in the crotch of the main altar. The right ear of a sheep is also severed in the *konchotun* ritual, a sort of blood brotherhood, which may occur during *ñillatun,* in which the two participants swear lifelong friendship and mutual obligation on the sheep's blood.

There seems to be a clear enough association between good phenomena and the right hand, so that ancestral spirits, shamans, *tren tren* (the magic mountain), day, and life itself may be placed on the right and, their complementary opposites, *wekufe,* sorcerers, *kai kai* (usually an evil serpent or sea bird), night, and the death in which forces of evil deal, on the left. In these instances there is always some association between rightness and leftness and, respectively, good and evil. Many other sets of symbolic values may also be ordered with reference to a right-left dichotomy.

While all the above-mentioned entries would seem to serve well as a clearcut ordering of symbolic values associated with good and evil, there are other pairs of opposites which, while linked in Mapuche thinking, are not clearly good or evil, either to the Western "mind" or to the Mapuche themselves. Yet they are classifiable as either right- or left-hand symbols by analogy to the previous list, and by their relatively superior or inferior qualities, as these are verbalized by the Mapuche. Most of these entries have special significance for ritual occasions and, in this context, are commonly verbalized with regard to right-left associations (table 2).

This list concerns mostly natural elements and directions, as these are ordered into a dualistic scheme. There are earth, land, sacred soil, known and unknown land; sky, "heaven," and celestial bodies; colors. West, north, winter, cold, below, blue, sin, outside, are all in some way connected to death and, therefore, analogically related to the evil forces which cause it and the leftness which symbolizes it. East, south, summer, warm, land, above, yellow, white, expiation, altar, and ceremonial field are associated with good and the right hand. In some cases the association is direct and literal but, in all cases, these sets of opposing yet complementary values are analogically connected with right and left. Sun, blood, ritual speech, and priest are all associated positively with ancestral spirits and the gods. East is the orientation for all ritual action and, ideally, the entrance to Mapuche houses should face east. West is asso-

TABLE 2. OTHER MAPUCHE RIGHT-LEFT ASSOCIATIONS

Right	Left
east	west
south	north
summer	winter
warm	cold
sun	moon
blood	(water)
ritual language	speech
land	ocean
above	below
yellow	blue
white	black
priest	layman
expiation (ritual)	sin
ceremonial field	(outside)

ciated with death, as is the ocean which ancestral spirits must cross before arriving safely in the afterworld. The ocean is the spirit's final barrier in its journey to *nomelafken* (*lafken,* ocean; *nome,* other side) or as it is sometimes rendered *wenumapu* (*wenu,* above; *mapu,* land). The north is the origin of cold, harsh winter rains, starvation, and general hardship. It is also the place of origin of the Inca and the Spaniards, the collective *winka.* Moon is placed in opposition to sun and in the left-hand column because of its connection with female menses. Below and above are literally inferior and superior categories which serve to qualify the characteristics of many phenomena, and they are analogically compatible with evil and good, left and right. *Minche* (below) *mapu* (land) refers to the grave, similar to the way in which *reñu* (underworld) refers to the subterranean region inhabited by witches and all forces of evil. Minche connotes as well defeat in either physical or supernatural combat. Wenu (above) is clearly associated with sun, the haven of ancestral spirits, the domain of the gods, and so forth, and is placed on the right by analogy to good connotations. Black and blue (not always differentiated) are associated with rain and/or death. Black and dark blue banners symbolize rain in the *ñillatun* agricultural fertility rite; white banners and sky-blue banners with yellow figures symbolize sun and good weather. The funeral wake (*kurikawin,* black assemblage) and mourning in general are symbolized by black. The cold, rainy, death-dealing month of August may be called *kurikuyen* (black month or black moon). Certain relatives of the affinal category may be called *kuripapai* (black women), and so on.

The following sets of complementary opposites involve, for the most part, categories of inferior (left) and superior (right) statuses, although, with respect to *winka* (outsider) and incest, we are again confronted with notions of evil. I have grouped categorical sets separately into table 3 in order to present them as the final step in demonstrating that the same dualistic principle inheres in the ordering of social phenomena as that which has been shown to characterize the complementary opposition of symbolic values. Many "problems" of interpretation are cleared up or at least placed in new perspective by applying this conceptual scheme to Mapuche values and their social correlates. The right-hand column contains inferior categories relative to the left-hand column.

TABLE 3. MAPUCHE INFERIOR-SUPERIOR AND LEFT-RIGHT HAND ASSOCIATIONS

Right	Left
man	woman/child
lonko	*kona*
senior	junior
dominant lineage	subordinate lineage
gift-giver	gift-receiver
wife-giver	wife-receiver
marriage (with MBD)	incest
Mapuche	*winka*
ritual congregation	reservation

There is a differential evaluation of the sexes in Mapuche society which is consistent with a left-right (woman-man) dualistic set of symbols. There are many indications of male superiority and association with the right, as well as with good and the sacred. Ancestral spirits, for example, are dealt with as though they all were male (elders and chiefs, *lonko*), and these have a close working relationship with the sons of the gods. Female ancestors are soon dropped from the roster of propitiated ancestral spirits and are eventually subsumed into the general ancestral category, *kuifiche*. It is the male of the god-set who is propitiated and supplicated first; then prayers are directed to his wife, who is propitiated only once or at least much less often than her divine husband. None of this seems incongruent with a patrilineal, patrilocal, and patripotestal society.

There are other indications of male dominance and a clear association between females and inferiority, if not evil. But there is a relativity of symbolism involved here which should not be overlooked. Women, for example, are barred from participation in the council of elders (males) which discusses procedural plans for *ñillatun* and which offers private (i.e., among themselves as representatives of their respective lineages) prayers to ancestral spirits during the preparatory phase of fertility ceremonies. Women are clearly associated with sorcery and are considered the most able sorcerers by virtue of being females, and, by analogy, may be placed on the black, cold, death-ridden side of the conceptual universe.

An interesting matter of the relativity of these sets of values enters at this point. It is that male shamans are not considered fully masculine by the Mapuche. Some are suspected of being homosexual. All or most dress in women's clothing (cf. Needham 1960b: 26–27) during their performance. Others are blind, crippled, or mentally unstable. All of these characteristics are nonmasculine in Mapuche eyes and, furthermore, are associated with the occult part of the universe of which sorcery is a part. But this is not to say that shamans are viewed as aligned with the forces of evil. For the Mapuche, shaman-sorcerer comprises a logical set of complementary forces symbolizing, respectively, good and evil, with right and left associations. It is inconsistent with Mapuche thought to include males in shamanistic roles, even *thungulmachin* (the shaman's male helper) having occult powers which are not wholly masculine. Therefore, male practitioners are attributed female characteristics. The shaman is not the logical opposite of the ritual priest *(ṇ̃illatufe)* in Mapuche thinking, even though shamans sometimes complement the activities of the *ñillatufe* in *ñillatun*. The *ñillatufe* has quite a different relationship to the supernatural than the shaman; he does not enter the spirit world, but is tied to it formally by virtue of birth into a particular patrilineal descent group and in the line of succession of chiefs. He is, therefore, at the same time political, lineal, and spiritual leader of the dominant lineage of his natal reservation, the group which is most clearly responsible for the staging of *ñillatun,* caring for invited participants and honored guests, and bearing heaviest responsibility of a moral nature for the successful enactment of the ceremony. The shaman has a quite different role.

The *kona-lonko* dichotomy also points up the relativity of these sets of complementary categories. *Lonko* (chiefs and other elders) are clearly in a socially superior position with respect to their male kinsmen. Formerly, they exacted tribute from them and others in their following and, even today, receive obligatory presentations on certain ritual occasions. They are also accorded the privilege of attending work parties in which they appear as titular heads, doing little or no work themselves. The *lonko* who is also *ñillatufe* receives abundant quantities of food, not as payment for his services to the congregation (as is the case with the shaman), nor as a gift, but rather as his due levy—with the understanding that this food will be distributed for ritual purposes.

Kona and *lonko* are related as junior and senior, but the junior-senior dichotomy is expressed in a number of other ways as well. The use of kinship terms expresses the superiority of the senior members of Mapuche society (uncles, fathers, grandfathers) to whom respect is accorded by all others. The same kinship idiom is extended to groups of relatives in the marriage alliance system. Males of the wife-giving unit are called *weku* (maternal "uncle"), which is a respectful designation, whereas males of the wife-receiving group are called *ñillan* ("the one who has purchased"), at best a designation of inferior social status.

Titiev mentioned that there was a feeling of "latent hostility" with respect to *ñillan,* and that this "person" is considered as a "potential traitor" (1951: 48). I would say that these facts might be interpreted to greater advantage as indicating that certain wife-receiving groups or segments of any large wife-receiving group are placed in a relatively suspect social position in which more than mere social inferiority is implied. These are the wife-receiving groups which have not maintained sustained marriage ties in the matrilateral system, or those just initiating such alliance, and which, because of that, might be suspected of actually practicing homicidal sorcery. It is members of such receiving groups who *must* put in an appearance at funeral ceremonies of the lineage who formerly provided them with wives or else bear the brunt of general suspicion and possible retaliation. It is their failure to meet the former obligations of ritual participation which lays suspicion upon them, just as the fulfillment of such obligation has the opposite effect with respect to units which maintained sustained and multiple intermarriages over several generations. In their obligation to bury inmarried women in the same ground as lineal ancestors is symbolized a dualistic separation of the two descent groups and the commitment of the socially inferior group to sustain the responsibility and cost which burial entails.

With respect to the subordinate lineage-dominant lineage set, little more need be said. The subordinate lineages are localized on the reservation by sufferance of the dominant one. Members of subordinate lineages look to the dominant one for political and ritual leadership (on well-functioning reservations) and, in any case, are forced to trace descent back to the time of the original chief in order to validate certain of their reservation rights. The greater rights of the dominant lineage have worked their effort on both the size and the composition of dominant and subordinate lineages throughout Mapucheland, and it will be easily understood that it is from the subordinate lineages that most young people emigrate to the cities and farms of Chile and Argentina, being accorded fewer real opportunities than members of dominant lineages to gain a living on their natal reservation. In some cases, when feelings run high, members of these subordinated lineages are called by the opprobrious name *winka,* usually reserved for whites.

The superiority of gift-givers to gift-receivers is not absolute, although in any particular situation gift-receivers are in an inferior position, momentarily at least. With respect to ceremonies such as *trafkin* and *konchotun,* in which gift-giving is important, the persons involved alternate periodically (yearly) as giver and receiver. But the recipient at any phase of the cycle is under moral obligation to return the gift at the next juncture, placing himself in an inferior position until the completion of the next phase of the cycle; symbolizing a mutual though cyclically asymmetrical obligation. Since a gift must be reciprocated, the receiver is in a position of formal obligation to the giver. When the return is made the other party becomes recipient in turn; and so on.

When gifts are placed in the coffin, a practice called *rokiñ,* the obligations of the living to the dead are expressed, but the proper bestowal of *rokiñ* binds the departed spirit to watch over the living. The relative, and shifting, inferiority-superiority of gift-receivers and gift-givers is an integral part of the network of marriage alliances.

Let us turn to a brief consideration of wife-giving and wife-receiving. Titiev's assertion that there is equal exchange of marriage wealth (1951: 101) is wholly inconsistent with Mapuche values and their social correlates. The inferiority of the group which pays bride-price is symbolized in a number of ways (see Faron 1961c; 1962). Rather than being equal, there is a great, symbolically significant, and obligatory imbalance in goods transferred at the occasion of marriage, consistent with the relative inferiority of the wife-receiving group.

There is no direct exchange of women between Mapuche lineages, the system being one of generalized exchange, strong preference accounting for the vast majority of marriages being contracted with matrilaterally linked groups (see Faron 1961c). On the face of it, this is a triadic structure in which are involved one's own lineage, one's wife-giving lineage, and the wife-receiving group into which one's lineage sisters marry. This relationship is symbolized in the kinship terminology, in which wife-receivers are designated as *ñillan* ("the one who has purchased") and wife-givers as *weku* (maternal "uncle"). One's own lineage consists of brothers, fathers, etc. The terms used for one's own lineage members are potentially extensible to all Mapuche who do not fall into a marriage-linked category which, more than a sentimental attachment to fellow Mapuche, expresses the structural boundaries of the marriage system. But the necessarily triadic structure involved in this kind of exchange system reduces to dyadic component relationships with respect to any marriage-linked units, affinals always standing in either the *ñillan* or the *weku* category, as wife-receiver and wife-giver, with respect to each other.

Now for the problem of why the Mapuche insist that marriage with mother's brother's daughter is the ideal union, one which they say was law *(admapu)* a generation or so ago. As I have indicated elsewhere (Faron 1961 a,c), genealogies do not show that marriage with a real mother's brother's daughter takes place with significant frequency, that it is in fact a rare occurrence. Since all marriageable women are called by the same term, *ñuke,* men marry, in the absence of exact genealogical knowledge, classificatory mother's brother's daughters in a generalized system of exchange. Therefore, the anthropologist's acceptance of this statement as literal truth is unfortunate (cf. Titiev 1951: 38 et passim). But what does the Mapuche expression of this ideal marriage form mean? Elsewhere (Faron 1962) I have suggested that this is a cultural device for expressing a relationship of great importance in the most intimate familial terms possible, the implication being that this is a mechanism for achieving or expressing solidary relationships. This is only a partial explanation of what such expression might mean to the Mapuche. A fuller explanation now suggests itself; one which relates to the notion of incest and which is understandable in terms of the dualistic ordering of the social system. It is simply that the cultural ideal of mother's brother's daughter marriage symbolizes complete observance of the matrilateral rule *(admapu)* by which marriage is not only preferred between two stable, intermarrying lineages but is proscribed between males and the groups into which their lineage sisters, daughters, and granddaughters marry. Mother's brother's daughter marriage is a shorthand or symbolic expression of both lineage exogamy and matrilateral preference, in complementary opposition to incest, which would result from its infraction.

I have already indicated the general sense of the concept *winka,* a term reserved especially for non-Mapuche, although sometimes used in anger or fear with respect to nonrelated or out-group Mapuche. For the Mapuche, all the indigenous peoples of the world are Mapuche; all colonizers, *winka.* Their questions about "Mapuche" in the United States or in other countries call this to the anthropologist's attention. There seems to be a fairly clear-cut dichotomy here.

Related to the concept of outsider or stranger, however, is the notion of geographical divisions in Mapucheland itself, that is, among Mapuche. The word Mapuche means "people of the land," and all Indians classified as Araucanian call themselves Mapuche, standing as each does in the center of his own little world. Mapuche residing to the north are referred to as Picunche (*picun,* north), to the south, Huilliche (*huilli,* south), to the east, Puenche, and to the west, along the coast, Lafkenche *(lafken,* ocean). Some writers have taken these geographico-directional classifications to mean that fixed political and ethnic divisions existed among the prereservation Mapuche. There seems no good evidence in the literature in support of this conclusion. Rather, these are clearly relative terms by which all Mapuche are able to orient themselves and sort out blocks of other Mapuche if necessary. Non-Mapuche are never classified in these terms—are never called *che* (people)—remaining an undifferentiated totality, *winka.* This, then, is the wide-angle view: there are Mapuche on the one hand and *winka* on the other. There are also regional or geographical orientations among the Mapuche themselves. And within the ritual congregation there are other important classifications made: one's lineage mates, one's wife-receivers *(ñillan),* and one's wife-givers *(weku).* Figure 1 depicts this conceptualization of structural categories in Mapuche-land.

The correspondence between region and ritual congregation is great, if not always complete. The reservations are alien political and economic constructs of Chilean derivation to which the

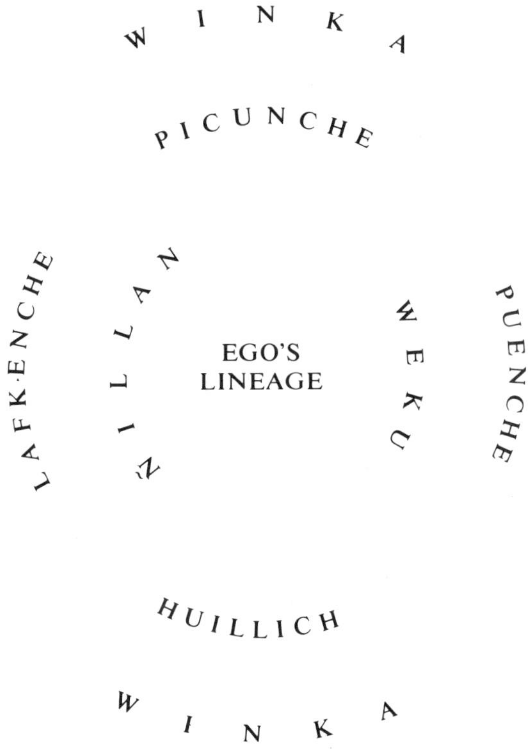

Fig. 1. Geographic orientations of the Mapuche

Mapuche have made accommodations. The region, however, is the seat of ritual responsibility, the locus in which matrilateral marriage alliances form their tightest web for any person or group, the stage on which the drama of life and death is enacted (see Faron, 1961c, chaps. 8, 9). The region as ritual congregation has moral unity, offers protection against the most malevolent forces of evil, is the center of ritual sacrifice to ancestral spirits. It is the center of the

Mapuche world. Its dimensions are unknown to the outsider; it is sacred to its membership. It is fundamental to the continuity of Mapuche religious morality.

Notes

1. I express my thanks to Rodney Needham for introducing me to the Hertzian scheme and for giving the manuscript of this paper a critical reading.

2. While the historical sources do not contain detailed enough data useful to the kind of interpretation attempted here, one repeatedly reads that shamans used to forecast the outcome of military and other ventures according to the flight of birds. Could these have been Hawks of the Sun? Could their flight have constituted the right-left gyrations alluded to above?

References Cited

Durkheim, E.
n.d. *The elementary forms of the religious life*. Glencoe: Free Press.
Faron, L. C.
1956 Araucanian patri-organization and the Omaha system. *American Anthropologist* 58: 435–56.
1961a The Dakota-Omaha continuum in Mapuche society. *Journal of the Royal Anthropological Institute* 91: (1:)11–22.
1961b On ancestor propitiation among the Mapuche of Central Chile. *American Anthropologist* 58: 824–30.
1961c *Mapuche social structure*. Urbana: University of Illinois.
1962 Matrilateral marriage among the Mapuche (Araucanians) of Central Chile. *Sociologus* 12: 54–66.
Hertz, R.
1960 *Death and the right hand*. Translated by R. and C. Needham. Glencoe: Free Press.
Needham, R.
1958 A structural analysis of Purum society. *American Anthropologist* 60: 75–101.
1960a Alliance and classification among the Lamet. *Sociologus* 10: 97–118.
1960b The left hand of the Mugwe: an analytical note on the structure of Meru symbolism. *Africa* 30: 20–33. [See chap. 7 above.]
Radcliffe-Brown, A. R.
1952 *Structure and function in primitive society*. Glencoe: Free Press.
Titiev, M.
1951 *Araucanian culture in transition*. Occasional Contributions, Museum of Anthropology, no. 15. University of Michigan.

Order in the Atoni House

11

Clark E. Cunningham

The house, like ritual, may be an effective means to communicate ideas between generations in a preliterate society. The Atoni of Indonesian Timor do not build houses to express abstract notions: they build homes. However, they do so in a way taught and managed by elders, according to rules regarded as a vital part of their heritage, and houses follow patterns, not individual whim.

When studying Atoni houses,[1] I was told how parts, sections, and appurtenances are made and used. Villagers are equally explicit, however, concerning another aspect of the house, the *order* in which things are placed and used. To the question why a particular order is necessary, one simple answer predominates: *Atoran es ia* ("this is the *atoran,*" the order or arrangement).

In this paper I consider what this just-so question of "order" involves. I believe that order in building expresses ideas symbolically, and the house depicts them vividly for every individual from birth to death. Furthermore, order concerns not just discrete ideas or symbols, but a system; and the system expresses both principles of classification and a value for classification per se, the definition of unity and difference.

The Atoni of Indonesian Timor number a quarter of a million, speak a Malayo-Polynesian language, have named patrilineal descent groups, and grow maize and rice by shifting cultivation on mountainous terrain.[2] Few villages have easy access to a road and an exchange, rather than a market, economy is the rule. Atoni

---

Bijdragen tot de Taal-, Land- en Volkenkunde 120 (1964): 34–68. Revised version, reprinted with the permission of the Koninklijk Instituut voor Taal,- Land- en Volkenkunde.

share many elements of a common culture, though there are variations over the ten princedoms. Atoni princes are among the few "native rulers" still recognized within the Indonesian republic, and the princedom is the maximal native political unit and the limit of society for most people. Christianity, Dutch and Indonesian administrations, and education came less intensively to Atoni than to nearby peoples, beginning only in the second decade of this century. Most Atoni still live by their traditions in a village environment, though outside influences increased after Indonesian independence.

The house *(ume)* is the residential, economic, and ritual unit at the base of Atoni society. It is inhabited mainly by an elementary family, which eats and sleeps there, and guests are entertained in the house. There are no communal houses for lineages or hamlets. Grain from the fields of a household is smoked on racks over the hearth and stored in the attic. There are no communal granaries for local lineages or hamlets, and there is a minimum of economic cooperation between households. There is, however, obligatory participation in life-cycle activities and ritual for agnates, affines, and hamlet-mates, and a general agreement on the value of aid within the hamlet in time of need.

The house is a ritual center for prayer, sacrifice, and feasts. Ritual of the life-cycle is conducted normally at the house of those immediately involved, and sacred heirlooms are kept there. A house (with its *sacra*) should endure; an heir should maintain and eventually inhabit it. Prayers may be directed from the house to the Divinity *(Uis Neno)*, the Powers *(pah meni)*, the ancestors *(nitu)*, and to special tutelary spirits; and diviners *(mnane)* normally work at the house of a client. Agricultural ritual begins and ends at the house.

In the following discussion I consider mainly the rectangular type of house found in the princedom of Amarasi, where I stayed the longest.[3] Space does not allow analysis of two different types found in other areas. Suffice it to say here that common structural principles and symbols underlie these variations, and these are my concern. Also limited space forbids discussing house-building ritual, though I appreciate its relevance.

The Amarasi House

Atoni say that the door should be oriented southward, the direction they call *ne'u* (right). North is *ali'* (left); east, *neonsaen* (sunrise);

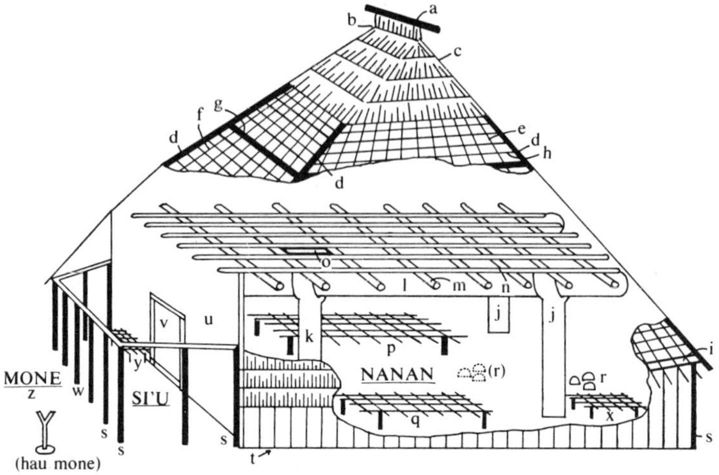

Fig. 1. The Amarasi house

key:

a	*fuf manas*	sun cranium	n	*nesa'*	rafter
b	*fuf ai*	fire cranium	o	*toi*	entrance (attic)
c	*hun*	grass (thatch roof)	p	*harak ko'u*	great platform
d	*suaf bidjae-kase*	horse spar	q	*harak tupa'*	sleeping platform
e	*suaf benaf*	*benaf* spar	r	*tunaf*	hearth
f	*suaf susuf*	*susuf* spar	s	*ni manu*	chicken post
g	*aka'nunu*	pillow	t	*haef*	foot
h	*tak pani*	cross-spar	u	*piku*	wall
i	*tnat oe*	'hold water' cross-spars	v	*eno*	door
j	*ni ainaf*	mother post	w	*toi*	entrance (outer section)
k	*ni ainaf (nakan)*	mother post (head)	x	*harak man-ba'at*	agreement platform (serving platform)
l	*atbat*	beam	y	*harak*	platform
m	*kranit*	cross-beam	z	*mone*	outside; male (yard)

west, *neontes* (sunset). The word *neno* (*neon* in metathesis) may mean sun, sky, or day, the reference here being sun. It is forbidden to orient the door directly east-west, say informants, "because that is the way of the sun" or "because the sun must not enter the house." In fact, houses are oriented variously, though rarely (in my experience) directly east-west; yet the front (or door) direction is called *ne'u* (right *or* south). Within the house, orientation is normally established as a person faces the door from the inside—

just as Atoni compass directions are fixed facing "sunrise"—and again *ne'u* and *ali'* (right *and* left) sides of the house are determined.

The metaphor *ne'u ma li'* (right and left *or* south and north) is a common Atoni one for "good and evil." East (sunrise) is the direction where prayers are made to the Divinity, *Uis Neno* (Lord of the Sun, Sky, or Day), a divinity who, though not otiose, is little concerned with moral issues. East is considered to be the direction of origin where the "ancient hill, ancient hamlet" *(fatu mnasi, kuan mnasi)* of each lineage is located, but the "way of the deceased" *(ran nitu)* upon death is toward the west or the sea. Noble lines have myths of origin and migration from the east which are recited at their festivals, but there are tales told surreptitiously in most princedoms that the ruling line actually came from some other direction and usurped power and then authority. In color symbolism, east is associated with white; south with red; west with black; north with yellow. The native cloth worn by men is red and white (the colors of south and east); the traditional woman's cloth is black (the color of west). Yellow is not used as a main color in cloths, but the color is associated with witches *(araut)* who may be termed *mat molo* (yellow eye). Rulers are associated with white; warriors with red; and village headmen with black in their costumes. In their totality, rulers may be termed *uis mnatu, uis muni* (gold lord, silver lord) in opposition to commoners who are termed *to' muti, to metan* (white commoners, black commoners).

The Amarasi house consists of the following elements, sections, and appurtenances. (The numbers in parentheses refer to figures. The figure number precedes the colon; the reference in that figure follows it.)

nanan (inside *or* center): inner section (2:a)

Ume nanan (house inside *or* house center) may refer to the inner section or to the whole area under the roof, depending upon contexts which I discuss later. *Nanan* may mean inside opposed to outside; the inner part opposed to the outer part of an area; or the center part opposed to the periphery of a circle. (However, *nanan* does not mean "center point" which is *mat,* eye, or *usan,* navel.)

The *nanan,* or inner section, is reserved for agnates of the householder, while the *ume nanan,* house center—the whole area under the roof—is for agnates, affines, and guests. Guests should not enter the inner section through the door (2:b), though they may enter

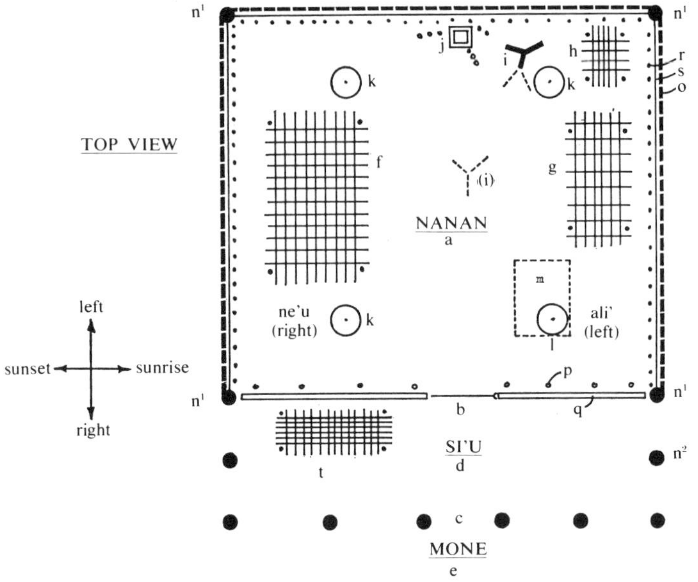

Fig. 2. Plan of interior

key:

a	*nanan*	inside; center (inner section)	(i)	*tunaf*	hearth (alternate place)
			j	*nai oe teke*	fixed water jar
b	*eno*	door	k	*ni ainaf*	mother post
c	*toi*	entrance	l	*ni ainaf (nakan)*	mother post (head)
d	*si'u*	elbow (outer section)	m	*toi*	entrance (attic)
e	*mone*	outside; male (yard)	n¹	*ni manu*	chicken post (corner)
f	*harak ko'u*	great platform	n²	*ni manu*	chicken post
g	*harak tupa'*	sleeping platform	o	*haef*	foot
			p	*haef mese*	first foot
h	*harak manba'at*	agreement platform (serving platform)	q	*piku*	wall
			r	*rusi*	inner wall post
			s	*rupit*	wall slat
i	*tunaf*	hearth	t	*harak*	platform

freely the outer section *(si'u)* through the entrance (2:c). Guests are not entertained in the inner section, though wife-giving affines may be received there on occasion. A wife has access to the inner section of her husband's parents' house only after initiation to his descent group ritual. Affines or guests may not sleep in the inner section, but a married daughter may do so if she returns alone to visit her parents. If her husband comes too, they sleep together on a platform in the outer section. Unmarried sons and daughters sleep in the inner section, but a boy on reaching his late teens may sleep in the outer section. All of the residents normally eat in the inner section when there are no guests. The mood is relaxed and the door is closed, and it is considered impolite to interrupt a family meal.

si'u (elbow): outer section (2:d)

This section, also covered by the roof and ceiling, is used to receive guests and for work by householders. It may be open (as in figs. 1 and 2) or enclosed by walls, an option of the householder. There are one or more fixed platforms *(harak)* in the outer section where guests sleep, eat, or sit (2:t). When guests come, the men eat in this section and are served by young people or women, and the women eat in the inner section. (A man of some social importance may eat here regularly, being served by his wife or children who crouch in the doorway while he eats and talk with him.) The right side of the outer section is used first for receiving guests, and there is often only one fixed platform, at this side. If there are many guests, persons of higher rank sit at the right and their food is served there. During the day, women may use the outer section for work such as weaving, spinning, basketmaking, or pounding corn and rice. More often though, since light is poor under the roof's shade, they work in the yard which is termed *mone,* a word meaning both "outside" and "male." This yard (1:z or 2:e), normally bounded by stones and sometimes by a fence, is often slightly elevated and paths should not cross it.

harak ko'u (great platform) (2:f)

This is the principal and largest platform in the house, in the inner section. Though I use the pale word "platform," a *harak* may serve as a bed, bench, couch, table, or rack. The form is always the same, but the use varies as may the appellation. The "great platform" is always on the right side within the inner section. Tools, household possessions, and pounded corn and rice are kept here, usually stored in baskets. Babies may sleep here, but children and youths should not. They sleep on mats on the floor by the hearth. Informants stipulate that neither women nor affines may sleep on the "great platform."

harak tupa' (sleeping platform) (2:g)

This platform, smaller and lower than the other, is always on the left side of the inner section. The elder male and female of the household sleep here, and a partition of split-bamboo may enclose this bed to give privacy for their sleep and personal possessions. Parents should not sleep on mats on the ground, consistent with all other daily and ceremonial usages in which a place on a platform signifies superior status.

harak manba'at (agreement platform): serving platform (2:h)

This platform, smaller than the others, is near the hearth on the left side and holds cooking utensils and dishes, and cooked food is placed here. (It is improper to serve directly from a pot on the hearth.) Women may be placed here when they give birth. A fire then burns under them during confinement and they are bathed in hot water from this fire which is tended by the husband. The word *manba'at* is a substantive from the verb *manba'an,* "to agree, arrange, or put in order." I return later to consider this name.

The use of three platforms, as described above, is common in Amarasi, but not essential. Often there are only two, in the places of what are here described as the "great platform" (2:f) and the "sleeping platform" (2:g), and the two then bear these names. The rules for their use remain the same. The former is used for storing household goods, food, and tools, and as a seat for men and elders of the household or wife-giving affines on occasion. The latter is reserved as a bed for the elder couple, and a woman gives birth there. The "sleeping platform" may also be used for serving food, especially when there are guests, or else a flat stone may be placed by the hearth for this purpose. Thus the "agreement platform" is combined with the "sleeping platform."

tunaf (hearth) (2:i)

The fire should be kept lit all the time by women, except during their confinement, when the husband is responsible. The hearth ideally consists of three stones, two at the back and one at the front. The back two should point toward the posts called *ni manu* (chicken post) (2:n[1]) and the front one toward the door, "so that the heat may go out." The hearth may also consist of five stones, two at the front and two at the back, all pointing toward corner "chicken posts," and one at the center pointing toward the door. The hearth may be at the center of the inner section or at the back, but not forward; it may be on the center-line of the house or to the left, but not to the right.

nai oe teke (fixed water jar) (2:j)

An earthenware jar must stand at the back of the inner section by the wall. It is normally opposite the door, though informants say it may be left of center. (Like the hearth, it may not be to the right.) The jar is set with ceremony when the house is consecrated, and it must not be moved. If a new house is built, the jar must be moved with ceremony to the new house.

According to informants, the door, water jar, hearth, and the two platforms are the main points of *atoran,* order, in the house. Their positions are invariable—or variable within the fixed limits I mentioned—and known to nearly all people. Items of European furniture, such as tables, chairs, and wardrobes, are rarely found in the inner section, though some houses have them in the outer section, which is otherwise bare except for one or two platforms. (If these items are found in the inner section, they do not upset the "order" described.) These elements, I believe, are not the only ordered ones: nearly all aspects of the house express *atoran.* However, it is significant that Atoni view these points as fundamental—the door, water jar, hearth, and the two platforms—and I shall return to this point.

ni ainaf (mother post) (2:k)

Four "mother posts" of equal size support the rafters and the ceiling (which is also the attic floor). The so-called head *(nakaf)* is the mother post at the front and left (2:1). The attic entrance is by this post: when villagers are asked why this post is called the "head," they say, "because it is by the hatch to the attic." This head mother post has a flat stone altar at its base and sacred objects of the ancestors may be tied to it. It is forbidden to put a nail in this post or to hang tools or other daily objects from it, and none of the mother posts is decorated by carving.

ni manu (chicken post) (2:n^1,n^2)

Twelve "chicken posts" help support the roof at its outer extremity. The four at the corners of the house (2:n^1) touch the four main roof spars which are termed "horse spars" *(suaf bidjaekase)* (1:d). The remaining chicken posts (2:n^2) surround the outer section. These may be decorated with carved designs or pictures.

haef (foot) (2:o)

The "feet" are peripheral wall posts, slightly smaller than the chicken posts, on which the roof spars *(suaf)* rest. These "feet" enclose the inner section. (The four ribs on each side of the partition [2:p] are also called "feet.") I was told that there should be 120 feet to 12 chicken posts. This proportion seemed to be maintained in most Amarasi houses. Many people did not know this fact, which I was told by elders, but counting generally verified it. It is appropriate, in terms of other fixed numbers for house parts and for the general importance of numbers in Atoni ritual, that some proportion is established and that the totals are multiples of four, the numerical expression of unity for Atoni.

These tightly-packed "feet" form a low wall about three or four feet high, but they are not conceived as the unit which our term "wall" implies (and which Atoni would term *piku*). On the inside, and parallel to these "feet," is a row of smaller posts called *rusi* (2:r), and between these rows are slats called *rupit* (2:s). (I do not know any other meanings for these words.) This form—two concentric rows of posts with horizontal slats between—is the same as the fence which surrounds Atoni swiddens, corrals, and hamlets. Rulers and warriors are likened, in ritual speeches, to these posts of a fence which surrounds and protects. As will be seen, this fence form is repeated in the roof.

piku (wall) and *eno* (door) (2:q and 2:b)

A wall separates the inner and outer sections, but does not support the ceiling or roof. A heavy wooden door *(eno),* either solid or of fitted slabs, is found at the center of the partition. The hinges are fixed so that the door swings onto the left side of the house, toward the "sleeping platform," thus giving entrance to the right. The doorway is rectangular, with separate pieces for the lintel, jambs, and threshold. The lintel, termed *eben,* may be straight or arched, ideally the latter, say informants, but usually the former. The name is related to *ebe,* the term for the moonshaped silver comb worn by women (which may also be termed *funan,* moon). The jambs are both called *su'tai* which means "to support," usually in the moral sense "to be responsible for." (*Su'* alone means "to carry on the head.") The threshold is termed *teri,* the verb "to step on" used as a substantive.

atbat, kranit, and *nesa':* the ceiling beams and rafters (1:l, m, n)

Each of the four "mother posts" has a curved fork at the top supporting two large beams termed *atbat* (1:l) which are parallel to the center-line of the house. Lying above and across them are beams called *kranit* (1:m) which are each the same length and of which there are 8, 12, 16, or 24, depending upon house size. The rafters, *nesa'* (1:n), lie above and across these, parallel to the *atbat,* and there are usually the same number of them as of the *kranit.* These rafters project over part of the outer section and their front ends may be decorated. The *atbat* and *kranit* beams are located over the inner section and are not decorated. A ceiling, usually split bamboo, rests on the rafters and also forms the attic floor. The attic *(po'af)* is used for storing unpounded maize and rice and also contains an altar stone termed *mekuf* (to press down; retain). (This stone is placed at the center of a field during agricultural ritual.) Entrance to the attic is forbidden to anyone who is not an agnate of the householder. Atoni say that the presence of another person in the attic "makes the soul of the rice and maize flee." The elder male and female in the household usually manage it, sometimes with the help of a son, but daughters rarely go there.

hun (grass): the roof (1:c)

The thatched roof, called simply "grass," is conical in appearance and extends almost to the ground. Seen from the outside, the Atoni house appears to be one great roof.[4] From the inside, however, the substructure of the roof is rectangular. It consists of small spars *(suaf)* all around and four main corner spars called "horse spars" *(suaf bidjaekase)* (3:d). The small spars are divided in two groups: *suaf susuf,* in the front and back (3:g^1, g^2), and *suaf benaf,* on the right and left (3:f^1, f^2). These two groups are subdivided into *susun*

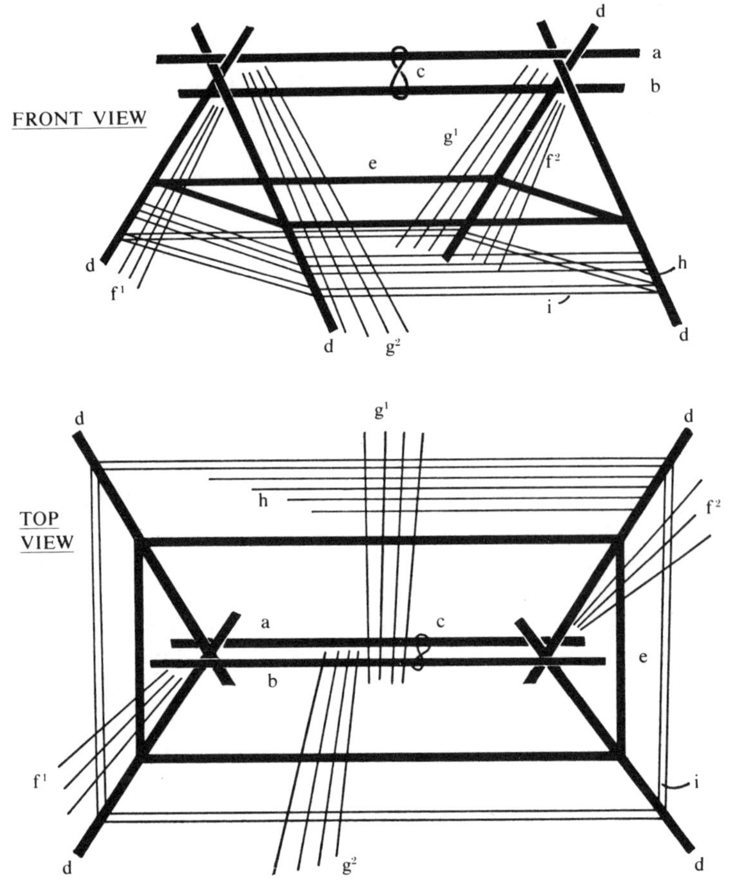

Fig. 3. The roof

key:

a	*fuf manas*	sun cranium	f^2	*benaf koitne*	outside *benaf*
b	*fuf ai*	fire cranium	g^1	*susuf pin*	lower *susuf*
c	*mausak (maus)*	a type of liana (things)	g^2	*susuf faof*	upper *susuf*
d	*suaf bidjae-kase*	horse spar pillow	h	*tak pani*	cross-spars
			i	*tnat oe*	hold water
e	*aka'nunu*	centre-point			
f^1	*benaf mat*	*benaf*			

pin (lower susuf) and *susun faof* (upper *susuf*), *benan mat* (centre-point *benaf*) and *benan koitne* (outside *benaf*). The *benaf*, which are placed first, should have a somewhat greater diameter than the *susuf*. I return later to the meaning of these two words.

All of the roof spars converge along the top between two horizontal beams, the *susuf* spars forming a cross between them. These beams are termed *fuf manas* (sun cranium) and *fuf ai* (fire cranium) (3:a,b). The former is larger and above, and its ends show after the summit thatch decoration is tied. These beams are tied at the middle by a rope termed *mausak* (a type of liana), though the rope need not

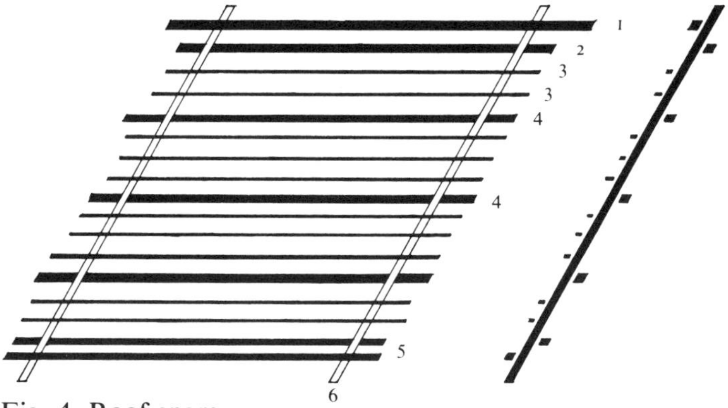

Fig. 4. Roof spars

key:

1	*fuf manas*	4	*aka'nunu*
2	*fuf ai*	5	*tnat oe*
3	*tak pani*	6	*suaf*

be made of *mausak* (3:c). One old specialist on the Amarasi house told me, "These two beams guard the sun *(manas)* and guard the fire." When *manas* is used for "sun," it refers specifically to the "heat of the sun."[5]

At the periphery of the roof are two parallel and tied cross-spars termed *tnat oe* (hold water) (3:i) which encase the roof spars *(suaf)* and encircle the roof. Further up are one or more larger cross-spars termed *aka'nunu* (pillow) (3:e), and up and down the roof are smaller cross-spars termed *tak pani* (3:h) to which bundles of thatch are tied.[6] The reader will note that the spars running between the "sun cranium" and "fire cranium," the "pillows" and the *tak pani*, and the "hold water" cross-spars reproduce a fence form (fig. 4), to which I return later.

Having given ethnographic detail, I now consider the structure of the Amarasi house and its symbolism in greater depth.

The Division of Space

A striking aspect of Atoni house structure is the cross pattern. The use of the number four, expressing unity, and regularly intersecting lines characterize this pattern, which consists of the following elements:

1. The four points of the Atoni compass (5: 1–4)
2. The four corner "chicken posts" (5: 5–8)
3. The four emphasized points of "order": water jar, sleeping platform, door, and great platform (5: 9–12)
4. The four "mother posts" (5: 13–16)
5. The central hearth (5: 17)

The configuration of these elements can be represented in two ways, both of which continually recur in Atoni symbolism, ritual usages, and conceptualizations of the social and political order: *(a)* concentric circles, and *(b)* intersecting and concentrically arranged crosses in the form + and ×. Figures 5 & 6 illustrate these patterns. In figure 5, each circle represents a step nearer the centre of the house. Figure 6 illustrates the way in which the + and × alternate with each circle. The regularity in this pattern might be fortuitous, but the ethnographic details argue the contrary. These figures represent a model of the house.[7]

A second striking aspect of Atoni house structure is the division of wholes into halves and the intersection of these divisions with units which are halves of greater wholes. The complete house under the roof, the *ume nanan* or "house center," is divided in two parts in opposition to the yard termed *mone* (male; outside), and both in turn are on an elevated area in opposition to a further "outside" *(kotin)*.[8] The first division within the house creates right and left sides of the inner and outer sections; the second divides the house back and front into inner and outer sections. The inner section is divided, by the arrangement of its fixed elements and their symbolic associations, into "male" and "female" (or "right" and "left") halves in opposition to the empty outer section. (When guests come to the outer section, however, they may be seated right and left in

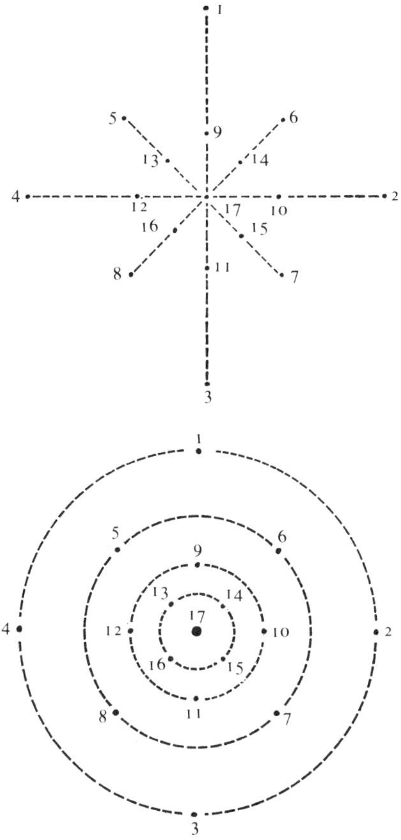

Fig. 5. Orientation and spatial order of house

key:

1–4 compass points

5–8 corner "chicken posts"

9–12 water jar, sleeping platform, door, great platform

13–16 mother posts

17 hearth

terms of seniority.) The inner and outer sections (*nanan* and *si'u*) form halves in opposition to the undivided attic *(po'af)* which covers both.

This type of division is conceived by Atoni to apply to the cosmos. Earth (*pah pinan,* lower land *or* land base) is divided into the "dry land" *(pah meto)* and the "sea" *(tasi)* in opposition to the

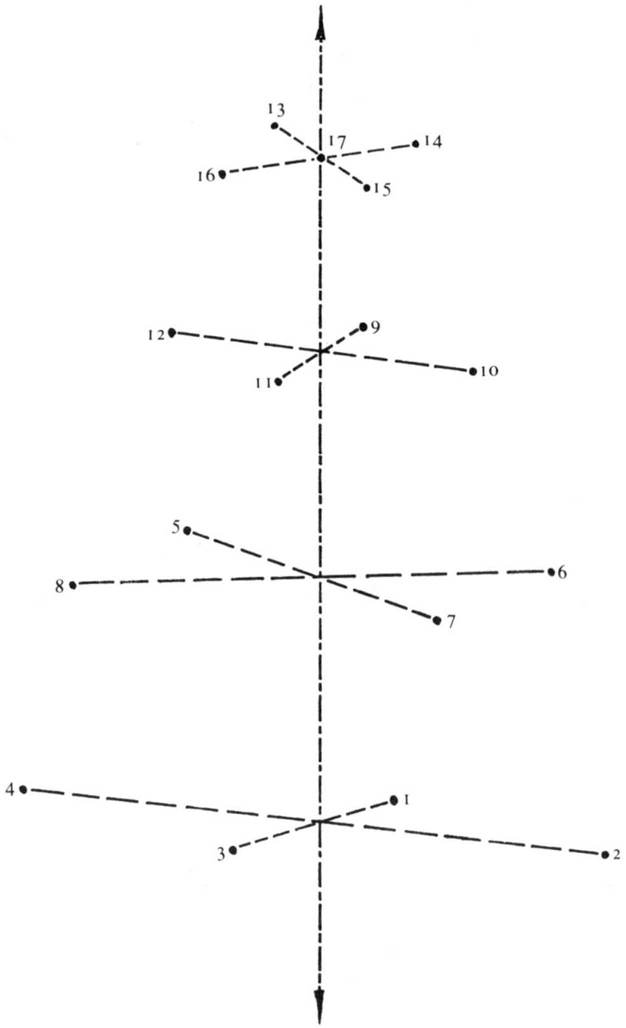

Fig. 6. Alternation of spatial pattern in house

"sky" *(neno)* which is conceived as a dome over them. (The Atoni call themselves *Atoin Pah Meto,* People of the Dry Land. Their origin is believed to have been originally from the sky; they have myths of migration over land, but not over the sea with which they eschew contact.) The sea, in turn, is conceived to be in two parts, the "female sea" *(tasi feto)* and the "male sea" *(tasi mone)*. The former is the inner circle of sea near the coast (and bays), appropriate to other associations of "inner" and "female." The latter is the distant circle of sea. Both parts stand opposed to the "dry land." In all of these oppositions—dry land and sea to sky, male sea and female sea to dry land, right and left sides of the "house

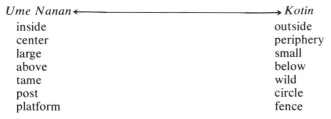

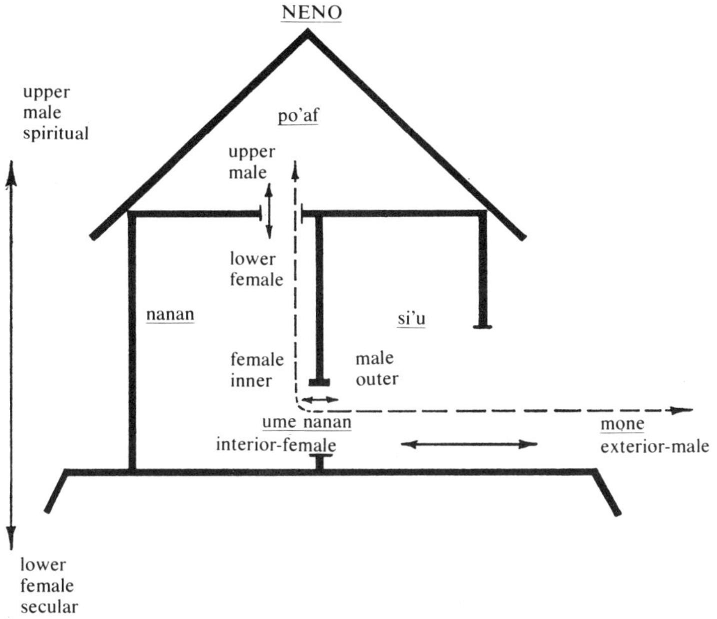

Fig. 7. Parts of the house (side section)

Ume Nanan ⟵	⟶ *Kotin*
inside	outside
center	periphery
large	small
above	below
tame	wild
post	circle
platform	fence

center" to the yard, right and left sides of the inner section to the outer section, and inner and outer sections of the house to the attic—a conceptually subordinate pair is opposed to a superordinate unit.

Atoni believe that all human activity should take place on "dry land." They avoid the sea, which is believed to be inhabited by monsters, crocodiles, and large snakes, and the "way of the deceased" *(ran nitu)* is toward the sea. The dome-shaped sky is under the authority of the Divinity (*Uis Neno,* Lord of the Sky), who in ritual may be referred to as *"Uis Neno aobet, abenit, aneot"* (Lord of the Sky, the dome-shaped, the protecting, the overshadowing) (Middelkoop 1960: 14). (A human prince is termed *uis pah,* lord of the land, and is said to be *naneom, namaf,* "the shadowing one, the shading one.") I noted that the attic is ritually proscribed and access is allowed only to certain persons. Atoni conceive the Divinity also to be isolated from man and approachable only through prayer and sacrifice at designated places (normally marked by a stone and a post), but not otiose. Divinity is concerned with rain, sun, and fertility of the land, and with the formation of the human being, both as creator and preserver, originally and in any birth. It is not fortuitous, or merely practical, I believe, that the attic of a house is devoted only to rice and maize, produce of the fields; that the altar stone for agricultural ritual is kept there; and that entrance is restricted in a ritual idiom. Dome-shaped as it is, it represents *neno* and all that it implies.

Given this point, it is understandable why in some Atoni areas the roof thatch is termed *unu.* This word may be used for "eldest" (e.g., *tataf unuf,* eldest older brother); in Taebenu, the "head mother post" is termed *ni unuf;* and a cognate, *un-unu,* is invariably used by Atoni for the "distant past." This distant past refers to the time, in mythical history, when an original order was fixed (e.g., when political authorities became established; when a place was founded; when certain clans first settled an area; when men obtained certain plants or animals). In this period, the ancestors established rules or customs which guide behavior at the present, and the ancestor spirits *(nitu)* now guard their perpetuation by sanctions on the living. Appropriately, when an individual recounts events which are said by others to have occurred later, and are therefore not an ultimate precedent, they are said to have occurred *tnana',* i.e., in the "inner" (or middle) past, an inferior recent time.[9]

In one sense, therefore, the Atoni house is a model of the cosmos. However, it is more than simply analogous to the universe; it is integrated within it. Prayers are made to the Divinity facing sunrise from the *hau mone* (male tree *or* outside tree), a ritual post set in the yard. Thus the Atoni compass is ordered as I described earlier, with south = right, north = left. The house must not face east-west, say informants, "because that is the way of the sun" or "because the sun must not enter the house." These reasons, or better, symbolic statements express the notion that the house is set in opposition to the sun, sky, or day (all *neno* in Atoni). It is segregated from all three, windowless and dark, and even in daytime its light and heat are generated by the perpetual fire. The door orientation symbolically blocks the "sun's way" *(ran neno),* and the pervasive interior division, right and left, is then made facing the door. The next division, back and front, is made by a line parallel to the sun's way, the partition. After that, the next beams, the *atbat,* are perpendicular to this "way," the *kranit* parallel, and so forth up to the two summit beams, the "fire cranium" and the "sun cranium." The naming of the two summit beams is appropriate: it concerns an opposition of "heats," one of the hearth fire *(ai)* and the other of the sun *(manas).* The two "heats" are symbolically opposed or separated by these beams, just as door orientation blocks the way of the sun. (The reader will remember that one reason for orienting the door southward was "because the sun must not enter the house" and that the hearth stones are oriented toward the back corners and the door "so that the heat may go out.")

The opposition of the house to the sky is illustrated further in the naming of the two linked cross-spars at the roof edge, the *tnat oe* (hold water). These cross-spars do not literally "hold water" but they symbolically keep rain water (for which most prayers to the Divinity are made) from touching the ground by the house. A respectful separation between sky and earth is implied. The association of the roof with a superordinate and supernatural sphere and the connotation of rain as a prestation is also implied in the naming of these "hold water" *(tnat oe)* cross-spars. The word *tnat* is an abbreviation of *atnatas,* "to hold in giving or receiving in the ceremonial context when a formal gift is made," e.g., tribute, bridewealth, or food to a host at a feast. The tying of thatch and its trimming along these spars is the final step in house-building. The trimming (*atref,* to cut) is a ritual act done by a representative of the wife-giving affines and is said to make the house "cool" *(mainikin),*[10] again a ritual counteracting the sun's heat. (Appropriately, it is considered physically dangerous for men to work on a house during the rain.)[11] Thus, heat and water from the "sky" *(neno)* are controlled ritually, and domestic heat and water (the hearth and fixed water jar) become elements of "order" inside the house. Interestingly, the latter elements become associated with the symbolically subordinate (left and back) parts of the house.

The idea of a gift, or ritual tie, introduces another important point in Atoni house symbolism, the linking of opposed areas and the stress on mediation. In a house the posts termed *ni* link the lower section with the attic, and the "head mother post" is the main place of ritual according to informants "because it is by the entrance to the attic." Forked posts, in the *ni* form and with a flat stone *(fatu)* or a ring of stones *(baki)* at the base, are used by Atoni in all prayer and sacrifice, i.e., in communication with the supernatural. Where such posts are used outside the house, they are termed *hau,* wood *or* tree, an example being the *hau mone* in the yard.

The notion of a link between opposed spheres is represented by the rope termed *mausak,* or *maus* for short, which ties together the "sun cranium" and "fire cranium" beams at the roof summit (3:c), whose symbolic opposition I noted earlier. This rope is not essential structurally, but it serves an important symbolic function. *Maus* has two meanings in Atoni: "a type of liana" and "things." In ceremony, *maus* may refer to tribute, bridewealth, or an inheritance,[12] all of which are "things" which unite in political, affinal, or descent contexts. Descent group ritual is termed *nono,* also a type of liana. Binding together, represented by a liana, is appropriate to house symbolism where the mode of opposition is complementarity not separation. The association of gift, "things," a liana, and a binding in this term *maus*—with its use at the important summit of the house—represents a vivid Atoni symbol of the "total prestation," as Mauss (1954: 3) termed it.

Right and Left, Male and Female

I shall now consider further the dyadic categories symbolized by "right-left" *(ne'u-ali')* and "male-female" *(mone-feto),* in relation to the house and the social order.

Within the Atoni house, male activities and symbols are regularly associated with the right side generally, the outer section, the right side of the inner section, and the attic; female activities and symbols are associated with the inner section (or back) and, particularly, the left side of the inner section. These associations are ubiquitous in Atoni symbolism and are coordinate with superordination and subordination respectively. Limited space allows mention of only a few examples.

The door, as I said, is conceptually oriented "right" (or "south") *(ne'u)* and men predominate in the outer section *(si'u)*. They receive male guests and eat there, whereas women remain in the inner section. Teenage boys sleep there, but girls do not. This pattern is analogous to that of the traditional Atoni princedom where a sacral lord called the *atupas* (sleeping one) remained at the center of the princedom in a palace area called *ba'af* (root). Though the sacral lord was always a man, he was called *feto* (female). As one informant said, "The sacral lord, the sleeping one, was female. He only knew how to sleep and eat." The rest of the princedom was divided in four "great quarters" *(suku naek)* at the cardinal points, and each was headed by a secular lord termed *monef-atonif* (male-man).[13] The secular lords were responsible for warfare, tribute to the sacral lord, adjudication, and public order and they had warrior chiefs who guarded the gate and the way of the princedom, controlling the movement of persons and tribute. The four secular lords were ordered by seniority in a pattern analogous to the color symbolism mentioned earlier, i.e., from east clockwise to north.

In village wars, men went outside the hamlets, whereas women remained behind to play drums and gongs and conduct ritual. In wars of the princedom as a whole, the symbolically "female" sacral lord remained at the center to conduct ceremonies. It should be noted that the secular lords (the "male-men" are on the periphery but within the circle of the princedom. Similarly, the symbolically male area in a house—the *si'u*—is outer, but within the circle of the "chicken posts" and under the roof. In neither case are the males "outside" *(kotin)*, which is another sphere entirely.

Within the inner section, there is a division right and left which is perpendicular to the *si'u-nanan* division. The door swings toward the left, thus favoring entrance to the right, a pattern also consistent with the symbolism of the *si'u* section and which honors a guest with superordinate (i.e., "right" or "male") status. The right side of the inner section contains the "great platform" where males, elders, and wife-giving affines are seated, all with superordinate status. The main provisions and tools of the household are also kept there, including the pounded corn and rice for meals. Thus the right side of the inner section, like the attic, is devoted to food supplies for which men are primarily responsible; the left side is devoted to their preparation, for which women are responsible. (In both collection and preparation of food in certain contexts, both sexes may play a part. When they do, either their activities or the items handled are classified as appropriately "male" or "female." For example: in the fields women may weed or gather crops by hand, but men must handle the knife; at ritual meals, women cook rice with chicken broth while men cook beef, buffalo, or pork at separate hearths.)

On the left and/or inner section are the hearth, fixed water jar, and "sleeping platform." These elements are permanent aspects of *atoran,* order, stressed by informants. Within the Atoni princedom, the sacral lord called *atupas* (sleeping one), who was considered "female" and who occupied the "inside" or "center" *(nanan)* position in a palace area called the "root," is a symbolic correlate of the woman and her position in the house, on whose side (the left) is located the hearth and "sleeping platform." Informants said of the sacral lord, "He only knows how to sleep and eat," and these are the two secular activities of the left side or back of any Atoni house. The door *(eno)* is opposed to these points, at the front in the male section. Appropriately, in the princedom the secular lords (the "male-men") were responsible for guarding the "door" (or gateway) to the princedom.

This complementary symbolism—of which "right" and "left," "male" and "female" are expressions—is clearly exemplified in the naming of the roof spars and the house posts. The uppermost roof beam, the "sun cranium," is opposed to the "fire cranium" below it; furthermore, it is opposed to the "hold water" cross-spars at the outer extremity of the roof. Here, in symbolic terms, "fire" and "water" stand together, below, in opposition to "sun," as the hearth and water jar stand together permanently in the left and back side of the inner section, and fire is more central than water in both cases.

The roof spars are also opposed. I mentioned earlier that the roof spars, the *susuf-benaf,* are divided respectively as "upper *susuf*" and "lower *susuf,*" "center-point *benaf*" and "outside *benaf,*" the former in each case being slightly larger. The terms *benaf* and *susuf* are cognate, I believe, with *benas,* the machete which only men may use, and *susu,* milk, which women both handle and provide.[14] This interpretation is consistent with the symbolic pattern in the betel-nut basket *(oko)* which women make and carry: the upper part is called *suin* and the lower part *aina*. The former word is *suni* (in common Atoni metathesis), the "head-hunting sword" carried by men; the latter word, "mother."

The main roof spars, the "horse spars," rest on the "chicken posts." Though horses and chickens play little part in Atoni ritual, they are associated with males and females respectively in several contexts. Only men tend horses (though both sexes may ride), and warriors were formerly trained to manage them and to hunt and fight from them. (Also, a horse accompanies the corpse of a prince to the grave and subsequently is given to the chief representative of the wife-giving affines.) Women care for chickens and prepare the chicken broth served with rice at feasts, while men cook the other meat. This symbolic use of large "horses" over small "chickens" is appropriate to the general superordinate characterization of the roof and attic over the lower part of the house.

The posts which surround the inner section, which are smaller, shorter, and more numerous than the four main posts, are opposed to them in the same dyadic idiom. In Amarasi, the "mother post" : "chicken post" :: a large female animal : small animal. In another area, Taebenu, the posts are termed *ni inaf* (mother post) and *ni ana* (child post), the two terms being applicable to animals or humans. Since the main posts are characterized in a "female" idiom, the outer posts are characterized in a similar, but lesser, idiom.[15]

A similar pattern is found in the opposition of the main posts and roof to the jambs and lintel of the doorway, each representing a supported dome or arch. (In Insana, there are only two main roof spars, rather than four as here, thus stressing the arch idiom in the roof more clearly.) These two structures are opposed as inside/outside, greater/lesser, male/female, and sun/moon in their size and symbols. I have already discussed "male" associations of the roof, a dome-shaped symbol of the "sky" or "sun," *neno*. The lintel *(eben)* is related in name and arch form to the woman's comb *(ebe)* which is made of silver and shaped like a half-moon. This same type of opposition was found by Middlekoop (1960: 23) applied to two ritual posts *(hau mone)* in one village: they were termed "tall Divinity" and "short Divinity," and villagers said they were like the sun and the moon, or, alternatively, the moon and morning star. The opposition of gold and silver, sun and moon, is common for Atoni, and may be used also for the sacral lord and the secular lords respectively in contexts where the superordination of the former is expressed.[16] It would be inconsistent within Atoni symbolism to give either the outer posts of the house or the door jambs and lintel conceptually equal size to the main posts and beams or a symbolically "male" characterization.

Inside and Outside

In Atoni, *nanan* may mean either "inner" or "center." In both meanings, "female" symbolism is used in the house; but in different contexts the question of superordination or subordination may vary. I have shown how inner and outer parts of the house or the princedom are opposed with "female" and "male" symbols and subordinate and superordinate characterization respectively. However, I have noted also the concentric pattern in which the larger and higher elements are found at the center of the house, the smaller on the periphery, and I have said that the further into the house one moves, the greater the rights and obligations. This apparent inconsistency can be understood, I believe, by viewing other Atoni social categorizations and the contexts in which superordination is expressed.

Agnates of a householder have full rights in the house, which is believed to be guarded by ancestor spirits and which contains sacred objects used in the descent group ritual termed *nono,* a type of liana. The households of a lineage form a community of worship, and the descent group may be referred to as *nono*. Atoni said that the symbol implies that ritual practices encircle (or perhaps ensnare) the members of a descent group as a liana does a tree. Descent group membership is referred to as *su' nono* (carry the descent group ritual on the head), with the implication that it is both a shelter and a burden. Birth ritual is said to *ansae noño* (elevate the *nono*), and an equivalent ritual is held for a newly married wife so that she may enter the inner section of her husband's parents' house and the couple may have a house consecrated for themselves.

All Atoni have continuing obligations toward their father's lineage, the *nono mnuke* (young *nono*), and their mother's lineage, the *nono mnasi* (old *nono*), and a boy should marry a girl from the latter. Marriage with a cross-cousin, whom a boy calls *fe ranan* (wife way), is termed *matsau ume nanan* (marriage within the house), the affinal alliance of the lineages of a mother and father having placed the groups conceptually within a house. The house thus symbolizes the balanced interests of agnation and affinity. The wife-giving affines are superordinate in daily and ceremonial affairs, which their *nono* designation as "old" denotes. Their representative, usually the mother's brother, is termed *atoni-amaf* (man-father), both terms expressing superordination and their conjunction emphasizing it.[17]

Though the norm and idiom of Atoni descent is patrilineal, in fact many people gain their lineage affiliation through their mother. They are then said to *su' nono mnasi* (carry the old *nono* on the head). In doing so, however, they hold subordinate status in the lineage, their position having the qualities of a wife-taking affine vis-à-vis their "agnates" in that lineage. Thus most lineages are said to have a "male house" *(uem mone)* and "female house" *(uem feto),* i.e., people who gain membership through the father or the mother.[18]

Any local lineage is considered the center of the social world and, as I said, its members have greater rights at the center of the house. In expressing this lineage-centric view, Atoni refer to either the lineage or household group as the *uem tuan* (house master) and to its affines as "male child" *(an mone)* and "female child" *(an feto),* the former wife-givers and the latter wife-takers. The use of "male" and "female" here indicates both the child whose marriage formed the affinal tie and the symbolic character of the wife-givers as superordinate, wife-takers subordinate. When affines are invited to any feast by the "house masters," they are termed collectively the *ranan* (way), i.e., the way to marriages. The reference to affines as either "child" or "way" indicates their subordination to the "house masters." At a feast, all other guests—either affines of affines or other people—are termed collectively *kotin* (outside), i.e., outside affinity or agnation.

Respect must be shown to all guests at a feast, and they are seated in special places. The wife-givers are seated in the *si'u* section and served by the householders. If the wife-takers are received there too, they are seated on the left, the wife-givers on the right. Sometimes, at small gatherings, wife-givers are received in the inner section and seated on the "great platform" at the right. The wife-takers are then seated in the outer section. All other guests, those classified as *kotin* (outside), are seated at temporary platforms outside the house. Thus the agnates of the household and their affines are seated inside under the roof, and it is their marriages which are said to be "marriage within the house."

This seating pattern expresses covertly the importance, unity, and closeness of those nearer the "house center." However, respect to guests is mandatory, and the hosts must strive to reverse this primacy of the "house center" by stressing the *nanan*, as subordinate "inner" opposed to outer rather than superordinate "center" opposed to periphery. The hosts must abase themselves, remain at the left or in bowed positions, and serve others. They claim that their food and gifts are inadequate in quantity and quality—and the guests may agree and demand more—though all know that the hosts are exhausting themselves to provide their best. The claims about the poor food are particularly important in this reversal, since feeding is pre-eminently an obligation of a superior to an inferior. Significantly, the wife-givers may not be called "male child" on these occasions; they must be called *atoni-amaf* (man-father). The "male" symbolic character of the "great platform" and outer section ensures that this reversal will be complete.

This leads to the next related point. The "inner" section is the ritual center and the "head mother post" is located on the inner left. Given the symbolic connotations of "left" and "female," this would seem to associate the ritual (or supernatural) with a subordinate sphere. The same would appear true in the princedom where the sacral lord had the same associations: the four secular lords, "male-men" in the outer area (which might be called the *si'u* of the princedom), were predominant in daily affairs. They even had the authority to beat the sacral lord and his guardians if they left the palace area without an escort and the permission of the secular lords. The association of ritual or supernatural concerns with a subordinate sphere is not, however, the case; spiritual matters are considered superior to secular ones. When spiritual matters are at hand, the idea of *nanan* as "center" is expressed, and the symbolically "female" becomes pivotal in the relation of Man to Divinity.

The presence of the "head mother post" on the left illustrates this fact within the house. As "head" it is foremost; the route to the attic (which has symbolic superordination) and to the supernatural, being the place for prayer and certain sacred heirlooms. This post may not be adorned or decorated. Only the "chicken posts" and the front ends of the *nesa'* rafters in the outer section are decorated. Thus, the nearer the "center," the greater the purity, a symbolic pattern identical to that in great Indian monuments of Southeast Asia such as the Borobudur. It is the left side of the house which is the way to the supernatural for Atoni men who would pray to Divinity or their agnatic ancestors. The same was true for the secular lords, the "male-men" in a princedom, who would pray for fertility or rain for their land crops. They had to do so through the sacral lord, the symbolically female "sleeping one" at the center of the territory.

This symbolically pivotal position of females, or the "female" category, is not limited among Atoni to ritual. The mother *(ainaf)* or sister *(fetof)*, like the wife *(fe)*, in a household or lineage is socially pivotal as mediator to the two types of affines, the groupings called "way." As "mother," she is mediator to her natal patrilineage which stands superordinate to that of her husband and from which her son should obtain his wife. Furthermore, it is this wife-giving group —appropriate to their superordination—which is responsible for major ritual elements in the life-cycle of their wife-takers. Without their service, the placenta cannot be cut from a newborn child and removed from the house; a bride and rights to her offspring cannot be secured to perpetuate the lineage; the roof cannot be placed on a house, its construction and ritual "cooling" being the duty of the wife-givers; and the soul of the deceased cannot be sent on its way in death-ritual to join its ancestors.

Given the points and symbols I have sketched, it is not surprising that the bridewealth given to the wife-givers consists of live animals *(muit)* and paddy *(ane)* or pounded rice *(mnes)*, while the counter-presentation from the wife-givers consists of cooked meat *(sisi)*, cooked rice *(maka')*, and woven cloth *(tais)*. The former items within the house are associated with the "great platform" and attic, the latter with the left side of the inner section and woman's hand. The former are raw, the latter cooked; the former derive directly from the fertility of the land (Divinity's concern), the latter are worked by human hands; the former are alive when given, the latter dead. These associations in the prestations are made explicitly by Atoni, and the symbolic character of the gift always suits the status of the group to which it is given. Thus the link between Man and Divinity (or ancestors) through the symbolically "female" side of the house, and the type of gift given—live animal sacrifice and the sprinkling of pounded rice *(mnes)* during prayer—is analogous to the link between a lineage and its wife-giving affines through the mediation of the woman received in marriage. As mediator at feasts, she must be referred to by her natal clan name (though she has been initiated to her husband's *nono* ritual) and she must go out to escort her natal agnates as they arrive.

In referring to females as pivotal, I am translating the Atoni idea expressed in the continual association of the *nanan,* or center, of the house and the princedom with female elements and symbols. In secular concerns, females are jurally subordinate, as the *nanan-si'u* usages or the secular organization of the princedom illustrate. Like a sacral lord, a woman in a household may be ordered about or beaten by men, her husband and brothers. In ritual, however, the reverse is true. In war dances, the main Atoni dance, women stand still and beat drums and gongs while men circulate and brandish swords, imitating the flying of a cockatoo, the head of which decorates the sword handle. Furthermore, Atoni consider women to be more fixed generally than men, more trustworthy and more stable in personality. Women control the purse-strings, and children in a home (particularly a broken home) gravitate toward the mother. Children commonly follow a divorced mother, in time if not immediately, even though the children remain agnates of their *genitor* or *pater,* and the completion of a stage in bridewealth transfers jural rights over a child from the mother's patrilineage to the father's.

This pivotal position of females is illustrated in the naming of the *harak manba'at* (agreement platform) (2:h) which is used by women to serve guests at the common meal concluding every ritual. *Manba'an* means "to agree; to put things in order by mutual agreement; the give and take needed in agreement on division of labor when some common activity such as a feast is planned." It is appropriate, given the Atoni view of the female position, that women are associated with such an activity in the naming of this platform which is for women's use in the house. Correlatively, women are forbidden the knife, and formerly they remained in the village to conduct ceremonial dancing and cooking for the feast to welcome back the warriors. (I have mentioned the importance of tying in ritual, with cutting its opposite.) Middelkoop mentions that "the ritual cooking is called dancing *(anbilu am nasbo)*" (1960: 23), i.e., circle dancing, and the one type of song and dance which does not express unity, the *ne si'u* (elbow quatrain)—a reproach against people in a hamlet who have misbehaved, in which they are metaphorically "elbowed out"—is linked in name with the outer section of the house where men predominate.

Having discussed dyadic symbolism and the pivotal position of the "center," I wish to mention two other usages which recur in

Atoni ritual and conceptualizations of their social and political order, the door *(eno)* and the way *(ranan)*. Related to this is the issue of the cross.

The traditional Atoni princedom had four "doorways" *(eno-ranan)* at the outer periphery and also between the outer and inner circles (the "great quarter" of the secular lords and the "root" area of the sacral lord respectively). At both points officials from assigned lineages guarded the doorway, and passage was attended by elaborate protocol (cf. the amusing description by Forbes 1885: 442). The officials who guarded the outer gates were warriors termed *meo naek;* those who guarded the gates between the sacral lord's center and each "great quarter" were called *atoin mnasi, bife mnasi* (old man, old woman). In the warrior costume, animal and plant symbols are frequent, and these warriors were called *meo naek* (great cat). The other gate guardians, the "old man, old woman," were the only officials whose title combined a male and female term. Thus the two types of gate guardians were symbolically either therianthropic or hermaphroditic, appropriate to their positions between opposed areas, the former between the circle of the princedom and the wilds, the latter between conceptually "male" and "female" areas.

In Atoni usage, an "open door" denotes peace and good relations; a "closed door," enmity. Marriage is initiated by gifts said to "open the door." As long as the door is open, gifts are exchanged between the prospective parents-in-law and a couple may conduct courtship. This culminates in marriage, after which the groom serves for a time in the house of his bride before they remove to his own area and their own house. A break in marriage negotiations is said to "close the door"; gifts no longer move and the door of the girl's house is literally closed to the boy. Any continuation of the affair must be done *kotin* (outside), i.e., in the forest or orchards.

Alliance (affinal or political), the movement of gifts, and mutual visits are inseparable, as are the reception of guests in a house, their seating at designated places, and the passing of betel. "Closing the door" in any social or political situation denotes disruption, epitomized in the Atoni word *lasi* (enmity; legal dispute; fight; conflict). Death, the great divide, is termed either *lasi nitu* (enmity of the ancestors) or *lasi neno* (enmity of the sky), the two supernatural spheres. Avoidance of *lasi,* enmity, and the maintenance of a "way" are important concerns for Atoni in all contexts. The reader will remember the earlier point about the *tnat oe* (hold water) cross-spars (3:i), the word *atnatas* meaning "to hold in giving or receiving a gift." This term *atnatas* is also used for spars at each end of a rack on which coffins are carried; the rack (with its four assigned carriers at each corner, two wife-giving affines in front and two agnates behind) is built like a platform *(harak)*. The leading of the corpse to the grave by the wife-givers is a prestation from the living to the supernatural which serves to heal this "enmity of the sky" or "enmity of the ancestors." The deceased is still considered to be "alive" *(ahoni)*, appropriate to other live prestations to a superordinate noted earlier. He is considered "dead" *(mates)* only after a ritual following burial.

At its broadest level, "order" *(atoran)* in the Atoni house structure expresses two simple, but pervasive, concerns—unity and difference—and their continual interpretation. The central structure, the "mother posts" and the web of beams they support, is identical to a platform, and the names for parts of a platform recur in its various uses. This platform structure contrasts with the fence form of the outer wall and roof. The repetition of these two forms—the only two the Atoni use in building—symbolizes, I believe, the concerns which underlie any system of classification: unity and difference. The platform is invariably used to express status difference, whether in seating elders over younger people, nobles over commoners, rulers over headmen, guests over hosts, or rice and meat over corn. The fence form, on the other hand, encircles spheres which possess some kind of unity and which Atoni call *ain* (tame *or* domesticated) in contrast to those outside called *fui* (wild). It is thus, for example, that civil wars within a princedom are with a *mus ain* (tame enemy) while wars with another princedom are with a *mus fui* (wild enemy). The wall and roof, in the fence form, mark the unity of a house and the social groups it comprises, and the house, viewed from without, is an almost solid circle and dome with no windows and one small entrance. Viewed from within, however, the house is a constant web of intersecting sections and beams, all symbolized as complementary, appropriate to the Atoni view of any structured social or political grouping in which the premise of inequality is pervasive.

The patterns of concentricity and intersection in the "order" of the house continually concern what spheres, or groupings, are to be included or excluded. The circle (or quadrangle) and the cross are ubiquitous in Atoni material culture, I believe, as symbols of this basic concern, and decoration (like house-building) follows repeated patterns. It is not without reason that these patterns mainly decorate cloths, door frames, outer house posts, betel and lime containers, and baskets and mats used on ceremonial occasions, all of which are used in gifts, or the point of meeting, between groups. Similarly, the figures representing men and animals are normally composites of quadrangles or circles and crosses. It is significant, perhaps, that often one cannot tell whether a pattern of crosses or a pattern of quadrangles is intended; the two fuse in expressing unity and opposition, or unity and difference.

These points explain, perhaps, why the resolution of conflict in Atoni society demands an oath made by drawing a cross on the ground and eating a bit of earth from the point of intersection. The cross marks the transgression; the point of intersection, the resolution. (Many people say that the ceremony should be done at a crossroads, but this is not strictly maintained.) Whether settling disputes over land, possessions, adultery, contract-breaking, or fights, this form of resolution is the same, and transcendental justice is believed to support the oath.

The reader will remember that the *susuf* spars (3:g) of the roof—with a symbolically "female" association—form a cross at the summit between the two "cranium" beams, this cross marking a point of segregation between the heats of the sun and hearth (or sky and earth). The *mausak* rope then links the segregated spheres. I believe (though no Atoni said so) that this usage is related to that of cross patterns in tattoos which old Atoni women have on their hands and faces. The usual explanation of these tattoos is that "they are used to trade for fire in the afterworld," though the just-so character of this explanation is such that Atoni cannot elaborate on it and many find it incomprehensible or ridiculous though they repeat it. I noted earlier the association of women with fire in the house and the symbolic importance of segregating "heats." Again, in regard to the tattoos, the role of women is pivotal in approaching the afterlife, and the item they trade for fire in the transition to death bears cross symbols.[19]

At ceremonies, it is always the young people who must serve, just as in the past it was a young person who took food out to the hut in the fields where head-taking warriors were secluded from women and the village before a purificatory ceremony allowed them to re-enter. Atoni say that a young person was selected, "because they did not yet know the difference between good and bad"; or, to use the Atoni metaphor, "they did not yet know right and left": that is, they were not yet polarized in a society where social relationships and loyalties depend upon membership in one group and alliance or opposition toward others. A common tale of origin for Atoni noble lines vividly illustrates this idiom. The following tale concerns the sacral lord of Insana, but it is also told for other princely lines:

> The sacral lord came alone to Maubesi and was impressed by the fine coconut and areca palms already planted there. He had a very handsome face; but when he came, his face and the rest of his body were blackened with charcoal. He visited a spring and saw a child of the ruling line, Afenpah, fetching water. He asked for a drink, but the child would not give the ruler's water to such an ugly man. Taking a leaf, he washed away the charcoal, revealing his handsomeness. The child then ran home, telling what had happened and describing the handsome face. He said that the man was the true *ane-pena tuan* (paddy-corn master). When the people heard this, they came to see the man and acknowledged him as their sacral lord. He then established himself with his secular lords at Maubesi.

Again, the child is the mediator in the discovery, and the idiom of the tale is transition. Two aspects of "order" in the inner left side of the house, fire and water, are first associated with the man who is blackened by charcoal at the spring. His transformation involves the elimination of these associations, his handsome face marking him as the proper "head," and he can then be acknowledged "master" and be given the tribute of the fields. The young, in these contexts, are like the symbolically therianthropic or hermaphroditic gate guardians of the princedom; they mediate and hence combine (or, correlatively, are free of) the associations of the sides they mediate.[20]

In conclusion, I would like to repeat that the house—with its constituent parts, divisions, form, symbols, and prescriptions concerning order, arrangement, and the behavior of those included and excluded—may be like a model of the cosmos as conceived by a people. The Atoni explicitly express "order" in the house, and much in their social and political order is related in form and naming to it. However, the references extend beyond the social order: space and time, man[21] and animals, man and plants, and man and supernatural are conceived to be ordered by principles related to those expressed in the house, and symbols involving all of these occur in the house.

Hertz said that "dualism marks the entire thought of primitive men."[22] In so saying, he was delimiting a common principle of classification, though his formulation may appear broad and also one-sided in the context of the Atoni house, stressing expressions of difference over those of unity. In using the house to consider ideas of order in Atoni society, I do not mean to imply that the house need necessarily be a basic reference, even for Atoni. The principles of categorization, not their expression, are important. However, as I said, the house is one of the best modes available to a preliterate society to encapsulate ideas, given the absence of literature and the sporadic occurrence and varying degree of participation in ritual. In addition, the house illustrates more than particular principles of classification; it illustrates the value of classification per se.

A comparative sociology of the house might begin with this question of unity and difference and its expression in architectural forms, with particular attention to the relation between the symbolic and social order.[23] The house form, expressing these concerns and exhibiting over the world so many common aspects of structure, is certainly an example of a cultural universal, to which anthropologists have been urged to attend. I hope that this discussion contributes to the effort and also places the houses of the remote Atoni within such great and ancient traditions as Hindu-Buddhist architecture and ancient Asian, Near Eastern, and Latin American cities.

Notes

1. My thanks to the Ford Foundation for support of field research in Indonesian Timor (1959–61). I am grateful to Dr. P. Middelkoop for supplementary information and valuable discussion, and to Dr. Rodney Needham for the stimulus to study the house, though the data and interpretation are my own. Sheila G. Lehman helped by doing the drawings.

2. Atoni (man; people) is short for *Atoin Pah Meto* (People of the Dry Land), their designation for themselves, and the group is usually called the "Timorese" in Dutch sources (e.g., Middelkoop 1950; 1960). For a survey of Indonesian Timor, see Ormeling 1956, which includes an extensive bibliography. A sketch of social and economic life in an Atoni village is found in Cunningham 1967b.

3. There are three types of Atoni house: beehive (or round), rectangular, and rectangular-with-*lopo*. The beehive hut is the classic Atoni form found

in the remoter territories of Amfoan, Mollo, Amanuban, and Amanatun, and in Portuguese Oè-cussi. The rectangular type is found in Amarasi, Fatu Le'u, and the coastal areas near Kupang, and the third type is found in Insana and Beboki. All three types are described and illustrated in Cunningham 1963: 329–442, and will be considered in a subsequent monograph.

4. This is especially true for beehive types not described here, where the roof reaches the ground. In Amarasi, the "feet" are visible from the outside. However, this does not invalidate the points made later on symbolism, since the outer wall and roof are symbolically associated.

5. *manas:* probably cognate with Malay/Indonesian *panas* (hot). The m/p shift is common between Malayo-Polynesian languages.

6. I could find no root meaning for the name *tak pani,* nor could Dr. P. Middelkoop, whom I asked. The same is true for the names *kranit, atbat,* and *nesa'* mentioned earlier.

7. Limited space forbids discussion of similarities between this model and that of the Atoni princedom which the reader may see in Cunningham 1965.

8. In Atoni, *mone* refers to "the outside part within a given area"; *kotin* means "outside any given area."

9. *tnana',* "between" (Dutch *tussen*) (Middelkoop 1950: 383), an abbreviation of *atnanan* which is used in ritual language for "center" (e.g., in the ritual parallelism, in *usan,* in *atnanan:* its center-point, its center-area).

10. As in many languages, "cool" *(mainikin)* denotes "auspicious" or "ritually purified," "warm" *(maputu)* the opposite. This explains, I believe, why women sit over a fire and are bathed in hot water during confinement, a time of ritual danger, the water being said to give them strength. Confinement ends when a woman goes outside the house to bathe in a cool stream.

11. Kruyt (1923: 452–53) reports this for Amarasi, and my informants said the same.

12. I heard *maus* used metaphorically in all of these contexts. Middelkoop (1950: 509) reports its use "generally as possessions, goods" in translation of Malay *harta* which also may imply "inherited goods." Schulte Nordholt (1947: 56, n. 9) reports *maus* for "tribute" though he defines the word as "a palm tree."

13. The first description of this political system appeared in Schulte Nordholt 1947: 54–67. I discussed it further in Cunningham 1965, and Schulte Nordholt 1966 expands upon it greatly. The relationship between dyadic symbolism and social organization on Timor was first stressed in van Wouden 1935, though the house was not discussed.

14. As Middelkoop (1950: 392) notes, "the / *f* / as suffix consonant serves to indicate a general notion."

15. Perhaps it is relevant that the wood prescribed for the *atbat, kranit,* and *nesa'* beams of this central structure is *usapi* (Schleichera oleosa), and that the palace of the symbolically "female" sacral lord was termed the *usapi* palace. Though this wood is sturdy, other woods would serve as

well. The "mother posts" are made of eucalyptus *(hau huel)* which plays little role in Atoni symbolism despite its frequency on the island. The practical value of eucalyptus is that it is large and strong and remains thirty to forty years in the ground without rotting, while the other type rots sooner.

16. The adjacent Tetun people probably share these symbolic associations. Note in Vroklage 1953, vol. 3, photos 161 and 162, the man with a sun tattoed on the right arm, a half-moon on the left.

17. The relevance and significance of this term, a title in the traditional Atoni polity, is described in Cunningham 1965.

18. This form of recruitment and male-female symbolism is described in detail in Cunningham 1967a.

19. Cross and crossroads symbolism marking points of transition is ancient and widespread, and not limited to Atoni culture or houses. European doors still, in most cases, retain the cross, or double cross, pattern. This pattern in Caucasian and Persian rugs is related to the European door. These "rugs" originally were door-hangings (not floor-coverings) as the colored corner tassels at one end survive in many cases to indicate.

20. This issue is discussed in greater detail in Cunningham 1964.

21. Human body symbolism in the house (e.g., "cranium," "head," "pillow" for the head, "elbow," "foot") is common in Amarasi. It is even more detailed in other Atoni house types where "jaw," "top-knot," "arms," and "ear-rings" also appear.

22. 1960: 96.

23. Any comparative study must begin with Lebeuf 1961. See also Needham 1962: 87–90.

Bibliography

Cunningham, C. E.

1963 *People of the Dry Land: a study of the social organization of an Indonesian people.* Doctoral Dissertation. University of Oxford.

1964 Atoni borrowing of children: an aspect of mediation. In *Symposium on new approaches to the study of religion,* edited by M. E. Spiro, Seattle.

1965 Order and change in an Atoni diarchy, *Southwestern Journal of Anthropology* 21: 359–82.

1967a Recruitment to Atoni descent groups, *Anthropological Quarterly* 40: 1–12.

1967b Soba: an Atoni village of West Timor. In *Villages in Indonesia,* edited by Koentjaraningrat. Ithaca.

Forbes, H. O.

1885 *A naturalist's wanderings in the Eastern Archipelago.* London.

Hertz, R.

1960 *Death and the right hand.* London.

Kruyt, A. C.

1923 De Timoreezen. *Bijdragen tot de Taal-, Land- en Volkenkunde van Nederlandsch-Indië* 79: 347–490.

LEBEUF, J. P.
1961 *L'habitation des Fali.* Paris.
MIDDELKOOP, P.
1950 Proeve van een Timorese Grammatica. *Bijdragen tot de Taal-, Land- en Volkenkunde* 106: 375–517.
1960 *Curse-Retribution-Enmity.* Amsterdam.
NEEDHAM, R.
1962 *Structure and Sentiment.* Chicago.
ORMELING, F. J.
1956 *The Timor Problem.* Groningen-Djakarta.
SCHULTE NORDHOLT, H. G.
1947 Nota betreffende de zelfbesturende landschappen Miomaffo, Insana en Beboki. Kefamenanoe (unpublished).
1966 *Het politieke systeem van de Atoni van Timor.* Driebergen.
VROKLAGE, B. A. G.
1952–53 *Ethnographie der Belu in Zentral-Timor.* Leiden.
WOUDEN, F. A. E. VAN
1935 *Sociale Structuurtypen in de Groote Oost.* Leiden. [English edition, translated by Rodney Needham with a preface by G. W. Locher: *Types of Social Structure in Eastern Indonesia.* Koninklijk Instituut voor Taal-, Land- en Volkenkunde Translation Series, no. 11. The Hague: Martinus Nijhoff, 1968.]

A Contribution to the Problem of the Pre-eminence of the Right, Based upon Arabic Evidence

J. Chelhod

12

I

The pitiful fate of the left hand is frequently evoked, at times with a certain lyricism. Considered as weak and incapable, it is condemned to a kind of confinement. By contrast, the right hand is strong and able; attention is lavished upon it and all privileges are accorded it. It is the sovereign; the other is its vassal; it acts, expands, exerts itself; the other assists it passively and wastes away through inaction. The supremacy of the one contributes to the inferiority of the other and vice versa. This undeniable superiority, a fact perhaps contested by right, is also recognized for all the parts of the body which possess the fortunate hand; it even extends to all the beings and things which are assigned a place on the same side. But as it focuses essentially on one member, we infer from the pre-eminence of the right hand,[1] somewhat prematurely, the pre-eminence of the right, establishing in this way a causal connection between a particular organic aptitude and the hierarchization of space. Contrarily, there is the possibility that it is precisely the polarization of space that has somehow brought about corporeal asymmetry.

It is well known that, in many cultures, the right enjoys a favored position: the good thief was to the right of Christ; the place of honor is to the right of the master of the house. Language gives evidence of this superiority: an able man is said to be dextrous; in the opposite case he is maladroit or gauche in manners.

"Contribution au problème de la prééminence de la droite, d'après le témoignage arabe," *Anthropos* 59 (1964): 529–45. Reprinted with the permission of the editors of *Anthropos*. Translated by James J. Fox.

Among the Arabs and in Islam, this marked preference for the right gives rise to all kinds of beliefs, customs, and injunctions. The Black Stone, that pearl of paradise sent by God to serve as the cornerstone of his sacred dwelling is, Muhammad is reputed to have said, "the right [hand] of Allah upon the earth."[2] The auguries drawn from the movement of birds are good or bad depending upon whether the flight is directed toward the right or toward the left. In the Koran, the elect are on the right of the Lord and the damned on his left (Koran 56: 9, 27, 41, 91; 15: 18 ff). On the day of judgment, the condemned will say to those who have led them into error, "Truly, you should come to us from the right side,"[3] that is, from the auspicious and beneficent side by which friends approach. In ancient Arab belief, prophets and diviners are inspired by their familiars. But whereas the former hear the word of their invisible companions at their right ear and are disposed to wear white, the latter are approached from the left side and are required to wear black.[4] According to Moslem tradition, God struck Adam's back and drew forth from him all his progeny. The men predestined for heaven came forth from the right side in the form of pearl-like white grain; those doomed to hell came forth from the left side, in the form of charcoal-like black grain.[5] Tabari tells us that Allah has nothing left-handed about him, since both his hands are right hands.[6] Tahir ibn al-Ḥusayn was nicknamed *dhul-yaminayn,* that is, the man of two right hands.[7] One must neither eat nor drink with the left hand, says a *hadîṭh,* for these are Satan's manners.[8] But one spits to the left[9] and holds the genitals with the left hand.[10] When a Moslem goes to the mosque, the theologian Ibn al-Hajj instructs us, he will leave his home and set forth with his right foot; he must go out with his left foot forward when he has to relieve himself.[11] On his arrival at Mecca, the pilgrim who reaches the Great Mosque enters with his right foot.[12]

Arabic also attests to the favored position of the right. *Yamîne* derives from the verb *yamana,* which includes the ideas of prosperity, of fortune, and of blessing. To take an oath, the right hand is used; hence the linguistic confusion: oath and right, both words are designated by the same term, *yamîne.* By contrast, the left, *šimâl,* is the harbinger of misfortune and the left hand is the bearer of ill omen.[13] The verb *ša'ama,* "to be inauspicious," used in the sixth form, *tašâ'ama,* signifies both "to receive a bad augury" and "to place on the left." Finally a left-handed person is called *'a'sar* from the verb *'asara* which means "to render difficult, arduous, troublesome, irresolvable." [14]

It is a fact of some importance that the word *yasâr* signifies both left and prosperity. Similarly, the term *maysarat,*[15] which designates the left side or the left flank of an army, is taken in the Koran to mean "ease": "If your debtor be in difficulty, *'usrat,* interpose a respite until he be at his ease, *maysarat*" (2: 280). Finally, *yusra,* left, is opposed to *yumna,* right; [16] but the Koran interprets these terms in an entirely different way, since it gives to *yusra* the meaning of "supreme ease" (87: 8; 92: 7) and opposes it to *'usra* (92: 10) "supreme difficulty." This also conforms with the etymological meaning of the roots, *'asr* and *ysr.*[17] Since the people doomed to *'usra* are misers filled with self-conceit, who regard the reward in the hereafter [18] as an illusion, it would be proper to place them with those of the *maš'amat* or of the left who reject the preaching of the Koran.[19] By contrast, *yusra,* where those who are generous and believe in the divine word are destined to go, would be situated on the right, in the *maymanat.*[20] But if *'usra* conforms with what we know of the left and the difficulties which it represents, then *yusra,* which denotes linguistically the same evil side of space, is here associated with the notions of prosperity and of well-being. The same is true of the words, *yasâr, maysarat* and *yusrat* which denote the left, but which are etymologically associated with ease and comfort. We are, therefore, evidently confronted with ambivalent terms which juxtapose collective representations of opposite meaning. The left, among the Arabs—and in other cultures as well—gives evidence of a certain instability,[21] in regard to its underlying mystic significance, in contrast to the right, which is not subject to similar variations. The vexing difficulty, it seems, is to find a satisfactory solution to this problem which is not unique to the Arab world. Ought we to direct our investigations to the realm of magic, recalling that the sacred, the *ḥarâm,* designates strictly the forbidden and that the reason for this prohibition can be sanctity as well as impurity, the religious as well as the magical? [22] If we recollect at the same time that an inversion of values is common in sorcery,[23] then *yasâr* would be the side of the body associated with the impure sacred. Because of this, it would enjoy greater effectiveness. We put forward this labored explanation with considerable hesitation and in its place prefer another: The different uses of the root, *ysr,* for designating the left, may be regarded as simple euphemisms involving a superstitious desire for a good omen. This is why the Arabs customarily refer to someone who is seriously wounded, or fatally bitten by a snake, by the word *salîm* which means "safe and sound," "in good health." For the same reason, in order to presage its safe return, the caravan is called *qâfila* from the verb *qafala,* "to return." However, in the precise case with which we are concerned, the etymology makes sense when the two verbs in question are taken together. An ambidextrous person is called *'a'sar-yasar,* literally "difficult-easy," "left-handed-right-handed." And it is always the case that, despite the ambivalence we referred to above, *maysarat* and *yusra,* when they are taken to mean "supreme ease," are located on the right. This once again confirms its supremacy.

There would seem to be no great interest in giving further evidence of the belief in the pre-eminence of the right among the Arabs, since historical and ethnographic evidence tends to prove that this is generally widespread. As in many societies, the right hand is the organ of possession and power (it symbolizes, then, the person)[24] and is made the object of careful and attentive training. The right is considered the good side, charged with *baraka,* whereas the left is regarded as evil because it is synonymous with ill omen. The empty, isotropic space of geometry is replaced by the mystic, asymmetric space of the collective representations.

Rather than multiply examples, it would be appropriate, then, to come to grips with the explanation for this strange phenomenon. Without having too many illusions about the value of the solution which we envision, it would perhaps be useful to add other, more or less recent, Arabic documents to the already voluminous record on this question.

The different hypotheses[25] which have been put forward can be reduced to the following question: is the pre-eminence of the right a fact of nature or of culture or of both at the same time? In other words, is a human being better disposed, by his organic structure, to utilize one side of his body rather than the other, or has he deliberately favored one part of his body rather than the other because of the influence of beliefs, training, and practice, reinforced in the long run by some hereditary predisposition?

II

For a long time and even today,[26] the attempt has been made to link the predominance of the right hand with the asymmetry of the organism. In man, the left cerebral hemisphere is indeed more developed than the right and it is known that each hemisphere innervates the muscles of the opposite side. Broca said: "We are right-handed because we are left-brained." To which Hertz justly retorted by reversing the terms of the proposition: "We are left-brained because we are right-handed."[27]

The progress made in the last thirty years, in neurology as well as in psycho-physiology, has not invalidated this objection of Hertz. Certainly research on the working of the brain has helped to resolve many of its enigmas, and the arguments in favor of an organic explanation for the predominance of the right hand have been revived. But while the data on this problem are better understood, the way in which it is formulated remains obviously the same. The same difficulties also confront it. "The left hemisphere," write J. de Ajuriaguerra and H. Hécaen, "has long been considered the superior hemisphere. By demonstrating the prevalence of the left brain, the study of aphasia has tended to confirm the significance of corporeal dexterity considered as a statistical norm from the point of view of motor control, but likewise valorized from a psycho-social point of view."[28] The pre-eminence of the right hand is, as is stated, again related to the predominance of the left hemisphere. But once again precisely what needs to be established is the cause of this cerebral superiority. As the psycho-physiologist C. T. Morgan has admitted, research "has led to numerous hypotheses but has achieved few positive results." Moreover these results are held to be all the more deficient as long as the general attempt is made to explain one organic predominance by another, equally organic, predominance (i.e., the greater development of one side of the body, the better blood circulation of one hemisphere) which, in turn, needs to be explained. As Morgan also candidly concludes: "Despite a number of interesting data, we are not yet able to give a clear solution to the problem."[29]

Actually, in spite of its titles, cerebral physiology appears to be ill suited to resolve the thorny problem of corporeal dexterity. In fact, what is involved is a specifically human phenomenon. Research should be directed toward that which, from the outset, distinguishes man from the other higher representatives of the animal kingdom, in other words, toward the foundations of cultural life. Doubtless, lateral predominance is found also in apes and even in other animals. But there is no question at all of a quasi-absolute pre-eminence of the same side of the body, common to an entire species. Rather there is a tendency to make use of either the right or the left extremities, a tendency which would appear to be nothing more than the result of habit and of an economy of nature. Laboratory apes sometimes make use of their right hand exclusively, in performing tasks as complicated as writing.[30] But would this not be the product and result of imitation? In experiments conducted by Finch on thirty chimpanzees, it happened that the three types of motor behavior with which we are familiar (i.e., utilization of the right hand, of the left hand, and of both hands) occurred among them with equal frequency. Yerkes, who reports these results, asks quite correctly how one ought to explain "the fact that man is usually right-handed and the chimpanzee as often left- as right-handed." Since their organic structures are appreciably similar, he feels that the preference in favor of the right hand cannot be attributed to psychological factors but should be explained by cultural causes.[31]

A similar point of view has been adopted by E. E. Evans-Pritchard in the introduction to the English translation of two essays by R. Hertz. "I am not competent to say whether or to what degree, or even in what sense, there can be said to be an organic asymmetry between the hands. Dr. J. S. Weiner has very kindly given me the gist of some recent papers on the subject, from which I gather that the question is a very complex one, since it is partly a matter of age and situation; but it would appear that the cultural and social element is, as Hertz held, a most important, perhaps the dominant factor in determining the degree of final disparity." [32]

The hypothesis of organic asymmetry, however updated, cannot therefore withstand a critical examination of the facts. If right-handedness were physiologically controlled, there would have been no need to impose it by training and coercion. At birth, a human being should be more or less disposed to make equal use of both his hands. This is why he is constantly called to task first of all by his parents and later by teachers. Furthermore, as Hertz observed, even if one admitted the existence of a vague tendency toward right-handedness, it "would not be enough to bring about the absolute preponderance of the right hand if this were not reinforced and fixed by influences extraneous to the organism." [33] And it is precisely to establish the nature of these influences that Hertz devotes his important article.

III

He establishes, first of all, that a fundamental dualism divides all nature into two contrary spheres: sacred/profane, light/dark, high/low, male/female; in short, a noble sphere, esteemed, strong, and active, and a plebeian sphere, common, weak, and passive. "How could man's body, the microcosm, escape the law of polarity which governs everything?" Does the human organism alone enjoy symmetry?[34] In the subsequent examination of the characteristics of the right and the left he states that they correspond to the same functional antagonism of the universe: one is the sacred side, the seat of beneficial powers; the other is the profane and evil side.[35]

To this point, Hertz has done no more than describe the facts, without, however, explaining them. The whole problem is indeed to know why a favored position is invariably attributed to the right side. But it is surprising that, after having rightly discarded the anatomical thesis, Hertz finally finds nothing else to propose but a baffling return to organic asymmetry. "An almost insignificant bodily asymmetry," he specifies, "is enough to turn in one direction and the other contrary representations which are already completely formed."[36] To this it is possible to respond that it remains precisely to be demonstrated that man possesses, naturally and not culturally, one side which is stronger and more able than the other. The anthropoid apes also live in a more or less polarized universe[37] to which they are unable to remain entirely indifferent. Yet they do not exhibit any special tendency to right-handedness because no social or religious coercion hinders the free development of their bodies. Hertz deserves great credit for rejecting the organic hypothesis and for forcefully stressing the decisive role of society in the quasi-universal belief in the superiority of the right hand. But he was still compelled to appeal, in the last resort, to anatomy to explain how the opposition of sacred and profane also applies to man's body. Rather than make this altogether unexpected concession, he could have avoided some inconsistency if he had materialized things on the ground, instead of extending a general antagonism to organic structures. In fact, the opposition of the sacred to the profane, of day to night, of high to low, of male to female, involves this other antinomy no less strikingly: that of the sun and the shade, of the south and the north. Certainly, according to Durkheim and Mauss, the classification of things by clans and their totems is held to procede the classification by direction.[38] But it might, perhaps, be appropriate to revise this judgment, since today the reality of totemism [39] has come to be suspect and its vogue has been compared to that of hysteria.[40] However one considers this particular problem of collective representations, the primordial character of orientation seems evident. The erection of a tent, the construction of a house, the building of a temple or a sanctuary, the very position of man in space, all are dominated by a constant concern: whether to expose oneself to the sun or to protect oneself from it according to the time of the day and the temperature of the season. The opposition of hot and cold, of light and shadow, of north and south, must have impressed itself very early on man's attention. This opposition is at least as primitive as that of the sacred and profane. It would therefore be surprising if man had not sought to integrate it within a framework of universal antagonism and, in projecting it into space, had not discovered a right and a left, in other words an auspicious side and an inauspicious side.

IV

Hertz reconsidered the naturalist hypothesis and, somewhat hastily, rejected it, since he felt that it revealed outmoded conceptions.[41] Doubtless he was right in so far as it is concerned with explaining a complex of religious notions by a spontaneous worship of the forces of nature. But in the case which concerns us it would not be absolutely necessary to invoke a solar cult; it would be sufficient to assert that the sun is the dispenser of the light without which the earth would be plunged into eternal darkness. The deification of the sun has doubtlessly contributed greatly to reinforcing the beliefs in an asymmetric space, charged with occult powers. In addressing his prayers to the rising sun, the devotee automatically positions himself in accordance with the cardinal points. The south is to his right, the north to his left, the west is behind him. We repeat, however, that this type of cult does not seem absolutely indispensable to the polarization of space. A recognition of the inestimable benefits of solar light would be sufficient. The north, deprived of it, is evil in contrast with the south, the seat of beneficial powers. In any case, the Arabic evidence seems to lead us to an analogous hypothesis.

Situated on the western face of the Arabic peninsula, the Ḥijaz, the cradle of Islam, is bounded on the north by Syria and on the south by Yemen. Now it is altogether remarkable that the Arabic word for Syria should be Sam, which is unquestionably related in etymology to *šu'm,* "unhappiness," "misfortune," "ill augury," and *maš'amat* which the Koran uses to designate the left.[42] We have already seen that the verb *ša'ama* has in fact two meanings, "to bring bad luck" and "to turn left"; it is now relevant to mention a third meaning, "to go to Syria."[43] The ancient Arabs therefore tended to confound the left with the north. The fact that the word *šimâl* indicates the north and also designates the left side makes this supposition a certainty.[44] Furthermore, in keeping with this association, the northern region is fraught with sorcery. The wind from the north brings famine with it. The author of the *Tâj-al'arûs* informs us that when it blows for seven consecutive days across Egypt, the inhabitants prepare their shrouds, for it is by nature analogous to death: dry and cold.[45]

In contrast, the south is laden with blessings. The south wind is the bearer of prosperity and fertility; it is also synonymous with good relations.[46] The south is the Yemen, the flourishing land, the Arabia Felix of the classics. Its etymology is taken from the root *ymn* which implies ideas of success and happiness, and from it are derived the terms *yumn,* "felicity" or *baraka,* and *yamîne,* "right." Here again geographical location is intimately bound to man's position in space and is subject to the same mystic influences.

V

The associations of left and north on the one hand and of right and south on the other are not confined to Arabic. The same mutual associations are also recorded in Hebrew, where the word for left is applied to the north and that for right indicates the south.[47] In the royal archives of Mari, there is a question about several nomadic groups the most important of which are the *Benjaminites.* As Georges Dossin has remarked, it would be better to call them the *Yaminites,*[48] since this would emphasize better their association with the right. That it is from the north that these nomads "arrived at Mari and that they are always described to the north of Mari"[49] is a fact of some importance. Now their name, *Benjaminites,* is clearly west-Semitic and fixes these bedouins as "the sons of the right," i.e., the "sons of the south." There is hardly a doubt that this is the interpretation to give them, since the tablets of Mari also allude to another tribe, the *Sim'alites*—the "sons of the left," i.e., "the sons of the north."[50] At the time of their arrival at Mari, the Benjaminites therefore introduced themselves by a name geographically associated with their former homeland situated in the south. We are not particularly concerned here with whether these nomads are to be identified with the Israelite tribe of Benjamin[51] or with another primitive Semitic group, perhaps from south Arabia. What seems essential, in this case, is to demonstrate the existence of an evident connection between a geographical location and man's position in space. And this is precisely what the name for these bedouins, mentioned in the archives of Mari, proves.

VI

This evidence is interesting in itself, but its importance in regard to the Arabs would become clearer if we knew by what reference point the Yemen and Syria were positioned right and left. A brief remark by Ibn Manzur, the author of *Lisân al-'arab,* specifies this for us: "The Yemen is called Yemen because it is situated to the right of the Ka'ba; similarly Sam is called Sam because it is to the left."[52] This information still leaves us with some doubts. The landmark which gives rise to this orientation must be located precisely. Now since the sacred Haram of Mecca has become the center of the Islamic world, the faithful are obliged to say their required prayers facing in the direction of the Ka'ba. One of the corners of this religious edifice possesses a sacred power greater than the other three. This is the eastern corner in which is set the Black Stone. When facing this, the positions of the Yemen and of Sam are reversed. The first is to the left and the second to the right of the Meccan sanctuary. But the position would be restored if, instead of placing oneself in front of the Black Stone, as Moslems do,[53] one turned one's back to it and looked in the same direction as the corner into which it is wedged, namely, toward the east. This would thus establish one of the essential functions of this stone (which, according to traditional sayings, was formerly white) in the primitive cult. The stone would indicate the exact direction of the rising sun and would be the simulacrum of it. In any case, it would make it difficult for us to concede that this orientation was the result of a simple accident. Like many ancient sanctuaries, that of Mecca must have been constructed according to the axes of the cardinal points.

The architecture of the Ka'ba seems to us to offer further evidence in favor of this oriented construction. We know, in fact, that this sanctuary resembles a cube [54] and that its name may be derived from it. To explain the unusual form of this edifice, some authors have considered it "an extension of the cube of stone which represented the divinity." [55] Although, however, more than one pre-Islamic divinity was nothing more than a great rocky block, the sacred enclosure constructed in its honor did not merit the name of Ka'ba.[56] We might perhaps find a better explanation when we recall that this cube was the *bayt,* the abode of the divinity, and when we compare it to the ancient dwellings of the settled people of Mecca. Now, according to Azraqi, these were round. The chronicler tells us that the houses at Mecca were circular out of respect for the Ka'ba. "The first person who constructed a square house," he adds, "was Ḥumayd ibn Zubayr. The Qorayš then say: Humayd gave to his house a square form, it is either the [great] life or death." [57] Philology would confirm this account. The Arabic word for house is *dar,* from the verb *dara,* "to turn." The ancient Meccans would, therefore, have reserved their square or rectangularly based buildings for their gods, or rather for the most exalted of their gods, since they recognized only one Ka'ba. Although we cannot affirm that this sanctuary was a temple of the sun, it does seem certain, as we shall see shortly, that it was at least associated with a solar cult. Hence a concern to mark the four cardinal points seems to account for its quadrilateral base.[58] The angle of the Black Stone indicated the direction of the rising sun.

VII

Admitted, as Gaudefroy-Demombynes has already noted, the actual Ka'ba is not clearly oriented.[59] Snouck Hurgronje's [60] remarkable works show that the eastern corner is today no longer on an east-west axis, but is slightly turned toward the south. It is possible to impute this slight change in orientation to numerous reconstructions, following fires and floods. The Spanish traveler Ibn Jubayr, a particularly acute observer, specifies in the account of his *Riḥla* done in 1183 that "the blessed black stone is inserted in the corner which looks toward the east." [61] On the other hand, we possess numerous examples of ancient monuments—the pyramids of Egypt, the Temple of Jerusalem—which, though perfectly oriented at the time of their construction, today show considerable deviation. As J. B. Dumas has aptly remarked: "the landmarks that we have believed firm and constant . . . give evidence of their instability after many successive centuries. . . . The polar axis which we know is constantly affected by tremors and shifts has varied in its relative angle."[62] One of the important consequences of this displacement in the direction of the axis of rotation is that "it becomes necessary, after a certain number of centuries, to alter the polar star."[63]

If a sanctuary as old as that of Ptolemy's ancient Mocoraba today shows some slight change in orientation, there is no need for surprise. Yet, despite numerous reconstructions and the variation of the axis of the poles, the corners of the Ka'ba are still designated by the names of the countries toward which they are turned. The Iraqi corner and Syrian corner are on the left façade; the eastern corner and the Yemenite corner are on the opposite façade. Because of its association with the right, the sanctity of the latter corner appears as great as that of the corner in which the Black Stone is set. The two are paired to such an extent that they are simply called "the two Yemenite corners,"[64] that is, those that look to Yemen or the right.

VIII

We find ourselves thus confronted with two sacred sources which contribute to the same polarization of space. On the one hand, the sun divides it notably into north and south, into an auspicious and an inauspicious region; and on the other hand, the Ka'ba apportions it into right and left and confers the same values upon it. Indeed, if this temple produces similar mystic effects, it is because it is itself a microcosm, a condensed image of the universe whose potentiality it projects. In fact, according to Islamic traditions, the Ka'ba is the tent of heaven; a hollowed hyacinth sent by Allah to Adam to console him on the loss of paradise. It is also the center[65] and the navel of the earth;[66] its site was the first thing created by God who thereafter extended the earth from this point.[67] Hence it is mystically related to the rest of the world, and over the world it directs its radiance and its *baraka*. "When water falls on the Iraqi corner, rain, fertility and abundance reign in Iraq; the same is true for Syria, if it is the Syrian corner which the fertile water touches. If it were to rain on all the corners, the whole earth would probably be fertile."[68] Islamic tradition also teaches that the Ka'ba is the highest place on the earth; its spatial position corresponds to the polar star: "no place on earth is closer to heaven than Mecca."[69]

This is why prayers said in its sanctuary are heard better.[70] As the navel of the world, it is perhaps regarded as "the supreme point, the place that procures nourishment for the entire earth; [it] forms the mediating link between the upper world and the lower world." [71] We recognize in these various traits the essential characteristics of the symbolism of the center which reduces the universe to the dimensions of a sacred edifice. Doubtless, most of the facts reported above are of Jewish origin; as Hamidullah has already noted, they do not appear either in the Koran or in the *Ḥadîth*.[72] But it seems imprudent for us to conclude that the ancient Arabs were not familiar with similar beliefs, since they are found, in more or less different forms, in most cultures, both classic and primitive. The polarization of space and the values given to the regions, according to their location in relation to the Ka'ba, prove that the symbolism of the center was known to the ancient Arabs. The Koran asserts that "the first temple which was founded for men is surely that situated at Bakka [= Mekka]" (Koran 3: 96). This assertion about the archetypal character of the Meccan sanctuary [73] is written in the same context of ideas.

An oriented sanctuary symbolizing the universe, the Ka'ba reflects, as we have seen, the spatial values of the macrocosm. Consequently, if the polarization of space was, as we suppose, due to the mystic influence of the sun, this ought to be apparent also in ancient Meccan beliefs and more particularly in the primitive ritual of the Ka'ba. Now it does seem certain that this temple was associated with a solar cult. The Koran also alludes to the worship of the sun by the Arabs (Koran 27: 24; 41: 37) and this fact is also attested by certain theophoric names. A. J. Wensinck draws an interesting parallel between the triple tunic *(kiswa)* with its red, yellow, and white of the rising sun and the covering of the Meccan sanctuary which formerly was also multicolored. This oriental scholar feels that this might be derived from a mythological conception of the god Šams dressed in his cloak. Although he is suspicious of "the speculations about the Ka'ba as a solar sanctuary," he declares nonetheless that "other traditions allow a glimpse of some connection between the Ka'ba and the sun, as indicated for example by the 360 idols around the Ka'ba which [Muhammad] is reputed to have destroyed at the time of the conquest [of Mecca]; Al-Azraki reports that even in Islamic times there were images (probably gold and silver discs) of the sun and the moon in the Ka'ba. A sun of gold, encased in pearls, hyacinths, and emeralds, appears among the gifts which the Caliph al-Mutawakkil presented to the house of Allah." [74] It is also relevant to recall that in the beginning the Meccan sanctuary had no roof; in addition, it was strictly forbidden to enter it at night.[75] These prohibitions can only be satisfactorily explained in terms of a solar cult. Consecrated to a daytime divinity, the Ka'ba would have been constructed in such a way as to receive the maximum sacred emanation; on the other hand, all acts of nocturnal worship were forbidden in it. But *tawâf* or circumambulation appears to furnish especially convincing evidence. We know, in fact, that this essential rite of the pilgrimage and of the *'umra* [76] consists, for the faithful, in circling the sacred dwelling seven times, beginning in the east, or more precisely at the corner of the Black Stone. The pilgrim is enjoined, by the Prophet's example, to embrace this fetish or, if he is unable to do this because of the crowd, to direct a kiss and a greeting toward it. Now it is laid down that the ritual rounds be extremely elaborate and that they correspond to the apparent journey of the sun. The believer who circles this microcosm, the Ka'ba, believes he is imitating the sun in its rotation around the earth. The circular direction observed in Islam is, without a doubt, sinistral; in other words, it is contrary to the seemingly clockwise movement of the sun.[77] But following his general rule of conduct, Mohammed is supposed to have adopted the reverse of the pagan ritual.[78]

If the Ka'ba, as we believe we have demonstrated, was associated with a solar cult, it must have contributed to the polarization of space. In the monotheistic view of Islam this space should be almost homogeneous. In fact, God is not only the Lord of the sacred temple of Mecca; he is also the absolute Master of the universe. To him "belongs the east and the west; wherever you turn there is the face of Allah." [79] Space is therefore freed from the ancient forces that inhabited it and disputed their spheres of influence. Certainly, there still exist here and there within the household trouble spots of animistic origin. These are, however, subordinate powers subject to the supreme authority of Allah and they serve his designs. The earth is dominated by the infinite transcendence of God and by the blessings of his sanctuary. By contrast, Arab paganism considered that these same blessings diminished in proportion to one's distance from the manifestation of the divinity and that they ceased at the actual or magical boundary of the city. Beyond that was the domain of chaotic and inimical forces. The ancient religion would have affirmed the heterogeneity of space. This space is sacred or profane and is placed under the aegis of powers, sometimes friends and sometimes foes. In a general way, the former are on the right, the latter on the left. The Ka'ba, the center of the world, would divide it into two opposed groups. The auspicious regions are those situated on the right; the inauspicious regions are on the left.[80]

IX

Thus the facts would confirm the hypothesis that the pre-eminence of the right does not depend on the structure of the organism, but on an asymmetric and mystic conception of space which forms part of a vast universal antagonism. Yemen is happy, as the ancients said, not because of some sporadic prosperity, but rather because it is located to the right of the Ka'ba. By contrast, Syria, although it enjoys a distinctly milder climate, is inauspicious because of its position to the left of this sanctuary, in a malevolent region populated by ghosts and shades.[81]

For Hertz, an hypothesis of this kind is today outdated by sociological evidence. According to him, "there is nothing to allow us to assert that the distinctions applied to space are anterior to those that concern man's body. They all have one and the same origin, the opposition of the sacred and profane; therefore they are usually concordant and support each other; they are nonetheless independent."[82] In reality, there is nothing to allow us to postulate the anteriority of beliefs that concern the polarity of the body. And since the privileges of the right hand by no means appear to be the result of a supposed anatomical predisposition, we are therefore forced to seek their origin outside the organism. Now the opposition of light and shade is, without a doubt, as primitive as that of the sacred and the profane. Our immediate attempt has been to coordinate it within the structure of an universal antagonism and to concentrate upon relations on the ground. It is, therefore, not surprising that we should perceive its effects on the corresponding parts of the body, since that body is in a posture of orientation (or of prayer addressed to the rising sun).

The "naturalist" hypothesis is certainly not free from criticism, and Hertz raises several objections to it which he considers decisive. Doubtless the most important is that its application to the Australian hemisphere requires the reversal of right and left. "But the Australian and Maori right coincides with ours."[83] At first sight, the argument appears weighty. But a glance at the map of the world shows that the major part of the habitable surface of our planet, the different centers of the great classical civilizations and perhaps also the cradle of humanity, is found in the northern hemisphere. It is from here that great waves of migration would have set out. These have allowed man to establish himself everywhere upon the earth and to populate the world's most isolated corners. Therefore it seems quite normal that well-established notions should accompany man in his gradual trek across the northern regions and should be preserved in the south, although they no longer conform with the new system of orientation. There are, indeed, many instances that illustrate the tenaciousness of beliefs and customs when it has become perfectly evident that they are inconsistent with new collective representations.[84] Besides, it is unnecessary to its validity and universality for a custom to have been invented in the same area where it is practiced. Rituals, like myths, are capable of a considerable extension of their area of influence, thanks to war, exchange, and peaceful expansion. A notion such as *baraka* is essentially Arab in origin but it is now instilled in most parts of the Islamic world.[85] The belief in the pre-eminence of the right by no means postulates, as Hertz asserts, the universality of a system of orientation from which this pre-eminence proceeds. Nor should it imply that it be known by all men at all times.[86] It appears intimately connected with beliefs concerning the mystic and beneficent power of the sun and with a certain deification of the sun. It owes its quasi-ecumenical character to the diffusion of a solar cult through the greater part of the northern hemisphere from whence it spread over the entire earth. It would, in the end, be so deeply implanted in custom, by prejudice, coercion, and training that it would have succeeded in becoming independent of the religious infrastructure that gave birth to it. History shows us that it still plays an important role in emotional life, despite the many changes that disorder the collective representations.

Certainly, there is no point in disguising difficulties or in maintaining that the amended "naturalist" hypothesis admits no exceptions. We simply consider that the explanation which it proposes for the pre-eminence of the right is at least as valid as that based upon a dubious organic asymmetry. In any case, Arabic evidence shows us that the predominance of the dextrous hand is intimately connected with the idea of a mystic and polarized space the values of which are related to the solar cult of the Ka'ba.

Notes

1. In 1962, the Institute for the Study of Human Relations in Paris devoted a conference to this problem, under the title "Norm and Laterality." The works of the participants are not yet published.

2. Ibn Jubayr 1959: 67; cf. Gaudefroy-Demombynes 1923: 41. The Black Stone symbolizes God's presence in the Ka'ba.

3. Koran 37: 28.

4. Abu Faraj al-'Isfahâni 1929: 125 ff.

5. Ṭabari 1879–1901, 1: 136 ff.

6. Ibid., p. 156.

7. Jâḥiz, 1323h.: 18.

8. Cited by Ibn Taymiya 1950: 141.

9. Houdas and Marçais 1903–14, 1: 153 ff. "The Prophet gave preference to the right side as far as possible, in [regard to] the performance of ablutions, putting on shoes, and the loosening of the hair" (ibid., 3: 656). Muhammad slept on his right side (ibid., 4: 241). It is customary, in putting on shoes, to begin with the right foot and, in taking off shoes, to begin with the left foot (ibid., p. 113). For other recommendations concerning personal hygiene, see ibid., 1: 71.

10. Ibn Rušd 1355h., 1: 52; cf. Houdas and Marçais 1903–14, 1: 71.

11. Ibn al-Ḥâjj 1329h., 1: 24, 41.

12. Duguet [Firmin] Paris 1932: 84.

13. The left hand is called *al-śa'mâ'*, from the word *šu'm*, misfortune; cf. Ibn Manẓûr 1300h., 15: 208.

14. Cf. Koran 2: 185; 9: 117; 74: 9.

15. Ibn Manẓûr 1300h., 7: 161.

16. Ibid., p. 160.

17. The Koran frequently opposes *'usr* and *yusr* (2: 185; 65: 7; 94: 5, 6), *'usra* and *yusra*. The verb *'asara* and its derivatives express difficulty, discomfort, something harsh and uneasy to endure; by contrast, *yasara* and its derivatives are used, almost exclusively, in the sense of well-being and ease.

18. Cf. Koran 92: 7, 8.

19. Cf. Koran 90: 19; 56: 9.

20. Cf. Koran 92: 7; 90: 12–18.

21. The instability of meaning for the left does not always occur. Cf. E. E. Evans-Pritchard, Introduction to R. Hertz, *Death and the right hand,* p. 22.

22. The ambivalence of the sacred does not at all mean, as is commonly repeated, that the primitive confounds holiness and impurity. W. R. Smith's thesis was repudiated more than fifty years ago by J. Lagrange (1905: 141 ff.) and is unreservedly rejected by E. Dhorme (1937: 308). In any case, no such confusion is recorded among the Arabs (cf. Chelhod, *Les*

structures du sacré chez les Arabes, 1965, chap. 1; cf. Chelhod 1961: 67 ff).

23. Hubert and Mauss 1902–3: 47.

24. Koran: "That which your right hands possess," 4: 24, 25, 33, 36: 24: 33; 30: 28 . . .

25. It is not within the scope of this article to expound the different hypotheses or to analyze the innumerable studies which raise the problem of the pre-eminence of the right hand. R. Hertz 1928 gives some good references. J. E. Downey (1933: 109–42), who discusses the contemporary state of the question, also provides an important bibliography. It contains no less than 219 titles, generally by American authors, for the single period 1924–33. It is relevant to add that with their well-known penchant for tests and statistics, the researchers on the other side of the Atlantic [U.S.A.] have, above all, endeavored either to measure the degree of lateral predominance or to count the number of right-handed, left-handed, and ambidextrous individuals in a given population. They have also studied the tendency to sleep on one side of the body, the way people applaud, and other facts of the same sort. Lateral predominance has been related to the aptitude for speech, manual ability, visual pre-eminence, the length of the humerus and of the foot, etc. However useful these researchers may be, they contribute only slightly to a real explanation of right-handedness. That right-handedness is correlated with sight, hearing, the leg or the foot, etc., does nothing but remove the question a step further, since it involves precisely the question of determining the nature and cause of this new preponderance which is supposed to have brought on the first. And therefore it leads, more or less directly, to the hypothesis of organic asymmetry to which we shall return later.

26. Van der Leeuw 1948: 202.

27. Hertz 1928: 100. Hertz's article was first published in the *Revue philosophique* 68 (1909): 553–80, under the title "La prééminence de la main droite: étude sur la polarité religieuse." It will be advantageous to consult E. E. Evans-Pritchard's introduction to the 1960 English translation in *Death and the right hand.*

28. De Ajuriaguerra and Hécaen 1949: 24. It is relevant to add that the data on the problem are presented with a great deal of qualification. If, in a general way, the predominance of the left hemisphere is verified, it should be stressed that it has by no means the fixity of character which is classically accorded it. This amounts to saying that the right hemisphere predominates perhaps in some instances, as is the case among left-handers. In fact, what is involved is a "functional cooperation in which the less important of the two executants can predominate under abnormal conditions and assume more or less satisfactorily the functions of the prevailing hemisphere" (ibid.). And the same authors add: "Besides, there is the question of variable hemispheric dominance depending on each cortical function" (ibid., p. 25). They recognize that "the problem of hemispheric dominance is therefore far from being solved." Indeed, present observation already shows that there exists an interaction between the two parts of the brain, so that whatever is required for one part is also advantageous to the

other. Therefore the left hand can perform tasks for which the right hand alone was trained. This phenomenon of transfer is further evident when there occurs a partial or total destruction of the predominant hemisphere. The patient is, then, induced to use the other side of the body. Lashley has proved this with experiments on rats and monkeys. Zollinger's observations are even more interesting. This surgeon had to perform a decerebration of one side of the suprathalamus on a "woman of 53 affected by a tumour of the left hemisphere which caused a complete paralysis of the right side accompanied by the loss of articulate speech." The patient survived for 17 days after this operation. And "not only did the psychic functions not appear diminished . . . but emotional expressions became more differentiated. . . . the speech trouble partially lessened" (Lhermite 1936: 77). If aphasia emphasizes the prevalence of the left hemisphere, Zollinger's experience shows that, even in so precise a case, the predominance is relative and that it is often relevant to keep in mind K. Goldstein's theory of cerebral totality (1951).

29. Morgan 1949, 2: 455 ff.

30. Guillaume 1941, vol. 8, no. 2, fig. 81: The ape imitates the child and, like him, uses his right hand for writing; fig. 67: with the right hand, he inserts one tube in another; fig. 68: he holds a stick with the right hand; figs. 64, 65, and 76: the left hand wields the square, the lever, and the stick. Cf. Rollet, 1889: 198.

31. Yerkes 1945: 113 ff. According to Tsai and Mauer's experiments rats are reputed to be right-handed. But these experiments conflict with Yoshioka's research. Of the 200 rats he studied, a few were ambidextrous; the rest were divided equally between right-handers and left-handers (see Downey 1933: 131 ff.).

32. Evans-Pritchard, Introduction to Hertz 1960: 19, n. 2.

33. Hertz 1928: 102.

34. Ibid., pp. 106–9.

35. Ibid., pp. 116–25.

36. Ibid., pp. 126–27.

37. In particular, the oppositions—day/night, male/female, high/low, friend/enemy—could not elude them.

38. Durkheim and Mauss 1901–2, 6: 40 ff.

39. Lévi-Strauss 1962: 22.

40. Ibid., Introduction, pp. 1–3.

41. Hertz 1928: 126.

42. Koran 56: 9; 90: 19.

43. Ibn Manẓûr, 1300h., 15: 208.

44. In order to differentiate the left from the north, the Arabs have had to establish a phonetic distinction. They therefore distinguish between *šimâl* and *šamâl,* the two words being derived, after all, from the same root. But Zabidi's phrase, in the *Tâj al-'arûs,* leaves no doubt about the possibility of reversal: *"šamâl* [north]," he writes, *"bil fatḥ wa yuksar"* (1306h., 7: 396).

45. Ibid.

46. Ibid., 1: 191, s.v. *jnb.*

47. G. Dossin 1939, 2: 983; Kupper 1957: 68.

48. Dossin 1959: 49.
49. Kupper, 1957: 81.
50. Dossin 1959: 49.
51. Kupper notes that this problem is still debated (1957: 81, n. 1). For Dussaud, the hypothesis would not be out of the question (1955: 182).
52. Ibn Manẓûr 1300 h., 17: 356.
53. Doubtless, the *imam* takes the *maqâm 'Ibrahîm* (the sacred stone upon which Abraham is believed to have stood) for *qibla* when he directs the prayer within the enclosure of the mosque of Mecca (Gaudefroy-Demombynes 1923: 107, 109). It is situated facing the door of the Ka'ba, in front of the side which is marked by the Black Stone (east) and the Iraqi corner (north). But the power of the eastern corner is attested by the importance of its role in the ritual circuits. Prayers are recited facing the Black Stone; and the pilgrims turn toward it when they drink the water of Zam-Zam (Duguet 1932: 85, 87).
54. In reality, it is an irregular cubic building, which originally had no roof; its earlier dimensions are unknown.
55. Gaudefroy-Demombynes 1923: 26, n. 2.
56. We know that the Arabs before Islam had other religious edifices with a cubic shape to which they also gave the name of Ka'ba. Unfortunately, we have very little information about these sanctuaries. Cf. Hamidullah 1960: 132 ff., n. 12.
57. 'Azraqi 1858: 196; Nuwayri 1923–55, 1: 313.
58. According to Gaudefroy-Demombynes, the prototype of the Ka'ba may have been recovered. "The excavations carried out in 1937–38 by the British mission to Huraïda and Hadramout have brought to light the ruins of a temple consecrated to the lunar god *Sin* and forming a quadrilateral 12.5 meters by 9.8 meters in width; it was oriented like the Babylonian temples, on the axis of the cardinal points, the façade being to the southwest. These are the dimensions and orientation of the Ka'ba except that its façade is turned to the north-east" (1957: 34). Hamidullah explains this change in orientation of the Ka'ba's façade by the desire of Abraham "to protest against the paganism of his former countrymen" (1960: 128). And he adds: "But before we talk of a 'prototype,' it ought to be established that the temple of Huraïda is older than the Ka'ba." This last remark is evidently inspired by the Koran 3: 96.
59. Gaudefroy-Demombynes 1923: 27.
60. Snouck-Hurgronje 1888–89.
61. Ibn Jubayr 1959: 59 ff.
62. J.-B. Dumas 1938: 18 ff.
63. *La Grande Encyclopédie,* s.v. Orientation, p. 562.
64. Of the four corners of the Ka'ba, the "two Yemenites" are incontestably the most honored; but the holiness of the eastern corner, in which the Black Stone is set, is even greater. Cf. Gaudefroy-Demombynes 1923: 212.
65. Ancient and modern maps make the Ka'ba a center around which the countries of the world are arranged (see Wensinck 1916; Hamidullah 1959, 1: 21 ff.; id. 1960: 103–4, a map with the following caption: "Mecca, center of the world").

66. Gaudefroy-Demombynes 1923: 30. The author notes that there exists "in the middle of the Ka'ba, a spike (?) which is called the navel of the world." Some pilgrims uncover their bellies, extending themselves on the ground so as to place their navel on that of the earth (ibid., p. 69).

67. Ibid., p. 30; Wensinck, article: "Ka'ba" in *Encyclopédie de l'Islam;* cf. Hamidullah 1960: 91 and notes pp. 129 ff.

68. Gaudefroy-Demombynes 1923: 5.

69. Wensinck, article: "Ka'ba," p. 628.

70. G. E. von Grunebaum 1951: 20.

71. Wensinck, "Ka'ba," p. 628.

72. Hamidullah 1960: 92; cf. Wensinck, "Ka'ba," p. 627.

73. Cf. Chelhod 1962: 66–90.

74. Wensinck 1928: 268 ff.

75. Qalqašandî 1913, 1: 356: "innal qa'bata lam tuftah laylan qatt."

76. Chelhod 1955: 66 ff., 71.

77. We know that the normal direction is beneficial, whereas the sinistral direction is associated with the funeral cult.

78. This is the most generally accepted thesis. The ingenious solution proposed by G.-H. Bosquet needs to be confirmed by other observations of ritual circuits performed in the tropics (Bousquet 1949: 106). Nor ought we to lose sight of the fact that the two great pre-Islamic festivals fell in the spring and autumn, that is, outside the critical period of 46 days, singled out by Bousquet, when the sun and its shadow turn, at Mecca, in a counterclockwise direction.

79. Koran 2: 115.

80. In reality, the Islamic conception of space is otherwise so rich and varied that one should not imagine this as an adequate outline of the problem. For precise details see Chelhod, *Les structures du sacré chez les Arabes* (1965), chap. 7.

81. The *ẓill* is the double of man, the specter of the *jinn;* see ibid., p. 115.

82. Hertz 1928: 126 ff.

83. Ibid., p. 126.

84. We cite as good examples: Friday the thirteenth, an unlucky day; walking under ladders, etc. In Egypt, the overflowing of the Nile's waters provides the occasion for very ancient practices.

85. Chelhod 1955: 68–88.

86. According to J.-B. Dumas, "it was not always so; the stone implements of the Chellean period show us," he writes, "that many men of this time mainly used their left hand, because their tools were so fashioned that they could not be used except with their left hand" (1938:5).

Bibliography

Abu Faraj al-'Isfahâni
1929 *Kitâb al-'Aghâni,* edited by Dâr al-Kutub. 4 vols. Cairo.

Ajuriaguerra, J. de, and Hécaen, H.
1949 *Le cortex cérébral.* Paris.

'Azraqi
1858 *'Aḫbâr Makka,* edited by Wüstenfeld. Leipzig.

BOUSQUET, G. H.
1949 *Les grandes pratiques rituelles de l'Islam*. Paris.
CHELHOD, J.
1955 *Le sacrifice chez les Arabes*. Bibliothèque de sociologie contemporaine. Paris.
1955 La baraka chez les Arabes. *Revue de l'histoire des religions* 148: 68–88.
1961 La notion ambiguë du sacré chez les Arabes et dans l'Islam. *Revue de l'histoire des religions* 159: 67–79.
1962 Le mythe chez les Arabes. *L'Homme* 2: 62–90.
1965 *Les structures du sacré chez les Arabes*. Paris.
DHORME, E.
1937 *La religion des Hébreux nomades*. Brussels.
DOSSIN, G.
1939 Benjaminites dans les textes de Mari. In *Mélanges syriens offerts à Monsieur René Dussard*, 2: 981–96. 2 vols. Bibliothèque Archéologique et Historique, vol. 30.
1959 *Les bédouins dans les textes de Mari*. L'Antica Societa Beduina, Studi Semitici, vol. 2. Rome.
DOWNEY, J. E.
1933 Laterality of function. *Psychological Bulletin* 30: 109–42.
DUGUET, F.
1932 *Le Pèlerinage de la Mecque*. Paris.
DUMAS, J.-B.
1938 La droite et la gauche. Unpublished. Press mark Bibliothèque Nationale de Paris: Fol Z 1329.
DURKHEIM, E., AND MAUSS, M.
1901–2 De quelques formes primitives de classification. *Année sociologique* 6: 1–72.
DUSSAUD, R.
1955 *La pénétration des Arabes en Syrie avant l'Islam*. Institut Français d'Archéologie de Beyrouth, Bibliothèque Archéologique et Historique, vol. 59. Paris.
GAUDEFROY-DEMOMBYNES, M.
1923 *Le pèlerinage à la Mekke*. Annales du Musée Guimet, Bibliothèque d'Etudes, vol. 33. Paris.
1957 *Mahomet*, L'Evolution de l'humanité, synthèse collective, vol. 36.
GOLDSTEIN, K.
1951 *La structure de l'organisme*. Paris.
La Grande Encyclopédie, s.v. Orientation. Paris.
GRUNEBAUM, G. E. VON
1951 *Muhammadan festivals*. New York.
GUILLAUME, P.
1941 La psychologie des singes. *Nouveau traité de psychologie* 8, pt. 2: 257–335. Paris.
HAMIDULLAH, M.
1959 *Le Prophète de l'Islam*. 2 vols. Études Musulmanes, no. 7. Paris.

1960 *Le pèlerinage à la Mekke.* In *Les pèlerinages,* pp. 89–138. Sources Orientales, vol. 3. Paris.

HERTZ, R.

1928 La prééminence de la main droite. In *Mélanges de sociologie religieuse et folklore,* pp. 99–129. Translated by R. and C. Needham, *Death and the right hand.* London, 1960.

HOUDAS, O., AND MARÇAIS, W.

1903–14 *Les traditions islamiques.* 4 vols. Publications de l'École des Langues Orientales. Paris.

HUBERT, H., AND MAUSS, M.

1902–3 Esquisse d'une théorie générale de la magie. *Année sociologique* 7: 1–146.

IBN AL-ḤÂJJ

1329h. *Al-Madḥal.* 3 vols. Cairo.

IBN JUBAYR

1959 *Riḥla,* edited by Sâdir and Bayrût. Beirut.

IBN MANẒÛR

1300h. *Lisân al-'arab,* 20 vols. Bûlâq, Cairo.

IBN RUŠD

1355h. *Bidâyat al-mujtahid wa nihâyat al-muqtasid,* edited by Halabi. 2 vols. Cairo.

IBN TAYMIYA

1950 *'Iqtiḍâ' al-sirâṭ al-mustaqîm, muḥâlafat 'aṣḥâb al-jaḥîm.* Cairo.

JAḤIẒ

1323h. *Al-Buḥalâ'.* Cairo.

KUPPER, J.-B.

1957 *Les nomades en Mésopotamie au temps des rois de Mari.* Bibliothèque de la Faculté de Philosophie et Lettres de l'Université de Liège, no. 142. PARIS.

LAGRANGE, M.-J.

1905 *Étude sur les religions sémitiques.* Paris.

LEEUW, G. VAN DER

1948 *La religion dans son essence et ses manifestations.* Paris.

LÉVI-STRAUSS, C.

1962 *Le totémisme aujourd'hui.* Paris.

LHERMITE, J.

1936 *Les mécanismes du cerveau.* Paris.

MORGAN, C. T.

1949. *La psychologie physiologique.* 2 vols. Paris.

NUWAYRI

1923–55 *Nihâyat al-'arab fî funûn al-'adab.* 18 vols. Cairo.

QALQAŠANDÎ

1913– *Ṣobḥ al-'a 'sâ fî ṣinâ 'at al-'inša.* Bibliothèque Khédiviale, vols. 1–14. Cairo.

ROLLET, E.

1889 La taille de grands singes. *Revue scientifique* 44: 196–201.

SNOUCK HURGRONJE, C.
1888–
89 *Mekka.* 2 vols. The Hague.
ṬABARI, MUHAMMAD IBN JARIR
1879–
1901 *Annales,* edited by M. J. de Goeje. 15 vols. Leiden.
WENSINCK, A. J.
1916 *The ideas of the western Semites concerning the navel of the earth.* Verhandelingen der Koninklijke Akademie van Wetenschappen te Amsterdam, Afdeeling Letterkunde, n.s., Nieuwe, vol. 17, no. 1.
1928 Quelques remarques sur le soleil dans le folklore de sémites. In *Mémorial Henri Basset,* 2: 267–77. 2 vols. Publications de l'Institut des Hautes-Études Marocaines, vols. 17, 18. Paris.
______. Ka'ba. Article in *Encyclopédie de l'Islam.* 1st ed., 2: 627 ff.
YERKES, R. M.
1945 *Chimpanzees: a laboratory colony.* New Haven.
ZABÎDI, MOHAMMAD MORTAḌA
1306h. *Tâj al-'arûs.* 20 vols. Cairo.

Dual Symbolic Classification among the Gogo of Central Tanzania

Peter Rigby

13

Since the work of Durkheim and Mauss on systems of classification,[1] it has generally been recognized that there is some structural relationship or "concordance" between the social and symbolic orders of any society.[2] The present analysis establishes a system of dual symbolic classification for an East Africa people and further indicates the widespread incidence of this type of classification in Africa (cf. Needham 1960a; Beidelman 1961; Wieschhoff 1938; Werner 1904; Evans-Pritchard 1953, 1956; and others). It also provides a closer ethnographic comparison with the neighboring matrilineal Kaguru, with whom Gogo share some linguistic and cultural features, and whose system of symbolic classification has been described by Beidelman (1961).[3]

I

I first present an outline of certain aspects of Gogo social organization. This is necessary because no such description is as yet readily available elsewhere, and because it is desirable to set the background against which I propose to analyze the series of symbolic oppositions which constitute Gogo dual symbolic classification.[4]

Every Gogo belongs to one of about eighty-five patrilineal clans (*mbeyu,* lit. "seed"). Clans are dispersed, non-corporate and non-exogamous, but each is associated with one or more small ritual areas (*yisi,* "countries") through the possession of the rainstones (*mabwe gemvula* or *"zimvula"*) which establish ritual precedence and authority within a defined territory. However, this determines

---

Africa 36 (1966): 1–16. Reprinted by arrangement with the International African Institute.

only the residence of the shallow-depth agnatic group directly concerned with the inheritance of the stones and succession to the office of ritual leader *(mutemi)*,[5] theoretically by the rule of patrilineal primogeniture. The majority of the members of any clan are dispersed throughout the Gogo area, and hence the population of any one ritual area includes members of a great variety of clans.

There is a high residential mobility of homestead-groups, primarily the result of difficult ecological conditions and the exigencies of pastoralism and the hoe-cultivation of sorghum and bulrush-millet.[6] This mobility is facilitated by the fact that land for cultivation and grazing is not inherited, controlled, or distributed by any political officeholder.

Each ritual area contains one or, more usually, several neighborhoods *(matumbi)*. Neighborhoods are composed of anything up to fifty or so homesteads *(kaya)*, clustered about a named geographical feature but lacking definite physical boundaries.

Several groups of full- and half-brothers ("the sons of one man," *wana wamunhu monga*), living together in homestead clusters (*vitumbi*, lit. "little neighborhoods") linked to one another by a wide variety of cognatic and affinal ties, basically comprise the population of each neighborhood.[7] Agnates of wider relationship than full- and half-siblings seldom live near each other or maintain ties of cooperation. Fission within agnatic groups of greater depth than this is facilitated by a well-defined house-property system for the inheritance and deployment of livestock, which allocates the property to the sons of one mother (i.e., "one house," *nyumba imonga*) before the death of the husband/father. Because land is not inherited and residential mobility is relatively high, the localization of large-depth agnatic groups is irrelevant.

The homestead *(kaya)* is the most fundamental residential unit in Gogo society and it is one of the primary units with which cosmological ideas and values (such as geographical orientation) are concerned. The role of homestead-head (*munyakaya* or *muzenga-kaya*) is the only one in Gogo society which enables a man to achieve complete jural and political maturity. The status of homestead-head confers *ipso facto* the status of elderhood in the community and the right to participate in the informal elders' courts which constitute the primary judicial bodies of Gogo society.

Depending upon the stage it has reached in its developmental cycle, the domestic group normally consists of an elementary, polygynous, or patrilineal extended family, frequently living together with several other categories of kin and non-kin.[8] Competition between a father and his mature sons over the control and use of livestock for bridewealth and subsistence frequently results in tension and conflict.[9] Fission within the domestic group occurs early and adult married sons, sets of full-brothers, with their mothers, wives, and children, may break away and set up separate homesteads. If this does not happen (and it is considered morally reprehensible), fission between sets of full-brothers occurs soon after the death of the homestead-head/father. They then become independently mobile homestead units in their own right, jurally and ritually independent of other like units (see below).

When such fission occurs, homestead-heads move to areas where they have kin and affines, and Gogo express the choice as being one between living near agnates (in which there is considerable tension and potential conflict) or near affines and matrilateral kin, particularly "mother's brothers" *(wakuku)*. These processes, combined with a highly selective marriage pattern within a restricted *spatial* range, result in the kinship structures which I describe later in relation to the system of dual symbolic classification.

II

In Gogo, as in many other "Bantu" languages, there is an explicit and direct relationship between the terms for right and left, and those for male and female. The right hand is called *muwoko wokulume,* and the root *-lume* denotes "male": e.g., *mulume,* "man" or "husband," or *nhume,* "male animal." The left hand is *muwoko wokucekulu;* the root *-cekulu* denotes "female": e.g., *mucekulu,* "wife" or "married woman," *ng'ombe nhyekulu,* "female cattle." Alternative terms which are seldom used are: *muwoko womulilo* (lit. "the hand used for eating," from *kulya,* "to eat")[10] for the right hand, and *muwoko womuciji* for the left. The root *-ciji* has no other connotations than a very specific one for ritual status, which I describe later.

Although the right hand is usually associated with "strength" *(vilungo)* and the left with "weakness" *(wusocele),* and many of the oppositions described below involve the right hand in "better" associations than the left, there are no generalized conceptions of "good" and "bad" under which all the other oppositions may be alternatively subsumed. The emphasis lies rather in the complementarity of the opposition than in any consistent "superior/ inferior" connotations.[11]

The contextual relativity of the "superior/inferior" opposition is indicated in the Gogo classification of the right and left as "clever" *(-sugu)* and "stupid" *(-lele)*. During the preliminaries to sexual intercourse a man should lie upon his right side and use his left hand in play with the woman's genitalia (cf. Beidelman 1961: 253). A man, explaining this to me, said:

> This left hand of ours is clever *(musugu)* in one way, and this (the right) is foolish *(mulele)* in this circumstance. And that is when you go to the sleeping skin *(ncingo)* of your wife; then you see that you have reversed *(mapitucila)* the normal order. . . .[12]

I explore further the relativity of the relations between left and right and bad and good respectively, and the more general problem of reversal, when I describe the special ritual status of left-handed people in Gogo values.

Nevertheless, it is true that many actions which are considered polite and good can be performed only with the right hand, and many of those considered "unclean" or bad must be performed with the left. All gifts and food must be accepted with the right hand and food should be eaten only with the right hand, except in the case of left-handed people. Tobacco (and sometimes beer), however, may be given and received with the left hand and no offense is implied. The left hand is not mutilated or weakened in any way [13] and left-handed children are not physically coerced into being right-handed, although all social values encourage right-handedness. The generally easy attitude with which Gogo regard left-handedness is possibly linked with the special ritual status accorded left-handed people. It may further be linked with the fact that Gogo omens (*ndeje,* lit. "birds") are not generally associated with the opposition of the left and right, as they are among many other peoples.[14]

[Carnell (1955: 36) notes several of the oppositions mentioned above. Gogo state that some witches and sorcerers set "traps" *(kutega mapeli)* in paths so that unwanted and unsuspecting visitors may be harmed. Carnell relates this to the opposition of right and left as follows: "The *'mapeli'* . . . works in such a way that a woman will be bewitched if she steps on it with her left foot, and a man only if he plants his right foot on it. To counteract this danger, a woman will wear an amulet on her left arm, and a man on his right." I did not confirm this information myself, but it is certainly consistent with the general series of Gogo symbolic oppositions.]

Other symbols and activities are associated exclusively with men or women, but again the emphasis is upon the complementarity of the oppositions rather than their "superiority" or "inferiority." Thus the bow *(wupinde)* is a male symbol, and is the main object which symbolizes the inheritance and succession of the principal heir at an inheritance ceremony *(ipinde)*.[15] The principal heir must, of course, be a man, and is usually the eldest son of the senior wife. The calabash *(nhungu)* appears as the female symbol in many contexts.

The two parts of fire-making sticks *(mhejeho)* are also thought of as male and female. The stick with a wedge-shaped incision in it which is placed flat upon inflammable material is the "female" *(nyhekulu)*, and that spun upright in the hands is the "male" *(nhume)*. This is a purely logical opposition in Gogo thought and does not necessarily involve any further associations. The type of explicit association illustrated here may be thought of as a metaphorical one, rather than as mere analogy. An elder told me:

> We "guessed" *(caganiciza)* that they *should* be such, because one fire-stick lies flat and the other stands up. So we said, this one flat on the ground is the female, and this one which stands up is the male. Even in the case of cattle it is the male which mounts the female.

Fire-sticks are used primarily in a ritual context relating to the protection of the homestead from supernatural attack, and I discuss this in some detail in the following section.[16]

In agricultural activities most tasks are carried out by both men and women, although in these joint activities there are strongly marked symbolic oppositions of left and right. The only agricultural activities which are completely separated by cultural norms between the sexes are bush-clearing *(kutemanga mbago)* and threshing *(kutowa uwuhemba)*, carried out exclusively by men, and seed-planting *(kuhadika mbeyu)* and winnowing *(kukwera mawaje)* by women.

The dead are buried in different ways according to the complementarity of the sexes. In both cases the body is stretched out. But men are buried on their right sides with the head pointing to the east and the feet to the west; women are buried on their left sides with the same orientation.[17] The geographical orientation of burial in most of Ugogo links directly with the well-defined series of oppositions which characterize the wider aspects of Gogo cosmology, and it is to these that I now turn.

III

All Gogo homesteads are geographically oriented according to very fixed and explicit rules, although at the present time one may occasionally come across wrongly oriented homesteads. But these are always remarked upon by elders with a proper knowledge of Gogo custom.

Gogo homesteads are composed of long, low, mud-roofed structures arranged about a cattle-byre. The latter is formed by the courtyard in the middle of several wings, all of which are usually joined together at the corners. Each wing *(itembe)* is normally composed of one set of two rooms, an inner *(kugati)* and an outer *(ikumbo).* This unit is called a "house" *(nyumba),* and is the domain of one married woman. Only one doorway *(mulango)* from each "house" leads from the outer room into the courtyard-byre.

In any homestead the first wing constructed runs in a line north–south, with the door on the west, and becomes the eastern wing of the completed homestead. All subsequent wings are built on to this at either end, running westward from it. The eastern house *(nyumba yecilima)* is the senior one, and is occupied ideally by the homestead-head's mother or, if she is dead, his senior wife. Other wives are not ranked and hence the other *nyumba* of the homestead are not oriented in relation to each other by rank.[18] Gogo give two reasons for the construction of a homestead in this manner: *(a)* because the "wind" *(mbeho)* blows from the east *(icilima)* and *(b)* that if you build otherwise, you would "cut the country" *(kudumula yisi),* which is "bad." Both reasons are closely connected.

It is true that throughout the protracted dry season of seven or more months a year, the wind *(mbeho)* does almost continuously blow from the east. But the physical discomfort that this can bring is not the sole or even the major reason for the orientation of Gogo homesteads, which of course have no doorway on the east. The primary reason is that *mbeho* also means "ritual state," and it is with this that Gogo are most concerned. For example, before initiation ceremonies can begin in a ritual area the elders must await the correct ritual and physical conditions, a "good ritual state" *(mbeho swanu).* If a calamity befalls a ritual area, such as storms which destroy the crops, this is due to a "bad ritual state," as well as perhaps a violent wind (both of which are *ibeho).*[19]

The ritual state of the country or ritual area is in general the responsibility of the ritual leader *(mutemi)* in conjunction with the diviner he regularly consults, and the knowledgeable elders of the community. But just as the country has a "ritual state," so too has each homestead in it, and this is the concern of the homestead-head. For example, when he builds a new homestead he must make a new fire with newly made fire-sticks, and then bury them with medicines in the cattle byre. This helps ensure the health and fertility of the homestead's occupants, both human and animal.

Disease and infertility can come into the country (or homestead) from any direction, and space has six aspects (*malanga mutandatu,* lit. "six windows") in Gogo cosmology. Four are the cardinal points, north *(sukuma),* south *(takama),* east *(icilima),* and west *(mwezi);* the other two are "above" *(kucanya)* and "below" *(hasika).* In ritual action, however, these are reduced to five. For medicines placed in the center of the country *(hagati yesi)* and the cardinal points of the geographical boundaries can "close" or "surround the country" *(kupilimila'si).* But these aspects are further subsumed under two opposing categories in the control and manipulation of the ritual state of any area of space.[20] In this context, east is associated with light, fertility, plenty; west with darkness, death, sickness. These associations appear in many values and actions which contain a ritual component, but are not always explicit. When analyzed in terms of an analogical series of oppositions, generally associated with left and right, it is possible to gain a much deeper insight into their meaning than is otherwise possible.[21]

I have noted the orientation of burial in relation to the east–west dichotomy, and the orientation of Gogo homesteads has been described. The eastern wing of the homestead, the "house" of the senior married woman and the "owner" of the homestead, is the locus of the ritual security and fertility of the whole homestead. It is the "house" in which all wives newly married into the homestead reside until their own *nyumba* are built, and each is anointed with oil and medicines (made from the bark of the tree, *mukulo*[22] provided by the senior woman in the eastern *nyumba.* This not only has a pleasant aroma, but also ensures the fertility and health of the new marriage.

In a ritual leader's homestead the rainstones and the stool upon which they are kept are in the eastern *nyumba*. When a delegation of elders visits a diviner (who is usually resident in another ritual area) in connection with the ritual prosperity of the country, they return straight to this *nyumba* with their instructions and medicines. There they are "cooled" *(kupoza)* of the ritual dangers of the journey by the senior wife. When a homestead-head dies it is in this *nyumba* that his bow, stool, and personal accoutrements (collectively termed *ipinde*), which will be inherited by his principal heir, are kept and protected from witchcraft and sorcery attack. And when he is buried in the cattle byre with his head lying towards the eastern *nyumba,* the grave should be aligned with a particular building pole *(isumbili)* in this *nyumba*. This post is called the "nose of the homestead" *(mhula yakaya)*. Beer offerings to the spirits of the dead *(milungu)* are poured in a trough *(mulambo)* molded around this post.

Hence, it may be seen that it is from the eastern *nyumba* of the homestead that the potentialities and properties of its ritual security, health, and fertility flow. All the other parts of the homestead must lie to the west of it. It should be noted also that the midden heap *(cugulu),* on which all the dirt and debris of the homestead are thrown, always lies to the west of it. The location of the midden heap also features in ritual and ceremonial activities. The task the women have of sweeping the living spaces of the homestead and throwing away the rubbish on the midden to the west has ritual dangers and consequent prohibitions attached to it.[23] The critical association here is that the midden lies to the west of the homestead.

When a hoeing party is working over a field which lies on flat ground, they move in a line, shoulder to shoulder, starting on the western boundary and facing east. In this procedure is embodied one of the least obvious expressions of Gogo symbolic and ritual action, at least at the present time. Many Gogo deny that they hoe fields in this manner. However, of twenty-one work parties in which I participated and observed in detail, thirteen (62 percent) were carried out in this way. When I discussed it later some elders admitted that this was normally the case. But if the field is on sloping ground, the party always moves uphill. Thus "up" and "east" are directly (if only implicitly) associated in one series, as opposed to "down" and "west."[24]

Turner has admirably demonstrated[25] that symbolic meanings may be seen upon at least three "levels": the exegetical, operational, and positional. Hence symbolic meaning may not only be seen in the actors' own concepts of ritual action. They may on occasion be unaware of them when, for instance, the symbolic meaning is implicit in the ritual action itself: that is, it has an operational meaning, not an exegetical one.[26] In such cases, interpretation must be esoteric, as only specialists or very perceptive individuals may be consciously aware of the symbolism involved.

The Gogo hoeing pattern, almost unconsciously associated with the geographical dichotomy and conceptual opposition between east and west, is more explicitly associated with the opposition of the sexes and the left and right hands. When the hoeing party moves across the field in a line, the women should (and usually do) make up the "left" (northern) end, and the men the "right" (southern) part of the line. Furthermore, as the length of the hoeing line is seldom enough to cover the whole field, several traversals from west to east are necessary. The usual pattern is for the party to begin along the northern boundary; thus, each subsequent swath is cut to the south of the previous one. If this pattern is adhered to it is evident that the women are always on the end of the line abutting the already "cultivated part" *(wulime)* of the field, the men on the "uncultivated," "wild" part *(ilale).*

The reason given by Gogo for this procedure is that men are supposed to go first over the thick weeds *(musote)* which surround the crop, and cut the first "swath" *(muvizi, nghuwo).* The noun *nghuwo* is derived from the verb *kukuwa,* which means "to wear a new path," "bring into common use," or "domesticate." At the next traversal, the women go over again what the men have already covered (now called *nheje*) while the men open a new swath from the uncultivated part of the field.[27]

A perceptive elder, when discussing these hoeing patterns in company with others, explicitly related them, by analogy, to the other Gogo concepts of orientation and opposing aspects of space which I have described:

> We should not hoe a field from north to south, because in our Gogo custom *(cigogo cetu)* we cannot divide a field along a north–south line . . . (. . . *sicidahile dumula mugunda cipinga, itakama nesukuma*). Do we not also, in our Gogo custom, begin building a homestead at the east? . . . Also, it is because women should always stand on the left side. Now, if they were on the

> south (of the hoeing line) would they not be on the right hand? And would they then be able to cut the first swath itself *(muvizi weneco)?* It is the "bulls" (*zinghambaku,* i.e., young men) who cut the *muvizi*. . . .

Later in the same discussion he went on to link these ideas with the opposed uses of the left and right hands by men and women during sexual intercourse *(vide supra)*.

We have here then a complex set of ideas and values which can only be explained and understood when integrated by analogy into two series of complementary oppositions. The basic oppositions left/right and female/male are linked with opposed values relating to the various spatial aspects of Gogo cosmology. Thus, east, south, up, men, and the right hand are associated with life, light, and fertility; west, north, down, women, and the left hand provide the opposing categories. Men bring the "wild," "untamed," and "undomesticated" into use, by performing the "difficult" tasks of bush-clearing, cutting the first swath, and so on. Women are associated with the "domesticated," "easier" tasks, linked with "cultivated" fields, seed-sowing, and so on.[28]

There are other contexts in which the same sets of oppositions occur. In *nindo* dancing, which takes place during the dry season after the main harvest and is intimately associated with love-making and potential marriage alliances, men always dance on the east, in a line facing the girls on the west. The two lines dance towards each other and away again, but their orientation does not change. During boys' circumcision and initiation ceremonies *(sona zacigotogoto)* the circumcision enclosure *(cibalu)* built in the bush has an entrance only on the west side (in some cases, I was told, it may also be on the south). At any rate, during the operation, the initiate sits with his back towards the east and against a medicated "stump" *(isici),* placed in the center of the camp. In this position the boy is clasped around the chest and over the legs by the operator's assistant, who sits behind and thus to the east of him. The operator *(munghunga)* kneels facing east, while at his back, over the entrance to the enclosure, are further protective medicines.

A most important indication that the west is associated with disease, catastrophe, and death, is embodied in the various purification rituals which take place in ritual areas or neighborhoods from time to time. On all these occasions (which are accompanied by ritual role reversal, women dressing as men, herding the cattle, and performing other "male" tasks) the sickness or ritual contamination is "danced" *(kuvinira)* out of the country to the western boundary and "thrown away" *(kutaga),* preferably into a pool of water or swamp.[29]

Yet further oppositions of left and right in the ritual context may be observed. For example, during the rain-making ceremonies held yearly by the ritual leader, a black ox *(nghongolo nhitu)* is slaughtered at a special ritual and dance *(cidwanga).* All those present are given a fragment of skin *(cigowe)* from the sacrificial ox. Men wear this on their right wrists, women on their left.

Again, all trees and shrubs and plants in Ugogo fall into one of two exclusive and opposed categories: *mupolo* and *mukali. Mupolo* means "non-bitter," "gentle," "non-poisonous," and it is from plants of this category that most medicines *(miti),* ritual fire-sticks, and so on should be made. *Mukali* on the other hand means "bitter," "poisonous," "sharp," and into this category all poisonous and harmful shrubs are classed, although a few medicines may be derived from them.

Color oppositions are not strongly marked or easily related to the two series. "Black" is the ritually auspicious color in Ugogo. Ritual leaders wear it, it is the color of rainclouds *(mavunde)* and the sky (*wulanga:* not only when there are rainclouds, for the color "blue" is in Cigogo included in the category "black," *wutitu*). Black oxen and sheep are slaughtered on all ritual occasions. When the delegation of elders returns from the diviner with instructions and medicines for the rain and crops, they sit on the skin of a black ox to be "cooled" *(kupozwa)* from the ritual dangers of the journey. On some occasions both black and white are required for symbolic purposes, as when a diviner asks (and this is frequent) for a speckled chicken *(nghuku yawusanze).*

The only context in which black has unfortunate connotations is in the expression *mutima watukuwala,* literally "the 'heart' has become black." It denotes a mental state which is a blend of despair and disgust.

The color with primarily dangerous connotations is red *(wudunghu).* It is related explicitly with ritually "hot" *("moto")* states, and hence ritual danger. It also denotes witchcraft and sorcery. Nevertheless, this does not prevent the redness of sacrificial blood from "cooling" ritually dangerous states; it is not necessarily the intrinsic quality of the color itself which denotes danger in Gogo thought, but the context in which it acts as a symbol.

White, on the other hand, is used to symbolize separation and isolation from the community. Thus all initiates, both boys and girls, smear themselves with white clay *(ilongo)* throughout the protracted period of initiation and are ceremonially cleansed of it upon their final reintegration into the community. Either white or black may be used in a burial shroud; the only condition is that it should not be of mixed colors.

The association of white with semen and red with menstrual blood, very frequent in other parts of Africa, is not marked in Ugogo. But in keeping with theories of procreation found in many patrilineal societies, Gogo stress that the whole physical being comes from the father; blood *(sakami),* bones *(mafupa),* skin *(nghuli),* and all. The mother, the "womb" *(muda),* is likened to a round bark-box *(mutundu)* or "something to put things in" *(muwici).*

IV

I have mentioned that left-handed people suffer no disabilities in Gogo society, and that in fact they are considered as occupying a rather special status in certain ritual contexts. We can deepen our understanding of the character of Gogo symbolic classification if we examine in more detail this special status of the left-handed.

A left-handed person is called *munhu wanciji,* literally "a person with the characteristic *nciji*" (cf. the use of *muciji* for the left hand, above). Such a person's left hand is thought of as if it were his right. Thus he is permitted to eat with it and perform other actions with his left hand which are normally associated with the right. I have seen some embarrassment shown by a youth eating with his left hand; this is probably due to the general emphasis on right-handedness. However, no other person would comment upon this or think it undesirable.[30] The parents and kin of a child who has clearly shown himself to be left-handed *(mwana wanciji)* do not feel embarrassed. On the contrary, there is an implication of ritual auspiciousness, in a rather vague and ill-defined way. This derives directly from the following factors.

Very frequently, when a diviner prescribes medicines and ritual action to ensure the safety and fertility of a ritual area (or any other spatial unit), he includes instructions that only left-handed persons, men and women or boys and girls, should carry out certain important procedures. In a typical example of this:

> The ritual delegation *(wanyalamali)* were instructed by the diviner to whom they had gone for rain, fertility, and protective medicines, to place five snail shells *(nghonze),* filled with certain objects, at the five spatial aspects of the country: the east, west, north, and south boundaries, and in the centre. He went on: "The people who are to bury these shells must be a young man and woman, both of whom are left-handed. . . .[31] And when they have finished, they should sleep at the ritual leader's homestead. They should not be elders, but youngsters only *(wadodododo du)* . . . and the ritual leader should slaughter a black sheep for them, so that they stay at his place and do not go home (until the other medicines have been distributed to the population)."

Interpretation of the value placed upon left-handedness in this ritual context, within the more general situation of the "pre-eminence" of the right hand, can best be sought in terms of Needham's analysis of the pre-eminence of the left hand of the Mugwe among the Meru. Needham shows that status and authority among the Meru are divided into two opposed but complementary categories: secular-political power on the one hand, and religious-ritual authority on the other. The former lies in the hands of the elders, the latter in the office of the Mugwe; and these oppositions are in turn related to other complementary dualisms, such as political moieties, groupings of clans, and so on. It is in this context that the left hand of the Mugwe, whose office is characterized by values ascribing it to the "left hand" (and therefore in other contexts "inauspicious") side of the series, stands for his special status which is primarily ritual in character. It is the special nature of his status and authority that is symbolized in the left hand of the Mugwe (Needham 1960a: 31).

Similar factors lead to the Gogo concept of the special ritual status of the left-handed; although in this case the ritual "pre-eminence" of the left hand is not confined to a particular ritual *office*. In Gogo society the right hand symbolizes, in the normal (or "profane") context, maleness, virility, power, and hence authority, albeit in a highly egalitarian society. The right hand is pre-eminent. So a "naturally" left-handed person is ascribed a special status in the ritual (or "sacred") context.[32] The implication here, which I think is a reasonable one, is that for the proper functioning of critical ritual processes and relationships, they should be untrammeled by the strains and potential conflict of secular authority relationships, or those symbols which represent them. Not all societies separate these functions by ascribing them to different social categories; but in those which do, it is possible that the most obvious and frequently used model for their symbolic opposition is that provided by the left and right hands.[33] Furthermore, I suggest that in Gogo society the complementary dualism in "authority" is directly linked with certain oppositions between two broad categories of kinship relationships when viewed upon a certain level.

V

The Gogo kinship system is characterized by a patrilineal descent ideology which is closely interrelated with Gogo concepts of clanship, avoidances, and so on. However, Ego classes all his kin into one broad category, *ndugu,* as opposed to "non-kin" (*wewisa,* sing. *mwiwisa*). *Ndugu* includes affines. Another broad category, *wandelwa* (sing. *mundelwa*),[34] includes all cognates of his own generation but excludes affines and certain lineal kin or those to whom he is related by filiation (such as "father" or "mother"). Thus all kin and affines are *ndugu,* but not all *ndugu* are *ndelwa* as well.

All *ndugu* belong, in certain contexts in which kin and affines are involved, to one of two categories: *wosogwe* or *wokulume* ("those of the father's side" or "those of the male/right side"); and *wokucekulu* ("those of the female/left side"). The former includes all kin related to Ego by agnatic ties only; the latter all kin *(ndugu)* who fall outside the other category. Hence *wokucekulu,* in the few contexts in which these categories are relevant (see later), denotes matrilateral, uterine, and affinal kin. Even male Ego's own affines are included in this category, for to his children they are matrilateral kin and, in a patrilineal descent system, "those whom we marry" *(welizenjere).* Therefore into the category *wokucekulu* are most commonly classed "mother's brothers" (*wakuku,* whom Ego addresses—and by whom he is addressed—as *"bulayi"*); "wives' kin" (*wakwe* and *walamu*), who may also be referred to collectively as *"welizenjere"* ("those whom we marry and build with"); and matrilateral cross-cousins *(wahizi wokucekulu).* At funerals and weddings, or the settlement of disputes among close kin, the two categories *wokulume* and *wokucekulu* are differentiated but referred to jointly as *"wezimbavu zose,"* lit. "those of both sets of ribs *(mbavu)."*[35]

In situations where clan affiliation is relevant, clans are conceived of as linked to each other as joking partners *(watani)* or in "perpetual kinship relationships," usually between the categories "mother's brothers" and "sister's sons" *(wakuku/wehwa)*.[36] But in Gogo concepts of kinship, joking partnerships *(wutani)* between clans arise out of "cross-cousinship" *(wuhizi)* in the past, which in turn, of course, arises out of a previous marriage between the clans. Hence the category *wokucekulu* can also classify in the more general sense the members of all clans linked with Ego's as joking partners, in perpetual kinship relationships, and as affines, irrespective of genealogical ties. In this context the members of all these categories subsumed under *wokucekulu* stand opposed to all members of Ego's own patrilineal clan, *wosogwe* or *wokulume*.

But I have noted that patrilineal descent groups of any depth do not function as corporate groups in Ugogo. Neither are clans and lineages unambiguously exogamous.[37] Hence these terms do not denote corporate kin groups related to one another in various ways, but categories of kin which are Ego-oriented. There is no system of affinal alliance linking patrilineal descent groups, although marriage with the category "matrilateral cross-cousin" *(wuhizi wokucekulu)* is theoretically "preferred." I stress "theoretically," because marriages are seldom if ever founded upon this relationship, and quite other factors determine the choice of spouses in the Gogo marriage system.[38] As in all nonpreferential and nonprescriptive marriage systems, locality and spatial propinquity become the critical factors involved.[39] Cross-cousin marriages are therefore a function of the restricted spatial range of marriage, although the relationship may later be used to justify the marriage on a *logically* satisfying basis, given the patrilineal descent ideology.

Contrary to the situation which exists among many patrilineal peoples (particularly in Bantu-speaking Africa), the shallow agnatic group of the "sons of one man," made up of sets of full-brothers, rely heavily upon close affinal and matrilateral kin, rather than more distant (and dispersed) agnates, in all major spheres of social action. Thus, in spite of the generally modifying influence of a high residential mobility, Gogo live near their close affines. And of course the close residence of affines in one generation leads to the close residence of cross-cousins in the next. This, combined with the continually restricted spatial range of marriage in each generation, results in the pattern outlined.

Despite the ideology of patrilineal descent, then, Gogo are constantly dependent to an almost equal extent upon close agnates, close affines, and matrilateral kin, particularly "mother's brothers." This shows itself in all spheres of action, economic, political, and ritual. "Mother's brothers" contribute one-quarter to one-third of the large bridewealth *(cigumo)* for the first marriages of their "sister's sons," and receive the same proportion from the marriages of their "sister's daughters." The rest are provided and accepted by agnatic kin. The part of the bridewealth passed between the agnatic kin of the spouses is called *"zokulume"* ("the [animals] of the male/right side"), and those which pass between the matrilateral kin are *zokucekulu* ("those of the female/left side").

"Mother's brother" also provides and receives the ritual *itambi* goat, an essential part of the bridewealth transaction. But these obligations are fulfilled only if the relationship between particular persons in the categories "mother's brother/sister's son" has been sustained by consistent prior cooperation. This cooperation is manifested in many ways, including the provision by the "mother's brother" of a beast for ritual slaughter during his "sister's son's" circumcision ceremony, which is deemed essential for the latter's recovery. So too, the "sister's son" must later provide a special sheep *(ngholo yakwemera uwupinde)* on the death of his "mother's brother," before the latter's son (the former's cross-cousin) can inherit his father's bow *(ipinde);* and so on.

Therefore, if these relationships with matrilateral kin are to survive as active relationships, the cooperation of close affines is essential. It also implies a close and continuing relationship between brother and sister, particularly full-siblings, and this indeed is the case in Gogo society.

Hence a person sees the close kin and affines upon whom he is primarily dependent for most of his life, and later for his children, as a close-resident set of persons in various kinship and affinal categories, but who are also grouped into two fundamental and opposed categories, "those of the male/right side," from whom he traces descent, derives his status, and inherits property; and "those of the female/left side," upon whom he depends in various economic and ritual transactions.[40] With his close agnates there is always tension (except perhaps with full-siblings), deriving from competition over authority and the deployment and use of livestock and scarce resources. Sorcery and witchcraft accusations are frequent between fathers and sons, and between half-siblings. With his matrilateral kin there are no such tensions; despite the difficulties inherent in such relationships (some of them are joking relationships), there appear frequent ritual interdependence and affective ties, in accordance with the jurally defined rights and conventional attitudes involved. The only close kin between whom witchcraft and sorcery accusation can never occur are those who stand in the relationship categories "mother's brother/sister's son."

The dual and complementary categories *wokulume* and *wokucekulu* further subsume members of clans linked with Ego's in various ways. So Ego may view his total "universe of kin" (whether "close" and cooperating or "distant" and potential) as belonging to one of two opposed, yet complementary, categories; but only on a certain limited level and in restricted contexts, which have already been described. The dual classification does not order or "inform" the total kinship and marriage system as it does in systems of asymmetric prescriptive alliance. But on the level of their limited structural relevance, the two kin categories described are directly linked with the series of oppositions which constitute the Gogo system of dual symbolic classification.

VI

The total series of oppositions may be represented in tabular form as follows:[41]

right *(kulume)* (hand, side)	left *(kucekulu)* (hand, side)
male	female
man	woman
hand used in eating *(mulilo)* ("clean" hand)	hand used after defecation ("dirty" hand)
hand used in taking or giving food or gifts	hand used in taking or giving tobacco
strength	weakness
"superior"	"inferior"
"clever" *(-sugu)*	"stupid" *(-lele)*
side on which a man lies in sexual intercourse	side on which a woman lies in sexual intercourse
side on which men buried	side on which women buried
hand *woman* uses in sexual play	hand *man* uses in sexual play ("clever" in this context)
bow	calabash, drum
fire-stick used in standing position	fire-stick used in "lying" position
bush-clearing	seed planting

threshing	winnowing, grinding
east	west
south	north
"up"	"down"
side of homestead ("eastern house") from which ritual properties flow	side of homestead at which midden is placed
"uncultivated" parts of fields *(ilale)*	"cultivated" parts of fields *(wulime)*
"new" swath in hoeing *(muvizi, nghuwo)*	"old" swath in hoeing *(nheje)*
fertility, health	death, sickness
——	evil spirits, sorcerers, witches
"cool"	"hot"
plants which are *mupolo:* "medicines"	plants which are *mukali:* "poisonous"
black	red/white
——	*-ciji:* left-handedness, auspicious in ritual contexts
"older people"	"younger people"
hand upon which men wear skin of sacrificial ox at rainmaking . . . *(cigowe)*	hand upon which women wear skin of sacrificial ox at rainmaking *(cigowe)*
senior woman of homestead (mother or first wife: *munyakaya)*	junior wives
"father" and all kin "on the man's/right side" *(wokulume)*	"mother" and all kin "on the woman's/left side"; affines *(wokucekulu)*
dominance, political authority, property	certain economic and ritual transactions in life-crises
spirits contacted through father's gravestone	ritual interdependence in life-crises
bridewealth which is the concern of patrilineal kin	bridewealth and the ritual *itambi* goat which are the concern of matrilateral kin

It is evident that the ascription of certain terms to one or other of the series is surrounded by ambiguity in some contexts. The foregoing analysis, however, shows that this in itself is a confirmation of the basic principles underlying the classification into dual symbolic categories.

Notes

1. Durkheim and Mauss 1903, translated by Needham (1963). All references are collected at the end of this paper.
2. Cf. also Lévi-Strauss 1958, chap. 15, passim; Hertz 1909.

3. The data on which this paper is based were collected during a period of field-work among the Gogo people of Central Tanzania, from September 1961 until the middle of 1963. The first part of the study was carried out under the auspices of the then Colonial Social Science Research Council, and thence as a Research Fellow of the East African Institute of Social Research, Makerere University College, Kampala. My later work on the material has been facilitated by a Crawford Studentship at King's College, Cambridge. I owe much to my friend and assistant, Mr. Madinda ala Mutowinaga, without whose help most of the material here presented would not have been recorded.

4. There is a considerable literature on the Gogo, dating from the middle of the nineteenth century onwards, but little of this material is of use in a systematic sociological analysis of Gogo society. A select bibliography is given in Rigby 1964. Some aspects of Gogo social organization are discussed in Rigby 1966, 1967a, 1967b, 1967c, 1968a, 1968b.

5. I must make it clear that I am talking here about the "traditional" system of Gogo political organization, which still exists, although it has been overlaid by other systems since colonial penetration in the area in the 1890s, and subsequent changes since Tanganyikan independence in December 1961. The ritual leader is what Gogo call "the one of the stool" *(mutemi weligoda)* or "the owner of the stool" *(munyaligoda)* upon which the rainstones are kept, as opposed to the "government chief" *(mutemi wesirikali)* of the British colonial régime: an office created by the colonial administration. Cf. Rigby 1971.

6. Rainfall averages just over 20 inches a year in most of Ugogo. It is erratic and localized. Droughts occur somewhere in the area with frightening regularity, once every 10, 6, or even 3 years (cf. Rigby 1964: 19–22), causing recurrent famines.

7. In one neighborhood of 45 homesteads, the homestead-heads were related to one another by 126 significant ties of kinship and affinity. Of the total, 89 (or 70.7 percent) were affinal ties of one kind or another, mainly between "brothers-in-law" *(walamu)*. Only 17 (13.4 percent) were agnatic ties.

8. The average population of Gogo homesteads in 1962–63 was about nine persons, both adults and children. But the variation in numbers is large, ranging from two persons to over fifty; and in one or two cases, over a hundred persons. Homestead groups were probably larger in the past than they are today.

9. Polygyny is highly valued in Gogo society, although as in most polygynous societies only 30–35 percent of married men have more than one wife living with them at any one time. Bridewealth is comparatively large and is ideally over 20 head of cattle and about 16 small stock; in 1962–63 bridewealth averaged 15 head of cattle and 11 small stock.

10. Cf. Beidelman 1961: 252, n. 3.

11. Cf. Needham 1960a: 26; Beidelman 1961: 252; Hertz 1909, trans. p. 97.

12. Another informant suggested that this was in fact the reason why the left hand was called the "female hand" and the right hand the "male." He

said: "The reason is love play, because when you sleep with your wife, you sleep on your right side and use the left hand, and the wife sleeps on her left and uses the right."

13. As among the Nuer, for example; see Evans-Pritchard 1956: 235.

14. For example, see Wieschhoff 1938: 209 et passim; also Beidelman 1963: 46–49.

15. Among the Ngulu and Kaguru the bow is also primarily a male symbol, but may on occasion represent female, depending upon the context (cf. Beidelman 1964: 370, 372–73).

16. Gogo rainstones *(zimvula)* are of three types: round, bored stones; round, unbored stones; and long "phallic-shaped" stones, sometimes with a hole bored in one end. In spite of these stones being labeled "male" and "female" by some observers (cf. Hartnoll 1932 and 1942) this association appears to have been imposed from outside. All the Gogo ritual leaders and elders I asked about this denied that there are "male" and "female" rainstones. All are referred to simply as *"zimvula,"* "the rains."

17. In Cinyambwa in western and southwestern Ugogo men and women are buried on their right and left sides respectively as elsewhere in Ugogo, but the deceased's head is pointed in the direction from which his or her clan is said to have come to Ugogo originally. The numerous Gogo clans claim to have originated from one of many surrounding peoples. Thus burials take place with the head pointing towards any of the four cardinal points, depending upon the clan affiliation of the deceased.

18. In some cases, when the homestead-head's mother has been living in his homestead before she dies, a junior wife may move into the eastern *nyumba,* the senior wife preferring to remain in the house she has previously occupied. But this is the only case when the eastern *nyumba* is not occupied by the senior woman of the homestead, who may also be called *munyakaya,* "the owner of the homestead."

19. The complexities of the concept *mbeho,* its manifestations, and the ways in which it can be influenced and controlled, are explained more fully in Rigby 1968a.

20. Cf. Littlejohn 1963: 9 et passim.

21. Part of the function of a useful conceptual scheme, or tool of analysis, is to relate what might otherwise appear to be isolated and inexplicable phenomena and, by thus relating them, to suggest explanation and facilitate understanding. Evans-Pritchard (1960) states in his Introduction to Needham's translation of Hertz (1909), p. 15: "Hertz's essays exemplify . . . (a) . . . descriptive integration, the meaning of the facts being shown to lie not in themselves, considered as separate facts, but in their interrelation; the art of the anthropologist being to reveal this and hence their meaning."

22. I was unable to obtain a specimen of this for identification. But the plant used must certainly belong to the broad class *mupolo* ("non-bitter," "gentle," "non-poisonous") in Gogo classification (see below).

23. For example, it is forbidden *(mwiko)* for a woman who has swept her house and is carrying the rubbish to the midden to greet, or be greeted, by

anyone else. Breach of this rule has been known to be taken to the local elders' courts for compensation, which is usually of a symbolic or ritual kind. Perhaps the offending woman is made to bear the enactment of the same offense against her by the woman she has offended. This is called *kwilipila ndole* (lit. "to pay each other the finger").

24. Cf. Littlejohn 1963: 9.

25. Turner 1961, reprinted 1965: 82–83; 1962: 124–25.

26. Cf. Turner 1964: 28–29, 41, 47–48.

27. The only exceptions to this pattern are: *(a)* when a field is hoed uphill, as already mentioned, although the women are still on the left of the men and the basic procedure is the same, and *(b)* when the field abuts another on the *southern* boundary and bush or uncultivated land on the north. In this case the women may begin on the southern end of the line (near the "cultivated land": *wulime*). The whole spatial orientation would then be reversed.

28. The associations that the matrilineal Kaguru give in this context are opposite to the Gogo ones and are linked by Kaguru with their values about the "nature of women" (cf. Beidelman 1961: 255–56). The pattern which occurs in Gogo society may also seem odd when it is compared with attitudes displayed towards "in-marrying" wives among other *patrilineal* Bantu-speaking peoples. Women marrying into the localized lineage group are "strangers," "distant" both in terms of relationship as well as residence, and therefore suspected of disrupting the cohesion of the lineage while at the same time providing it with its only means of continuity. But in Gogo society, in fact, women married are not "strangers," and the unity of the "lineage group" is a minor consideration because of its lack of political significance.

29. A full analysis of some Gogo purification rituals is given in Rigby 1968a.

30. Cf. Evans-Pritchard 1956: 235–36; but Gogo do not mutilate the left hand as Nuer youths do for a short period with the *thiau* rings (ibid., p. 235).

31. It should be noted here that a further opposition in Gogo values is between odd and even numbers. Even numbers are auspicious and required in most ritual contexts; odd numbers are rejected as the opposite. Thus the delegation which goes to the diviner should ideally be composed of any even number of men, usually about six. These ideas may be derived by the Gogo from the Baraguyu, who live in areas throughout Ugogo. The Gogo word *wanyalamali,* used for the ritual delegation, is derived from the Baraguyu term *olamal,* which means any group or delegation which goes to consult divination, usually on behalf of an age-set (cf. Beidelman 1960; Fosbrooke 1948: 18; Gulliver 1963: 27). Many rain diviners in Ugogo are Baraguyu, but the majority are Gogo. The opposition of odd and even numbers also appears in the Gogo interpretation of omens.

32. By the use of these terms I am not suggesting that I subscribe totally to the Durkheimian dichotomy of the sacred and the profane as two universal, opposing, and exhaustive categories.

33. This explanation of the ritual status of left-handedness is confined to one level only. I suggest that there is another dimension to the problem, which may be explored only through the analysis of the broader question of "reversal" and "role reversal" in ritual contexts. However, this is a problem of a complexity which requires separate treatment, and I propose to explore the Gogo material relevant to it in another publication (Rigby 1968a). But cf. Gluckman 1949 and 1963; also Needham 1960a: 27, n. 3.

34. The term *mundelwa* is derived from the verb *kulela,* "to bear a child," in its passive form *kulelwa,* "to be born." It denotes "those who are born of (related by filiation) kin" in all lines; (bilateral) filiation is stressed, rather than (unilineal) descent.

35. The reference here is to both sides of the rib-cage of sacrificial animals killed at these ceremonies; but the Gogo do not divide up the meat of such animals among kin with reference to the "sides." Age differentiation is more important in this situation.

36. Ribgy 1964: 84–85.

37. Ibid., pp. 227–30.

38. Of 203 marriages, past and present, only 45 (22.2 percent) were between kin of any kind. Of these 45, only 11 (24.3 percent of kin marriages) were between classificatory cross-cousins, and another 13 (28.8 percent) were with persons already "affines" *(welizenjere)* in some way: cf. Ibid., pp. 228 ff.

39. Cf. Fortes 1962; also Harris 1962 and La Fontaine 1962 in the same volume; Rigby 1964: 272–3 ff. Marriage is both normatively and statistically patri-virilocal in Ugogo.

40. This does not mean that there is no ritual interdependence among close agnates. In fact, it is usually the necessity of contacting the spirits of the dead *(milungu)* through the gravestone of their father *(citenjelo)* that keeps sets of full-siblings residentially near their half-brothers, and cooperating in certain fields, after their father's death. It is in the ritual context of "life crises" such as initiation, marriage, and death, that dependence upon the *wokucekulu* is greatest, and in which specific ritual functions are allocated to them. This, I have suggested, is analogically related to the ritual connotations of left-handedness in the contexts I have already described.

41. The methodological desirability for thus tabulating the pairs of symbolic oppositions is indicated by Needham 1960a: 25; 1958: 97, 99.

References

Beidelman, T. O.

1960 The Baraguyu. *Tanganyika Notes and Records* 55: 244–78.

1961 Right and left hand among the Kaguru: a note on symbolic classification. *Africa* 31: 250–57.

1963 Kaguru Omens. *Anthropological Quarterly* 36: 43–59.

1964 Pig (Guluwe): an essay on Ngulu sexual symbolism and ceremony. *Southwestern Journal of Anthropology* 20: 359–92.

CARNELL, W. J.
1955 Sympathetic magic among the Gogo of Mpwapwa district. *Tanganyika Notes and Records* 39: 25–38.
DURKHEIM, ÉMILE, and MAUSS, MARCEL
1903 De quelques formes primitives de classification. *Année sociologique,* 1901–2 (1903). Translated by R. Needham, *Primitive classification*. London, 1963.
EVANS-PRITCHARD, E. E.
1953 Nuer Spear Symbolism. *Anthropological Quarterly* 26: 1–19.
1956 *Nuer religion*. Oxford.
1960 Introduction to Hertz 1909. Translated by R. Needham, *Death and the right hand*. London, 1960.
FARON, L. C.
1962 Symbolic values and the integration of society among the Mapuche of Chile. *American Anthropologist* 1151–64. [Above, chap. 10.]
FORTES, M.
1962 Introduction in Fortes, ed., *Marriage in tribal societies*. Cambridge Papers in Social Anthropology, no. 3, Cambridge, 1962.
FORTES, M., and DIETERLEN, G., (eds.)
1965 *African systems of thought*. London.
FOSBROOKE, H. A.
1948 An administrative survey of the Masai social system. *Tanganyika Notes and Records,* vol. 26.
GLUCKMAN, M.
1949 The role of the sexes in Wiko circumcision ceremonies. In M. Fortes, ed., *Social structure: studies presented to A. R. Radcliffe-Brown*. Oxford.
1963 *Order and rebellion in tribal Africa*. London.
GULLIVER, P. H.
1963 *Social control in an African society*. London.
HARRIS, G.
1962 Taita bridewealth and affinal relationships. In M. Fortes, ed. *Marriage in tribal societies*. Cambridge, 1962.
HARTNOLL, A. V.
1932 The Gogo *Mtemi*. *South African Journal of Science* 29: 737–41.
1942 Praying for rain in Ugogo. *Tanganyika Notes and Records* 13: 29–60.
HERTZ, R.
1909 La prééminence de la main droite: étude sur la polarité religieuse. *Revue Philosophique* 68: 553–80. Translated by R. and C. Needham, in *Death and the right hand*. London, 1960. [Above, chap. 1.]
LA FONTAINE, J.
1962 Gisu marriage and affinal relations. In M. Fortes, ed., *Marriage in tribal societies*. Cambridge, 1962.
LÉVI-STRAUSS, CLAUDE
1958 *Anthropologie structurale*. Paris. Translated by Claire Jacobson

and Brooke Grundfest Schoepf, *Structural anthropology*. New York, 1963.

LITTLEJOHN, J.

1963 Temne space. *Anthropological Quarterly* 36: 1–17.

NEEDHAM, R.

1958 A structural analysis of Purum society. *American Anthropologist* 60: 75–101.

1960a The left hand of the Mugwe: an analytical note on the structure of Meru symbolism. *Africa* 30: 20–33. [Above, chap. 7.]

1960b Alliance and classification among the Lamet. *Sociologus* 10: 97–118.

1963 Introduction to Durkheim & Mauss, *Primitive classification*. London.

RIGBY, P. J. A.

1964 The Gogo: cattle and kinship in a semi-pastoral society. Ph.D. dissertation, Cambridge (MS.).

1966 Sociological factors in the contact of the Gogo of central Tanzania with Islam. In I. M. Lewis, ed., *Islam in tropical Africa*. London: Oxford University Press for the International African Institute.

1967a Changes in local government and the national elections. In Lionel Cliffe, ed., *One-party democracy*. Nairobi: East African Publishing House.

1967b Time and structure in Gogo kinship. *Cahiers d'études africaines* 28: 637–58.

1967c The structural context of girls' puberty rites. *Man*, n.s., 2: 434–44.

1968a Some Gogo rituals of purification: an essay on social and moral categories. In E. R. Leach, ed., *Dialectic in practical religion*. Cambridge Papers in Social Anthropology, no. 5. Cambridge: Cambridge University Press.

1968b Joking relationships, kin categories, and clanship among the Gogo. *Africa* 38: 133–54.

1969 *Cattle and kinship among the Gogo: a semi-pastoral society of central Tanzania*. Ithaca, N.Y., and London: Cornell University Press.

1971 Politics and modern leadership roles in Ugogo. In *Profiles of Change: African Society and Colonial Rule*, edited by V. W. Turner. London and New York: Cambridge University Press.

TURNER, V. W.

1961 Ritual symbolism, morality and social structure among the Ndembu. *Rhodes-Livingstone Journal*, Manchester. Reprinted in Fortes and Dieterlen, eds., *African systems of thought*, vol. 3. London, 1965.

1962 Three symbols of *Passage* in Ndembu circumcision ritual. In M. Gluckman, ed., *Essays on the ritual of social relations*. Manchester, 1962.

1964 (written 1957). Symbols in Ndembu ritual. In M. Gluckman, ed., *Closed systems and open minds: the limits of naïvety in social anthropology*. London, 1964.

WERNER, A.
1904 Note on the terms used for "right hand" and "left hand" in the Bantu languages. *Journal of the African Society* 13: 112–16. [Below, Appendix.]

WIESCHHOFF, H. A.
1938 Concepts of right and left in African cultures. *Journal of the American Oriental Society* 53: 202–17.

Temne Right and Left: An Essay on the Choreography of Everyday Life

14

James Littlejohn

I

The Temne, who live mainly by cultivating rice, inhabit the rain forest area of northern Sierra Leone. They are divided into autonomous chiefdoms in which the basic (landowning, etc.) group is a short-depth patrilineage, called *makas*. Mother's lineage is recognized with the name *makara,* but there is no matriline in the sense of perpetual lines of descent used as the principle of recruitment into enduring groups or for the transmission of stipulated property or statuses. The data on left and right I collected seem perhaps not too promising. There are no moieties, no trace of a formal dual organization, and no association of left and right with mother's and father's line or with females and males.

When asked about the different everyday employments of the two hands, Temne merely say that the right hand is stronger than the left, and that is why it is the more active one and the left used merely to support its activity, e.g., by holding objects steady. This state of affairs they say is "of God" *(tei ta Kuru),* a phrase they often use in contexts where we would normally say "natural," indicating that the speaker sees nothing problematical about the state of affairs so designated. The term they use to designate strength is *ofoso,* which as in our everyday use of the words "power" or "strength" can mean several different sorts of effectiveness—physical strength or power, political or social power, and the sort which, because we do not believe in it, we usually qualify as "supernatural" or "magical." The whole matter is much more

A shorter version of this article appeared in *New Society,* 9 February 1967, pp. 198–99. The permission of the editor of *New Society* to reprint much of the material in that place is gratefully acknowledged.

complex than their first explanations would suggest, and it is best to begin with the ground of distinction between left and right.

II. The Ground of Distinction

Since there is no such thing as left and right "in space," these regions being relative to the direction an individual faces, the ground of distinction must first be sought in the human body. It must, to meet the logical requirements of a ground of distinction, by uniting make possible the separation of left and right on the body and it must confer a primary meaning on the two halves. This ground I suggest must be a fixed, in a sense absolute, and directed straight line. It must be fixed, for otherwise there could be almost no end to the subdivisions of left and right; e.g., each hand could have a left side and a right side, and so on. The line must be directed, represent a sort of vector; otherwise left and right on the body could change sides depending on which end of the line was taken as a starting point, the point of departure for viewing a body. Moving from the feet up, left is on our right-hand side and right is on our left-hand side. Evidently the vector is a movement from head to feet, from "high" to "low."

Apart from vectorial quality such a line does exist, called in Western medicine the median line. On it lie important organs on some of which it is visible. These are the nose, mouth, navel, genitals, and anus. I do not know if the Temne recognize a median line in quite the same sense as Western physiologists do, but the line of organs on it as conceived and treated by them seems to me to qualify for the epithet "sacred" much more than either hand does; not because these organs are any more important than hands in maintaining life, but because they are the object or means of more intense ritual. At any rate, whether the line is sacred or not it is from their functions with respect to it that Temne left and right hands receive their primary meanings. Before going on to show this, a few brief references to the place of these organs in everyday life and in ritual will underline their importance.

In Temne the one word, *neysem,* means both life and breath, inhaled through the nose and mouth. Ancestors sometimes communicate directly with descendants by means of the nose; if one sneezes while eating, that is a sign the ancestors want more of the meal than the small share one threw aside for them before beginning. In so far as ritual announces position in society, this function is performed more by eating than by any other performance, by the company one eats with and the foods one is forbidden or permitted to eat. Adult men eat with each other, normally agnates, children with children, and co-wives with each other. Each clan has its tabooed foods, special persons such as chiefs or twins are prohibited certain foods, and each rite of passage is marked by its own food restrictions.

The placenta is secretly buried by mother or grandmother, as both mother and child are vulnerable through it. The umbilical cord is buried along with the seed of a tree, preferably a kola. This is done publicly within or near the father's village so that "everyone" knows the tree belongs to the person whose cord was buried there. It becomes the legal testimony to the owner's right to land in that village; a common question asked of litigants in land dispute cases is "Where is your cord buried?" Also, in adult life the individual takes pride in giving presents of kola nuts from his own tree. The place of kola nuts in West African prestation is too well known to need further description.

The place of the genitals in ritual also does not require extended description. Boys are circumcised and girls undergo clitoridectomy as a necessary step towards adult status. The parts excised are considered extremely powerful. The collected crop of foreskins from a cohort of male initiates is buried under water to cool them off and to ensure that they are not used to make harmful attacking medicines. Temne explain the presence of a boy's father or uncle at his initiation as being required to prevent his foreskin falling into the wrong hands. Should a doctor use it to make medicine there would be the danger that the medicine, instead of attacking wrongdoers as intended, would attack the person whose blood is a component of it. Apart from ritual matters, the Temne regard the penis as a specially powerful organ because they hold that all veins converge in it, and that blood is a major component of life and an endowment from the ancestors.

The clitoris is thought to be even more powerful in medicine than the foreskin. I have heard two accounts of its use; one that the Digbas (the women empowered to excise clitorises) eat them to "acquire power and fame," the other that the Yambas (the best male doctors) buy them from the Digbas to make medicine with. For various reasons I think the second is the more usual.

I have never heard the Temne calling this line of organs the "line of life," but there is good reason to believe they think of it in these terms, for it has a correlate in physical space which is explicitly called the "line of life." This is the east-west line. For the Temne, east provides the primary orientation; it is "where you take direction from." The ancestors live in the east, all sacrifices to them must be done facing east. Life, they say, started in the east. West is associated with death, e.g., cemeteries are on the west of the town or village. The Poro bush where young men "die" at initiation is also on the west of town, and when they return after "rebirth" they do so by the east road. East like the head is "up" and "high," while west like the anus is "down" and "low." "We think of the east as rising up like a hill, of everything going up to the east," Temne say. The adverb for "up" *(rokom)* is often used in place of the word for east *(rotoron),* and west *(ropil)* is often used for "down." "Up" and "down," "high" and "low," can be drawn upon in Temne as in English to make all sorts of invidious comparisons between people with respect to degrees of knowledge, power, and social status.

East and west are also located in time, east being the past and west the future. Temne regard the past as in a general sense "good" and the future as "bad." As proof of this they point out how much better the ancestors were than they are. This movement of time from good to bad will someday culminate in catastrophe, when the world will be destroyed and a new one created afresh by God. It has already happened once, this being the second world. When it happens the world rotates on its axis until east becomes west.

Since facing east is the primary orientation, north and south are on the left and right respectively. The adjective for left, *mero,* with the prefix *ka* means north, and the adjective for right, *dio,* similarly forms *kadio,* south. North like west is considered dark and south like east is light. Thunder and lightning are prepared in the north. South is a region of "good breezes," and a doctor may recommend a trip south for a convalescent patient. I must also report however that north is spoken of as "up" and south as "down." I do not know the reason for this; it is possible that it is a case of reversal (see below), but more likely that here there is a switch to a purely geographical frame of reference; north is spoken of as "up" always as far as I know in the context of going on journeys; North Sierra Leone is mountainous, as all Temne are aware.

III. Right and Left Hands

It is out of their relationship to the central line of organs on the body that hands receive their primary meanings. The rule is that the right hand serves the upper half, particularly the mouth, and the left hand serves the lower half, particularly the genitals and anus. Food must be conveyed to the mouth only by the right hand, and when washing the region of the mouth after a meal again only the right hand may be used. As far as possible, in the preparation of food women must avoid handling it with the left hand. When cleaning the anus only the left hand may be used. Also, in the case of men engaged in sex play only the left hand may touch the woman's genitals. From these activities right and left hands are sometimes said to be "clean" and "dirty." No one on that account contemplates depriving himself of the left hand.

What is really dirty in Temne eyes is to use one hand for the activity appropriate to the other. "Clean" and "dirty" as applied to hands are secondary, weak meanings. The primary meanings the hands have can only be discovered by examination of the significance of eating, excretion, and copulation. Such examination reveals a basic social dualism which, though not a formal feature of Temne social structure in the sense in which moieties are in those societies which have them, is yet the social dualism corresponding to that of the hands. The dualism is that of being-in-proper-relation-with-others and not-being-in-proper-relation-with-others.

Eating among the Temne is not only a most sociable act, the men of a household eating together with right hands out of a common bowl; it is also an earnest of one's good faith towards co-eaters. They say, e.g., "you only eat with people you are friends with"; "if you ask a man to eat with you and he refuses you know that man harbors evil thoughts against you"; "in your book who was it who wouldn't eat with Jesus?" Peace and social harmony are associated with the right hand. For example to bring a quarrel to an end the junior (son, wife, commoner, etc.) should ask forgiveness of the senior (father, husband, chief, etc.), who grants it simply by placing his right hand on the junior's head. Similarly at sacrifices to ancestors each participant should touch the sacrifice with his right hand or as a minimal gesture extend his right hand over it. Sacrifice should and, in important ones, does end in a common meal. Appeal to the ancestors is efficacious only if all participating have peace in their hearts towards each other.

Sometimes one has to affirm unequivocally one's adherence to the moral imperatives of one's society. Thus sometimes in Temne court cases litigants or witnesses swear to tell the truth, and in doing so must touch an instrument called *ansassa* with the right hand, or a stick held in it. It is also much used by husbands for controlling wives; a suspicious husband will demand of a wife to swear on an *ansassa* that she has no lover. Sometimes one has to signal one's good intentions towards others, particularly in greetings. Like us, Temne do so with the right hand. It is also obligatory to offer and receive gifts with the right hand.

Defecation, on the other hand, is always performed alone, as is cleaning the anus afterwards. The individual is in intense interaction with himself. Sex play, if not quite solitary, is an intense interaction of two who are not under surveillance by the community. The Temne are extremely suspicious, to say the least, of activity not under surveillance by the community. An individual who engages in too much solitary activity, or even simply rejects everyday sociability too much, is suspected of witchcraft, an evil and illegal activity. The witch is the prototype of the secretive, hence evil, person. I have been present when a villager was denounced as a witch by the whole community just because he had deliberately hidden the fact, by wearing long trousers, that he was suffering from a boil on the leg. In the villagers' view, had it been an ordinary boil he would have consulted a doctor and let everyone know about it. That he hid it meant that the boil was caused by anti-witchcraft medicine; hence he must be a witch. Witchcraft is explicitly connected with the left. Witches are known to grow a special organ low down on the left-hand side of the trunk, called *ankunto*. This is the region of the body where hate develops; it is hate which makes *ankunto* grow, and this is the source of the remarkable and evil power of the witch.

These primary meanings, of inclusion in and exclusion from normal community life, are the basis of the meanings of right and left as omens, with right as auspicious and left inauspicious. If on setting out on a journey you stub the toes of the right foot your project will be successful, if the left it will be unsuccessful. In explaining this, Temne are often explicit about what going on a journey implies; they will say, e.g., "if you stub the toes of the left foot the person you are going to see won't be at home." One journeys to "see people," to trade, fix politics, arrange marriage, etc.; right indicates one will make one's contacts, left that one will not. While on the road a bush rat jumping across one's path similarly announces success (from left to right) or failure (right to left). Similarly, if the muscles around the right eye start twitching involuntarily, that means you are being gossiped about in a reputation-enhancing way: if those round the left eye, in a denigrating way—acceptance and rejection by the community.

There are many modes of not-being-in-proper-relation-with-others; another one the Temne take account of is technical or aesthetic awkwardness. If one handles a tool in such a way as to inconvenience workmates, or sings so out of tune as to irritate others, one is liable to be told that one is behaving left-handedly.

It is consistent with these meanings of left and right that the right hand should be the more conspicuously active of the two in everyday life. Most Temne most of the time are law-abiding people at peace with kinsmen and neighbors. Wrong use of the left hand by a child should be severely punished. He is first of all rapped on the kunckles, and if he persists the hand is tightly wrapped with rags so that it cannot be used. A naturally left-handed person whose instincts survive this treatment is allowed to use implements—hoes, hammers, etc.—in a left-handed way, but he must still employ right and left hands as other people do for the activities described above.

However, despite the treatment accorded a too-active left hand in infancy, despite the inconspicuous role of the left hand in everyday life, and despite their initial assertion that the right hand is the stronger, Temne will eventually say in any sustained discussion of the matter that the left hand is the stronger.

IV. Reversal

In the totality of existence a Temne individual passes from the state of being alive to that of being dead, in which he continues to exist though in another mode. Alive he existed as *wuni* (person), dead he exists as *anina* (spirit). At death his everyday relationships with other persons are dissolved, he passes out of normal community relationships at best to become an ancestor, at worst to be forgotten. Once he is removed from normal relationships with others his left hand becomes stronger than his right. The right hand dies while the left talks to God, giving him a true account of the individual's life. (Temne "expect" that God punishes evildoers but do not seem to have any developed dogma about it.) Neither the mouth nor the right hand can talk to God; he would not listen to them because they cannot give a true account of the individual's life—they would merely speak well of him. They—mouth and right hand—are, as the Temne point out, "accomplices."

It is not, however, because it starts talking to God that the left hand becomes the stronger; the presence of God is merely the situation in which the activity of the left hand comes to articulate expression. For all the time that the right hand has been prominently active the reserved left hand has been a "witness" *(maseri)*. The left side of the body as a whole is a witness, Temne say; that is why if you find yourself on a journey having to sleep among strangers you should sleep on your right side, left uppermost, "So that if they murder you there you will have a witness to God."

There is another situation in which the individual retreats from the common world into his own, that is in sleep. Here again Temne say the left hand becomes the more powerful of the two. As proof they observe that if in sleep your left hand falls on your chest you wake up groaning under the impression that you are being crushed by a terrific weight. There is probably here also a linkage with dreams, though I have no Temne statements illustrating one. But dreams, Temne hold, are a sort of gift from God; they are at any rate "sent from God," and as the witness to God the left hand must be more trustfully intimate with him, perhaps even receiving these messages from him.

Secondary reasons given for the power of the left hand are that it has more courage than the right in daring to touch those parts of the body which the right may not and that the right hand uses up all its strength in activity while the left hand conserves its.

Sleep and death are situations in which a total reversal occurs with respect to activity and the most general attribute Temne confer upon the hands, i.e., power. There is one instance of ambiguity in the relation between the hands arising from the possibility of ambiguity in one's situation within the social dualism in relation/not-in-relation with the community. At any given moment it may be to one's own advantage not to enter into too close relations with others. An itch in the palm of the hand presages money; if in the left palm it means you will get money which you can keep to yourself, if in the gift-giving right palm you will get money but have to disburse it to others. Temne do not decide here which is the auspicious omen and which inauspicious, but as it were with a wink indicate that one often prefers "left-handed" money. At the same time too much "left-handed" money lays one open to, at worst, accusations of witchcraft and, at least, the petty calumnies motivated by jealousy.

The power of the left hand is put to work in Temne medicine. The instrument mentioned above, *ansassa,* is employed to attack malefactors, especially witches. It is a bundle of heterogeneous items—leaves, needles, powdered hornet's nest, etc.—wrapped in red or black cloth or animal skin. The left hand from a corpse is a specially powerful ingredient, or any equivalent of it, e.g., nails, skin, powdered bone. Such an *ansassa* will certainly kill whomever it is aimed at; others may kill or merely inflict illness. (One doctor reckoned that the left hand of a chimpanzee does just as well, while the left leg of a chicken will send the culprit crazy—"he will walk anywhere." Otherwise animals "have no left and right." There is, however, an indirect linkage in the case of animal sacrifices. Whichever side is uppermost when the animal falls is the side one distributes in gifts.)

Another instrument used against thieves only is *anwanka,* employed in a protective manner. It is placed in the vegetable garden or on trees, usually fairly conspicuously to inflict disease or deformity on anyone who tries to steal from them. The most dreadful one inflicts tetanus. There are various kinds, and some contain leaves which should be plucked with the left hand. When being set the *anwanka* should be laid or conspicuously handled by the left hand.

I do not know exactly what virtue is being incorporated into the employment of these objects through the left hand. Such statements as I have on the matter amount only to the assertion that a medicine incorporating the left hand in any way will certainly harm someone, the emphasis being on harming, as against, e.g., medicine to charm an employer or a girl. It could be the association with death or darkness, or it could be the power of the witness. These instruments act only against unknown malefactors, hence require the power of the witness or detector. Or it may be that since the malefactor has by his evil deed put himself outside normal community relations one can best get at him outside normal community relations.

At any rate the main point of the Temne account of the left hand is that though weak in everyday activity it is all the time a witness, and in sleep and after death becomes more powerful than the right. The reversal is a familiar one. Each hand has the weakness of its strength and the strength of its weakness. The strong right hand by its activity is led into sin. Not that Temne think activity is necessarily sinful, but they think it necessarily ensnares us in sin.

Life, they say, has three main stages: childhood during which one is innocent, old age during which one is blameless, and in between the period when one is most active, hence they say most sinful. A favorite illustration of the connection they cite is animal sacrifice. "You always kill an animal with the right hand. So it's the right hand that commits the sin. The left only holds the animal." They also point out that it is the right hand which steals. Meanwhile the weak left hand by its inactivity remains the immaculate witness, and in its own times has its own power.

The unity of opposites each exhibiting this oxymoron is a commonplace of Temne thought, enshrined in a proverb. By itself the proverb is incomprehensible; the exemplary tale which renders it intelligible is as follows. A cotton tree (a very large species) boasts to a tiny termite mound at its roots that the mound owes its existence to the protection of its mighty self (protection from sun and rain); the mound replies that the mighty tree owes its existence to the protection of its tiny self (protection from animals and insect parasites).

The tropes in terms of which Temne conduct their rhetoric of right and left are perfectly familiar to us, as is the social dualism which I suggest generates the meanings put in correspondence by them. Also the notion of "left" as witness, though perhaps fading from general consciousness, is not unfamiliar to us. For those to whom St. Matthew addressed the injunction not to let the left hand know what the right does when it gives alms, "left hand" was a metaphor for "witness." It is clear from the context that he was exhorting them not to advertise, i.e., contrive witnesses to, their deeds of charity. He is even more explicit: advertisement is hypocritical and otiose, for God witnesses all in secret. "Left" as final and true witness figures in at least one of our current rhetorical schemes. In Jung's dream analysis "left" is a symbol of the unconscious, that phase of the self which captures the true meanings of our actions, meanings which pass unnoticed by the conscious mind in the wordless stages of infancy or the bustle of adult activity but which press for recognition in sleep.

It is apparent how close this is to the Temne view of the left hand becoming more powerful in sleep, having the capacity to exert a crushing weight. Weight is for them a virtue of truth or of the power which becomes equivalent to truth, as it is for us a metaphor for them ("his words carry weight"). Sometimes an ambitious man or an already powerful man will hang a piece of iron in some inconspicuous corner of the roof, "so that all the words spoken in the house will have weight."

Evidently the Temne could not subscribe to the Durkheimian notion that, God and society being one, truth must be the constraint society exerts upon the individual mind. In so far as justice is the mode in which truth exists in society, not-being-in-proper-relation-with-others is for them a condition of perception of truth. On the evening before his coronation a Temne chief disappears from his capital and is said to have "gone to Futa." In a grove he undergoes the final transformation from citizen into chief and next day is carried to the boundary of his capital. When he walks in to be crowned he is said to have "come from Futa." The Temne are known to have been driven from Futa Jallon in Guinea by the Fulbe people, and these ceremonies have been interpreted as commemoration of history. My informants were emphatic that the meaning of these ritual journeys is that "the chief comes as a stranger, for only from a stranger can you expect justice."

ACKNOWLEDGMENTS

As any anthropologist writing on this subject must be, I am greatly indebted to the essays by R. Hertz and by R. Needham, and to the chapter on spear symbolism in his book *Nuer Religion* by E. E. Evans-Pritchard (Oxford: Clarendon Press, 1956), chap. 9.

Right and Left in Nyoro Symbolic Classification

Rodney Needham

15

Comment espérer atteindre l'esprit de finesse dans l'enquête psychologique sans une richesse suffisante du symbole, sans une forêt de symboles?

Gaston Bachelard 1942: 214

I

The aims of this analysis are: (1) to investigate a puzzle in Nyoro ethnography; (2) to make a further contribution to the understanding of secular-mystical diarchy or complementary governance; and (3) to carry out a routine exercise in the structural analysis of symbolism, in a continuing attempt to isolate its general principles.[1]

Sources. The published ethnography on the Nyoro is usefully large and covers over a century. Four authorities in this substantial corpus of evidence are central to the present enterprise and deserve special notice.

Exact investigation begins with Emin Pasha, the founder (though oddly neglected since) of Nyoro ethnography, in 1877, when the remarkable German doctor visited King Kabarega and acutely recorded many details of Nyoro custom and belief which have later been amply confirmed. He was, moreover, the first European to be able to converse fluently with the Nyoro in their own language (Emin 1879a: 184; 1879b: 259), and his reports are in the main of unchallenged reliability.[2]

In addition to Emin's material, the factual data for the present paper are taken primarily from Roscoe's impressive and admirably

Africa 37 (1967): 425–51. Reprinted by arrangement with the International African Institute.

precise monograph, *The Bakitara* (1923). It will be necessary, however, for the reader to keep in mind, since the judgment affects the essential reliability of this major fund of evidence, that a modern expert on the Nyoro rates this work as merely "interesting if not wholly accurate," and as "old-fashioned and superficial" (Beattie 1960: 86; 1965: 4).[3]

A source of comparable importance is Mrs. Fisher's invaluable collection of Nyoro traditions, *Twilight tales of the Black Baganda* (1911). This work is singularly authoritative in that chapters 6–13 (pp. 69–178), dealing with the Cwezi and the period down to Kabarega, are translations of accounts which were written, with the aid of their "witch doctors," by Duhaga, "ce prince intelligent" (Gorju 1920: 63), the king of Bunyoro, and Kasagama, the king of Toro (pp. v–vi). Mrs. Fisher reports that she has tried as far as possible to translate the text literally, but she adds the dismaying qualification: "Heaps of non-essential details have had to be cleared away, and in many cases modifications have been made, or passages entirely discarded, to purify the story and render it suitable reading to the general public" (p. vi). Attempts to trace the original manuscript, through the publishers, the Church Missionary Society, and surviving relatives, in an endeavor to retrieve what may have been invaluable information, have proved unsuccessful.

Gorju's account of the Nyoro (1920), finally, has proved to be of decisive value, though once again it is a source which has been strangely neglected in later writings on this society.

The history of Bunyoro-Kitara has been well set out by Dunbar (1965), and an ethnographic survey has been compiled by Taylor (1962).

There exists no complete bibliography on the Nyoro, though the International African Institute list (Jones 1960: 33) forms a useful introduction, and Dunbar includes an extensive list of sources (pp. 229–39) which is by far the fullest yet published. The bibliography appended below, which includes a number of items not commonly referred to in other publications on this society,[4] may provide a serviceable introduction to the study of Nyoro mystical ideology and symbolism.

II

The puzzle is that left-handed people in Bunyoro are "hated," and nothing may be given with the left hand (Roscoe 1923: 50),[5] yet that in divination by the casting of cowrie shells, which is by far the commonest technique resorted to whenever Nyoro are in trouble, the diviner holds the shells in his left hand (Beattie 1964: 48, 49). That it is the left hand is explicitly stated by the Nyoro informant whose account is reproduced by the ethnographer.

This report poses a theoretical problem because the beneficial left hand of the diviner is contrary to our general expectations about the symbolic values of right and left (cf. Hertz 1909), and is apparently inconsistent with the characteristic features of Bantu symbolic classification (cf. Beidelman 1961; Needham 1960; Rigby 1966). Yet we may suppose that this seeming contradiction, when placed in its proper ideological setting, will be seen to accord after all with the principles of Nyoro symbolic classification. The unexpected capacity of the left hand to preserve or rescue from trouble presumably has a meaning, and it is the task of the social anthropologist to discover what this may be. Some encouragement to think that it may be possible to do so has already been provided by the investigation of an initially similar situation elsewhere in East Africa, concerning the left hand of the Mugwe among the Meru of Kenya (Needham 1960). It is in any case a methodological imperative, now that the general pre-eminence of the right has been so definitely established, to seek out apparently contrary cases which may at once test and extend our understanding of the meaning and structure of ideas about right and left.

III

A general survey of Nyoro symbolism, in terms of right and left, intensifies the puzzle and makes the apparent contradiction of the diviner's left hand emerge as a more glaring contrast; for in the crucial events of life, and the major institutions of the society, the right is pre-eminent and auspicious while the left is inferior and inauspicious. Let us begin by establishing a range of symbolic connotations of the sides.

Birth. After the birth of a child the father digs a hole in the floor of the house near the door, on "the right side" if the child is a boy, and on the left if it is a girl (cf. Emin, 1879a: 393; Felkin, p. 144). The mother places the afterbirth in this hole and covers it with leaves; among certain classes of person the leaves from a kind of tree used in brewing are employed in the case of a boy, and those from a tree used for cooking if it is a girl (243; cf. Gorju 1920: 329).

Women carry their babies "straddling their right hips" (Casati 2: 59).

Initiation. Young princes are initiated into manhood by a ceremony in which the six front teeth of the lower jaw are extracted (168). Other authorities, e.g., Stuhlmann (p. 433 n.), say that four teeth are taken out; Emin says four, and sometimes six, including the neighboring canines (1879a: 393). The operator begins with the first tooth on the right, and then removes the others. The youths are taken to a special place where they remain until the gums are healed, and on their way they have to expectorate "only over the right shoulder" (168). Ordinary boys of the pastoral class undergo the same operation, and the description of this makes it clear that after extracting the first tooth on the right the operator proceeds to the next one, and so on from right to left (261).

Dress. In one of Roscoe's photographic plates the king has his right arm wholly free and exposed, whereas his left arm is shrouded and concealed from shoulder to wrist. Conversely, the three milkmaids in his company—who stand, incidentally, to his left—have their right shoulders and arms thus wrapped around and hidden from view, and the two of them who hold certain appurtenances do so with their left hands (Roscoe 1923, facing p. 64). Both Emin and Junker describe Kabarega as wearing a cloth over his left shoulder (Emin 1879a: 184; Junker, p. 584).

A photograph by Buchta, later reproduced by Casati with the caption "Relatives of King Chua [i.e., Kabarega] in their finery" (2: 91), shows two young women, completely covered to the neck in what appears to be dark barkcloth; the cape covers the shoulders and arms completely, and in each case is held together in front by the left hand, which alone is exposed (Buchta 1881a, vol. 2, p. 69; cf. Thomas, p. 117).

Another picture shows a Nyoro girl with her right shoulder and arm covered, and the left exposed (Buchta 1881a, vol. 2, pl. 68; cf. Junker, p. 583). A photograph in Vandeleur shows a chief with his cloth passed under his right arm, which is prominently in view, and knotted on the left shoulder, partly concealing the left arm. One of his followers, apparently dressed traditionally in barkcloth, has his left arm quite covered; though another, on the fringe of the group depicted, has his cloth knotted on his right shoulder (Vandeleur, facing p. 66).

Royal etiquette, etc. The queen and other members of the royal family greet the king by touching him on the forehead, and then under the chin, with the fingertips of the right hand (103); princesses greet him by placing the fingertips of the right hand on his shoulder (which one is not reported) and then on the arm (109).

When a chief or freeman has committed some offense, he is not dishonored by being put in the stocks, but the king instead has him put under legal constraint by having a band tied around the offender's right hand, marking him as the king's prisoner (62).

The royal bow (Nyapogo) is restrung at the king's coronation with sinews removed from the right side of a certain man who has been kept in a condition of purity (133–34, 329).

At the conclusion of a war of succession among princes, the victor visits the late king's body and sticks his spear into the ground near the right hand of the corpse (Felkin, p. 163).

Sacrifice. At a sacrifice to the "god of plenty" a bull is killed, and the right shoulder of the animal is presented to the officiating priest (23). At the ceremony of blessing the country, a cow and a sheep are sacrificed and their right shoulders are cut off and cooked (111). A bull is kept in a herd until it is too old and has to be replaced; it is then ceremonially killed near a sacred fire, and the right shoulder and leg are "carefully cut off" and hung over the doorway of the owner's house (193). At a feast which forms part of the marriage ceremonies, a cow is killed and the bride's father and his relatives are given the right shoulder (264, cf. 277).

Augury. If the king feels ill, or if there is any report of danger or calamity, or if he wishes to send out an expedition, he asks an augur what steps should be taken. The throat of a fowl is cut and the flow of blood is observed: if the stream runs more freely from the left artery than from the right, it is a bad omen; if it runs freely from both arteries or more freely from the right than from the left, the omen is good (35).

Blood pact. When two men have formed a friendship so close that they wish to cement it in a manner that will bind them "for the rest of their lives," they conclude a blood pact.

They sit opposite each other and each makes several incisions "near the navel," catches a few drops of blood in his right hand, rubs half a coffee bean in the blood, and gives it to his partner with the right hand (45). (The very awkwardness of these movements emphasizes the importance which is attached to using the right.) Emin reports that the blood is taken from a light incision over the fifth rib on the right side (1879a: 223; cf. Felkin, p. 173); Grant says that the incision is made to the right above the navel (p. 271); Beattie, apparently following Roscoe, writes merely that it is "near" the navel (1958: 199). After the exchange of blood, each in turn seizes the other's right hand and taps it gently against his stomach (Beattie 1958: 199).

Baker seems to have committed a symbolic solecism in making an incision in his left arm when concluding a blood pact with Ruyonga, though the latter, presumably with political advantages in prospect, would appear not to have been deterred (Baker 1895: 404). Beattie regards the ceremony as "unorthodox" on the ground that it was the arm from which the blood was taken (1958: 203), though Felkin reports this as a normal mode of concluding a blood pact (p. 173).

Ordeal. A man who pleads innocent of a charge may have to submit to an ordeal in which a hot iron is run down his right leg; if the skin comes off, he is shown to be guilty (Fisher 1899: 8; cf. Gorju 1920: 254).

Milking. The milking of cows is not a task of merely nutritional significance but is governed by strict and even ritual procedures. The care of cattle is considered of such importance that the king's own sons are sent away, at the age of six or eight, to be brought up for some years by a royal herdsman who teaches them all about cow-keeping; they learn to herd, milk, and treat the illnesses of cows (166–67).

Certain sacred cows which provide for the king's nourishment are milked from the right side (97). In ordinary herds also the milkman squats at the right side of the cow (187), and when a boy is first instructed in the care of cows he is told that milking has to be done from the right side (26).

Hunting. The right tusk of an elephant that is killed is the perquisite of the chief in whose territory it is taken (318); the right shoulder of a wild buffalo that is killed goes to the owner of the land (320). In each case the hunter gets the left portion (cf. Emin 1879a: 394).

Sexual intercourse. The man lies on his right side "when sleeping" and the woman on her left (Beattie 1961: 173). This would seem to imply that the man's left hand alone is free for sexual play (cf. Beidelman, p. 253; Rigby, p. 3).

Death. At the death of the king his body is buried lying on its right side (Ingham, p. 144), and the hands are placed "under the right side of the head" (121). When the queen's body is prepared for burial, however, her hands are placed palm to palm "under the left side of her head" (143). Again, a prince has his hands folded together under the right side of his head, and some beans which are used by his son in a rite of heirship are placed in his right hand (173–74). A chief similarly has his hands under the right side, and is, moreover, buried on the right side of his house as one looks from the door (292), lying on his right side (293).

In general, the body of a man is buried lying on its right side, and that of a woman lying on its left (Beattie 1961: 173). In one case reported, the wife of a wealthy man was buried, not only with her hands placed under the left side of her head, but also on the left side of the house (296). Wieschhoff, citing Roscoe (1923), has it that "ordinary men *and women* are buried with their hands under the right side" (p. 204, italics supplied), but this is a mistake (cf. Felkin, p. 162).

The right is thus associated, according to context, with the king, chiefs, landowners, men, masculine tasks, civil behavior, and good omens; the left is associated with the queen, subjects, interlopers, women, feminine tasks, sexual activity, and bad omens. The right is superior and esteemed; the left is "of less importance" (33), inferior, and hated. Specific confirmation of these opposed kinds of meaning is provided by the words of a "witch-doctor" (diviner) at another kind of consultation: he places a wand on the left shoulder of the client and says, "Sickness be gone . . . sorrow be gone, barrenness be gone"; then he places the wand on the right shoulder and says, "Come wealth, come children, come long life, . . . come all goodness . . ." (Fisher 1911: 56). In a creation myth, Ruhanga ("God") points up with his right hand and says, "This is heaven"; he points down with his left and says "This is earth" (Fisher 1911: 69). In these respects Nyoro symbolism is perfectly straightforward, and in a comparative context even commonplace. It exhibits, in its own cultural idiom, a general contrast of symbolic values associated with right and left which has indeed a worldwide distribution.

But if this is so, how are we to interpret the inconsonant fact that the left hand is deliberately resorted to in the most common form of divination, and precisely when the Nyoro are in trouble from which they desire release?

IV

The beginnings of an answer can be seen in some of the very situations which have provided the normal or ideal values of lateral symbolism among the Nyoro, viz., birth, milking, and death.

Although the placenta of a baby girl is buried on the left side of the door, this is not donc in thc case of a princess; her placenta is buried on the right (158).

Whereas the queen, like ordinary women, is buried with her hands placed under the left side of her head, a princess is buried with her hands under the right side (143, 175).

When an ordinary Nyoro is buried, the children of the deceased sprinkle the first earth into the grave; they may scoop it up with their hands, but traditionally they first brush a little earth in with their elbows, men using their left elbows, women their right (Beattie 1961: 174). Gorju writes that the relatives throw four clods of earth with the back of the hand, four with the palm (1920: 356). Roscoe, describing the burial of the body of a chief in a dung-heap, says that the heir and the chief relative throw the first two lots of dung into the grave with the right hand; he reports the pushing of earth with the elbows, but does not specify which (175, 293).

Cows must normally be milked from the right side, but when the king dies a special cow is milked from the left side, and some of the milk is poured into the mouth of the corpse (121).

These usages show that divination with the left hand is not a solitary instance in which the values of right and left are subverted or manipulated, but that the Nyoro in certain circumstances conventionally resort to symbolic reversal. The customs in question are of the same type, thus defined, but they can be distinguished secondarily as relating to either *(a)* situations, or *(b)* social status; one kind of reversal is relative and temporary, the other is absolute and permanent. Let us examine these exceptions in an ascending scale of theoretical interest.

The milking of a cow from the left can readily be seen as a situational reversal; it distinguishes the situation by the formal employment of the side which is expressly associated with death and which is otherwise shunned and regarded as ill-omened. The ultimate in the inauspicious (namely, death) has taken place, and this event is recognized by an appropriate lateral symbol.[6]

The use of normally inappropriate sides of the body, when pushing the earth into the grave with the elbows, is also an instance of situational reversal, but rather more complex. In this situation the participants do not adopt in common a ritual which has generally inauspicious or mortuary connotations, for while the men use the left (just as they might occupy the left side in milking the funeral cow), the women, who are already associated with the left, have recourse instead to the right. In doing so, the sexes first align themselves, as it were, with their respective "sides" of the symbolic classification, men with right and women with left, and they then adopt opposite postures. What they are doing, in other words, is temporarily to override the distinctive meanings of the symbolism of the sides in favor of a relational definition of the situation. It is no longer the specificity of the opposed connotations of right and left that counts, but the very relation of opposition which, more fundamentally, is manipulated in order to express the reversal. This also is easily recognizable as a common symbolic process, for there are many reports from other societies of the belief that the state of death is in various particulars a continuation of life under an opposite sign.

The Batak of Sumatra, for example, believe that the way of life of certain spirits, *begu,* including the ghosts of the recently dead and the spirits of distant ancestors, is materially the same as on earth, only everything that they do is reversed: when they go down steps they climb *(klettern)* head first; when they carry a burden they do not face forwards but instead go backwards; they hold markets and council meetings, but only at night; they sleep by day and go about at night (Warneck, pp. 83, 74; cf. p. 82).

Among the Ngaju of southern Borneo it is thought that the language spoken in the afterlife is the reverse of the language in this: "right" there becomes "left," "straight" is "crooked," "sweet" means "bitter," for "stand up" one says "lie down," and so on (Hardeland, p. 308, s.v. *liau;* Witschi, p. 159).

The Toraja of Celebes believe that everything the dead do is the opposite of the practice of the living: not only do they use words in their opposite meanings, but they even pronounce them backwards; they use the left hand all the time when the living use the right, and accordingly the living employ the left whenever they do something for or in connection with the dead (Kruyt, pp. 342, 343, 344, 345).

These particular and contingent beliefs held by Indonesian peoples are not reported to be held or closely paralleled by the Nyoro, but there are nevertheless certain interesting indications of a connection in their culture between death and reversal.

When the king pronounces a death sentence, if he touches the offender's body with a spear the person is beaten to death; whereas if he touches him with a stick he is speared to death. As Baker acutely observes, "Thus the instrument used to slay the criminal was always contrary to the sign" (1867: 189).

When the king dies, the "drum of State" is turned upside down (Fisher 1911: 96, 125).

As a sign of mourning, women put on their dresses upside down, and for a woman to do so during her husband's lifetime would be taken to show that she desired his end (Gorju 1920: 357, 325 n. 1).

It may be, too, that an avoidance of "reversal" lies behind the belief that it will bring misfortune to return by the same path as that on which one goes out (Buchta 1881b: 88).

A relational similarity thus appears to exist between the Indonesian ideas and Nyoro customs and indicates a logic of symbolism which has a more essential significance than have mere differences of tradition.

We may now turn to the absolute mode of reversal, that in which lateral symbolism permanently marks a social status in a way opposite to what might be thought appropriate to the occupant of that status. The example is the princess; the factual signs are that her placenta is buried on the right (masculine) side of the door, and that her corpse is buried (presumably lying on the right side) with the hands under the right side of the head, just like that of a man.

Roscoe tells us expressly, in connection with the burial of the placenta, that "a princess was always considered and spoken of as a prince and treated as a boy" (158). Moreover, in the general treatment of children "no difference was made between princes and princesses: they were both called prince and received the same honour from the people" (161). Princesses are treated "much as princes" and are allowed more liberty than women usually have; although they are not allowed to milk cows, they learn much of men's work and they herd cows as princes do, for they are regarded as "unsexed by their rank." They even take their places with the princes at the initiation ceremony, and likewise have their teeth extracted (168–69). Princesses are forbidden to marry, and although they may have sexual liaisons with their half-brothers they may not become pregnant; if they do so, the birth is concealed from the king and normally the child is killed (171). They are "really encouraged to live promiscuously with their half-brothers," but intercourse with a commoner is punished with great severity, and to bear a child to a commoner would entail being put to death (171–72).

It is because princesses are treated like princes, "that is, as if they were men" (175), that when they die their hands are placed under the right side of their head. In all this they stand opposed to the queen, who of all the princesses is the only one to be allowed to marry;[7] she is fully feminine in this regard, and accordingly is buried with her hands under the left side of her head.

Here, then, is a class of person who, in spite of being physically entirely female (as is fully recognized in the sexual relationship with princes), is socially masculine. This social status is marked symbolically by a special application of lateral symbolism; although the individual is female, and thus normally to be associated on this ground with the left, the person (the social status) is masculine, and is therefore marked by symbols of the right.

This clear example of an absolute symbolic reversal, in which a social status is permanently qualified by sex-linked symbols opposite to those associated with the sex of the occupant, permits us to return to the diviner.

V

The obvious possibility now is that the diviner, who in his characteristic activity is marked symbolically as associated with the left, is a counterpart to the princess. He is physically male, but through his left hand he is symbolically associated with the feminine.[8]

This inference is derived analogically from the association of masculine with right and feminine with left, a dual association which is decisively borne out by the status and attributes of the princess, but presumably there will be other means of determining the symbolic status of the diviner. The left hand, used so prominently and so often, is indeed an unequivocal sign of the feminine connection, but so far it is all that we have been able to identify. A well-recognized feature of symbolism, however, is its redundancy (cf. Durand, p. 10), i.e., that it conveys meaning by repetition, by differing vehicles, and by circuitous but ultimately convergent routes. When we seek confirmatory evidences of the postulated connection between the diviner and the feminine, therefore, it is not merely to satisfy ourselves that we have really arrived at a correct identification, but also because, knowing of the feature of redundancy, we may suspect that we have not properly grasped the symbolic message until this condition is satisfied. It appears generally to be the case that the degree of redundancy is directly proportional to the recognized social importance of the object, and the Nyoro diviner clearly has an importance to which a fairly high degree of such symbolic emphasis would be appropriate. There are in fact a number of symbols, of various types, which complement the lateral indication of the diviner's character and which will permit us to develop and expand the analysis.[9]

Colors. When the diviner prepares to cast his cowries he lays out a black goatskin, and in one consultation reported he demands a fee of a black he-goat and some money (Beattie 1964: 49).[10]

On the fourth day after the birth of a child to the king, he sends a cow or a bull to the mother for her food; the skin of this animal is worn by her for a time and is then passed on to the child; it can be "of any colour except black" (159). When the king gets out of bed, he steps over a man who sleeps on the floor; this man is "always very black," and in stepping over him the king is supposed to leave "the darkness of night" upon him (92). No black cow is ever admitted to the royal herd (113). The king, at a ceremony performed every morning, passes the evil of the past night into a black cow—significantly, through a white spot on its forehead against which he places his head (Roscoe 1922: 205).[11] "Nothing black must ever be offered to the Bacwezi," and a black hair in the tail of a sacrificial beast can nullify the rite (Fisher 1911: 59, 62). The death of the king is proclaimed with the cry, "Darkness has come in the daytime . . ." (Ingham, p. 138). Witches, who eat human flesh, fly about at night (Emin 1879a: 185). There appears to be a significant connection among the Nyoro words *ira,* "grow dark," *iragura,* "be black," and *iragwe,* "place where diviners *(embandwa)* meet" (Davis, p. 51, s.vv.) A rain-maker wears black barkcloths (29). If a man is possessed by evil spirits, a black goat and a black fowl are sacrificed to them (Fisher 1911: 57). Smoke-blackened barkcloths signify sorrow, and black banana fiber is worn as a sign of mourning (Fisher 1911: 141, 166; Gorju 1920: 357). After a death the house is pulled down, and from its remains a temporary shelter is made which is called *kyiragula*, "the black" (Gorju 1920: 358). There is a class of spirits which are called "black"; they are nontraditional, individualistic (and therefore unsocial), and are commonly associated with alien and intrusive powers (Beattie 1960: 78). Everything in "hell" is black; the couch and eating utensils of Nyamiyongo, "the king of hell," are "all covered with soot," his food is smoked, and his milk is taken from a black cow; his guest room is strewn with singed grass and charcoal, spread over with black hides (Fisher 1911: 82–83). To have a "black belly" means to harbor evil intentions (Baker 1867: 63). Black therefore connotes night, death, evil, and danger.

On the color white we have more abundant information, which also better indicates by contrast the significance of black. The man who is to provide the sinews for the royal bow is "purified" and wears white barkcloth; in addition to his sinews, those of a bull are also used, and this animal has to be white (329). In general, sacrificial beasts are white, e.g., the cow, sheep, and fowl at the ceremony of blessing the country are all white (111). White cows are offered to the king as a sign of fealty (Fisher 1911: 154), and Kabarega presented Baker, after the battle of Masindi, with a peace-offering of "two beautiful white cows" (Baker 1895: 372).[12] White or "piebald" goats are sacrificed to the demigods (Fisher 1911: 59). White clay is used as a sign of purification and fasting (96), and of the virginity of the royal milkmaid (98); the royal cook is purified for the duration of his duties and is half covered with white clay (102); princes and other participants at the coronation ceremonies are purified by sprinkling with white clay (128); at the ceremony of bringing out royal twins, the king, the mother, and the king's representative have their heads smeared with clay as a conclusion to the purifying ceremony (164); cows, too, are smeared with white clay after a certain salt drink which is considered necessary to their health (191).[13] The king, when he drinks the first milk of the day, is reported to sit on a stool covered with nine white cow-skins (98); photographic illustrations actually show leopard skins (e.g., Roscoe 1922, pl. facing p. 150), which are reserved to the king (Gorju 1920: 270), though the general color is none the less white. The predominant color in the royal regalia is white (Fisher 1911, pl. facing p. 109). The Nyoro verb *ēza* has the instructive meanings: "to make white, whiten; make holy, sanctify; make fruitful, ripen"

(Davis, p. 32, s.v.); *era,* which similarly means to "be white," also has the significant meaning, when said of the king, of to "laugh" (p. 29, s.v.). To have a "white belly" means to have good intentions (Baker 1867: 63).[14] A piece of the hide of a white rhinoceros makes a man invulnerable (Emin 1879a: 224; cf. Felkin, p. 174). The new house erected after the termination of mourning is called *kyera,* "the white" (Gorju 1920: 358). White is thus associated with purity, blessing, the sacred, the kingship, and the gods.

A neat illustration of the opposed meanings of black and white is provided by the legend of King Dubongoza. He was fleeing from the Baganda, and escaped to a barren island in the middle of Lake Albert. For four days he had nothing to eat or drink. A milk cow was ferried across to him, but as it was black the king's men "feared" to give him its milk. Seeing that he would otherwise starve to death, they painted the cow with "red earth" and rubbed (white) chalk on its horns. "When . . . the evil spirits saw that the cow was no longer black, they left it, so the milk was given to the king, and his life was saved" (Fisher 1911: 150).[15]

Numbers. The diviner casts nine cowrie shells. Beattie says that nine is a "ritually auspicious" number in many contexts (1960: 72), but the many particulars on the significance of numbers which are to be found in Roscoe's work and in other sources make it appear that this characterization may be neither wholly exact nor complete. It is true that in the blood-pact ceremony there are nine coffee beans (Beattie 1958: 199), and that the number nine does appear in other important contexts, but there is more to the Nyoro symbolism of numbers than this.

In divination by the casting of leather squares, the complete set consists of nine pieces, but only three are actually cast (39); Beattie, who has not seen the procedure, says that "two or three" pieces are cast (1964: 46–47), but symbolic considerations, which will emerge as we proceed, make this imprecision seem questionable. At the new moon the king is secluded with his "wizards and magicians" for three days (Junker, p. 582). Nyoro spit three times if they happen to see a falling star (Emin 1879a: 224). A man who believes himself to suffer from the evil eye spits three times in the face of women thought to be responsible, and is relieved of the affliction when he thus encounters the one who actually did it (Buchta 1881b: 88). Alternatively, a woman who has cast the evil eye on someone can relieve the consequent pains by spitting three times on the body of the sufferer (Emin 1879a: 186). The birth of triplets is "a dreadful event . . . bringing with it all kinds of evils"; the king sends some of his personal guard, who take the mother with her children and parents to a deserted place, where they spear them and leave the bodies for wild animals to devour; the father has his eyes gouged out so that he cannot look upon the king, "for his gaze would bring evil" (257).

After a normal childbirth, the woman goes to bed for three days if the child is a girl, four if it is a boy (243–44; cf. Gorju 1920: 328–29). When a newborn child is taken out of the house for the first time, a blade of grass is passed round its body; three times for a girl, four times for a boy (Gorju 1920: 330). At the marriage ceremony the bride is washed three times, the groom four (Gorju 1920: 312). A number of days after a burial, lumps of smelted iron are placed on the grave; three days after for a woman, four days for a man (Beattie 1961: 174).[16]

Four appears in a number of distinctive contexts: e.g., the virgins who guard the throne are on duty for four days at a time (77), and so are the royal cook (84) and the royal milkmen (96); four days is the test period upon entering a new kraal (185), and the first fire in a new house must not be allowed to die out for four days (213); milk only is drunk for four days after initiation by tooth-extraction (262); a newly installed chief sits four times on his stool (301); a couple just married are aspersed four times (272), and the bride is secluded for four days before final recognition as a wife (273; Gorju 1920: 314); when twins are brought to the king, he asperses the mother and her party four times, and each child is placed four times on his lap (164); twins are marched four times round certain sacred trees (165); the definitive part of the marriage ceremonies centers on four ripe fruits (Gorju 1920: 312).

There are seven royal huts, and the seventh is "even more sacred than the others" (81). In one method of seeking augury seven pots of water are employed (Roscoe 1922: 215).

Nine, finally, is indeed prominent. The crown is placed nine times on the head of the king (130) and of a chief (300); the royal ceremony of the new moon lasts for nine days (107–8); a human victim, impersonating a dead king, is killed after nine days (126–27); the queen takes nine sips of sacred milk at a ceremony following her installation (139); and a new chief takes twice nine sips (300).[17] There were nine Cwezi (demigods); Ndahura makes gifts to his father, Isimbwa, nine of each kind, "for this was the number relating to the gods" (Fisher 1911: 99, 95); an initiate into the Cwezi cult of spirit possession is anointed nine times (Beattie 1957: 153); a spirit medium's pipe has nine bowls (Gorju 1920, pl. facing p. 224). The fee for divination by the leather squares is nine cowries (39), and in another method of divination nine augury sticks are used (40).[18] Nine small pots, filled with water, are used in divination; nine dishes of embers are used in rain-making; goats and cowries in multiples of nine are given to a priest for relief from sickness (Fisher 1911: 58, 59).

This numerical symbolism allows, in the first place, a further identification of the diviner's status. Three is feminine, four is masculine; the diviner is once directly associated with three, and more often with nine (three times three), which hints again at the feminine connection. Whether odd numbers should be referred to as "auspicious" is something of a question, for they are certainly said to be "bad" for a young married couple at least (272), and Roscoe's index refers in this connection to "Odd numbers, danger of . . ." (361). The feminine contexts which are explicitly characterized by the number three[19] make it dubitable that any odd number should be regarded as propitious.

A general impression is that odd numbers tend to be associated, not only with feminine (three), but also with the contingent, the extraordinary, and the assumption or restoration of mystical status; whereas even numbers tend to be associated, not only with masculine (four), but with regularity, formal action, public office, and the assumption or confirmation of social status.[20] There are indeed occasions of the latter type in which nine appears; but it may well be that it has a place in them because odd numbers in general are associated with the sacred, mystical, or spiritual, and because in such ceremonies the number nine symbolizes precisely this aspect of the proceedings. However this may be, odd numbers appear to connote, not the auspicious, but a connection with mystical agents or influence, and thus with a kind of danger.[21] The diviner, at any rate, is typically associated with odd numbers; and through the number three, as through his left hand, he is more particularly associated with the feminine.

Spirit-voices. A final and more specific indication of the diviner's nature is found in divination by recourse to spirits. The diviner is possessed, and the account of one séance reports that he begins to speak "in a small falsetto voice, like a woman's"; it is of special importance that this is not the ethnographer's gloss but is part of an account dictated in English by a Nyoro informant (Beattie 1964: 55). Two other accounts also describe the diviner's voice as "tiny" or "small" and as "falsetto" (ibid., pp. 55, 57).

Even the explicit comparison with a woman, however, does not necessarily ascribe any feminine characteristics to the diviner himself, for very commonly in ethnographic accounts from other cultures the spirits twitter and gibber, just as Roscoe writes that a ghost "squeaks" (1922: 191); and it is not to be inferred from the Nyoro accounts that these spirits, whatever they may sound like, are feminine, or that the diviner, being possessed by them and uttering their words, is thus again associated with the feminine. All the same, it is very interesting, and might to an expert on the Nyoro be diagnostic, that a diviner is said by a Nyoro informant to speak in a voice like a woman's, and that other accounts should be consistent with this description.

The diviner's office is thus cumulatively defined by the distinct but concordant terms of lateral, color, and numerical symbolism. That he should employ his left hand, in at least one kind of divination, is not in itself a decisive indication of his symbolic status, but may now be seen as a partial revelation of a character which the combined action of other symbols more clearly displays. The left connects the diviner not only with the feminine but also with other values which themselves are connected, either by direct association or by analogy, with the feminine.[22] Black, evil, danger, the inauspicious, and death (perhaps, too, the destructive and impure aspect of sexuality)[23] all conjoin to make of the diviner what the Nyoro themselves may well conceive as an agent of the powers of darkness, and the left hand is the readiest symbol of this condition.[24]

VI

The evidences which lead to this conclusion may make a persuasive enough impression, but it could be thought that they do not quite justify a positive assertion that this is the answer to our problem.

What provides a firmer confidence is not such specific ideological material but the structural comparison with the status of the princess. This comparison demonstrates that Nyoro symbolism exerts on two otherwise disparate persons a similar yet opposite effect.

In each case the individual in question is displaced from a normal status, defined socially by the criterion of sex, into an opposite and exceptional status, defined symbolically also by sex. In their several associations, the princess becomes a man, and the diviner becomes a woman.

But these inverse displacements do not merely exemplify a process in Nyoro symbolic classification; they lead us to a conclusive and fundamental opposition. The princess, possessor of the masculine prerogatives of a prince, is decisively accorded (by her title, initiation, and near-complete association with cattle)[25] a political rank in the kingdom. She is not simply called a prince; she is a prince. The diviner, correspondingly, is professionally and obviously a medium of mystical influence, a party to spiritual powers, agents, and danger. The mystical is very commonly associated with the feminine, and in other cultures there are express proofs that men, through accomplishing a sexual reversal (by homosexuality, feminine accoutrements, putative child-bearing, or by other less dramatic means), are believed to acquire a special power in this dangerous sphere. Further indications that Nyoro ideas may conform to collective representations of this type are provided by the facts that Nyoro women are thought especially to possess the "evil eye" (Emin 1879a: 186; Buchta 1881b: 88), and that the word *mutende,* which means "handmaid, concubine, king's dairymaid," also means "pupil of *embandwa* [diviner]" (Davis, p. 166, s.v.; cf. p. 92). The term *mbandwa* itself is said to be related to a family of words found as far south as Tanganyika and possessing a common root *nda,* breast, from which Gorju derives the associations, for the diviner's office, of "begotten, born, initiated" (1920: 216, n. 1); cf. Nyoro *nda,* "womb" (Davis, p. 122, s.v.). More than all this, however, there is a decisively specific parallel among the Nyoro to the mystical transmutations of sex alluded to above.

At the ceremony of initiation into the Cwezi cult the novice is given to believe that he must demonstrate his genuine possession by the spirits by *becoming a woman.* He endures long torments while his initiators overbear him with accusations that he must be lying about his spiritual fitness, since he has not changed sex. He is not thought actually to pass this test, in any respect, for when he is admitted as an *mbandwa* the chief officiant asks him ironically whether he really imagines that a man can change into a woman

(Gorju 1920: 215), but the important point analytically is that such an idea is in fact subscribed to and acted out by the Nyoro.[26] Even more interestingly, a woman candidate must correspondingly submit to the furious reproach that she has not become a man, which shows in another context the type of complementary displacement seen in the temporary situation of men and women at a funeral and which marks permanently the relationship of princess and diviner. The latter persons may be seen as exemplifying, through their remarkable reversals of symbolic status, the perennial relation of the complementary functions of secular power and mystical authority.[27] In their turn, also, and within the hierarchy of Nyoro society, they may prefigure a more consequential complementary opposition between chiefs and clan priests, and ultimately between the king and the "priests of the nation" (22). In the end, perhaps, we may thus isolate a definitive principle of order in Nyoro ideology and social organization.

VII

There is a legend which further confirms the significance of dual symbolic classification among the Nyoro, and which demonstrates the analytical application of this relational approach to their collective representations. It tells of Mpuga Rukidi, the first king of the Bito dynasty. Let us begin with a standard version, and supply glosses as we proceed to analyze it.

The narrative begins in the time of the Cwezi, during the reign of Wamara, and with an attempt at augury from the entrails of an ox in order to find out why things have been going badly in the kingdom and to discover what the future holds. When the beast is killed, it is seen to be quite empty. A diviner called Nyakoko, dressed in the skins of wild animals, arrives from the land of Bukidi and offers to interpret this mystery. He splits open the head and the hooves with an axe, and the missing organs fall out. He explains the empty belly as meaning that the rule of the Cwezi is over, and that the land is void: the entrails found in the head mean that the Cwezi will nevertheless continue to hold power over mankind; and those in the hooves mean that they will wander continually over the earth.

A smut flies out of the fire and settles on the intestines. It resists both washing and scraping, and cannot be removed (Fisher 1911: 107); according to another account, a black spot is discovered on the intestines (Vanneste, p. 149).[28] This spot is read as an evil omen, meaning that a "black man" will come to usurp the kingdom (Fisher, p. 107; Vanneste, p. 149).[29]

The Cwezi depart from the land, and the diviner, Nyakoko, returns to his own country. There he meets a man called Mpuga Rukidi and his younger brother Kato, who in one tradition are twin sons of a Cwezi, Isimbwa (Fisher 1911: 111; cf. K. W. 1935: 156). Mpuga Rukidi is a hunter, "ignorant and savage." Nyakoko asks what fortune he has had, and Mpuga shows him a curious animal which he has shot: "part of it resembled a colobus monkey and the other part a lion, and when they skinned it the animal still lived and ran about" (p. 111).

Nyakoko persuades Mpuga to seize the throne of the rulers of Kitara, and he does so. One version, related by King Kabarega himself, says that he gains the throne because the queen falls in love with him and poisons her husband (Casati, 2: 39; cf. Vanneste, p. 154). The inhabitants of Kitara regard the stranger with contempt: he is dressed in a sheepskin; he has long hair, plaited and greased, hanging to his shoulders; and he is particolored, such that "one half of his body was white and the other part was black" (Fisher, p. 114; cf. Vanneste, p. 152).

Nyakoko, who has promised Mpuga that he will initiate him into the customs of the country, has him instructed in court etiquette. His long hair is shaved off, he is smeared with butter, and clothed in two barkcloths (Fisher, p. 117; Bikunya, p. 42). Mpuga Rukidi mounts the throne, taking the royal name Nyabongo (cf. Derscheid, p. 253; Vanneste, p. 150), and becomes first king in the Bito dynasty whose line of succession has continued until this day.

This myth can be interpreted historically, as Vanneste has done (1950), and may thus permit inferences about the origin and route of immigration of the Bito, and about the ethnological relations of the Nyoro to the surrounding peoples. Alternatively, it can be read in textbook functionalist style as a "mythical charter" for the social and political order. Thus Beattie says of the series of myths to which that of Mpuga Rukidi belongs that they establish a "genealogical link" between the recognized dynasties of Nyoro rulers:

> . . . We may suppose that historically the genealogical link was important for the immigrant Bito, who lacked the prestige of the already existing Huma aristocracy, and needed the enhancement of status which this "genealogical charter" provided.

> So the main function of Nyoro mythical history is the establishment of Bito credentials to govern, by emphasizing the distinction and antiquity of their genealogical antecedents.
>
> According to the myth, the present Mukama [king] is descended in an unbroken patrilineal line from the very beginning of things . . . (1960: 16).

Yet again, however, the myth of the first Bito king can be explicated in a quite different way, as a coherent and highly condensed allegory. An astonishing variety of semantic components are impacted in this brief tale, and with a degree of mutual reinforcement such as to make it appear almost as a deliberate elaboration of a symbolic paradigm.[30] Let us examine some of the more prominent of these mystagogical features.

To begin with, Nyakoko is culturally and politically an outsider, and this character is appropriate to his role as diviner, by which calling he is identified with what is alien, unknown, and dangerous. There is no exigency of the plot which necessarily makes him a stranger of such a kind, but that is what he is, and there must be a meaning to it. For the present, we may see him as at least an arresting chorus to the drama, a harbinger of extraordinary things to come. This setting is completed by the disquieting circumstances of the augury: the entrails, essential to the inquiry, are out of place —and as far out of place as they could possibly be, in the head and in the hooves. That they are in these places, and that the belly should be void, can indeed be reasonably interpreted, and Nyakoko does so; but, more fundamentally, what is important is not the three interconnected predictions but the fact that they are produced by a precise and local inversion of right order.

The culmination of this opening scene is the appearance of the black spot. We already know the many inauspicious connotations of black, and the fact that here the vehicle of the color is a smut from the fire intensifies the dread meaning. There are indications in the ethnography that fire, as the generator of extreme heat, is the symbolic embodiment of danger: e.g., the sun is associated with withered grass (pasture), death, and malaria (Fisher 1911: 38). The inimical quality of heat appears in other contexts: "The natives of Unyoro will not eat red pepper, as they believe men and women become barren by its use" (Baker 1867: 169); women may not eat a certain antelope, *nsa,* because it "heats" the body too much (Gorju 1920: 325, n. 1).[31] Ashes are used to bewitch people; they are sprinkled about a house as a sign of mourning; charcoal and ashes are a symbol of a spiritual curse. When the first Bito king died—after he had reigned, it may be noted, for nine years—his son milked the funeral cow into a "sooty" pot (Fisher 1911: 152, 158, 161, 166, 58–59). Wrigley glosses the name of Nyamiyonga, ruler of the land of ghosts (whose black realm has been described above), as "Old Sooty, or the Lord of Ashes" (1958: 11), and Beattie as "he of the black smuts" (1958: 201). We can easily understand, therefore, impressed by the semantic redundancy of this event, that the omen is evil. For the Cwezi the point is re-emphasized by the prediction that a "black" man will usurp their power: this cannot be a purely physical distinction, though the Kedi (Kidi) are said to have indeed "a very black complexion" (Johnston, 2: 595), but again is a symbolic term distinguishing the future intruder, and the fearful train of events that he will initiate (Fisher 1911: 107), from the "white" Cwezi (Nyakatura, p. 67; cf. Oliver, p. 136) and the continuance of their reign.

What we might call the premise of opposition qualifies Mpuga himself as well. There are at least five versions of his ancestry:

He is the son of an unknown man who seduced a girl called Nyatolo under a *bito* tree (Gorju 1920: 59; cf. Crazzolara 1950: 106; Vanneste, p. 153); he is the son of Kyomya, Isimbwa's son, who seduced the girl in the same circumstances (Gorju 1920: 58–59; Crazzolara 1950: 106); he is, by an implication only, which Crazzolara rejects (1950: 106), the legitimate son of Kyomya (K.W. 1935: 159–60), though Kyomya is otherwise reported to have only one recognized son, namely, Kagoro (Gorju 1920: 47; cf. Dunbar, p. 18); he is the son of Isimbwa himself, who seduced the girl in Bukedi (Wilson, in Johnston, 2: 595; cf. Bikunya, p. 37; Vanneste, p. 152); or he is the son of Olum (Vanneste, p. 150), i.e., Olimi in Nyoro (Crazzolara 1950: 110).

The uncertain parentage of Mpuga Rukidi is emphasized by other features of his biography. Although the identity of his father—in this patrilineal society—is unknown or uncertain, we are told a great deal about his mother: she belonged to the Bakwonga or the Bachwa and was the daughter of a Kedi man who lived on a hill called Gulugulu, near which there was a cave called Nyalaki, in the territory of Tolo, next to Ganyi, on the western flank of Mt. Elgon. Moreover, Mpuga's mother belonged to the totem *(muziyizo)* of *ngabi*, bushbuck (whence, according to Vanneste [p. 153], her designation *okwero gabi*)—which is actually the "royal totem," that of the Bito themselves (Gorju 1920: 59, 271; Roscoe 1923: 14).

The constant burden of tradition, therefore, is that Mpuga Rukidi is illegitimate. This is supported, moreover, by the Acholi versions of the legend, in which Labongo (i.e., Nyabongo, or Mpuga Rukidi) is said to be either illegitimate, of an unknown father (Bere 1934: 65–66), or to be probably the illegitimate son of Olum (Bere 1947: 1; cf. p. 3). Dunbar says that the Nyoro do not differentiate between legitimate and illegitimate children (p. 43, n. 4), but this scarcely accords with the purificatory ceremonies which traditionally are required after the birth of an illegitimate child, or with the report that an unacknowledged illegitimate child is regarded as a slave (Roscoe 1923: 67–68). Possibly the underlying fact is that the Nyoro do not care whether a child is born in or out of wedlock just so long as its paternity is acknowledged by the payment of bridewealth. In any case, whatever the precise connotations and social consequences of illegitimacy in the eyes of the Nyoro, it scarcely seems tenable, in this regard, that the myth should provide a "genealogical link" emphasizing the "prestige" and "distinction" of Bito antecedents. There may indeed be an unbroken patrilineal line down the chain of succession from Mpuga, but a line traced backwards from any later king is abruptly broken when it reaches this indisputably alien, and almost certainly illegitimate, ancestor. Nor, for that matter, can the alleged unbroken patrilineal line be traced "from the very beginning of things" (Beattie 1960: 16), before Mpuga, for among the five kings from Isaza to Mpuga Rukidi there was only one (Wamara) who was qualified by direct patrilineal descent to succeed to the throne (fig. 1).

Mpuga is not a son of the previous king, and is thus not eligible for the throne (Crazzolara 1937: 16). What is more, he is a twin, i.e., a person born in a state of abnormality which causes "general consternation" (Fisher 1911: 51; Gorju 1920: 342–47). As if this were not enough, he is one of twin brothers, i.e., his birth is of the relatively disfavored kind which is believed to entail that the "presiding god" aids the father—who in this very case is not in fact the social father at all—and bears some "grudge" against the mother and her clan (250). The combination of illegitimacy and twin birth decisively labels Mpuga as abnormal, a person born contrarily to right order. More than all this, he is the elder brother, and even the eldest son of the king is "never allowed to reign" (Fisher 1911: 125), so that in this respect as well, whatever his paternity, he is quite disadvantaged as a possible claimant to the throne.

In other respects also Mpuga is the embodiment of opposition to Nyoro values. He is a naked[32] hunter (see also Casati, 2: 39;

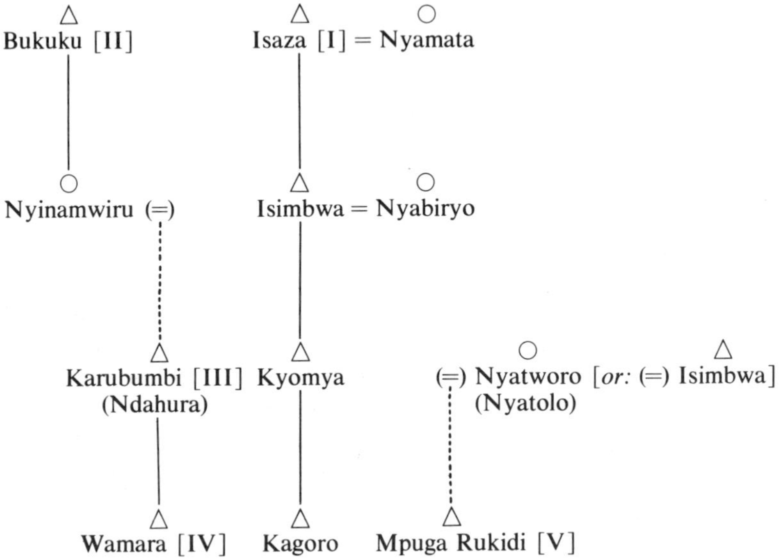

Fig. 1. Genealogical antecedents of the Bito and succession to the throne

Note. Equation signs in parentheses indicate sexual liaisons; a broken line of descent indicates illegitimacy. Roman numerals in brackets indicate order of succession.

Bukuku, who was a drum-keeper or a gate-guardian, proclaimed himself king when Isaza was trapped in the underworld by Nyamiyonga. Karubumbi speared Bukuku and seated himself on the throne. Ndahura by one account abdicated in favor of his son Wamara (Gorju 1920: 49; Morris, p. 7); in another he refused to be succeeded by Wamara because the latter was so selfish and would destroy the kingdom, and appointed instead his deputy Mulindwa—but Wamara nevertheless seized the throne (Dunbar, p. 18). See text (sec. VII) for other versions of Mpuga Rukidi's paternity. Contrast what would indeed have been "an unbroken patrilineal line" of succession, viz., Isaza–Isimbwa–Kyomya–Kagoro.

Johnston, 2: 598), living practically without possessions in a state of nature,[33] whereas the kingdom which he is to seize is the realm of demigods, with their court, elaborate civilization, and vast herds. He cannot even speak Lunyoro, or understand any of it, but instead is served by an interpreter (Fisher 1911: 115; K. W. 1936: 75). It can readily be imagined how outlandish this ignorance proves him to be, and all the more so for the Nyoro, among whom the pastoral aristocrats are recognizable not only by their features but also by a class accent (Gorju 1920: 3, n. 1) and a distinctive form of speech (Emin 1879b: 259). He will not drink milk, either, for he does not know what it is (Fisher 1911: 123); as Gorju particularly remarks, it is interesting to see the Bito thus continuing to affirm that their ancestor did not drink milk, when by this single fact they testify to their savage origin (Gorju 1920: 61). His adornment and clothing inevitably provoke the contempt of the inhabitants of Kitara. His hair hangs long instead of being properly shaved (Fisher 1911: 6; cf. Emin 1879a: pp. 180, 185; Grant, p. 286; Roscoe 1923: 180). He even wears a sheepskin, which can be worn only by women (198, 210) or by young boys (Fisher 1911: 14). Sheep are especially associated, too, with augury and sacrifice, and are the favorite beasts for ceremonial offerings (197). The king is not allowed to eat mutton (Roscoe 1915: 10), Ruyonga did not eat mutton (Buchta 1881b: 88), and in general no prince of Bunyoro does so (Fisher 1911: 151). No one, after eating mutton, may approach the king for a certain period (209). There is a specific association with death, moreover, in that a rich man may be buried wrapped in the skin of a newly slain sheep (Gorju 1920: 355). Furthermore, while Mpuga possesses no cattle, he does have some chickens (Fisher 1911: 112; Vanneste, p. 152), but these creatures (odd, in any case, for a wandering hunter to possess) give no claim to status: they are kept for purposes of augury, and in daily life are affected by many prohibitions and bad omens (210); the king in particular does not eat poultry (Casati, 2: 44; Felkin, p. 147); thunder and lightning are supposed to be caused by a fabulous fowl, Nkuba (Davis, p. 129, s.v.; cf. Fisher 1911: 102–3). Finally, Mpuga, pretender to the throne, is described as the underling or servant, *mwiru,* of Nyakoko, the diviner, and the latter is clearly described as his master, *mukama* (Bikunya, p. 37; cf. Gorju 1920: 48)—a relationship the reverse of the normal.

What kind of game does this strange hunter get? A "curious animal," an anomaly: half monkey, half lion. Bikunya emphasizes its curiosity by writing clearly that one "side" *(orubaju)* is monkey and the other side lion (p. 37). It is half a tree-borne, semi-flying kind of animal, and half firmly terrestrial, a grotesque combination of the very small and the very large, the timorous and the valiant, an affront to any classification. It has been killed, but it still lives; it has even been skinned, but it continues to run about, confounding the ultimate distinction between life and death. Its colors, too, may be significant. The monkey is black and white; the lion, we may conjecture, is "red." In one creature, therefore, there are mixed the three prime symbolic colors which in ritual must be distinct. The juxtaposition may be wrong, furthermore, in that white should be joined not to black but to red; compare the colors of Dubongoza's cow (above, sec. V), and the red and white flag of Kabarega's bodyguard (Stuhlmann, p. 324 n.). Everything, it seems, is wrong and incomprehensible about this creature, just as culturally everything about the hunter himself is repellent.

But he is not repellent to the queen. She conceives a passion for him which is not only adulterous but perverse, for by all the standards of her rank, class, and nation he is everything that she ought to shun. A princess discovered in a love affair with even a Nyoro commoner has all her property confiscated and is reduced to abject poverty; she is never allowed to see the king again, and her lover, the chief responsible for her, and her nurse are all put to death (172). Yet in the myth the queen herself falls in love with a misbegotten intruder, an "ignorant and savage" hunter from the wilderness of a distant and uncivilized country; and she does so because he is splendidly built and she is overwhelmed by desire for him (Casati, 2: 39), thus loosing the destructive and disorderly power of sexuality.

A prince may sometimes rebel against the king and try to seize the throne, but it is important to him to have the support of the chief who is his guardian. This course may plunge the country into civil war, but it is a recognized possibility which is subject to institutionalized checks and other conventions (313–14). But Mpuga is no prince and has no guardian to whom he can turn for support in a plot; he cannot enlist other chiefs as allies, and he cannot muster Nyoro followers. He does not even confront the king in personal combat, as a prince may challenge the designated successor to the throne after the king's death (123). Instead, the queen gains the throne for him by the foul treachery of poisoning her husband.[34]

Now that we have examined the body of the myth,[35] and have grasped its main features and processes, we may return to a very prominent element which has not so far been expounded. Mpuga is half white and half black. What does this mean?

Let us first establish the facts. Even without later sources than Fisher we could be confident that it is sides that are in question, not the upper "half" and the lower "half" of the body, as some of the accounts could be taken as saying. The royal milkman has his head and shoulders whitened, and the princesses who attend the milking have "the upper part of their body whitewashed" (Fisher 1911: 124; cf. Roscoe 1922, pls. facing pp. 146, 148; 1923: 98); the royal cook is whitened on his face, chest, arms, and hands (102). If the colors on Mpuga were distributed in this way, he would then correspond in appearance to an everyday Nyoro ceremonial convention, which would be wholly inconsistent with his character, actions, and setting.

In fact, Roscoe says plainly that "one side of his body was dark and the other light" (1915: 9; 1923: 327). Bikunya also writes specifically that Mpuga had one "side," *orubaju,* white, *era,* and the other "side" dark, *nanata* (p. 37). Nyakatura says that one side was white "like his fathers, the Bacwezi," and the other was black "like his mother's people, the Abakidi" (p. 67). Dunbar, however, says: "Mpuga means patchy, because he had patches on his skin and this is thought to indicate his descent from the Bachwezi" (p. 32).

Roscoe provides us with a decisive clue, when he writes that Mpuga was so named "because" one side of his body was dark and the other light (1915: 9); and this is confirmed by Gorju, who says that it was because Mpuga was half white and half black that he was given his name by the Nyoro (1920: 60). Now the Nyoro word *mpūga* does mean "patches on cattle . . . ; cow, etc. with large white patches," which fits with Dunbar's reference to a patchy skin; but it also means "spear blade which is polished on one side only" (Davis, p. 97, s.v.)[36]—which better explains the preponderant references to Mpuga as having one side light or white and the other side dark or black.

The lateral image is further confirmed, and the symbolic activity better delineated, finally, by King Kamurasi's statement to Speke: "Formerly our stock was half-white and half-black, with one side of our heads covered with straight hair, and the other side frizzly" (Speke, p. 536).

Beattie, without mentioning any particular sources, writes that "half of Mpuga's body was black and half white," and seems to follow Nyakatura when he says that this feature is "a reference to his [Mpuga's] mixed descent" (1960: 15). By this he refers to Mpuga's father, who in the version he gives is Kyomya, son of a Cwezi, Isimbwa, who "married"[37] in a country to the north of the Nile, and presumably it is this mixture that is alluded to. Doubtless the white may signify the Cwezi part of Mpuga's ancestry, but in the light of what we now know about the symbolic importance of sides and colors it seems a rather superficial explanation. Even less satisfactory is Gorju's report that he has himself seen negroes who were half-albino, with its hint at the possibility of a natural origin for the hero's appearance (1920: 59–60; cf. Emin 1879a: 186; 1879b: 265, s.v. *námagsj*)—though, since actual albinoes are supposed to bring misfortune (Felkin, p. 140), such a physical feature would be symbolically correct also in that it would only put Mpuga further beyond the pale.

There seems indeed to be a more radical elucidation of this central feature of the myth. The rationale of Nyoro symbolic classification, well seen in the myth itself, is complementary dualism, and the defining relation is opposition. Black and white are outstanding and general symbols, in Nyoro tradition and ritual, representing two sets of quite contrary meanings. In that Mpuga is both colors, he symbolizes in his person both the principle of opposition itself and the alien, uncategorized, and essentially disorderly nature of his own condition and intent. A patchy skin would serve this purpose, but a clearer and more informative means is for him to be black on one side and white on the other. None of the authorities cited, from Speke to Beattie, thinks to tell us which side is which color, but it does not seem that we can now be in any doubt. Mpuga's right side will be white, his left will be black.[38]

Here we may conclude this rather rapid and compressed analysis of the myth. It abundantly confirms the dualistic structure of Nyoro symbolic classification, in terms of which we have interpreted the diviner's left hand; but does it really confirm that the main function of Nyoro mythical history is the establishment of Bito credentials to govern? There is certainly no conventional or obvious sense, at any rate, in which it could usefully be described as a "mythical charter" for the social and political order, for it would be a charter which set out precisely the opposite of what was intended. Alien origin, illegitimacy, twin birth, menial status, savage ignorance, usurpation, adultery, misalliance, and accession by treacherous murder at the hand of a woman are hardly the instruments to confer aristocratic prestige or to emphasize the "distinction and antiquity" of Bito antecedents. These scandalous and sinister origins cannot establish any credentials to govern, for they are worse than spurious: they are, significantly, the very negation of all valid credentials.

If the myth of Mpuga does so at all, then, it conveys Nyoro precepts by way of a moral and hierarchical representation in which everything is reversed and inverted, the opposite of right order. Rather than look for some banal social function, we should take seriously the principle of order which Nyoro collective representations not only exemplify but state, i.e., the relation of complementary opposition. But this does not mean simply that Nyoro values are reflected in the myth by an ultimate contrast with their opposites. The myth is a chronological expression of an ideological and symbolic scheme which is defined in its entirety by opposition and made unitary by analogy (see "Scheme of Nyoro Symbolic Classification," below). The narrative describes a transition from nature to culture: it states the perennial and complementary opposition between order and disorder.

Within this scheme of representations there is an ideological opposition which for its special theoretical interest is worth isolating, namely, that between secular and mystical values. This is seen not only in the structurally complementary statuses of princess and diviner, but can now also be discerned in the relationship between the forceful figure of the hunter Mpuga Rukidi and the diviner Nyakoko. They gain their joint end by an alliance between the secular action of Mpuga's physical incursion into the kingdom and Nyakoko's action in reading the augury.[39]

Why the Nyoro myth possesses its particular form and character, apparently stressing the triumph of the negative and disorderly, is a question which cannot be answered within the terms and values of Nyoro culture alone. It is a problem which embraces many similar situations, reported widely in history and from around the world, in which societies or institutions or persons are brought into being by precisely those means which are actually most abhorred (cf. Durkheim and Mauss, pp. xxxvii–xxxix), and of which a specially good example is descent from incestuous mythical unions (cf. Moore 1964). In Nyoro tradition itself, in fact, mankind origi-

SCHEME OF NYORO SYMBOLIC CLASSIFICATION

right	left
normal, esteemed	hated
boy	girl
brewing	cooking
giving (social intercourse)	[sexual intercourse]
king	queen
man	woman
chief	subject
good omen	bad omen
owner of land	hunter
health	sickness
joy	sorrow
fertility	barrenness
wealth	poverty
heaven	earth
white	black
security	danger
life	death
good	evil
purity	impurity
even	odd
hard	soft
princess	diviner
political rank	mystical office
Kitara-Unyoro	Bukidi
legitimacy	illegitimacy
normal birth	twin birth
cattle	chickens, sheep
milking	hunting
clothed	naked
shaven hair	long hair
barkcloth	animal skins
Nyoro language	alien dialect
civilization	savagery
royal endogamy	misalliance
fidelity	adultery
personal combat	murder
moon (beneficent)	sun (maleficent)
culture	nature
classified	anomalous
order	disorder

nates from the intercourse of a man and his sisters, children of the first man and the first woman (Emin 1879a: 182). The theme of dual classification is exemplified, also, by the facts that there are two sisters, and that one bears a chameleon (the bringer of death) and the other bears the moon (the embodiment of beneficence, the remover of sickness and hunger, and the source of milk, food, and health [Fisher 1911: 38; cf. Roscoe 1922: 213]). These indeed are fundamental issues, and they demand (as do all the most intriguing questions in social anthropology) logical and psychological answers of a correspondingly radical kind. The present sketch can be taken as little more than a demonstration that Nyoro mythology provides an additional instance of such a type of symbolic narrative, and as an example of a preliminary method of analyzing it.

VIII

This investigation has brought us some way from the bare report that a Nyoro diviner holds cowrie shells in his left hand, but the analysis has described a fairly direct progress, directed from point to point largely by the explicitness of the material itself, and has composed for the first time (with however little authority)[40] an integrated account of the principles and certain aspects of Nyoro symbolic classification.

It should be possible to test this proposed interpretation by seeing whether it helps us to pose other resoluble problems, or to understand what might otherwise appear to be isolated and arbitrary oddities of custom.

For example, the injunction that a newly married couple must "always sleep face to face and never back to back" (273) may plausibly be interpreted as the symbolic affirmation, during a definitive and formative period, of the relative moral "positions" of man and wife as expressed through lateral postures. Other questions raise themselves in the ethnography, and may well be seen, by someone familiar with the culture, under a new aspect when related to the dual structure of Nyoro symbolism. For instance, with which hand, and for what reason, do the Nyoro cover the mouth when expressing astonishment (Felkin, p. 139; Baker 1895: 335)? What does it mean to say that the hair of animals turns *hinduriza,* "the wrong way" (Davis, p. 43, s.v.)?[41] Why is there a special "low partition" *(ndamurano)* on the right side of the bed (Davis, p. 122, s.v.)? What are the facts, and what is the explanation, of the report that the king must not leave his bed "on the wrong side," but rather at a particular place (92)? What is the meaning of the daily ritual, when the king is to arise, that a young virgin dips barkcloth in her own urine and then touches the king's feet with it, "first one great toe and then the other on the underside" (92), and in what order is this done? Bukuku's daughter, Nyinamuiru, had "only one eye and one ear,"[42] but on which side? Kalīsa is an "imaginary monster with one eye, arm, leg, etc." (Davis, p. 60, s.v.)—but on which side are these organs developed?[43]

These problems all hang together, in their reference to the symbolism of the sides. In this respect, it seems very likely that the investigation of any of them would involve the establishment of the symbolic scheme which we have arrived at here. Indeed, it is an indication of the "total" character of Nyoro symbolism that one would be directed to this scheme by the governing ideas in Nyoro ethnography whether one started from the diviner's left hand or from any one of the problems above.

But it is not only lateral symbolism which makes this point. The connotations of red, for example, which it has not been feasible to investigate properly here, would provide another fascinating avenue into Nyoro symbolism. Color symbolism, in its turn, also emphasizes that it is not only Nyoro culture that is in question. A comparative study of the meanings attached to colors in Bantu cultures makes it seem probable that there is in some respects a common Bantu color symbolism, which in an historical perspective makes an interesting contrast with the great variety of types of descent system, economy, political organization, and so on. By a concentration on the fundamental and enduring features of Bantu symbolism (relating to space, colors, numbers, etc.) it may thus be possible to reconstruct, in Africa also, an "archéologie de représentations" (Dumézil 1949: 43) which could provide an entirely new foundation for local studies such as the present paper.

There would then remain the larger task of a universal and radical comparison, aimed at the discernment of the most general images, terms, and principles of symbolism. It might then be possible to say something useful about why the Nyoro, in East Africa, conceive the one-sided figures of Nyinamuiru and the monster Kalīsa, together with the lateral imagery of Mpuga's body—and why the Ngaju, in southern Borneo, tell of their mythical character Silai, son of a god and a mortal woman, who was "born with limbs developed on only one side of his body" (Schärer, p. 205).

On this note we may well conclude our examination of the particular culture and problem at issue here. There is, however, a more general consideration of certain points which we may yet indicate, and which has to do with other fundamental features of symbolism.

In the Nyoro case, as usually elsewhere, we have discovered our crucial evidence in the circumstances of birth, the relations between the sexes, and death. Moreover, the very kinds of "trouble" with which the Nyoro approach their diviners are related to these matters: barrenness, impotence, miscarriage, loss of marital affection, and sorcery (Beattie 1964: 45). They also ask about the identity of thieves, and presumably about a host of lesser afflictions as well, but their foremost troubles derive from the critical human situations of birth, copulation, and death. It is both methodologically instructive and intellectually exhilarating to appreciate, through even a summary structural analysis, the extreme contrast between the rich complexity of the culture which governs these passionate concerns and the slender logical and symbolic resources on the basis of which Nyoro collective representations have been elaborated in the creation of an ordered existence.

Very briefly, the interest is that we have in the main, and recurrently, been concerned with only four terms (right, left, male, female) and two types of relation (opposition, analogy). That is, we have been dealing with an elementary logical opposition (right/left) and a basic empirical contrast (male/female), two distinct kinds of antithesis, made coherent by analogical association. The former is a conceptual reflection of a necessary element in the structure of thought; the latter is an affective expression of genital nature. These components are reinforced most importantly by conceptions about numbers and colors: the former give cosmological significance to the cognitive category of quantity; the latter ascribe meaning to a mode of perception, equally ineluctable, of the phenomenal world. In these respects we may claim that we have been trying to understand, through the cultural categories of an African society which happened to be convenient for the purpose, certain primary factors of human experience.

Notes

1. I wish to acknowledge the reassurance afforded by my friend Dr. T. O. Beidelman, especially in view of his scholarly command of East African ethnography, who was so good as to read and approve the first version of this paper. My obligation in respect of this encouragement is the more particular in that Dr. Beidelman had, as I then learned, already long

felt that the Nyoro material called for such an analysis and had himself decided to write one.

Since regrettably I cannot read Lunyoro, I am deeply indebted to Mr. Y. M. K. Gwayambadde, B.Litt., of St. Peter's College, Oxford, who very kindly and patiently translated for me certain crucial pages in Bikunya (1927) and Nyakatura (1947).

2. At the end of the century he was still well remembered: "He was a good man and knew our language" (Fisher 1899: 14). This information comes from an account entitled "Bunyoro, Book XII," by the late Rev. A. B. Fisher, an early missionary in Bunyoro and husband of the author of *Twilight tales of the Black Baganda*. The account, which is based on Mr. Fisher's diaries, forms part of a collection of his papers held by the Church Missionary Society, London. No anthropologist, it is reported, has previously consulted these papers, but although they contain indeed little of ethnographic value they have a considerable interest, as reminiscences of the early years of European settlement in Bunyoro, and are well worth investigation by anyone interested in that country.

3. Dr. J. H. M. Beattie, who has made a re-study of the Nyoro and has published a number of papers on them, was invited to write a paper on right and left in Nyoro symbolic classification for inclusion in this handbook, but he declined. He was abroad on sabbatical leave when the present paper was written (August 1966), and it was considered a fairer test of the method that the analysis be made quite independently. He has no personal connection with the paper and is not answerable for anything in it but the facts and evaluations which he has published.

4. It has been thought useful, for this reason, to list certain works not cited in the paper. Blok (1951) is purely linguistic and contains no ethnographical material; Liesenborghs (1939) discusses Fr. Crazzolara's theory about the origin of the Babito and the possibility of a historical connection between the Watutsi and the Nyoro; it has not proved possible to consult Emin (1900), but it appears from the particulars to be only a secondary report or commentary.

5. This source will in future be referred to by page numbers alone; it is cited, as are all the other works drawn upon, in the ethnographic present.

6. Cf. the drill of reversing arms at a military funeral.

7. [In the original place I wrote also "and to bear children" (p. 432). I regret that this was incorrect. Roscoe indeed writes that there was "no law forbidding her to have children by the king"; but he further states that "for long it has been an accepted rule that the queen never bore children," and that if she found herself pregnant it was customary for her to take drugs and to bring on an abortion (Roscoe 1923: 140–41).]

8. There are women diviners as well, as we shall see below, but typically diviners are men.

9. "Toute interprétation juste d'un symbole doit être marquée par une complexité croissante, c'est-à-dire suivre une véritable loi d'accroissement des rapports analogiques et d'approfondissement de leur raison" (Alleau, p. 57).

10. Once again, the report is a direct rendering by the ethnographer of

a written account by a Nyoro informant. (The goatskin is mentioned in Beattie 1960: 72, but the color of it is not specified there.)

11. Three months after his coronation the king sends black cattle to a "great priest," Mihingo, but what this means is not reported (135).

12. Baker would seem to have understood something about the meaning of colors, or at least to have been well advised. Among his many gifts to Kabarega he included "one pound long white horsehair" (resembling, one supposes, the long white hairs of the colobus monkey which are so prominent in royal attire), but nothing in his long list seems to have been black; and he concluded an alliance with Ruyonga's people by making presents of "red and white beads" (1895: 284, 405).

13. Cf. "*kabunu,* a white strongly smelling stick used . . . as medicine" (Maddox, p. 100, s.v.).

14. The declaration of a white belly, on Baker's part, was to lead to the conclusion of a blood pact.

15. The king gives to a priest, Kyagwire, cattle which are white on one side and red on the other (135)—which more than whets analytical curiosity. There is also a royal ceremony involving black cows with white and red patches (Roscoe 1922: 205), which demands expert interpretation. A red or black hen may be used in augury (Emin 1879a: 224). The verb *tona* poses a problem: it means "to paint with black mud" (Maddox, p. 121, s.v.), but no explanation of this usage is supplied by the source; perhaps it is related to the ritual of progressive purification, a splendidly efficient and pleasing example of Nyoro symbolism, by which a person is rubbed all over with black ashes, then rubbed down with sand in a swamp, and finally washed in a clear, flowing stream (Fisher 1911: 45).

16. Two kinds of ore are used in iron-smelting: hard, which is called "male," and soft, which is called "female" (218). Beattie does not mention this, but it would seem likely that the appropriate qualities of stone are selected for the respective graves.

17. Cf. the possible influence of symbolism on history in Kabarega's claim that he was the eighteenth in line of succession from the first king (Casati, 2: 39), whereas it appears that he was in fact twenty-third (Dunbar, p. 35). Similarly, Ndahura is said to have had a huge house with "eighteen" doors (Johnston, 2: 598; K. W. 1935: 159).

18. Beattie refers to divination by means of "five twigs" (1964: 47), a different total but still uneven. He himself suggests that the number may be at the option of the diviner.

19. In one tradition, however, Inchia (i.e., Nkya), the first man, is said to have had three sons (Liesenborghs 1935: 212), and there is the possibility, to judge from the context, that this number may have a different symbolic basis apart from the consideration that these sons are held to have founded the three major classes of Nyoro society (cf. Fisher 1911: 72). There may be some significance also in the "brass tripod" captured by Thruston and said to have formed part of Kabarega's regalia (Thruston, p. 232).

20. Cf. "To Ngulu, the number four is an auspicious number representing the repetition gained only through orderly, stable relations" (Beidelman

1964: 379). [A subsequent publication indicates that this general impression, though consistent with the ethnographical literature cited, may not accord so widely as appeared might be the case. John Nyakatura, in his *Aspects of Bunyoro customs and tradition,* translated, annotated, and with a preface by Zebiya Kwamya Rigby (Kampala: East African Literature Bureau, n.d. [1970]), makes many scattered references to symbolic numbers, and although the sexual connotations of three and four are abundantly confirmed, not all of the contexts of five, six, seven, eight, and ten can readily be assorted by the particular criteria that I proposed. There are, however, certain usages which appear to distinguish more widely between odd and even numbers, on grounds more general than those implicit in the sexual contrast, and which may be subsumable under the classification that I have inferred. It may be significant, too, that the discordant instances which are most difficult to interpret come from within the field of divination (see esp. pp. 78–84), where the mystical/secular opposition is largely irrelevant to the character of the proceedings.]

21. Is it, for example, merely fortuitous that King Kamurasi kept Speke waiting for an audience for a period of nine days (Speke, pp. 498–511)? The first Europeans to enter Bunyoro, led by Speke, were thought to be the Cwezi returned (Fisher 1911: 156–57); Kamurasi would certainly have consulted his diviners about confronting Speke, and it would be readily understandable if they had counseled him to effect the meeting after *nine* days.

22. "'La Femme' dans un text mythique ou rituel n'est jamais la 'femme'; elle renvoie au principe cosmologique qu'elle incorpore" (Eliade, p. 353; cf. Needham, p. 26).

23. An iron-worker abstains from sexual intercourse on the night before seeking stones for his hammer and anvil (221); he must be continent while making the bellows, or else they will not work (223), and so must a drum-maker while making a drum (230); the man whose sinews are extracted for the royal bow is first purified and has to abstain from women (329).

24. It might make an interesting comparison, incidentally, if LoDagaa ideology were analyzed in this respect. See Goody's unexplained observation, in a footnote: "*gobr* means left-handed man . . . ; the term is also applied to diviners" (p. 256 n.).

25. It is understandable enough that she, like ordinary women, may not milk cows (cf. Felkin, p. 148); being mistress to her half-brothers makes sure of that, for in this role she is uncompromisingly an agent of feminine sexuality—and of this alone, not fertility.

26. Beattie reports nothing of the kind in his paper "Initiation into the Cwezi spirit possession cult" (1957); but he nowhere refers to Gorju's description of the ceremony either, and thus understandably does not consider the matter.

One crucial item of information, not to be found even in Gorju (or in any of the other sources cited), is how a diviner is buried. (The immediate presumption is that he will be buried lying on the left side with the hands under the left side of the head.)

27. See references in Needham (p. 32). I shall eventually publish a

special study, inspired chiefly by Dumézil's admirable work *Mitra-Varuna* (1948; cf. Needham, 1960), of this quite basic social and ideological relationship.

28. The late Fr. Vanneste's account does not expressly cite Mrs. Fisher's, but it is plain from certain precise parallels in wording that he has incorporated parts of her version into his own. It seems similarly plain, however, that what he had learned among the Nyoro in the area to the west of Lake Albert and the Semliki river, in the former Belgian Congo (cf. Stuhlmann, pp. 324, 554, map: "Ethnographische Übersicht der Völker des äquatorialen Ost-Afrika"; Emin 1916–21, vol. 1, map following p. 128: "Völkerstämme im Nil-Kongo-Zwischengebiet"; Liesenborghs 1935: 209, 217, map), so closely corresponded to the Uganda narrative that he had no hesitation in subscribing the latter.

29. Beattie, who otherwise appears in the main merely to repeat Mrs. Fisher's version, adds the dramatic touch that the black smut foretells the advent of "dark-skinned strangers" (1960: 15). Dunbar writes "a black man," in the singular, but he explicitly declares that he relies on Mrs. Fisher's account for the chapter in which this incident is narrated (pp. 8, 19). The dynastic history written by "K. W." (1935), i.e., Sir Tito Winyi, the present king (Dunbar, p. 7), does not include this legend.

30. Nyoro ethnography in general makes this quasi-articulate claim on our attention, and with its recurrent and insistent references to horns, crossroads, directions, lemon-grass, water, urine, blood, fire, ashes, times of the day, phases of the moon, and so on, might be said to be full of symbols screaming to be let out.

31. There is one apparent contradiction. At a certain ritual, the king is washed with a mixture of hot water and cold water; the hot is said to be "male," and the cold "female" (94), which is the reverse of what might be looked for.

The burning of scars on the temples and forehead, as a tribal marking according to Stuhlmann (pp. 325, 58), and elsewhere on the body for aesthetic purposes according to Gorju (1920: 331), is a custom which evidently requires another kind of elucidation.

32. The Kidi do not wear "any covering around the loins" (Grant, p. 290); the name WaKedi means "naked people" and they wear "absolutely no clothes" (Vandeleur, p. 74); Bukedi is described as "the Land of Nakedness" and the name "Bakedi," applied to the inhabitants, is said to mean "the naked" (Johnston, 2: 595); "Rukidi means the naked one, because he came from Bukidi, the land of nakedness" (Dunbar, p. 32).

33. Chaillé Long's map designates the area the "Kidi Wilderness" (facing p. 1).

34. This is made the more shocking, perhaps, by the fact that the king of Bunyoro is a "divine king," and that taking poison is the proper means by which the king himself secures the safety and continuation of the throne when he is incapacitated (121). Poison is also the means by which the king has other people killed, such as a defecting chief (Thruston, p. 198 n.).

35. The mythical aspect of Mpuga Rukidi is perhaps further indicated by the fact that there appears to be no royal shrine *(egasani)* for his jaw-

bone. K. W. says that his "tomb" is at Gulu (1936: 77), whereas Gorju says that the shrine is at Kichunda and contains only a shield in any case (1920: 110); but Ingham's survey reports no shrine for Mpuga, and none in fact before Winyi I, who was fourth on the throne (map following p. 144; cf. Dunbar, p. 35).

36. This, incidentally, is not the only connection in Lunyoro between spears and cattle: *muhimba* means both "blade of a spear before it is beaten out" and "swelling on side of fat cow" (Davis, p. 103, s.v.).

37. But this, as we have seen above, is actually a dubitable point of some consequence for the understanding of the myth. Even K. W. says only that Kyomya's twin sons were "got from a lady Nyatworo" (1935: 160).

38. There must be thousands of Nyoro who could say whether this simple inference is right or not. Cf. Wieschhoff, p. 214: "among many [African] tribes right is associated with light (white) and left with dark (particularly red)."

Postscriptum. Mrs. Zebiya Rigby, herself a Nyoro by birth, has made inquiries into the question and most kindly writes, in a personal communication (26 October 1966), which she permits me to reproduce, as follows: "The name Mpuga means 'He who has two colours.' A cow with darker patches on one side is also called *mpuga*. The first Mpuga had one side of his face and body darker than the other; he was lighter on the right side and darker on the left."

39. This relationship is confirmed in a later incident, when Nyakoko reads the omens of the drums, which decisively forecast Mpuga's accession (Fisher 1911: 177).

40. To any who may find it remarkable that an orientalist should investigate an African culture in this way, it may be responded that (1) social anthropology is comparative or it is not a discipline at all, and (2) what counts in this subject is not so much a mere knowledge of factual material (let alone direct acquaintance with the field) but the perception of problems, and then the theoretical interest of the analysis of them.

In the present case, moreover, it will be seen that I ally myself squarely with Dr. Beattie, who has a privileged acquaintance with Nyoro ideology, in his forthright contention that "the sensible student of myth, magic and religion will . . . be well advised to recognise that their tenets are not scientific propositions"; and I trust he may approve my attempt to put into effect, for the Nyoro, his persuasive and well-phrased exhortation that "as symbolic statements, they [i.e., the tenets] are to be understood by a delicate investigation of the levels and varieties of meaning which they have for their practitioners, by eliciting, through comparative and contextual study, the principles of association in terms of which they are articulated, and by investigating the kinds of symbolic classification which they imply" (Beattie 1966: 72).

41. Among the Sumbanese, who have a highly developed dual symbolic classification (cf. Onvlee 1949), whorls in the hair of cattle are thought to be auspicious or otherwise according to whether they turn to the right or to the left (field inquiries, 1954–55).

42. By one account, she was born so (Fisher, p. 84); in another, she is thus mutilated by her father in order to prevent her bearing the son who is destined to kill him (cf. Dunbar, p. 17). In the Ankole version she is deprived, at her father's orders, of "one breast and one eye" (Morris, p. 7).

43. Cf. the Lugbara spirit Adro: "He is said to be formed like a man, and very tall and white; but his body is cut down the centre and he has only one eye, one ear, one arm, and one leg . . ." (Middleton, p. 254).

References

ALLEAU, RENÉ
1958 *De la nature des symboles*. Paris: Flammarion.
BACHELARD, GASTON
1942 *L'eau et les rêves*. Paris: Corti.
BAKER, SAMUEL W.
1867 *The Albert N'yanza, Great Basin of the Nile, and explorations of the Nile sources*. 2 vols. London: Macmillan.
1895 *Ismailïa: a narrative of the expedition to Central Africa for the suppression of the slave trade*. London: Macmillan.
BEATTIE, J. H. M.
1957 Initiation into the Cwezi spirit possession cult in Bunyoro. *African Studies* 16: 150–61.
1958 The blood pact in Bunyoro. *African Studies* 17: 198–203.
1960 *Bunyoro, an African kingdom*. Case Studies in Cultural Anthropology. New York: Holt.
1961 Nyoro mortuary rites. *Uganda Journal* 25: 171–83.
1964 Divination in Bunyoro, Uganda. *Sociologus* 14: 44–61. [Reprinted in J. Middleton, ed., *Magic, witchcraft and curing* (pp. 211–31). Garden City, N.Y.: Natural History Press, 1967.]
1965 *Understanding an African kingdom: Bunyoro*. Studies in Anthropological Method. New York: Holt, Rinehart, and Winston.
1966 Ritual and social change. Malinowski Memorial Lecture, 1965. *Man*, n.s., 1: 60–74.
BEIDELMAN, T. O.
1961 Right and left hand among the Kaguru: a note on symbolic classification. *Africa* 31: 250–57.
1964 Pig *(Guluwe)*: an essay on Ngulu sexual symbolism and ceremony. *Southwestern Journal of Anthropology* 20: 359–92.
BERE, R. M.
1934 Notes on the origin of the Payera Acholi. *Uganda Journal* 1: 65–67.
1947 An Outline of Acholi History. *Uganda Journal* 11: 1–8.
BIKUNYA, PETERO
1927 *Ky'Abakama ba Bunyoro*. London: Sheldon Press.
BLOK, H. P.
1951 Iets over de Zogenaamde "Geïntensiveerde" Fonemen in het Ganda en Nyoro. *Kongo-Overzee* 17: 193–220.

BUCHTA, RICHARD
1881a *Die Oberen Nil-Länder: Volkstypen und Landschaften.* 2 vols. Berlin: J. F. Stiehm.
1881b Meine Reise nach den Nil-Quellseen im J. 1878. *Petermann's Mittheilungen* 27: 81–89.
CASATI, GAETANO
1891 *Dieci anni in Equatoria e ritorno con Emin Pascia.* 2 vols. Milan: Dumolard.
CHAILLÉ LONG, C.
1876 *Central Africa: naked truths of naked people.* London: Sampson Low, Marston, Searle, and Rivington.
CRAZZOLARA, J. P.
1937 The Lwoo people. *Uganda Journal* 5: 1–21.
1950 *The Lwoo,* Part I: *Lwoo migrations.* Museum Combonianum, no. 3. Verona: Istituto Missioni Africane.
DAVIS, M. B.
1938 *A Lunyoro–Lunyankole–English and English–Lunyoro–Lunyankole dictionary.* Kampala: Society for the Promotion of Christian Knowledge.
DERSCHEID, J. M.
1935 The Bakama of Bunyoro. *Uganda Journal* 11: 252–53.
DUMÉZIL, GEORGES
1948 *Mitra-Varuna: essai sur deux représentations indo-européennes de la souveraineté.* 2d ed. Paris: Gallimard.
1949 *L'héritage indo-européen à Rome.* Paris: Gallimard.
DUNBAR, A. R.
1965 *A history of Bunyoro-Kitara.* East African Studies, no. 19. Nairobi: Oxford University Press for the East African Institute of Social Research.
DURAND, GILBERT
1964 *L'imagination symbolique.* Paris: Presses Universitaires de France.
DURKHEIM, EMILE, and MAUSS, MARCEL
1963 *Primitive classification.* (1st ed. 1903.) Translated from the French and edited with an introduction by Rodney Needham. Chicago: University of Chicago Press.
ELIADE, MIRCEA
1964 *Traité d'histoire des religions.* Nouvelle édition. Paris: Payot.
EMIN PASHA [EDUARD SCHNITZER]
1879a Journal einer Reise von Mrúli nach der Hauptstadt Unyóro's, mit Bemerkungen über Land und Leute. *Petermann's Mittheilungen,* 25: 179–87, 220–24, 388–97.
1879b Wörtersammlung des Kigánda und Kinyóro. *Zeitschrift für Ethnologie* 11: 259–80.
1900 Emin Pacha dans l'Ounyoro. *Congo Belge* 5: 68–69.
1916–21 *Die Tagebücher von Emin Pascha.* Herausgegeben . . . von Dr. Franz Stuhlmann, 6 vols. Brunswick: Georg Westermann.

FELKIN, ROBERT W.
1893 Notes on the Wanyoro tribe of Central Africa. *Proceedings of the Royal Society of Edinburgh* 19: 136–92.
FISHER, A. B.
[1899] Diary: Sept. 18–Nov. 20, 1899. [London: Church Missionary Society archives.]
FISHER, A. B. (MRS.)
1911 *Twilight tales of the Black Baganda*. London: Marshall.
GOODY, JACK
1962 *Death, property and the ancestors*. Stanford: Stanford University Press.
GORJU, JULIEN
1906 *Essai de grammaire comparée: du Ruganda au Runyoro et au Runyankole*. Maison-Carrée (Algiers): Imprimerie des Missionnaires d'Afrique.
1920 *Entre le Victoria, l'Albert et l'Edouard: ethnographie de la partie anglaise du Vicariat de l'Uganda*. Rennes: Imprimeries Oberthür.
GRANT, JAMES AUGUSTUS
1864 *A walk across Africa: or, scenes from my Nile Journal*. Edinburgh-London: William Blackwood.
HARDELAND, AUG.
1859 *Dajacksch-Deutsches Wörterbuch*. Amsterdam: Frederik Müller.
HERTZ, ROBERT
1909 La Prééminence de la main droite: étude sur la polarité religieuse. *Revue Philosophique* 68: 553–80. [Above, chap. 1.]
INGHAM, K.
1953 The *Amagasani* of the Abakama of Bunyoro. *Uganda Journal* 17: 138–45.
JOHNSTON, HARRY
1904 *The Uganda protectorate*. 2 vols. London: Hutchinson.
JONES, RUTH
1960 *East Africa*. African Bibliography Series. London: International African Institute.
JUNKER, WILHELM
1891 *Reisen in Afrika, 1875–1886*, vol. 3: *1882–1886*. Vienna: Eduard Hölzel.
K. W. [Sir Tito Winyi]
1935 The kings of Bunyoro-Kitara. *Uganda Journal* 3: 155–60.
1936 The kings of Bunyoro-Kitara, part II. *Uganda Journal* 4: 75–83.
KRUYT, ALB. C.
1941 Rechts en Links bij de Bewoners van Midden-Celebes. *Bijdragen tot de Taal-, Land- en Volkenkunde van Nederlandsch-Indië* 100: 339–56. [Above, chap. 5.]
LIESENBORGHS, OSWALD
1935 Enkele Nota's over de Bale en Banioro van Belgisch Kongo. *Kongo-Overzee*, 1: 205–18.

1939 Nog over de Banioro. *Kongo-Overzee* 5: 82–84.

MADDOX, H. E.

1938 *An elementary Lunyoro grammar.* (1st ed., 1901.) London: Society for the Promotion of Christian Knowledge.

MIDDLETON, JOHN

1960 *Lugbara religion: ritual and authority among an East African people.* London: Oxford University Press for the International African Institute.

MOORE, SALLY FALK

1964 Descent and symbolic filiation. *American Anthropologist* 66: 1308–20.

MORRIS, H. F.

1962 *A history of Ankole.* Kampala: East African Literature Bureau.

NEEDHAM, RODNEY

1960 The left hand of the Mugwe: an analytical note on the structure of Meru symbolism. *Africa* 30: 20–33. [Above, chap. 7.]

NYAKATURA, J. W.

1947 *Abakama ba Bunyoro-Kitara.* St. Justin, Quebec, Canada.

OLIVER, ROLAND

1953 A question about the Bachwezi. *Uganda Journal* 17: 135–37.

ONVLEE, L.

1949 Naar Aanleiding van de Stuwdam in Mangili. (Opmerkingen over de Sociale Structuur van Oost-Soemba). *Bijdragen tot de Taal-, Land- en Volkenkunde* 105: 445–59.

RIGBY, PETER

1966 Dual symbolic classification among the Gogo of Central Tanzania. *Africa* 36: 1–16. [Above, chap. 13.]

ROSCOE, JOHN

1916 *The Northern Bantu: an account of some Central African tribes of the Uganda protectorate.* Cambridge: Cambridge University Press.

1922 *The soul of Africa: a general account of the Mackie Ethnological Expedition.* London: Cassell.

1923 *The Bakitara or Banyoro.* Cambridge: Cambridge University Press.

SCHÄRER, HANS

1963 *Ngaju religion: the conception of God among a South Borneo people.* Translated from the German by Rodney Needham. The Hague: Martinus Nijhoff.

SPEKE, JOHN HANNING

1863 *Journal of the discovery of the source of the Nile.* Edinburgh-London: Blackwood.

STUHLMANN, FRANZ

1894 *Mit Emin Pascha ins Herz von Afrika.* Berlin: Dietrich Reimer.

TAYLOR, BRIAN K.

1962 *The Western Lacustrine Bantu.* Ethnographic Survey of Africa, ed. Daryll Forde: East Central Africa, Part XIII. London: International African Institute.

THOMAS, H. B.
1960 Richard Buchta and early photography in Uganda. *Uganda Journal* 24: 114–19.
THRUSTON, A. B.
1900 *African incidents: personal experiences in Egypt and Unyoro.* London: John Murray.
VANDELEUR, SEYMOUR
1898 *Campaigning on the Upper Nile and Niger.* London: Methuen.
VANNESTE, M.
1950 Nyabongo, de eerste Bito-Koning: Werkelijkheid en Legende. *Kongo-Overzee* 16: 148–54.
WARNECK, JOH.
1909 *Die Religion der Batak: ein Paradigma für Animistiche Religionen des Indischen Archipels.* Religions-Urkunden der Völker, herausgegeben von Julius Boehmer, Abteilung IV, Band 1. Leipzig: Theodor Weicher.
WIESCHHOFF, HEINZ A.
1938 Concepts of right and left in African cultures. *Journal of the American Oriental Society* 58: 202–17. [Above, chap. 4.]
WITSCHI, HERMANN
1938 *Bedrohtes Volk: von den Ngadju-Dajak an den Urwaldströmen Süd-Borneos.* Stuttgart-Basel: Evang. Missionsverlag.
WRIGLEY, C. C.
1958 Some thoughts on the Bacwezi. *Uganda Journal* 22: 11–17.

On Bad Death and the Left Hand: A Study of Rotinese Symbolic Inversions

James J. Fox

16

That they carried them out of the world with their feet forward, not inconsonant unto reason: As contrary unto the native posture of man, and his production first into it.
Sir Thomas Browne, *Urne Buriall* (1658)

I

On the basis of a series of four exemplary ethnographic reports written by the Dutch missionary Heijmering in 1843, Hertz, in his essay "The Collective Representation of Death" (1907), was able to advance the following observations on certain funeral procedures of the Rotinese, an island people of Eastern Indonesia:

> On the island of Roti, the same day as the soul departs for the land of the dead, a palm leaf is cut in a particular way and is sprinkled with the blood of a sacrificial animal; this object (called *maik*), which hence forth bears the name of the deceased, is then attached to other identical ones, representing those who died previously, and is hung under the roof; this ceremony, we are told, is equivalent to a canonisation of the deceased. When the *maik* disappears, due to wear and worms, it is not replaced; two classes of spirits *(nitu)* are distinguished, those of within, who still have their *maik* and to whom sacrifices are offered inside the house, and those without, whose names no longer live in the memory of the living, and to whom sacrifices are made outside. Thus the domestic cult is concerned only with the closest ancestors; after a certain time the souls are lost in the collectivity of souls common to the whole village. (Hertz 1960: 139, n. 207.)

An original study written especially for this volume.

This distinction which Heijmering originally observed and correctly recorded, between that class of spirits confined within the house, the *nitu nai dalek,* and the contrasting class of spirits outside the house, the *nitu nai deak,* remains as fundamental to an ethnographic description of the Rotinese today as it appears to have been at the time when Heijmering wrote his "Zeden en gewoonten op het eiland Rottie." The intention of the present paper is to return to this important distinction, to describe and elaborate on the contrast between these two classes of spirits, and to examine the principal means by which individual ghosts, through their death and burial, come to join one or other of these classes.[1] My treatment of these spirits, in the interests of exposition and analysis, as divided into classes should not, I hope, obscure the fact that these same classes might, more graphically, be described as opposing and hostile camps engaged in a struggle to which the living are themselves subject. Certainly this would convey something of the seriousness with which, on occasion, the Rotinese and especially the elder Rotinese regard the *nitu.*

II. The Orientations of Outside and Inside: *Deak* and *Dalek*

The orientation categories of outside and inside share, with a limited number of other terms of orientation, a position of such prominence in Rotinese thought that they must be regarded as primary coordinates in Rotinese classification. As coordinates within a system these categories are applicable at various levels of Rotinese classification. They rarely indicate an absolute orientation; each application of these coordinates must be considered relative to a certain view and level of reference. Since even the spirits are subject to this orientation, I propose to discuss briefly a few applications of the categories of outside and inside.

At the level of the individual, a Rotinese will often preface some well-considered opinion or reflection with the remark that it comes from "within" *(neme dale-na)* or that this is something he has "pondered on within himself" *(afi nai dale-na).* In this sense, *dale* refers to the inner core of a man, his person, what Jonker (1908: 72) translates, not incorrectly, as the "heart" (although, in fact, this inner sentiment may be physically located within the stomach, *teik*). A common Rotinese admonition to be sincere and trustworthy is *Boso ma-dale dua ma boso ma-tei telu,* which, translated literally, advises "Do not have two hearts and do not have three stomachs." There are any number of other compound expressions (Jonker 1908: 72–74) that utilize this sense of the word *dale*—with *malole* (good), *dale-malole:* "to be good hearted," "friendly"; with *sala* (wrong), *dale-sala:* "to be greedy," "envious"; *dale-hi:* "to desire intensely"; *dale-loloa:* "to comfort," "console someone"; or *nata-dale:* "to be glad," "overjoyed."

In contrast to this use of *dale* is the conscious, often artful show of words in which all Rotinese delight. But this verbal play does not belong to the essential inner level of things "of the heart." It manifests itself for example in what, to the observer, appears as interminable disputes and law cases. Not to be involved in some dispute is hardly to be Rotinese. In fact, the Rotinese have gained the reputation of being the most disputatious people of the Timor area. To the Dutch colonial administration, the island was indeed a trial and testing ground for young administrators. Yet to the Rotinese, it seems, the point of many disputes lies in the conduct of the argument itself.[2] All forms of this externalized verbal display from minor quarrels to major court cases, heard by the lord of a domain, are described as *dedeäk.* They are classified, in some way, as things of the outside. Conflict, in this sense, belongs to the realm of things of the outside.

Many Rotinese folktales involve trickster-like heroes. Much of the humor lies in the listener's knowledge of both what the hero thinks to himself *(nai dale-na)* and what he says *(dedeä)* to achieve his deception. At a different level of reference the categories of outside and inside are applied to the house. The house is an exceedingly complex symbolic structure and I confine myself here to these two simple coordinates. The house proper is an enclosed rectangular structure raised on poles, above the ground. The roof forms an oval dome over this square form. On three sides, this roof slopes steeply to within a few feet of the ground, while, to the front, the slope of the roof is gentle and it encloses beneath itself a wide forecourt, before the ladder that leads up into the house proper. All houses are oriented lengthwise in an east-west direction and their entrances are either from the north or the south. From the outside, the impression is of an immense haystack under which one stoops to enter.

On entering, there is first the forecourt around which are raised a number of long broad wooden platforms, perhaps three feet high, often covered with pandanus mats, on which, sitting or reclining, a

Rotinese entertains his guests. The host occupies the platform on the east side of the house while guests always range themselves to the west of their host. Rarely, except in the case of a funeral, will a guest be allowed to climb the ladder into the house proper.

The house proper is divided into two partitioned halves. The west side of the house, with the cooking fire, the water-pot, the *pule sio* or "nine seeds" of the agricultural cult, the ladder into the loft, and the never empty pot of lontar syrup (the *bou nitu inak*) is the women's half of the house and is called the *uma dalek,* the "inner house." The east side of the house, with its male implements, sword, spear, and parang, and possibly an offering of red coconut oil to *Tou mane,* the "Male-man," Lord of the Lightning at the *di kona,* the "right post" in the southeastern corner of the house, this side is the man's half of the house and is called the *uma deak,* the "outer house." This division is never, however, a perfect bisection; the *uma dalek* must always be somewhat larger than the *uma deak.*

The categories of inside and outside have innumerable further applications. Here I wish to consider a few common usages of the term "outside," *deak.* The island is divided into eighteen independent states or domains each ruled over by a lord *(manek)* who maintains his own court to judge cases according to the local customary usage *(hadak).* The word for these domains is *nusak.* A man of a particular *nusak* regards the other domains of the island as *nusa-dea* and other strange Rotinese *(hataholi feëk)* as *hataholi nusa-dea,* "men of the outside nusak." This is sufficiently clear but the same man applies the category *deak* to any uninhabited wood or grassland, any area of his own domain removed from human settlements. Here the meaning is the "bush," the wilderness in which it is possible to encounter wandering spirits.[3] *Deak* has the further sense of "in back of" or "behind." A man's back is his *deak;* "to turn back" or "return" is *fali deak;* the clients and followers of a lord are referred to as *mana-tunga deak,* "those who follow behind." In certain contexts, *deak* has the added meaning of something "secret," something done "behind the back." One defecates *nai deak,* at some distance from the house, and a more polite expression for the verb to defecate *(tei)* is *nanga-deak,* which can be translated as either "to make outside" or "to make backward." In yet another common usage, the open sea, as opposed to the shore lines along which the Rotinese fish and sail, falls within this category of *deak.* Not unexpectedly, the Rotinese are wary of sailing out into the open sea, and they leave deep sea fishing to small colonies of Badjo-Laut on the island.

There is, however, one particularly interesting usage of the term *deak*. As a noun, this word refers to the stony fish walls or weirs which the Rotinese erect in the shallows of the shore to trap fish as the tide goes out. Each tide takes its name from the time of the day or night at which its waters begin to recede, allowing the Rotinese to fish their *deak*. Certainly, these *deak* may be conceived of as physically "the back" of the land, the boundary between the land and sea, but they are also eminently a resort of the spirits. The Rotinese regard the sea depths as a separate realm of life, not unlike a Rotinese domain, but ruled over by shark and crocodile. This realm to which, according to the ritual texts, the Rotinese are allied by marriage, is a source of both bounty and adversity and is intimately associated with the realm of the dead. It is not surprising therefore that the midnight tide, in which the Rotinese fish their *deak* by torchlight, is called the *meti-nituk,* "the tide of spirits," and that in folktales a fish-wall at night is a common meeting place of man and spirit.

III. Spirits of the Inside and Spirits of the Outside: *Nitu nai Dalek/Nitu nai Deak*

The spirits of the inside are referred to in various ways. They are the *nitu bei-baï,* "the spirits of (the male and female) ancestors" or they are the *nitu dalek,* "the inside spirits," "the center spirits." Their most common name is *nitu uma,* "the spirits of the house." Heijmering, in his short account of a Rotinese funeral (1844: 365–67), has given a good description of how, at the end of the funeral rituals, the individual ghost is incorporated within the house and represented by a lontar-leaf *maik* joined to other such ancestral *maik* hung under the inside roof of the house. In the domain of Termanu or Pada, this ceremony is called *kekela maik,* "the cutting of the *maik,*" and should be performed on either the third or ninth day after the burial, depending upon the elaborateness of the funeral procedures.

In Termanu, the *maik* are usually hung in the southeastern corner of the house, but like the dialects of the island, the rituals vary from domain to domain. In the domain of Korbaffo, which borders with Termanu, ritual procedures are similar to Termanu, although the *maik* are frequently referred to as *ola*. The southern domain of Thie (Ti) presents an interesting variation. Here there are two distinct lontar-leaf representations. When a person is old enough to marry, a lontar leaf is made and hung in the house. This is called a *lais,* a noun formed from the term *lai,* meaning "above," and hence a *lais* might be translated as "an above." It is to feed this *lais* that a woman returns on about the seventh month of her pregnancy. Finally, at death, when the major death ceremonies are concluded, this *lais* is simply thrown away. This is described as *sele lais,* "planting the lais." Then on the fortieth day after burial, a *maik,* called the *soe-maik,* the "skull-*maik,*" is made and, as in Termanu, hung in the *uma deak*. In the western domain of Dengka, on which unfortunately I have little first-hand information, the *maik* are called *baä,* but here the distinction is made between the *baä* that represent the male ancestors and are hung on the east side of the house and the *baä* of the female ancestors which are hung on the west side of the house. This distinction follows the fundamental division of the house observed in Termanu.

The *maik* I have observed were all over a foot in length and made by removing a section from the full fan of the lontar leaf, splitting this, folding and then knotting the split portions to form a three-pronged forklike object. The number three is essential and propitious. The *maik* is three-pronged and is like the special three-sided lontar leaf containers *(fifiluk)* which hold the rice used to feed the spirits.[4]

As a class, the spirits of the inside are clearly defined. They are a circumscribed class of named beings, the immediate lineal ancestors of the living. These spirits are represented as the protectors of their descendants, but if they are neglected, they are capable of causing illness. The Rotinese describe many houses as *uma nitu,* "spirit houses." The sense of this designation depends upon the referent to which the term is applied. Any house or household able to support the expense of a burial feast is necessarily an *uma nitu.* In this sense, an *uma nitu* defines a descent group of limited extent. Two brothers, who have divided an inheritance on the death of their father, may be regarded as having separate *uma nitu*. The youngest son, however, inherits the house of his father and initially it is his inherited cult of *nitu* which is regarded as the more powerful. Frequently, in practice, long after the division of an inheritance elder brothers remain dependent upon the *uma nitu* of their youngest brother. In the folktales, it is the younger of two brothers who has the closer relation to the world of the spirits.

In the larger clans, certain houses whose owners possess or exercise a claim to the cult of an apical lineage ancestor are regarded as particularly powerful *uma nitu*. The owners of these houses are spoken of as *mane nitu,* "spirit lords," or *manasongo nitu,* "those who offer to the spirits." Often, although not necessarily, these titles are coincident with the title of *maneleo,* "lineage lord," or the title of *manesio,* "lord of nine." For those clans that possess a *hus* or origin feast, the term *uma nitu* is applied to the house to which all ancestors of the clan are called during the night of drumming *(bapa)* before the "running" of the *hus*. To the lord of each domain, as the possessor of the most important of these *hus*-feasts, belongs the most powerful of all *uma nitu*. What one encounters on Roti is not simply a hierarchy of ancestral houses (which may be regarded as descent groups) but also a hierarchy of *nitu*.

The *nitu* of the more powerful spirit houses are no longer represented by a *maik* within the house. Hertz interpreted Heijmering in Durkheimian terms to mean that the *nitu* who lack a *maik* "are lost in the collectivity of souls common to the whole village." This is slightly inaccurate. Since within a village area there may be members of any of a number of clans, it might be more accurate to say that these "souls" become the common property of their clan. Yet even this would be somewhat incorrect because while their names are remembered and recited, these *nitu* still possess some individuality and the Rotinese genealogies which record these names are of considerable depth. The genealogy of the present lord of Termanu, for example, requires the recitation of thirty-one ancestors. The genealogy for the commoner clan of Kiu-Kanak has a similar depth.

Certain Rotinese claim the ability to see *nitu*. On occasion women who faint, in fits of intense mourning at a funeral, wake to describe the *nitu* they have seen. This ability, which some Rotinese women have by nature, men must seek by technique. To see the *nitu,* one must stand beneath the floorboards of the house and wash one's face three times with the water poured out during the ritual washing of the corpse. I pressed one of my best informants for a description of one of these eyewitness accounts of the spirits. He told me that the *nitu* can be seen hovering over the corpse within the house. They look much like what they did when they were alive, except that they lack heels to their feet and are forced to walk on their toes.[5] They have school notebooks now, like some of their more modern, living descendants, and they record every gift made to the deceased and report its arrival to the *nitu* who are no longer present within the house. (In a conversation with another informant, I was told that the gifts given to the deceased by others are intended for conveyance to ancestral spirits of gift-givers. The *nitu* of the deceased is only the medium for the transmission of gifts to one's own *nitu*.) The *nitu* of the house can be seen coming and going on their journeys to the absent *nitu*. For these other ancient *nitu*, the term used is *nitu mate basak*, the "spirits who have completely died."[6] As Hertz originally observed, death in Indonesia is not a moment but a process.

Another characteristic of the *nitu* of the inside is their accessibility to invocation.[7] At the *hus*, the ceremony of invocation is *bapa*, the persistent beating of the drum which must be done with the palm of the right hand, while the ancestral names are recited. This or any other naming of the spirits is described as *lona bei-baï*, "the bringing down of (male and female) ancestors." But to mention the ancestral names outside a ritual context, I was frequently told, and without proper sacrifice is particularly dangerous. Without discussing the complexities of personal names, it may be sufficient to note that most Rotinese in childhood are given the name of an ancestor who then becomes that person's lifelong *tamok*. Since, however, the ordinary mention of ancestral names is rigorously avoided, a variety of what are called *nade manganaü*, "soft names," are substituted to suggest but never state the name of the *tamok*. To speak a man's *nade balakai*, his "hard name," is regarded as an insult and a serious breach of Rotinese proper behavior.

The *nitu nai dalek*, we have seen, are a class of named ancestral spirits who are seen as the guardians of the house; the closest of these mediate with the more remote in a hierarchy of spirits. By contrast, the spirits of the outside are conceived otherwise. The expression *nitu nai deak*, or *nitu dea*, is applied to all the odd spirits with which the bush, the forests, and the sea and especially the crossroads are all too abundantly populated. Unlike the spirits of the inside, these *nitu* are unnamed. They form a disordered collection of individual roaming spirits. Above all, they are dark creatures of the night.[8]

Toward these spirits, the Rotinese consistently apply two terms.

These spirits are said to be *nitu maka-tataü*, "spirits who frighten" or "terrify" men. Christians on the island often translate *naka-tataü* with the Indonesian word *menggoda;* these spirits (also referred to in Indonesian, as *iblis* or *setan*, "devils" or "satans") come to "tempt" or "hinder" men.[9] The other term applied to the *nitu* is *ma-nufak*. Jonker (1908: 408) translates this as "disaster-bringing." Certainly *ma-nufak* has this sense but, in fact, the term suggests a whole complex of ideas which the Rotinese have about dangerous *nitu*.

Nufak is a word borrowed from the dyeing of woven cloths. Rotinese native ikat-cloths are red and white with what one could call a "black" background. This black background is produced with an indigo dye, called *tau* in Rotinese. *Nufak* is the first stage in the process of *tau*-dyeing. The tied threads *(futus)* of the cloth are soaked for a week in a mixture of the finely ground oily seeds of the *nitas* (Indonesian: *kelumpang;* Sterculia foetida) tree and a bark called *loba* (which does not grow on Roti but is imported to the island by Buginese traders). *Nufak* is done as preliminary so that "the threads are strong in absorbing the *tau*." *Tau*-dyeing requires at least a month; the dyeing itself must be done at night. Each day in the late afternoon the tied cords of the *futus* are submerged in the indigo solution and in the morning removed to dry in the sun. Pots of *tau* are never taken into the house, and the dyeing is usually done out of doors because, as the Rotinese say (and I can well confirm) the smell of the dye *(tau isi)* is particularly pungent. (The Rotinese themselves describe the smell as putrid like the stench of rotting meat.) A cloth that has been properly dyed for a month can be described as black. The Rotinese themselves often describe their cloths as black *(nggeo)*, but they also characterize these same cloths as *momodo*, a color category which crosscuts our own delineation of the spectrum and includes the colors from blue through green to certain yellows. (This color *momodo* and its association with the spirits are discussed below.)

I suggest that the spirits of the outside are called *nitu maka-tataük* and *nitu ma-nufak* because they are conceived of not only as "terrifying" but also as "blackening" (strictly speaking in Rotinese, "blueing" *momodo)* spirits.[10] They threaten always to blacken man. This also locates the spirits (as I intend to discuss below) within one quadrant of another Rotinese symbolic order.

One must recognize what V. Turner (1967: 286) has described

as "fictitious etymology" which in this case achieves homonymy by "increasing the senses possessed by a word by adding to them those of a word of the same form but different derivation." This seems an important method of accomplishing the integration of symbolic systems. Etymologically, the roots *taü,* meaning "to fear" or "frighten," and *tau,* indigo plant, are unrelated. *Taü* is related to the Indonesian word *takut,* "to be afraid" while *tau* is related to the Indonesian word for indigo, *tarum.* But both of these words by a similar process of linguistic development (in this case, omission of middle and final consonants) have come to resemble each other. That there is this association of indigo and the spirits is further confirmed by the fact that wild indigo plants are described as *tau nituk,* the "indigo of the spirits." [11]

Another defining characteristic of the spirits of the outside is that, besides being deformed, they are inverted creatures. About this the Rotinese are explicit. The outside spirits travel about upside down with their hands on the ground and their feet in the air. The very name *nitu dea* (in distinction to *nitu nai deak*) implies also that these spirits are "backward" or "reversed" spirits. Their behavior may equally be characterized as the inverse of human behavior. They crave the essence of human flesh, prey upon the livers of men, and are one of the principal causes of illness, death, and disaster on the island. But here one cannot dissociate these spirits from the sorcerers who use them. A sorcerer, I was assured, can encounter and gain control of individual spirits of this kind and can send these spirits to do his bidding. I return to this point shortly; here I want to observe that an essential part of Rotinese curing is intended to *na-fuli,* "drive away," these spirits of the outside. At funerals, the spirits of the outside (in contrast to the spirits of the inside who are attracted by the *bapa* of the drum) are repulsed by noise of nine gongs *(meko sio).* This noise forms a boundary round the celebrating Rotinese.

An observation the Rotinese make about the spirits of the outside is that they have died a bad death *(nisa lalak).* Bad death may not explain the existence of all the sundry spirits of the outside, but it is the only origin the Rotinese offer.

IV. Bad Death: *Mamate Nisa-lalak*

To die a good death, the Rotinese say, is "to die in the house and home" *(mate nai uma-lo).* Alternatively, a good death is described as "an ancestral death" *(mamate bei-baï)* or "a death of the [good] spirits" *(mamate nituk)*. By contrast, a bad death is sudden, violent, and inauspicious. In central and much of eastern Roti, the term for bad death is *mamate nisa-lalak;* in southern Roti (beginning in the domain of Thie) and in western Roti, the term is *mate-tandek.*[12] Death in childbirth, although it occurs within the house, is classified as a *mamate nisa-lalak.* The following is a list of the principal categories of bad death (dialect of Baä): [13]

1.	*tuda tua*	to fall from a lontar palm
2.	*nana-tatik*	to be cut/killed [by a man]
3.	*kamba foik*	to be gored by a water buffalo
4.	*tatas tek*	to be speared by lightning
5.	*fa nenik*	to be carried by a flood
6.	*bai kak*	to be bitten by a crocodile
7.	*bolo tasi*	to drown in the sea
8.	*ketu funik*	to sever the placenta

1–4. Tuda Tua, Nana-Tatik, Kamba Foik, and Tatas Tek

Of these four kinds of bad death, *tuda tua,* "falling from a lontar," is the most frequent, for the majority of Rotinese men are lontar-tappers and they tap their palms in the dry, gusty winds of the east monsoon. These winds reach their height in July and August, at which time many Rotinese suspend tapping, adding that the agitation of the *haik* (the lontar leaf containers for catching the juice of the palm) produces an inferior *tuak.* Other Rotinese continue to tap but concentrate on only a few trees. It is in July and August that *tuda tua* is most likely to occur.

There are certain simple ritual procedures to be followed when a man has fallen to his death. I have not seen these procedures nor am I certain whether they are performed specifically in the case of *tuda tua* or generally whenever the corpse is recovered of a person who has died in bad death.

Whoever encounters the corpse of a bad dead beneath the tree must first jump over the body three times. Then, in Termanu, several blades of gewang leaf *(tula)* are tied to form a rope; this is bound around the wrists and ankles of the deceased; but once bound, the gewang-rope is immediately undone. This is called *seï tula,* "loosing the gewang," from which the procedure takes its name. I never learned the significance of this performance but its end, it was said, was to prevent the spirit of the dead from "troubling" *(na-nufa)* the living. In Baä, a neighboring domain to Termanu, jumping over the corpse three times is also required but in place of *seï tula* is an equally simple ritual called *te nodok* in which coconut milk is sprinkled about on the corpse and those present "to cool them" *(lini-do makasufu)*. As in other periods of ritual crisis, everything that has to do with bad death is regarded as ritually "hot" *(hanas)* and potent.[14]

Nana-tatik (being killed by sword or machete) includes murders, executions, deaths in feuding and formerly deaths in head-hunting. Head-hunting, when it was practiced, was regarded as a male occupation of the outside and, if successful, as resulting in the creation of further dangerous outside spirits. In the domain of Termanu, there is still the persistent expectation of head-hunters *(nako langas)* toward the end of the dry season in September and early October.

While falling from a lontar palm is common, being gored to death by a water buffalo and being "speared" by lightning are rare occurrences. My many informants remembered only two instances of goring and none of "spearing" by lightning. The Rotinese distinguish deaths in categories 1–4 from those in 5–7 by the fact that in the former the body of the deceased is recovered and must therefore be disposed of, whereas in the latter the body is often lost in the sea and presents no further problem.

5–7. Fa Nenik, Bai Kak, Bolo Tasi

The category *fa nenik* can include all deaths by drowning on the island but it refers specifically to being swept away by the flash floods that suddenly swell Rotinese rivers after heavy rain. It is possible, given the rocky bareness of the island's surface, for any dry coastal river bank to become a torrent almost without warning after rains in the hills.

To be devoured by a crocodile, *bai kak,* is highly inauspicious because the crocodile is addressed as ancestor or ancestress (*baï* or *bei*) and stands in a special relationship to man. The Lord of the Sea Depths known by his dual name *Dangalena Liun ma Manetua Sain* is represented as the crocodile (and shark).[15] Several Rotinese of commoner descent have assured me they may enter crocodile waters without danger.

Bolo tasi, to drown in the sea, is the most frequent of all bad deaths, since the Rotinese, while keeping close to the shore, will risk the voyage to Timor in small overloaded perahus *(lete-lete)* at the very height of the east monsoon. As is the case with falls from the lontar palm, it is usual to expect deaths by drowning in July and August.

8. *Ketu Funik*

Death in childbirth, despite the fact that it occurs in the inner house *(uma dalek),* is nevertheless a bad death. Because it has occurred within the house, it requires special ritual procedures. On women who have died in childbirth the Rotinese are explicit. They become *buntiana* spirits and take the form of owls. Alternatively they are spoken of as *ina ketu-funik,* "women with several placentas." The *buntiana* is one of the most feared of the *nitu-dea* and to prevent the return of a woman who has died in childbirth the Rotinese bury her with needles in the fingers of her hands and eggs under her armpits to prevent her from developing wings and flying. The *buntiana* attack other women in childbirth and may cause their deaths but there is a close connection which, for some, amounts to an identity between the *buntiana* and the *nitu kak.* The *nitu kak* (or *buntiana*) is a creature who can take the form of a beautiful woman but is so inverted that her teeth line her vagina and in this way she seduces men to their destruction. The Rotinese give an interesting elaboration to this traditional Indonesian belief. There exist two *buntiana* or possibly two aspects (conceived of as either man and woman or husband and wife) of the one *buntiana.* These are the *buntiana touk* (the "man *buntiana*") and the *buntiana inak* (the "woman *buntiana*"). The "man *buntiana*" attacks women in childbirth and in general brings all manner of illness. The "man *buntiana*" is nevertheless described as a woman who brings illness in the shape of fire issuing from the genitals. The "woman *buntiana,*" on the other hand, attempts to seduce men. She is always recognizable by the whiteness of her skin ("white as cotton") and a man who encounters this spirit in the bush must stop, lower his head, and remain silent while performing the symbolically appropriate gesture of *tucking his thumbs into his closed fists.*[16]

One of my closest Rotinese acquaintances claimed to have been skeptical of the "woman *buntiana*" until one night he encountered one who came upon him swiftly from behind, taking the shape of the girl he favored at that time. When the spirit was level with him, she tore off the cloth he was wearing, clawed at his belly, and disappeared. He returned home and lay ill in his house for weeks. The man who eventually cured him recognized his illness by means of the deep owl-talon marks he bore on his belly.

Children who die at birth become separate spirits called *ndafe*. A distinction is made in practice between the still-born child or the child who dies with its mother (and must therefore be classified as a bad death) and the child who survives for some time after birth and can be given a proper, if somewhat abbreviated, funeral feast. A child who dies before the age of three months may be buried beneath the ladder of the house and an older child (up to about the age of a year) is wrapped in white cotton and buried in proximity with a kind of cotton plant called *modo-kapa-oek* (Calotropis gigantea, R. Br.). This plant is said to possess a symbolic water buffalo's milk *(kapa-oek)* which nourishes the child. Poetically, the Rotinese say that the cotton tufts of the *modo-kapa-oek* are carried away by the wind in the same way as the child is carried off from its mother by a *buntiana* spirit. In general, however, the spirits of all dead children are spoken of as *ndafe*. They are no danger to adult men but can be of considerable danger to their mothers and to any children born after them.[17]

The Rotinese, as I have already indicated, have the reputation in Eastern Indonesia of being extremely argumentative. Among themselves, they are addicted to endless verbal dueling and they have developed a wide-ranging, conventional vocabulary of mockery and cursing *(dedeăk aăli-oŏlek)*. Terms of this mockery are directed not only toward men but toward all domestic animals as well. Some of this vocabulary consists of wishing one's opponent a bad death. Most of the terms for bad death I have already listed can easily be used as terms of mockery. *Bolo tasi,* "drown in the sea," and *tuda tua,* "fall from a lontar," are very common and I have also recorded *bei sik,* "may a crocodile rend [you]" and *bei kak,* "may a crocodile bite [you]." Other expressions for wishing an opponent illness or death mention the *nitu: nitu tati bak,* "may a nitu slash your lungs"; *nitu tatik,* "may a nitu slash you"; *nitu mbaak,* "may a nitu bind you"; *nitu lembak,* "may a nitu take you on its carrying stick." A frustrated lover can say to a girl, *kailu nituk,* "may a nitu get you pregnant," since all unusual swelling of the abdomen in women are described as *mailu nituk,* "nitu pregnancies." The expression *ketu funik,* "sever the placenta," is never, in my experience, used toward a woman. The expression is regularly used, however, as mockery to drive away an owl in the night. This expression and the throwing of an onion is sufficient to drive away even the most dangerous of *buntiana* spirits.

V. Order and Orientation on the Island of Roti

Roti is a long narrow island lying to the southwest of the larger island of Timor. In the ritual language, the island is said to have a head *(langa)* and a tail *(iko)*. In fact, in the rituals, head is synonymous with east *(dulu)* and tail is synonymous with west *(muli)*. The island may be conceived of as a crocodile, a water buffalo, or even a man, since these three are sacrificially commutable. By this analogy, north is left and south is right. The word *ki* in Rotinese means both "left" and "north," and the word *kona* means both "right" and "south." In this way, all distinctions between right and left are integrated with and inseparable from the categorization of the four quarters. The Rotinese possess aphorisms which state in near syllogistic form that heaven is superior to earth, east is superior to west, and normally south/right is superior to north/left. To give one such example of this type of aphorism: *Dulu nalu muli, te-hu ledo neme dulu mai, de dulu bau lena muli,* "The east is as broad as the west, but the sun comes from the east, therefore the east is greater than the west." The right hand is the *lima malelak,* "the knowing hand"; the left hand is the *lima nggoa,* "the foolish" or "ignorant hand." Those with a natural bias for the left hand are mockingly called *kode-ki,* "monkey left"-handed persons. To the Rotinese, these persons are as left-handed (ignorant of proper human order) as monkeys.

To the four quadrants there corresponds a congruent system of color categories. East is white *(fulak);* west is black *(nggeo);* south is red *(pilas);* and north is blue-green-yellow *(modo)*. My concern here is with the color *modo* (reduplicated form: *momodo*).[18]

For most of the year Roti presents a picture of relentless, uncompromising brown. This the Rotinese classify as *pilas*. For a brief period, if the rains do not fail altogether, the land suddenly grows green. The category of *modo,* like that of *pilas,* does not conform to our conventional color discriminations. *Modo* may refer to the colors from dark blue through green to various shades of yellow. The grassland becomes *momodo,* the ripening rice is *modo,* the color of the sea can be *modo;* the deepest indigo dye is still *momodo*. It is worth noting that the outside *(dea)* becomes *momodo* while the Rotinese house with its lontar thatch and surrounding courtyard retains its fundamental *pilas*. But the gardens near the house *(osi)* do become *momodo* and it is hardly surprising therefore that in many ritual chants these same gardens are the favorite haunts of the spirits of the outside.

Modo, however, has a wide range of other meanings and referents. Specifically, tobacco is *modo,* but generally, as in the expression *modo ai-dok, modo* refers to all plants, herbs, and roots used in curing. The term includes poisons as well *(modo mamates)*. The distinction between witch and sorcerer is of limited practical relevance to the Rotinese. In the folktales, there are women who are witches. They are cannibals, *mana-naä ate,* "eaters of men's livers," but apart from these occasional folk characters, Rotinese thought is almost exclusively concerned with sorcerers who are invariably men (although women too may become sorcerers). These sorcerers are *mana-tao,* those who do their work by means of charms, plants, and magical techniques (the breaking of a chicken's leg, for example, to lame someone). All this knowledge must be sought and bought. This quest for magic is *tadi modo*. Sorcerers of the worst kind are also able to control and direct *nitu* familiars. Besides the borrowed Indonesian word *suangi,* all sorcerers are called *mana-momodo,* "those possessed of *modo.*" Just as it is context alone which determines whether the declinable verb *na-modo* means to poison or to cure, so, too, there is little distinction between the sorcerer and the curer. The curer is the *mana-puli momodo*. In the parallelism of ritual language, the curer is the *mana-puli kunik do mana-lae modo,* "he who applies the (yellow) turmeric or he who rubs the (green) tobacco/plants."

Modo, as I have already indicated, is the color symbolically assigned to the north while black is the color assigned to the west. The Rotinese orientation system with its corresponding color categories is a system for ordering, locating, and judging. It was inevitable that the Dutch, during their period of government over the island, should be located within this system, but since the Dutch claimed to originate from the northwest, they came to be associated with the two inferior segments of the system. They were associated with the fertile black of death and the wonderous blue-green-yellow of curing but also sorcery. This period of rule reversed the orders of symbolic primacy, making the north or left superior to the south or right. Jonker (1913: 613) recorded the symbolic syllogism of the time (dialect of Oepao): *Ona bau i boe, te hu Koponi nai i, de i bau lena ona,* "The south (right) is as great as the north (left), but the Company is in the north, therefore the north (left) is far greater than the south (right)." It is instructive also to read the folktales which Jonker recorded because in many of them the Dutchman *(tou Olana)* plays the part that one might expect of a sorcerer. Sometime after I had adopted Rotinese dress, I was told, with some hesitation, the four-line poem that the Rotinese applied to the Dutch. The poem locates the Dutch simply but descriptively within the northwest quadrants of the compass:

Mana-sepeo nggeo	Those with black hats
Mana-koe modok	Those with blue-green socks
Sila o lalo boe,	They too die,
Sila o sapu boe.	They too perish.

As one old, nearly blind chanter from the domain of Baä explained: "With independence power returned to the south."

VI. Order and Its Inversion in the Funeral Rituals

On Roti, death has its proper order, its ritual provisions for the conduct of the deceased. In the funeral chants the coffin is described in the dual couplet, *tona-ofa ma balu-pao.* The coffin is the "boat and canoe" of the deceased and it sails over shark-infested, crocodile-swarming waters in the direction it is pointed. The mother's brother or his direct lineal descendant, the *toö-huk,* as a last ritual service prepares this ship for his sister's child while the mother's mother's brother or his descendant, the *baï-huk,* must dig the grave. A description of Rotinese funeral ritual will eventually require a separate monograph; here I am concerned only to mention the elements of a proper Rotinese funeral which can be contrasted with those accorded someone who has died a bad death.

The coffin is brought to the house amid a great uproar. It is made from the hollowed-out trunk of a tree and must be borne forwards so that its "head" (the higher end of the tree trunk) is to the front and its "tail" is to the back. The coffin is invariably set down outside the house but parallel to it, on the west. This position is the *pepeda kopak,* the place for "resting the coffin." (The house is oriented lengthwise in terms of the primary directions. The *uma deak* or male half of the house is on the east; the *uma dalek* or female half is on the west.) The coffin is then raised, carried under the roof, through the forecourt and up the ladder, into the house. The corpse is laid in the *uma deak,* with head to the east, and feet to the west. The coffin *(kopa)* is the symbolic ship of the dead and like a ship, with its keel *(ofa kenik),* the under half of the coffin is its keel *(kopa kenik).* Similarly within the *uma deak,* the middle beam running east and west which supports the floorboard is called the *lolo kenik.* Before the arrival of the coffin, the corpse must be laid directly above the *lolo kenik,* facing upward toward what is structurally and symbolically the spine of the house. Over the adult dead, there is hung a cloth (a *patola* cloth, if this is available) called the *tema lalais,* "the broad cloth of heaven." When the corpse is laid within the coffin, this same position is maintained; the head of the corpse is at the "head" of the coffin; his feet at the "tail" and the *kopa kenik* is made to coincide with the *lolo kenik.* Usually, but not always, a short time before burial, the closed coffin is brought down from the *uma deak* and laid lengthwise on the east side of the forecourt but still beneath the sloping roof of the house.

In carrying the coffin out of the house, the same scrupulous attention is given to directions. Coming out from the house, the tail of the coffin is carried first and the head last, and in this way the body is conducted in a noisy stampede to the grave. The graveyards of the Rotinese are always near the house, often at no more than a dozen yards remove. Formerly burial was beneath the house, but this practice was forbidden by Dutch authorities for reasons of health and sanitation. Some of the more substantial houses I have visited on Roti still have the graves of ancient dead beneath them. All graves are dug lengthwise running east to west. At the side of the grave, the coffin is turned so that now the corpse is headed westward and in this position the coffin is lowered into the grave for its journey to the land of the dead in the west.

It is only in contrast to this proper order that we can understand the inversions accorded the bad dead. The striking feature in the burial of the bad dead is the absence of ceremony but the simple provisions which are taken for the disposal of the deceased are characterized by a reversal or inversion of the proper funeral order.[19]

Nowadays, there exists a genuine disagreement about the coffin for those who have died a bad death. The sternest upholders of Rotinese custom assured me that the bad dead should not be afforded a coffin and no payment should be made to the mother's brother and the mother's mother's brother for their ritual services. But most Rotinese now, despite these protests, do bury the bad dead in coffins and sometimes make token payments for simple ritual services. For a man who has fallen from a tree, it is customary to fell the offending lontar for his coffin.

There is a rule that the bad dead should not be brought into the house proper. Usually the body is placed in a hastily erected structure covered over with coconut fronds. If—as occurs nowadays—the body is brought under the roof, it is not laid on the east side of the forecourt but on the west side. A woman who has died in childbirth remains within the house. Instead of being laid east to west along the *lolo kenik* in the *uma deak,* the corpse is positioned north to south in the *uma dalek* and is later carried down from the house proper and laid temporarily on the west side of the house. In the carrying of the coffin to the grave there is a further inversion. Instead of being carried out "tail" first, the coffin is carried out "head" first. The graves of the bad dead are called *lete nisa-lalak* or *lete-lalak* and are kept separate and usually a considerable distance from ordinary Rotinese graves. These graves are not dug running east to west but north to south. The coffin is lowered into the grave "headed" north or as might equally well be said in Rotinese, the coffin of the bad dead is headed left. I have already indicated that blue-green is the color of the north/left and I have argued that the root *taü* which means "to terrify" and is always used in connection with the terrifying spirits of the outside is associated with the term *tau,* meaning indigo dye. I have given various reasons for this connection but the best evidence of this comes from the last act in the burial of the bad dead. According to a reliable old informant, it was the practice formerly to pour an entire pot of indigo dye on the grave of a bad dead before departing. This act clarifies the otherwise curious Rotinese expression for the "paying of blood-money." To pay blood-money in compensation for killing another is *tifa tau,* "to pay [for] the indigo dye."

There is a further simple ceremony to drive away the bad dead. After an ordinary funeral, the odd remains from the feast, especially the blood-soaked lontar leaves on which raw meat was cut, are taken to any crossroad or forked path *(eno singok)* and there thrown away with some sirih-pinang and tobacco for the spirits of the outside. After the burial of a bad dead, a similar quantity of sirih-pinang and tobacco is taken to a crossroads and the ghost of the deceased is told bluntly in ordinary language to be gone: *Hataholi tulu hataholi leo-leo ndian, de o nai salak-ka dalek, de ami mai mafuli o, te hu o boso tungga ami* (dialect of Termanu), "So man helps man, but you are in a state of evil *(salak)*, therefore we come to drive you away, do not follow us." This procedure is so simple and terse that it is hardly a ceremony at all.

The question remains of how the Rotinese themselves interpret the inversions they perform in the burial of the bad dead. According to what I have been told, these inversions "cause" the spirits of the outside themselves to be inverted. In a proper burial, the corpse is carried out of the house feet first and therefore his spirit will walk the world upright while the corpse of a bad dead is carried out head first and therefore the spirit will wander about upside down. Here I should quote verbatim the explanations of these inversions I was given by a friend and informant, M. Fanggidae. This discussion, although somewhat repetitious, contains a number of interesting arguments:

> When it is time for the burial, they carry the coffin out of the house to the grave; they allow the "tail" to go forward and the "head" to be behind. Therefore in carrying the coffin, the custom is thus followed. The object is this: that the man walks on his feet, but not on his head. If they carry the "head" forward, then he [will] terrify men. Were the man to walk on his head, then [he would be like an evil] spirit. But for the bad dead, they carry the coffin head forward and the "tail" of the coffin behind. If for the bad dead, they carried the tail forward, he would terrify men. Therefore in Bàà, for the good dead they carry the coffin tail forward. And [for] the bad dead, they carry the coffin head forward.

The arguments set forth here are *(a)* that to invert the coffin of a good dead would cause the dead man's spirit to terrify men and *(b)* that to carry the coffin of a bad dead in the normal fashion of the good dead would also cause the dead man's spirit to terrify men. What is left unstated is that, despite the inversion of the coffin of a bad dead, a man's spirit nonetheless becomes a spirit of the outside capable of terrifying men. It would seem that these ritual procedures are less capable of effecting the fate of the deceased than they are of locating the spirit of the deceased within an established conceptual order. Treating a good dead in inverted fashion may locate or actually transfer this spirit to the spirits of the outside but treating a bad dead in the normal fashion does not remove this spirit from the class of outside spirits. If this were so, it would be conceivable for the Rotinese, by their ritual alone, to do away with all spirits of the outside.

VII. Two Instances of Bad Death

During my stay on Roti, I had only two encounters with the rituals (or lack of ritual) accorded the bad dead. While I was in the village of Ufa-Len in Termanu, a young girl of about six drowned in a few feet of stagnant water on the otherwise dry river bank of the Ufa-Len. This happened about a hundred yards from our house. The girl was a noble and this was the first day of her visit to the village. Her body was found at dusk and the alarm immediately went around the village area. When I arrived, I discovered that apart from the beating of the gongs, nothing was being done. The body of the girl had been taken in beneath the roof but was placed on the west side of the house. (The proper position should have been upstairs on the east side of the house.) The word had been sent to the girl's parents, and everyone waited until late in the night for their arrival. There were no animals sacrificed for a feast as would certainly have been the case at a proper funeral. After several hours of waiting, I announced I was going home, whereupon two young Rotinese with blazing torches were assigned to escort me the short distance to the house, something that would have been thought unnecessary if I were to leave an ordinary funeral. The girl's relatives eventually came and removed the body to a distant village to the south of Ufa-Len. I received no invitation to attend a funeral and apart from the relatives with whom the girl was visiting and the man who had fished the body out of the water, no one bothered to accompany the corpse to her village. For months after this death, I was told that the terrifying spirit of the poor girl haunted the river bank that divided the village. As proof of her presence, my friends noted the unusual restlessness of the dogs on certain nights and those living on the opposite side of the Ufa-Len river temporarily interrupted their nightly visits to our house.

My second encounter with the rituals accorded the bad dead occurred in an area of southern Roti that clings tenaciously to all forms of the traditional adat. I was invited to attend a marriage feast in Thie when the word came that a young girl had died shortly after childbirth. In spite of her parents' opposition, she had been living with a boy of her own moiety and it was the implicit assumption of my companions that the girl's death was a consequence of her incestuous union. The boy in turn had fled. When I arrived, there was a discussion on whether it would be possible to bury the body immediately. The door of the house proper was closed to all visitors and I was informed that the body was indeed laid out in the *uma dalek* (as opposed to the *uma deak*). No mourners were admitted into the house as is always the practice at a proper funeral. After some argument it was finally decided that the girl would be buried in a coffin and the burial was postponed until the following day. When I returned the next day (after attending the marriage feast to which I had been invited) the coffin was laid out on the west side of the house beneath the roof. Shortly after I arrived, the coffin was carried out in great confusion in the inverse fashion and burial was, as I have described, with the head of the coffin pointing north. Before the coffin was lowered into the earth, a Rotinese Christian preacher prayed over the grave because the girl was a Christian and because, as the Rotinese themselves are quick to make clear, Christianity does not recognize the traditional distinction between auspicious and inauspicious death.

VIII. Definition of the Spirits of the Outside and the Spirits of the Inside

It is possible now to characterize the contrast between the spirits of the outside *(nitu nai deak)* and the spirits of the inside *(nitu nai dalek)* by means of a series of symbolic contrasts.

The *nitu nai deak* are:

1. *ki*	sinister spirits of the north
2. *deak*	outside and backward
3. *lenik langa lao*	inverted (literally: "walk on their heads")
4. *mate nisa-lalak*	have died a violent, bad death
5. *momodo (tau)*	symbolically blue-green (covered in indigo dye)
6. *laka-tataü*	terrifying

By contrast the *nitu nai dalek* are:

1. *muli*	spirits of the west
2. *dalek*	incorporated within the house
3. *lenik ein lao*	upright (literally: "walk on their feet")

4. *mate nituk* have died a good death
5. *nggeo* black
6. *la-nea* protecting

In this paper, I have concentrated my discussion on the spirits of the outside. This shorthand characterization of the spirits inside is incomplete. A full discussion of these spirits would carry us still further. Here I mention two other characteristics of the *nitu nai dalek.* The youngest child, who inherits the house and with it the ancestral cult represented physically by the lontar *maik,* has a particularly close relationship to the spirits in the west. The term for youngest [son] is, in fact, a homonym of the word for west: both are *muli.* It is therefore not surprising to learn from the folktales that the blood of two brothers is different. The blood of the eldest is red, the blood of the youngest is black. Earlier I referred to the spirits of the inside as the fertile spirits of the west. While the west is associated with death, it is nevertheless the source of fertility, both physically and spiritually. The west monsoon brings the rains and there is some resemblance between the word for west, *muli,* and the verb *moli,* "to grow," which is used of plants and the moon. From among the recent ancestors, one ancestor is chosen (formerly by divination with the spear) to become the *tamok* of his descendant. This descendant assumes the name of his *tamok* and should at some point in his or her youth hold a small feast to reaffirm this bond. This feast is said to *naka-momoli tamok* (literally: "continue to make grow the *tamok*-ancestor"). Similarly the spirits of the west make grow the life of the Rotinese.

Notes

1. The present paper forms part of a longer study on Rotinese conceptions about the spirits and the spirit world.

The research on which this paper is based was supported by a Public Health Service fellowship (MH-23, 148) and grant (MH-10, 161) from the National Institute of Mental Health and was conducted, in Indonesia, under the auspices of the Madjelis Ilmu Pengatahuan Indonesia and the Departemen (Lembaga) Urusan Research Nasional.

I am grateful to Dr. Rodney Needham, Dr. C. Hooykaas, and Dr. J. Finnis, who have read and commented upon an earlier draft of this paper.

2. There are numerous references, in the literature, to this Rotinese love of litigation. The ethnologist and naturalist, Dr. H. F. C. ten Kate (to cite one example), during a brief tour of the island in 1891 justly observed: "Nearly everywhere we went on Roti, there was a *perkara* [litiga-

tion or dispute] over this or that. The native, to wit the Rotinese, can ramble on over trivia like an old Dutch granny. I believe that his loquaciousness is partially to blame for this, for each *perkara* naturally provides abundant material for talk" (1894: 221).

3. The Rotinese also express this contrast by means of the common expression, *aek do fuik,* "tame or wild." The *dae fuik,* the "uninhabited or hostile land," the *bana fuik,* "wild animals," and *hataholi fuik,* "enemies," are contrasted with the *dae aek,* "settled land," *bana aek,* "domestic animals," and the *hataholi aek,* "friends."

4. It is important to note that while certain *maik* remain secure within the house, the Rotinese make similar lontar leaf representations of the spirits inside, which they hang outside to serve, they say, as protection against other threatening spirits. I have seen single *maik* tied beside the fires for cooking lontar syrup and strings of *maik* hung around fields of ripening rice, or across roads and paths. In times of illness, I was told, it is customary to hang a string of *maik* across rivers at their mouth to close these paths from the sea.

5. One might interpret this lack of a heel as an indication of the spirits' similarity to birds. They are said to fly as well as perch on the rafters of the house.

6. Riedel in a brief note on Roti (1889: 646) writes: "Les *nitou* sont divisés en *nitou dok* [*nitu dok*], esprits des morts qui ont déjà disparu au firmament, et en *nitou beouk* [*nitu beuk*], esprits des morts qui protègent encore les vivants." I have not heard precisely these terms applied to the spirits, but the distinction which they indicate is one which I have often heard expressed in other words. The *nitu beuk,* the "recent *nitu,*" act as mediators between the living and the *nitu dok,* the "long-gone or distant *nitu.*"

7. Heijmering (1844: 365) states that after the cutting of a *maik* to represent the soul of the deceased, the right ear of a sacrificial animal is attached to the *maik*. The right ear is chosen, he says, because it is "the symbol of hearing." I have never seen this rite performed and I cannot confirm Heijmering's statement. It is, however, entirely consistent with the Rotinese insistence on the sensitivity to invocation which the spirits of the inside are said to possess.

8. Strictly speaking, the spirits of the outside are reported to roam and wander only at night. During the day they are said to sleep at or in particular trees—behavior in itself the inverse of normal human behavior.

9. Christianity is effecting a change in Rotinese spirit conceptions. The Indonesian word, *setan,* has come to be applied to the *nitu* indiscriminately and has led to the condemnation of all *nitu* as devils. As one Rotinese somewhat hesitantly explained to me: "The spirits *(nitu)* whom we call devils *(setan)* are really our ancestors *(bei-baï).*"

10. I once urged a Rotinese to explain how one knows about the presence of these terrifying spirits. His explanation was that if a man walking along in the night were suddenly overcome by fear, this would be evidence of the presence of terrifying spirits. In other words, the emotion of fear does not arise within oneself but is caused from without. In this sense, the

nitu maka-tataü are "fear-causing spirits," the external cause of an internal emotion. When this emotion occurs, it points to the spirit's (unseen) but certain presence.

11. Fictitious etymology is of great importance to the Rotinese. This single instance is illustrative but not demonstrative of the use made of these etymologies in Rotinese speculations. I intend to devote a long paper to this subject. In the case of *tau/taü,* I have maintained Jonker's transliteration of these two words, although the discrimination between them is of limited relevance. *Taü* might better be written as *ta'u.* The diaeresis, in Jonker's script, is not indicative of a sound change, but rather of the occurrence of metathesis or of the omission of an intervocalic consonant (usually *k* or *t*). Nevertheless, *tau* and *taü* are distinctive words.

12. Linguistically, I am unable to analyze these terms, although clearly *nisa* in the expression *mamate nisa-lalak* is the third person singular of the declinable verb *(isa, misa, nisa . . .)* meaning to "murder" or "kill." This would imply that bad deaths are conceived of as murders. According to van de Wetering (1922: 315–16) bad deaths are regarded as thefts by the Lord of the Sea Depths.

13. This is a Rotinese list and is itself illustrative of Rotinese modes of classification. Each type of bad death is expressed in couplet form, although strictly speaking *nana-tatik* is one word, *nana* being a prefixed (third person) particle. To judge from other similar category lists, the list should properly have nine categories. The missing category is, I suspect, death by burning.

14. There is also some association of bad death with the heat of the dry season, the *fai hanas*. Statistically, the majority of bad deaths each year do occur during the dry season.

15. It was often suggested to me that the danger of bad death originated from the sea depths and came by way of the rivers. In the ritual chants for the good dead, both shark and crocodile are described as dangers every man faces in his voyage to the realm of the dead.

16. Rotinese practices and beliefs about the *buntiana* are similar to many of the widespread traditional Indonesian conceptions about this *pontianak* or *matianak* spirit. Winstedt reports that among the Malays a woman who has died in childbirth is buried with eggs under her armpits and needles in the palms of her hands (1925: 20), and Sell in his comprehensive survey on conceptions of bad death among the Indonesian peoples has also remarked on this practice of "fettering" the *pontianak* spirit (1955: 47). Interestingly Arndt reports the existence of a distinction between the male and female *pontianak* in Larantuka in east Flores (1951: 32).

17. Were a woman to lose several young children, this would be evidence of the work of an *ndafe* spirit, but the loss of a single child is not a cause for alarm. On the contrary, the child, buried beneath the ladder of the house, may be a source of good fortune. Auspicious offerings of a white chicken with white rice in a white bowl are made to the child, either to induce it to return or to bring good fortune (Kruyt 1921: 297–98).

18. These are the primary color terms upon which, through combination and comparison, the Rotinese are capable of extremely fine color discrimination. Indonesian-speaking Rotinese use the word *kunik* (Indonesian: *kuning*) for shades of yellow that would once have been covered by the word *modo*. According to Jonker (1908: 258) *kunik* originally referred to turmeric. In ritual language, *kunik* and *modo* form a dyadic set.

19. W. J. Perry, in a remarkable early article, "The orientation of the dead in Indonesia" (1914), called attention to the proper and the inverted directions of burial among a number of Indonesian peoples, the Karo Batak of Sumatra, the Galela of Halmahera, and the Belu of Timor among others. He recognized that in burial "distinct categories of persons receive distinct directions of orientation" and he admitted the possibility "that psychological causes are at work to produce the separation of the two or more categories." Yet his final explanation for this practice was, disappointingly, the diffusionist one "that the assignment of different directions of orientation to different categories of persons is a result of the complexity of cultures, the category comprising those persons who have died a natural death being typical of the immigrant culture which has overlain that typified by the category of infantile or unnatural deaths" (289–90).

Bibliography

Arndt, P.
1951 *Religion auf Ostflores, Adonare und Solor.* Vienna-Modling: Verlag und Druck der Missionsdruckerei St. Gabriel. Studia Instituti Anthropos, vol. 1.

Heijmering, G.
1843–44 Zeden en gewoonten op het eiland Rottie. *Tijdschrift voor Nederlandsch-Indië* 5: 531–49, 623–39; 6: 81–98, 353–67.

Hertz, R.
1960 *Death and the right hand.* Translated by R. and C. Needham. London: Cohen & West.

Jonker, J. C. G.
1908 *Rottineesch-Hollandsch Woordenboek.* Leiden: E. J. Brill.
1911 *Rottineesche Teksten met Vertaling.* Leiden: E. J. Brill.
1913 Bijdrage tot de kennis der Rottineesche tongvallen. *Bijdragen tot de Taal-, Land- en Volkenkunde van Nederlandsch-Indië* 68: 521–622.

Kate, H. F. C. ten
1894 *Verslag eener reis in de Timorgroep en Polynesie.* Leiden: E. J. Brill.

Kruyt, A. C.
1921 De Rotineezen. *Tijdschrift voor Indische Taal-, Land- en Volkenkunde* 60: 266–344.

Perry, W. J.
1914 The orientation of the dead in Indonesia. *Journal of the Royal Anthropological Institute* 44: 281–94.

RIEDEL, J. G. F.
1889 Note sur l'île Rote. Compte-rendu du IV Congrès Internationale des Sciences Geographiques à Paris.

SELL, H. J.
1955 *Der schlimme Tod bei den Völkern Indonesiens.* The Hague: Mouton and Co.

TURNER, V.
1967 Themes in the symbolism of Ndembu hunting ritual. In *The forest of symbols,* pp. 280–98. Ithaca: Cornell University Press.

WETERING, F. H. VAN DE
1922 De afkomst der Roteneezen van het Eiland Rote. *Mededeelingen van wege het Nederlandsch Zendeling-Genootschap* 66: 312–26.

WINSTEDT, R. O.
1925 *Shaman, Saiva and Sufi.* London: Constable & Co.

Some Categories of Dual Classification Among the Lugbara of Uganda

17

John Middleton

I

Dualistic classifications of the world and society have been reported from many peoples, and there is a large body of published material on this topic. It has sometimes been thought that a dualistic classification is merely due to an innate desire or need of human beings to classify the world in which they live in such a way as to produce a sense of neatness and completeness when its members survey it. People classify other people into males and females, and various things and actions are said to belong to or to be associated with the right or with the left, and so on. It has been suggested that this may reflect the organization of the brain into right and left hemispheres or the fact that human beings happen to have two hands or two eyes.[1] But if these facts were relevant—and I am not at all sure that they arc—they would explain only an innate necessity to organize experience in this particular way; they would not explain the varying ways in which dualistic classifications are made in different cultures. Social classifications are social facts and need analysis in terms of their functions as social facts. Each classification needs to be seen in its relationship to the remainder of the particular culture of which it is a part; it is of little value merely to list examples of such a widespread phenomenon apart from their cultural contexts.

In this paper I give an account of dualistic categories used in various situations by the Lugbara, a people of Uganda, in East Africa. The Lugbara classify various types of persons, things, and

History of Religions 7 (1968): 187–208. Reprinted with the permission of the editors.

activities in opposed, contrasted, or complementary pairs. I first present an outline of the structure of their society, the framework in which the classification is used; then I present the various dual categories and their social and ideological implications. These can be understood only by discussion of the symbols and items used. Essentially these categories refer to the distinction between good and evil. Any society must make this distinction and must have some means of expressing it, and also have some means of relating good and evil to social actions and social relations. The Lugbara also use these categories to express relations between men and women which are based upon those of power and of authority—I use "authority" here in the sense of legitimate and recognized power. Power and authority relations are essential to any conception of society and its functioning. Indeed, it is hard to see in what other terms any people can conceive of the structure of their society. In addition, these categories are used by the Lugbara to express relations of social stability and social change. In this paper I build the symbols used into a formal classificatory schema; the Lugbara do this only by implication, each symbol being used to elicit certain associations with other elements of the schema.

II

The Lugbara are a Sudanic-speaking people of northwestern Uganda and the northeastern Congo, and number about a quarter of a million. They occupy the watershed between the Nile and the Congo rivers, some four thousand feet above sea level, and are sedentary agriculturalists, keeping some livestock. The country is fertile and watered by both a well-distributed rainfall and many permanent streams, and the density of population in the central areas is as high as two hundred persons per square mile.

The basic residential and economic group is a cluster of elementary, compound, and joint families, which I call a "family cluster." It is formed round a core provided by a three- or four-generation patrilineal lineage, the minimal lineage.[2] The genealogically senior man of this lineage is the hereditary head of the family cluster. I refer to him as the "elder"; Lugbara call him *'ba wara* ("big man"). He has complete authority, outside trivial domestic situations, over all the members of his family cluster. His authority is sanctioned mainly by the fact that he is regarded as the living representative of the dead members of the lineage and of the wider lineages of which it is a segment. Lineages are segments of subclans, of which there are about sixty. The subclan is the localized core of a clan, a dispersed unit comprising all the patrilineal descendants of the clan-founder; the clan-founders were the sons of the two hero-ancestors of the Lugbara people. Elders act as representatives of their lineages and make sacrifices to the dead of the lineage on behalf of their living kin.[3]

Traditionally there were no chiefs. Although today there are government-appointed chiefs, they play relatively little direct part in the everyday life of the ordinary Lugbara peasant. There were, however, and still are, rainmakers, the senior men of the senior descent lines of subclans; they exercise considerable ritual authority. They also had rudimentary political powers, but today these are of little significance. There are also men of influence, known as "men whose names are known," who may be called to arbitrate at disputes and who are consulted for advice on various matters outside the control of ordinary elders.

III

The Lugbara believe that the world was created by Spirit, a divine power which stands above and outside men.[4] Spirit is omnipotent and timeless; it is beyond the control of men, and its purpose may be known only through particular manifestations of its power or by the intervention of diviners, prophets, and other figures. One of its forms or aspects is known as *Adroa* or *Adronga,* often qualified as *Adroa 'ba o'bapiri* ("Spirit the creator of men"), *Adroa 'bua* ("Spirit in the sky"), or *Adroa onyiru* ("good Spirit"). *Adroa* is linguistically a diminutive form of the substantive term *Adro* and is regarded as being remote from men, in the sky, in the wind, everywhere and invisible. It is not personalized, and Lugbara say that no one can know whether it has a physical form or not.

At the beginning of the world *Adroa* created a man and a woman, Gborogboro and Meme. They were placed on the earth at a place called Loloi, to the north and outside the Lugbaraland of today. Meme was created pregnant and gave birth to the wild animals of the earth. Later she conceived a boy and a girl after goat's blood had been poured over her legs by her companion Gborogboro. These siblings in turn produced another pair of siblings, and there were several generations of such pairs, who were all ignorant of the obligations of kinship and of marriage. Finally one pair produced two men, Jaki and Dribidu, whom I call the "hero-ancestors." After many wanderings during which they lived by hunting, after many acts of cannibalism of their own children, and after performance of many miracles, Jaki and Dribidu entered Lugbaraland. They impregnated leper women who were already living there, married them, and settled down to farming. By these women they begot the sixty or so founders of Lugbara clans. The descendants of these clan-founders were in their turn the founders of lineages and are at the apex of lineage genealogies.

Longer accounts of this corpus of myth have been published elsewhere.[5] Here I need say only that the myth has a particular thematic pattern. Before the formation of Lugbara society the various mythical personages (the sibling pairs and the two heroes) are given characteristics which I have called "inverted." They behaved in ways which are the opposite of the ways expected of normal socialized persons in Lugbara society today. They were at first ignorant of sexual intercourse; the blood of Meme's first menstruation was not human blood; they committed incest; they ate their own children; they did not know of kinship or marriage; they were inhuman in appearance; they could perform miraculous acts; they lived by hunting.

The concept of "inversion" represents the presocial period (in our sense of placing mythical events in a time sequence) before there was an ordered society, when there was, instead, a world of social disorder or chaos. It had been created by Spirit, but its human inhabitants were unsocialized, amoral, and "natural." After the advent of the heroes and their begetting sons, order was established, and the ideally unchanging pattern of social life came into being. This was not the work of Spirit directly, but of its creatures. Before was a time of primordial disorder, afterward a time of order; before there was no recognized authority among men, only uncontrolled and divine power; afterward was the recognition of properly constituted social and moral authority.

A similar pattern may be seen in what we would call spatial terms. At the center of the field of social relations of any particular family cluster are the closely related lineages and neighboring groups of the same subclan affiliation. Beyond that lie various other groups which tend to be characterized by being believed to be sorcerers and magicians. Beyond them, along and over the horizon, are thought to live incestuous cannibals, who are said to walk on their heads and to commit almost unimaginable abominations. In brief, the same thematic pattern emerges in terms of spatial relations as in terms of temporal relations, as we would conceive them. Fairly direct social relations are conceived and chartered in terms of genealogy: those beyond are conceived and chartered in terms of myth and inversion. Together the two dimensions represent a total field of morality.

This set of notions provides a means of conceiving the development of settled society, of order springing from disorder, of authority from lack of authority, and of genealogy from myth, in a single schema. Lugbara society is based upon a segmentary lineage system, and relations of authority and social order are validated by genealogies, which are formulations of actual relations of authority. This basic dualism runs through much of Lugbara thought about the nature of society and the world and the relationship of man and divine spirit. It may be represented:

Order	Disorder
Man in society	Man before and outside society
Genealogy	Myth
Authority	Power
Normality	Inversion
Social, moral	Asocial, amoral
Kinship and marriage	Incest and cannibalism
Lugbaraland	Alien lands
Farming, livestock herding	Hunting wild animals

The concepts in the two columns are both opposed and complementary. The elements of the first column compose the representation of society within a wider world, a sphere of order within a universe of disorder, and also a development of social man from natural or primeval man. These elements all refer essentially to social and moral relations among people.

IV

Lugbara conceive of the universe as consisting of three spheres, realms, or levels of existence. In each of them the duality between what I may for the moment continue to refer to as "order" and "disorder" is distinguished. The three spheres are the realm of the surface of the world, the realm of time and space as distinct from the immediate area of a given locality, and the realm of the individual organism.

The first realm, the surface of the world, is the place on which men dwell. It is known as *oroo. Oroo* has a social implication that is lacking in the word *nyaku* ("earth" or "soil"). Living persons are *'ba oroo dria* ("people on the surface of the world"); the dead are *'ba nyakua* ("people in the earth"). In the center of the world's surface, for any given person, family, or lineage, are the huts and compounds of the family cluster and the wider groups of which it is a segment. Beyond them are the cultivated fields, first the home fields under more or less permanent tillage and beyond them the outside fields under shifting cultivation. The compound or cluster of compounds is known as *aku* or *'buru,* both of which are used literally to refer to the compound. *'Buru* is used also for the home where people live and where the shrines of the dead are placed; and *aku* can be used for a wider sense of "home" to include the whole settlement and its cultivated fields. Beyond the *aku* in this latter sense are the bushland and grassland, together known as *ase* ("grass"). The words are used antithetically. For example, domestic animals are *anyakpa akua* ("beasts in the home"), while wild animals are *anyakpa asea* ("beasts in the grass"); men are often referred to as *'ba akua* ("persons in the home"), women as *'ba asea* ("people in the grass").

The settlement is not only the place of living people. It is also the place of the ancestors of the lineage, who are usually buried in the center of the settlement and for whom shrines are erected in the compounds of their living descendants. The shrines of the dead are the visible foci of lineage perpetuity and lineage authority.[6]

Whereas the settlement is the domain of men, the grassland beyond is the domain of wild creatures and of Spirit in the aspect known as *Adro. Adro* is the term of which the diminutive form is *Adroa,* "Spirit in the sky," *Adro* is immanent on the surface of the world. *Adro* lives in streams, in bush and grassland, and on hills and mountains. Whereas *Adroa* is everywhere "in the wind" and "in the sky," *Adro* is everywhere on the surface of the world outside the settlements and cultivated fields. But whereas *Adroa* is formless and unpersonified, *Adro* is attributed the form of a human being, tall, white in color, and cut in half lengthwise, with one leg, one arm, half a face and head. I have never heard *Adro* attributed genitalia, and the term *agule* ("like a man") used for *Adro* has no definite sexual connotation. It hops about on one leg—Lugbara are unsure whether right or left leg—and can harm, or even kill by eating, any human beings who are so rash as to go into its domain in the evenings or at nighttime. It is not thought to be so harmful in daytime, when it retreats to the hills and bushland. *Adro* is the inverted being par excellence. It is commonly referred to as *Adro onzi* ("evil Spirit") and sometimes as *Adro 'ba o'dupiri* ("Spirit the taker away of men").

With *Adro* dwell spirits known as *adroanzi* (literally: "spirit children" or "Spirit's children"). They live in places in the bushland and may take the form of water spirits *(yii adro),* tree spirits *(pati adro),* or rock spirits *(uni adro).* They may all harm people who enter their domain, and it is believed that these spirits may take the form of little men and women at nighttime in order to guard rain groves. *Adroanzi* are the elements known as *adro* of dead human beings.[7]

In the realm of the individual organism there is a distinction made by the Lugbara between an asocial, natural human being and a socialized person. A fully socialized person comprises several elements which separate at death. Besides the body, which after death becomes a corpse, there are certain immaterial elements. There is first the soul *(orindi),* which is the element that acts responsibly, especially in kinship relations; after death it leaves the body and goes to the sky, the place of *Adroa.* Later it is contacted by a diviner and brought down to a shrine placed for it in the compound of a son. It then becomes a ghost *(ori)* and acts responsibly as protector and guardian of lineage interests and morality. There are also the elements known as *adro* and *tali.* Both are closely connected with Spirit. *Adro* is itself the word for Spirit, and *tali* is the word used for manifestations of Spirit in the world of men: it is the skill of divination given to a woman by her possession of Spirit, it is used for a place struck by lightning, and so on. Whereas only men, and adult men at that, are thought certainly to possess a soul, men and women, old and young, all have *adro* and *tali,* although their strengths increase during their possessor's lifetime. At death the *adro* leaves the body and goes into the bushland to become one of the spirits known as *adroanzi,* which I have already mentioned. The *tali* stays in the compound and becomes part of the collectivity of lineage *tali,* for which a special shrine is erected.[8]

These three elements of a man together constitute a totality which represents his total social personality. The soul is that part of a man concerned with kin and lineage responsibility. The *tali* is that part of a man which gives him influence over other people, whether related or not; a man with strong personality has a powerful *tali*. Both soul and *tali* are "good," in the sense that they behave responsibly; it is therefore logical that after death both should remain associated with a man's descendants, his lineage, and his compound. The *adro* is rather different. Men are different from animals, and Lugbara sometimes say that men are also different from women and children in having souls, that is, as being socially responsible people. But people are also different from animals in being created directly by Spirit, whereas animals were born by Meme. There is spirit in all living persons, what might be called a "divine spark," something that is separate from man as a purely social being. It is a sign of man as a divinely created being, in the sense that the mythical siblings were divinely created but existed prior to the formation of society by the hero-ancestors. That is the significance of *adro*. When its possessor dies, *adro* leaves the body and becomes a spirit of the wild and so again part of Spirit. Unlike the soul and *tali* it is not associated with a descent line, nor is it associated with any kind of social grouping. It is that element responsible for idiosyncratic behavior, behavior which marks one man out as being distinct from other men.

I have translated the words *Adro* and *Adroa* as "Spirit." Despite the use of the diminutive, Lugbara do not explicitly distinguish between them except as aspects of the same power. This power links the three spheres or realms I have mentioned: *adro* that of the individual, *Adro* that of the surface of the world, and *Adroa* that of the whole universe. These realms are linked into a single moral system, in which Spirit is in each case in some way both opposed and complementary to other concepts:

The individual soul, associated with lineage relations and responsibility	*adro,* the divine part of a man, unassociated with lineage relations
The homestead and settlement, home of lineage members and domesticated animals	*Adro,* in the bushland away from the settlements, the place of wild animals
The world of men	*Adroa,* in the sky, above, outside and remote from men

Since the concepts in the right-hand column are expressed by the single term *Adro-Adroa,* we might expect those in the left-hand column to be linked also in Lugbara thought. The former concepts have in common that they represent the power of Spirit, which stands outside men living in their petty communities. Spirit created the world *ex nihilo,* thus creating order from primordial disorder. This relation, between order and disorder, is that which Lugbara express by the use of these opposed concepts. We may now picture this:

Order	Disorder
Within social control	Outside and lacking social control
Social persons	Individuals
Men and maleness	Women and femaleness
Socialized genealogical beings	Asocial, morally ignorant mythical beings
Settlements and cultivated fields	Bush and uncultivated land
Domestic animals	Wild animals

We may now perceive a further factor. I have said that these concepts are opposed and complementary. But they are not true opposites. Disorder is not the true opposite of order but an incomplete form of order, made into order by the action of Spirit. The mythical sibling pairs were incomplete men and women, in a moral sense. They were ignorant of sexual intercourse, an activity which represents the essence of the complementary nature of men and women; they later became social persons by miraculous means, and they then begot and bore their children as do men and women today. They were ignorant of kinship and marriage, an ignorance represented by incest; their incest was in this sense a sign of incompleteness. Uncultivated land is incompletely used land; wild animals are incomplete animals from the point of view of their use to men. The leper women were physically incomplete, lacking fingers and toes, but were made complete by being cured by the heroes. In each case, the distinction is between what we might call natural things and behavior, on the one hand, and social things and behavior, on the other. Lugbara refer to this very distinction when they speak of babies and of clients, people who settle with wealthy patrons. Babies are said to be *afa* ("things") and to become complete persons after socialization by the society into which they are born. Clients may also be called *afa* when they first enter a settlement, and they may then even be killed; but later they become persons *('ba)* after they are adopted into the settlement and their patron gives them a daughter as a wife.

There are two additional points briefly to be mentioned here. One is that the complementarity of the pairs is a necessary one for the continuity of a divinely created and ordered cosmos. Uncultivated land and its wild animals are as necessary for economic life as is cultivated land with its domesticated animals. Women are necessary for the continuity of the patrilineal lineage, even though this is controlled by men. The other point is that in the myths there are two categories of women: the sibling women and the leper women. The former seem to represent the female principle rather than women as wives. They vanish from the scene when it shifts to Lugbaraland; only the heroes enter there, and their link with the siblings is a weak one (the two myths are rarely told together and are linked only by the existence of the heroes, who feature in both of them). The women of the second myth became wives and mothers at the formation of Lugbara society.

V

This duality is fundamental to an understanding of the cosmology of the Lugbara and to their comprehension of their social structure. It provides them with a means of conceiving and giving meaning to their world and the ways in which it, and society within it, came into being. It also provides them with a way of comprehending change in the world and society. Lugbara conceive of their society as ideally unchanging and as unchangeable by the actions of ordinary men. Yet clearly change does occur, and for Lugbara to be able to live in any kind of ordered social life, change must somehow be accommodated in their thought. They are aware that there is always change or development of a regular or repetitive kind, as part of normal social life. This is due to the birth, maturation, and death of men and women; to the cycle of development of family and lineage; and to the evil activities of witches and sorcerers who disrupt the even flow of ordered social life. They are aware, too, of change of a more radical kind, in which the very structure of their society is threatened and may be altered. Regular development can be accommodated without a breakdown of the social structure: the actual pattern of relationships of authority may vary from day to day, but the basic structure of these relations does not. Lugbara myth gives an explanation of this pattern. But when the basic structure does alter, then new myths are added to the existing corpus. In this way change can be accepted as part of an ideally unchanging order and the paradox resolved.[9]

Lugbara conceive of their society as a field of ordered relations in the dimensions of space and time, and also in a moral dimension.

They see it as an area of order surrounded by disorder, the latter the domain of asocial and amoral chaos and of unpredictable power uncontrolled by members of society, whether living or dead. The occurrence of change in this field of order is seen as the entry of this external disorder into the sphere of order. External order may impinge upon, weaken, or threaten ordered relations. In addition, certain persons may leave the sphere of order and enter that of disorder, and others come from the sphere of disorder into the realm of ordinary men, as agents of the power of Spirit.

There are, that is to say, certain situations in which Lugbara see confusion between the elements of this cosmological classification. In the remainder of this paper I shall describe some of them briefly. They are:

1. The possession of a woman by Spirit to make her a diviner
2. The occurrence of certain sicknesses thought to be sent by Spirit
3. The part played by Spirit at sacrifices to the dead
4. Birth
5. Death
6. The activities of witches and sorcerers
7. The activities of specialist craftsmen and of hunters
8. The appearance of epidemics, droughts, and famines
9. The appearance of Arabs and Europeans at the turn of the century

There are other situations, but a discussion of these will suffice.

All these situations are associated in Lugbara thought with evil, danger, moral inversion, and to some degree with pollution. The word *onzi* is used to refer to them, although its use is wider. It means "evil," "bad," "dangerous"; it refers to activities or events which disturb or threaten to disturb the orderly exercise of authority, and in particular that of lineage authority. Lineage authority lies at the basis of their social organization. Some societies have as a basic principle of organization the allegiance of subject to king or the submission of man to God. For Lugbara it is the recognition of parental and ancestral authority in the lineage, and the recognition of the duties and respect that this entails. Despite their seemingly near anarchy and fragmentary social organization, the unity and perpetuation of the agnatic lineage are for them the most important goals for the mature and responsible person to achieve. The dualistic classification of things, people, and events into the spheres of order and authority, on the one hand, and disorder and uncontrolled power, on the other, is a crucial one. The two spheres, by their very nature of being complementary, should be kept apart in both thought and experience. Any merging of them is evil and dangerous.

Lugbara have fairly explicit notions as to the nature of the persons who are in various ways associated with breaches in the classificatory schema. They regard them as uncanny, dangerous, often specifically evil, and as incomplete beings. The confusion of order and disorder is seen as the confusion of authority (which is moral, responsible, controlled, and predictable) and power (which is amoral, perhaps immoral, irresponsible, uncontrollable, and unpredictable). The people associated with this confusion have in common the characteristic of themselves being incomplete and so representing the essential nature of disorder itself. These people are diviners, prophets, witches, rainmakers, elders in certain situations, and certain women.

VI

In this section I present, very briefly, an account of those situations in which the moral classification of the universe becomes confused and a description of the roles of the persons associated with this confusion.

1. *The possession of diviners.* Diviners are usually women who are possessed by Spirit *(Adro)* before or at puberty. They are taken by a fit or trance and typically run off into the bushland, often for several days, wandering crazily. They may throw away their apron of leaves and run about naked. Their close kin will watch them and follow them at a distance to protect them from serious physical harm but otherwise leave them alone. On their return they are said to have the mystical power *(tali)* of divination and healing. Not all women so possessed do in fact practice divination, and those who do go through a form of initiation at the hands of other diviners. But all erect a special shrine, known as *Adro jo* ("*Adro* house"), which they place under the eaves of their huts. Women who do divine sometimes start to do so after marriage, but most of them divine only when past the menopause. Contact with Spirit thus usually occurs before puberty and after the menopause, when they lack the power of procreation (itself known as *adro*) and so are said to be "like men" *(ekile agule).* I believe that those women who divine before the menopause are in fact barren, but I am not certain

on this point. Diviners transmit their power to their eldest daughters. Diviners tend to be feared; they practice in the semidarkness of their huts, and not outside in public, and are regarded as uncanny and dangerous.[10] It would be too strong to say that they are polluting, but certainly they remove pollution in others. There are also male diviners, but I have never met one; they are said usually to be unmarried, and accounts given to me suggest that they may be homosexuals; but this is uncertain.

2. *Sickness sent by Spirit.* Disorder may affect the well-being of the individual in the form of certain sicknesses thought to be sent by Spirit. These are not the sicknesses sent by the dead, which are considered specifically to be a consequence of the commission of sins, acts which harm the well-being of the lineage by threatening the accepted distribution of authority within it. Sickness from the dead is followed by sacrifice and purification, both of which are lineage rites and performed by lineage elders.[11] Spirit also enters into them to some extent, and I deal with this below.

Sickness sent to an individual by Spirit is different. It is believed that, should a person wander into the domain of Spirit *(Adro)* in the bushland and near streams, away from the settlements, particularly in the evening or at night, he may see, touch, kick, or tread upon Spirit or one of the spirits known as *adroanzi.* He is later sick with sharp pains. This sickness has no moral content as far as lineage authority is concerned. A person who suffers it has shown merely that by his (literal) wandering away from the domain of men into that of Spirit he has shown that he does not accept the proper cosmological boundaries. He goes to a diviner, who treats him by removing the sickness in the physical form of pieces of rock or metal from his body. The victim is regarded as dangerous and tends to be avoided. It would be too much to say that contact with him is polluting, but certainly there is an element of pollution in his condition. This element is quite lacking in the condition of a person made sick by the dead.

There are also sicknesses whose symptoms are trembling and shaking, which are sent by spirits called *yakan* and *kalia.* These are spirits which come "in the wind" and which are associated with Spirit *(Adroa).* They are treated by diviners. Again, these are purely individual sicknesses, without moral content.[12]

3. *Spirit and sacrifices made to the dead.* Sacrifice is made to the dead as a consequence of sin, an action committed against lineage

authority. In all sacrifices to the dead, Spirit *(Adroa)* is also concerned, to a greater or lesser degree. The sacrificial animal is consecrated for sacrifice by being led counterclockwise around the sick man's compound, and if it urinates this is taken as a sign of the approval of Spirit. If at the sacrifice itself it rains or the sky grows dark, this is a sign of the disapproval of Spirit, and the rite must be postponed to a later occasion. The sacrificial beast is usually a goat or bull; but in some cases a sheep, a "beast of Spirit," is used instead. These are situations which concern the segmentation of the lineage, and thus the rearrangement of lineage authority, rather than the everyday maintenance of lineage authority. Segmentation occurs typically after the death of an elder rather than after that of an ordinary man, and the Lugbara liken it to the creation or recreation of social units by Spirit.[13]

An important sacrifice is made by the elder of the minimal lineage concerned. Before making it he observes certain taboos: he must not have sexual intercourse with his wife the night before, and he must not wash his face and mouth on the morning of the rite. It is said that then his breath will be powerful and also that it is still "like nighttime." When he makes the actual offering to the dead he goes alone to their shrines and places meat, blood, and beer in and on them with his left hand. The right hand is said by Lugbara to be the hand of men, and the left that of women. At these times he stands alone, and other men fear to touch him or even to stand too near him. He is temporarily leaving the realm of men and entering that of Spirit. He marks the duration of this period during the rite by holding certain sacred leaves in his left hand before and after performing the actual oblation; these leaves come from the bushland and are said specifically to be associated with Spirit.

4. *Birth.* At birth a new being is created, specifically by *Adroa 'ba o'bapiri* ("Spirit the creator of men"). A person's soul develops in the course of his lifetime. But it is at birth that the element known as *adro* enters a person, as a sign of his divine creation: the external power of Spirit enters the realm of the individual. This makes him a creature of Spirit, still to some extent outside the realm of men (and called "thing," *afa,* as I have mentioned above) until he becomes socialized and a full person. Birth is regarded as dangerous and polluting and is called "evil," *onzi.* It is marked by taboos. Men are prohibited from entering the compound where the birth is taking place. Midwives include diviners and those women of the

household who are past the menopause. The placenta is buried secretly in the bushland by a diviner and is thought to be highly polluting to men. The paths to the compound are closed by placing eggs on them; eggs are associated in Lugbara thought with sterility, in that a woman fears to become sterile by eating them.

5. *Death.* Death is caused by *Adroa.* At death there is a movement, between the spheres of order and disorder, of certain of the elements that compose a man. They are linked during his lifetime and separate at his death. As I have mentioned above, the elements of *adro* and *tali* leave the body, which merely becomes a corpse. The soul *(orindi)* leaves the body and goes to the sky, the realm of *Adroa.* It remains there while on earth the elaborate mortuary rites are performed, at which the network of relationships of authority formerly centered upon the lineage status of the dead person is reformulated. After the end of the mortuary rites the soul is contacted by a diviner, who summons it to earth and places a shrine for it. It then becomes a ghost *(ori),* and sacrifices are made to it.[14]

Death, like birth, is associated with pollution in Lugbara thought. A corpse is highly polluting and should be handled by sisters' sons, men of other lineages, who are afterwards purified. A widow is segregated in a specially built hut and later purified.[15] In former days, when feud and warfare were frequent, the corpse of a man killed by enemies was collected by women of his lineage from the bushland where he had been killed. They had to observe taboos, of which the most important is said to have been against sexual intercourse the previous night.

6. *The activities of witches and sorcerers.* A further situation of confusion between the spheres is that of the activity of witches. Witches, in Lugbara, are men who possess lineage authority which they pervert for their personal ambitions. They use their mystical power of kinship to harm people against whom they bear a grudge or whom they envy. They turn to the use of antisocial power instead of being content to use their lawful and responsible authority. They are considered "evil" *(onzi)* and are given the attributes that I have called inverted. They are regarded as incestuous and are associated with night animals; a man thought to be impotent or homosexual is said to behave as a witch does. A man who is sick from witchcraft goes to a diviner, as only diviners can tell the identity of witches.

The various kinds of sorcerers believed to exist by Lugbara are similar in certain ways. They are associated with night and night animals, and they harm others for their personal ambition. Some of them are women, and all use magical "medicines." Sorcery sicknesses are thought to be of various kinds, but all are similar in being identifiable and curable only by diviners.[16]

7. *The activities of specialist craftsmen and hunters.* Specialist craftsmen in Lugbara include blacksmiths and potters, and hunters may be classed with them in this context. They are all part-time specialists only. Smiths are never Lugbara, but are Ndu, a Sudanic-speaking tribe living to the southwest of Lugbaraland, almost all in the Congo. There are families of Ndu smiths scattered across Lugbaraland. They intermarry and are fairly rigidly differentiated from Lugbara in everyday life, although they are not regarded as being inferior. When actually smithing, their hearths are surrounded by taboos, and women, especially menstruating women, must not come too close or the smithing will be unsuccessful. They are able to curse people and fields, and Lugbara will not willingly approach their compounds at night. They are said specifically to be associated with Spirit *(Adroa),* as the work they do is considered almost miraculous, their skill being known as *tali.*

Something of the same awe surrounds the Lugbara women who make pots. They are usually past the menopause, and a menstruating woman who enters their compounds may cause the firing to go wrong and the pots to crack. However, their skill is not mystical: it is known as *ondua,* not *tali.*

The position of hunters is significant. Today hunting is of very minor economic importance in Lugbara, as most of the game has been hunted out. None the less, there is great ritual importance attached to it. The horns of animals caught are placed in or near the shrines under the granaries and are especially associated with those shrines known as *drilonzi* ("bad luck"). Hunters are men who venture into the realm of Spirit *(Adro):* before going they may not have sexual intercourse, and on their return they undergo a form of ritual purification by diviners to rid them of the dangers of revenge by the "kin" of the animals they have killed.

8. *The appearance of epidemics, droughts, and famines.* Spirit may enter into the affairs of men by the sending of epidemics, drought, famine, and other disasters; they are all sent by *Adroa.* They affect all members of a community equally and are not re-

garded as a consequence of sin by its members. The response is for a rainmaker to take a white ram and to lead it around or at least through the territory of his subclan. and then to drive it across a stream into the bushland beyond. I have been told that the ram is thought to go into the mountains, where it becomes a leopard and so becomes rain, or causes rain, in some mysterious manner. Sheep, unlike other animals, are associated in particular with *Adroa*.

Rainmakers are the genealogically senior men of senior lineages of subclans and have great authority and influence. They are regarded as very different from ordinary men. They are generally both respected and feared, and their rain groves, into which only they may go, are places much feared and said to be protected by the *adroanzi*. Rainmakers are buried differently from other people; unlike ordinary people, who are buried in daylight, they are buried at nighttime, in silence. It is said that this is because the elements called *adro* and *tali* have left them from the time when they began to practice the mystical power *(tali)* of rainmaking, a power given to the clan-founders in the remote past by *Adroa*. They are, as it were, partially dead, already joined with Spirit outside the sphere of social order. They are also closely connected with leopards and are said to become leopards when they die. Leopards, like hyenas, are greatly feared night animals and are closely associated with Spirit.

9. *The appearance of Arabs and Europeans*. Spirit has also entered the sphere of order in situations of radical change brought about by outside agents—Europeans and Arabs. Europeans are known as *Adro* (it is said because they are white and eat people). The end of the last century and the first twenty years of this one were marked both by severe epidemics, particularly meningitis, and by the advent of Europeans. These were considered closely related events, and the response was for the Lugbara to accept the ritual leadership of prophets. The prophets came from the Kakwa, the tribe immediately to the north of the Lugbara. They and their cult, centered on the drinking of magic water, were related in Lugbara thought to the power of Spirit *(Adroa)*. Prophets were the emissaries of Spirit, and today they are remembered as personages with mythical attributes which mark them as outside the sphere of social order. The principal prophet, Rembe, is said to have introduced the practice of divination with a divining gourd,

which was later taken over by the women diviners. He was regarded as "not a man" and as "like a woman." He left no children (as far as the Lugbara know) and is often said not to have slept with women. He wandered about the bushland as do adolescent girls when possessed by Spirit. He was neither a full man nor a Lugbara, and his exploits are related in mythical terms.[17]

VII

There are two points to be discussed that arise from the data presented so far. One is the dual classification itself; the other is the nature of the persons I have listed who can move between the spheres of order and disorder.

It is useful to draw up a list of paired elements, as they have been presented above. They include (1) things, people, and events; (2) directions and relationships; and (3) abstract concepts.

The items shown under (1) and (2) are those mentioned explicitly by Lugbara; those shown under (3) are concepts that I have myself drawn from the Lugbara data, in the sense that the Lugbara do not have specific terms for them. It is these concepts, of course, that Lugbara are representing by the items listed under (1) and (2). All the items in the right-hand column have certain attributes, opposed and complementary to those in the left-hand column. The opposition is expressed in certain concepts: incompleteness becomes complete by man's social action; chaotic and unpredictable power becomes controlled by social action; evil is made into good by social action; and so on. In each case there is a notion of the process of a thing or event being socialized and made moral, good, controllable, predictable, comprehensible.

The list does not in fact exhaust the number of antithetical elements in Lugbara thought. There are, for example, the social categories of the groupings known as High People and Low People and those known as Lu and Ma'di, which I have described elsewhere.[18] But as far as I know these are not brought into the schema I have described (and I do not assume that this schema is complete). Perhaps they should be; certainly I could force them into it without much difficulty, merely because they are antithetical, but I have never heard them associated by Lugbara with the other elements I have listed. This, of course, raises an important problem in the interpretation of symbols – whether or not the observer may use his own interpretation even where the people do not themselves

Dual Classification among the Lugbara of Uganda

	Order	Disorder
1.	Men	Women
	Adults	Babies
	Domesticated animals	Wild animals
	Ordinary men	Witches and sorcerers
	Co-wives	Sorceresses
	Persons	Things
	Soul	Spirit
	Ordinary places	Places called *tali*
	Elders	Prophets and rainmakers
	Oracles	Diviners
	Shrines inside homestead	Shrines outside homestead
	Ghosts	Spirits
	Persons	Individuals
	Life	Birth
	Life	Death
	Kinship and marriage	Incest and cannibalism
	Wives	Leper women
	Farmers	Hunters
	Ordinary "amateur" craftsmen	Blacksmiths
	Ordinary housewives	Pottresses
	Ancestors	Heroes
	Lineage members	Clients
	Lugbara	Europeans, Ndu
	Ordinary blood	Menstrual blood
	Smelted iron	Iron ore
	Fired clay	Raw clay
2.	Right	Left
	Male	Female
	Home	Bush
	Earth	Sky
	Lugbaraland	Loloi, Congo, Sudan
	Genealogy	Myth
	Daytime and light	Night and darkness
	Sexual intercourse	Sexual abstinence
3.	Good	Evil
	Moral, social	Amoral, asocial
	Authority	Power
	Normality	Inversion
	Moderation	Immoderation
	Change	Stability
	Cosmos	Chaos
	Completeness	Incompleteness

offer it as a valid one. But I shall not discuss this matter here. I am merely presenting certain data which may be of comparative interest.

The second problem, that of the persons whom I shall call "liminaries,"[19] is one that demands far more space than I can devote to it here. It will be the subject for a later paper. These are people who, either because of certain inherent attributes or because they temporarily acquire certain attributes, are thought to move between the spheres of order and of disorder. These attributes have one thing in common: they are negative. The liminaries take on a characteristic which is the opposite of a main characteristic of their social status. They take on, permanently or temporarily, a characteristic which gives them a "no-status," if the phrase be permitted. By this I mean that essentially they hold a paradoxical or anomalous social status. The obvious example is that of the diviner: she is either a girl who has not yet menstruated, a woman past the menopause, or a barren woman. She is a female but not a woman. The main statuses in Lugbara society are determined by the three principles of social organization of sex, descent, and ethnicity. The liminary may be a "no-man" or a "no-woman"; or he stands outside the descent system proper, as does a rainmaker or a prophet without family or children; or he is a non-Lugbara, as was the prophet Rembe. Sex is used by Lugbara as the most obvious principle of organization in this regard. Since people must be either male or female, it would seem obvious to take sex as the most basic feature. There is not the space here to expand on this important and pervasive theme in Lugbara thought, but it may be pointed out that women act as liminaries in situations of repetitive change, whereas men do so in situations of radical change and at sacrifices, where the act of sacrifice is in certain ways a re-creation of order from disorder.

These beliefs and concepts are used in several situations: they have more than one social function in Lugbara culture. They provide both a classification of experience and a way of conceiving change; and they also provide a way of conceiving and accommodating the varying ambitions and wishes of individual people.

The set of concepts establishes ideal relations between various categories of persons in a single consistent pattern of authority: men and women, adults and babies, living and dead, living people and Spirit, elders and ordinary men, ordinary men and rainmakers, ordinary men and diviners, lineage members and clients and neighbors. It also brings into place the occupations of craftsmen and hunters, cultivators and ritual specialists, and relates the events of birth and death to ordinary life.

But more than this is the point that by these concepts and their organization into a classificatory schema the Lugbara can conceive of the basic principles of their society (as of any society), the arrangement of patterns of authority and power. They have a model of their social system as one that is ideally unchanging and one that is unchangeable by ordinary human endeavor. Change is seen as involving the incursion of an external disorder, an evil, unpredictable, uncontrollable power. Social change involves change in the patterning and generally in the scale of social relations, which are themselves relations of authority and power. The concepts referred to in this paper symbolize these relations.

The concepts that Lugbara call "evil" *(onzi),* those that have the characteristics of inversion or incompleteness, are either events, places, relations, or persons. The events are those of change; the places are usually outside the compound; the relations are distortions of proper relations between people; the persons are in some way incomplete, either sexually or socially or both. The sexually neutral liminaries are given these attributes because they are dealing with power that is uncontrolled by men. To control it, to drive it away or to canalize it and turn it into legitimate authority, they must themselves become part of it, they must step out of social space and time into spacelessness and timelessness.

NOTES

Fieldwork among the Lugbara was carried out between 1949 and 1952 with aid from the Worshipful Company of Goldsmiths and the Colonial Social Science Research Council, London. Initial writing up of my research material was made possible by grants from the Wenner-Gren Foundation for Anthropological Research, New York, and from the Coltart Scholarship Fund, Exeter College, Oxford.

I am grateful to Dr. J. H. M. Beattie, Professor T. O. Beidelman, Mr. W. R. G. Horton, Dr. P. M. Kaberry, Miss L. Kalinich, Professor C. H. Long, Dr. R. Needham, and Professor V. W. Turner for discussing early drafts of this paper.

1. See Robert Hertz, "The Pre-eminence of the Right Hand: A Study in Religious Polarity," *Death and the Right Hand,* trans. Rodney and Claudia Needham (London, 1960).

2. Details of this system are given in my *The Lugbara of Uganda* (New York, 1965) and my "The Political System of the Lugbara of the Nile-

Congo Divide," in J. Middleton and D. Tait, eds., *Tribes without Rulers* (London, 1958).

3. The cult of the dead is described in my *Lugbara Religion* (London, 1960).

4. In *Lugbara Religion* I referred to Spirit as "God"; I now realize that that is a somewhat inappropriate term.

5. See my "Some Social Aspects of Lugbara Myth," *Africa* 24 (1954): 189–99; *Lugbara Religion,* chap. 5; "Three Lugbara Myths," in W. Whiteley, ed., *A Selection of African Prose* (Oxford, 1964), 1: 128–34; and Father J. P. Crazzolara, *The Lwoo* (Verona, 1954), 3: 350 ff.

6. Not all people are buried in their compounds. Lepers and certain other persons who die through the sudden and direct intervention of Spirit are traditionally thrown out into the bushland.

7. I have heard it said that *Adro,* despite its sexlessness, has a wife and the *adroanzi* are their children. But this belief seems to be unimportant, and I think it was introduced into a discussion by informants for the sake of logical consistency and to emphasize the anthropomorphic features of *Adro.*

8. I have discussed these concepts at greater length in *Lugbara Religion.* There, however, I used the term "guardian spirit" for *adro:* I think the simple term "Spirit" is better.

9. I have given an account of the myth of the coming of the first Europeans elsewhere—see n. 5. This myth, which deals with events of the early years of this century that were therefore witnessed by some of my informants, is put by them into the same thematic pattern as the myth of creation.

10. This is in contrast to operators of oracles, who are men who practice in daylight and in public and are regarded as "good."

11. The cult of the dead is discussed in detail in *Lugbara Religion.*

12. See my "The Yakan or Allah Water Cult among the Lugbara," *Journal of the Royal Anthropological Institute* 93 (1963): 80–108.

13. The points alluded to here are discussed in detail in chap. 4 of *Lugbara Religion.*

14. These rites are described in some detail in chaps. 3 and 4 of *Lugbara Religion.*

15. See my "Myth, History and Mourning Taboos in Lugbara," *Uganda Journal* 19 (1955): 194–203.

16. For an account of Lugbara witches and sorcerers, see my "Witchcraft and Sorcery in Lugbara," in J. Middleton and E. H. Winter, eds., *Witchcraft and Sorcery in East Africa* (London, 1963).

17. I have given a description of the prophets and their cult in "The Yakan or Allah Water Cult among the Lugbara."

18. "Myth, History and Mourning Taboos in Lugbara."

19. The word was suggested to me by Professor V. W. Turner.

The Right-Left Division of South Indian Society

18

Brenda E. F. Beck

According to historical sources, South Indian society was explicitly divided into "right" and "left" halves for almost nine centuries, roughly A.D. 1000 to 1900. This partition served to classify a large number of localized and occupationally specific kin groupings into two over-arching and ritually opposed social categories. Though this overt division has declined rapidly in recent years, and few villagers think of their society in these terms, many subtle social markers of a traditional bifurcation persist to the present day. In the following pages the nature of South India's previous dual organization is discussed, and several important social differences still identified with it are described. Several reasons for the recent decline of this right-left opposition are also suggested.*

The first known mention of a partition of South Indian society into ritually contrasted halves can be found in inscriptions dating from the first half of the eleventh centuty A.D.[1] With time, the strength and importance of this division appears to have increased.[2] By the time the British and French reached Madras in the seventeenth century, the ritual prerogatives associated with membership in one community or the other were considerable. Quarrels usually focused on ritual usages: such matters as one division's right to wear a red ribbon, to take a procession through certain streets, or to display certain banners and temple flags at festivals.[3]

The literature on South India contains only scattered references to this old right-left division. Enough is clear, however, to establish that the "right" bloc of castes was dominated by a body of rural

Journal of Asian Studies 29 (1970): 779–97. Reprinted, with additions, by permission of the editors.

landlords. Allied with them were several groups who were economically dependent on land, especially castes who could claim a share of the harvest of a particular area in return for ritual services rendered to a local peasant community.[4] The "left" bloc, by contrast, was led by the artisans. This division included a number of communities who lived mainly by marketing their skills and who were paid by the individual job. They were the "specialists" who learned and practiced some particular inherited occupation rather than the "generalists" whose fortunes were linked directly to agricultual production.

In the initial period, the economic differences between the castes of the right and those of the left appear to have been relatively clear. The communities labeled right occupied the nucleated, rural areas, where intensive agricultural production was the major economic concern. Those labeled left, on the other hand, were largely urban-based groups. Brahmans, interestingly enough, were considered above the division and were members of neither bloc. Inscriptional records also suggest that in some areas the castes closely allied with Brahmans, namely the VēLāLār or wealthy landlords (and perhaps the accountants too?) also tried to remain above the conflict.[5] The bifurcation of South Indian society, therefore, began with the middle range of castes. In time it came to affect all (or almost all) of the groups below them.

This early picture, already difficult to clarify in detail, was soon complicated by later developments. Territory located in upland and previously forested areas was rapidly cleared and brought under the plow. Tillers for these new agricultural tracts were frequently recruited from groups that were peripheral to the established society of the nucleated areas. Many of these settlers initially belonged to left division communities and were not always allowed to change their bloc affiliation at a later date to accord with their new occupations.[6] Warriors, generally members of the left, also acquired some land as a reward for important victories. At the same time, the sons of some right division landlords strove to set themselves up in business, generally a left division occupation. Local mythology suggests that in such circumstances a man always retained the same bloc membership as his ancestors had, but such stories are no doubt intended to conceal such movement from right to left as did occur. Certainly there were changes in bloc affiliation resulting from intradivision quarrels, for some of these have been recorded by early

British observers. Given such uncertainties, it is very important to avoid a rigid view of the membership of these two groups over time. Only in the most general sense may one speak of the opposition of land-tied peasants to mobile labor, or of agricultural generalists to craftsmen specialists, particularly in later centuries.

Identification of the Castes of Each Division in a Local Area

In Koṅku[7] (as elsewhere) the right-left division has become sufficiently obsolete as to prevent the fieldworker from learning which castes belonged to which bloc by simple random questioning. Furthermore, there is no easy way to identify a particular caste as a member of one bloc or the other by virtue of some overt marker such as a name or a traditional occupation. It was only the old men of an area, particularly those who were recognized as authorities on traditional matters, who I found could still provide local lists of bloc membership. The list of castes (actually subcastes) discussed later in this paper was obtained with the help of such specialists.

I considered a qualified informant for such an inquiry to be someone who could remember the ceremonial division of castes on certain important occasions in his childhood (fifty to sixty years ago). In discussions with these men there was always agreement that certain castes belonged together as a bloc. Individual castes were not assigned to one division in one informant's list but to another division in the lists of others. My five commentators consistently grouped all the castes of their area (except Brahmans and accountants) into two categories. Some disagreement did occur, however, in the labeling of the two blocs, once they were clearly identified. The majority (three) agreed that the dominant peasant caste of the area and their ritual dependents bore the label "right." Two men, however, reversed this picture and called the peasants and their followers "left" and the members of their own bloc "right." It is interesting to note that both these men belonged to castes (Kammāḻaṉ and Cakkiliyaṉ) which are unambiguously identified as members of the left division in historical descriptions.[8] For the analysis of the data in this paper, therefore, I have accepted the opinion of the majority of my informants that the peasants and their associates did indeed belong to the "right." This decision agrees with much textual and inscriptional evidence.

The Significance of Right and Left as Social Categories

For any discussion of the right–left division it is important to know which castes belonged in which category for the area under study. This identification of specific castes, however, is only the starting point. The more important question to be raised concerns the nature and the significance of such an opposition. Why were there two rival blocs of castes, and were the members of these two groups socially distinct? These are the problems to be addressed in this section.

From my field material, an initial characterization of the social contrasts between the two divisions can be easily accomplished. All the castes responsible for providing the peasants with specific ritual services are drawn from one bloc. They bear a striking resemblance to one another in ritual matters and, furthermore, they have an elaborate system of service exchange. These same castes are also the ones whose presence and participation are essential at the celebration of a yearly festival for the local *kirāmam* goddess.[9]

Complementing or balancing those allied with the peasants are a second grouping of castes. These share a different selection of features. For example, they have a common allegiance to certain nonlocal deities, they share a mythology which in describing certain events hints at their common history, and some of them exchange special services on the occasion of weddings and funerals. Third, there are the Brahmans and the accountants, who remain largely above the division and provide services to the more prestigious castes of both groups. Lastly, a few peripheral, migrant communities such as the gypsies (Nāri Kuravaṉ) also fall "outside" the position, or depending on one's perspective, below it.

Given these descriptive details of the contrast, the question remains: What underlying principles could have been responsible for maintaining this right–left division for so many centuries? The answer lies in understanding the connection between these specific similarities which bind the castes of each bloc together and the larger social and political patterns of the Koṅku region. In this area the Brahmans are a small and relatively poor community. It is a large agricultural caste called KavuNTar (previously referred to by the term "peasant") which exercises political control and supervises the distribution of rural wealth. Members of this community are known in legend, in ritual, and even by title, as "kings" of the area.

As everywhere in India, the Brahmans of Koṅku are considered to occupy the top of the social hierarchy. Thus they are accorded higher status than KavuNTars in all contexts where ritual interaction is required.[10] On the other hand, the land-based power of the KavuNTars enables them to dominate in a more material realm. Wherever an exchange of goods or services is taken as the criterion of status,[11] the Brahman priests are reduced to a secondary position. They are an impoverished minority who perform at the KavuNTar's convenience.

Given this basic frame, all castes below that of Brahman and KavuNTar have a choice. They may either compete for social position in ritual terms, emphasizing caste purity and ceremonial orthodoxy, or they may compete for political power and attempt to dominate over others using KavuNTar techniques. The later choice involves a concentration on productivity rather than purity and on this-worldly, instrumental activity rather than on otherworldly, ritualistic seclusion. In short, some Koṅku castes actively flout certain details of the Brahman ideal in order to symbolize their connection with territory[12] and a local elite. Others, by contrast, give priority to the rules of orthodoxy. The former bear the traditional label "right" and the latter the label "left." Each group makes its choice in an attempt to tip the scales of social prestige in its own favor. The symbolic overtones of this rivalry are discussed in the following section.

The Terms "Right" and "Left" as Labels for the Two Divisions

A brief analysis of the terms used to identify the two divisions can provide some further insight into the debate underlying this opposition. The terms *idaṅkai* and *valaṅkai*[13] have generally been translated as "left-hand" and "right-hand," respectively. The English term "hand," however, is misleading. Unlike English, the Dravidian languages do not make a critical distinction between arm and hand, or between leg and foot. The term translated above as "right-hand" can equally mean "right-arm." The same holds true of the complementary terms for left limbs. The use of the term "hand," furthermore, introduces an immediate problem of relative ritual rank, since the left hand throughout India is considered polluted and inferior to the right. The ranking of these two caste divisions, however, has always been in dispute. It makes more sense, therefore, to interpret the terms as referring to the "left" and the "right" sides of a social body. To avoid possible misinterpretation the terms "right" and "left" alone are used as labels for these divisions throughout this paper.

When the interpretation "sides of a social body" is considered, further suggestive implications emerge. In Indian tradition the sides of the human body are clearly identified with the two sexes, the left interpreted as being female and the right as male. The clearest statement of this association of sides with sexuality is the frequent iconographic representation of Siva as Ardhanarisvara, or as male and female joined in one body. In bronze images portraying this form of Siva, the right side of the figure has the hip, shoulder, and chest of a man, while the left side is fashioned with the thighs, waist, and breast of a woman.[14]

Consideration of this association of the two sides with the two sexes, however, does not solve the question of relative rank. Though not as clearly ranked as hands, the male or "right-sided" sex is taken as superior in India under most conditions.[15] In order to understand the ambiguity in the ranking of the two divisions, therefore, one must further consider the relation of the categories male and female to the four caste categories or *varna*. According to this all-pervasive theory of society, Brahmans are ranked first and Kshatriyas second. Furthermore, Brahmans are male in relation to Kshatriyas (implicitly female). Metaphorically, these two *varnas* are husband and wife. When Kshatriyas are described vis-à-vis the lower Vaishya *varna,* however, then the Kshatriyas are spoken of as male.[16] The right and left caste divisions are in a sense a new set of labels for the old Kshatriya and Vaishya categories. Thus the Kshatriya may alternately be female or male, inferior or superior, depending on which *varna* this group is contrasted with.

In the previous section it was noted that in collecting the lists of castes in Koṅku belonging to the two blocs, some informants reversed the labels. All informants who tried to do this were attempting to label their division as "right" and KavuNTar-allied castes as "left." This is not so surprising when it is remembered that the dominant values of the former group rest on an orthodox or Brahman model. Their claim to be "male" or Brahman in contrast to the Kshatriya set of values makes sense in these terms. To a KavuNTar, however, the opposed bloc do not resemble Brahmans, but rather Vaishyas or Shudras. Hence, from a KavuNTar perspective, this group is "left" or female in contrast to their position as "male" or "right." This tendency for the left bloc of castes to deny their title "left" appears to have also been something of a problem in identifying the two blocs in the past. In general, however, it seems that the land-tied, peasant-allied group was able to dominate in this matter and that the term "right" for their division prevailed.[17]

A Diagram of Subcaste Differences in the Koṅku Region

In previous sections a distinction has been developed between a ritualistic and an instrumental orientation in the efforts of a group to raise (or affirm) its status. These two value schemes define a dimension which is not limited to caste rivalry. Indeed, it appears as a very widespread feature of Indian culture. In the ancient texts, for example, the contrast is expressed in the opposition of *dharma* to *artha* and of Brahman to Kshatriya. Similarly, in Koṅku today one clan or descent unit often inherits ritual privileges, while an opposed group inherits the headmanship of secular affairs. At the family level in Koṅku, furthermore, cognates are responsible for the basic financing of their members' life-cycle ceremonies, but affines provide gifts and certain essential ritual services. Finally, the ritualistic-instrumental contrast can occur in local sibling rivalry, where one brother serves as a family priest, or a religious devotee, and another as director of a family's mundane concerns. Though it is important to recognize these "parallels" in the society at large, the focus of this paper is on the opposition of these two orientations at the level of subcaste organization alone.[18] This level has been chosen for analysis in detail because it was here that this dichotomy of values became overtly institutionalized in the right-left opposition.

In order to study the dynamics of the rivalry described, ten aspects of social custom among sixteen subcastes in Koṅku will be examined in detail.[19] Each of the ten items was selected for two reasons: because it served as a conscious marker of subcaste identity and because variations in each were amenable to some sort of scoring along a ritualistic-instrumental continuum. The items used include diet,[20] clan deity, formal clan organization, kin terminology, clan terminology, wedding ritual, style of the wedding necklace, direction of wrapping the sari, use of the sacred thread, and the color of a widow's garments. All of these except the last also bear some relation to the distinction between Brahman and Kshatriya in the classical texts.[21]

For the purpose of this initial effort at measuring subcaste variation, actual Brahman behavior in the region was taken as defining the end point of the ritualistic scale and actual KavuNTar behavior as defining the end point of the instrumental scale. This technique of using the behavior of an actual community as the end point seems justified in the instrumental case by the fact that the castes who identify with this ideal do so by forging important ritual and economic ties with an already prominent or "kinglike" group.[22] Instrumental behavior is not so much an abstract ideal outlined in traditional texts as it is a practical route to dominance according to the local customs of a particular area.

The ritualistic orientation, on the other hand, is treated at length in the classical literature without any direct reference to customary behavior in a particular area. The end point of this scale, therefore, should ultimately be defined in terms of some compilation of statements concerning ideal behavior as specified in the classical corpus to which local groups refer, via scholars, bards, and other mediators.[23] The present study defines the end point in terms of actual Brahman custom in a particular area only because the author does not have the classical training needed to establish a behavioral scale on the basis of the textual tradition alone. If one were to do so one would certainly find that present-day Brahman communities do deviate significantly from such a composite ideal. The complacency of many Brahmans and the wide variation among subcastes have provided repeated opportunities for the claims of reformist groups that their behavior conforms more closely to ritualistic, textual ideals than the habits of the Brahmans in their own community.

For each caste, the ten items described above have been combined to form an estimate of the group's general position on the ritualistic-instrumental dimension. The score on each item represents a judgment about the degree to which a subcaste resembles Brahman or KavuNTar social custom in that particular. This dimension is used to define the horizontal axis of the graph (fig. 1). The vertical axis, on the other hand, is defined as a measure of caste rank.[24]

The graph summarizes a great deal of information about social custom and the position of the right and left blocs. Several points require commentary. First, the higher the general rank of a community in Koṅku, the more definitive is its association with one of the two opposed ideals. The lower a caste in the social hierarchy, on the other hand, the more its customs represent a compromise or balance of behavior which draws on both value schemes. It would seem that low-ranking groups are torn in selecting between these ideals or are at least less particular about combining the incongruous details of both. This finding may also indicate that castes that do not have the economic power or social prestige needed to conform to all the details appropriate to either ideal will tend to adopt at random whatever social markers are easily obtainable.

Fig. 1. Social custom and ritual rank among castes in the Koṅku region

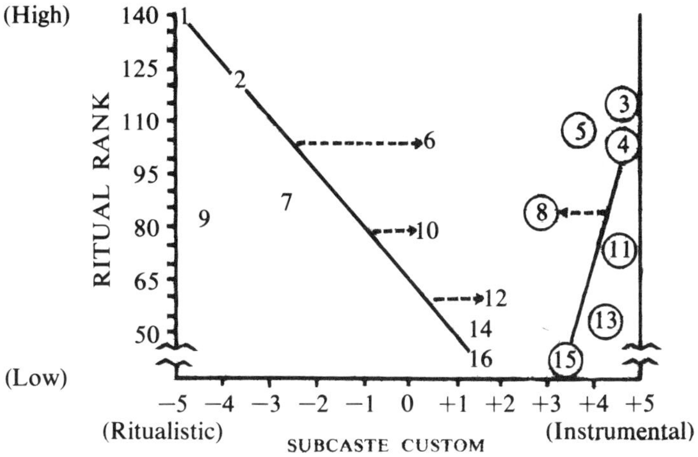

For an identification of individual castes (nos. 1–16) and a discussion of this graph construction, see the appendix (p. 406 below). Circled numbers identify castes which traditionally belonged to the right division.

A second important feature of the graph is the grouping of castes. On one side of the diagram fall the KavuNTar agriculturalists and all the communities which provide ritual services for them. These communities were all right-bloc members by tradition. Those castes who have chosen to emulate Brahmans, on the other hand, are all grouped on the left. They are largely comprised of skilled castes, groups who live by their professional expertise. Significantly for this analysis, all the castes falling on this side of the graph are traditionally members of the left division.

Third, it may be observed that the base of the V falls to the right of the graph's center point. This means that the lowest castes in the hierarchy are not really neutral but tend toward the KavuNTar end of the scale. This can be explained by the fact that these low-ranking castes subsist largely by providing agricultural labor for KavuNTar landlords and only in addition to this do they practice a particular trade. They are closer to the land than the higher members of the "left" division who support themselves by their professional skills alone. In daily activities, the lowest members of the left bloc interact more frequently with the KavuNTars than with many of the castes in their own division. Their position to the right of a center point, therefore, is not surprising.[25]

Finally, it is clear from an examination of the slope[26] of the regression lines that the right one is considerably steeper than the left one. This indicates a considerably greater degree of homogeneity in social behavior among castes who emulate the KavuNTars than among those who emulate Brahmans. The former constitute the "in" group or the "allied castes." They maintain a position of considerable power and prestige by close association within their ranks. At the same time they insist on their distinctiveness vis-à-vis other groups. The left division of castes, those who emulate the Brahman model, show all the characteristics typically associated with an "out" group. They are united in their refusal to recognize KavuNTar supremacy and in their attempt to bypass it with varied claims to caste purity. In terms of actual social customs, however, these castes show much more variation than those who fall on the right. Indeed, this finding fits the more general pattern described by observers of political behavior in other fields, namely, that groups united only by their opposition to current leaders tend to be more diverse than groups that hold established positions of power.[27]

The value of the V diagram lies in the clarity with which it summarizes a great number of social details and displays an important general pattern which underlies them. In the Koṅku area there are two very prestigious castes, Brahmans and KavuNTars. These groups have radically different life styles and customs. All of the other castes in the area are aware of the contrast presented by these two social "models." The higher a caste in the social hierarchy of the region, the more decisively it has patterned its behavior after either the Brahman or the KavuNTar community. The lower the caste, on the other hand, the more ambivalent and difficult the choice between these two patterns appears to be.

One question which arises from this finding is: If the lowest castes were the most ambivalent of all in their choice between the two models, why should the untouchables have been the ones who were the most vociferous in the right-left disputes?[28] The explanation of this situation appears connected with two factors. First, a common response to the experience of ambivalence is to make an extreme outward show of commitment.[29] And second, those who rank low in a social hierarchy are very often concerned to show that there exists some other group or person who ranks still lower. Arguments about right- and left-bloc prerogatives among low-ranking groups appear to have been of this nature.

Extent of the Right-Left Division Elsewhere in India and in Southeast Asia

The V diagram above is incomplete in so far as it summarizes data from only one region. What of a very different area of the south, like Tanjore, where the Brahmans constitute a much larger proportion of the population (some 6 percent) and own large amounts of land? My impression is that VēLāLās in Tanjore (the KavuNTar equivalent elsewhere in Madras) do not differ nearly as much from Brahmans as their counterparts do in Koṅku. It would seem that in the former area there has been a behavioral convergence of these two high-ranking castes, perhaps resulting from their common concern with agricultural production.[30] When Brahmans become *jajmans* (a "boss" for whom men of many other castes provide labor) they usurp the highest position in the socio-economic sphere without ever losing their equivalent placement in the ritual hierarchy. To become a landlord a Brahman must relinquish a certain degree of personal purity,[31] but not enough to lose his ascribed caste status.

If a similar diagram could be constructed with data collected from Tanjore, I would predict that the results would be significantly different. There the V should be narrow, perhaps absent, because of the convergence in this region of the otherwise competing life-styles outlined above. In its place the predominant pattern would be a gentle slope where high-ranking Brahman customs fall in one corner of the chart, and low-ranking castes lie across the diagonal.

This hypothesis is supported by historical evidence indicating that the right-left division was, indeed, less intense in the Tanjore area than elsewhere.[32] Roughly similar findings should characterize Kerala.[33]

Why this moiety-like development in the south failed to stretch beyond the Dravidian-speaking area into North India, however, is a question that cannot be adequately answered with the existing data. In areas of the North where non-Brahman landed castes are very distinctive, notably in parts of Maharastra, Gujarat, Rajasthan, western Uttar Pradesh, and the Punjab, detailed research would probably show a social division exhibiting many similarities with the right-left division in the south. Even though the opposition of ritualistic and instrumental styles has not acquired the same institutionalization in the north, certain details present a striking similarity. For example, throughout the subcontinent the artisan communities have attempted to counteract the power of the landed castes with the assertion of superior status on the grounds of the exclusiveness of their caste customs and the orthodoxy of their ritual.[34]

Suggestions concerning the possible extension of a right-left division beyond the borders of India into Ceylon and Southeast Asia are intriguing but remain largely unexplored. The inscriptions on the pillars of the Council Hall in Polonnaruva, for example, indicate that the chiefs of state there were once divided into a right and a left group.[35] Furthermore, the association of a king's right side with temporal power and his left with the professions is clearly reminiscent of the pattern of division as it has been described for South India. A similar right-left opposition exists in Siamese and Cambodian court ritual. Until more detail is available, it seems reasonable to explain these organizational similarities in terms of cultural diffusion resulting from the movements of traders. Certainly the existence of right-left symbolism in the regal ceremony of various groups in Southeast Asia could be due to the emulation of prestigious foreigners, rather than to more general social and economic parallels with South India. In the case of both Ceylon and Thailand, however, there are hints that a right-left partition may have been characteristic of much larger segments of these societies in earlier centuries.[36] If further research indicates that this was the case, then an explanation of the similarity must be sought in social and economic parallels along the lines already suggested for North India.

The Decline in Importance of the Right-Left Division

During the late eighteenth and early nineteenth centuries the quarrels between the right and left factions seem to have reached a peak of intensity. The right group of cultivators and their dependents were incensed when the British tried to treat them and their left division rivals as equals. The East India Company records and early court documents of this period are full of accounts of bitter disputes over this issue.[37] The most plausible explanation of the decline of feeling in recent decades rests on the changes in the definition of land-based rights in South India during the subsequent period.

In the pre-British era the prevailing system of land tenure focused on territorial divisions, rather than on individual "ryots" or cultivators.[38] Rights to participate in cultivation and to a share in the harvest thereof were inherited. Those who did not possess such rights lived by their professional skills. By specializing in the latter type of occupation some merchant and artisan communities were able to amass considerable wealth and thereby to claim a high rank in the social order. With the exception of forced upheavals due to military adventurers,[39] however, rights of land management rarely passed from one caste to another. Land and moneyed assets existed side by side, but constituted separate, rival paths to social status.[40]

By the middle of the nineteenth century, however, the furor over the right-left division had begun to recede. The energy behind the disputes had been spent and the public began to lose interest in this overarching social division. Today most peasants no longer remember the division names, or their significance, though many details of social custom, as we have seen, still mark the two groups. In the following I will try to explain the decline in overt importance of the right-left partition by reference to changes brought about by the British rule. Comparison with a similar change in English society in the eighteenth and nineteenth centuries will also be pursued.

With the introduction of the British ryotwari system in the Madras presidency, the separation of land-based rights and capital assets became much less clear. Though Zamindaris persisted in some areas, land in general acquired a mortgageable value. This meant that what was once only the right to regulate the production and distribution of produce on a piece of land now expanded to include the right to alienate land and thus to convert it into capital. Large amounts of land gradually came on the market in this way and were purchased by wealthy members of the professional castes as a speculative investment. This new trend was warmly approved of by nineteenth-century English liberals who counseled Parliament on Indian policy. In their eyes the separation of land from man was a vital part of the utopian concept of a market economy.[41] Furthermore, the human population of the Madras presidency rose by over 300 percent during the nineteenth century,[42] thus greatly altering the man/land ratio.

Under the new British administration, each ryot had to pay his land tax to the government in cash, and this enabled the money lender to gain an effective control over village landlords for the first time.[43] Meanwhile, the British began to recruit civil servants for coveted government jobs on the basis of education and not (in principle, at least) on the basis of caste affiliation, as had previous rulers. All this, plus the development of new markets and a rapid increase in transportation and communication facilities, served to multiply the possible routes to prestige and power. Land rights and capital were no longer distinct alternatives. The right-left opposition was clearly built on an earlier economic base. As this base widened and diversified, so did the social superstructure. The former social division into right and left caste blocs, therefore, no longer characterized the increasing diversity of possibilities for attaining a respected social position. For this reason, I argue, the social concern with that division gradually became outmoded and less salient to the local populace.

Some additional support for the above hypothesis can be brought to bear by examining a similar social development in a very different cultural context: the Whig-Tory division in the eighteenth-century British Parliament. The Tories, in this period, were identified with the landed interest, while the Whigs were engaged largely in trade and banking. A gentleman of the day was someone who derived his income from his rural holdings, not from commerce, industry, or a salary. Unlike India until recently, however, outsiders could be absorbed, provided that they purchased land and used the income from their property in a "noble" fashion. Furthermore, the younger sons of nobles and squires often went into business. Thus the distinction between those with access to land and those with professional skills was never as rigid in England as it was in India. Nonetheless, the prominence of the English gentry is fundamental to an understanding of social ranking in that period.[44]

The Tory and Whig alliances were built on a network of loyalties existing between smaller units where kin and social ties were important. These smaller units bear a suggestive resemblance to castes, and in particular to subcastes. The two alliances had a shifting membership in day-to-day matters but were always represented by opposed blocs in Parliament on ritual occasions. When both houses met to hear the royal message at the end of a session, for example, the place to the right of the king was taken by the lord keeper and the marquis who bore the "cap of maintenance," while to the left stood the treasurer, the "earl who bore the sword," and the ladies.[45] This division was followed in traditional seating arrangements as well. Furthermore, in political campaigns the Tories and Whigs were distinguished by the use of different colored rosettes,[46] a parallel with the insistence of each division in South India that it display certain colors of ribbons and temple flags. Clearly there was a tendency, in both cultures, to express a basic economic opposition in a ceremonial medium.

This English comparison serves to illustrate how a symbolic and ceremonial division similar to the right-left partition in India could develop elsewhere, in a different cultural and historical context. In both examples temporal power was strongly associated with landed wealth, and to oppose it a second route to status developed, backed by moneyed interests but couched in philosophic, religious, and reformist terms. This challenge, furthermore, became ritualized into a formal ceremonial opposition of the two interest groups and led to intense rivalry on certain occasions. Finally, in England, just as in India, the interest in this ritual opposition declined when land came on the market in quantity and cash resources became a major means to acquiring rural acreage.[47] This change, coupled with the development of new routes to prestige made possible by industrial expansion and improved communication, "broke the back" of the older status system.

Though the cultural terms of the opposition were different in the two contexts these two dichotomous superstructures rested on similar economic bases. As these bases began to diversify and develop, the social categories dependent on them also began to shift. Thus the English example serves as a first step toward the confirmation of a more general hypothesis concerning the possible development of corresponding social patterns in culturally different (but economically similar) contexts.[48] Furthermore, this parallel helps to substantiate the argument that it was essentially the economic changes in South India, traceable to the period of British administration, which led to the decline of overt interest in the right-left division. Nonetheless, social customs and patterns of prestige change more slowly than economic realities. Thus in some areas of South India many of the traditions associated with this earlier dual organization still endure.

APPENDIX

The appendix which follows provides the details from which the V graph in the text was constructed. The chart below contains the

DETAILS OF SCORING USED IN THE CONSTRUCTION OF THE V GRAPH, BY SUBCASTE

Ritual Rank	Division Membership	Subcaste Name (and the number which identifies it in the accompanying graph)	Relative Score on Ten Items of Behavior: 1 2 3 4 5 6 7 8 9 10	Combined Subcaste Custom Score (average of columns 1 through 10)
138		1. Aiyar Pirāman (Brahman)	−5 −5 −5 −5 −5 −5 −5 −5 −5 −5	−5.0
118		2. KarūNīkal PiLLai (accountant)	−5 −3 −5 −5 −5 −5 −5 −5 −3 +5	−3.6
112	R	3. Koṅku KavuNTar (agriculturalist)	+5 +5 +5 +5 +5 +5 +5 +5 +5 +5	+5.0
108	R	4. Koṅku CeTTiyār (merchant)	+5 +3 +5 +5 +4 +5 +3 +5 +5 +5	+4.5
107	R	5. OkecāNTi PaNTāram (non-Brahman priest)	+5 +1 0 +2 +5 +5 +5 +5 +5 +5	+3.8
103	L	6. Kaikōlan Mutaliyār (weaver)	+5 −3 −5 −2 −1 −5 +3 +5 +5 +5	+0.7
90	L	7. KōmuTTi CeTTiyār (merchant)	−5 −3 −5 −5 −4 +5 −5 +5 −4 −5	−2.6
89	R	8. Koṅku UTaiyār (potter)	+5 +1 0 +2 +1 +5 +5 +5 −3 +5	+2.6
81	L	9. CōLi Ācāri (artisan)	−5 −3 −5 −5 −3 −5 −4 −5 −4 −5	−4.4
81	L	10. Koṅku Ācāri (artisan)	+5 −3 −5 −5 −1 +5 −1 +5 −3 +5	+0.2
79	R	11. Marамēri NāTār (toddy tapper)	+5 +3 +5 +5 +2 +5 +3 +5 +5 +5	+4.3
62	L	12. VaTakku Nāyakkaṉ (well-digger)	+5 −1 −5 −2 +2 +5 −1 +5 +5 +5	+1.8
53	R	13. Koṅku Nāvitaṉ (barber)	+5 +1 0 +2 +5 +5 +5 +5 +5 +5	+3.8
51	L	14. VaTaku VaNNaṉ (washerman)	+5 +1 0 +2 0 +5 −1 +5 +5 −5	+1.7
2	R	15. Koṅku Paṟaiyaṉ (drummer)	+5 +1 0 +2 +5 +5 −1 +5 +5 +5	+3.2
2	L	16. Moracu Mātāri (leather-worker)	+5 −1 +5 −2 +1 +5 −1 +5 +5 −5	+1.7

full set of scores from which the subcaste positions on the graph were plotted. Following this is a detailed description of the ten items used and an explanation of how each scale was defined. Finally, a few difficulties in the construction of the graph are discussed.

Description of the Ten Items Used in Constructing the Social Behavior Score

1. *Diet.* The main contrast in diet, in Koṅku, is between vegetarian and nonvegetarian subcastes. Although there is some prestige-grading according to types of meat eaten (beef and pork are low-ranking foods), no significant distinction is made between a partial (egg- or fish-eating) vegetarian and a full vegetarian. For this reason it was thought best, for the purpose of contrasting a Brahman and a KavuNTar model, to assign only two scores, +5 for nonvegetarian and −5 for vegetarian groups.

2. *Clan deity.* There is considerable variation among subcastes in Koṅku as to the clan or descent-group deity worshipped during life-cycle ceremonies. Brahmans generally make offerings to all-India deities on these occasions while KavuNTars propitiate divinities which bear some relation to local territory. This Brahman/KavuNTar contrast could be expected in the light of the ritualistic and philosophical concerns of the Brahman as compared with the local landed interests of KavuNTars. A continuum of possible deities, defined by these end points, has been scored in the following fashion:

All-India deity (Shiva or Vishnu)	−5
General South Indian deity (Aṅkālammaṉ or Murukaṉ)	−3
Generalized South Indian folk hero (Maturaivīraṉ)	−1
Generalized local deity (Māriyammaṉ)	+1
Caste hero whose story is localized (ANNaṉmār)	+3
Clan hero whose story is highly localized (usually the name of a legendary ancestor)	+5

3. *Strength of clan organization.* Local clan groupings can be classified according to their complexity and importance. For some subcastes the organizational complexity is marked, for some it is

moderate, and for others it is tenuous. These three possibilities were defined and assigned a score as follows:

> *Marked:* Clan divisions are found to be closely associated with local landownership and/or residence. Clan exogamy regulates marriage and can override the niceties of terminological reasoning. Furthermore, these clans may (though not necessarily) be organized into an all-encompassing two-section system. Clan temples and clan ceremonial rights are well developed. Stories about the clans are extensive, but at the same time, generally localized. Such stories refer infrequently, if at all, to the events recounted in the great *puraNa*(s). Clans are frequently subdivided and there are temples and legends to correspond to each subdivision. +5

> *Moderate:* Clans are frequently associated with a *nāTu* area, but a link with a particular *kirāmam* or *ūr* is uncommon. In other words, territorial associations are very general. Clan temples occur here and there, but do not form a a regular pattern. Clan ceremonial rights at particular temples are infrequent, but can sometimes be identified. Some clan stories show links with the great *purāNa*(s), others are localized. Clans are rarely subdivided. Clan exogamy may be a factor in regulating marriage, but there is considerable hesitance in contracting unions which go against the logic of the kin terminology. 0

> *Tenuous:* There is no tradition of clan temples (as distinct from places of general pilgrimage), clan territory, or clan ceremonial rights, although odd shrines to family ancestors can be found. Clan groupings have no bearing on everyday affairs. People have difficulty in recollecting clan names and marriage is regulated solely in terms of the logic of the kin terminology. Clan stories are consistently linked to the events recounted in the great *purāNa*(s), and unassociated with specific territorial locations. Clans are not sub-divided. −5

It is interesting to note that clan strength seems to bear no relationship to actual land ownership. The KarūNıkal PiLLai or accountants, a high-ranking subcaste which owns land, have tenuous clans while the Moracu Mātāri, a group of untouchables with no land at all, have a marked development of clan organization.

4. *Term used to designate clan.* There are four terms generally used to designate a clan grouping in the Koṅku area. These terms

vary by subcaste, not by individual speaker. For scoring purposes they have been translated in accordance with local usage rather than by reference to dictionary definitions. The scale places familial purity, reinforced by claims to descent from a classical sage, at one end, and localized economic rights in land at the other. The minus scores, therefore, refer to the degree to which a term serves to link a mythology of familial purity to textual tradition and the plus scores refer to the degree to which the term associates a group with a large territorial unit *(nāTu)* or a smaller tract of land *(kirāmam)*.

Kōtiram	Those whose clan name carries the connotation of generalized purity and orthodoxy and implies descent from a specific classical sage	−5
KuTTam	Those whose clan name connotes a tradition of tight intermarriage (e.g., of localized purity) but does not link the group directly to textual tradition	−2
NāTu	Those whose clan name connotes a tradition of shared rights (of a ritual nature) in a large territory *(nāTu)*	+2
Kulam	Those whose clan name connotes a tradition of shared rights (of an economic nature) in a specific local area *(kirāmam)*	+5

This was the most difficult scale of all to construct and different word usages might make comparison with data from other areas difficult. Possibly one could validate what is here a subjective judgment of word meaning by asking a series of respondents in a given area "What does (clan term) mean to you?"

5. *Marriage ceremony*. In order to gauge the degree to which various subcastes resembled KavuNTars or Brahmans in their marriage ceremony, ten items present in the Brahmans ceremony but not in the KavuNTar ceremony were noted. Similarly, ten rituals included in the KavuNTar but not in the Brahman ceremony were listed. The details are too elaborate to give in full here. However, in general it may be said that the ten Brahman items are rituals described in the classical texts on marriage, and that the ten KavuNTar items have no such textual source. The KavuNTar rituals, by contrast, gain significance by reference to local territory, to agricultural abundance, and to various details of the social obligations existing between close relatives.

In scoring, each item in a subcaste's marriage ceremony which resembled the Brahman list was worth −0.5 point and each item present which resembled the KavuNTar list was worth +0.5 point. The points were totaled and rounded out to the nearest whole number. The result of this calculation is entered as the subcaste's score on this item.

6. *Kin terminology.* One item of variation in the kin terminologies of castes in the Koṅku region is the presence or absence of a distinction between mother's father and father's father. The presence of the distinction is in keeping with an emphasis on territorial alliances between lineages in the KavuNTar community, and the absence accords with a tight-knit kin circle undifferentiated by descent group in the Brahman community. All subcastes who make the distinction were given a score of +5. Those who do not make the distinction were given a score of −5.

7. *Style of the wedding necklace.* The style of the wedding necklace varies considerably among the various subcastes of the Koṅku region. The pendant on this necklace is double in the case of Brahmans, but is single and worn in an inverted or "upside down" position in the case of KavuNTars. This reversal or inversion can be understood as an expression of the rivalry of these two groups in the Koṅku area. Furthermore, in the general culture there is a tendency to equate double with male and single with female. The KavuNTar inversion, therefore, may suggest a reversal in the usage of these other categories as well.[49] Various necklace styles in use in the area have been scored as follows:

Necklace Styles—Pendant Only

Double image with specific pattern	−5
Double image with a pattern slightly different from the Brahman style, above	−4
Circular image, plain; reminiscent of the wedding necklace tied to temple deities	−1
Inverted single image, small size	+3
Inverted single image, large size	+5

Elsewhere in South India a single image, not inverted, is used by many subcastes. Though this particular pendant does not occur in the Koṅku data, it would seem tentatively reasonable to assign such a style a score of −3 (to contrast with the +3 for an inverted single image). In Andhra the circular image (double or single?)

appears to be the pendant design of some Brahman groups. This difference would have to be taken into account in a larger study utilizing this particular scale.

8. *Direction of wrapping the sari.* In South India a woman's sari can be wrapped either clockwise or counterclockwise. (Directions are given as if the woman were looking down on herself.) This choice can be observed in the Koṅku area in the wrapping of eight- and nine-yard saris (in contrast to the modern six-yard sari which is always wound counterclockwise). Older women still wear these longer cloths and all women in the south did so until recently. Brahman women wrap their traditional sari clockwise and the KavuNTar women their traditional dress counterclockwise. The scoring on this feature of behavior was done as follows:

Sari wrapped clockwise	−5
Sari wrapped counterclockwise	+5

9. *Sacred thread.* The investiture of a young boy with a sacred thread is one of the classical rites of the twice-born castes. It is clearly associated with the Brahmans. Though technically Kshatriyas and Vaishyas were expected to go through the investiture ceremony too, they were to do so at a later age. In fact, it seems, most people of the latter two categories did not bother with sacred threads in actual practice.[50] The scoring on this feature was done as follows:

Special investiture ceremony, sacred thread worn all the time	−5
Used to be a special investiture ceremony and a sacred thread was subsequently worn at all times; now only some members of the subcaste bother with this detail, while others have given it up	−4
Sacred thread worn only at weddings and on other ceremonial occasions; no special investiture ritual	−3
No use of the sacred thread whatever	+5

10. *Color of the widow's sari.* The color of the widow's sari has become a detail of great social importance, though there does not seem to be any reference to this matter in the Sanskrit texts.[51] In the Koṅku region (and all over the south?) the Brahman widow does not wear a truly white sari, but rather a cloth of a light tan color (turmeric dye?) with a narrow, reddish border. KavuNTar widows, by contrast, wear pure white. Other castes vary in this matter, though those who permit colored garments do not neces-

sarily restrict them to a particular color as the Brahmans do. My notes contain sufficient detail only to make the color/pure white contrast. The scoring on this feature was done as follows:

Pale tan or colored sari worn by widows	−5
Pure white sari worn by widows	+5

Comments on the Construction of the Chart

The original draft of the chart included indices on only six items of behavior. As more data were marshaled by sifting field notes, and by writing to a research assistant in India, however, the number of items was gradually expanded to twelve. In the final draft two of those twelve were cut (rate of literacy and average marriage distance) on the grounds that information on these was incomplete, and because it seemed that these particular indices were strongly associated with the wealth of an individual caste and the strength of its local population, and only indirectly with a choice involving the opposition of ritualistic and instrumental life-styles. Thus, it was reasoned, their relevance to the question of contrasting ideals was not easily separated from their dependence on other factors.

Both of the axes of the graph are defined in terms of ordinal scales. The discussion of the relative slope of the two regression lines, however, assumes that they are also equal interval scales. There are two reasons for arguing that this is a reasonably accurate assumption:

1. Despite the variation in the number of items used in three trial runs (and an attempted weighting of items in one case) the graph which resulted turned out to be essentially the same shape in each case. The slopes of the two lines were never significantly affected by these manipulations of the basic data. In sum, it was found that the form of the graph was roughly invariant over a number of lineal transformations. Measuring ritual rank on an inverse logarithmic scale also leaves the graph virtually unchanged.
2. Though the intervals on the social behavior scale are not necessarily uniform, the fact that the scores used in plotting subcaste position are the result of averaging ten different items mitigates against any severe effect due to variation in the units themselves.

On the basis of these arguments it appears justifiable to discuss a general contrast in the slopes of the two lines. The actual regression curves were drawn by eye, rather than computed. A calculation of the exact slope assumes the use of strictly equal interval scales and seems too exacting a method to use on the data available at present. Furthermore, considerations of this nature are not relevant to the general issues addressed by this paper. If this method were to be adopted by others for more extended use, some refinement would certainly be required.

Added Comment: A Reanalysis of the Foregoing Data Using a New, Nonmetric Method

Soon after the publication of the foregoing discussion the author became acquainted with a new, nonmetric technique for the computerized analysis of categorical data. This method, termed Multidimensional Scalogram Analysis (hereafter MSA), has been recently developed by Guttman and Lingoes[52] for the analysis of sociological detail of the type just presented in the foregoing article. The great advantage of this new approach to observed variations within a population is that the reduction of categorical distinctions to a numerical code is not required. Hence previous worries about the introduction of ordinal and interval assumptions in the discussion of nonmetric data can now be avoided.[53] This brief addendum will reanalyze the data, using MSA. The sounder methodological grounds on which the restudy rests, coupled with startling results, are believed to make this additional commentary worthwhile.

The first task is to recode the data presented, reducing them to the form in which it was collected. This is done in the table below. All that is necessary is to indicate what categorical contrasts between population elements (subcastes) can be observed with regard to each characteristic (custom) judged relevant. Furthermore, with an MSA Program the number of distinctions used can be allowed to vary for each category or characteristic (two styles of sari wrapping, but six types of clan deity) without constraining the analysis.

Once the data have been so coded, the computer is asked to arrange the population elements provided in a space of X dimensions in the way that best allows that space to be partitioned to take account of the distinctions between elements for each characteristic studied. Since the computer can supply an answer in any number of dimensions (up to the number of elements originally included), it is up to the analyst to decide which representation of his data is most appropriate. In the present case the coefficient of contiguity reached .985 in two dimensions and .986 in three dimensions. Hence the solution in three dimensions represents an insignificant improvement in mathematical terms over that in two, but since the arrange-

DETAILS OF SCORING USED IN THE CONSTRUCTION OF THE V GRAPH, BY SUBCASTE *

Subcaste Name (and the number which identifies it in the accompanying graph)	Characteristics 1	2	3	4	5	6	7	8	9	10
Population elements:										
1. Aiyar Pirāman (Brahman)	a	a	a	a	a	a	a	a	a	a
2. KarūNikal PiLLai (accountant)	a	b	a	a	a	a	a	a	c	b
3. Koṅku KavuNTar (agriculturalist)	b	f	c	d	i	b	e	b	d	b
4. Koṅku CeTTiyār (merchant)	b	e	c	d	h	b	d	b	d	b
5. OkecāNTi PaNTāram (non-Brahman priest)	b	d	b	c	i	b	e	b	d	b
6. Kaikōlan Mutaliyār (weaver)	b	b	a	b	d	a	d	b	b	b
7. KōmuTTi CeTTiyār (merchant)	a	b	a	a	b	b	a	b	c	a
8. Koṅku UTaiyār (potter)	b	d	b	c	f	b	e	b	b	b
9. CōLi Ācāri (artisan)	a	b	a	a	c	a	b	a	c	a
10. Koṅku Ācāri (artisan)	b	b	a	a	d	b	c	b	d	b
11. Maramēri NāTār (toddy tapper)	b	e	c	d	g	b	d	b	d	b
12. VaTakku Nāyakkaṉ (well-digger)	b	c	a	b	g	b	c	b	d	b
13. Koṅku Nāvitaṉ (barber)	b	d	b	c	i	b	e	b	d	b
14. Vatakku VaNNaṉ (washerman)	b	d	b	c	e	b	c	b	d	a
15. Koṅku Paṟaiyaṉ (drummer)	b	d	b	c	i	b	c	b	d	b
16. Moracu Mātāri (leather-worker)	b	c	c	b	f	b	c	b	d	a

* Recoded without recourse to ordinal or interval assumptions.

ment of elements in the former spoke more directly to the theoretical issues previously raised (contrasting models, dominance, the internal solidarity of rival blocs, and rank) the three-dimensional solution was chosen as the more relevant.

A perspective drawing of this three-dimensional solution is provided below (fig. 2), plus a two-dimensional view of the location of points when this arrangement is viewed from each of three sides (fig. 3).[54] Each of the three views will be discussed in turn and a theoretical interpretation of each of the dimensions supplied. It will be seen that the first two dimensions discussed provide striking support for the previous analysis while the third dimension suggests an important modification of the earlier discussion.

The distribution of points along axis 1 supports the earlier finding: i.e., that Brahman (ritualistic) and kingly (instrumental) life styles compete as models for local behavior. The KavuNTars or local landowners fall far to one end of this axis (+100) just as the Brahmans can be found at the other extreme (−100). As predicted earlier, all the other six subcastes which were traditionally labeled members of the "right" division are also found far over on the positive side of this axis. By contrast, the two subcastes traditionally defined as neutral (plus one deviant left-division group) are alone in clustering around the axis's negative extreme. All the other six subcastes traditionally defined as "left" are found in a middle area, reinforcing the earlier conclusion that the left group is internally more diverse, and its members seemingly more ambivalent about choosing between life-styles than are their right-division rivals. The fact that five of the seven "left" subcastes are in fact located on the positive side of this axis suggests that these groups may indeed be more influenced by KavuNTar norms than was previously recognized.[55]

The distribution of points along axis 2 suggests that a second factor which can tentatively be called "ability to dominate interaction" also sorts out the three traditional groups—neutral, right, and left—quite clearly. Here the Brahmans fall closest to the positive end of the scale, while the other neutral subcaste (professional accountants) ties with the landowners for second place.[56] All other groups traditionally classed as "right" fall just beneath the KavuNTar landlords. Although these groups cannot be said to "dominate" many interactions, they do enjoy considerable cooperation and protection from their overlords. The subcastes traditionally classified as left, by contrast, do not serve or interact regularly with any leading groups. They are ignored and scoffed at by neutral subcastes and landowners alike. Hence on this scale they appear near the minus end. Note that no. 14 lies higher and further towards the positive end of axis 1 than any other "left" group. This is the one subcaste of this division which has recently begun to interact

Fig. 2. Multidimensional Scalogram Analysis: a perspective view on three axes of an analysis of population elements in Konku

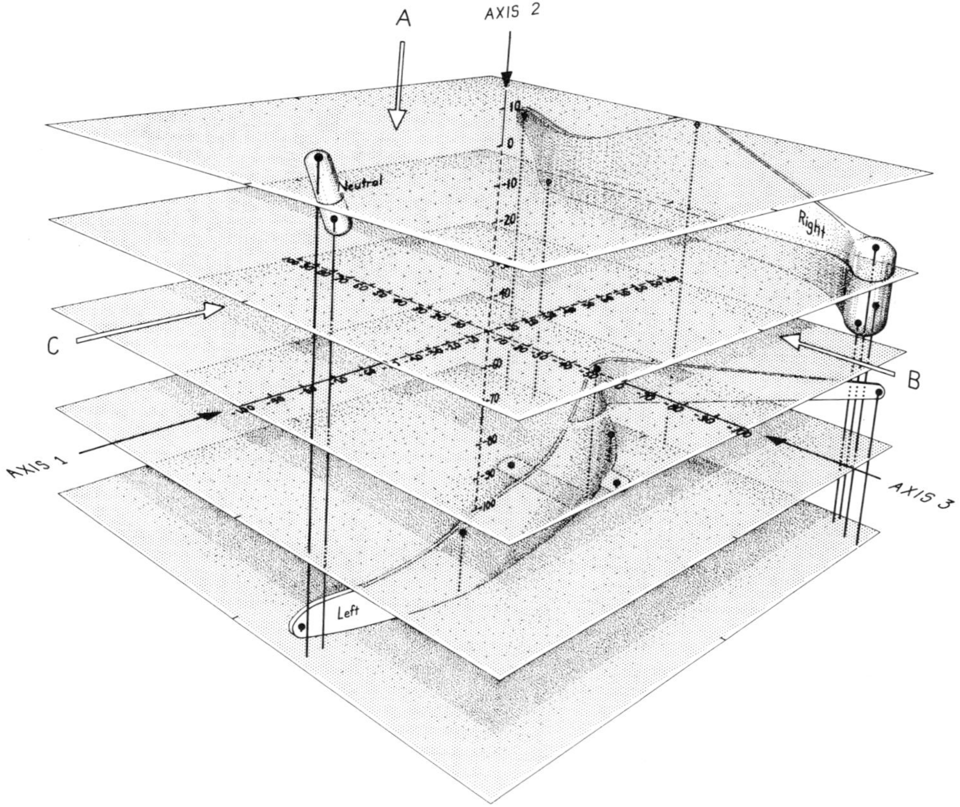

regularly with important families in the KavuNTar community.[57] Dominance of daily interaction, then, serves to define one end of this vertical axis, while the opposing end is defined by the most severely dominated, plus those who have opted out of interaction entirely or who in some other way insist on their individuality.[58]

Axis 3 suggests a final dimension in the sorting of the data. Significantly, this dimension was not apparent in the previous analy-

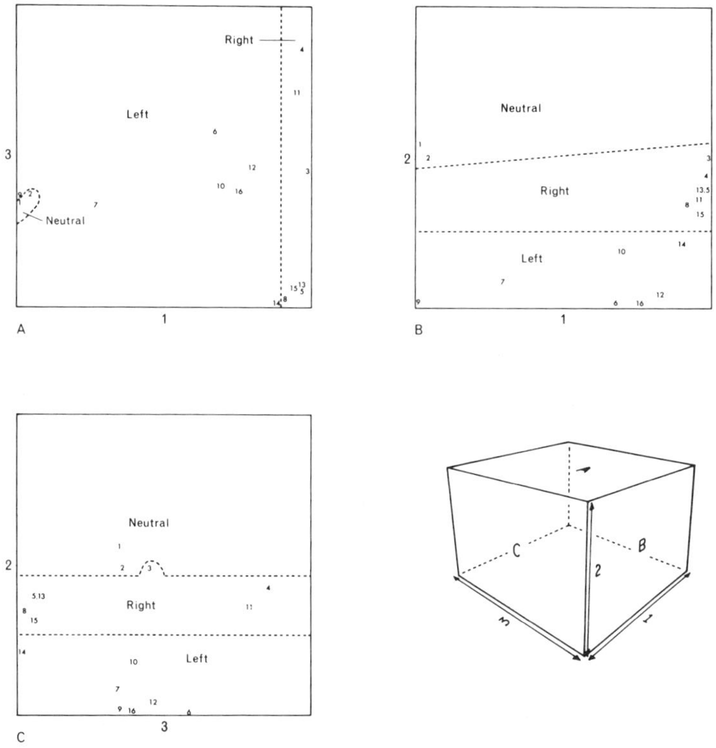

Fig. 3. Location of points when arrangement depicted in figure 2 is viewed from each of three sides

sis. On this axis both the neutral and left subcaste groups cluster in the center area, while the right division members (with the exception of the KavuNTar leaders) fall at two extremes. At the positive end are the two subcastes who enjoy direct rights to land or to trees in return for intermittent payments of produce and service.[59] Those on the negative end of the scale, by contrast, all provide ritual services for the KavuNTar community and are in the position of being intimate subordinates. This distinction between intimate service (ritual interdependence) and formal cooperation (economic interdependence) seems to form the essential key to the third dimension. Note that it is only relevant in distinguishing the different types of bonds which exist between the several members of the right division. Members of left-division subcastes and members of neutral subcastes, by contrast, cannot be differentiated in these terms.

This new technique of analysis has served to confirm the main argument of the earlier paper: that a clear opposition in models of behavior in the Koṅku area does exist and that clarifying this antithesis helps to explain the diversity of caste customs in this region.

At the same time that this reanalysis has placed the former conclusion on a sounder methodological footing it has also served to modify the initial argument in certain respects. One can no longer say that adherence to one or the other of these models is linked directly to caste rank. It is now clear that this dimension of rank is better broken into two: dominance vs. submission, individuation, or withdrawal on the one hand, and economic vs. ritual interdependence on the other. Furthermore, it appears that all three dimensions may be interdependent and that an increase in variance in one is likely to result in a decrease of variance in others. Hence one could expect an increase in the concentration of dominance at the hands of a single group (the Brahmans) in other areas of the south to lead to an increase in variance by subcaste along axis 2, and a decrease in variance by subcaste along axis 1. Together these three dimensions make for a more complex picture than that formerly provided by the V diagram, but at the same time for a more rigorous model which should prove more readily capable of comparison with data collected elsewhere.

Notes

* This description of current customs draws upon field work conducted in the Coimbatore District of Madras State during 1965 and 1966. Historical statements, unless otherwise specified, refer to the area of South India covered by the present states of Mysore, Andhra, and Madras. Literary sources rarely specify an area more precisely than this. This paper has used a scheme of letter by letter transliteration from written Tamil. With the following exceptions, common English letters are used as direct equivalents for Tamil ones:

a) The capital letters L, N, and T represent retroflex sounds in the middle of a word.
b) n and n̲ distinguish two Tamil letters, both pronounced like the English n.
c) ṅ is equivalent to the English ng.
d) ā, ē, ī, ō, and ū represent long as opposed to short vowels.

A guide to accurate pronunciation necessitates a long list of rules, and would require too much space to provide here. Only two difficult words recur frequently in the text. The first is the name of a region, Koṅku, which should be pronounced like "Kongu," and the second is the name of a caste, KavuNTar, which should be pronounced a little like "Gounda(r)."

1. M. Arokiaswami, *The Kongu Country* (Madras: Madras University Press, 1956), p. 272.

2. The roots of the division were probably economic, but evidence suggests that the initial separation of social groups on these grounds became blurred with time. Not surprisingly, the ritual rivalry of the two blocs appears to have gradually increased to compensate for this sense of confusion. By the time the British arrived in South India petty bickering between the divisions was intense, while the cause of the opposition left these foreign observers bewildered. See B. Stein, "The Integration of the Agrarian System of South India" in R. Frykenberg, ed., *Social Structure and Land Control* (Madison: University of Wisconsin Press, 1968) for a general discussion of the conflict and its development.

3. Henry D. Love, *Vestiges of Old Madras* (London, John Murray, 1931), 2: 25 ff., 142–43; P. J. Bertrand, *La mission du Maduré* (Paris: Librairie de Poussielgue-Rusard, 1947), pp. 78, 81; R. Frykenberg, *Guntur District, 1788–1848* (Oxford: Clarendon Press, 1956), p. 144; and C. S. Srinivasachari, "Right and Left Hand Caste Disputes in Madras in the Early Part of the 18th Century," *Indian Historical Records Commission: Proceedings of Meetings* 12 (Calcutta: Government of India, 1930): 68–76.

4. The term "peasant" refers to anyone directing agricultural activities on a day-to-day basis, whose instructions are normally decisive in the final division of the produce. "Peasant" in this sense refers to a powerful, landed community, not to field laborers.

5. Burton Stein, "Brahman and Peasant in Early South Indian History," *Adyar Library Bulletin,* vols. 31–32, 1967–68, "Dr. V. Raghavan Felicitation Volume."

6. Burton Stein, "The State and the Agrarian Order," lecture delivered at the University of Chicago, 31 March 1969.

7. Koṅku comprises most of the District of Coimbatore, plus the southwestern part of Salem and parts of Tiruchirappali and Madurai. It consists of one large upland plain, surrounded by mountains and watered by the upper reaches of the river Kaveri.

8. Locally the Kammālan̲ are referred to as Ācāri and the Cakkiliyan̲ as Mātāri. Indeed only one of my five informants (a second Cakkiliyan̲) was content to label his own bloc as "left." This suggests that the labels do carry overtones of rank and that "right" is the preferred and implicitly

superior category. The probable reasons which lie behind these conflicting claims are discussed further in the next section. One may note also that the tendency to reverse the labels of two opposed divisions, where the reversal favors one's own group, is not unique to my data. See, for example, Paul Radin's description of the phratries of the Winnebago tribe. Two of Radin's informants (one from the "upper" and one from the "lower" phratry) gave him inverse descriptions of the position of clan lodges. Each placed the leading clan of his phratry in the southernmost (most prestigious) location. See D. Maybury-Lewis, "The Analysis of Dual Organizations: A Methodological Critique," *Bijdragen tot de Taal-, Land- en Volkenkunde* 116 (special issue entitled *Anthropologica,* 1960): 18–19.

9. The *kirāmam,* a territory some five to ten square miles in size and containing several discrete settlements, is the traditional economic and ritual unit in rural areas. It corresponds in significance (if not always in exact dimensions) with the *panchayat* territories of post-independence reorganization. It is the unit into which British land records were subdivided and within which a local government appointee was responsible for revenue collection. Current usage of the term "village" is ambiguous, since some authors use it to refer to a unit like the *kirāmam,* and others to refer to a discrete settlement *(ūr).* Much argument over the significance of the Indian village as a unit of study has been generated by this confusion.

10. This point is discussed at length in Louis Dumont, *Homo Hierarchicus* (Paris: Gallimard, 1966).

11. See McKim Marriott's extended treatment of this situation in "Interactional and Attributional Theories of Caste Ranking," *Man in India* 39, no. 2 (1959): 92–107, and "Caste Ranking and Food Transactions: A Matrix Analysis" in Milton Singer and Bernard Cohn, eds., *Structure and Change in Indian Society* (Chicago: Aldine, 1968), pp. 133–72.

12. This choice is beautifully symbolized by the act of plowing. According to orthodox Hindu doctrine, plowing land is a polluting activity since overturning the soil threatens life within it. (See, for example, W. Crooke, *The Tribes and Castes of the N.W. Provinces and Oudh,* vol. 1 [Calcutta: Government of India, 1896], p. cxlix.) On the other hand, plowing is an essential agricultural activity, directly linked to high productivity. A Brahman will never plow himself but always hire a man of another caste to do this task for him. A caste which has opted to contest its rank in these worldly terms, by contrast, will plow and do so with pride. Steve Barnett of the University of Chicago has recently collected data of great interest on this point. He worked with a caste who stand just below the Brahmans in ritual status. This caste attempts to compete both in orthodox, ritual terms and in this-worldly terms as landowners. Their decision about the plow balances the two views as delicately as would seem possible, yet ultimately opts for the orthodox position. They will touch the plow during an annual ceremony, yet will not use it actually to turn over earth in cultivation. The KavuNTars in Coimbatore, by contrast, boast of their plowmanship to the point where a recent book about the caste published by one of its leaders has a vivid color picture of a man wielding a plow on the front cover.

13. These are the Tamil terms. There are equivalents which can be given the same English translation in Kanada and Telugu, the other two principal languages spoken in areas where the right-left division was once prominent.

14. Other examples of this are a local saying to the effect that "if the breath be taken in through the right nostril at conception the child will be male; if through the left a female," and the popular belief that bodily features such as moles and muscular tics are auspicious when they occur on the right side of a man's body, or on the left side of a woman's. Furthermore, a woman is sometimes asked to use her left foot or hand to contrast with the male right in rituals where both sexes participate.

15. Indeed, it is difficult to find any conceptual antithesis which is truly symmetric except in a formal sense. Nearly all such oppositions have some evaluative connotation implying a superior-inferior relationship. It is not surprising, therefore, to find this problem of relative value or rank intruding at the level of social groupings wherever such a pair of terms has been used to describe them. This point has been made previously by Maybury-Lewis, "Analysis of Dual Organizations," p. 42.

16. A. K. Coomaraswamy, *Spiritual Authority and Temporal Power in the Indian Theory of Government* (New Haven: American Oriental Society, 1942), pp. 1–3.

17. See Abbé Dubois, *Hindu Manners, Customs and Ceremonies* (Oxford: Clarendon Press, 1966), p. 25. Burton Stein, in a personal communication, mentions that he has found similar examples of attempts at reversal of the two labels in early temple inscriptions which he has studied. Furthermore, in the eighteenth and nineteenth centuries the Brahmans brought several lawsuits against the artisans in an attempt to dampen their exalted claims to Brahman-style knowledge and status. See Gustav Oppert, *On the Original Inhabitants of Bharatavarsa or India* (London: Westminster, 1894), pp. 58–63.

18. Subcaste is a very difficult concept to define. Here the term will refer to a group within a general occupational or social category which identifies itself by an additional modifying adjective (usually one with ritual significance) and which attempts to impose sanctions on marriages across its boundaries. Subcastes are primarily kin groupings and only secondarily occupational units.

19. Up to this point differences between the two divisions have been described by reference to castes as the basic social unit. This was done in order not to confuse the reader with a caste-subcaste distinction prematurely. Strictly speaking, however, the observations contained in this paper refer to subcastes. It is here that detailed markers of ritual and social custom take on their importance and it is at this nodal point where identification with one division or the other was ultimately affirmed. According to available historical sources, when switching between blocs took place members of a subcaste moved across the divide together.

20. A particular diet, either vegetarian or nonvegetarian, and including specific restrictions on certain animals, is socially sanctioned by a subcaste as a whole. This is asserted as the norm when ranking the group

vis-à-vis outsiders, though individuals within the subcaste may at times deviate from the rule in practice.

21. See P. V. Hare, *History of Dharmasastra* (Poona: Bhandarkar Research Institute, 1941), 2, pt. 1: 274–96, 583–636.

22. The term KavuNTar is related to the Sanskrit *grama kuta,* a title meaning "village or regional chief of Shudra origin." See M. B. Emeneau and T. Burrow, *Dravidian Borrowings from Indo-Aryan* (Berkeley: University of California Press, 1962), p. 21.

23. In such an undertaking one would have to take account of local, regional, and all-India sources, and of the considerable disagreement within as well as between such materials. Nonetheless, such work must form the critical base for the initially seminal, but currently vague and overworked concept of "Sanskritization." For work to date on Sanskritization, see M. N. Srinivas, *Social Change in Modern India* (Berkeley: University of California Press, 1966).

24. The rank of a caste was determined by analyzing the results of twenty-five systematic interviews with members of thirteen castes. In the interviews one male and one female from each caste (with one exception) were asked to evaluate all the others in terms of restrictions they applied to those communities concerning house entry, seating, acceptance of food, and bodily contact. The fewer the restrictions the higher the score assigned to any particular caste evaluated. For details of the ranking procedure see my doctoral dissertation, "Social and Conceptual Order in Koṅku: A Region of South India," Oxford University, 1968, pp. 460–64. The method used closely resembles that described by Pauline M. Kolenda in her article "A Multiple Scaling Technique for Caste Ranking," *Man in India* 39, no. 2 (1959): 128–47.

25. The service castes are not adequately represented in my field material and their full complement, therefore, does not appear in the chart. Traditionally these service groups, particularly barbers, washermen, and drummers, were divided. Some subcastes served the right bloc of castes and the other subcastes served the left. Presumably if the sample were larger, subcastes identifying with each division would follow the same pattern and fall on the same half of the chart as do those they traditionally served.

26. See the appendix for a discussion of how the regression lines were drawn and for a justification of the contrast in relative slope.

27. Theodore Riker, *A Theory of Political Coalitions* (New Haven: Yale University Press, 1962).

28. Many sources indicate that this was the case. See for example, Dubois, *Hindu Manners,* p. 25, and N. Subba Reddi, "Community Conflict among the Depressed Castes of Andhra," *Man in India* 30, no. 4: 1–12.

29. The current stress on "Black is Beautiful" may be an example of this.

30. Various details which are cited in the literature about Tanjore support this conclusion. See, for example, E. K. Gough, "Brahman Kinship in a Tamil Village," *American Anthropologist* 58 (1956): 827 and 49.

31. Being a landlord requires more worldly interaction with men of other castes than is seemly for a priest. It also limits the amount of time one can spend in ritual-related activities.

32. Burton Stein, personal communication.

33. Joan Mencher indicates, in a recent article, that the Nayars of central Kerala resemble the Nāmbudiris very closely indeed. See her "Nāmbudiri Brahmans: An Analysis of a Traditional Elite in Kerala," *Journal of Asian and African Studies* 1 (1966): 183–96. An explanation of the absence of a right-left division in Kerala lies, perhaps, in the unusual position of the Nāmbudiri Brahmans in this area. Unlike their counterparts in other areas of the South, the Nāmbudiris of Kerala have a tradition of "marriage" with the Nayar community whose social position falls just beneath their own. This intimate linkage of the two groups has reinforced Brahman pre-eminence in the region. Furthermore, in much of Kerala the Nāmbudiris are the major landowners and in areas where they do not control land directly their customary behavior continues to serve as an uncontested model for the region. For further detail see Eric Miller, "Caste and Territory in Malabar," *American Anthropologist,* vol. 56 (1954); Adrian Mayer, *Land and Society in Malabar* (Oxford: Oxford University Press, 1952); and E. Kathleen Gough, "The Nayar" in David Schneider and E. K. Gough, eds., *Matrilineal Kinship* (Berkeley: University of California Press, 1961). The possible connection between Nayar hypergamy, Brahman emulation, and the absence of a right-left division was initially suggested to me by David J. Elkins, Department of Political Science, University of British Columbia.

34. Artisan groups all over India refer to themselves as "Visvakarma Brahmans," a term that refers both to the god Visvakarman or "world-creator" of the *Rig-Veda* and to the demigod Visvakarman or "craftsman-creator" of the *Ramayana*. Use of the term today plays on this double meaning, indicating that group members see their status as craftsmen in this world as a counterpart to that of divine creator in another. Because of their insistence on familial purity and their refusal to accept food from other high-ranking communities, they tend to be difficult to place in a unidimensional hierarchy. In some places they are also associated with extremist and puritanical sectarian movements. See such studies as Adrian Mayer, *Caste and Kinship in Central India* (London: Routledge & Kegan Paul, 1960); David Pocock, "The Movement of Castes," *Man* 55 (1955): 71–72; and Dev Raj Channa, "Sanskritization, Westernization and India's Northwest," *Economic Weekly* 13, no. 9 (4 Mar. 1961): 409–14.

35. The heir, the viceroy, the general and the president stood on the right, while the master of ceremonies and the minister of commerce stood on the left. A. M. Hocart, "Duplication of Office in the Indian State," *Ceylon Journal of Science,* sec. G, vol. 1, pt. 4 (1928): 208.

36. Ibid., pp. 208–9; and Nur Yalman, "Dual Organization in Central Ceylon," *Journal of Asian Studies* 24 (1965): 197–223.

37. Dubois, *Hindu Manners,* p. 25. Also J. H. Nelson, *The Madura Country* (Madras: Government Press, 1868), pt. II, p. 4.

38. N. Mukherjee, *The Ryotwari System in Madras* (Calcutta: Muk-

hopadhyay, 1962), pp. 332–33, 346. See also Dharma Kumar, *Land and Caste in South India* (Cambridge: Cambridge University Press, 1965), p. 34.

39. Ibid., p. 9.

40. This appears to be a very old and persistent characteristic of Indian society. There are references to a similar separation as early as the second half of the first millennium B.C. (Romila Thapar, "The Elite and Social Mobility in Early India," paper read at the University of Chicago, April 1968, pp. 9–11).

41. Karl Polanyi, *The Great Transformation* (Boston: Beacon Press, 1944), p. 178.

42. Dharma Kumar, *Land and Caste,* p. 192, and Frykenberg, *Guntur District,* p. 2.

43. Thomas R. Metcalf, *The Aftermath of Revolt* (Princeton: Princeton University Press, 1964), p. 178.

44. See Lloyd Rudolph, "The Meaning of Party: From the Politics of Status to the Politics of Opinion in Eighteenth Century England and America," unpublished Ph.D. dissertation, Harvard, Department of Government, 1956, pp. 83–86; Bulmer-Thomas, *The Growth of the British Party System* (London: John Baker, 1965), 1: 9; and Austin Mitchell, *The Whigs in Opposition, 1815–1830* (Oxford: Clarendon Press, 1967), pp. 10–17.

45. This description is actually for the end of the sixteenth century, but it is said that the rituals which were associated with Parliamentary sessions persisted nearly unchanged in later periods. See J. E. Neale, *The Elizabethan House of Commons* (London: Jonathan Cape, 1949), p. 421. It is interesting that when the House of Lords met alone the representatives of the church stood on the right of the sovereign and the temporal peers on the left. With only the landed present, the church was given the place of honor, just as the Brahmans take ritual precedence over kings in India.

46. Bulmer-Thomas, *British Party System,* p. 7, and Love, *Old Madras,* 2: 143. It is interesting that the landed group, in both cases, preempted the color red, possibly because of its ready association with physical prowess and military valor.

47. Mitchell would date the beginnings of change from the period of the great Reform Bill of 1832, *Whigs,* p. 4. See also Polanyi, *Great Transformation,* p. 180.

48. Some researchers have suggested that all societies depend to a greater or lesser extent on a set of core themes, and that these themes are generally expressed in terms of a few elementary dichotomous categories. If this is the case, then the question becomes why these themes, so common at an ethical and linguistic level, find expression in the actual organization of some societies, but not in others. More specifically, examples of dichotomous social organization (as opposed to dichotomous categories of thought) come largely from "primitive" or at least pre-industrial societies. This paper suggests, implicitly, that such a finding can be connected with economic facts. Societies which support themselves by means of a few relatively discrete and straightforward economic activities often have

the kinds of basic social cleavage (due to specialization in easily contrasted activities) which lend themselves to symbolic elaboration. As the economic base of a group becomes more complex, however, it would appear that these dualistic aspects of social organization "fit" less well with reality. At the same time, such practical complexity does not lend itself as easily to symbolic manipulation. It is hypothesized, therefore, that a pattern of dual organization (where previously existent) will tend to disappear under conditions like those described in this paper. For detail on the general assertion concerning the dualistic nature of major cultural themes see Emile Durkheim and Marcel Mauss, *Primitive Classification,* trans. Rodney Needham (London, 1963), and Robert Hertz, *Death and the Right Hand,* trans. Rodney Needham (London, 1960).

49. For further discussion of the possible symbolism involved see Coomaraswamy, *Spiritual Authority and Temporal Power,* pp. 1–2, and Beck, "Social and Conceptual Order in Koṅku," pp. 359–60.

50. See P. V. Kane, *History of Dharmaśāstra* (Poona, 1930), p. 296.

51. Ibid., pp. 583–636.

52. James C. Lingoes, "An IBM 7090 Program for Guttman-Lingoes Multidimensional Scalogram Analysis—I," *Behavioral Science* 2 (1966): 76–78. I am greatly indebted to Milton Bloombaum of the University of British Columbia for introducing me to this technique of analysis and for spending many hours discussing the results of this particular application.

53. In developing the foregoing method of interpreting the data I was well aware of the difficulties and dangers of numerical reduction, but did not then know of a way to circumvent them.

54. View A of the three-dimensional model closely approximates the two-dimensional solution provided by the computer. Hence no separate discussion of that output is necessary.

55. The position of no. 14, which lies closest of all to the positive extreme of the axis, is easily explained by the fact that this is a left subcaste of washermen who have recently begun to provide ritual services for groups of the right due to the absence (in the recent past) of a washerman traditionally identified with this bloc. No. 14 is the only left-division group in the sample which is in this unusual position.

56. It is interesting that the computer did not make use of the full range of this scale in locating members of the population studied. It is possible to speculate that the full range of possibilities (from 100 percent dominant to 100 percent dominated, or isolated) is not utilized in regions of India where ritual eminence and economic power are enjoyed by two very distinct subcaste groups. In an area where the Brahmans hold both trump cards to themselves, by contrast, one might expect more of a spread along this axis and concurrently less along axis 1.

57. Subcaste no. 10, because of their adoption of the regional term "Koṅku" and their stepped up interaction with KavuNTars, also fall higher on this axis than do any of their other division colleagues.

58. This concern for self-definition or individuality suggests a possible effort to opt out of the system of dominance by some subcastes, a theme

which has appeared recurrently in Indian history and was particularly strong in earlier centuries during the heyday of the Lingayat movement in Mysore.

59. Actually subcaste no. 4 own their own lands outright and serve primarily as economic allies of the KavuNTar landlords.

Note on the Terms Used for "Right Hand" and "Left Hand" in the Bantu Languages

Alice Werner

APPENDIX

I have been led to look into this subject, in trying to discover whether it would throw any light on the prevalence or absence of ambidexterity among the Bantu tribes. The results of my inquiry are, so far, very incomplete; yet they are interesting, philologically, and, I hope, may furnish a starting-point for further investigation by better qualified observers. On the whole, the evidence of language seems to indicate a decided preference for the right hand, though a remarkable point which we shall have to notice in the case of Nyanja, tends to make this less certain than might at first appear. What is more important for our present purpose (since we are concerned merely with the linguistic phenomena) is the fact that, while the epithets given to the *right* hand are usually descriptive, or at least have some obvious meaning, derived from some real or supposed attribute, function, or resemblance, the word for *left*, in many, if not most, instances, can be traced to no other meaning, and is probably a root denoting "the left hand." In other cases, a depreciatory meaning can be more or less plainly traced.

We may summarize results as follows:

1. The *right* hand is frequently named from some action performed by it—usually that of eating.
2. It is often called "the male hand."
3. It is sometimes, but less frequently, called "the strong," or "great hand," or by some name equivalent to "*the* hand," par excellence.
4. A few words for *right* I am unable, with the means at my command, to explain.
5. The *left* hand is sometimes, though apparently not so often as (2) would lead one to expect, called "the female."
6. The name for *left* sometimes implies inferiority.
7. In a number of cases the word for *left* does not appear to bear any other meaning.

Many of these words, but not all, can be traced to one root. Of the 37 languages which I have examined for this purpose 18 (or possibly 21) use

---

Journal of the African Society 13 (1904): 112–16. Reprinted with the permission of the Royal African Society.

the expression "eating hand" for right hand. They are as follows. Those marked with an asterisk (*) employ other forms as well. (The names are given without prefixes.)

* Zulu
*Chwana
Chopi (or Shilenge, or Gitonga, of Inhambane)
Zwina (also called Chino, spoken in Mashonaland)
Yao
* Nyanja
Hehe
Konde
* Nyamwezi
* Swahili
Chaga
Kikuyu
Ganda
Nyoro
Bemba
Rundi
Sukuma
Mwera (inland from Lindi)

I do not know whether the Kimbundu word *madilu* (which seems to be a noun: *mbandu ya madilu*) should be included in this category. Two other doubtful items are:

* Kami (mdilo)
Zaramo (kudila)

The latter I should certainly have included, but for the fact that in this language "to eat" is *ku ja.* Perhaps, however, it should be written *ku dia,* or *ku dya,* and *ku dila* is the applied form. Some languages use the verb in this (as Swahili: *kulia,* for *kula*), others in the simple form; some (as Nyanja: *dzanja la kudya,* and *kudyetsa*) have both.

In Zulu, we also have *isandhla sokuponsa,* "the throwing hand."

The following use the expression, "male hand." Those marked (†) also call the left "female hand."

Pokomo
Shambala
†* Swahili
* Nyamwezi
Gogo
† ? * Nyanja (Dr. Henry gives *Njira ya kutshikazi,* but I have not met with this expression elsewhere.)
Makua
† Lomwe
† Suto
* Chwana

Congo (*Fiote [rare]; Bangi [*mobali,* "husband"]; Lunkundu? [*elomi,* "male"])
Duala (*mome,* "male")
* Kami
Taveta

Of words meaning "great," or the like, we have:

Chwana: *seatla se seolo,* "the great hand" *(olo-kulu).* Another expression used is *se siamen,* from the verb *siama,* which means "to be right, to be straight" (cf. our own word "right"), and corresponds to the Zulu *lunga.*

Herero: *okuoko oku-nene.* This root, *nene* = great, is also found in several of the Congo languages.

Zulu: *isandhla soku-nene (= sauku-nene).* This must be the same root; but it is not used in Zulu in the sense of "great," and *uku-nene* is only used for "the right hand." Colenso (*Dictionary,* p. 355) [1] says: "The word seems to mean, as in English, the hand where a man's strength lies."

Fiote: *koko kwanene,* "the great hand."

Nyanja: *dzanja la manja,* "hand of hands," and *dzanja la kwene* (Likoma), "real," or "very hand." Perhaps we may add the word *nkononkono* for "right" in the Sena dialect of this language. It is evidently from *mkono,* which seems properly to mean the forearm, including the hand.

The following words I do not know how to explain:

Swahili: *mkono wa kuvuli.* Has it anything to do with *uvuli,* "shade"? – "the hand which carries the umbrella"?

Tswa (a dialect of the Thonga language of Delagoa Bay): *shineneni.*

Lolo (Middle Congo): *ebomi.*

The left hand is called "the female hand" in Swahili, Nyanja (not common, seemingly), Lomwe, Suto, Fiote (but rarely), and perhaps some others.

Molema, in Chwana, appears to be a word denoting inferiority. The Rev. John Brown, L.M.S. *(Secwana Dictionary,* 1895, p. 381), says: "*Molèma.* The left. Seatla sa molèma, a left hand. . . . E molèma, it is crooked horned, one horn pointing up, and the other down. O molèma, he is spoilt. . . ." But it is possible that these unfavorable meanings may be derived from an attribution of ill luck to the left hand, as in the case of the Latin *sinister,* the etymology of which is uncertain.

The Zulu *ikohlo (isandhla sekohlo) may* be connected with the idea of forgetfulness or neglect – cf. *kohla,* "to slip the memory," *kohlwa,* "to forget," *u(lu)-kohlo,* "anything dried up or shriveled"; but of this I have at present no satisfactory evidence.

The following fifteen languages appear to have some form or other (though in one or two cases this is very doubtful) of the root – *moso.*

* Pokomo: *a kumosho*
Shambala: *a moso*
Kikuyu: *a kwomotho*

Nyamwezi: *moso*
Makua: *wimushi*
Herero: *moho*
(?) Kimbundu: *kiasu*
(?) Bemba: *uku-so.* (The Rev. W. Govan Robertson tells me (letter of 29 April 1904) that he does not know the meaning of this word.)
Nyoro: *moso* (*kwa nkento,* "female," sometimes used)
Fiote: *monso*
Bangi: *mwasi* (*nkoso* also used)
Lolo: *enso* and *eso*
Duala: *a dimose*
Taveta: *a ku moso*
Sukuma: *mosho*
Mwera *(mkono wa): moso*

I should be very grateful to any Bantu student who would throw any light on the identity of the above root, and also on the following expressions:

Ganda: *omukono ogwa'kono.* This looks as though it were analogous to *dzanja la manja,* which seems strange in the case of the *left* hand. But the Rev. H. Barnes (*Nyanja Vocabulary,* 1903) points out that in Nyanja the expressions translated as "right" are really applied to the most used hand, whichever that may be, and conversely.
Pokomo: *a dsondso* (cf. *Zeitschrift für afr. Sprachen,* 1, 3: 224)
Swahili: *a ku shoto*
Gogo: *a kučekulu*
Yao: *a mchiji*
Nyanja: *a manzere* (dialectically, *manjele*)
Sena: *a bzele*
Zwina: *a munzere*
Chopi: *nyambade*
Tswa: *šimatseni*
Konde: *a kimama*
Hehe: *a kuñiki* (also, *kunena*)
Rundi: *wamfu*

For the last-named language I am indebted to P. Van der Burgt's magnificent dictionary, just published by the Société d'Illustration Catholique at Bois-le-Duc (Holland).[2]

Notes

1. [John William Colenso, *Zulu-English Dictionary* (Pietermaritzburg, 1861).]
2. [J. M. M. van der Burgt, *Dictionnaire Français-Kirundi* (Bois-le-Duc, 1903).]

Authors

BECK, BRENDA E. F. Born 1940, U.S.A. Educated at University of Chicago (B.A., 1962); Somerville College, Oxford (Diploma in Anthropology, 1963; B.Litt., 1964; D.Phil., 1968).

National Science Foundation Fellowship, 1962–67; Fellow, American Institute of Indian Studies, 1964–66; Faculty Research Fellow, University of Chicago, 1968–69. Assistant Professor of Anthropology, University of British Columbia, 1969–

Publications: "Colour and Heat in South Indian Ritual," *Man,* 1969; *Peasant Society in Koṅku: A Study of Right and Left Subcastes in South India,* 1972.

BEIDELMAN, THOMAS O. Born 1931, U.S.A. Educated at University of Illinois (B.A., psychology, 1953; M.A., anthropology, 1956); University of California at Berkeley; University of Michigan; Trinity College, Oxford (D.Phil., social anthropology, 1961).

Assistant Professor of Social Anthropology, Harvard University, 1963–65; Fellow, Center for Advanced Study in the Behavioral Sciences, Stanford, California, 1965–66; Associate Professor of Anthropology, Duke University, 1966–68; Associate Professor of Anthropology, New York University, 1968–72; Professor, 1972– .

Author of *A Comparative Analysis of the Jajmani System,* 1959; *The Matrilineal Peoples of Eastern Tanzania,* 1967; *The Kaguru: A Matrilineal People,* 1971; numerous papers on the ethnography of Africa, symbolism, folklore, etc.

Editor, *The Translation of Culture: Essays to E. E. Evans-Pritchard,* 1971.

CHELHOD, JOSEPH. Born 1919, Syria. Educated Faculté des Lettres, Université de Paris (Licencié ès-Lettres, 1948; Docteur ès-Lettres, 1952).

Centre National de Recherche Scientifique, 1952– . Chargé de conférences, Ecole pratique des Hautes Etudes, 1960–62; Chargé de cours complémentaires, Faculté des Lettres, Paris, 1967–68.

Publications: *Le Sacrifice chez les Arabes,* 1955; *Introduction à la sociologie de l'Islam,* 1958; *Les Structures du sacré chez les Arabes,* 1965; *Le Droit dans la société bédouine,* 1971; numerous articles in learned periodicals.

Cunningham, Clark E. Born 1934, U.S.A. Educated Yale University (B.A., 1957); Exeter College, Oxford (Rhodes Scholar), Diploma in Anthropology, 1958; B.Litt., 1959; D.Phil., 1963.

Research Associate and Lecturer, Department of Anthropology and Southeast Asia Studies Program, Yale University, 1962–63, 1965–67; Assistant Professor of Anthropology, University of Illinois, 1963–64; Associate Professor and Professor, University of Illinois, 1968– .

Evans-Pritchard, E. E. Born 1902, England. Educated at Exeter College, Oxford (M.A., history, 1924); London School of Economics (Ph.D., anthropology, 1927).

Lecturer in Anthropology, London School of Economics, 1928–31; Professor of Sociology, Egyptian University, Cairo, 1931–34; Leverhulme Fellow, 1935–36; Research Lecturer in African Sociology, Oxford, 1935–40; Honorary Research Assistant, University College London, 1935–40; Reader in Anthropology, Cambridge, 1945–46; Professor of Social Anthropology, Oxford, 1946–70. Fellow of All Souls.

Publications: *Witchcraft, Oracles and Magic among the Azande,* 1937; *The Nuer,* 1940; *The Sanusi of Cyrenaica,* 1949; *Kinship and Marriage among the Nuer,* 1951; *Social Anthropology,* 1951; *Nuer Religion,* 1956; *Essays in Social Anthropology,* 1962; *The Position of Women in Primitive Societies, and Other Essays,* 1965; *Theories of Primitive Religion,* 1965; *The Zande Trickster,* 1967; *The Azande, History and Political Institutions,* 1971; numerous papers on ethnography of Africa and social anthropology in learned periodicals.

Faron, Louis C. Born 1923, U.S.A. Educated at Columbia University (A.B., 1950; Ph.D., 1954).

Research Associate in Anthropology, University of Illinois, 1955–59; Assistant Professor of Anthropology, Los Angeles State College, 1959–62; Associate Professor, 1962; Associate Professor of Anthropology, University of Pittsburgh, 1962–64; Professor of Anthropology, State University of New York at Stony Brook, 1964– .

Publications: *Native Peoples of South America* (with Julian Steward), 1959; *Mapuche Social Structure,* 1961; *Hawks of the Sun,* 1964; *The Mapuche Indians of Chile,* 1968.

FOX, JAMES J. Born 1940, U.S.A. Educated at Harvard University (A.B., 1962); University College, Oxford (Rhodes Scholar; Diploma in Social Anthropology, 1963; B.Litt., 1965; D.Phil., 1968).

Visiting Assistant Professor of Anthropology, Duke University, 1968–69; Assistant Professor of Social Anthropology, Harvard University, 1969– .

Publications: "Semantic Parallelism in Rotinese Ritual Language," *Bijdragen tot de Taal-, Land- en Volkenkunde,* 1971; "A Rotinese Dynastic Genealogy: Structure and Event," in T. O. Beidelman, ed., *The Translation of Culture,* 1971.

GRANET, MARCEL. Born 1884. Chargé de mission scientifique, China, 1911–13; Directeur d'études pour les religions d'Extrême-Orient, Ecole des Hautes Etudes, Paris; President, Institut français de Sociologie. Died 1940.

Publications: *Fêtes et chansons anciennes de la Chine,* 1919; *La Polygynie sororale et le sororat dans la Chine féodale,* 1920; *La Religion des Chinois,* 1922; *Danses et légendes de la Chine ancienne,* 1926; *La Civilisation chinoise,* 1929; *La Pensée chinoise,* 1934; *Catégories matrimoniales et relations de proximité dans la Chine ancienne,* 1939; *La Féodalité chinoise,* 1952; etc.

HERTZ, ROBERT. Born 22 June 1881, Saint-Cloud, France. Educated at Lycée Janson de Sailly; Lycée Henri IV, Paris, 1898; Ecole Normale Supérieure, Paris, 1900. Agrégation de philosophie, 1904. Research at British Museum, 1904–5, 1905–6. Assistant master (philosophy), Lycée de Douai, 1906–7. Lecturer, Ecole des Hautes Etudes, Paris, 1907. Killed in action at Marchéville (Meuse), 13 April 1915.

Publications: "Contribution à une étude sur la représentation collective de la mort," *Année sociologique,* 1907; "La Prééminence de la main droite: étude sur la polarité religieuse," *Revue philosophique,* 1909; "Saint Besse: étude d'un culte alpestre," *Revue de l'histoire des religions,* 1913; "Contes et dictons receuillis sur le front parmi les poilus de la Mayenne et d'ailleurs (campagne de 1915)," *Revue des traditions populaires,* 1917; "Le Péché et l'expiation dans les sociétés primitives," ed. Marcel Mauss, *Revue de l'histoire des religions,* 1922.

KRUYT, ALBERTUS CHRISTIAAN. Born 1869, Java. Educated at Rotterdam. Missionary of the Nederlandsch Zendeling Genootschap, to central Celebes, 1890; comparative ethnographical investigations on Mentawei,

Nias, Sumba, Roti, and Timor, 1905–6, 1920–21. Retired to the Netherlands, 1932. Died, The Hague, 1949.

Publications: *Het Animisme in den Indischen Archipel,* 1906; *De Bare'e-sprekende Toradjas van Midden-Celebes* (with N. Adriani), 1912–14; *De West-Toradjas op Midden-Celebes,* 1938; many articles on Indonesian ethnography in learned periodicals.

LA FLESCHE, FRANCIS. Born 1857, U.S.A. Son of Estamaza, or "Chief Joseph," La Flesche, himself son of a French trader and an Omaha woman, and an Omaha mother. After separation of his parents, chose to grow up among the Omaha; took part in the annual buffalo hunt, and at the age of fifteen covered a hundred miles in eighteen hours, discovering the first herd of the season; participant in traditional ceremonial life.

As interpreter, and representative of the cause of the Indians, attracted attention of Secretary of the Interior and given post in the Office of Indian Affairs. Educated at the National University; graduate in law, 1893. Bureau of American Ethnology, 1910–29. Member of the American Anthropological Association; President, Anthropological Society of Washington, 1922–23; Hon. D.Litt., University of Nebraska, 1926. Died, Nebraska, 1932.

Publications: many articles on the Omaha and Osage.

LITTLEJOHN, JAMES. Born 1921, Scotland. Educated at Glasgow University, 1940; London School of Economics (Diploma in Anthropology, 1948; Ph.D., anthropology, 1955). Assistant Lecturer, University of Edinburgh, 1948–50; Lecturer, 1950–62; Senior Lecturer, 1962–72; Professor, 1972– .

Publications: *Westrigg: The Sociology of a Cheviot Parish,* 1963; "The Temne House," *Sierra Leone Studies,* 1960; "Temne Space," *Anthropological Quarterly,* 1963.

LLOYD, G. E. R. Born 1933, U.K. Educated at King's College, Cambridge (B.A., classics, 1954; Ph.D., 1958).

Fellow of King's, 1967– ; University Lecturer in Classics, Cambridge.

Publications: *Polarity and Analogy: Two Types of Argumentation in Early Greek Thought,* 1966; *Aristotle: The Growth and Structure of his Thought,* 1968; *Early Greek Science: Thales to Aristotle,* 1970; many articles in classical and other scholarly periodicals.

MIDDLETON, J. F. M. Born 1921, England. Educated at University of London (B.A., English, 1941; University of Oxford (B.Sc., social anthropology, 1949; D.Phil., 1953).

Lecturer in Anthropology, University of London, 1953–54; Senior

Lecturer, University of Cape Town, 1954–55; Senior Lecturer, Rhodes University, 1955–56; Lecturer, University of London, 1956–64; Professor, Northwestern University, 1964–66; Professor, New York University, 1966–72; Professor, School of Oriental and African Studies, University of London, 1972– .

Publications: *Lugbara Religion,* 1960; *Land Tenure in Zanzibar,* 1961; *The Lugbara of Uganda,* 1965; *Zanzibar: Its Society and Its Politics* (with Jane Campbell), 1965; *The Effects of Economic Development on Political Systems in Africa,* 1966; *The Study of the Lugbara,* 1970.

Editor or co-editor of: *Tribes without Rulers,* 1958; *Witchcraft and Sorcery in East Africa,* 1963; *Spirit Mediumship and Society in Africa,* 1969; *From Tribe to Nation in Africa,* 1970.

NEEDHAM, RODNEY. Born 1923, England. Educated at School of Oriental and African Studies, University of London (Chinese, Malay), 1947–48; Merton College, Oxford (Chinese, social anthropology), 1948–53; University of Leiden, 1950. Diploma in Anthropology, B.Litt., M.A., D.Phil., D.Litt. (Oxon.).

Visiting Lecturer in Anthropology, University of Illinois, 1956; University Lecturer in Social Anthropology, University of Oxford, 1956– . Fellow, Center for Advanced Study in the Behavioral Sciences, Stanford, California, 1961–62; National Science Foundation Senior Foreign Scientist Fellow, University of California at Riverside, 1970–71. Fellow of Merton College, Oxford.

Publications: *Structure and Sentiment,* 1962; *Bibliography of A. M. Hocart,* 1967; *Belief, Language, and Experience,* 1972; *Remarks and Inventions,* forthcoming; numerous papers on the ethnography of Indonesia, social organization, symbolism, and classification.

Editor, translator: *Death and the Right Hand* by Robert Hertz, 1960; *Primitive Classification* by Emile Durkheim and Marcel Mauss, 1963; *Totemism* by C. Lévi-Strauss, 1963; *Ngaju Religion* by H. Schärer, 1963; *Yoga and Yantra* by P. H. Pott, 1966; *The Semi-Scholars* by Arnold van Gennep, 1967; *The Development of Marriage and Kinship* by C. S. Wake, 1967; *Types of Social Structure in Eastern Indonesia* by F. A. E. van Wouden, 1968; *The Elementary Structures of Kinship* by C. Lévi-Strauss (with J. H. Bell and J. von Sturmer), 1969; *The Life-Giving Myth* (second impression) by A. M. Hocart, 1970; *Kings and Councillors* by A. M. Hocart, 1970; *Rethinking Kinship and Marriage,* 1971; *Imagination and Proof* by A. M. Hocart (forthcoming).

RIGBY, P. J. A. Born 1938, India. Educated at University of Cape Town (B.A., 1958); King's College, Cambridge, 1960–64 (Ph.D., 1964).

Lecturer in Social Anthropology, The Queen's University of Belfast,

Northern Ireland, 1964–65; Lecturer in Social Anthropology, Makerere University College, Kampala, Uganda, 1965–67; Adjunct Associate Professor, New York University, 1967–68; Senior Lecturer in Social Anthropology, Makerere University College, 1968–69; Professor of Sociology, Makerere University, 1969– .

Publications: *Cattle and Kinship among the Gogo,* 1969; "Some Gogo Rituals of 'Purification': An Essay on Social and Moral Categories," in E. R. Leach, ed., *Dialectic in Practical Religion,* 1968; "The Symbolic Role of Cattle in Gogo Religion," in T. O. Beidelman, ed., *The Translation of Culture,* 1971; number of articles in learned periodicals.

WERNER, ALICE. Born 1859. Educated at Cambridge, 1878–80.

Lecturer in African Languages, King's College, London, 1901; recognized as Lecturer, University of London, 1910; Lecturer, School of Oriental and African Studies, University of London, 1917–21; Professor, 1921–30. Died 1935.

Publications: *Native Races of British Central Africa,* 1906; *The Language Families of Africa,* 1916; *African Mythology,* 1925; *Structure and Relationships of African Languages,* 1929; *African Stories,* 1932.

WIESCHHOFF, HEINRICH (HEINZ) ALBERT. Born 1906, Hagen, Germany. Educated University of Frankfurt, Dr.Phil. 1933. Emigrated to United States in late thirties; Instructor in Anthropology, University of Pennsylvania. United Nations Secretariat, 1946–61. Died September 1961, with Dag Hammarskjöld, in an airplane crash at N'Dola, Congo.

Major publications: *Die afrikanischen Trommeln und ihre ausserafrikanischen Beziehungen,* 1933; *The Zimbabwe-Monomotapa Culture in Southeast Africa,* 1941; *Colonial Policies in Africa,* 1944; *Anthropological Bibliography of Negro Africa,* 1948.

Index

RIGHT AND LEFT

Essays on Dual Symbolic Classification

Edited by Rodney Needham

In 1909 Robert Hertz, a young French scholar who was to lose his life in World War I, published his now classic essay, "The Pre-eminence of the Right Hand," the pioneering work on dual symbolic classification from which almost all the essays in this book developed. Hertz's theme was not merely right vs. left or even the dark side of humanity, but that of polarity or opposition as basic to human expression.

RIGHT AND LEFT: *Essays on Dual Symbolic Classification* is the first book to be published on right and left dualism as systematically revealed by the study of varied cultures. In addition to a new translation of Hertz's seminal work by Rodney Needham, RIGHT AND LEFT contains seventeen essays, both literary and ethnographical, on this subject. They are arranged in chronological order to show the successive theoretical influences, from 1909 to 1971, and the increasing intensity of the investigations. Together they reveal the many manifestations of dual symbolic classification, such as right and left, male and female, order and disorder, north and south.

Diverse societies categorize the world in terms of the division between right and left. Ranging from ancient Greece to African and Indonesian cultures, the articles have been chosen to illustrate the worldwide ramifications of right-left dualism. In his "Introduction" to this volume, Dr. Needham counters certain methodological criticisms, elaborates on points of analysis, and indicates the intrinsic significance of this mode of classification.